Understanding Global Financial Markets

Nikiforos T. Laopodis

Routledge
Taylor & Francis Group
LONDON AND NEW YORK

Designed cover image: LaymanZoom / Getty Images

First published 2026
by Routledge
4 Park Square, Milton Park, Abingdon, Oxon OX14 4RN

and by Routledge
605 Third Avenue, New York, NY 10158

Routledge is an imprint of the Taylor & Francis Group, an informa business

British Library Cataloguing-in-Publication Data
A catalogue record for this book is available from the British Library

ISBN: 978-1-041-14995-8 (hbk)
ISBN: 978-1-041-14994-1 (pbk)
ISBN: 978-1-003-67716-1 (ebk)

DOI: 10.4324/9781003677161

Typeset in Sabon
by codeMantra

Access the Support Material: www.routledge.com/9781041149941

This textbook is dedicated to my later mother, Helen, and my father, Socrates, for their incessant and loving guidance throughout my personal and professional life.

Contents

Detailed table of contents

Figures

Tables

Boxes

Sidebars

Preface

I have been teaching the subject of financial markets, institutions and instruments for over twenty years. I have used a number of different textbooks to deliver the workings of the money and capital markets, financial institutions and financial instruments. All of these textbooks have adopted roughly the same approach, which is to present the material from the financial institution or financial manager's point of view by exploring their operational details and roles. In addition, in many textbooks one can see detailed discussions of the central banks and monetary policy, which is typically the material for textbooks in Money and Banking and related courses. This textbook is different or, in many respects, unique. The focus is on the retail (individual) investor such as a student or a novice investor in the financial markets.

More specifically, this textbook has grown out of the need to provide students with the workings of the global financial markets from a *practical*, *intuitive* and *hands-on* perspective. In addition, the focus is on the *retail* (individual) *investor* and not on the financial institutions as most existing textbooks emphasize. Typically, existing textbooks begin with the theories of financial markets (and related topics such as instruments and institutions) and finish with some applications/examples and real-world news. What they lack or, at least, do not offer to the desired level, is analysis of the thinking process by an agent in exploiting the financial markets. Specifically, students are guided in interpreting and using the information available or emerging in the global financial markets in the most efficient and effective manner. For example, when we hear about increases in interest rates, we should not just think the immediate obvious (such as that the cost of money has increased or that this will depress our wealth or asset values) but also ways to benefit from these rate increases. In addition, when a student in the medical or law fields hears about these rate increases they should also know how these are related to their respective disciplines. For example, doctors may think that the cost of drugs or prescriptions may increase following an interest-rate increase and thus need to advise patients about alternative drugs and/or economize on prescription costs. Lawyers also need to understand that rate increases may raise the cost of consulting, litigation, and legal expenses in general, and thus suggest ways of containing potential higher costs to their clients.

Let us examine what happens when tax rates are raised in an economy. Tax rates may also increase for capital gains and dividends. Apart from the obvious effects such as lower disposable incomes, lower savings, lower consumption and investments, you need to understand the other effects which may not be so apparent or you may recognize them but ignore them thinking that they do not apply to you. Let us identify some of them. First, if currently you do not (want to) hold a particular stock which pays dividends (for various reasons, which will be discussed in the chapters ahead) you may not care that, other individuals who hold dividend-paying stocks pay higher taxes on their (earned or unearned) dividends. What if now the company (again, for various reasons to be explained in later chapters) decides to eliminate dividends what would you do? Would you buy the stock now betting on higher capital gains (even if you pay higher taxes) or ignore the stock again? If the company uses debt instead of equity for its financing this may endanger the company (in terms of becoming riskier and leading to bankruptcy) and thus your potential dealings with it (as a consumer, supplier or just a general stakeholder). Furthermore, such distortions (from higher taxes on capital gains and dividends) may generate overinvestment and hence an inefficient allocation of financial and real resources in the economy. All these situations will negatively affect you and in various ways. Therefore, as you see you may not realize that you will be affected indirectly from tax rate raises and as a result this textbook will teach/show you how to think properly and protect yourself.

Therefore, this textbook is not like the other textbooks in financial markets, instruments and institutions and its structure is different. Specifically, the theories will not take center stage but they will be discussed in brief, either in boxes or within the text. What forms the main body is *the thinking process* and *economic/* financial *analyses of global events* that have to do with the financial markets and the *agents' behavior*. We will discuss how one should interpret an event and what its possible consequences and hence appropriate course(s) of action would be. Plenty of real events will be analyzed, abundant examples (real and hypothetical) will be discussed and lots of applications from related business disciplines (economics, management, marketing, accounting) as well as others such as the medical and law fields, besides finance, will frame each chapter. In addition, in many chapters there will be applications of most of the financial/economic principles discussed with real data and extant empirical evidence of them. Another novelty of this textbook is the presentation and interpretation of important econometric methodologies which can be used to test the theories and/or create predictions about economic and financial magnitudes. These are mainly discussed (with outputs and graphs) in the online Appendix. One more novelty of this textbook is the application (or relationships) of financial markets and instruments to the fields of management and marketing. You may think that these two are separate, isolated from finance disciplines, but reality is that they are very much linked. You will discover the many ways these areas are interconnected through the *boxes* that appear in all (but Chapter 11) chapters and explain how financial markets are linked to marketing and management concepts. Finally, several concept checks ("Test your understanding" boxes) with real and hypothetical scenarios and *sidebars* – for a more in-depth analysis of selected concepts – will be scattered throughout each chapter to check and ensure comprehension of the material.

The many innovations of the textbook are listed in bullet points below.

- The emphasis is on the individual investor who strives to comprehend and navigate through the complex and constantly innovating global financial markets.
- The writing of the material is made from the economics, practical and intuitive perspectives so the reader can understand the functions (roles) of the various

financial markets, their instruments and their institutions so as to equip the reader with the information to avoid the dangers of the financial markets and, at the same time, exploit them profitably.

- The first few chapters convey mundane insights from economics, financial management, and investments so the student can understand the significance of the material pertaining to the financial markets.
- Each chapter presents the material using economics, finance (corporate finance and investments), and econometrics to enable readers to truly understand the nature of the global financial markets and realize that they are an integral part of these markets.
- There are also a few appendices with information (and practice with real data) about standard econometric methodologies so the student can apply many concepts and be able to create forecasts (a useful feature absent from leading existing textbooks).
- In each chapter, a number of additional insights are included: a couple of *sidebars* with additional information on the relevant topics, two (or three, sometimes) "Test your understanding" boxes, one in the middle of the chapter and the other at the end, and *boxes* linking the material to marketing and management disciplines.
- Several chapters include examples with real data, presentations and discussions of real economic and financial situations (unlike other textbooks which discuss examples mostly relative to exchange rates), and examples of how to trade in selected financial markets.
- This textbook includes chapters that most traditional (and current) textbooks do not, such as the derivatives markets, the commodities market, financial technology and global risks.
- Finally, this textbook is flexible enough to be used for various courses such as Money and Capital Markets, Global Financial Markets and Institutions, Financial Markets, Instruments and Institutions (there are so many different titles for the same course) at both the undergraduate and Master's levels.

The plan of the book

This textbook has only fourteen chapters in the spirit of permitting instructors to finish the entire book within one semester. Each chapter is comprehensive in the sense that it contains theory, real events/scenarios and analyses, applications and selected empirical evidence. Below, a brief description of each chapter is given.

Chapter 1, titled "Essential economic concepts", is unique since no such chapters exist in current textbooks in financial markets. The chapter begins with some important assumptions and continues with a number of economic, financial and psychological fallacies that must be borne in mind when analyzing and attempting to exploit the tools of the financial markets.

Chapter 2, titled "Essential notions in finance", discusses important concepts from corporate finance (financial management) and investments. Additional sub-topics include risk management and how the disciplines of management, marketing, and accounting are connected to the global financial markets.

Chapter 3 is titled "Overview of the global financial environment". It discusses the various financial markets, instruments and intermediaries, presents the central banking system and monetary policy, and concludes with how a retail investor can exploit these financial markets using specific real-world examples.

Chapter 4, titled "The characteristics and globalization of the money market", provides a look inside the global money markets, elaborates on their economic functions, analyzes the global trends in the money markets and concludes with how investors use the money market.

Chapter 5, titled "Money market instruments and intermediaries", concludes the money market by presenting the instruments in the money market, the various financial intermediaries and ends with a look oh how individual investors exploit the money market instruments.

Chapter 6, titled "Investment companies and investment banks", highlights the capital market characteristics by analyzing the investment company and investment banking industries, traces the implications of their roles for a retail investor, continues with a discussion of the insurance companies and pension funds, and ends with some perspectives on the use of these financial institutions by an individual investor.

Chapter 7, titled "The equity market", presents the various equity investments, the markets characteristics, offers some guidance on how a novice investor can invest in the equity markets, continues with some equity valuation methods and concludes with some trends and developments in the global equity market.

Chapter 8, titled "Analyzing and exploiting the equity market", concludes the discussion on the equity market. It begins with some basic analyses of the equity market, proceeds with the interpretations of equity-market instruments, shows how a retail investor can exploit opportunities in the equity market using actual examples, continues with the presentation of basic small investor investment strategies and their underlying theories and ends with a demonstration of how one should build an efficient asset portfolio.

Chapter 9, titled "The fixed-income market", continues the discussion of the capital market. It begins with a discussion of what the fixed-income market is and its features, its functions and the types of securities that are traded in that market, continues with some valuation (of a bond) methods and concludes with an analysis of what your role (as a retail investor) is in this market.

Chapter 10, titled "How do investors exploit the global bond market", concludes the discussion of the fixed-income market. It starts with a presentation of how investors can profitably exploit the global bond market. It illustrates how an individual investor can build a bond investment portfolio and offers some specific examples of bond portfolios, shows how one can assess a bond portfolio and ends with a discussion on how retail investors can interpret and act upon various news.

Chapter 11 is titled "The derivatives and commodities markets". The chapter explains what these markets are, their characteristics and determinants, explains why and how investors trade in these markets, offers some real examples of hedging and speculating in these markets and concludes with a discussion of the roles of management and marketing in the derivatives and commodities markets.

Chapter 12, titled "The foreign exchange market", lists and explains the characteristics of the market, discusses how exchange rates are determined using established economic theories, provides several examples of foreign exchange transactions and strategies and ends with an illustration of how one can do foreign-exchange forecasting.

Chapter 13 is titled "Financial technology and financial markets". This chapter discusses at length the major innovations in financial technology (fintech), the categories of fintech products, the key relationships between fintech and financial markets, the linkages between fintech and financial services worldwide, the role of fintech in developing nations and women and ends with a list of additional risks in the fintech revolution.

Chapter 14, the last chapter in this textbook, is titled "Global risks affecting the financial markets". The chapter identifies a number of global risks and their implications on financial markets, economic and non-economic alike, classifies them into short-term and long-term (shocks) and discusses their implications for the investment instruments, and ends with some analysis of how retail investors can cope with these global risks.

Ancillary material

This textbook has three supplementary materials. A *Solutions Manual,* a set of fourteen (14) *Powerpoint slides* and an *Appendix* with the explanation and illustration of selected, yet important, econometric techniques. The econometrics Appendix and the answers to the "Test your understanding" questions are placed online (by the Publisher), at the textbook's website.

Acknowledgments

I would like to thank the Finance faculty of The Gabelli School of Business at Roger Williams University for its enthusiastic response when I announced to them that I was writing this textbook. I also wish to thank my students for their general comments on earlier drafts of selected chapters and the university for its technical and technological support.

My sincere appreciation to Editor Michelle Gallagher and Chloe Herbert at Taylor & Francis for their effective guidance throughout the process.

I would also like to thank my Finance and Economics colleagues at The American College of Greece for their valuable comments and suggestions on the main idea of the textbook.

Finally, I wish to acknowledge the support and advice I have received from my dear friend, Dr. Eleftheria Kostika, at The Bank of International Settlements, on earlier drafts of selected chapters.

Part I

Notions in economics, finance and financial markets

This part contains some very important concepts from economics and finance which are essential in understanding the material that follows in the other parts of the textbook. Although not all notions in economics and finance are covered in this part, some basic ones needed to carry out fundamental economic and financial analysis are presented. The rest are discussed in the relevant chapters. There are three chapters in Part I.

The first chapter deals with basic economic principles such as laws and fundamentals, some pitfalls (fallacies) in economic thinking and a few assumptions in conducting economic analysis. The second chapter involves financial concepts that a student typically encounters in courses such as investments, portfolio management and corporate finance, as well as finance-related disciplines such as management, marketing and accounting. Some of these concepts are treated mathematically, graphically and practicably in that chapter. Finally, Chapter 3 presents a very general overview of the global financial environment by presenting the major types and functions of the financial markets, the instruments, the players (financial intermediaries and other players), and in general why we need to study the global financial markets.

DOI: 10.4324/9781003677161-1

Chapter 1

Essential economic concepts

Introduction

This chapter relates to financial markets a number of assumptions, economic, financial as well as psychological fallacies, that render the thinking process and ultimately the decision made either incorrect or invalid. Several well-known and useful economic laws or principles are presented. Since humans make decisions (even when one argues that machines make decisions one needs to think who programs them) it is natural to think that they are being influenced by various environments (personal, economic, social, global etc.) and thus they are prone to making errors. Humans may blame others, ignore real conditions or even believe rumors or fads. In general, humans may be 'contaminated' by information and attempt to explain or extrapolate events based on observations by making assumptions that either may not hold or may be unrealistic under a similar future scenario.

First we discuss some very important economic assumptions in order to properly study economic events and phenomena and 'predict' the outcome from one or many changes in the variables. These basic, implicit economic assumptions are necessary when discussing economic/financial news and events and when involving entities, markets and individuals. Next, we will present several fallacies or biases that humans have suffered from, all of which lead to incomplete, incorrect or even misleading decisions. We categorize them into economic, financial and psychological aspects. Obviously, the list is not exhaustive but many important ones related to financial markets are presented below. We end the chapter with some important economic laws and principles which will guide us in understanding the functions and operation of the global financial markets and the place and behavior of agents within them.

DOI: 10.4324/9781003677161-2

1 Assumptions in economic analysis

A fundamental assumption in economics and finance, when discussing the impact of one magnitude on another (or others) is the *ceteris paribus* assumption. This Latin expression means 'other things being equal'. It is an important assumption to invoke implicitly when we want to isolate the impact of one variable on another without the interference of the other variables. The classic example offered in economics textbooks is about the laws of demand and supply. If the demand for a product increases (that is, its entire demand curve shifts to the right), then the price of the product increases, *ceteris paribus*. This further means that the supply curve remains unchanged. If it did change, the price change could be indeterminate and depend on the magnitude of the shifts in the supply curve. Another example from finance is about interest rates. If interest rates are raised, investment (and consumption and demand for debt) would go down, *ceteris paribus*. Again, this outcome is based on the implicit assumption that there is no expected increase in the supply of money or that companies do not have profitable projects (ones that yield a positive Net Present Value) or when companies simply (rationally) slow down their growth.

A related yet opposing notion is *mutatis mutandis*, which involves analysis of several variables and their effects on each other in unison rather than in isolation, as *ceteris paribus* implies. More plainly, *mutatis mutandis* means permitting other things to change accordingly. So, the difference between *ceteris paribus* and *mutatis mutandis* is that the former assumption isolates causation (or correlation) whereas the latter assumption assumes correlation. *Mutatis mutandis* are used extensively in economics (policymakers must account for other things changing in the economy when proposing/implementing policies), finance (project managers must include all relevant stakeholders when designing a business plan), law (clauses in contracts with several provisions) and other disciplines. See the nearby *sidebar* on *impact assessment* and the significance for both assumptions.

IMPACT ASSESSMENT

Does the restriction in economic reasoning and prediction caused by the *ceteris paribus* assumption render economics useless as a tool of policy analysis? No!

Impact assessment offers the methodology and specific techniques for identifying and evaluating the effects of policy decisions. The contributions of impact assessment can be the tools that enable economic analysts to evaluate all of the economic effects of a change in the system.

Mason, Thomas W. (1988). Economics and Impact Assessment: *ceteris paribus* or *mutatis mutandis*. *Impact Assessment* 6(3–4), 165–171.

There are many more assumptions in economics and finance that one can search online or find in standard textbooks. We will highlight a few more here. We begin with the concepts of scarcity and opportunity cost. Recall from your economics courses that scarcity refers to the limited availability (by default) of resources, in general. For example, on this earth we have limited quantities of raw materials, arable land, workers, and so on. Be attentive here! When demand for a product exceeds its available supply, we have excess demand not scarcity! The former derives from our want/need to have (buy) more of that product while the latter is there by nature. But since our wants, as humans, are insatiable (unlimited) we clash with the limited quantities of resources. The solution is to make a choice, by prioritizing our wants. This means that we must give up something in order to get something else, which refers to the opportunity cost (or trade-off). What is your opportunity cost of reading this textbook? What could you have been doing instead!

Economics is all about the efficient use of scarce resources. Efficiency has many definitions. In finance and financial markets, it means that in a financial asset's price all past and current information has been incorporated and thus its price is fair or the right one. To an economist, however, efficiency means simply the avoidance of waste of resources. As mentioned earlier, a related concept to scarcity is the appearance of opportunity costs. How society uses its resources affects the society itself (and other societies through foreign investments and trade) and thus we can relate it to the saying that 'There is no such thing as a free lunch'. Everything has a cost.

Other assumptions worthy of mention here are rationality, utility/profit maximization and responding to incentives. Neoclassical economists were working with the fundamental assumption that people act rationally or have rational preferences about outcomes that have some value. In other words, it is assumed that people possess well-defined references (transitive and time-consistent), are able to process all necessary information in order to maximize utility without cost and make the best choice, are not subject to psychological biases, and think about the long term.[1] Obviously, you understand that such an assumption is very strong and individuals almost never apply such a principle. But we consider this assumption as a good starting point for understanding human decision-making and it informs us about people's idiosyncratic and random behaviors.

The utility maximization assumption, whether applied to individuals (consumers) or firms, states that agents attempt to maximize their utility, if consumers, or profits, if firms. Recall from your microeconomics course that utility maximization states that consumers allocate their dollars so that the last dollar spent on each product purchased is equal to (or yields) the same amount of marginal utility. You can think of something similar for profit maximization. As an example of how consumers (or borrowers, here) use utility is to state that as utility increases from the purchase of a financial asset with debt (borrowed funds), the more willing the buyers are to borrow money to increase their utility. So, do we always maximize utility in our day-to-day actions? Economists use the term *bounded rationality* to describe that people have a limited capacity to anticipate, solve complex problems, or identify all options. As a result, they may not make the best choice and thus not maximize their utility. Since neither rational behavior not utility maximization is often encountered in real life, economists have advanced the notion of behavioral finance and economics, which concerns itself with the cognitive and other biases an individual has that affect his/her behavior. We will discuss this concept in Chapter 8.

Finally, responding to incentives is important to work with because incentives motivate a person to do or not do a particular thing by giving them a reward for their action. Rationality is assumed here as well. People compare the costs and benefits of a particular action and decide only if the marginal benefit exceeds the marginal cost. This assumption is also applicable to policymakers, public and private, as they should not ignore incentives, given that many policies change the costs and/or benefits that people face and, therefore, influence behavior.

1.1 Some real examples

One can find numerous applications of the above assumptions in financial and legal documents, thereby highlighting their importance in today's globalized and complex world (of finance). One example, about the *mutatis mutandis* assumption, can be found in an (online) document about the 2007/8 Global Financial Crisis. The following excerpt highlights this (words in brackets are the author's addition): "Setting aside the precise characteristics of the derivative involved [regarding the Long-Term Capital Management hedge fund], the same sequence of events can be observed, *mutatis mutandis*, for the energy derivatives proposed by Enron."[2] Another example is Europe's regulatory system and its applicability to other emerging markets and reads as follows: "*Mutatis mutandis*, this line of argument applies to other prominent emerging market economies. For the foreseeable future, then, the EU is thus likely to remain one of two polesin global financial regulation."[3]

Finally, one application of the term in law is this: 'Claims for repair or replacement are subject to a statute of limitations of 12 months calculated from the start of the statutory statute of limitations; the same shall apply *mutatis mutandis* in the case of rescission and reduction.'[4]

Schredelseker (2021) argued that we should not expect investors, analysts or market agents, in general, to behave in some expected pattern where all act alike. He provided examples such as that an incompetent analyst may systematically outperform a highly skilled one, or if the quality of financial reporting is improved, its recipients may not be better off, and so on. Shantha and Ram (2019) found that investors tend to give attention to news only when it affects their portfolio or investment strategy, and that investor inattention occurs when information is irrelevant to their portfolio and investment objective, and when it runs contrary to their beliefs or goals.

On the concept of utility and the manner in which agents attempt to maximize it, Barth, Kraft and Wiest (1977) examined total asset portfolio adjustments by individual commercial banks in response to changing relative interest rates. The authors assumed that a bank maximizes utility subject to its balance sheet constraint, with utility being dependent upon asset levels. Hence, this resembles a situation where bank borrowing from the Federal Reserve is determined by the minimization of disutility from borrowing and selling securities. When discussing investments and portfolio theory, we typically assume that the investor tries to maximize his utility – expected return or reward – subject to some constraints as well as risk. Hence, a representative utility function is expressed from which the formulae to maximize return, given risk, are derived and then applied. We will encounter this in Chapter 2.

What about firms and their utility maximization principles or objectives? What is the main objective of the firm, when we examine the firm in a financial context? Maximization of shareholder wealth. In economics, the objective is to maximize profits. Hart and Zingales (2017) suggested that company and asset managers should pursue policies consistent with the preferences of their investors. Friedman (1970) argued that corporate executives, as employees of the owners of a public company, have a responsibility to conduct the business in accordance with their owners' desires, which will generally be to make as much money as possible.

Financial and non-financial incentives can help shape and sustain a rapid performance improvement in all aspects of the economy including the financial markets and institutions. Financial incentives such as bonuses, higher salaries, merit pays or stipends can create a higher level of energy and excitement across an organization and boost the personal and team efforts of employees. Non-financial (on non-pecuniary) incentives can also work very well within an organization. For example, searching for new talent, retaining high performers or promoting high-qualified individuals must be a top priority for the organization's executives. In his 2018 speech at the US Chamber of Commerce, Washington DC, William C. Dudley, President and Chief Executive Officer of the Federal Reserve Bank of New York, emphasized the need to focus on the incentives facing banks and their employees. Misaligned incentives contributed greatly to the financial crisis and continue to affect bank conduct and behavior. Regulators and/or policymakers should do more to make the regulatory regime more efficient and transparent, he suggested.[5]

1.2 Some comparative statics

In this section, we will use graphical analysis to explain the behavior of one magnitude when one or more magnitudes change at the same time. We will apply the analysis to financial variables such as interest rates, quantity of money and the factors that affect their demand and supply. Let us begin with the determinants of the demand and the quantity demanded of assets. An *asset* is simply a real or a financial resource such as land, machinery, money, stocks, and bonds.

At this point, it is important to distinguish between a shift in the demand (curve) and a change in the quantity demanded. The former implies shift or change in the entire curve, either to the right or to the left, whereas the latter implies a movement along the given demand curve, either upwards or downwards. A rightward shift in the demand (or supply) curve means that there is an increase in the demand for or supply of the asset, while a leftward shift in these curves implies a decrease in the demand for or supply of the asset. Finally, note that the only factor that causes a movement along the demand or supply curve is the price of the asset, whereas anything else causes a shift in the demand or supply curve. Let us start showing these concepts.

1.2.1 Shifts in demand and supply curves

When investors need to select (purchase/hold) an asset or to buy one asset instead of another, the following factors are at play:

a. *Expected return*, the return expected over the next period on one asset relative to other assets
b. *Risk*, the degree of uncertainty associated with the return on one asset relative to other assets, and
c. *Liquidity*, the ability to convert an asset into cash relative to other assets
d. *Income (or wealth)*, the total resources owned by the investor

Now, let us begin tracing the impact of the change in each of these factors on the demand for the assets. In this context, we assume the entire market for the asset and hence its demand and supply. You should have guessed that these factors are not the price of the asset and thus any changes in each factor would cause the demand curve to shift (to the right or to the left). We begin with return expectations.

In general, expectations can be for many financial magnitudes such as interest rates, alternative (or substitute) assets, inflation and so on. Assume that the expected return on IBM's stock rises relative to expected returns on alternative stocks, *ceteris paribus* (or holding everything else constant), then it is more desirable to purchase the IBM stock, and the demand curve increases, that is, shifts to the right. This happens because the investor expects lower future interest rates which would mean that stock prices would be expected to rise more than originally anticipated, and the ensuing higher expected return today would raise the quantity demanded at each stock price and interest rate. This is shown in Figure 1.1, panel (a), where price is on the vertical axis and quantity on the horizontal axis. D_0 is the original demand curve and D_1 the new curve, which lies to the right of D_0.

Furthermore, changes in expected returns on other assets such as bonds can also shift the demand curve for stocks. If investors are becoming more optimistic about the bond market and begin expecting higher bond prices in the future then both expected capital gains and expected returns on bonds will rise. With the expected return on stocks held constant, the expected return on stocks today relative to bonds will fall, lowering the demand for stocks and shifting its demand curve to the left (as in panel (b) in Figure 1.1). Finally, a change in expected inflation is likely to alter expected returns on real and financial assets which, in turn, affect the demand for stocks. For example, if expected inflation goes from, say, 4% to 7%, this would lead to higher prices on real assets such as automobiles and houses in the future and hence higher nominal capital gains. The subsequent rise in the expected returns today on these real assets will lead to a fall in the expected return on stocks relative to the expected return on real assets today and thus cause the demand for stocks to fall.

Risk is also another factor that affects the demand for an asset. Risk is also known as *volatility* or the sharp ups and downs in the returns of a financial asset. So, if prices in the stock market become more volatile, the risk associated with stocks rises, and stocks become less attractive relative to other assets. Consequently,

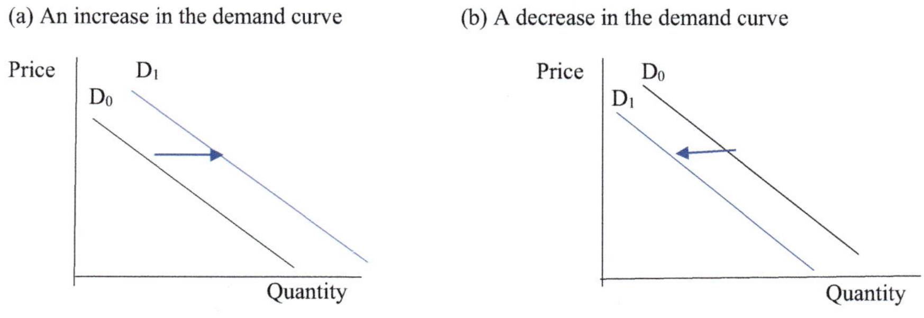

Figure 1.1 An increase and decrease in the demand curve

an increase in stocks' riskiness causes the demand for stocks to fall and the demand curve to shift to the left or decrease (as in panel (b) in Figure 1.1).

Now assume that more investors start trading in the stock market hence providing higher liquidity which would make it easier to sell stocks. An increase in liquidity would cause an increase in demand for stocks resulting in a rightward shift of the demand curve. Stated differently, higher liquidity causes the quantity of stocks demanded at each interest rate to rise. Finally, wealth shifts the demand for stocks to the right, if wealth in the economy and in individuals increases, that is, causing the quantity of stocks demanded at each stock price to increase. Note that wealth does not occur only when the economy prospers (or expands) but also because individuals might save more, pay less taxes or hit the lotto hence boosting their ability to buy more stocks.

The key point from the above analysis is that every time we wanted to predict the change in one asset, stocks here, we assumed that the other variables (see also p. 11) remained unchanged, the *ceteris paribus* assumption. This is the only way we can assess how a magnitude can move in response to movements in one of these factors. If all factors, from both sides, were allowed to change (the *mutatis mutandis* assumption) then we would not have been able to predict the new resting equilibrium because there would be several possible ones. We show that at the end of this section's discussion.

Now, let us discuss some factors that affect the supply curve for stocks to shift. These are the expected profitability of investment opportunities, expected inflation and government budget deficits. A rightward/leftward shift in the supply curve means that it has increased/decreased. Figure 1.2 shows these two shifts in two panels, (a) and (b).

Again, when we change one factor we assume that the others are held constant. When the economy is expanding, it not difficult to see that investment opportunities (for both investors and companies) become available and more profitable hence causing firms to want to invest more. To invest, in turn, firms can either use debt (that is, finance the projects via bond issuance) or equity (via new stock issuance). Therefore, in a rapidly growing economy, the supply of stocks (and bonds) increases causing their supply curves to move to the right.

Governments (either federal, state or local) also need to finance their expenditures and thus incur budget deficits (the gap between revenues and expenditures). For example, when the US Treasury incurs large deficits, it sells bonds causing the supply for bonds curve to shift to the right. Finally, expected inflation affects the

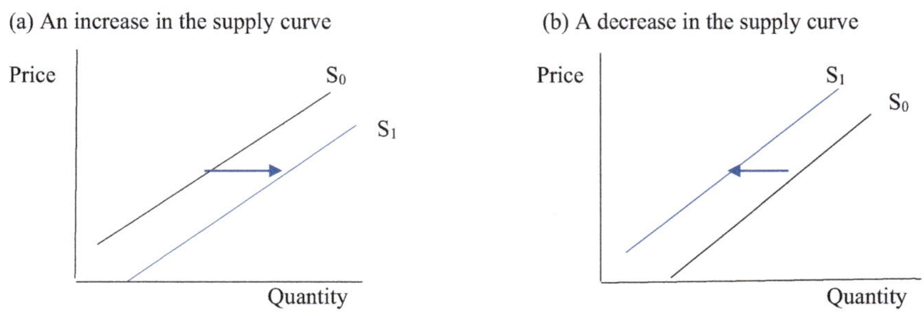

Figure 1.2 An increase and a decrease in the supply curve

supply of bonds. When expected inflation increases (for a given interest rate and stock price), the real cost of borrowing falls thus causing the quantity of stocks supplied to increase at any given stock price. Therefore, an increase in expected inflation causes the supply of stocks to increase and the supply curve to shift to the right.

Finally, what if more than one factor changes at the same time? What would be the new equilibrium point? Currently, you own 100 shares of IBM stock which you paid at $1000. The equilibrium is at point A, as shown in Figure 1.3. Suppose now that you experienced an increase in your income (or wealth) and at the same time the IBM company increased its new share offerings in the market. What would be the new equilibrium point? There could be three possible new equilibria and three different prices. In all cases, quantity rises.

a. If the demand curve shifts more than the supply curve, then the price would be higher.
b. If the demand curve shifts less than the supply curve, then the price would be lower.
c. If the demand curve shifts as much as the supply curve, then the price would be the same.

Each of these results are shown in Figure 1.4, in the three panels, (a), (b) and (c), respectively. The original equilibrium is shown in black whereas the new equilibrium is in blue. Hence, the *ceteris paribus* assumption is critical when we wish to predict the resulting equilibrium following changes in the factors.

In addition to the above analysis, it is possible that both curves could move in opposite directions to each other precisely so as to leave the quantity demanded

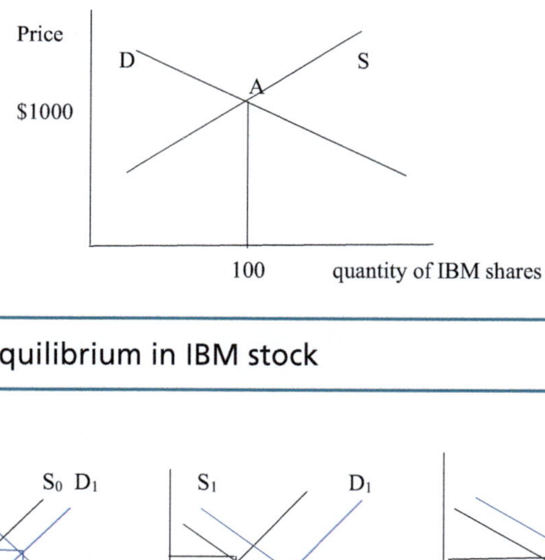

Figure 1.3 Equilibrium in IBM stock

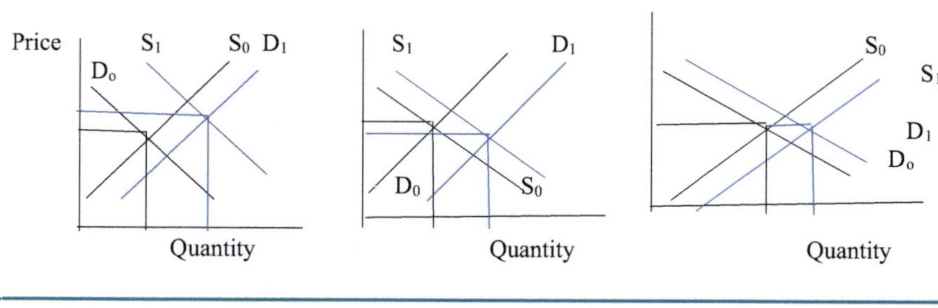

Figure 1.4 Multiple equilibria

the same and increase or decrease the price. Specifically, we may have an increase in the demand curve and a corresponding decrease in the supply curve. In this case, the price rises but the quantity remains the same. Similarly, we could have a decrease in demand and a corresponding increase in supply resulting in the same quantity but a lower price. There are additional possible shifts in each curve but these cases and their graphical illustrations are left for the reader.

1.2.2 Changes in quantity demanded and supplied

Now, let us examine what happens to the price and quantity demanded of a single financial asset when its price and other factors change. The factors that are relevant here are:

Price of the asset
Expected return
Risk
Interest rates
Liquidity

In these cases, we talk about a movement along a curve, either upward or downward, as in the two panels in Figure 1.5. An upward movement along a demand curve (D) signifies a decrease in the quantity demanded, whereas a downward movement along the same curve signifies an increase in the quantity demanded (see panel (a)). An upward movement along the supply curve (S) of an asset means an increase in the quantity supplied, whereas a downward movement along the same curve means a decrease in the quantity demanded.

So, if the price of a financial asset increases/decreases, people would tend to buy more/less of it, *ceteris paribus*. When a financial asset's expected return (a concept we wil analyze in a later chapter), relative to other assets, increases, investors would tend to buy more of it or increase the quantity demanded. Similarly, when the risk of a financial asset (by risk we mean the asset's standard deviation, a concept we will also encounter in later chapters) increases, relative to other assets, this causes the amount demanded of that asset to decrease and thus they hold less of it.

When interest rates rise, this would cause the value of the financial asset to decline and thus quantity demanded (or supplied) changes as a result of a change in the price of say, a bond (equivalently, a change in the interest rate). This would

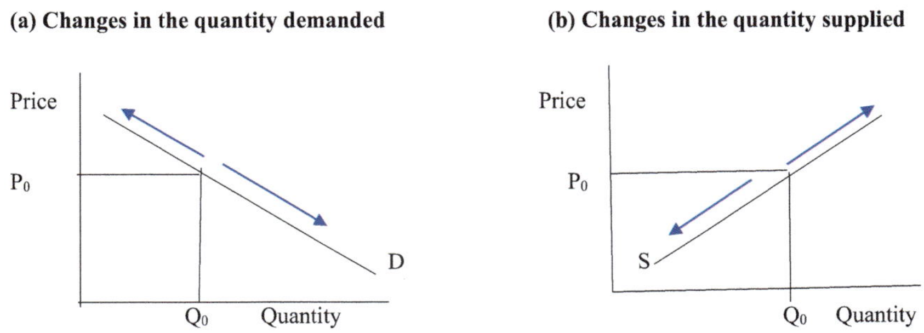

Figure 1.5 Changes in the quantity demanded of an asset

cause a movement along the demand (or supply) curve. Finally, when the liquidity of a particular asset declines, relative to other assets, then investors would demand less of it at the current price, which would entail an upward movement along the asset's demand curve.

So, to summarize we talk of a movement along the demand (or supply) curve, when quantity demanded (or supplied) changes as a result of a change in the price of the asset, whereas a shift in the demand (or supply) curve occurs when the quantity demanded (or supplied) changes at each given price of the asset in response to a change in some other factor besides the asset's price. We can also have the interest rate on the vertical axis instead of the price and conduct analogous analysis (but in this case we would talk about changes in the demand for and supply of money with quantity of (loanable)funds in the horizontal axis).

Test your understanding 1

1. If people saved less, what would the impact be on the demand for bonds?
2. If there is an increase in the riskiness of alternative assets, what would be the impact on the demand for bonds?
3. If a government ran budget surpluses, how would that impact the market for bonds?
4. If a stock's price decreased, how would that impact that stock's purchases?

Solutions appear at the textbook's website.

2 Economic fallacies

It is known that economic relationships are often complex and involve many different variables either related or unrelated among themselves. It is easy to get confused about the correct cause behind events or the impact of policies on the economy. Therefore, in order to reason (think) economically, in addition to making the assumptions we discussed earlier, it is important to avoid certain pitfalls. Although there are dozens of pitfalls in economic or every day thinking, here we will discuss only some of them next.

2.1 The fallacy of composition

The fallacy of composition is when one assumes that what holds true for one person also holds true for everyone. For example, if there is fire in a theater you and others are in, it would take only a couple of seconds for you to get out and be saved but not the same time for all the others. Or, when you assume that what is true for the part is also true for the whole. However, in economics, we see that the whole is not equal or the same as the sum of the parts. In both cases above, you are committing the fallacy of composition. Here's a classic example from economics of this fallacy. If one farmer has a bumper crop, his income would grow. However, if all farmers produce a record crop, farm incomes will fall.

What about instances of this fallacy encountered in financial markets? Consider this statement made by Sabine Lautenschläger, Member of the Executive Board of the ECB and Vice-Chair of the Supervisory Board of the ECB, in a speech she made for the Dutch Banking Day, Amsterdam, February 15, 2018: "if each bank is safe and sound, the banking system must be safe and sound as well. By now, we have learnt the hard way that this might indeed be a fallacy of composition".[6] Why is that? She elaborated on it with an example which goes as follows. Assume that a particular asset that all banks hold suddenly becomes riskier. If one bank acts alone, then it will simply sell that asset. However, if all banks attempt to do the same thing at the same time, they will drive down the asset's price. This, in turn, would amplify the initial shock, might affect other assets, and a full-blown crisis might result. So, the message is that even though each bank has acted prudently, their collective behavior has led to a crisis.

Another real example, taken from the headings of the financial press, involves banning short sales in the US in 2008 during the 2007 global financial crisis. The rationale of the US regulators at that crucial time was that banning short-selling of financial stocks would lessen the downward and steep drive in stock prices during the crisis. So, was the goal accomplished? A 2012 paper by the Federal Reserve Bank of New York stated that such a restriction did not actually work and that stocks subject to short-selling restrictions performed worse than stocks free of such restraints.[7]

THE FALLACY OF COMPOSITION

"The ... composition fallacy is committed when one infers that a whole has a certain property from the premiss that every constituent part of that whole possesses the property in question". Examples of the fallacy of composition (parts–whole type) are: (1) all the parts of this machine are light; therefore, this machine is light. (2) all the parts of this machine are small; therefore, this machine is small. Are these arguments fallacious or not? Yes, they are!

Rowe, William L. (1962). The Fallacy of Composition. *Mind*, New Series, 71(281), 87–92.

Finally, Hirakata, Kido and Thum (2020) in a paper on systemic risk and the role of Japanese regional banks found that fee- and commission-related activities of these banks exerted positive and significant effects on systemic risk by generating higher co-movement among banks despite reducing standalone bank risk through portfolio diversification. The marginal effect of an increase in common risk factors on systemic risk is larger when other banks are already highly exposed to common risk factors. They interpret the results as suggestive of the fallacy of composition, since an individual bank's behavior could be prudent (optimal) but collectively had an unfavorable systemic effect. See the nearby *sidebar* for more historical discussion on this fallacy.

2.2 The post hoc fallacy

The post hoc fallacy occurs when we assume that, because one event took place before another event, the first event caused the second event. Hence, it refers to the (wrong) deduction (inference) of causality.[8] Sometime you may hear that fallacy as causal fallacy. Here's a classic example of this fallacy. When we hear the rooster crow, we expect the sunrise. Hence, we tend to conclude that the rooster was responsible for the sunrise! Another example would be when one sees two cars colliding at an intersection, one may deduce that the first car was responsible because he saw this car running into the other. Finally, when we see the economy improving and observed that the government reduced taxes, we are inclined to infer that this was due to that particular governmental action. However, a lot must happen for the economy to kick-start again not just government policies.

James Tobin (1970) stressed the fallacy underlying the Latin phrase "*post hoc ergo propter hoc*". His point was that a causal relation, in his paper between money and income, must rely on something more than time precedence. Stravelakis (2014) wrote that the existing financial and economic literature explains the ensuing depression as a cause of the 2007/8 financial crisis which preceded it. He argues to the opposite, that the depression resulted from weak production growth reflecting weak profitability and showed that under this reasoning, financial crisis episodes are highly probable, serving as the trigger of depressions.

A related pitfall is to tend to oversimplify things in order to understand them better. Here's an example. If you water your flower regularly and you see that the flower blooms, you tend to associate watering with blooming, forgetting that the sunlight, soil and pesticides may also be responsible for the flower blooming.

Let us discuss a current event within the context of the post hoc fallacy. In September 2022, the US Federal Reserve Board will meet again and most analysts expect another interest-rate hike, given a number of them took place during the year. There are voices, however, advising the Fed to hold off from another rise in the key interest rate, the federal funds rate, because its hikes have slowed the economy (and the housing sector) and have brought inflation down. Although proponents praised the Fed for having accomplished these tasks, other observers say that the Fed should adopt a "wait-and-see" policy until a more reliable appraisal of the situation is available. Was the tight monetary policy responsible for such results in the US economy? Stiglitz (a Nobel laureate in Economics) and Baker, in an article on September 12, 2022, in the *ProjectSyndicate* online magazine, stated that such an argument commits the *post hoc ergo propter hoc* fallacy and confuses correlation with causation. They went on noting that most of the main factors behind today's inflation have little to do with reducing demand (due to the previous rate hikes). It was mostly supply-side constraints that drove inflation higher, and now supply-side factors are bringing inflation back down.[9]

2.3 The straw man fallacy

This fallacy describes making a rebuttal more convenient (or to discredit it) by distorting an opponent's argument or view. In other words, when we take someone's words out of context, we can quote them in a way that can make their position look weaker than it really is. This is common in financial press coming from commentators and politicians. Examples include statements about a major policy such as opposing the death penalty, whereby one may be accused of being soft on crime, campaign ads/attacks by politicians going after an opponent using unfair tactics, or in supporting the legalization of drugs one may be accused of accepting drugs.

Finally, an example out of financial markets is the advice that portfolio advisers or even robo-advisers give to their clients in preferring one investment strategy, say the passive, to another, the active. The problem is that they rationalize that because interest rates are very low, hence making very high equity valuations, that passive investment strategies do not pay off anymore and should switch to active investment management.

2.4 The hot hand and the gambler's fallacies

The first fallacy refers to the use of the past to extrapolate the future and the belief that a continuous streak of positive results will continue into the future. For example, if one believes that because an investment strategy was successful in the past it will continue to be so in the future, one commits the hot hand fallacy. By contrast, the gambler's fallacy refers to people's inclination (or cognitive bias) to overweight an outcome simply because it has not occurred yet. For example, you may believe that a recent (and sustained) increase in a particular stock is at odds with the past and thus be tempted to predict that it will fall in the future. You may have noticed that these two fallacies are the opposite of each other. So, the gambler's fallacy is to expect a negative correlation in a random process, whereas the hot hands fallacy is to believe that another positive/negative event is more likely after a run of positives/negatives. As another example, investors affected by the gambler's fallacy tend to sell their stocks when the prices are at their peak, and if affected by the hot hand fallacy, they buy stocks when prices are rising. Similarly, when investors follow those fund managers with good past performance, they commit themselves to these fallacies signifying their irrational choices.

In general, these fallacies fall within what the financial (and behavioral) economists call "heuristics" or rules of thumb. This refers to decision-making with a few representative points (small sample) because it is assumed that this sample accurately reflects/represents the population. This is another case of a cognitive bias. But, even statistics teaches us that the sample size is important and must be reckoned with to avoid these and many more biases, such as finding that there is high risk that observations will be due to chance, using the wrong confidence interval, not abiding by the normal distribution and more. However, studies using much larger samples can detect tiny or small associations but might not be important or relevant to the question at hand. Nelson and Kim (1993) found that predictive regressions suffer from two small sample biases: (1) the coefficient estimate is biased if the predictor is endogenous, and (2) asymptotic standards are biased downward. Both biases work in the direction inflating the t-ratios and affect standard inference in favor of predictability when none is present. The authors cautioned that these biases are large enough to affect inference in practice, and should be heeded when studying predictability.

The hot hand fallacy was first described and explained by Gilovich, Vallone, and Tversky (1985) in an article which focused on the origin and validity of the hot hand and streak shooting in basketball. The authors stated that people believe that a player's chance of hitting a shot is greater if the previous shot is a hit. Empirical evidence, however, has proved no positive correlation between the results of successive shots. Croson and Sundali (2005) found that casino gamblers betted more often after winning than after losing, which is incorrect (they committed the gambler's fallacy), but they did so because they thought that they had greater chances of winning than before. Williams wrote an article on the various fallacies in financial economics (in honor of James R. Thomson) where he gave an overview of finance, economics and their relationship and how they had evolved over time.[10]

In general, even though financial advisors are trained to avoid such fallacies and strive to give the best advice to their clients (emanating from what we call "fiduciary responsibility"), it is always best for the investor to use rational thinking and logic before investing. Perhaps, you could ask your advisor to provide you with a greater history of the performance of the assets you are interested in investing in so you gain a broader perspective of their history or plan to rebalance your portfolio less often (unless it is called for by major market shakeups).

3 Some well-known economic laws

Let us now present very briefly some important economic principles/laws that will be useful in studying the financial markets and understanding/shaping the behavior of an individual when confronted with financial problems. The idea is to be aware of the issues surrounding financial markets (and institutions) and act in the best possible manner (that is, rationally). We begin with the law of demand (which we presented extensively in Section 1).

3.1 The law of demand

Also known as the law of the downward-sloping demand curve, this postulates an inverse relationship between price and quantity demanded. That is why it is sloping downwards. Hence, as consumers demand more of a good, the lower its price will be, *ceteris paribus*. We had explained this earlier as a movement along the demand curve or the changes in the quantity demanded in response to changes in price. However, there is no "law of supply"! Such a law would require a particular shape of the supply curve, typically upward sloping. But supply curves tend to have various slopes as they can bend backwards (after a certain price or reward), be vertical and horizontal (as is the case for the demand curve), convex or even downward-sloping (we call these perverse curves).

An example of a backward-bending supply curve would be in the case of the worker's value (level) of the wage rate. The higher his wage rate, the more work they will supply, but beyond a certain point, they will substitute labor for leisure and thus decline working more hours. After all, there are 24 hours in a day and we need some sleep and other time for other things or even to enjoy leisure (higher level of welfare). In addition, this backward bend effect can be created when interest rates are high enough so that people start saving less. An example of supply curves being convex comes from research by Boehm and Pandalai-Nayar (2022) proving that industries' supply curves are flat at low levels of capacity utilization and steep at high levels of capacity utilization, hence convex. They showed that such a curvature can be economically large meaning that industries that produce close to their capacity respond to a positive demand shock by raising their prices by six times as much as industries that produce far below their capacity, while their production response is cut by half.

3.2 The law of diminishing marginal utility

This law states that as more and more of a good is consumed (at a given point in time, not over time), the extra (marginal) utility the person obtains diminishes. As you might have guessed, this observation led to the formulation of the law of downward-sloping demand. How is this principle related to finance, which comprises the interrelated areas of corporate finance, investments and financial markets? To give a simple answer to the question, we need to graph and explain a consumer's utility function (or curve), U. This is shown in Figure 1.6.

The utility curve is concave to the wealth axis because as wealth increases, the utility of it initially increases fast but beyond some point it decreases fast. Just look at the slope of each point on the curve, steeper at wealth levels of 10 and 100, and flatter at wealth levels of 200 and 250. Hence, we observe a diminishing marginal utility of wealth, which implies that the additional or extra satisfaction (reward) from each extra dollar of wealth is smaller than the pleasure from the previous dollar. As we will encounter in later chapters, an individual whose utility function is concave to the wealth axis is risk averse. A *risk-averse* individual is one who refuses to take a fair bet. What is a *fair bet* (or a risky situation)? An example of a fair bet is one in which you pay a dollar, if a flipped coin comes up tails, and receive a dollar if it comes up heads. Since we expect a 50–50 chance of either outcome occurring, the expected value of this bet is zero [= (0.5 x 1) + (0.5 x –1)]. We will explain in greater detail these concepts in later chapters.

A related law, which is more relevant to this textbook's material, is the *law of diminishing returns*. Instead of using the utility function, we can use the production function. A *production function* provides information about the relationship between inputs of production (labor, capital, etc.) and output. It shows the amount of inputs needed to produce a given level of output. The law of diminishing returns states that a firm will produce less and less extra output when it adds units of an input, *ceteris paribus* (here meaning holding other inputs fixed). Stated differently, the marginal product of each unit of input will decline as the amount of that input increases, *ceteris paribus*. An example of the application of this law is on the wealth or poverty of many nations. In many low-income countries such as Bangladesh, living standards are poor because so many workers are crowded in limited land and marginally add less and less to overall production. One can apply this principle to investments. For example, if investment in a particular area increases,

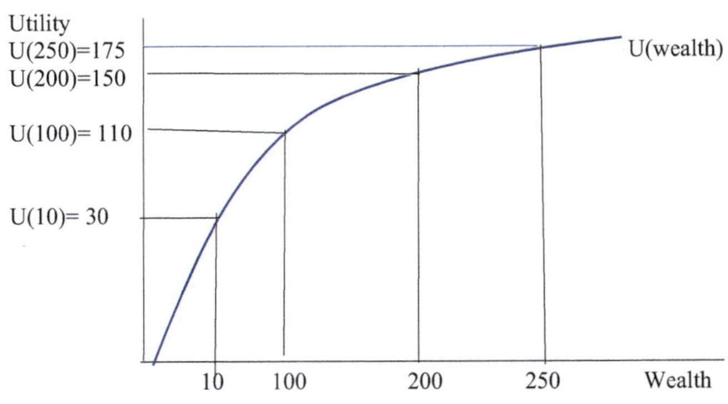

Figure 1.6 The utility curve

the profit rate initially will increase but after a certain point, it will start decreasing (and in fact it may become negative to the community/society), if other factors remain constant.

Here's a real application of the law of diminishing returns, one from the cryptocurrency market. Undoubtedly, you know that this digital (financial) asset has gained tremendous popularity since the late 2000s and more recently, it has become an investment category. As a result, many investors, retail (i.e., small) and institutional alike, have heavily invested in that currency, primarily the Bitcoin. However, according to *barchart.com* as early as recently (since 2021), the cryptocurrency market (cryptos, for short) has experienced declining returns.[11] Why was that? Well, at the end of 2011 the market capitalization (in billions USD) was 0.03, and by the end of 2013, it rose to 9.17. This implied a 304% increase! From then, it rose to 616.26 by the end of 2017, representing a rate of increase of 66%. Finally, from that date to the end of 2021, the market cap reached 2369, reflecting a change of 4-times (4x) higher. So, as you see the rate of increase initially was very high but then over time it declined reflecting the law of diminishing marginal returns.

3.3 The law of diminishing marginal product

This law is very much related to the previous law and refers to the decreasing extra production resulting from using one extra unit of a variable input, usually labor, *ceteris paribus* (or when land and other inputs are held constant). So, in this case we can speak of the diminishing marginal product of labor, since labor is the variable input. However, we do not want to commit the error that Thomas Malthus committed (in 1798) when he predicted starvation in a country if population was left unchecked and grew faster than food production because the quantity of land was fixed. He reasoned that the fixed amount of land would lead to a diminishing marginal product of labor, so output would not rise more than in proportion to the increase in land workers. What he did not take into account was technological progress (innovation) as well as better use of other inputs such as fertilizers, high-quality seeds which would enable the inputs of production to be more productive and efficient.

3.4 The law of one price

This law applies to international trade and states that if two countries produce an identical good, and transportation costs, free competition and trade restrictions are negligible, the price of the good should be the same everywhere. If the price was different, given these assumptions, then arbitrage opportunities would arise and a trader would buy the good in the low-price country and immediately sell it in another country at a higher price. He would then realize a riskless, net profit. *Arbitrage* refers to the notion that identical products should sell for the same price everywhere. This law has wide applicability in financial assets as well (we will see this again in Chapter 2).

Commodities is an example. Commodities are traded across various markets in the world using a variety of financial instruments such as futures and/or forwards. Since commodity prices are typically homogeneous across the markets, this law is responsible for that (and, according to some economists, the basis for much of financial economics). Lamont and Thaler (2003) offered evidence of several violations of this law, including closed-end country funds, dual class shares, and corporate spinoffs. They concluded that such deviations emanated from some limits on the extent to which rational arbitrageurs can intervene.

Another law stemming from the previous law, is the theory of *purchasing power parity* (PPP), which states that exchange rates between any two countries' currencies will adjust to reflect changes in the price levels of the two countries. This theory is basically an application of the law of one price to national price levels rather than to individual prices. The theory has two versions, the absolute (as defined on p. 19) and the relative (which implies that price level changes across countries should be the same after adjusting for the change in the exchange rate, and may still hold if relative price changes across countries are identical). For this, see Chowdhry, Roll and Xia (2005).

To understand the (absolute PPP) theory, assume that the euro price of European wine rises by 5% (to 1.05 euros) relative to the price of American wine (at $1). If this law holds, then the exchange rate must rise to 1.05 euros to the dollar, or a 5% appreciation of the dollar. Thus, we should expect that the European price level rises by 5% relative to the American price level and the dollar will rise in value (appreciate) by 5%. In conclusion, PPP suggests that if one country's price level rises relative to another's, its currency should depreciate (and the other country's currency should appreciate).

An alternative way to see this is to employ the *real exchange rate*, the rate at which domestic goods can be exchanged for foreign goods. In essence, the real exchange rate is the price of domestic goods relative to the price of foreign goods denominated in the domestic currency. Using the real exchange value (of 1) from the previous example, if a burger in Washington, DC, costs $3 and the same burger costs $4 in Athens, Greece, the real exchange rate is 0.75 (= 3/4). Hence, since this is lower than 1 this means that it is cheaper to buy the burger in Washington, DC than in Athens, Greece.

It is interesting to mention that this type of cross-country comparison formed the basis for the well-known "Big Mac" index (since 1986), which is published by the *Economist* magazine and calculates PPP exchange rates based on the McDonald's sandwich that sells in nearly identical form in many countries around the world.[12] Here's an actual quote from the webpage: "A Big Mac costs £3.69 in Britain and US$5.15 in the United States. The implied exchange rate is 0.72. The difference between this and the actual exchange rate, 0.83, suggests the British pound is 13.8% undervalued."

3.5 The law of comparative advantage

This related law states that a country has a comparative advantage in producing a good if the opportunity cost of producing that good in terms of other goods is lower in that country than it is in other countries. Put differently, a country should specialize in producing and exporting those commodities which it can produce at relatively lower cost (because it has an abundance of them) and that it should import those goods which it produces at relatively high cost. Note also that there is the related notion of absolute advantage. *Absolute advantage* implies that, say a nation X is able to produce two goods more efficiently than nation Y. Just because nation X holds absolute advantage in both goods, it does not necessarily imply that it can export these goods to nation Y. Hence, this (version of the) theory does not imply international trade. That is why trade occurs on the basis of comparative advantage and not on absolute advantage.

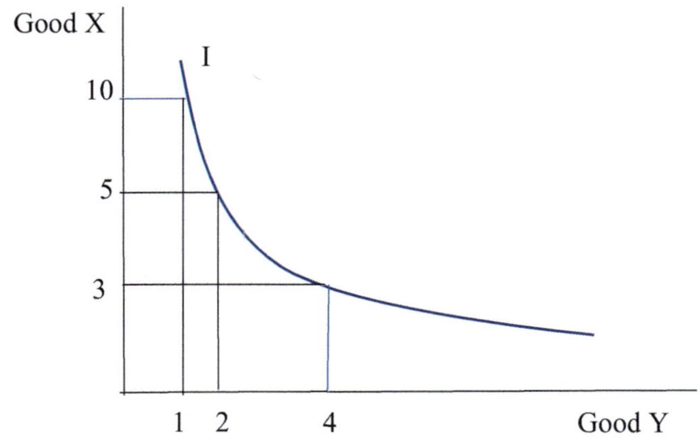

Figure 1.7 An indifference curve

3.6 The law of substitution

This law is based on the concept of a consumer's indifference curve. Recall from your microeconomics course that an *indifference curve* refers to a curve (or schedule) which shows various consumption bundles for which the consumer is indifferent because their utility is the same. Put differently, this is because all combinations of say, goods X and Y, are equally desirable. An indifference curve, *I*, is shown in Figure 1.7.

In this graph, we see that the goods X–Y bundles, 10–1, 5–2 and 3–4, are equally preferred by the consumer because their utility remains constant. This also refers to *I*'s slope and represents a movement along the curve. Note that the convexity of the indifference curve follows from the law of substitution, which says that as you get more of a good, its substitution terms (ratio), or the indifference curve's slope, diminishes. Hence, the slope of the indifference curve is the measure of the goods' relative marginal utilities (also known as the *marginal rate of substitution*). Note also that as you move downward and to the right along the curve, it becomes flatter. Finally, you should know that, in theory, a consumer has an infinite number of indifference curves, known as the indifference map, and the objective would be to move to the rightmost-lying one because this would entail a better (in terms of quantities of both goods) consumption bundle. Hence, a northwestern movement in the indifference map would mean higher utility. As we will see in Chapter 8, the indifference curves are related to the risk/return tradeoff, a central element in financial markets and instruments.

3.7 The diversification principle

This principle or law states that you should not put all your eggs in one basket. The idea is that you should spread or diversify your financial assets into various places (asset classes) so as to reduce overall risk and, hopefully, maximize (or enhance) your return. Keep in mind that the main goal of diversification is not to maximize one's portfolio returns, rather to limit the impact of volatility on the portfolio. This is a principle that we will be using extensively in this textbook. As a simple example, financial institutions such as banks or mutual funds in managing their assets, must attempt to lower risk by diversifying or investing in many different types of assets (government securities, corporate securities, etc.).

3.8 Say's law of markets

Proposed by the French economist Jean-Baptiste Say in 1803, this law states that overproduction cannot occur by default or that supply creates its own demand. Stated differently, because of flexible (non-sticky) wages and prices, any excess demand or supply is quickly absorbed and full employment is restored. That law held in classical economists' times because there were no macroeconomic stabilization mechanisms to restore imbalances in the real economy. This law holds only in *a barter economy*, in which commodities are exchanged for others without the use of money. According to a columnist in Forbes magazine, this law went through several tests and refutes, first by "Thomas Malthus in 1820, refuted again by John Maynard Keynes in 1936, un-refuted by Henry Hazlitt in 1959, and re-refuted by Paul Krugman as recently as February 10th of this year."[13]

3.9 Okun's law

Formulated by Arthur Okun, this law shows that when actual GDP declines 2% relative to the potential (or full-employment) GDP, the unemployment rate increases by about 1%. This occurs because as output falls, firms need fewer labor inputs and so there are no new hires and current workers are laid off. How does this law apply to global financial markets? A study by the *International Labour Organization* estimated the Okun's coefficients derived during the 2007/8 global financial crisis and found that they had displayed considerable variation across countries. This indicates the heterogeneity in the responsiveness of unemployment across countries. For example, in the United States, Canada, Spain and other economies, the coefficient increased sharply, whereas in countries where unemployment had remained subdued, such as Germany and the Netherlands, the coefficient had fallen dramatically.[14]

3.10 The Phillips curve

This curve shows the relationship between the unemployment rate and inflation. Specifically, when the economy is growing and output is high, unemployment falls, and thus prices and wages tend to rise more rapidly. This tradeoff is evident in the short run and does not hold in the long run. In the long run, the *Phillips curve* is vertical, not downward-sloping which suggests that in the long run there is a minimum unemployment rate that is consistent with steady inflation. The latter is referred to as the *nonaccelerating inflation rate of unemployment* (NAIRU). How does the economy move from the short run to the long run? The idea is that when price changes are unexpected, the short run Phillips curve tends to shift up or down. Following the initial surprise (or shock or unanticipated change) in inflation, market participants revise their expectations thus shifting the curve upwards (in the graphs, inflation is on the vertical axis and unemployment on the horizontal axis) where the level of unemployment remains the same (the NAIRU level).

3.11 The law of large numbers

Put forth by Swiss mathematician Jakob Bernoulli in 1713, this law suggests that when a large number of people are insured, the probability distribution of the losses will resemble the normal probability distribution. This inference is important and makes an insurance company's forecasts relatively accurate and allows them to price the policies so as to earn a profit. Using statistical terms, the law of large numbers (or the large numbers theorem) states that if we repeat the same experiment many times, the average of the results of the trials should be close to the expected value.

In corporate finance, this law posits that as a company grows, its previous growth rates become unsustainable. As a result, the company's growth rate declines as it continues to expand. If applied to traders and investments, then a larger number of trades, with a positive risk-reward profile, will be more effective than a smaller number of trades. Hence, a trader should expect to carry out hundreds of trades before its effectiveness can be assessed within a larger strategy. Related to the above, if one invests in companies with good investment and growth potentials, ignoring companies with fewer investment opportunities, then you should be looking for companies with smaller capitalizations as potential targets, according to this law.

We end this chapter with an interesting question: what do economics, marketing and management have in common? We are sure that you know the answer and so, in general terms, we can state that Economics provides the theoretical and macro foundations, Marketing focuses on customer-oriented value creation, and Management translates theory into organizational practice. In general, all three disciplines share a common foundation in resource optimization, strategic decision-making, understanding human and market behavior and innovating. Box 1.1 lists four (although there are more) common elements among the three disciplines.

Box 1.1

Some common elements among economics, management and marketing

DECISION-MAKING: All disciplines make decisions under various states of nature such as uncertainty, risk, scarcity

OBJECTIVES: Maximization of some magnitude such as profits, wealth (value), sales, revenues, client base, organizational goals, employee output

ANALYSES: All disciplines engage in some sort of empirical analyses such as economic, market, environmental, and more

PERFORMANCE EVALUATION: All disciplines evaluate the performance of their systems and resources. For example, Economics attempts to optimize value creation or utility, human rational behavior, resource allocation; Management attempts to optimize the organization's performance focusing on resource (human) efficiency, cost-effectiveness, and achieving objectives; Marketing strives to optimize promotional (advertising) campaigns to sell products, establish a brand and secure clientele(s).

Test your understanding 2

1. Why does the law of one price fail, in reality? Can you provide some reasons?
2. Why does marginal utility declines with higher consumption?
3. Can you associate the law of diminishing marginal returns to the law of gravity? Which law is most likely to occur?
4. How can the law of comparative advantage contribute to a nation's welfare? Which actions the government could take that might prevent it?

Solutions appear at the textbook's website.

Summary

- We have made a number of assumptions when reasoning economically such as *ceteris paribus*, *mutatis mutandis*, scarcity, opportunity cost, rationality, profit and utility maximization and responding to incentives.
- We conducted some comparative statics with the demand and supply analysis and concluded that unless the ceteris paribus assumption holds we may have different equilibrium prices, when both demand and supply curves shift, always with higher quantity and with the same quantity but higher or lower prices.
- Shifts in a financial asset's demand and supply curves occur when factors except the price change (in which case we have a change in quantity demanded) such as incomes or wealth, risk, expected return, and liquidity change.
- We discussed a number of economic fallacies such as the fallacy of composition, the post hoc fallacy, the straw man fallacy and the hot hand and the gambler's fallacies.
- We then listed and explained some well-known microeconomic laws (principles) including the law of demand, the laws of diminishing marginal returns/utility/product, the law of one price, the law of comparative advantage, the law of substitution, the diversification principle, and the law of large numbers and some macroeconomic principles such as Say's law of markets and Okun's law.

Questions and problems

1. Is it plausible or real to invoke the *ceteris paribus* assumption?
2. Explain what happened to the demand for financial assets during the following periods: the *dot.com* or technology boom of the later 1990s and the global financial crisis of 2007/8.
3. Explain the impact of a savings surplus and low (real) interest rates on the market for risky assets.
4. Explain which fallacy is implied in the following statements:
    a. Stock market advisors make predictions based on a few coincidental indicators which, in the past, just happened to precede a rise or fall in prices.
    b. In a free capitalist economic system, each member of society must act in a way that will maximize their own economic interests. As a result, society as a whole will be better off.

   c. Investors tend to purchase funds or financial assets that were successful in the past, believing that the manager will be successful in the future.
5. Assume that the yen price of Japanese cars rises 10% (to 110 yen) relative to the dollar price of American cars (at $1). If the law of one price holds, by how much should the exchange rate change? If you apply this law at the country price level, which other, related law do we get?
6. Suppose that we are offered a game of coin-flipping and each time the coin comes up heads, we win $100, but each time it comes up tails, we lose $100. What is the expected value of this gamble? What is it called? Who would not take such a gamble and why?
7. If you were offered two portfolios, one comprising of all car stocks, and another comprising car, tech and food stocks, which one would you prefer and why?
8. Consider this argument: if the banking system functions efficiently, then savings would be channeled to borrowers thus, readjusting individual demand, while keeping the total demand unchanged. Which law is implied here and does it agree with the statement?
9. Barberis et al. (1998) note that agents believe that random movements of an asset price have two regimes, reversing (or mean-reverting) and trending (following the same trend). Associate each regime with the appropriate fallacy.
10. Explain the fallacy in each case.
    a. The problem with environmentalists is that they lack common sense and believe that protecting the environment for the gray wolf in the Western Great Lakes and the State of Wyoming is more important than allowing people to make a living clearing land in the wolf's habitat.
    b. If a high tariff is put on a product such as steel, the producers in that industry are likely to profit. However, if high tariffs are put on all products, the welfare of the nation is likely to be reduced.
    c. Some people may advocate stopping eating meat and, if a celebrity endorses that, they may say that you will end up looking like him.
    d. In a bull market, stocks advance and so people continue to earn higher returns, whereas in a bear market people believe that low returns will continue.
    e. Have you ever heard the traffic authorities' advice "come early and leave late" so road congestion be reduced or spread evenly over the day? Do you agree with that or not?

Notes

1. *Transitivity* means that a rational individual prefers good X to good Y and also prefers good Y to good Z, then he will also prefer good X to good Z. *Time consistency* means that a rational person will find it optimal to apply the plans that he made for the future.
2. https://www.degruyterbrill.com/document/doi/10.1515/ael-2013–0030/html
3. https://www.tandfonline.com/doi/epdf/10.1080/13501763.2014.884312?needAccess=true
4. https://www.jenetric.com/fileadmin/user_upload/Downloads/General_Terms___Conditions_-_JENETRIC_INC.pdf
5. https://www.bis.org/review/r180420c.htm

6. https://www.ecb.europa.eu/press/key/date/2018/html/ecb.sp180215_2.en.html#:~:text=One%20of%20them%20is%20known,of%20its%20parts%20%E2%80%93%20or%20less
7. https://www.newyorkfed.org/research/current_issues/ci18-5.html
8. This is the short version of "post hoc, ergo propter hoc," a Latin phrase meaning "after this, therefore because of this."
9. https://www.project-syndicate.org/commentary/fed-should-pause-rate-hikes-inflation-dampening-by-joseph-e-stiglitz-and-dean-baker-2022–09
10. https://www.stat.rice.edu/~dobelman/Dinotech/eew/Fallacies.EEW.formatted..pdf
11. https://www.barchart.com/story/news/8382990/cryptocurrencies-and-the-law-of-diminishing-returns
12. https://www.economist.com/big-mac-index
13. https://www.forbes.com/sites/louiswoodhill/2013/03/13/sorry-paul-krugman-but-we-still-need-says-law/?sh=7c3c13be7040
14. https://www.ilo.org/employment/Whatwedo/Publications/working-papers/WCMS_170782/lang--en/index.htm

References

Barberis, N., A. Shleifer, and R. Vishny (1998). A Model of Investor Sentiment. *Journal of Financial Economics* 49, 307–343.

Barth, James, Arthur Kraft, and Philip Wiest (1977). A Utility Maximization Approach to Individual Bank Asset Selection. *Journal of Money, Credit and Banking* 9(2), 316–327.

Boehm, Christoph E., and Nitya Pandalai-Nayar (2022). Convex Supply Curves. *American Economic Review* 112(12), 3941–3969.Chowdhry, Bhagwan, Richard Roll, and Yihong Xia (2005). Extracting Inflation from Stock Returns to Test Purchasing Power Parity. *The American Economic Review* 95(1), 255–276.

Croson, Rachel, and James Sundali (2005). The Gambler's Fallacy and the Hot Hand: Empirical Data from Casinos. *The Journal of Risk and Uncertainty* 30(3), 195–209.

Friedman, Milton (1970). The Social Responsibility of Business Is to Increase Its Profits. *New York Times Magazine*. September 13.

Gilovich, Thomas, Robert Vallone, and Amos Tversky (1985). The Hot Hand in Basketball: On the Misperception of Random Sequences. *Cognitive Psychology* 17(3), 295–314.

Hart, Oliver, and Luigi Zingales (2017). Companies Should Maximize Shareholder Welfare Not Market Value. *Journal of Law, Finance, and Accounting* 2, 247–274.

Hirakata, Naohisa, Yosuke Kido, and Jie Liang Thum (2020). Systemic Risk and the Fallacy of Composition: Empirical Evidence from Japanese Regional Banks. *International Journal of Central Banking* 16(4), 293–325.

Lamont, Owen A., and Richard H. Thaler. (2003). Anomalies: The Law of One Price in Financial Markets. *Journal of Economic Perspectives* 17(4), 191–202.

Nelson, Charles R. and Myung J. Kim (1993). Predictable Stock Returns: The Role of Small Sample Bias. *The Journal of Finance* 48(2), 641–661.

Schredelseker, Klaus (2021). There Is No Unique Rational Decision Strategy in Financial Markets. *The Journal of Portfolio Management* 48 (3), 153–163.

Shantha, Gowri B. and Vedantam, Seetha Ram (2019). Influence of news on rational decision making by financial market investors. *Investment Management and Financial Innovations* 16(3), 142–156.

Stravelakis, Nikos (2014). Financial Crisis and Economic Depression: 'Post Hoc Ego Propter Hoc'? Implications for Financial Asset Valuation and Financial Regulation. *MPRA* Paper No. 55944, 1–35.

Tobin, James (1970). Money and Income: Post Hoc Ergo Propter Hoc? *The Quarterly Journal of Economics* 84, 301–317.

Chapter 2

Essential notions in finance

1 Essentials of corporate finance

What is corporate finance? As the term implies, *corporate finance* is the way funds are raised and used best, that is, to maximize profits or shareholder wealth. Who runs a business (or a corporation)? The chief executive officer (CEO) with the assistance of the chief financial officer (CFO). The CEO is the top management of a business and in charge of the company and makes crucial decisions such as planning, organizing, staffing, controlling and so on, in an effort to run the company effectively and profitably. What is the specific role of the financial manager? In general, the *financial manager* performs two major functions within an organization: financing and investing. The financing decision is commonly called the *capital structure* decision, which involves a mixture of equity and debt, whereas the investment decision is known as *capital budgeting*, which refers to a listing of the major projects eligible for investment. Thus, the relevant questions are: (1) what should the corporation invest in, and (2) how should it pay for those investments. The first question refers to the spending of money, whereas the second question involves raising it. Are you also a financial manager in your daily life? Yes! This is so because you attempt to use your scarce resources (money and time, for example) efficiently to buy the goods and services that offer you the maximum satisfaction. So, relating this to the two questions above, where you should spend your money and how you are able to pay for the goods and services, are the two activities that both you and a financial manager engage in.

But, what is the financial manager's (and, by extension, financial management's) objective? To *maximize shareholder wealth* (equity) or, put differently, maximize the current value (per share) of the stock outstanding. This goal makes sense if the firm operates in an efficient financial market (see Chapter 3), where savings are effectively channeled to their best uses. If these (and a few other) conditions are met then the financial manager can strive to achieve their objective and thus increase

DOI: 10.4324/9781003677161-3

their company's market value. To reach this objective, the company needs to invest in real assets (such as plant and equipment) that produce more value than their cost. In what comes next, we will understand how one can value assets and how capital investments are made. We begin with the present value notion and its variant(s).

1.1 Present and future values

Equipped with the above notions, how do financial managers create value? Simply, by creating more cash flow(s) than they use. *Cash flow* is the amount of cash that is generated or spent by the company during a given time period. For example, when the firm pays dividends to its shareholders or makes coupon (interest) payments to its bondholders, these are types of cash flow. The idea now is to ensure that the cash flows paid to stockholders and bondholders exceeds the cash flows they put into the firm. So, cash flows play a central role in the notions of present and futures values, as we will see next.

What is the *time value of money*? It is the notion that a dollar today is worth more than a dollar tomorrow. For example, if you invest $100 in a bank account that pays interest of 5% a year, how much would you have at the end of the year? You earn interest of $5 and thus the value of your investment grows to $105 (=$100 + $100 x 0.05). If you left the money (untouched) in the bank for another year, *ceteris paribus*, how much would you have then? First, understand that the starting amount is $105 and second, that you will earn interest on it, as follows: $105 + ($105 x 0.05) = $110.25. Recognize also that the amount of $100 is the current or present value (PV) and that the ensuing amounts, $105 and $110.25, are the future values.[1] Now, let us formalize these calculations and derive the first important equation (formula), the *future value* (FV):

$$FV = PV\ (1 + r)^t \qquad (1)$$

where FV and PV are as defined earlier, r is the interest rate or the *compound rate* and t the time period, years in this case. You can verify that if you invest the original amount of $100 for two years instead, the result will be exactly the same as if we did the work year by year:

$$\text{FV} = \$100\ (1 + 0.05)^2 = \$100 \times (1.05)^2 = \$100 \times 1.1025 = \$110.25$$

Now, let us reverse the question and ask how much you need to invest today in order to earn $110.25 at the end of the second year. Put differently, what is the present value (PV) of the $110.25 payoff? Even though you know the answer to this question, let us prove it formally. You simply can reverse question (1) and solve for PV, as follows:

$$PV = FV\ /\ (1 + r)^t \qquad (2)$$

and so, you can divide the $110.25 by $(1 + 0.05)^2 = 1.1025$ and obtain $100. In the first case, you multiplied the payment by the $(1 + r)^t$ factor, the *compound factor*, whereas in the second case, you divided the future payment by the reverse of that factor, $1/(1+r)^2$, the *discount factor*, to find the present value of $100 received in year t.

The next important question to ask is how would a financial manager decide whether an investment opportunity is worth undertaking or not. Suppose you open up your own business, an office, out of which you render your consulting services. You estimate that the total cost of buying the land and constructing the office is \$100,000, but you read in the financial news that there is shortage of office space a year from now. You predict that you will be able to earn as much as \$150,000 next year. This is your future value or expected cash flow. What should you do? Go ahead with the project or not?

In general, it is rational to assume that you should go ahead with the project if the present value of the cash inflows exceeds the initial investment of \$100,000. You look up the financial pages and see that, currently, the interest rate (r) on safe government securities, the US Treasury notes, is 3% per year. This is your *opportunity costs of capital* or the rate you give up earning by engaging in the project instead. So, the PV of your office is:

$$PV = \$150{,}000 / (1 + 0.03) = \$145{,}631$$

The rate of return, r, is also called the *discount rate* or the *hurdle rate*, in addition to the opportunity cost of capital. But, what does this value mean? It means that if you decided not to run your business but sell your office today, you would value it at \$145,631 and that would be the price the market would bear (or, the price that *you* would be willing to pay someone else for it if you had not purchased it yourself).

Now, the office building is worth \$145,631 today, but that does not mean you are that much richer. You invested \$100,000, so the net present value (NPV) is \$45,631. This refers to the notion of net present value (NPV), which equals the PV *minus* the initial cash outflow (investment):

$$NPV = PV - \text{initial investment} = \$145{,}615 - \$100{,}000 = \$45{,}631$$

As you see, your office project is worth more than its cost, that is, it adds value and increases your wealth. To formalize the above, we have:

$$NPV = CF_1 / (1 + r) - CF_0 \qquad (3)$$

NPV vs. OTHER RULES

The NPV criterion is the optimal capital budgeting rule in efficient markets. Yet, in practice managers employ other simpler rules. Gitman and Forrester (1977) found that less than 10% of 103 large firms use NPV as their primary technique, while over 50% use the IRR rule, which avoids a cost of capital calculation. Graham and Harvey (2001) survey of CFOs also reported that the IRR rule is more widely used than NPV, and over 50% of CFOs use the payback period rule.

Gitman, L. and J. Forrester (1977). A Survey of Capital Budgeting Techniques Used by Major US Firms. *Financial Management* 6(3), 66–71.

Graham, J.R. and Harvey, C.R. (2001). The Theory and Practice of Corporate Finance: Evidence from the Field. *Journal of Financial Economics* 60, 187–243.

where CF_0 is the initial cash outflow (at time 0) and CF_1 is the expected cash flow(s).[2]

It is important to note that the expected cash flows are typically uncertain (they are forecasted) and thus, NPV calculations may be misleading. Hence, a related important principle is to recognize that a dollar in the future (or a risky dollar) is worth less than a safe dollar (today). The typical investor is *risk averse*, which means that he must be compensated extra in order to take more risk. Stated differently, the extra reward, compensation or return the investor would seek must be commensurate with the risk of the investment (or financial asset). This is another definition of a risk-averse investor that we learned in Chapter 1 and it is more convenient to work with when we discuss the concepts of risk and expected return in subsection 2.2.

Returning to the previous example, if you believe that this investment project of yours is risky, then you should use a different discount rate, one that is more relevant to a risky investment or financial asset, say the stock market. If the stock market (or investment in a portfolio of stocks) expects to yield 12% return, the new opportunity cost of capital, then our PV and NPV values change dramatically:

PV = \$150,000 / (1 + 0.12) = \$133, 928 and
NPV = \$133,928 – \$100,000 = \$33,928

Although the project still makes a net contribution to value, the increase in your wealth has declined than in the case where the projected cash flows from the project were risk-free.

If we generalize these concepts, we arrive at the discounting of future cash flows or the process known as discounted cash flow (DCF) analysis. The relevant formulae, for PV and NPV, can then be expressed as follows:

$$PV = \Sigma^{T}_{t=1} \{CF_t / (1+r)^t\} \quad (4)$$
$$NPV = CF_0 + \Sigma^{T}_{t=1} \{CF_t / (1+r)^t\} \quad (5)$$

where Σ is the summation operator, T is the (terminal) time frame and the rest as defined above. Recall that the CF_0 must be subtracted from the expected discounted cash flows and that the end NPV value may be negative. This would mean that the project should not be undertaken. As a rule, you undertake projects whose NPV = > 0 but not when NPV < 0.[3] The nearby *sidebar* discusses that use of this rule versus other, simpler project evaluation rules.

1.2 Capital budgeting

From the preceding discussion, one may infer that the decision to accept or reject a project is straightforward since one only needs to identify the (expected) cash flows, choose the discount rates and produce net present value. In reality, a number of problems may occur and generate misleading NPVs. For example, how does one identify good, value-enhancing projects for consideration? Further, when a manager is confronted with investment proposals, they must be able to evaluate the cash flow forecasts and infer possible slack or problems with them. Hence, managers typically (re)evaluate assumptions in investment projects, conduct break-even analyses, sensitivity analyses and other methods to determine possible problems early enough. We will explain the above methods very briefly below.

So, how can a manager 'trust' the NPV approach? One way is to conduct *sensitivity analysis* or 'what-if analysis', which explores how sensitive a particular NPV result is to changes in the underlying assumptions for revenues and costs. What are some of the assumptions/elements that underscore revenues? The price of the product and the company's market share (and/or the size of the relevant market). The costs are broken down into fixed – those that do not change with the level of output – and variable – those that do vary with output – costs. Sensitivity analysis uses changes or forecasts in all these inputs (and one at a time) and creates possible scenarios or outcomes. Such analysis reveals omissions in the magnitudes, erroneous forecasts (of optimistic and pessimistic scenarios) and the possible use of more information (so the whole analysis can be repeated). Sensitivity analysis has a few drawbacks, however. For example, it may produce ambiguous results when one does not interpret correctly what an optimistic or pessimistic scenario means. Also, it may instill contentment in the manager, making them incorrectly believe that there is no possible loss of money from the project and so on.

Continuing with the inputs to the sensitivity analysis, a related check is break-even analysis. *Break-even analysis*, as the term implies, involves finding that crucial quantity (or units) that would result in zero profits – break even – or when total revenues equal total costs (fixed and variable). So, the goal is to produce beyond that crucial quantity in order to start making profits. The formula is as follows:

Break even quantity = Fixed costs / (Sales price per unit – Variable cost per unit) (6)

From the formula, one can use the magnitudes in parentheses (Sales price per unit *minus* variable cost per unit) refer to the *contribution margin* per unit. For example, if a TV's selling price is $200 and its variable cost is $50 to produce that TV, $150 is the contribution margin per unit and contributes to offsetting the fixed costs. The contribution margin can then be expressed as:

Contribution margin = (sale price per unit – variable cost per unit) / sale price per unit (7)

Why is break-even analysis useful to an investor, existing and potential? First, existing investors need to know that their business is profitable and keeps rewarding them. Second, potential investors may not only want to know their investment's expected rate of return to expect. Third, potential investors will also want to know when that return may be realized because some companies may take years to turn positive profit or may lose money initially before breaking even. However, caution is advised on watching production costs, capital and (break-even) sales (which may be unrealistic or out of reach, given costs).

While sensitivity analysis (or, its variant, scenario analysis) considers the effect of a small number of probable combinations of variables (the "what if" question posed earlier), the *Monte Carlo analysis or simulation* considers the entire distribution of a project's outcomes.[4]

Since the details of this approach are beyond the scope of this textbook (you can simply look this up in any standard corporate finance textbook), suffice to say that we can compute a project's NPV by using the distribution of the cash flows for each future year and then discounting these expected cash flows at an appropriate (discount) rate. The three steps, before the calculation of the NPV, are shown below:

1.3 Financial statements

The financial manager must have a good working knowledge of the firm's financial statements to guide him/her to an effective decision. The three essential financial statements – balance sheet, income statement, cash flow statement – prepared by the firm's accountant, help the manager understand the firm's overall performance and some key financial ratios may alert them to potential current and future problems. Below, we will discuss each statement very briefly by highlighting their significance to not just the financial manager but also to an investor.

The *Balance Sheet* is a statement that shows the overall picture of the company at a particular point of time (typically on the last day of the year). In other words, it provides a snapshot of the company's assets at the end of a year as well as the sources of the funds that were used to buy those assets. The main components of a typical balance sheet are assets, liabilities and shareholders' equity. Table 2.1 depicts such a statement (of a hypothetical company).

The assets are divided into two categories, *current assets* (such as cash and marketable securities and inventories), *fixed assets* (such as plant and equipment) and *long-term assets* (investments such as vehicles). Next comes the liabilities side, or the money owed by the company. Those liabilities that need to be paid off in the near future are listed first, known as *current liabilities*. These include debts that the company must pay in the short-run to its suppliers as well as accounts payable. Note that the difference between the current assets and current liabilities is known as the *net working capital* and roughly reflects the amount of cash the company (potentially) has available.

Finally, the section labeled "Shareholders' Equity" shows the sources of the cash that was used to acquire the net working capital and fixed assets such as the issue of bonds that will not be repaid for many years. After all these long-term liabilities have been paid off, the remaining assets belong to the common stockholders, the equity. The company's *equity* is simply the total value of the net working capital and fixed assets *minus* the long-term liabilities. Part of this equity has come from the sale of shares to investors and/or from earnings that the company has retained and (re)invested on behalf of the shareholders. Note that the amounts in each side, total assets and total liabilities *plus* equity (or net worth) must be the same.

The *Income statement* shows the company's financial situation over the previous entire year. The income statement includes magnitudes such as net sales,

Table 2.1 Balance sheet of ABC company, as of 12/31/2024

Assets	
Current assets	
Cash and marketable securities	1,500
Accounts receivable	200
Inventories	5,000
Other	350
Total current assets	7,050
Fixed assets	
Property, plant, and equipment	17,000
Less accumulated depreciation	5,000
Net fixed assets	10,000
Long-term investments	300
Other long-term assets	400
Total assets	**17,700**
Liabilities and Shareholders' Equity	
Current liabilities	
Debt due	1,000
Accounts payable	3,500
Other current liabilities	2,000
Total current liabilities	6,500
Long-term debt	4,500
Deferred income taxes	450
Other long-term liabilities	900
Total liabilities	5,850
Common stock and other paid-in capital	700
Retained earnings and capital surplus	9,500
Total shareholders' equity	10,200
Total liabilities and shareholders' equity	**17,700**

Note: hypothetical company and data

depreciation, cost of goods sold, interest and net incomes. An important magnitude for all stakeholders of the company is the *Earnings before interest and taxes* (EBIT), the income from operations, defined as the difference between total revenues and costs and depreciation. It is an indication of how profitable the company is (or has been over the year). A related and equally useful financial metric is *EBITDA* (because it adds back depreciation, D and Amortization, A). Financial analysts prefer EBITDA because it better reflects the before-tax operating cash flow. Finally, another very important magnitude is *net income*, defined as total revenue *minus* total expenses. Net income reflects differences in the company's capital structure and taxes as well as operating income and its also known as the "bottom line". Shareholders and potential investors look closely at it because dividend payout and retained earnings are closely linked to net income.

The *cash flow statement* reflects cash flows from operating, investing and financing activities, that is, sources of cash (as positive numbers) and uses of cash (as negative numbers) over the year. It reconciles the items reported in the balance sheet and income statement. Investors feel that this statement is the most transparent of the three financial statements and so they tend to use it more often to infer the true performance of a company.

1.4 Financial ratio analysis

How can you use a company's financial statements? Simply, to assess its financial performance and current standing. What do you need to do? Compute a number of financial ratios that reflect the five aspects of the company's business: liquidity, profitability, debt, asset management, and market value. *Liquidity ratios* are intended to provide information on the firm's liquidity or short-term solvency. The idea is to infer the firm's ability to pay its bills over the short run without undue squeezes. Essentially, one looks at the firm's current assets and current liabilities by forming ratios such as the *current ratio* (current assets over current liabilities), *quick ratio* (subtracting inventories from current assets and dividing by current liabilities) and *cash ratio* (cash over current liabilities).

Debt ratios focus on the long-term solvency condition of the company to ensure that the firm is able to meet its long-term obligations or its *financial leverage*. Ratios include the *debt ratio* (total assets over total equity), *debt-to-equity ratio* (total debt over total equity), *times interest earned ratio* (EBIT over interest), and *cash coverage ratio* (EBITDA over interest). *Profitability ratios* are intended to measure the efficiency with which the firm uses its assets and manages its operations. A firm's profitability can be inferred by ratios such as *profit margin* (net income over sales), *return on assets* (net income over total assets), and *return on equity* (net income over equity). *Asset management ratios* look at how efficiently the company uses its assets to generate sales (sometimes, these ratios are called asset management or *utilization ratios*). Some ratios are the *inventory turnover ratio* (cost of goods sold over inventory), *receivables turnover ratio* (sales over accounts receivable), and *total asset turnover ratio* (sales over total assets). The final set of ratios is the market value measures such as *earnings per share* (EPS), defined as net income over the number of shares outstanding, the *price/earnings multiple*, PE, or the price per share divided by EPS, the *market-to-book ratio* (market value per share over the book value per share) and the *enterprise value* (EV) multiple, defined as the enterprise value over EBITDA.

In sum, apart from enabling an investor, existing or potential, to assess the current financial situation of a company, *ratio analysis* also permits analysts and managers to spot a trend, use it for forecasting, and for critical decision-making. Furthermore, ratio analysis can be employed to compare the strengths and weaknesses of each firm and help analyze whether the company has progressed, as well as compare a firm against the industry in which it operates.

1.5 The weighted average cost of capital

In subsection 1.1, we mentioned and defined the company's cost of capital as the right discount rate for investments that are much related to the company's overall business (and risk). In reality, however, a company's cost of capital is estimated as a weighted-average of the average rate of return demanded by investors in the company's use of equity and debt. From this discussion, it follows that a company's cost of capital can be defined as the expected return on a portfolio of all the company's existing securities, that is, debt and equity. Therefore, the cost of capital is estimated as a blend of the cost of debt (which is, actually, the interest rate that the company pays on borrowed funds) and the cost of equity (or the expected rate of return demanded by investors in the firm's common stock).

So, we can easily define the weighted average cost of capital (WACC) as follows:

$$WACC = w_D\, r_D + w_E\, r_E = (D/V)\, r_D + (E/V)\, r_E \tag{8}$$

where w_D is the weight of debt (D) relative to the sum of debt and equity or total firm value, V (D/V), w_E the weight of equity relative to V (E/V), and r_D and r_E are the cost of debt and equity, respectively. If the company additionally issues preferred stock, P, then equation (8) must be augmented to reflect that third source of capital, as follows:

$$WACC = w_D\, r_D + w_E\, r_E + w_P\, r_P = (D/V)\, r_D + (E/V)\, r_E + (P/V)\, r_P \tag{9}$$

where now V is the sum of Debt, Equity and Preferred stock.

It is often convenient to use the after-tax WACC, since interest on debt is text deductible, as follows:

$$\textit{After-tax } WACC = (1 - t)\, r_D\, w_D + w_E\, r_E \tag{10}$$

To summarize, the WACC is the minimum return a company needs to earn in order to satisfy its investors (bondholders, stockholders and preferred stockholders). One major application of WACC is its use as the discount rate for calculating the value of a company. Another is its use in evaluating investment opportunities, as it is considered to represent the firm's opportunity cost, or the hurdle rate. More generally, WACC can be employed to assess mergers and acquisitions and the acceptance or not of projects, via the *internal rate of return* (IRR). The IRR is used to determine the return a company can expect from a project's future cash flows. So, if a company's IRR exceeds its WACC, then the company should accept the project.

1.6 Dividend decisions

The third important function (role) of the financial manager is to decide if (and when) to return cash to the company's shareholders by paying a dividend or by repurchasing shares. This is a challenging task and there is controversy surrounding (if and) how dividend policy contributes to the overall goal of the maximization of shareholder wealth (or how such policy affects shareholder value). To understand dividend payout policy, payout decisions must be separated from investment (and borrowing) decisions. There is also a trade-off between the level of cash dividends and the issuance of new or the repurchase of common stock. The importance of this trade-off is based on two main reasons. First, because of the information content of dividends regarding the firm's profitability and second, because of their taxation (at higher tax rates than capital gains). There are other reasons too such as the feeling of investors that cash is wasted if not being put into profitable reinvestments.

Dividend cuts give off bad signals as investors predict financial trouble such as a cash or earnings shortfall. At the same time, managers know that cuts will be treated as such and thus they usually postpone dividend cuts until things get worse, which would then force them to act accordingly. A recent paper by Krieger, Mauck and Pruitt (2021) found that almost 1,400 dividend paying firms, 213 cut dividends and 93 omitted dividends entirely in mid 2020. In general, the authors found that the 2008 financial crisis was characterized by a high proportion of increased dividend cuts across all industries.

But it is not always true to assume that stock prices fall following an announcement of a dividend cut, at least not for a long time. On Tuesday, January 31, 2022, ATT's CEO announced that it would cut its dividend " pouring some of that cash back into the infrastructure of this business to [generate] returns at a higher level than what we pay out on the dividend. So it's time to make that transition for this company."[5] Figure 2.1 shows the path of the company's stock price on the day of the announcement. The opening price was $18.859, the high for the day was 19.290, the low for the day (following the announcement) was $18.595, and the closing price for the day was $19.259. The adjusted (for the dividend cut of $1.11) for the day was $18.147 (=$19.259 – $1.11).

.In general, when managers decide on dividend payments their main concern appears to be to give shareholders a fair return for their investment, either via cash

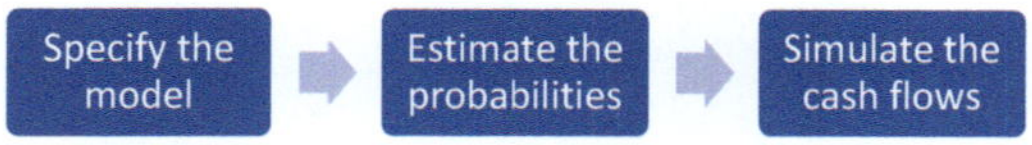

Figure 2.1 The three steps before the calculation of the NPV

Figure 2.2 ATT's stock price on 1/31/2022

payments (from common stock repurchases) or direct dividends. Assuming that the firm's investment decision and capital structure are constant, then payout policy becomes a "battle" between cash dividends and repurchase of stock. Put differently, should the company increase dividends and then issue new stock to replenish the equity capital? Or should the company retain and reinvest earnings and pay out any residual as cash dividends? Market imperfections and investor beliefs and preferences are responsible for such a battle or trade-off regarding a firm's dividend policy. Lastly, share repurchases are typically used to return undesirable cash to shareholders or to retire equity and replace it with debt.

1.7 Risk management

Risk is part of life and everyday business for a company. Consequently, the financial manager must be able to identify, avoid and manage risk. There are various ways a manager can deal with risk (which may emanate from both sides of the market, demand and supply) and we will mention some of them very briefly below.

Evidence on risk management, at both the retail (individual) and institutional levels, abounds. For example, many of us take out insurance against theft, fire, accidents and the like. Insurance companies specialize in assessing risks and can manage risk by pooling risks thereby creating a diversified portfolio of policies. When insuring against some potential loss, two situations complicate the matter for the insurance company. First, *adverse selection*, which refers to the inability to distinguish between "good risks" and "bad risks". The consequences of that is first, that only bad-risk people will seek insurance and second, that the company will (be forced to) increase premia (at the expense of good-risk insureds). Second, *moral hazard* which refers to conduct by the insured person to behave irrationally after insurance is adequate and thus raises the cost to the insurance company. Again, this is at the expense of the rational insured person who will care about his insured asset(s).[6]

Firms, by contrast, use more sophisticated instruments to ensure that the values of their portfolios do not decline (much) following adverse economic and financial conditions, that is, they *hedge risk*. Specifically, firms use financial contracts – part of derivatives – to manage risk. For instance, they may buy contracts that fix prices of some of their inputs or output or enter into long-term lease contracts for real estate, setting the price at which they acquire space many years before. Also, traders can use a *futures or forward contract*, which is an agreement to trade an asset on some future date, at a price that is agreed upon today.[7] In fact, managers regularly buy options on currencies, interest rates, and commodities to limit downside risk.

Here's a very simple example of hedging. Identify two highly related (ideally, perfectly correlated) assets, X and Y. Then, you can buy one and sell the other exactly in portions that minimize (or, ideally, eliminate) the risk of your net position. The challenge now is to find the *hedge ratio*, the number of units of one asset that is needed to offset changes in the value of the other asset. So, for example, if you know that a 1% change in the value of Y has been accompanied on average by a 3% change in the value of X, then the hedge ratio (also known as *delta*) equals 3. This practically means that in order to hedge 1 dollar invested in X, you need to sell 3 dollars of Y.

In general, *financial derivatives* enable parties to trade specific financial risks (such as interest rate risk, equity and commodity price risk, and many more) to other entities who are more willing to take or manage these risks. There are other ways to hedge risks such as *swap agreements* – exchanging a fixed cash flow for a floating cash flow in a contract – and its variants (interest rates, currency and so on).

Box 2.1 discusses the relationship between finance and marketing. You can see that many of the functions/activities that financial management deals with are relevant to marketing people as well. So, a marketing manager can relate to a financial manager.

Box 2.1

How is finance related to marketing?

BUDGETING: Involves setting financial targets, estimating costs and allocating resources to achieve your marketing objectives

FINANCIAL ANALYSIS: Involves examining key performance indicators such as return on assets, investment, costs etc.

RISK MANAGEMENT: Involves identifying key risks and mitigating them such as market volatility, changing consumer behavior and competition

RESOURCE ALLOCATION: Ensures that you allocate your budget wisely across various resources, promotional campaigns, and other marketing activities

FORECASTING AND PLANNING: Involves forecasting future revenues, expenses and cash flows in order to develop accurate forecasts to predict market trends and make informed decisions about resource allocation and budgeting

FINANCIAL REPORTING: Provides your stakeholders an overview of your marketing performance, financial health, and future company prospects

Test your understanding 1

1. If an asset is currently idle, is its opportunity cost zero?
2. What are the ways companies try to identify and evaluate the risks of a project's success? Link each one of them to the NPV approach.
3. What is the discount rate of a project, its assumption and the other ways of naming it?
4. What is the significance of using financial statements and ratios? List all classes of financial ratios.
5. Contrast the two ways of the dividend payout policy.
6. What are the main two reasons that prevent the efficient functioning of the insurance market? Explain.

Solutions appear at the textbook's website.

2 Essentials of investments

To effectively navigate through the complexity of the global financial markets, the agent (player) must also possess some knowledge about investing. It is assumed that the reader already has the basic investments background to understand the financial markets jargon. In what follows below, we will provide a very brief refresher of the main concepts in investments but many more will be encountered in later chapters. We begin the basic elements of investments: risk and (expected) return.

2.1 Risk and return

As you know, there is always some risk when dealing with financial assets (or investments, in general). When you *diversify* – create a portfolio with diverse assets – your risk decreases because exposure to risk by any individual asset may not affect the remaining securities in the portfolio. Hence, we face a risk–return trade-off in securities markets, that is, higher-risk assets offering higher expected returns are preferred to lower-risk assets. How do we measure risk and return? Let us begin with return.

There are various ways we can use to measure return of a financial asset. The most basic one is to take the simple rate of change (return), as follows:

$$Rate\ of\ return = (P_t - P_{t-1}) \,/\, P_{t-1} \tag{11}$$

But this method ignores distributions such as dividends and interest income (coupons). Hence, the augmented version is

$$Rate\ of\ return = (P_t - P_{t-1} + Distr.) \,/\, P_{t-1} \tag{11a}$$

This is also known as the *holding-period return* (HPR). However, the better method is to compute the *continuously compounded rate of return*, which simply means taking the log of equation (11a) or to compute the asset's log-return:

$$Rate\ of\ return = log\{(P_t + Distr.) \,/\, P_{t-1}\} \tag{11b}$$

Other, related and derivative measures of return are *excess return* – the difference between the actual nominal return (as expressed above) of an asset and the *risk-free rate* (the rate which does not have any risk such as Treasury bill or note) – *risk premium* – the difference between the expected HPR (as we will see next) on the asset and the risk-free rate – *risk aversion* – where we say that investors are risk averse in the sense that, if the risk premium were zero, they would not invest any money in stocks.

However, investors do not care so much about the historical, actual or earned return. They care about the *expected return* or the return they expect to earn in the future by investing in the assets. Hence, we need to measure the expected return. Since we are dealing with risk, we must use probabilities to estimate future magnitudes such as economic scenarios and the expected returns of each asset. In other words, since there is considerable uncertainty about financial-asset prices one year from now, you cannot be certain about your future HPR. Thus, you can set up your beliefs/expectations about possible outcomes for the financial asset by assuming various economic outcomes (scenarios) as well as estimate their probabilities. An example will clarify this (see Table 2.2, for the data and information).

In Table 2.2, we have identified the three possible economic scenarios (outcomes) such as a normally growing economy, a booming economy and a contracting economy and their associated probabilities (0.70, 0.10, 0.20) of occurrence, respectively. The last two columns refer to the expected (estimated) rates of return of two stocks, X and Y. We can compute the following (at least) from this information and data: each stock's expected return and risk. We begin with the computations of the stocks' expected returns.

Table 2.2 Outcomes, probabilities and expected returns

Outcomes	*Probability*	*Stock X*	*Stock Y*
Normal economy	0.70	10%	5%
Booming economy	0.10	20%	10%
Contracting economy	0.20	5%	–5%

The formula to calculate the expected return, $E(r)$, is

$$E(r) = \Sigma^{o} (pr(o)\ HPR(o)) \quad (12)$$

where o is the outcome, pr is the probability and HPR the holding period return of the stock.

Applying the formula, we obtain 10%, for stock X, and 3.5%, for stock Y:

$$E(r_x) = (0.70 * 10\%) + (0.10 * 20\%) + (0.20 * 5\%) = 7\% + 2\% + 1\% = 10\%$$

$$E(r_y) = (0.70 * 5\%) + (0.10 * 10\%) + (0.20 * -5\%) = 3.5\% + 1\% + -1\% = 3.5\%$$

However, a stock is risky and the actual return may be (a lot) more or less than its mean (expected) value. For example, in the above best-case scenario, X's return would be better, 20%, but in a contraction, the return will be a disappointing 5%. Even worse for Y, whose return could be negative in a contracting economy. How can we quantify this uncertainty? We can compute the stock's variance, σ^2, as the expected value of the squared deviations from the mean (or the expected squared surprises across scenarios), as follows:

$$\sigma^2 = Var(r) = \Sigma^{o} (pr(o)\ [HPR(o) - E(r)]^2) \quad (13)$$

where terms were defined above. The variance is also known as *volatility*. Typically, we compute also the square root of the variance to obtain the *standard deviation*, which we may name volatility as well as risk. Hence, in our example, the variance of stock X is 15, and for stock Y is 20.25, and computed as follows (omitting the %s):

$\sigma^2_x = 0.70 * [10 - 10]^2 + 0.10 * [20 - 10]^2 + 0.20 * [5 - 10]^2 = 0 +$
$10 + 5 = 15$
$\sigma^2_y = 0.70 * [5 - 3.5]^2 + 0.10 * [10 - 3.5]^2 + 0.20 * [-5 - 3.5]^2 = 20.25$

Taking the square root of each variance, we obtain 3.873% for stock X and 4.5% for stock Y, or the standard deviations, σ.Notice that in this case, we added the %s and so, as you probably guessed, we can interpret these numbers (but not variances because they are expressed in squared values). Their interpretation, as mentioned earlier, is the *risk* of each stock. And, as long as the probability distribution is roughly symmetric about the mean, the standard deviation is a reasonable measure of risk.

2.2 Diversification, covariance, correlation and utility

When you construct a portfolio – a collection of financial assets – that come from wide variety of sectors and assets, then we say that you have *diversified* your portfolio because you spread your risk across many securities. But, even though you may include all tradeable assets in your portfolio, you will never be able to eliminate risk! Hence, the total risk from a portfolio can be decomposed into *diversifiable risk* (or firm-specific or unsystematic risk) – the type of risk than can be completely eliminated because you have effectively diversified across many securities – and *non-diversifiable risk* (or market risk of systematic risk) – which is the risk component that remains and emanates from the general market. In general, you should aim for efficient diversification (not naïve) and so you need to take into account the following notions in order to construct the most efficient portfolio (among many other portfolios) that would enable you to reduce risk and maximize your expected return. We analyze the simple case of investing in the two stocks analyzed earlier, X and Y.

The actual or historical return of the two-stock portfolio, R_p, is defined and expressed as:

$$R_p = w_x r_x + w_y r_y \tag{14}$$

where w_x and w_y are the weights for each stock and r_x and r_y the actual returns of each stock, respectively. The variance, σ^2_p, of the same portfolio as

$$\sigma^2_p = (w_x \sigma_x)^2 + w_y \sigma_y)^2 + 2w_x w_y \, cov(r_x, r_y) \tag{15}$$

where $cov(r_x, ry)$ is the covariance between the two stocks. The covariance is, in turn, defined as:

$$\sigma_{xy} = cov(r_x, r_y) = \Sigma^o (pr(o)\{[HPR_x - E(r_x)] \, [HPR_y - E(r_y)]\}) \tag{16}$$

The covariance tells us how the two stocks co-move or co-vary, that is, positively, negatively or not at all (if zero).

Another, very important metric is the correlation coefficient, ρ_{xy}, which tells the extent or the degree to which the two stock move with each other. It is defined as:

$$\rho_{xy} = cov(r_x, r_y) / \sigma_x \sigma_y = \sigma_{xy} / \sigma_x \sigma_y \quad (17)$$

The numerical boundaries of the correlation coefficient are –1 (which implies that the two stocks are perfectly inversely correlated), 0 (no correlation between the two stocks) and +1 (perfectly positively correlated). Note that we could have replaced the covariance term in equation (15) with the correlation term ($\rho_{xy} \sigma_x \sigma_y$).

Recalling our earlier discussion on excess returns, we can say that it is possible to also create the excess return of a portfolio, as follows: $E(r_p) - rf$, where rf is the risk-free rate. Then, if we divide (standardize) this magnitude by the portfolio's standard deviation, σ_p, we have a very important metric known as the *Sharpe ratio* or the *reward-to-volatility ratio* or the *excess return per unit of risk*, as follows:

$$Sharpe\ ratio = reward\text{-}to\text{-}volatility\ ratio = (E(r_p) - rf) / \sigma_p \quad (18)$$

This ratio shows the risk-return tradeoff that an investor faces.

Now, let us apply these formulae to the data in Table 2.1. We begin with the (expected) return of the portfolio. Assume equal weights for each stock (in the absence of any specific mention about weights) and a risk-free rate of 3%.

$R_p = 0.50 * 10\% + 0.50 * 3.5\% = 6.5\%$
$Cov(r_x,r_y) = \sigma_{xy} = [0.70 *(10 - 10) * (10 - 3.5)] + [0.10 * (20 - 10) * (10 - 3.5)] + [0.20 * (5 - 10) * (-5 - 3.5)] = 0 + 6.5 + 8.5 = 15$
$Corr(r_x, r_y) = \rho_{xy} = 15 / (3.873 * 4.5) = 0.860$
$Var(r_p) = \sigma^2_p = (0.50 * 3.873)^2 + (0.50 * 4.5)^2 + 2 * 0.50 * 0.50 * 15 = 16.312$ *OR*
$Var(r_p) = \sigma^2_p = (0.50 * 3.873)^2 + (0.50 * 4.5)^2 + 2 * 0.50 * 0.50 * 3.873 * 4.5 * 0.860 = 16.312$
$Sharpe\ ratio = (6.5 - 3) / \sqrt{(16.312)} = 3.5 / 4.038 = 0.866$

So, what do all these values mean? First, the expected return of the portfolio is 6.5% and its risk 4.038%. Second, the two stocks appear to be co-moving positively with each other and their extent of correlation is 0.86. Finally, the investor seems to require 0.866 extra units of return per one unit of risk. Note that we will see these important formulae again in Chapter 8.

Finally, we assume that an investor can assign a utility (satisfaction, welfare) score to competing portfolios on the basis of the expected return and risk of those portfolios. Hence, higher utility values are assigned to portfolios with more attractive risk–return profiles. The objective, obviously, is to maximize utility (subject to some constraints). A typical utility function for a portfolio, *p*, is this:

$$U = E(r_p) - (1/2) * \sigma^2_p A \quad (19)$$

where *A* is the investor's degree of risk aversion or *risk tolerance*.[8] More risk-averse investors (those who have larger values of A) penalize risky investments more severely than less risk-averse investors.

So, there are three types or attitudes towards risk by investors: *risk-lovers* – those who enjoy taking on more risk and are willing to take fair games and gambles (with A values of < 0), *risk-neutral* – those who are indifferent to risk and focus exclusively on expected return (A value of 0), and *risk-averse* – as explained above (with A values of > 0).

The above principles comprise Markowitz's (1952) Modern Portfolio Theory which is also known as the *mean-variance model* and entails maximizing expected return while minimizing risk based on the efficient diversification principle.[9]

CAPM vs. REALITY

The CAPM faces several problems including the inability to identify the market portfolio, all returns are cast in expectations and hence unobserved and that coefficients are time-varying. Hence, academically speaking the model does not sit well. But, it is still used widely in practice such as by courts (to value corporations, infer a normal rate of return for firms, or involving bankruptices when in dispute by stakeholders), in real estate (to evaluate risk measures of property) and in financial modelling. See, for example, the article by *Forbes*.

https://www.forbes.com/sites/davidmarotta/2012/03/19/capm-the-first-factor-of-investing/?ctpv=-searchpage

2.3 Capital asset pricing model

The *capital asset pricing model* (CAPM) serves many functions such as providing a benchmark rate of return (required and expected rates of return) for evaluating possible investments and helping us evaluate the expected return on assets that are expected to be available (and traded) in the market such as an initial price offering. CAPM was suggested by Sharpe, Lintner and Mossin in three different (and independent) papers.[10] The model rests on several assumptions but the two most important ones are (1) that investors possess homogeneous expectations (based on the same information set, which is available for everyone) and thus are mean-variance optimizers (based on Markowitz's principles, as mentioned above) and (2) that markets are functioning well (i.e., efficient) with very few restrictions to trading.[11] The model, which describes the expected return–beta relationship, can be expressed as follows:

$$E(r_x) = rf + \beta_x\,[E(r_m) - rf] \tag{20}$$

where $E(r_m)$ is the expected excess return of the market, m, and β_x the beta of stock X. The *beta* of the stock is just the ratio of the covariance between the stock's and the market's returns over the variance of the market portfolio $(Cov(r_x, r_m)/\sigma^2_m)$ and measures the contribution of stock X to the variance of the market portfolio. So, if a stock has a beta greater/smaller than 1 (the market beta), then the stock is riskier/less risky than the market. This expected return–beta relationship tells us that the total expected rate of return is equal to the sum of the risk-free rate (the time value of money) *plus* a risk premium (the compensation for risky investments). It also gives us an idea about (the size of) the risk premium, which is the product of a reference (benchmark) risk premium (that of the market portfolio) and the relative risk of the particular asset as measured by its beta (its contribution to the risk of the overall risky portfolio).

To use or estimate CAPM, we must re-express equation (20) in an estimable form, known as the *single-index model*, for a stock *i*, as follows:

$$R_i = \alpha_i + \beta_i R_m + e_i \tag{21}$$

This model states that the *realized excess return* on any stock, R_i, is the sum of the realized excess return due to market factors, $\beta_i R_m$, a nonmarket premium (the *alpha of a stock*), α_i, and firm-specific factors embedded in e_i. CAPM's prediction is that for every stock, the equilibrium value of α_i is 0. The alpha of a stock is due to Jensen (1968, 1969) and sometimes it is referred to as *Jensen's alpha*. The logic is that the only reason for a stock to provide a premium over the risk-free rate is that the stock imposes market (systematic) risk for which the investor must be compensated. Hence, a positive/negative alpha implies reward without/with risk. Finally, the term e_i is also known as the error term (in econometrics) and is assumed to be zero when one has constructed a very well-diversified portfolio of securities.

The nearby *sidebar* discusses whether CAPM is still valid as well as some other uses of it in the real world, despite its deficiencies.

2.4 Arbitrage pricing theory

The single-index model just presented suggested that the only factor (magnitude) that affect the return on a stock (or portfolio) is the return on a broad market-index portfolio. Recall that we also decomposed stock variability into market or systematic risk, due largely to macroeconomic events, and firm-specific or idiosyncratic effects that can be diversified in large portfolios. However, risk premiums may also depend on other risk factors such as inflation, interest rates, volatility, market-risk premiums, aside from betas. We say *factors* in this discussion to mean surprises or innovations or unanticipated events (or magnitudes) as opposed to expected or actual events. For example, the inflation rate is an actual magnitude because it has been realized or observed. An inflation rate factor is the difference between the actual inflation and its expected magnitude.

If we re-express the single-factor model of excess returns (as described by equation 21 above) using *F* as the factor, we have:

$$R_i = E(R_i) + \beta_i F + e_i \tag{22}$$

where $E(R_i)$ is the expected excess return on stock *i*. Notice that if the macro factor has a value of zero in any particular period (that is, no surprises), the excess return on the security will equal its previously expected value, $E(R_i)$, plus the effect of firm-specific events only. As before, the nonsystematic components of returns, the e_is, are assumed to be uncorrelated across stocks and with the factor F.

From this discussion, it easily follows that models that allow for several factors – *multifactor models* – can provide better descriptions of security returns.

So, for example we can add macro variables as potential factors as in the model below:

$$Ri = E(R_i) + \beta_{iGDP}\, GDP_t + \beta_{iIR}\, IR_t + \beta_{iUR}\, UR_t + e_i \quad (22a)$$

where the unanticipated growth in *GDP*, the unexpected changes in interest rates *IR* and unexpected unemployment rate *UR* are the three factors. The coefficients, β_is, are sometimes called *factor loadings* or factor betas. For example, an increase in interest rates is bad news for most firms, and so we would expect interest rate betas to be negative.

Ross (1976) developed the *arbitrage pricing theory* (APT) along the lines of CAPM, so that APT predicts that a security's expected return is linked to risk and described by a factor model (as opposed to CAPM). An *arbitrage* opportunity arises when an investor can earn riskless profits without making a net investment. This notion is based on the law of one price (which we had discussed in Chapter 1). One crucial assumption (beyond the other ones) needed to derive APT is that we consider only *well-diversified portfolios* (where each asset's weight is small enough to render the portfolio's (*p*) nonsystematic variance, σ^2_{ep}, negligible).

The APT is an extremely appealing model and does not require that almost all investors be mean-variance optimizers. Instead, it is built on the realistic assumption that a rational capital market will preclude arbitrage opportunities. Further, the APT is very similar to CAPM because it also gives us a benchmark for rates of return that can be used in security valuation and investment performance evaluation.

2.5 The efficient market hypothesis

The *efficient market hypothesis* (EMH) posits that stocks already reflect all available information and thus their prices are fair or correct. The three forms of EMH are *weak* (where all past information is embedded in the current price of the stock), *semi-strong* (where, additionally, all currently public information is reflected in the current price of the stock) and *strong* form (where, additionally, all private information is incorporated in the current price of the stock). One major implication of these three forms is that the designated investment strategy is the *passive* – which attempts to establish a well-diversified portfolio of securities (from the top down such as an index fund or the market) without seeking to find under- or over-valued stocks – relative to *active investment strategy* – which does just the opposite (the "bottom-up" approach). Another implication is that trends, technical or even basic fundamental analyses are fruitless because there would be no additional information not already reflected in the current price of the stock. Let us qualify this (strong) argument, however.

Note that all three forms of the EMH assert that prices should reflect all available information. However, traders are human and thus some correctly and others incorrectly interpret available and incoming information. Hence, errors are bound to be made. The EMH states only that at the given time, using current information, we cannot be sure if today's prices would have been too high or too low relative to yesterday's prices. But, if markets are rational, we can expect them to be correct, on average. More discussion of the EMH in Chapter 8.

Test your understanding 2

1. If the risk premium were zero would investors invest or not in stocks? Explain.
2. Under CAPM, what would be the optimal (best) risky portfolio for any investor?
3. Suppose we have estimated the following two-factor model for ABC's excess returns: $R_{ABC} = 0.10 + 1.2(GDP) - .1\ (UR)$. Interpret each coefficient.
4. Evaluate each form of market efficiency for plausibility and applicability in the real world.
5. What is your definition of Jensen's alpha?

Solutions appear on the textbook's website.

3 Using the finance and investments concepts

As an investor, consumer, student or simply the average person strolling down the street, you need to know basic financial and economic concepts because you encounter them every day in your life. Below, we will give several examples of how you can use and exploit some of the finance and investments concepts (as well as some other, related ones) that we have just described above to show you that you need to know them and put them to work for your benefit. We will also show you how to avoid risks and keep yourself out of harm's way.

As a student, you take courses in finance, economics, statistics, mathematics, science and many others during your four years in college. Have you ever wondered why you had to take so many of them and from various disciplines? Have you ever wondered which concepts in general finance describe this wide learning approach? The fact that you take many courses from various disciplines highlights the concept of diversification! You acquire knowledge from a wide variety of subjects in order to be a full, all-rounded person upon graduation and be able to converse about many things in every day life. Furthermore, this ability enables you to reduce risk – the risk of not being employable or not being useful to a corporation – and, at the same time, maximize your reward or potential of success in life. So, there is what we call the risk–return trade-off, which means that the more education and investment in your future, the higher the (expected) reward.

Say you have an amount of money and you wish to deposit it in a bank. How would you go about selecting the best bank so you can get the max return on your money? Would you just go to any bank? No, of course not. You should be able to choose among banks based on objective and investment criteria some of which we mentioned next. First of all, you should know that the compound interest is better than the simple interest. While the annual interest amount remains constant with simple interest, the annual interest amount changes with compound interest. This has to do with the frequency of earning interest and so a bank that has compound interest should be preferred to another which promises simple interest. In addition, simple interest is preferred if you have a loan because the loan's cost remains the same throughout its life.

One way to determine which bank makes a better offer, is to compute the *effective annual rate* (EAR), defined as $(1+APR)^m - 1$, where m is the number of compounding periods and *APR* the *annual percentage rate*, defined as the interest rate divided by the number of periods. EAR is the real return on an interest-paying investment when the effects of compounding over time are taken into account. Here's an example. Assume that bank X offers you a credit card with an APR of 24% with monthly compounding, whereas bank Y offers you a credit card with a 26% APR but compounded semi-annually. Which bank's offer is better?

$$EAR_X = (1 + 0.24/12)^{12} - 1 = 26.82\%$$
$$EAR_Y = (1 + 0.26/2)^2 - 1 = 27.69\%$$

and so, we see that bank Y offers a better deal even though compounding is less frequent than banks X's.[12]

You walk down the street and a man approaches you with the following offer. If you pay me now $100, I will give you back $104 next year (assume that this is a certain outcome). What you say to his offer? To properly answer, you need to know your opportunity cost, that is, the next best alternative you have which, in this case, might be placing the $100 in a bank which, currently, offers a simple interest of 5%. How much money would you have a year from now in this case? Simply, $105 (=100 + 1.05). This amount, however, is less than the amount the man promised and so you should say no to his offer! If he were to offer you $105.5, then you would accept it and if he had offered you $105, then you should see no difference between the two alternatives. Understand that there's an opportunity cost associated with everyday choices you make in your live and thus, you should know what that is at all times!

You are in your armchair pondering your future, in general, your future family (which may include kids), your retirement and so on. Which decisions should you make now in order to be on track with your goals and be prepared for the future challenges? First of all, essential concepts from investments should help you a lot. First, begin with your long-range goal(s), overall strategy or mission in life. Say you wish to save to buy a house, or send your kids to college. You should then begin investing in assets (financial and real) so as to expect higher return for your invested funds. You may wish to consult a professional investment adviser to help you navigate the complex and ever-changing global financial landscape. Your adviser will assist you to identify the (classes of) assets to invest in (what we call, the *asset allocation* step in the whole investment process) such as stocks, bonds, cash etc., and then pick the best ones within each asset class (the *security selection* step). Markowitz's modern portfolio theory concepts (such as correlations, covariance, mean-variance and the ensuing CAPM) will be of relevance to the construction of the ideal investment portfolio (for you). In general, you do not want to build a portfolio with highly correlated (co-varying) assets and diversify assets as much as possible.

Next, your adviser will compute the fractions of funds that you should allocate to each individual asset (that is, the optimal weights) so at to maximize return and minimize risk. He may also run scenario analyses with this data, for example, to seek the maximization of the Sharpe ratio, which shows the extra return per unit of risk. Finally, your adviser should inform you of the progress of the investment (through monitoring and periodic performance evaluation of the portfolio) and, if needed, seek corrective actions, when short-term, temporary deviations from the aim are observed – known as *tactical asset allocation* – or long-run changes which may be more substantial in order to accomplish the mission or target – known as *strategic asset allocation.* Hence, you now realize that these basic investment concepts are very much used in real life and very much apply to everyone!

Suppose that you are interested in purchasing a private business and must pay a sum of money upfront. How would you value the business so as to pay the right price? In this case, the concepts discount rate, cash flows, financial ratios and more – from corporate finance – are relevant. Your first task is to forecast the company's *free cash flow* (*FCF*), defined as the amount of cash that the firm can pay out to investors after making all investments necessary for growth (here, we assume that the firm is all-equity-financed, no debt). Then, you need to forecast each year's free cash flow out to some valuation horizon, H, and assess the business's value at that horizon (PV_H). Finally, you need to discount the free cash flows at the after-tax WACC in order to give you the total value of the company.

So, for example, if we estimate the free cash flows until some year, say 5, we think growth is at a certain level and after that you expect the company's sales to settle down to stable, long-term growth starting in year 6, you can the discount them at a suitable weighted average cost of capital, you would have the following equation:

$$PV = FCF_1/(1+wacc)^1 + FCF_2/(1+wacc)^2 + \ldots + FCF_H/(1+wacc)^H + PV_H/(1+wacc)^H \qquad (23)$$

where $PV_H = FCF_{H+1}/(wacc - g)$ and g is the long-run growth rate. Hence, the sum of these two equations reveals the value of the business [$(PV_{business} = PV(cash\ flow\ years\ 1\text{–}5) + PV(horizon\ value)$].

Of course, there are quicker methods to find the value of a business such as the (earnings) multiples approach. A very important one is the *price/earnings (PE) ratio*, defined as the market value per share over the earnings per share of the company. So, for example, if the estimated earnings of the company for each of the next few years is $300,000 and the company's PE ratio is 15, then we can value the company at $4.5 million (=15 * $300,000). Keep in mind that there are several similar metrics that you can use to not just value a business abut also a company's stock.

Finally, another general metric is the *enterprise value* (EV), which is calculated by combining a company's debt and equity and then subtracting the amount of cash not used to fund business operations:

$$Enterprise\ Value = Equity + Debt - Cash \qquad (24)$$

Finally, let us say that you wish to buy shares of a company that seems to be hot right now (according to you and perhaps, your friends and relatives), without including it in a portfolio, as analyzed earlier, for the sake of discussing this activity within your circle. How can you determine if its price is fair or not? Remember the EMH we discussed earlier? It says that if you believe in it then you should not challenge the currently observed prices of individual stocks because you take them as correct. Notice, however, that what we are describing here is the exact opposite! In other words, when you are a firm believer in EMH, the construction of the portfolio is based on the top-down approach (as mentioned in subsection

2.6), but this purchase is based on the bottom-up approach. Hence, you challenge the market's assessment of the share's price and want to check if the price is right (or the market's wisdom is).

One important approach to value the stock, P_x, is the *Gordon model* or the *constant-growth model*, expressed as follows:

$$P_x = D_1 / (k - g) \tag{25}$$

where D_1 is the next period's dividend (the stock pays), k is the required rate or return – the familiar CAPM – and g, as defined in equation (23), represents here the growth rate of dividends.[13] So, if the next period's (year's) dividend is \$1.00, your required (or minimum acceptable) rate of return is 10% from the stock and g is 5%, the price of the stock would be $P_x = 1.00/(0.10 - 0.05) =$ \$20. If you observe that the current market price is \$22 then you would say that the stock was overpriced, and thus not buy it, but if it was \$18 then it would have been underpriced and thus a good bargain, *ceteris paribus*.

4 Some finance-related concepts from other disciplines

In order to understand the global financial market(s), we need to have (at least) a basic knowledge of the fundamentals of corporate finance, investments and other related disciplines such as management, accounting, marketing and so on. It is important to stress, at this point, that the intention here is not to present *all* notions in these disciplines and thus replace the standard textbooks dealing with these inter-related areas of finance. Instead, we will focus on these (select) principles and fundamentals that are crucial in dealing with the financial markets permitting you to function effectively and efficiently. As we move along with the material in subsequent chapters, many more notions from these areas will be encountered but they will be discussed at that time.

4.1 Management

The roles of the manager in a corporation are to plan, organize and staff, lead and control. Employees possess various traits which the manager must recognize, assess and exploit accordingly. For example, the diversity of personalities, attitudes, preferences, and work behaviors affect how managers deal with the above roles. Some companies use *personality testing* to evaluate existing employees or screen out candidates. Managers, in general, must understand the diversity among their employees and assign them to their best uses. The investments area also employs personality tests for potential investors known as risk tolerance tests. Such tests

ONLINE TESTS

For personality:

https://www.outof-service.com/bigfive/

https://cmoe.com/blog/personality-tests-develop-employees/

For risk tolerance:

https://investor.vanguard.com/tools-calculators/investor-questionnaire/questions

are designed to reveal the level of risk an investor can afford before constructing the appropriate portfolio. The nearby *sidebar* contains the links for two personality tests and one risk tolerance questionnaire.

People do not always make rational decisions, as we already mentioned earlier. The classical economists had assumed that man always acts rationally because he is able to gather all pertinent information, analyze it correctly, use it to make accurate calculations and finally make the right decision. When applying this principle to an organization, we see that people are not always rational, they are not always loyal to their workplace, and their preferences and motives may interfere with the organization's decisions. A more realistic model of decision-making – *bounded rationality* – is put forth by Simon (1955, 1957) in three dimensions: (a) a person does not seek maximization but other objectives (such as *satisficing behavior*), (b) they do not care about other viable alternatives and (c) they use heuristics to make a decision.[14] Satisficing behavior resembles rational decision-making, but it differs in that rather than choosing the best alternative the person saves resources by accepting the first alternative that meets some minimum threshold.

For example, many students or graduates do not conduct national or international searches for colleges to attend or for potential job openings but limit their searches to a limited geographic area and tend to accept the first offer in their chosen area, even if this is not the best (ideal) outcome. As another example from the investments field, although a professional portfolio manager may be competent in exploiting alphas and betas, a client may not consider these manager's (or investment adviser's) traits when selecting him or her and discussing the construction of the portfolio. Instead, the client may use heuristics or personal biases to determine quality and suitability of the investment portfolio. Such actions may actually translate into portfolio losses or suboptimal outcomes. Finally, it is worth mentioning that following the work by Kahneman and Tversky (1979) titled "Prospect Theory", which focuses on bounded rationality in decision making, a whole new (sub)field in finance has emerged known as *behavioral finance* and *behavioral economics*.

One component of planning is *strategizing*, which includes corporate and business strategies. Specifically, *corporate strategy* involves the question of which business we should be in and is a wider concept, whereas *business strategy* asks how the firm should compete and is a narrower concept. One element of corporate strategy is diversification, which entails participation in various diverse businesses that are distinct from each other. For example, think of the group of companies as an investment portfolio where an investor tries to include diverse investments in order to spread risk and maximize the expected performance of the overall portfolio. If on any given day an investment isn't doing so well it should be offset by one that is doing well. This is what corporate strategy tries to achieve. Business strategy focuses on how a given business needs to compete in order to be effective, survive and thrive.

Another linkage of strategy to investments is the accomplishment of the first step in the investment process, asset allocation. Asset allocation can be decomposed into *strategic asset allocation* – focusing on the broad mission or objective of the investment portfolio – and *tactical asset allocation* – which involves the fine-tuning of the portfolio to exploit market trends or economic conditions or even realign the portfolio's course with the mission. In general, the major activity in strategic planning is *business portfolio analysis*, whereby management evaluates the products and businesses that make up the company. Therefore, the expected actions would be to allocate strong resources into its more profitable businesses and reduce allocation or eliminate its weaker ones.

In management, two crucial inputs to strategy are *SWOT* (Strengths, Weaknesses, Opportunities and Threats) and *PESTEL* (Political, Economic, Social, Technological, Environmental and Legal) analyses. SWOT analysis is a way to improve the investment process (such as the investment policy, asset allocation, the monitoring and evaluation of the portfolio).[15] The PESTEL framework is used by management teams and consultants as an aid to their strategic planning processes, by financial analysts when they need to determine how these factors may influence the investment portfolio and financing decisions, and by marketers when they wish to analyze and monitor the macro-environmental (external environment) factors.[16]

We end this subsection with *Maslow's* (pyramid of) *hierarchical needs* which are physiological and survival, safety, social, ego and esteem, and self-actualization.[17] According to his theory, people first direct their attention to satisfying their basic needs (at the bottom of the pyramid) which are the physiological, safety, and security needs. The next level of achievement involves social needs and once these are satisfied, people focus on their ego and esteem needs, the top of the pyramid. This pyramid of needs is related to finance and investments, in particular, when one thinks of a person who has achieved some satisfactory level of income and all basic needs of him/herself or family have been met, and then can invest a discretionary amount of his income. Investors can select any stage in the pyramid according to their preferences and needs. For example, some investors wish to have safe and secure investments – corresponding to their physiological, survival and safety needs – while other investors (such as fund managers, retail investors, and some entrepreneurs) – to satisfy their ego and esteem – may undertake more complex investments and risky investments that would bring them attention, respect and success.[18] Finally, the last class of investors could be involved with the investigation of economic and financial phenomena in hopes of realizing their full potential and suggesting impactful and groundbreaking theories to achieve self-worth. So, depending upon the preferences of each investor, the ideal investment portfolio should contain various asset classes including cash investments and perhaps some more complex financial instruments (such as options or structured products) which, in this discussion, would be categorized into the self-actualization need as the person strives for personal growth and skills.[19]

4.2 Marketing

As you probably know, marketing is all about creating value for the customer. Hence, the *marketing process* involves the following steps: understand the customer and its needs; design a value-creating marketing strategy; build a value-enhancing marketing program; establish and grow profitable customer relationship; and capture value to generate profits. Hence, it is evident that the focus is on the customer – just like in investment management the focus is on the investor, the client – and on the construction of a value-creating marketing program – just like the creation of a return-maximizing investment portfolio in investment management. Also, just like a marketer tries to understand the customer, the investment advisor tries to understand the investor and his/her needs, as mentioned earlier via risk-tolerance tests, for example. Finally, when the marketer sets up their value-creating marketing strategy this is similar to a portfolio manager establishing the position of their investment portfolio within the competition in terms of assets, fees and achievable goals.

The first step in the marketing process also resembles SWOT and PESTEL analyses we mentioned earlier. Understand that marketing functions in a complex and changing environment where many factors such as suppliers, customers, competitors, and others may work with or against the company. In addition, environmental factors (demographic, economic, technological, political, and cultural) all are likely to shape marketing opportunities, pose threats, and impact a company's ability to engage customers and build lasting and value-enhancing customer relationships.

The *product life-cycle* is a theory that explains a product's sales (and profits) over its lifetime first suggested by R. Vernon (1966, 1979) and applied to international trade and then marketing.[20] The theory lists four stages in the life of a product: the development and introduction stage, the growth stage, the maturity stage and the decline stage. The *Introduction* is a period of slow sales growth as the product is being introduced in the market. Profits are non-existent because of the expenses of product introduction. The *Growth* stage is characterized by rapid market acceptance and increasing profits. The *Maturity* is a period of slowdown in sales growth because the product has become known, accepted and trusted by most buyers. Profits level off because of increased marketing outlays to support the product against competition. The final stage, *Decline*, is the period when sales fall off and profits drop and the only way to avoid getting out of the market is innovation.

This theory is very much relevant to the study of finance, investments and financial markets, in general. First, young companies do not make any distributions (such as dividends), they simply grow. So, investors should know that when including these companies in their portfolios. After some years, these companies become mature and then they may begin distributing dividends as profits become solid and expectations grow. Investors continue keeping these companies in their portfolios as long as they are capable of fending off competition, remain solvent and post solid profits as well as innovate in order to retain their presence in the market. These companies may revert to value companies given their long-run presence in the market. Using the product life-cycle theory in another way, picture what portfolio managers may do. Investment portfolio managers look at the stage a company is in when deciding how much money to allocate in their portfolio when revising them periodically. So, they may allocate a higher amount of funds to a given company (or industry) – that is, to over-weigh it – if they expect it to grow disproportionally (relative to their peers – which they under-weigh) and thus extract the additional return. Or, if they perceive a turning point in the general economy because of some sectors (or firms) become harbingers of extraordinary growth, then they may invest heavily in them to capture the excess return. This investment strategy is also known as *sector rotation*.

The *marketing mix* is a set of tools classified into four groups – called the *four Ps* of marketing – and are designed so that the firm can deliver on its value proposition. These are: product, price, place, and promotion. For example, the firm must first meet the need in the market (the product). Then, it must decide how much it will charge for it (the price) and how it will make the product available to consumers (the place). Finally, it must communicate about the product and persuade consumers of the product's merits or needs (the promotion). In general, the firm must blend each tool into a comprehensive marketing program that delivers the intended value to its target customers. By now, it should be obvious to you, that this mix or process is very much similar to the investment process we discussed in section 3. The investment adviser's role is to prepare the investment plan – also known as the *Investor Policy Statement*, in a broad sense – and then sell it to the investor. So, if the marketing manager does a good job with the first three steps in the marketing process, then this would set the stage for the next step which is building and managing customer relationships.

The same applies to the investment manager, who must first assess the needs and wants of the investor (the client), then build the suitable portfolio and then offer it to the client. Specifically, regarding the product in the marketing mix, the analogy with investments is that the financial services authorities (FINRA or SEC in the US or FCA in the UK) protect the investors by monitoring the transmission and execution of buy/sell orders, the management of portfolios, the underwriting of investments and so on.[21] As for the price, these authorities ensure that the prices of financial assets paid by investors are fair, the financial advice or research investors obtained is not fraudulent or misleading, as well as that the fees that investors pay are appropriate, and more. On the tool of place(ment), the financial authorities work to verify that private placements of financial assets (such as stocks and bonds) are legitimate and that the exchange process is fair and transparent. Finally, regarding the promotion tool of the marketing mix, the analogy with finance and investments occurs when the financial authorities check to see that when financial services firms promote their own or proprietary investment products or advertise about the superior successes of their investment managers or flaunt the prospects of their companies these are all legal, legitimate and free from hidden conflicts.

4.3 Accounting

One basic definition of *accounting* is that it contains three activities – it identifies the economic events pertinent to a firm, it records those events in order to provide a history of its financial activities, and communicates the economic events of an organization (in the form of reports or financial statements, which we discussed earlier) to potential users (internal or external). At this point, can you see the links between accounting and corporate finance and investing, marketing and management? A question such as whether the company has enough cash to pay dividends to shareholders or buy back some of its shares is relevant to corporate finance. Is this company generating enough profits and how is this company stacking up against its peers in the industry? These are questions from an existing and potential investor. Asking which price would be the one that would maximize the company's net income is a marketing question. Which product line of a company would be more profitable so it can be kept while the other be abandoned? Or can we pay higher salaries to our employees next year or not? These are all questions for the management!

Another, very relevant notion that is discussed in the accounting field, and not just there, is *ethics*. In accounting, ethics involves the ethical standards in reporting financial and accounts information. The financial press is continuously reporting financial scandals by companies such as Enron, WorldCom, AIG, and many others. Many advanced countries' regulatory authorities are very concerned that the economy would greatly suffer if investors lost confidence in corporate accounting because of unethical financial reporting. Ethical behavior is also related to investments since a client assumes that the financial adviser or portfolio manager will be straightforward with him regarding the information about the building and monitoring of his portfolio.

The basic *accounting equation – Assets = Liabilities + Owner's Equity* – is at the heart of finance and investments. For a corporation, the accounting equation is slightly modified by replacing the owner's equity with stockholders' equity. This equation is frequently used in investments when the investor needs to start a private business, or when he needs to compute the equity in an investment account (such as a margin purchase or a short sale), or if he needs to verify that certain business transactions (such as equity or debt financings) carried out by the company are being accurately reflected in its accounts and more.

Accountants must prepare the entries for many changes in the business' accounts and fundamentals (meaning plant and equipment, investments, tangible and otherwise, and more) and all these are reflected in financial ratios. These, in turn, can serve as inputs to managerial decisions on payout policy (cash or stock distributions), retained earnings and financial statement analyses including shareholders' equity analysis. In addition, the accountant is responsible for addressing investment decisions by companies. Specifically, why corporations invest, and, more importantly, how can the accountant account for debt and equity investments (in terms of recording the transactions), and how can he/she value and report investments.

Finally, the accountant must prepare financial statements which can be used, in turn, by investors to conduct comparative ratio, horizontal, or vertical analyses, and compute the bottom line magnitudes such as the earnings per share, dividends per share, the P/E ratio and more. *Horizontal analysis* (or trend analysis) evaluates a series of financial statement data over a period of time, whereas *vertical analysis* (or common-size analysis) evaluates financial statement data by expressing each item in a financial statement as a percentage of some base amount or magnitude such as assets.

Test your understanding 3

1. If you conducted a stock valuation exercise and found that the intrinsic value (price) of the stock is \$18, how would you characterize the stock and what would you do with it, that is, buy, sell of keep it (if you had it) when its current market price is \$20?
2. As an investor, why do you need to know which stage a firm or an industry is in?
3. How can an investor relate to Maslow's pyramid of needs?
4. How is the marketing mix relevant to an investor?

Solutions appear at the textbook's website.

Summary

- We presented a number of essential concepts from finance, namely, corporate finance and investments.
- From the area of corporate finance, we briefly discussed the concepts of presents and future values, capital budgeting (the NPV approach, Break-Even analysis and Monte Carlo simulation), the three financial statements (Balance Sheet, Income Statement and Cash Flow Statement), financial ratios (profitability, liquidity, asset management, debt management, and market values), the weighted average cost of capital, dividend policy, and risk management (adverse selection, moral hazard, financial derivatives).
- From the area of investments, we discussed the risk and return tradeoff (measurements of return and risk), diversification, correlation, covariance and utility (the Sharpe ratio, risk aversion, utility function and Markowitzs mean-variance analysis), the capital asset pricing model, the arbitrage pricing model, and the efficient market hypothesis (and its three forms, weak, semi-strong and strong).
- We provided some examples of the use of most of the above concepts by the average person as investor, consumer, or student.
- Concepts from the management discipline such as employee personality traits, bounded rationality and strategy were discussed and linked to finance and investments.
- Concepts from the marketing field of study such as the marketing process, the product life cycle and the four Ps.
- Finally, some very much related and needed in financial analysis concepts from accounting are ethics in financial reporting, the basic accounting equation, transactions reporting challenges and financial statement analyses.

Questions and problems

1. Since the market investment portfolio is composed of individual stocks, why does its variability not reflect the average variability of its components?
2. Assume the following information on two stocks.

Outcomes	*Expected return X*	*Expected return Y*	*Probabilities*
Bull market	20%	10%	0.50
Bear market	–5%	5%	0.20
Normal market	10%	8%	0.30

   Compute the following:
   a. Each stock's expected return, variance and standard deviation.
   b. The covariance and correlation coefficient.
   c. The portfolio's expected return, variance and standard deviation. Assume equal weights.
3. Corporations face two principal financial decisions: what investments to make and how to pay for them. Provide an example from your real life that applies these two decisions.

4. What are the steps in analyzing a proposed new $2 million investment? Be sure you conclude with how you can make a decision.
5. A bank offers two alternative interest schedules for a savings account locked in for *n* number of years: (a) a monthly rate of 1% and (b) an annually, continuously compounded rate of 10%. Which alternative should you choose?
6. What would be your required rate of return for a stock with a beta of 1.5? Assume that the risk-free rate is 3% and the expected return on the stock market is 8%.
7. What would be the price of a stock when its current dividend is $1.00, and the dividend growth rate is 3%? Assume that you require a 10% return from that stock in order to invest in it.
8. Out of these three rates of return for stock (or bond) – the holding-period return, the distributions-augmented and the log-return – which one(s) is (are) superior and why?
9. If your objective is to determine the risk-adjusted expected returns, which metric can you use? Can you also use it to evaluate investment managers?
10. What would be the minimum quantity that would generate zero profits for a business with fixed costs of $100, per-unit variable cost of $3 and price of $5? Verify this.

Notes

1. You understand that in the second case the $105 is also the present value, if you decide to reinvest it.
2. Note that in other formulae, the initial cash flow, CF_0, appears before the discounted cash flows, CF_t. In this case, the CF_0 value must be entered as negative.
3. As you may know, NPV is only one among the few alternative methods (such as the payback period, IRR and the average accounting return) to evaluate projects but these are beyond the scope of this textbook. The IRR is briefly mentioned in subsection 1.5
4. This approach is named after the known European casino in Monte Carlo because it draws a direct analogy of engaging in project analysis as one would analyze gambling strategies.
5. https://www.cnbc.com/2022/02/04/att-ceo-says-dividend-cut-reflects-shift-to-put-more-cash-back-into-the-business.html
6. More discussion and examples in Chapter 5.
7. When a standardized forward contract is traded on an exchange (called the *futures exchange*), it is called a futures contract. We explain derivative products in Chapter 11.
8. Note that risk aversion and risk tolerance are opposite notions.
9. Markowitz, Harry M. (1952). Portfolio Selection. *The Journal of Finance* 7 (1): 77–91.
10. Sharpe, William (1964). Capital Asset Prices: A Theory of Market Equilibrium. *Journal of Finance*, September. Lintner, John (1965). The Valuation of Risk Assets and the Selection of Risky Investments in Stock Portfolios and Capital Budgets. *Review of Economics and Statistics*, February. Mossin, Jan (1966). Equilibrium in a Capital Asset Market. *Econometrica*, October.
11. We present the Markowitz efficient portfolio in Appendix C.
12. For continuous compounding cases, use this expression: $1 + EAR = exp\ (r) = e^r$ where *r* is the compounding rate.
13. If you do not have the next period's dividend but the current dividend, then you should multiply the current dividend, D_0, by the growth rate, g, as follows: $D_1 = D_0(1+g)$.

14. Simon, Herbert A. (1955). A Behavioral Model of Rational Choice. *Quarterly Journal of Economics* 69(1), 99–118, and (1957). *Models of Man*. New York: John Wiley.
15. We present an application in Chapter 13.
16. We present an application of this analysis in Chapter 8.
17. Maslow, A. H. (1954). *Motivation and Personality*. New York: Harper, and Maslow (1943). A theory of human motivation. *Psychological Bulletin* 50, 370–396.
18. We present an application of Maslow's pyramid in Chapter 4.
19. Note that the field of behavioral finance relates much more to Maslow's pyramid of needs than this discussion reveals. Visit the Corporate Finance Institute at https://corporatefinanceinstitute.com/course/behavioral-finance/
20. Vernon, R. (1966). International Investment and International Trade in the Production Cycle. *The Quarterly Journal of Economics* 80 (May), 190–207, and Vernon (1979). The Product Cycle Hypothesis in a New International Environment. *Oxford Bulletin of Economics and Statistics* 41(4), 255–267.
21. FINRA stands for Financial Industry Regulatory Authority; SEC stands for Securities and Exchange Commission and FCA is the Financial Conduct Authority. How is finance related to marketing?

References

Jensen, Michael C. (1968). The Performance of Mutual Funds in the Period 1945–1964. *Journal of Finance* 23(2), 389–416.

Jensen, Michael C. (1969). Risk, the Pricing of Capital Assets, and the Evaluation of Investment Portfolios. *Journal of Business* 42(2), 167–247.

Kahneman, D., and Tversky, A. (1979). Prospect Theory: An Analysis of Decision under Risk. *Econometrica* 47(2), 263–291.

Krieger, K., N. Mauck, and S.W. Pruitt (2021). The Impact of the COVID-19 Pandemic on Dividends. *Finance Research Letters* 42, 101910.

Ross, Stephen A. (1976). The Arbitrage Theory of Capital Asset Pricing. *Journal of Economic Theory* 13(3), 341–360.

Chapter 3

Overview of the global financial environment

1 Overview of the global financial markets

You are definitely aware of what a financial market is! The fact that you have accounts in a bank, you are able to purchase items or services online and at a store using your credit card or even cash, you need to obtain a loan to buy or finance something and more, are all transactions that necessitate the use of a *financial intermediary* – an institution that comes between you and the other part – which is a component of the financial market. Your bank accounts, your credit card and your loan are all instruments created by the financial market. Formally, a *financial instrument* legally obligates one party to transfer something of value to another party at some future time frame under mutually stipulated conditions. Additional examples of financial instruments are stocks and bonds (which sometimes are called underlying or *primitive securities*). The essential role (function) of financial instruments is important, which is to transfer risk from one party to the other. Derivative securities such as options and futures and insurance (whose payoffs derive from an underlying security) are examples of financial instruments that are used to transfer risk.

If you purchase an item online or at a physical store and deal with the seller directly, then you would engage in *direct finance*, whereas if you went through a financial intermediary such as a bank (in the loan case), then you would practice *indirect finance*. The house or the car you would purchase with the loan is called your asset and the loan a liability. These instruments are all created thanks to the financial market. Therefore, the formal definition of the *financial market* is the institution or mechanism that brings together two agents, a buyer (you) and a seller (the bank or store owner). In other words, a financial market exists to facilitate the flow of funds from one group of players – the *surplus units* or the

DOI: 10.4324/9781003677161-4

suppliers of funds – such as you as consumer and investor to another group of players – the *deficit units* or demanders of funds – such as banks, businesses, the government and even you.

The nearby *sidebar* asks if direct finance is the future now that we are talking about financial technology (fintech) and suggests that you look it up further. Some other challenges to these two types of financing are adverse selection and moral hazard (we first discussed these in Chapter 2). Adverse selection problems – which entail the difficulty of distinguishing between good and bad risk entities – inhibit the development of direct finance which are still the main source of corporate financing in most countries. In addition, moral hazard problems related to debt and equity contracts are partly responsible for the predominance of indirect finance. Financial intermediaries can function as monitors, collecting information that limits the potential costs arising from moral hazard behavior and adverse selection problems. Therefore, financing through financial intermediaries is an effective solution to mitigate adverse selection and moral hazard problems that arise in transactions between lenders and borrowers.

DIRECT FINANCE

Have you ever wondered what Airbnb, Ebay, P2P and Etsy do? You know what Airbnb does (it allows property owners around the world to rent out their spaces directly to travelers looking for a place to stay), what P2P involves (it enables individuals to obtain loans directly from other individuals), and what Etsy provides (a global online marketplace, where people come together to trade unique items). Is this the future of finance, to bypass financial intermediaries? Research it!

Figure 3.1 illustrates the process in indirect finance, where funds are sent from the surplus units (the lenders) to the financial intermediaries and then to the deficit units (the borrowers), while financial intermediaries create claims or instruments for both sides of the market for funds.

Thus, *financial markets* are the places – physical or virtual – where financial instruments are traded (bought and sold) and represent the central highway of an economic system. Put differently, they assist in allocating resources, determining prices and restoring equilibria in the economy. Financial markets play many more roles than just transferring funds between parties and transferring

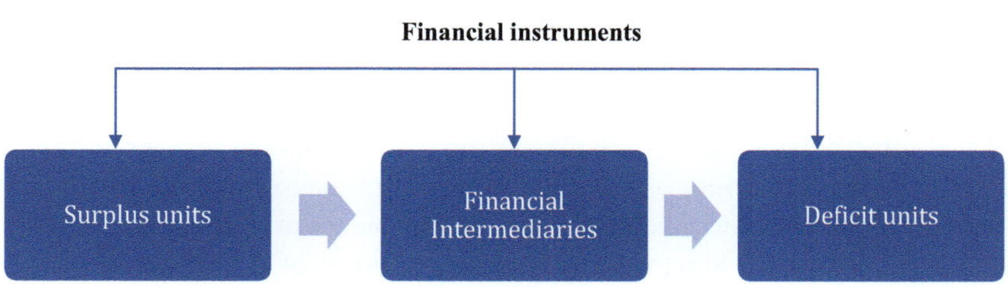

Figure 3.1 Indirect finance

risk. They provide liquidity to the market, disseminate information and permit inter-temporal consumption for agents. Specifically, when you need to convert your financial assets into cash rather fast, this is made possible by the financial market. Also, financial markets gather and report information about the issuers and buyers of financial instruments and reflect these into a price. Finally, when you do not wish to spend all your money but wish to enjoy more consumption in the future, the financial markets are there for you to accomplish that (via, perhaps, investments and savings at a bank).

1.1 Types of financial markets

There are many types of markets. Let us begin with the two main categories of the financial markets: money and capital markets. The *money market* is the market in which securities, whose life is less than a year, are highly liquid and have very low risk, are traded.

The main role of the money market is to facilitate the transfer of short-term funds from surplus units (individuals, corporations, or governments) to those with deficient funds thereby enabling participants to maintain liquidity. The *capital market* is a long-term market and the securities traded have (default) risk and offer lower liquidity. The main function (among many more) of the capital markets is to facilitate the movement of capital to productive areas to finance long-term investment and ultimately boost economic growth. *Disintermediation* is the process of facilitating a transfer of funds without a financial intermediary and leads to the creation of financial instruments (securities) such as debt or equity.

The capital market is sub-divided into primary and secondary markets. A *primary market* is one that negotiates the issuance and sale of new securities, whereas a *secondary market* facilitates the trading of existing (outstanding) securities. For example, when a firm re-issues shares or sells for the very first time (as in an *initial public offering*), this is a primary market transaction. But, when you wish to buy later shares of that company or any other company's shares, this is a secondary market transaction. Note that although primary market transactions provide funds to the initial issuer of securities (the firms), secondary market transactions do not. The seller of the security gets the funds in this case.

Further sub-classifications of financial markets include the *over-the-counter* (OTC) market – where transactions take place from virtually anywhere via electronic communication networks (ECNs) – *organized* market – where sellers trade from an actual physical location – *debt* and *equity markets* – where financial assets (claims) trade for immediate payment – and *derivative markets* – where financial claims are traded for execution at some later date.

A further classification of the global financial markets is the *international market* which comprises a number of types. For example, we have the international bond market, the Eurobond market and the Eurocurrency market. For example, the *Eurobond* refers to the market where a bond denominated in a currency other than that of the country in which it is sold, say, a bond denominated in US dollars sold in Germany. The *Eurocurrency market* involves foreign currencies deposited in banks outside the home country such as *Eurodollars*, which are US dollars deposited in foreign banks outside the US or in foreign branches of US banks.

1.2 Types of financial instruments

Financial instruments comprise pretty much the financial claims (or assets) that can be traded in the financial markets. We have *money-market instruments* for example. Examples of them are the US Treasury bill, Commercial paper, repurchase agreements (repos) and federal funds (which we will see again later in the chapter), and *capital-market instruments* such as equity (stocks and more), debt (bonds and more) and derivatives (options and futures). Money-market securities are commonly purchased by households, financial and commercial corporations and government agencies that have funds available for a short-term period. Money-market securities are typically sold in the secondary market and provide liquidity to investors. The money raised from capital-market instruments (through the primary market) is primarily used for the realization of investment projects by businesses in general as well as governments and individuals (for example, when they wish to buy a house).[1]

Other financial instruments include *cash instruments* – financial instruments with values directly influenced by the condition of the markets – such as bank deposits (and their variants) and loans, *derivative instruments* (besides options and futures) such as swap agreements and forwards, and *foreign exchange instruments* such as currency swaps and outright forwards. *Swap agreements*, in general, entail the exchange of one financial instrument, say, with a certain interest rate, with another similar instrument in different currency or standards. An *outright forward instrument* involves a currency agreement where the actual exchange of currency is done for the future and before the actual date of the agreement.

1.3 Types of financial intermediaries

Financial intermediaries fall into three categories: depository institutions, non-depository institutions, and investment intermediaries. *Depository institutions* or banks include categories such as commercial banks – which accept deposits, issue all types of loans, mortgages, and government securities – Savings and Loan associations, Mutual savings banks, and Credit unions. The category of *non-depository institutions* includes Life Insurance companies, Fire and Casualty insurance companies, and Pension funds. Finally, *investment intermediaries* comprise of Finance companies – which issue commercial paper, stocks, bonds and more – and Mutual funds and variants such as Money-market mutual funds and Exchange-Traded Funds (ETFs).[2]

Intermediaries can also be individuals (who typically work for a financial institution such as a brokerage house or investment bank) known as *brokers* and *dealers* and serve both sides of a market. For example, a real-estate agent is a type of broker. The person who minds (manages) your finances can also be a broker. Dealers and repo brokers act as financial intermediaries (for a fee) to create repurchase agreements for firms with deficient or excess funds. Federal funds brokers similarly serve as financial intermediaries matching up institutions that wish to sell (lend) funds with those that wish to purchase (borrow) them. Finally, specialized brokers, known as dealers for bonds (or stocks) serve as intermediaries in the secondary market by matching up buyers and sellers of Treasury bonds (but can also take positions in these bonds).

2 The central bank and the banking system

At the heart of the financial system is the banking system with its central banks and member banks. In the United States, the central bank is known as the Federal Reserve System (or the Fed), in most countries such as the United Kingdom or Greece it is the Bank of England or Greece, in Germany it is the Bundesbank and in New Zealand it is the Reserve Bank of New Zealand. However, in the European Union or the Euro area, the central bank is the European Central Bank. We begin with the central banks and their objectives.

2.1 Central banks

In general, all central banks have the responsibility for conducting national monetary policy in an attempt to achieve full employment (economic growth) and price stability (defined as low inflation). Central banks are solely responsible for conducting monetary policy (to be defined later) and print their national currency (coins and notes). However, not all central banks are structured the same. For example, the Fed has the following components: members (member banks and Fed district banks) and governance (the Board of Governors and the Federal Open Market Committee (more on that later) and some Advisory committees).[3] The Bank of England comprises the Governor, the Court of Directors, and three subcommittees (the Monetary Policy Committee, the Financial Policy Committee, and the Prudential Regulation Committee).[4] The Bank of Japan's structure includes the Governor (and Deputy Governors), Members of the Policy Board (the bank's decision-making body), Auditors, Executive Directors, and Counsellors. The European Central Bank is made up of the Governing Council (its main decision-making body), the Executive Board (which handles the bank's daily operations) and the General Council.[5]

Finally, there are some other central banks that contain a reserve system and are called "Reserve Bank of". Some examples are the Reserve Bank of Australia (RBA), New Zealand (RBNZ) and India (RBI). RBA's governance structure was established by the Reserve Bank Act of 1959 and is managed by the Governor. The Reserve Bank Board has an Audit Committee and a Remuneration Committee.[6] RBNZ is wholly owned by the New Zealand government but retains its independence and is run by the Governor. In many cases, central banks are called the *bankers' bank* because they supervise and assist member banks and cater to the greater financial system.[7] Finally, RBI began its operations in 1953 as a private entity following the enactment of Reserve Bank of India Act but in 1949 it was nationalized. The reserve bank is governed by a central Board of Directors appointed by the government.

2.2 Member banks

The only central bank system that includes district banks (12 in total) is the Federal Reserve System. A *Federal Reserve District Bank* serves a specific district in the United States and, along with the member banks, constitutes the operational arm of the Federal Reserve System. Of them, The New York district bank is considered the most important because of its location (at the heart of New York City) and its proximity to the largest banks in the US. Reserve Banks are quasi-public and thus, are federally chartered banks and private, nonprofit organizations, owned by the commercial banks in their districts. However, they are overseen by both the Fed's Board of Governors and their own Boards of Directors. Commercial banks can elect to become member banks as long as they meet specific requirements set by the Board of Governors. All national banks (which are chartered by the Comptroller of the Currency) are required to be members of the Fed, but other banks (chartered by their respective states) are not. Currently in the US, although about 35% of all banks are members they account for about 70% of all bank deposits.

Bank membership differs across central banks. For example, the central banks of all European Union countries own the ECB. Each member has a share in the ECB's capital (that is, provided a certain amount of money) in order to support ECB's goal of keeping prices stable across the eurozone. In a sense, the 20 national central banks (as of early 2023) of the Eurosystem play a role similar to the 12 regional Federal Reserve Banks in the US. Just like in the US, the President of the ECB chairs the Governing Council meetings in much the same way as the Chairman of the Fed's Board of Governors chairs meetings of the Federal Open Market Committee (FOMC, see section 2.3) that is responsible for formulating monetary policy in the US.

The Bank of England has twelve agencies across the UK and their agents are the eyes and ears of the central bank. Specifically, these agents collect information from all sectors of the economy (by holding one-to-one confidential conversations with businesses and community organizations in their area) and then convey it to the central bank. The Bank of Japan operates more as a head office than a federal system of central banks and is in charge of 32 domestic local branches and 12 local offices.

2.3 Monetary policy

Monetary policy constitutes the sole authority of a nation's central bank. *Monetary policy* is a set of tools designed to control a nation's overall money supply and achieve economic growth. In the US, the FOMC's goals are to achieve stable economic growth and price stability through the control of the money supply, which means being in charge of conducting monetary policy. The latter results in changes in interest rates – via its key short-term rate, the federal funds rate – and ultimately economic activity.[8] But how does the Fed achieve this? It uses three quantitative tools: open-market operations, reserve requirements, and the discount rate. Let us briefly explain each tool.

Open-market operations involve the buying and selling of government securities by the central bank in the open market on a daily basis (through its *Trading Desk* at the Fed Reserve Bank of New York). This constitutes the most important monetary policy tool because such trades change the banking system's federal reserves and interest rates. Specifically, an open-market purchase/sale causes the federal funds rate to fall/rise, because the money supply (curve) shifts to the right/left. In other words, when the Fed buys government securities from investors, the available money supply rises thus causing interest rates – and primarily the *federal funds rate*, the Fed's key short-term rate – to decline. The opposite occurs when the Fed sells government securities.

The second monetary policy tool is the *reserve requirement ratio*, which is the fraction of a bank's deposit accounts that must be held as required reserves (that is, in the bank's vaults). Specifically, a change in the reserve requirement ratio (rrr) changes the proportion of a bank's funds that can be invested (or lent out), and this affects the extent to which the money supply can grow. For example, assume the *rrr* is 10%, which means that out of $100 new deposits the bank must keep $10 in its vaults in cash (to meet daily operations or withdrawals). Assume now that the Fed raises the *rrr* to 20%. What is the impact on the money supply? The resulting change in the money supply would be the inverse of the *rrr*, *1/rrr*, known as the *money multiplier*. So, initially the money supply would grow to $1000 (1/.10 = 10 *times* the initial money injection of $100) but now it only grows to $500 (1/.20 = 5 * $100). Hence, the money supply would contract when the *rrr* is raised.[9]

The third and final quantitative monetary policy tool is the *discount rate* or the Fed's loan rate. The Fed typically provides short-term loans to banks (depository institutions) through, what is called, its discount window. Since 2003, this rate has been called the *primary credit lending rate*, which is set slightly above the federal funds rate (the rate charged on short-term loans between depository institutions). Banks take loans from the Fed only as a backup and that is why the Fed is also known as the Lender of Last Resort. Primary credit is available only to those banks that satisfy specific criteria reflecting financial soundness. In general, a discount loan leads to an expansion of reserves, which can be lent out leading to an expansion of the monetary base and the money supply.

A similar approach is used by the European System of Central Banks or the European Central Bank in that it signals the stance of its monetary policy by setting a *target financing rate*, which in turn sets a target for the overnight cash rate (which is similar to the federal funds rate for very short-term interbank loans). Thus, the monetary policy tools used by the ECB involve open market operations, lending to banks, and setting reserve requirements. Specifically, the ECB uses open market operations as its primary tool for conducting monetary policy. *Main refinancing operations* (MRO) are the predominant form of open market operations and are similar to the Fed's repurchase transactions. The MRO rate is the interest rate banks pay when they borrow money from the ECB for one week (with collateral to guarantee that the money will be paid back). Next, the ECB lends to banking institutions – which is conducted by the national central banks – and this lending takes place through a standing lending facility called the *marginal lending facility*. There, banks can borrow (against some collateral) overnight loans from the national central banks at the *marginal lending rate*. Finally, the ECB imposes reserve requirements (currently at 1%) such that all deposit-taking institutions are required to hold 1% of the total amount of checking deposits and other short-term deposits in reserve accounts with their national central banks.[10]

When would the Fed apply a restrictive or accommodative monetary policy? Assume the economy is contracting. How would the Fed reverse that trend? The Fed should apply accommodative (or stimulative) monetary policy. It can do it in a number of ways. First, it could buy Treasury securities from investors and give money in exchange, which will be deposited in the investors' banks (accounts). The immediate effect would be a decrease in the interest rates, which, in turn, would prompt investors to invest (borrow money) and consumers to spend more on goods and services. Then, the aggregate (that is, economy-wide) demand would increase and begin lifting the economy out of its declining trend. It is worth mentioning that these policies could have unintended side-effects such as the rise of inflation (demand-pull inflation) and the valuation of financial instruments. Second, it can lower the reserve requirements ratio (if it was a positive number before) which would then allow banks to have less money restricted (or kept in the form of cash) and increase lending out to investors and consumers. Finally, it can lower the discount rate so banks can borrow at a cheaper rate from the Fed and pass on these savings to their customers who, in turn, would begin spending more thus reversing the downward trend of the economy. Obviously, the reverse must occur (that is, the Fed must conduct a restrictive monetary policy) if it wants to apply the brakes to an overheating economy.

2.4 Economic indicators

Recall that the Fed's goals are to achieve low levels of inflation and unemployment in an effort to achieve economic stability. Given the Fed's goals, it must assess the economic indicators before determining its monetary policy. An *economic indicator* (or a set of economic indicators) is some macroeconomic piece of data that is used to assess current and future economic activity. There are three general types of economic indicators: *leading* – which predict the state of the economy in the near future – *lagging* – which trail or precede economic activity – and *coincident* – which coincide with the current state of the economy. Examples of leading indicators are the stock market, manufacturers' new orders and an index of consumer expectations; some lagging indicators are the average duration of unemployment and the consumer price index; and some coincident indicators are GDP, industrial production and non-agricultural payrolls. Therefore, the Fed monitors these indicators of economic growth (and many more, actually) because high economic growth creates a prosperous economy and can lead to lower unemployment, which the Fed also monitors.

The Fed also closely monitors price indexes and other indicators to assess the US inflation rate. There are several measures of inflation. The first is the *consumer price index*, which represents prices paid by consumers at the retail level. Another measure is the *producer price index*, which reflects prices at the wholesale level. A third measure, a broader one, is the *GDP deflator*, which represents the prices of goods and services produced in a country, including exports. As is evident, this inflation measure closely mirrors the GDP price index. Finally, there are other measures of inflation such as oil prices, wage rates and gold prices.

Panels A and B in Figure 3.2 depict the *business cycle* – the ups (peaks) and downs (troughs) in economic activity – for the United States, from 1967:I to 2025:III. In Panel A, the unemployment rate (quarterly data also) is superimposed, and in Panel B, the index of leading indicators is shown, to see how these magnitudes change with the recessions (brown bars) and expansions (clear regions). Looking at the first graph, we note that the unemployment rate rises when the recession begins, peaks during the middle (height) of the recessions, and then falls during normal, expansionary times. From the second graph, we observe that the leading indicators index rises while the economy is in a recession because it predicts the future course of the economy, which would be a rebound in economic activity or expansion. Note also that this index falls before the economy is hit with a contraction and later a recession, which also attests to this measure's name of being a leading indicator (of economic activity).

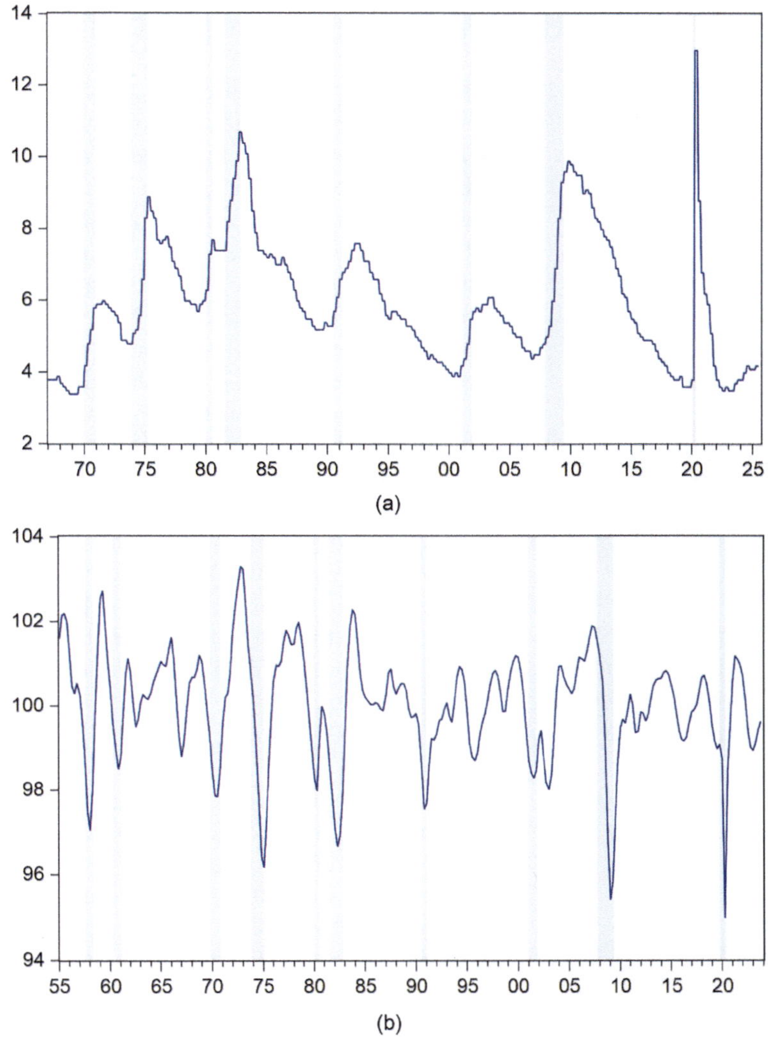

Figure 3.2 US Unemployment rate and Business cycles, 1967–2025

Test your understanding 1

1. What type of market player – deficit or surplus unit – would you be as a typical college student, salary earner (worker) and then retiree?
2. Do you think that financial technology will reduce (or eliminate) the need for financial intermediaries? Can you provide a for and against argument?
3. What would be the impact on the economy of an increase in the money supply?
4. As an investor why would you also closely watch some economic indicators?
5. How does monetary policy impact investments?

Solutions appear at the textbook's website.

3 Analyzing and using the global financial markets

TYPES OF INFLATION

There are several types of inflation: demand-pull (which arises because of excessive demand for goods and services), cost-push (due to rises in raw materials, tax rates and wage rates) government-induced (when the government engages in excessive spending), hyperinflation (when prices rise in excess of 50%), built-in (based on people's expectations about future inflation) and other variants such as galloping, creeping and so on.

In this section, we will discuss a number of current events that are closely linked to the above sections on financial institutions, instruments and monetary policy. We do not wish to give the idea to the reader that all current events – financial, economic, social, political and so on – are exhausted in this discussion! Many more will be presented and analyzed in depth in subsequent chapters. The goal here is to identify, discuss and analyze selected major current events (of the early 2023) that directly involve the above-mentioned topics in sections 1 and 2. The discussion will be framed as follows: first, the event will be presented and explained; then, it will be put in context with this chapter's topics and third, it will be analyzed, from the rational player's point of view, in terms of how (s)he would react to these events so as to exploit and/or shield her/himself from them. We begin with the Fed's interest rate hikes over the period of one year (March 2022 to March 2023).

3.1 Interest rate changes by the Fed

The United States' central bank – the Fed – has been increasing the federal funds rate from nearly zero in March 2022 to nearly 5% in March 2023, in a series of 25- or 50-basis point changes. A *basis point* is 1/100th of 1% or 0.0001. Figure 3.3 illustrates the path in the federal funds rate (FFR) since July 2025, on a weekly basis (week ending in Friday). Why did the Fed keep raising the interest rate during that period? The main reasons were the fight of inflation (which hit 6% during that year) and to slow down an overheating economy. Let us begin with inflation. For some additional information on inflation, please see the nearby *sidebar*, which presents some types of inflation.

What were the causes of inflation over the previous year? Economists generally agree on the following causes behind the high inflation that has defined the global economy over 2022. First, the COVID-19 pandemic, which shifted consumer demand away from services toward goods and left producers unable to keep up with rising demand along with factory closures because of that. Second, Russia's invasion of Ukraine caused a spike in oil prices, which increased the cost of both manufacturing and shipping, while also forcing up the price of wheat and other commodities thereby fueling food inflation. The economic rebound in 2022 further contributed to inflation (for example, resumed travel, outside dining, demand for housing etc.). Third, the US was dealing with a labor shortage, leaving many businesses unable to meet rising demand (which came from the government's stimulus payments) and gradually being able to open. Many countries as well including

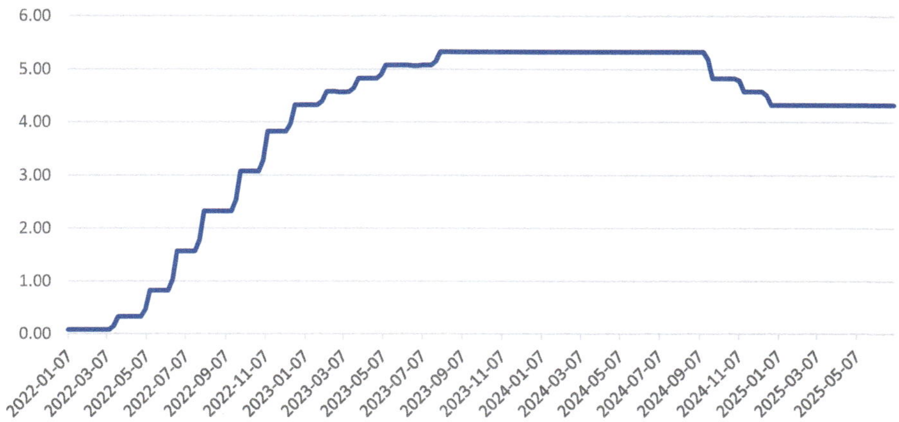

Figure 3.3 Federal funds rate, 01/01/2022–01/07/2025

the European Union funneled large sums of money to households and companies to ensure that they could manage lockdowns and layoffs. These actions surely increased the money supply and may have led to inflation.

The next question is what is the impact of inflation on you, as a consumer, investor or just average person? As you understand, there are two sides in everything, a losing and a gaining side. On the gaining side, you are now earning more (interest) on your savings and other banking products because of higher interest rates. Second, while interest rates were low you could benefit from stock investments – as the stock markets soared – as well as from some bond investments (such as the 10-year Treasury bond), whose yields are now higher. Third, if you are an existing long-term, fixed-rate borrower you do not need to worry as your mortgage rate is locked regardless of current (or future) rate increases. The same applies to owning and using a fixed-rate credit card. Fourth, companies also gain if they are able to cut real wages or own real estate or real assets (such as factories). Finally, if your income keeps up with the pace of rising inflation, then your purchasing power would not be affected.

Now, what about the losing side of inflation? First, you will now have to pay more for goods and services and your income's purchasing power would decline if prices of food, shelter and energy, for example, exceed the cost-of-living adjustments (from various sides such as income, investments etc.). Second, if you live off fixed income (if you are a retiree or a non-working student, for instance), then you would lose in purchasing power as well as potential income from fixed-income investments (Certificates of Deposits, interest income from bonds etc.). Third, you need to take on loans (mortgage, student, personal) or apply for a new credit card, then you will have to shell out more money now that interest rates are higher. Similarly, if you had opted for a variable-rate loan then you would have to pay more now per month to pay off your debt. Fourth, if you collect money (debt) then you would lose because the money now is worth less (but if you owe money then you would gain, as is the case of the government when it pays us with currently less-valuable dollars). Finally, export-oriented companies now find themselves on the rising-cost side because of the currency depreciation (in the presence of inflation which makes products more expensive now for foreigners to buy).

So, how do you protect yourself from these situations? One idea, although you still need to be careful, is to buy real assets (houses, land) and invest in inflation-hedging instruments (mainly commodities) such as gold and silver. For example, gold cannot be subject to the same inflationary pressures as paper money because it is not printed. Figure 3.4 shows the producer price index for gold and ore silver mining and consumer price index (inflation) since 1985 on a monthly basis. You will certainly observe that there were times where inflation (the red line) exceeded the commodity index (blue line). Research has shown that gold is not always a very good hedge against inflation.[11] Also, investing in Real Estate Investment Trusts (REITs) can provide reasonable inflation hedges. *REITs* are securitized real estate investments – or pooled with several individual real estate income-generating real estate such as housing buildings and commercial building – designed to provide large-scale (stable or fixed) income. Bahram et al. (2004) found that REIT investments – equity and mortgage – provided a reliable hedge against inflation.[12]

Another way is to invest in specific securities such as the US *Treasury Inflation-Protected Securities* (TIPS). As the term implies, TIPS are indexed to inflation to protect investors from a decline in the purchasing power of their money and thus, as inflation rises, TIPS adjust in price to maintain their real value.[13] Below is an example (see Table 3.1) to see how it works and why it is an effective (according to many analysts) inflation hedge. Assume that you invested in a 3-year, 3% coupon rate TIP security with a par (face) value of $1,000 at time 0. Assume also that the inflation rates were 2%, 3% and 1% over the year of the security. The mechanics of the various cash flows (coupon payments and principal) are shown next.

The par value at year 1 is found by simply multiplying the face value of $1,000 by the expected inflation rate of 2%. Then, the 1st coupon payment is found by multiplying the new, inflation-adjusted par value of $1,020 by the 3% coupon rate

Figure 3.4 Gold and silver price index and inflation, 1985:1–2023:3

Table 3.1 How TIPS work

Year	*Inflation in previous period*	*Par value*	*Coupon payment*	*Principal repayment*	*Total payment*
0		$1,000			
1	2%	$1,020	$30.600	$0	$30.600
2	3%	$1,050.600	$31.518	$0	$31.518
3	1%	$1,061.106	$31.833	$1,061.106	$1,092.939

($1,020 * 0.03) to arrive at $30.60. There is no principal repayment at that year because your investment horizon has not been reached yet. Hence, the only cash flow you would earn is the inflation-adjusted coupon payment. In year 2, inflation is expected to be 3% and so the security's (previous) principal will be adjusted again {$1,020 * (1 + 0.03)} to reach $1,050.60. The coupon payment will now be $31.518 (=$1,050.6 * 0.03) and so the only cash flow you will get is h = just that payment. Finally, in year 3 the same adjustments take place (both principal and coupon) and so the total payment will now include the principal repayment of $1,061.106 for a total of $1,092.939.

At this point it is instructive to ask the following question. What is the *real rate of return* you earned from this investment? Is it the 3% yield on the security? Did it really protect you against inflation? To determine this, you must first compute your nominal (not adjusted for inflation) rate of return (in the 1st year), using the formula below:

Nominal rate of return = (Interest income + Price change) / (Initial price) (1a)
= (Interest income + Initial price – Ending price)/
= (initial price) (1b)

Applying either of the above two formulae, we get

nominal return = (30.60 + 1,020 – 1,000) / (1,000) = 50.6 / 1,000 = 0.0506
= 5.06%

Now, you can compute your real return (also for the 1st year) as follows:

Real rate of return = {(1 + nominal return) / (1 + inflation)} – 1 (2)

and so, {(1 + 0.0506) / (1 + 0.02)} – 1 = 0.03 = 3%, which is exactly the yield on the TIP security. Using the same approach, you can calculate the nominal and real rates of return for the remaining years.

Finally, what does equation (2) also imply? You can find the nominal return by simply re-arranging it as follows:

Nominal rate of return = real rate of return + (expected) inflation (3a)
$(1 + i) = (1 + r) * (1 + \pi)$ (3b)

and this equation is the famous *Fisher equation* after Irving Fisher who proposed it. In (3b) i is the nominal rate, r the real rate and π expected inflation.

A very recent (as of 2022) '"'rival" financial asset to TIPS is the *Series I savings bonds* (known as *I Bonds*) where you earn both a fixed rate of interest and a rate that changes with inflation. I Bonds earn interest monthly. Interest is compounded semiannually, meaning that every 6 months the US Treasury sets the bond's interest rate to a new principal value. The new principal is the sum of the prior principal and the interest earned in the previous 6 months. Therefore, your 'bond's value grows both because it earns interest and because the principal value gets bigger. The full comparison between the two rival government investments can be accessed at the US Treasury's website.[14] In general, *I Bonds* are one of the best sources of safe, real yields available today, but the purchase limitations on I Bonds are so restrictive that for larger investors. TIPS are the only way to build meaningful inflation protection into their portfolios in a short period of time.

Finally, the stock market is another way of hedging against inflation. The stock market has traditionally been viewed as a typical inflation hedge by research. This is so because stocks compensate investors from inflation in two main ways: by paying dividends and by appreciating in value (price). Equity securities take up a sizable portion of a well-diversified portfolio and as such they serve as inflation hedges. However, the literature is split on the subject. Early work (Bodie, 1976; Ely and Robinson, 1997; and Tiwari et al., 2019, for example) did not conclusively find that common stocks are good (effective) inflation hedges, whereas recent work by Al-Nassar et al. (2019), Anari and Kolari (2001) and Luintel and Paudyal (2006) found support for inflation as a good inflation hedge.

3.2 Some financial consequences of raising interest rates

As we discussed earlier, the Fed engaged in a series of rate hikes for almost a year in an effort to combat (tame) inflationary pressures. However, as you learned in Chapter 2, as yields (or rates) rise, the value of the asset (based on its cash flows or face value) fall. This, essentially, means that the market value of your financial investment portfolio (which includes stocks, bond, debt etc.) declines. Such declines pose immediate (and very short-term) problems of liquidity and solvency, not only for investors but also for financial institutions. Further, continuing rate hikes would endanger the economy – real and financial alike – and send it to a steep contraction and then recession. Why is that? Well, as interest rates rise, investors will invest less in the real and financial economy and so the economy's productive capacity and liquidity will decline, consumers will spend less since the cost of buying goods and services is now higher and the government will have to pay more to finance its activities (and may raise taxes later) and hence some of the macroeconomic consequences will be not only inflation but also unemployment. Firms will have to lay off workers when they are not able to sell their products. In the past (in the early 1980s, early 1990s), when the fed funds rate soared, the US economy plunged into recessions.[15] Finally, a recent paper by Cecchetti et al. (2023) reviewed 16 episodes since 1950 when a central bank like the Fed raised the cost of borrowing to fight inflation, in the United States, Canada, Germany and the United Kingdom. In each case, a recession resulted.

Since the beginning of 2023, the Fed continued raising the fed funds rate (as mentioned on p. 68) and now may economists and market professionals worry that such high rates would steer the economy to a recession. The US (and global) financial press is calling for an end to rate hikes because the economy has begun seeing other serious financial consequences. First, the collapse of the Silicon Valley Bank (SVB) – a California-based regional bank – specializing in loans (investments) for startup, tech-sector companies. The huge money influx prompted the bank to invest heavily (disproportionally) in long-term US government bonds, including mortgage-backed securities. When interest rates kept rising, the value of the bank's portfolios fell and, at the same time, the tech sector found itself struggling for growth (stifled by higher interest rates or borrowing costs). In plain language, when short-term rates (which the banks use for borrowing) are higher than longer-term rates (the benchmarks the banks use for lending), this squeezes liquidity and hence profitability. Some very well-known companies (Amazon, Meta and Microsoft) announced massive layoffs. In addition, tech companies were increasingly moving to withdraw their bank deposits (including from SVB) and this quickly brought SVB to its knees. To meet the rising demand from depositors, the bank sold its government bonds ($21 billion) at a massive loss (of $1.75 billion), yielding it an average 1.79 percent well below the then 10-year Treasury yield of about 3.9 percent! Soon after this event, other US banks collapsed (Signature, First Republic and PacWest Bancorp). These bank runs prompted the Fed and the federal government to intervene to secure deposits and calm the fears of depositors by guaranteeing their deposits.

Further, global consumer confidence has been suffering a sharper decline than in the run-up to past global recessions. The world's three largest economies – the US, China, and the Euro area – have been slowing sharply. The World Bank proposed (in 2022) that economic policies – monetary and fiscal – should focus on boosting production in order to achieve low inflation rates, currency stability and faster growth. "Hence, there should be policies in place seeking to generate additional investment and improve productivity and capital allocation, which are critical for growth and poverty reduction."[16] Calls from reputable market experts and analysts (such as Elon Musk, Mohamed El-Erian and Nouriel Roubini or "Dr. Doom") are about the risks that rate hikes could hit banks, commercial real estate and government debt (says Musk), the confluence of

TURKEY'S INTEREST RATES

When all major central banks raise interest rates in order to combat inflation, Turkey's President Erdogan reduced interest rates! In early 2023, interest rates were slashed from 19% to 8.5% despite high inflation in the country. This policy led to a currency (Lira) crisis and sent inflation soaring, further eating away household savings. The main reasons for lowering interest rates were to support financial conditions to sustain the growth momentum in industrial production and the positive trend in employment. Another reason was the major earthquakes the country experienced in February 2023 and the country's authorities needed to look at the domestic economy and its exports rather than inflation.

financial stability, inflation and economic growth (says El-Erian) and call rate hikes a "'"megathreat" to the US economy (says Roubini). Also, worries are growing about liquidity in US Treasurys, which has been drying up due to the Fed's reducing its balance sheet. This "dysfunction" in the bond market could destabilize other areas of the financial system given the wide-reaching impact of Treasurys.[17]

The nearby *sidebar* discusses the consequences from a completely opposite course of action by Turkey's President to combat inflation. Specifically, at the time when major central banks raised interest rates to fight inflation, Turkey's central bank reduced interest rates!

Test your understanding 2

1. How would banks act following interest-rate hikes?
2. Can you mention some things that you can do as an individual consumer when interest rates rise? [Hints: discuss in terms of savings, credit cards and mortgage loans]
3. Explain the process of the reduction in the federal funds rate when the FOMC lowers its target for that rate. Concentrate on the Fed's most powerful monetary policy tool.
4. How do you feel when you hear about bank mergers (when one bank is taken over by another), bank profit losses or higher costs of banking and so on?

Solutions appear at the textbook's website.

3.3 Other global financial problems

Apart from inflation, high interest rates and the threat of recession, other global, financial problems contribute to the worsening of the global economy, which the financial markets and the central banks are called to moderate or solve. For example, some analysts are worried that real estate prices are too high, many financial institutions are likely to have large indirect exposures through loans, investments, and derivative exposures to firms and individuals (taking market risk), climate-related risks and issues such as pollution, land degradation and greenwashing, the rise of new and volatility in digital currencies (cryptocurrencies, stablecoins and central bank digital currencies, part of *fintech* or financial technology trends), and the threat of corporate insolvencies as a result of the COVID-19 pandemic.[18] We discuss financial technology and its implications on the global financial markets in Chapter 13. In addition, the nearby *sidebar* suggests that you should read regularly major financial articles by major organizations such as OECD and *The Economist*.

For example, the recent (as of March 2023) troubles of Credit Suisse bank (in Switzerland), Deutsche bank (in Germany) and British and French giants HSBC and BNP Paribas witnessed collapses of their share prices as investors panicked due to some of these banks' obscure investments and hidden management tactics. Specifically, Deutsche Bank agreed (in 2017) to pay a $7.2 billion fine to the US for its "irresponsible lending practices" in 2006 and 2007 that partially caused the Great Recession. Recently, the bank's 5-year CDS (credit default swaps) – intended to proxy for bondholders' beliefs in the health of the issuing institutions – just reached the highest level since 2019. A series of year-long scandals, top management shakeups, multi-billion dollar losses and a naïve investment strategy can be blamed for the mess in Credit Suisse, which was taken over by Switzerland's other major bank, UBS. French banks such as BNP Paribas rely on more expensive, market-sensitive wholesale funding because most of the deposits are from regulated savings accounts, and this potentially can put pressure on 'lenders' liquidity buffers in the event of a financial shock.

Next, global issues such as climate-related and corporate governance conflicts are getting serious. On the corporate governance issues and challenges we can mention a few. First, the US Department of Justice recently announced that it is accelerating efforts to enforce Section 8 of the Clayton Act, which prohibits officers and directors from serving with competing companies simultaneously.[19] Second, the SEC requires publicly traded companies to adopt policies allowing them to *claw back* incentive-based executive compensation if there were mis-reportings of the firm's financial statements or conditions (either by error or fraud) which subsequently required accounting restatement. Third, newly proposed SEC rules (and expected in early 2023) focused on the disclosure of board diversity as part of the corporation's good corporate governance practices.[20]

On climate-related challenges, the SEC's 2022 rulings would require ESG disclosures about management oversight and governance of material climate impacts, greenhouse gas emissions, as well as targets and transition plans.[21] In addition, there has been enhanced scrutiny of "greenwashing" over the past year, with private lawsuits alleging deceptive marketing, skepticism about sustainability-linked financing and additional SEC enforcement actions alleging misleading climate-related disclosures.[22] *Greenwashing* occurs when a firm conveys false or misleading information to overstate its environmental or sustainability practices. Some notable examples of companies accused of greenwashing are Volkswagen (which in 2015 the US Environmental Protection Agency discovered that the company cheated on federal emissions tests to make its vehicles seem less harmful to the environment than they were), the Swedish company IKEA (which was accused of illegally obtaining timber from Ukraine and Russia despite its green public image in 2021), several oil- and gasoline-producing giant companies such as BP and Exxon-Mobil (which, since 2019, promoted low-carbon energy products which were actually 96% from oil and gas or polluted the environment or campaigned that its experimental algae biofuels could reduce transport emissions) and many more companies.

OTHER FINANCIAL READINGS

If you begin reading academic and other journals, you will be able to understand many of the financial problems that are current and expected. Some topics you could explore from the OECD's *Financial Markets Trends* journal are: green financing and green bonds, macroprudential policies, portfolio investments and strategies, bank failures and more. One more website is the *Economist Intelligence Unit* (EIU) where many reports on the global financial trends are published routinely.

Finally, a number of national and international organizations, such as the World Bank, International Monetary Fund, World Economic Forum, United Nations and many more of them, worry that the 2020s will bring new challenges to the global economy. Some of these challenges include the following. First, coming out of the COVID-19 global pandemic and the resulting national recovery plans will place a much bigger burden on countries' national debts. This is particularly serious for emerging countries where economic and financial impacts are always greater than in developed economies. The most serious consequence of that would be poverty and social unrest. Governments are riddled with huge debts, which embeds the danger of defaults of non-repayments. In addition, private service companies (such as aviation, transportation, tourism) are in the same situation since there could be further supply-chain disruption and hikes in crude oil prices (primarily because of OPEC's decisions to cut output).

Second, geopolitical tensions among nations continue brewing. The Russia–Ukraine war aside, tensions build in the China sea, between China and Taiwan and China–US because of Taiwan. Apart from new military conflicts,[23] we will also witness mass migrations as the world (and particularly Europe) has witnessed in recent year. Another implication of geopolitical tensions entails big changes in cross-border portfolio investments, real investments (real direct investments) and bank allocations of global claims. Finally, other and related consequences are cybersecurity, data fraud/loss, new financial instruments and so on.

3.4 Your role in all this

In sum, what is your role and position in all this? How can you protect yourself? Although the answer to such questions are always difficult and challenging, we can offer some suggestions on how you can deal with some of these events assuming several capacities as an individual.

First, as a consumer you could, perhaps, change or adjust your preferences and prioritize anew your needs and wants. Try to acquire new habits that go along with these times and search for deals. Obviously, this is not easy for some people of age but if you are young then the chances of success and effective navigation through such times are high. It is also understood that by the time you read this, things have changed in your country as well as the world and so constant adaptation must take place. Your objective should remain the same – maximize your utility – but you need to find new ways of accomplishing this. As an educated person, you will be able to improvise and use your intellectual skills.

Second, as an investor you should consult professional advisers for investment advice and portfolio choices but you should always be the final decision-maker (we will discuss this in later chapters when we learn how to construct an efficient portfolio.) The complexity and constant growth of financial instruments will always complicate investments but you should be able to discern the "good" and "bad" investments and select effectively. For example, the trend towards *socially responsible investments* – investments that are made in companies that care about the environment, climate, people and so on – is now mature and there are plenty of them out there. This means that now you have the opportunity to shy away from companies that harm the environment, abuse workers and/or produce socially undesirable goods such as tobacco and firearms and concentrate on 'good' companies. Further, the risks of investments are now more and, in many cases, amplified by the evolving structure of the global economy. For example, we have new risks that involve geopolitics (as mentioned earlier), *sustainability risks* (ESG or environmental, social and governance events which, if materialize, could cause actual or potential negative impacts on the value of an investment), social issues (such as abortion rights legislation changes, LGBTQ+ rights, large-scale migrations and more) and *anti-ESG sentiment* (alarms about conservative attacks on socially conscious policies).[24] In general, keep in mind that there are more risks relative to expected return.

Finally, as a citizen you are witnessing fast-paced and drastic changes in the global financial landscape. You, as a citizen, you should organize actions and activities starting with your neighborhood and gradually extending then to the community, the town, city and so on. You should also cooperate with local and state authorities to enforce laws and regulations so as to begin a change from the bottom up. It is understood that the local and federal government should support your efforts. In turn, central government (federal) authorities should establish cooperation with other countries – advanced and emerging alike – to establish and supervise a global financial safety net.

In sum, you must be on top of things, constantly following the news and acquiring knowledge that you can use. You need to start discussing with the people around you on how best to address the current and emerging financial disruptions and turn them into opportunities rather than allowing them to become destabilizing risks for you. You should begin engaging on the global financial, social, political and more developments by participating or following global financial centers and economic powerhouses around the world. Read some influential articles/reports on how to make the global financial system work for all, how to foster economic resilience in a world of open and integrated markets and how to make business thrive in today's fast-changing world.[25]

Finally, it would be interesting to ask whether Management and Marketing are relevant to the global financial markets. If you study Management, would you know how financial markets are related to your major? Box 3.1 explains how the global financial markets connect with your discipline so you can understand how managers deal with them. For the Marketing majors, would you like to know how the four P's – price, product, place, promotion – are linked to the study of the global financial markets? Box 3.2 explains how.

Box 3.1

How is management related to the global financial markets?

GLOBALIZATION: The world is increasingly economically and financially integrated and that means that managers need to be alert on what is happening elsewhere in the world. Global managers need to have more skills to successfully engage in world business and financial markets, in particular.

CROSS-CULTURAL CHALLENGES: Managers need to understand other people's customs, cultures and mentality in order to remain competitive. Country-by-country differences can be vast even among advanced economies.

STAKEHOLDERS: Groups of people that affect the cost and availability of capital your company needs such as shareholders, bondholders, financial institutions, venture capitalists and many more. A manager needs to be able to communicate with them effectively in an effort to contribute to the maximization of the company's value.

STRATEGIC MOVES: Managers need to work with the global financial markets (and their constituents and instruments) in order to develop and successfully implement the company's strategic goals and mission.

Box 3.2

How are the four Ps related to the global financial markets?

PRODUCT: Financial markets trade financial products, foster innovation in new financial products (securitization, ESG investments, cryptocurrencies, Green technology etc.) to meet investor demand recognizing that the success of their financial products affects their cash flows, profitability and their stock prices.

PRICE: Pricing in financial markets is essential and all financial instruments are constantly repriced to reflect constantly changing economic, financial, social, political and more conditions in the global financial environment; central bank policies affect pricing strategies for the fixed-income and equity markets.

PLACE: Financial assets are traded in global exchanges because firms list their stocks in international exchanges, thus making location or place critical for investor access and liquidity; companies sell their products and raise capital in various markets worldwide.

PROMOTION: Financial markets are moved by information flows and thus companies promote or advertise their investment projects through calls, prospectuses and financial reports; financial institutions promote their successes through advertising and leadership in order to attract more investors.

Summary

- We offered an overview of the global financial markets.
- We discussed concepts such as financial intermediaries, financial instruments, direct and indirect finance.
- We listed the main roles of the financial markets.
- We discussed the types of financial markets, namely the money and capital markets.
- We outlined the types of financial instruments such as money-market and capital-market instruments.

- We presented the type of financial intermediaries, depository and non-depository financial institutions.
- We elaborated on a country's central bank and the banking system.
- We discussed the characteristics of central banks in many countries and the role of their member banks.
- We talked about monetary policy and its main tools, namely open-market operations, reserve requirements and the discount rate.
- We listed the main economic indicators and categorized them in leading, coincident and lagging.
- We next analyzed certain situations found in financial markets and learned how to exploit them and avoid dangers.
- Examples of such situations are the consequences of interest-rate changes by central banks (mostly the Fed), the concepts of nominal and real rates of return, and other global financial problems.
- Examples of the latter are climate-related issues, the rise of new transactions instruments (such as cryptocurrencies and stablecoins) and the threat of corporate insolvencies as a result of the COVID-19 pandemic.

Questions and problems

1. What are some of the challenges to indirect financing?
2. Which type of financial market – money or capital market – would an investors prefer?
3. Evaluate the following actual statements in terms of the type of monetary policy tool employed.
   a. In order to keep the liquidity in the banking system adequate at a reasonable level, the People's Bank of China conducted reverse repo operations in the amount of RMB2 billion through interest rate bidding on November 7, 2022.
   b. In line with its main objective of price stability and in the scope of efforts towards supporting financial stability and encouraging liraization, the Central Bank of the Republic of Turkey has strengthened its macroprudential policy toolkit and revised the reserve requirement regulation.
   c. The Governor and the Chairman of the Board of Directors of the Central Bank of Kuwait (CBK), Basel A. Al-Haroon, stated that the CBK Board of Directors decided to raise the discount rate by 0.50% from 3.5% to 4.0% effective January 26, 2023.
   d. The European Central Bank on Thursday confirmed its intention to hike interest rates at the policy meeting next month and downgraded its growth forecasts.
4. Classify the following economic indicators as leading, coincident and lagging. Provide a brief description of each.
   a. 'Manufacturers' new orders for consumer goods and/or materials
   b. Money Supply (M2)
   c. The change in labor cost per unit of output
   d. The average prime rate charged by banks
   e. Number of employees on non-agricultural payrolls
   f. Unemployment rate

5. Explain how raising interest rates affect home sales, business profits and consumer spending.
6. Can you identify some ways through which greenwashing affects the consumer and the investor?
7. Please identify some geopolitical risks on consumers and investors.
8. What is the impact of bad corporate governance practices on the society, in general?
9. What could be some implications of the trend towards greater technology in financial services (fintech) for consumers and investors?
10. Should the recent (as of early 2023) bank troubles and scandals make you less trusty of banks?

Notes

1. Money-market instruments are discussed in Chapter 4.
2. Financial intermediaries are presented in Chapter 5.
3. https://www.federalreserve.gov/aboutthefed/structure-federal-reserve-system.htm
4. https://www.rethinkeconomics.org/wp-content/uploads/2022/03/Understanding-the-Bank-of-England.pdf
5. https://european-union.europa.eu/institutions-law-budget/institutions-and-bodies/institutions-and-bodies-profiles/ecb_en#:~:text=The%20ECB%20has%20the%203,day%20running%20of%20the%20ECB
6. https://www.rba.gov.au/about-rba/governance.html
7. It is interesting to mention that the *central banks' bank*, at the global level, is the Bank for International Settlements (BIS) which itself is an international financial institution owned by central banks and fosters international monetary and financial cooperation (https://www.bis.org/)
8. More discussion on monetary policy implementation is found in Chapter 4.
9. The Fed's rrr (as of 2020) is set at 0%, which means that it has eliminated it. The Fed now focuses on managing the overall level of reserves in the banking system and influencing interest rates. https://www.federalreserve.gov/monetarypolicy/reservereq.htm
10. https://www.project-syndicate.org/commentary/central-banks-should-raise-minimum-reserve-requirements-by-paul-de-grauwe-and-yuemei-ji-1–2023-02
11. For example, Hoang, T.H.V., A. Lahiani, and D. Heller (Is Gold a Hedge Against Inflation? New Evidence from a Nonlinear ARDL Approach. *Economic Modelling* (2016) 54, 54–66) found that it is not a good inflation hedge in the long run for many countries such as the US, UK, China and India but a good hedge in the short-run for UK and US. On the other hand, Xu, Yingying, Su Chi-Wei, and Jaime Ortiz (Is Gold a Useful Hedge Against Inflation Across Multiple Time Horizons? *Empirical Economics* (2021) 60, 1175–1189) found that gold is a good inflation hedge in the long and short run. Finally, as regards silver, Bampinas, Georgios and Theodore Panagiotidis (Are Gold and Silver a Hedge against Inflation? A Two Century Perspective. *International Review of Financial Analysis* (2015) 41, 267–276) found that gold is a good inflation hedge (in the US and UK) but silver is not an inflation hedge in the US but marginally in the UK.
12. Bahram Adrangi, Arjun Chatrath and Kambiz Raffiee (2004). REIT Investments and Hedging Against Inflation. *Journal of Real Estate Portfolio Management* 10(2), 97–112,
13. https://www.treasurydirect.gov/marketable-securities/tips/
14. https://www.treasurydirect.gov/research-center/history-of-savings-bond/comparing-tips-to-i/
15. https://www.epi.org/publication/issuebriefs_ib148/
16. https://www.worldbank.org/en/news/press-release/2022/09/15/risk-of-global-recession-in-2023-rises-amid-simultaneous-rate-hikes

17. https://markets.businessinsider.com/news/stocks/fed-rate-hikes-growth-inflation-financial-stability-mohamed-el-erian-2022-10; https://markets.businessinsider.com/news/stocks/inflation-recession-fed-rate-hikes-economy-dr-doom-nouriel-roubini-2023-3#:~:text=The%20central%20bank%27s%20efforts%20in%20the%20name%20of,mass%20liquidity%20and%20solvency%20problems%2C%22%20the%20economist%20said
18. https://www.oliverwyman.com/our-expertise/insights/2022/jan/finance-in-2022-five-key-policy-issues.html#:~:text=Based%20on%20those%20discussions%2C%20here%20are%20five%20key,and%20central%20bank%20digital%20currencies%29%20Corporate%20solvency%2C%20post-pandemic
19. https://www.justice.gov/opa/pr/justice-department-s-ongoing-section-8-enforcement-prevents-more-potentially-illegal
20. https://www.sec.gov/news/public-statement/roisman-board-diversity
21. https://www.sec.gov/news/press-release/2022–46
22. https://corpgov.law.harvard.edu/2022/12/01/thoughts-for-boards-key-issues-in-corporate-governance-for-2023/
23. At the time of revised writing, the Israeli-Iran short-lived war erupted (June 2025).
24. https://news.bloomberglaw.com/esg/citi-valero-adt-flag-new-investment-risk-the-anti-esg-effect https://hbr.org/2023/04/why-business-leaders-must-resist-the-anti-esg-movement
25. https://www.globalfinancialgovernance.org/files/g20epg-full%20report.pdf; https://www.oecd.org/en/about/news/press-releases/2021/03/oecd-reports-to-g7-on-need-to-strengthen-economic-resilience-against-crises.html; https://www.weforum.org/agenda/2019/01/how-can-global-businesses-navigate-the-new-normal/

References

Al-Nassar, Nassar S., and Razzaque H. Bhatti (2019). Are Common Stocks a Hedge Against Inflation in Emerging Markets? *Journal of Economics and Finance* 43, 421–455.

Anari, Ali, and James Kolari (2001). Stock Prices and Inflation, *Journal of Financial Research* 24(4), 587–602.

Bodie, Z. (1976). Common Stocks as a Hedge Against Inflation. *The Journal of Finance* 31(2), 459–470.

Cecchetti, Michael E. Feroli, Peter Hooper, Frederic S. Mishkin, and Kermit L. Schoenholtz (2023). *Discussion of the Paper* "Managing Disinflations". The paper was presented at the US Monetary Policy Forum, New York, February 24.

Ely, David P. and Kenneth J. Robinson (1997). Are Stocks a Hedge Against Inflation? International Evidence Using a Long-Run Approach. *Journal of International Money and Finance* 16(1), 141–167.

Luintel, K., and K. Paudyal (2006). Are Common Stocks a Hedge against Inflation? *Journal of Financial Research* 29(1), 1–19.

Tiwari, Aviral Kumar, Juncal Cunado, Rangan Gupta, and Mark E. Wohar (2019). Are Stock Returns an Inflation Hedge for the UK? Evidence from a Wavelet Analysis Using over Three Centuries of Data. *Studies in Nonlinear Dynamics and Econometrics* 23(3), 20170049.

Part II

The money market

This section deals with the money market and its characteristics, its instruments and participants. The global money markets provide the funds of market participants such as households (consumers and retail investors), businesses (corporations and financial institutions including institutional investors), the government (federal, state and local) and the rest of the world to those participants, who are the same ones who provide the funds, when they need to cover short-term obligations. In this part, we will discuss a number of items that relate to the money market. First, we will describe the globalization and integration of the money market, the basic money-market instruments by issuer (government and businesses), the risk/return profiles of selected money-market instruments, the players (mainly intermediaries) of the money market and conclude with how these instruments are exploited by retail and institutional investors.

Specifically, Chapter 4 deals with the characteristics, internationalization and integration of the money market as well as the peculiarities found in selected financial markets. The chapter ends with a section on how one would exploit the international money market drawing on real examples.

Chapter 5 discusses in detail the instruments and the intermediaries of the money markets worldwide. Some valuation tools are also presented and a discussion on how a retail investor can exploit the money market is included.

Chapter 6 discusses the money market funds and the mutual fund industry as well as the investment banking industry. This chapter concludes with a section on investor investment perspectives (insights) in these two financial services industries.

DOI: 10.4324/9781003677161-5

Chapter 4

The characteristics and globalization of the money market

1 Inside the global money market

The *global money market* is an important financial market because it serves all market participants, nationally and globally. This market is typically used by financial institutions, large corporations, and national governments. Investments and financing – in major national currencies – made in the money markets are usually for a short period of time. The *International Money Market* (IMM) is a large-scale money market that allows many countries' central banks to conduct transactions – both lending and borrowing – from different countries. This activity takes place 24 hours a day and handles funds in trillions, with the main actors being central banks and major commercial banks.

At this point it is instructive to point out that there are many differences between *money market mutual funds* (MMMFs) or *money market funds* (MMFs) and a money market account in a bank. An MMMF or MMF account is considered an investment, and it is not a savings or checking account, even though some money market funds allow you to write checks. MMMFs are offered by brokerage firms and fund companies, whereas money market checking or savings accounts are offered by banks (which also are related with MMMFs) but abide by different rules and regulations. For example, MMMFs or MMFs are not protected by the Federal Deposit Insurance Corporation (FDIC), which we mention later in the chapter. Also, money market accounts may limit your monthly withdrawals (say, at an ATM) and have a higher minimum balance requirement than traditional savings accounts. Finally, you are able to write a limited number of checks directly

DOI: 10.4324/9781003677161-6

from your money market account, eliminating the need to transfer funds from savings to checking.

In the United States, the money market became noticeable in the early 1970s, when short-term interest rates rose above historic levels due to Regulation Q. *Regulation Q* set restrictions on the payment of interest on deposit accounts. From its inception during the Great Depression in the early 1930s to 1986, it also imposed a ceiling on the payment of interest on savings accounts and NOW accounts (see Chapter 5 for its description). As a result, a rapid outflow of funds from financial institutions in the late 1970s and early 1980s took place, which, in turn, resulted in massive failures of many savings and loan associations as well as banks. The funds simply went to money market funds and the first money market fund was established in 1971. The mutual fund industry has exploded in growth since then.

Global money market funds saw tremendous growth as of early 2023 primarily due to US high interest rates and bank collapses (such as the Silicon Valley bank and several more in the US). In essence, high interest rates caused depositors to move their funds out of banks and into money market funds including investment banks. Similarly, a lot of money was pulled away from global equity and bond funds – both from advanced and emerging economies – as investors feared another recession in early 2023. The deteriorating outlooks on US, UK, Canadian as well as some German banks implied significant uncertainty about the credit quality of this market and led to a contagion effect on money funds as global portfolios were concentrated in this financial sector.

What do such high interest rates mean for rate-sensitive cash investments such as bank accounts, CDs, money market funds and short-term Treasury debt maturing within one year? As you have probably guessed, there is an opportunity to take advantage of these high yields now, which, probably, are not going to continue for long. Large money market funds offered an average 4.64%, 7-day yield as of Crane's Money Fund Intelligence, while the annual percentage yields on high-yield savings accounts and one-year online bank CDs reached 4% and 5%, according to May 10, 2023 Crane Data.[1] Note that CDs stand for Certificates of Deposit and offer higher interest rates than traditional savings accounts. We discuss the CD market in Chapter 5.

Finally, one more reason for the recent explosion (as of 2023) in such funds was the strong US employment report which raised expectations among market participants that interest-rate hikes in the US were not over. Recall from Chapter 1 that there is an inverse relationship between unemployment and inflation – the so-called Phillips curve – and so when employment grows and thus, unemployment falls – inflationary pressures build up, triggering thoughts by the Fed to raise interest rates further.

The end result of all above events was for the yield on the 3-month US Treasury bill – an instrument we will discuss in Chapter 5 – and in which money market funds invest the most, to surge to near a 16-year high of 5.175% on April 13, 2023.[2] In Figure 4.1, the huge increase in that money market instrument's yield over the 2022–2024 period is clearly shown.

Money market rates globally differ as economies differ in many aspects namely, economic, financial and social. However, money market rates tend to move together over time as national monetary policies are aligned and mostly converging. Table 4.1 shows the correlation matrices for four major money market rates (US, UK, Eurozone and Japan) for each decade, 2000s (2000–2009), 2010s

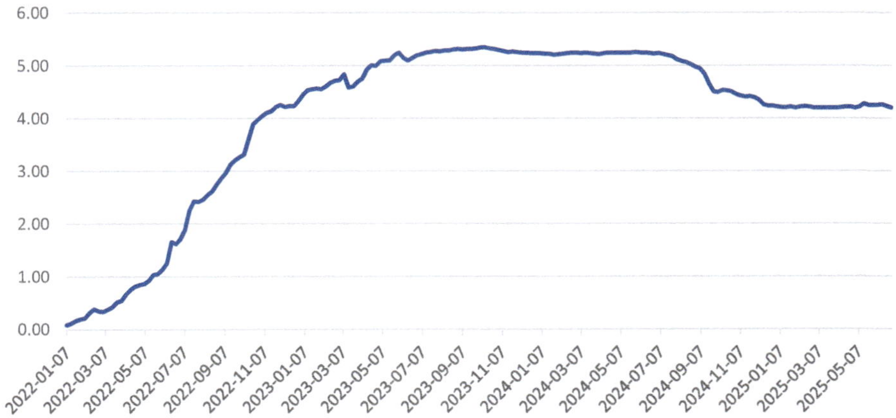

Figure 4.1 Growth of 3-month US Treasury bill, 2022:1–2025:7

Table 4.1 Correlations among major money market rates by decade, 2000s to 2020s

2000S

	US	*UK*	*EUROZONE*
UK	0.7773		
EUROZONE	0.6284	0.7365	
JAPAN	0.2870	0.2907	0.6006

2010S

	US	*UK*	*EUROZONE*
UK	0.4716		
EUROZONE	−0.5935	0.1104	
JAPAN	−0.8290	−0.0392	0.7397

2020S

	US	*UK*	*EUROZONE*
UK	0.9834		
EUROZONE	0.9656	0.9716	
JAPAN	−0.2325	−0.2652	−0.2552

Note: 2000s (2000:1 – 2009:12); 2010s (2010:1 – 2019:12); 2020s (2020:1 – 2023:4)

(2010–2019) and 2020s (2020–2023). From these correlations, we observe high positive correlations between US, UK and Eurozone money market rates in the 2000s and 2020s decades, but lower and a negative one (between the US and Eurozone) during the 2010s decade. In addition, US, UK and Eurozone rates have been weakly and negatively correlated with the Japanese rates since the 2010s decade.

The same picture is seen in Figure 4.2, where these rates are shown since 2000. Specifically, we note some positive co-movement (among the US, UK and Eurozone rates) prior to the 2007/8 global financial crisis, then a sharp drop in all of them during the crisis (2007–2009), followed by a tranquil period, where all rates were near zero. Then, beginning in 2016, the US money market rate began increasing but not closely followed by the UK or Eurozone rates until mid-2021 where all

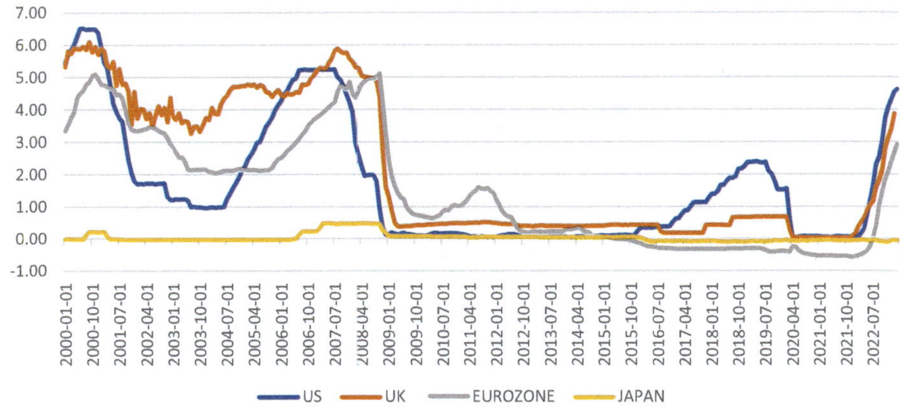

Figure 4.2 Selected money market rates, 2000:1–2023:3

three rates were sharply raised. Note also the lag that exists between the US and the UK and Eurozone rates with the latter two rates following the movements of the former rate. Finally, observe the Japanese rate which was mostly flat throughout the 20+ year period.

In general, a well-functioning money market is a trait of advanced economies. Most very low-income countries have limited financial systems in which money markets play no role. For example, in Africa expatriate commercial banks have substituted for a local money market and these banks met fluctuations in domestic loan demand by changing their balances at head offices overseas. Government policies have also encouraged these banks to develop domestic channels for temporary surpluses and deficits. Other issues responsible for stifling the growth of money markets in developing countries such as Latin America and Asia, are persistent inflation, the low incomes of people that leave no savings and the use of the money market as a primary government outlet for short-term funds. Hence, there was the birth of *unorganized money markets* (known as such because they are outside normal financial institutions) so as to escape government controls over interest rates but these do not function effectively because interest rates are high and contacts between localities and borrowers and lenders are limited.

In mature economies, money market interest rates are influenced by the demand for short-term funds by borrowers, relative to the supply of available short-term funds that are supplied by savers. So, if the demand for short-term funds (denominated in a particular currency) is high/low relative to the short-term funds that are available in that currency, the interest rates will be relatively high/low in that country.

2 Characteristics of the money market

In general, money markets provide easy access to one's money, allow very safe investments, higher rates of return than standard savings accounts; check-writing and money-transferring privileges; and very low minimum balance amounts are usually required. More specifically, the main characteristics of the money market are the following: short-term life and thus short-term funds, low risk and hence high liquidity; wholesale market (large size); global presence, secondary market and submarkets; organized banking system; determines interest rates. Let us briefly discuss each one of them in turn.

2.1 Short-term life

Money market securities have a life of one year or less. The shortest life (maturity) is one day but most money market instruments mature in 120 days or less. Because this is a market purely for short-term funds or financial assets, they are also called near money.

2.2 Low or no risk

Due to this market's short-term nature, its instruments carry very low risk of default but one specific instrument, the Treasury bill, or Tbill for short (which we will discuss in Chapter 5), has no risk of default at all. More specifically for the Tbills, even if the government runs out of money, it could simply print more to redeem them when they mature. In addition, the risk of unexpected changes in inflation is low because of the short-term to maturity nature of the money market securities.

2.3 High liquidity

Recall that a liquid market is one in which securities can be bought and sold quickly and with low transaction costs. Further, investors in such markets have little liquidity risk that they will not be able to sell (or convert) their securities (into cash) when they wish to. An investor can access his/her money whenever they need it, without penalty.

2.4 Wholesale market

A *wholesale market* means that most transactions are very large, usually in excess of $1 million and, as a result, retail investors are prevented from participating directly in the money markets. Instead, institutional investors including dealers and brokers, who operate in the trading rooms of large banks and brokerage houses, bring customers together to exploit the money market (via mutual funds, a topic we will start discussing in Chapter 5 and in later chapters). The majority of money market transactions are wholesale transactions that take place between financial institutions and companies. However, despite the wholesale nature of the money market, innovative securities primarily mutual funds, hedge funds and exchange-traded funds as well as trading methods such as program trading have been developed to give small investors access to money market securities.

2.5 Global presence

Money market transactions do not take place in any one particular physical location such as an exchange. Instead, traders usually arrange purchases and sales between participants electronically (via electronic communications networks or ECNs) or over the phone. Because of this feature, money market securities usually have an active secondary market. An active secondary market enables businesses and governments to satisfy their short-term financial needs (known as "*bridge financing*"). The money market is not a homogeneous market but part of the larger financial market consisting of numerous smaller sub-markets including federal government, corporate and other institutional agents. More specifically, the major sub-markets are the call loan market, the Tbill market, the collateral loan market, the acceptance market, and the foreign exchange market. All of these markets and more will be discussed in Chapter 5.

2.6 Organized banking system

At the center of this market are the commercial banks which, being the principal suppliers of short-term funds, serve as a vital link between the central bank and the various segments of the money market. In addition, a mature money market has the central bank which controls, regulates and guides the entire money market. It provides liquidity to the money market, as it is the lender of the last resort to the various participants of the money market.

2.7 Determination of interest rates

Money markets serve as channels for the execution and transmission of monetary policy, and as trading venues for the shortest-term instruments (namely, the Tbill) that affect the entire term structure of interest rates. Moreover, economically speaking money markets are instrumental for the allocation of capital, the efficient distribution of liquidity among financial institutions, and the hedging of short-term risks. Finally, these markets are central to the credit evaluation process and the settlement of the large-value payments systems. One principal, key interest rate is the federal funds rate which, as you recall, is the rate banks charge each other for loans of funds overnight. When the central bank conducts open-market operations, this key short-term rate is immediately and directly affected which, in turn, impacts other short- and long-term rates.

2.8 Some risks in the money market

The funds in the money market, known as money market funds (MMFs) as mentioned earlier, reside in between the capital markets and the banking system and provide private money-like (or near-money) assets that resemble bank deposits. As a result, they are vulnerable to bank runs that arise from liquidity changes, redemption waves and sudden changes in investor perceptions of the funds' ability to serve them. Many bank runs have taken place over the past three decades with the most recent one (in early 2023) in the US involving the Silicon Valley Bank (SVB), Signature Bank and more, and then some European banks including Credit Suisse and several other banks (HSBC, Deutsche bank and Barclay's) witnessed sharp declines in their stock prices. Bank runs occurred during the 2007/8 global financial crisis and the COVID-19 pandemic periods.

Other risks that exist for MMFs include the potential for losses of funds for investors because their accounts are not guaranteed by the Federal Deposit Insurance

Corporation (FDIC). The FDIC guarantees deposits up to $250,000 per depositor. Another potential source of risk is *volatility*, defined as the sharp ups and downs in returns, which can harm accounts if excessive. By contrast, if MMFs experience low returns there is a chance that they fall below the rate of inflation, thus providing negative real returns to investors (this is known as *inflation risk*). MMFs were a culprit in the global financial crisis in September 2008. Specifically, a leading fund (the Reserve Primary Fund) "broke the buck" – that is, took losses that brought its price below $1, due to its exposure to Lehman Brothers' debt. Investors' confidence was shattered as stress emerged in what was thought to be a safe asset class.

Further, interest rates can also go down reducing returns on money market investments (the so-called *interest-rate risk*). Although money market security values are sensitive to interest rate movements and move in the same direction as longer-term securities such as bonds, they are not as sensitive as bond values to interest rate movements. This lower degree of sensitivity is due primarily in the shorter term to maturity. Liquidity risk can also emanate from market volatility or from a lack of liquidity in underlying securities held by a fund.

An additional risk, inherent in MMFs, is credit ratings from various credit rating agencies. Such agencies provide reports not on the credit (default) risk of such funds but on their ability to preserve capital, and/or income and, naturally, liquidity. In other words, they do not get the typical ratings that capital instruments receive (the capital market will be discussed in Part III) but need the highest quality in such ratings (that is, the investment grade category). Investors can switch between no-risk securities – the Tbills – and riskier money market securities while weighing the higher potential return of the latter against exposure to credit risk. Investor perception of credit risk can change over time, which affects the required return and hence, the value (price) of money market securities. For example, the credit crisis of 2008 had a major impact on the perceived risk of money market securities.

Finally, some other risks include the cost of investing in the money market such as broker(age) fees, redemption fees and more which eat out of the MMFs returns. Other risks, emanating from the professional investment management industry, include frauds and Ponzi schemes, promising you exorbitant rates of return on your investments often more that 100 percent! The latest Ponzi scheme (reported on May 12, 2023) was from a professional manager who flaunted his expensive cars, famous paintings and billions of dollars in the bank as successful investor pooling average investors' moneys and promising returns in excess of 200 percent![3] Bear in mind that if interest rates increase, the value of a money market fund's investments generally declines, and vice versa. Hence, some securities (especially those with longer maturities) have greater interest rate sensitivity. We'll discuss these risks in later chapters.

Box 4.1 discusses how some marketing activities are related to the money markets. In general, marketing plays a crucial role in the functioning of money (and capital) markets by influencing investor behavior, shaping public perception, and facilitating the flow of capital. A company's marketing department is deeply connected to the financial markets by enhancing investor confidence, supporting capital raising, and differentiating the company in the financial markets. Strategic marketing is not just about selling products, rather it is about influencing stock prices, market perception, and financial growth.

Box 4.1

How is the money market related to marketing?

BRANDING AND SHAREHOLDER VALUE: A strong brand increases customer loyalty, revenue stability, and long-term growth potential, which attract investors and influence stock prices. Companies with strong marketing strategies tend to have higher market capitalization and lower capital costs. Just look at Apple and Nike.

INVESTOR RELATIONSHIPS AND COMMUNICATION: Marketing teams collaborate with investor relations to craft earnings reports, press releases, and investor presentations. In general, effective communication enhances transparency and investor confidence, affecting stock price volatility. As an example, consider Tesla whose earnings calls and social media strategy boosted investor engagement and stock performance.

CAPITAL RAISING: When a company goes public, its marketing department plays a key role in building brand awareness and generating investor demand. For example, digital and traditional marketing campaigns increase public excitement and institutional interest before stock offerings. Also, effective branding and financial stability improve a company's bond ratings and lower borrowing costs.

Test your understanding 1

1. Explain why we say that one characteristic of the money markets is that they are wholesale markets.
2. Why do we say that money markets serve the opportunity cost of holding idle cash?
3. What is the interest-rate risk in money market securities?
4. Explain how the interest rates in the money market are influenced by the demand for short-term funds by borrowers and the supply of short-term funds provided by savers.

Solutions appear at the textbook's website.

3 Functions of the money market

The money market plays important roles within an economy and, by extension, in the global financial markets. The main characteristics of the money market also serve as functions because they ensure low-cost and secure transactions, plenty of information, provide ample liquidity and enable an investor to easily sell the financial assets, and effectively transfer funds between savers/lenders and the investors/borrowers. In what follows below, we will present some additional roles of the money market.

Table 4.2 Selected money market instruments and rates, as of October 20, 2025

Money market instrument			
Federal funds (effective)	4.11	US government securities	
Commercial Paper		Treasury bills (secondary market)	
Nonfinancial		3-month	3.81
1-month	4.00	6-month	3.66
2-month	3.95	1-year	3.435
3-month	3.90	Treasury constant maturities	
Financial		1-month	4.15
1-month	4.01	3-month	3.97
Bank prime loan	7.25	6-month	3.78
Discount window primary	4.25	1-year	3.55

Source: https://www.federalreserve.gov/releases/h15/

3.1 Warehousing funds

Investors in the money market, who are not trying to earn unusually high returns on their money market funds, can temporarily park or warehouse their funds. They use the money market as an interim investment medium that provides a higher return than holding cash in banks. The reasons can be many, such as that the market conditions are not ripe for them to lock in their funds for a longer term (in the capital market), or expect market interest rates to go up so they can exploit other higher-yielding investments (such as bonds), or simply they may anticipate a need to use most of these funds for important purchases or emergencies. Table 4.2 displays the yields of selected money market instruments and shows that many instruments (defined in the next chapter) except some Tbills, offer higher yields. However, as we know holding idle money (cash) can be expensive for the investors because it represents an opportunity cost (that is, foregone interest income and decline in purchasing power due to inflation). Therefore, the money markets provide a means to invest idle funds and to reduce this opportunity cost.

3.2 Financing national and international trade

Short-term funds are needed by both local and international traders to fulfill essential trade functions such as payments for exports and imports. For instance, local traders as well as corporations, issue short-term paper (known as *commercial paper*, which will be discussed in the next chapter) to obtain short-term financing to meet daily operations such as to support or expand existing operations (to other national markets), to pay wages and salaries to their employees and for raw materials. Similarly, when an exporter that is sending goods to an importer, who is not known and whose credit(worthiness) is not known to the exporter, he contacts his bank to act as a guarantor. The bank, in turn, facilitates the transaction by accepting a draft which obligates payment at a specified point in time (this instrument is referred to as a banker's acceptance and is also discussed in the next chapter). The end result is for the order to be fulfilled and the payment to be made.

3.3 Monetary policy implementation

Central banks around the world could not conduct monetary policies without the assistance of commercial banks, which operate in the money market. For instance, the money market interest rates reflect the current conditions in the banking industry and can guide the central bank in developing an appropriate interest rate policy. Globally, integrated money markets help major central banks (the Fed, ECB, BoE, BoJ, for example) to influence the sub-markets and implement its monetary policy objectives. In Chapter 3, we learned the federal funds rate, which is the rate banks charge on federal funds transactions, and which is affected by the supply of and demand for funds in the federal funds market, and the Federal Reserve influences it by adjusting the amount of funds in depository institutions. This is one reason as to why all market participants closely watch that rate because the Fed manipulates it to affect general economic conditions and hence, conduct monetary policy.

3.4 Federal funds market

As mentioned earlier, the money market provides commercial banks with a ready market where they can invest their (highly liquid) excess reserves and earn interest. Further, whenever they are faced with liquidity problems, they can borrow from the money market (the federal funds market) on a short-term basis as an alternative to borrowing from the central bank. The advantage of this is that the money market may charge lower interest rates on short-term loans than the central bank typically does. Further, borrowing from the central bank may trigger scrutiny for the borrowing bank and possible penalties. The federal funds market – which we will discuss in some detail in Chapter 5 – consists of domestic unsecured borrowings by depository institutions from other depository institutions and government-sponsored enterprises (GSEs).

SAUDI ARABIA TAPS THE MONEY MARKET

Saudi Arabia in 2023 is looking to tap into the global money market to attract investments in its economy with new initiatives. People said that the country "is now one of the most attractive countries for investments as it has the right balance between risk and return, growth opportunities, as well as profitable opportunities." The Minister of Investment said that "We want to focus on the money market, insurance and lending, and we have initiatives that focus on this."

https://www.arabnews.com/node/2269136/business-economy.

3.5 Economic functions

A number of other functions are served by the money market such as facilitating a payments' clearing system, so that trades can be settled, and credit evaluations, so participants are aware of each other's creditworthy status. In addition, the money market is central to the efficient and effective capital allocation as funds are allocated to their best uses by financial intermediaries ultimately promoting economic growth (including investment). The financial market also performs the function of *price discovery* of the different financial instruments traded. The prices at which the financial instruments trade in the financial market are determined by the market forces, i.e., demand and supply. In general, the money market balances the supply and demand in short-term financial transactions and boosts economic growth by allowing businesses (and the government) to access funds quickly. The nearby *sidebar* contains the drive by Saudi Arabia to tap the global financial markets, and especially the money market, to attract investments and spur economic growth.

4 A detailed look at some money market functions

4.1 Monetary operations

The Fed (and particularly the New York Fed) conducts various monetary operations in US fixed income and money markets to support the Federal Reserve's monetary policy and financial stability objectives. The latter include price stability, maximum employment, and long-term interest rates. The first two are known as the Fed's "*dual mandate*" and produce the necessary environment to maintain moderate long-term interest rates. Monetary policy works by influencing the short-term interest rates to affect the economic and financial decisions businesses and households make such as the availability and cost of credit, asset prices such as stock and bond prices, and the exchange rate of the US dollar against foreign currencies. Ultimately, all these, affect economic activity and, ultimately, the Fed's dual mandate.

As regards the implementation of monetary policy, the Fed sets the policy and then the New York Fed plays a central role in implementing it through the FOMC (which we learned in Chapter 3). So, the FOMC announces the target range for the federal funds rate after each of the Committee's meeting (note that the Committee meets eight times per year). The New York Fed publishes daily the effective fed funds rate, which is computed as a (volume-weighted) median of the previous business day's overnight federal funds transactions. In addition, the Fed administers two rates at levels to help keep the federal funds rate well within the target range. The first rate, set by the Board of Governors of the Federal Reserve System, is the interest on reserve balances, and is the rate paid to banks and other eligible entities on their Fed account balances, or reserves. The second rate is the overnight reverse repo facility, is set by the FOMC and operated by the Trading Desk at the NY Fed bank, and refers to the interest rate the Fed pays for such an operation. The facility offers a broader range of money market participants an overnight investment that enhances their bargaining power on short-term private investment transactions. These rates help establish a floor under overnight interest rates, below which banks and other money market participants would not (be willing to) lend.

Related to the above, the Fed also conducts *liquidity backstops* and these tools play an important role in supporting the effective implementation of monetary policy. In essence, they limit the potential for pressures in overnight funding markets to push the effective fed funds rate above the FOMC's target range. These tools are: the discount window, which assists banks in managing their liquidity risks and helps support the flow of credit to households and businesses (primary credit is one of the key lending programs within the discount window); the standing repo facility, which is open to primary dealers and eligible depository institutions, is designed to limit the potential for pressures in the repo market from spilling over to the federal funds market; the Foreign and International Monetary Authorities Repo Facility under which approved account holders can enter into overnight repo transactions with the Fed against Treasury securities held in their custody accounts at the New York Fed; and the standing US dollar and foreign currency swap lines which help ease strains in global funding markets on the supply of credit to households and businesses worldwide.[4]

Who are some of the counterparties in the standing overnight repo transactions market (facility) and reverse repo facility?[5] First, to become eligible for joining the standing repo facility firms must be chartered or federally chartered banks or savings associations with total of US Treasury, agency debt and agency mortgage-backed securities holdings exceeding $2 billion. Some of such banks from the US, Canada, France, UK and Japan are: Bank of America, Citibank, Barclays Bank PLC, Canadian Imperial Bank of Commerce, Credit Agricole Corporate and Investment Bank, HSBC Bank, Mizuho Bank, Sumitomo Mitsui Banking Corporation. As regards the reverse repo counterparties, the eligibility criteria are that banks must be state- or federally charted, with foreign total assets of at least $30 billion, a government-sponsored enterprise (GSE) or an SEC-registered fund, with assets of no less than $2 billion or an average outstanding amount of reverse repo transactions of no less than $500 billion. Some additional banks (including those mentioned above) are Ally Bank, Royal Bank of Canada, some GSEs are Fannie Mae, Farmer Mac and AgriBank, FCB, and some funds are BlackRock Fund Advisors, BNY Melon Investment Adviser, Charles Schwab Investment Management, and Goldman Sachs Asset Management.

4.2 Shadow banking

Shadow banking refers to the activities of all financial intermediaries (and institutions) that do not belong to the traditional banking system. Examples of shadow banks are money market funds, pension funds and asset management firms. Even though they are not part of the standard commercial banking network, they are able to make loans to individuals and other institutional investors. Specifically, shadow banks raise (borrow) short-term funds in the money markets and use those funds to buy assets with longer-term maturities. Since they are not part of the commercial banking system, they cannot borrow from the Fed and do not accept deposits. Hence, they are in "the shadows", as Fed economist Paul McCauley coined in a 2007 speech of the Federal Reserve's annual meeting.[6] Shadow banking plays an important role within an efficient economic system but its large size in the European Union (reaching 30% of the total financial system) and close links to the traditional banking system have raised concerns about risks and possible regulation. Some risks include the ability of shadow banks to circumvent banking rules and regulations and the fact that they can foster high levels of debt in the financial sector.[7] Finally, it is now recognized that shadow banks were instrumental in the generation of the 2007/8 global financial crisis through the securitization process they had created. The huge amounts of credit intermediation provided by the shadow banking system contributed to asset price appreciation in (residential and commercial) real estate markets prior to the crisis. In addition, aggregate risk and asset price correlations were hugely underestimated by the relevant players in that markets such as credit-rating agencies, bank managers, investors and regulators.

According to an article by the New York Fed (Pozsar et al., 2013), the shadow banking is composed of three subsystems which intermediate different types of credit. The first one is the *government-sponsored* shadow banking subsystem, which refers to credit intermediation activities funded through the sale of structured products such as agency debt and mortgage-backed securities (MBS). The second subsystem is the *internal* shadow banking subsystem, which denotes the credit intermediation process of a global network of banks, finance companies, broker-dealers, and asset managers. The third type is the *external* shadow banking subsystem, which refers to the credit intermediation process of diversified broker-dealers and a global network of nonbank financial specialists such as captive and stand-alone finance companies and asset managers.[8]

According to the *Financial Stability Board*'s 2022 Annual Global Monitoring Report on Non-Bank Financial Intermediation, the non-bank financial intermediation (NBFI) sector exhibited strong growth in 2021, partly due to higher valuations and inflows into equity investment funds, which benefited from the economic recovery.[9] Growth in other investment fund assets (excluding hedge funds, real estate investment trusts/funds and money market funds), accounted for just over a half of the overall change in NBFI sector assets. Figure 4.3 exhibits the total global financial assets of NBFI from 2002 to 2021. The blue line shows the percentage growth of NBFI and clearly indicates an upward trend since 2008, after a short decline in 2020 due to the COVID-19 pandemic. The data cover 29 country jurisdictions that account for around 80% of global GDP. Finally, the FSB 2022 report stated that due to the war in Ukraine and the subsequent rise in inflation, the NBFI

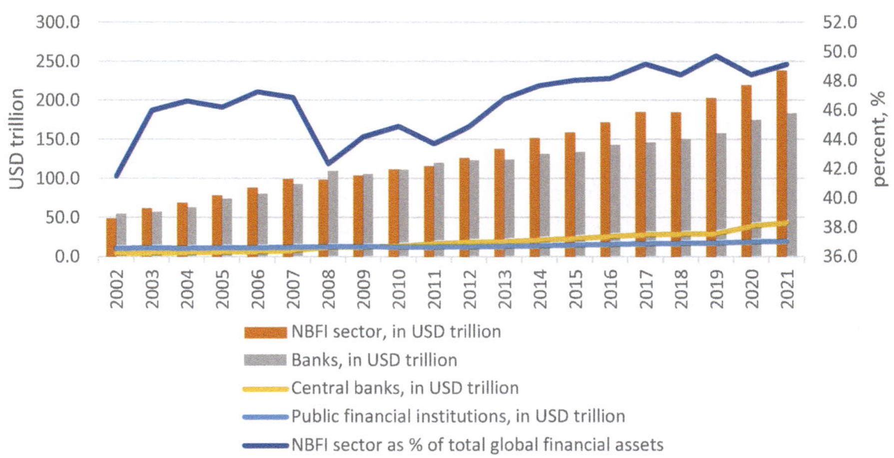

Figure 4.3 Total global financial assets, as of 2022

sector faced serious setbacks and challenges translating in declines in assets under management and other funds outflows.

4.3 Global trends in the international money markets

A number of economic, financial, social, cultural, environmental and more reasons are continuously shaping the nature and extent of the global money market. For example, pandemic eruptions, the war in the Ukraine, the ensuing higher commodity inflation and interest rates, environment degradation (leading to severe climatic changes that destroy property and make people poorer and starving), the deteriorating outlooks for major advanced countries' economies (and China's economy) and banking sectors, the shifting focus from "greed" to more social-responsible investments (under the general heading of ESG (Environmental, Social and Governance) and more have a profound impact on the functioning of the money markets world-wide with negative consequences on people and assets. According to Fitch's *Global Money Market Funds Outlook 2023*, the outlook for global money market funds is deteriorating, partly driven by deteriorating outlooks in some of the key banking sectors that these funds invest in and continued market volatility stemming from the global recessionary backdrop.[10] The *International Monetary Fund*'s 2023 Global Financial Stability Report also highlighted the buildup in vulnerabilities since the global financial crisis such as persistent inflation and higher sovereign debt levels.[11]

In a speech by Isabel Schnabel, Member of the Executive Board of the European Central Bank, in 2020, three long-term key forces that would impact the euro area money markets were identified.[12] First, the heightened awareness of counterparty risk, which prompted a shift towards secured and centrally cleared transactions. Second, changes in central bank policies and regulation have also had a significant impact on money market rates, creating a high level of excess liquidity (which may further reduce cash-driven activity in some market segments), leading to changing anchors for money market rates. The third long-term challenge refers to the introduction of regulatory relief measures for NBFI which could have implications for monetary policy implementation in the future.

A 2017 OECD article, based on the minutes in OECD's Financial Roundtable in 2017 by the members of the OECD Committee on Financial Markets, cited the key challenge for the global money markets which was *green financing*. That is, whether the financial system would be capable of providing capital reallocation consistent with the green transition in the long run. More specifically, to provide financing for companies and sectors to protect the environment by shifting energy production and related activities ways from fossil fuel sources to cleaner energy sources.[13]

According to the *Global Banking & Finance Review*, the future of global money movements will be shaped by a umber of developments/innovations such as financial technology (or fintech, for short) B2B's (Business-to-Business) increase in cross-border payments, the use of digital currencies such as Bitcoin and others, based on the Distributed Ledger technology and Blockchain technology, the risks associated with such currencies and digital wallets (for purchases' payments and money transfers) and the ensuing regulation of such transactions.[14] In general, fintech has a significant role to play in capturing the future of global money movement,and hence it may be necessary to foster partnerships within the industry and regulators so as to create a more efficient and secure global payments ecosystem that benefits individuals, businesses, and economies alike.

Finally, is there a relationship between the functioning of the international money markets (as well as capital markets, which we discuss in a later chapter) and the various religions in the world? You have certainly heard of Islamic Finance, usury laws, ethical treatments of people in financial transactions and related notions, and thus you should expect that religion may play an important role in finance in the coming years. Over the past decade, there has been a movement toward understating Islamic banking and finance, relative to traditional finance and banking, and is "based on a belief that money shouldn't have any value in itself. It's just a way to exchange products and services that do have a value.", according to the Bank of England.[15] More specifically, it is based on Shari'ah Islamic law's rules and principles, which do not permit interest payments, gambling, investments in tobacco, alcohol and other society-harming products and activities. Islamic Finance has gained popularity and acceptance in Muslim populations in the Middle East and Asia (aided by the global issuance of *Sukuk*, the Islamic equivalent of bonds) and is rapidly expanding. A recent book by Watkins (2022) highlights the place of religion within the global money markets by exploring the influence of Christianity, Islam, Judaism and Hinduism.

5 Using the money market

Any individual can use the global money market and its instruments (discussed in the next chapter) in order to fulfil his/her objectives or needs. For example, one may place one's unspent income in a short-term bank (savings or money market) product, where one can earn a bit higher interest rate, another may invest in the safe government security – the Treasury bill or Tbill – for up to one year, and yet another may buy (invest in) a money market mutual fund. Similarly, a corporation may borrow from the money market on a short-term basis by issuing certain short-term securities, to cover its temporary financial needs, a bank may borrow from another bank (from the federal funds market) on an overnight basis and finally, a dealer/broker or designated financial institution may engage in special repurchase agreements (known as repos, discussed in the next chapter) whereby a loan made one day is reversed the next day.

Why would an individual, with a one-year max investment horizon, place their funds in some money market instruments rather than in traditional bank savings accounts? We discussed some differences between the two options earlier in the chapter. Apart from the typical requirement that investments in certain money market instruments within an investment portfolio context (which we discuss in later chapters) must be made, let us present some additional reasons and then try to put them into an economic context. One reason is the higher yield. This makes good economic sense since the (expected) reward would be much higher than otherwise. This explains why investors poured $1 trillion into global money market funds in 2023 due to the best yields available in years. In addition, even if that yield is lower than riskier investments, investors may be more comfortable investing there because they believe that they will earn that yield. Perhaps, investors also think that the economy may be slowing down and thus longer-term instruments may not deliver what investors expect.

Another reason may be the safety promised by money market instruments. Tbills, for example, are backed by the full faith and credit in the US federal government, certain specialized bank accounts are also guaranteed by the banks offering them. This follows from the characteristic of the money market which refers to low or no risk in money market investments. Moving from risky securities into safer ones is known as "flight to quality" or "flight to safety". A third reason could be the ease of trading in such instruments and the low investment budget that is required to begin with. This implies that investors may be concerned with the volatility in financial markets and the inability to get rid of riskier and longer-term instruments during upcoming economic or financial crises. For example, a potential home buyer who sold his investments in anticipation of closing on a new home, or an investor who sells stocks in his portfolio, can use money market funds to earn dividends until the cash is invested elsewhere.

Finally, one more reason may simply be the mere preference of investors to remain in the short-term end of the market. Without saying too much about this preference (behavior) at this point, this will be explained in detail in Chapter 10 using some economic theories of the yield curve. Suffice to say that investors may expect to use their funds soon for other reasons or simply prefer to roll over their investments year after year and be content with the yields they earn. Put differently, the money market is an ideal place for investors with low risk (or very conservative) tolerance, for instance retirees.

What about the firms? Should they invest in the money market? We answer this question noting that we are not implying tapping the money market to raise funds, which is something that all firms do. One argument in favor could be the fact that firms need the money markets to earn the yield that may be necessary for their day-to-day operations, pay bills due in a short period of time as well as manage liquidity. Hence, if they do not hold any money market securities, they will frequently be forced to borrow more frequently to cover unanticipated cash needs which would raise the cost of such financing (the so-called *risk premium*). In addition, if they have holdings of money market securities, they can always sell them (at a negligible cost) to obtain the needed cash. Financial institutions such as commercial banks with uncertain future cash in- and out-flows generally maintain additional money market instruments for liquidity.[16]

The argument opposing investing in the money markets would be that firms should use their excess funds in such a way as to maximize the return to their shareholders. These yields will not make shareholders rich. Given that money market investments typically offer lower yields than capital-market investments, some shareholders may not be happy and abandon investments in these firms. In addition, the yields in such instruments although may seem high, may not adequately cover the rate of inflation (without considering taxes) and this may not sound acceptable to sophisticated investors. There are also more risks for firms associated with this market such as adverse conditions during financial market stress periods, according to a 2023 article in *The New York Times*.[17]

We end this section with an interesting question for the general readership. How is Maslow's hierarchy of needs related to the money (and capital) markets? From your Principles of Management course you learned that people rank their needs (hierarchy) from the most basic need to the utmost one. Specifically, humans first need to satisfy their physiological needs such as needs for living (food, shelter and basic living requirements). Then, once these needs have been satisfied, people tend to become concerned about safety (in work and environment) and reduce uncertainty. Then, come social needs, that is, needs to bond with other people, to be loved, and to form lasting relationships. Upon this need's fulfilment, human beings seek to build respect in social behaviors, feel a sense of being important and appreciated. Finally, the highest level of the pyramid (hierarchy) refers to self-actualization, which means that people become all they can be and advance in their skills and personal values. Box 4.2 links these five needs to the financial markets.

Box 4.2

Maslow's hierarchy of needs and money and capital markets

PHYSIOLOGICAL NEEDS: People strive to earn enough income to cover necessities (food and bills) and engage in basic budgeting activities and save – investing in money market funds, savings accounts and short-term bonds.

SAFETY: Humans seek job security (stability), save more and take out insurance while planning for a major purchase or retirement, in an effort to avoid future (potential) risks and uncertainty. They may begin investing in safe financial instruments such as Treasury bills/bonds, bank certificates of deposit, seek capital preservation investments.

RESPECT AND APPRECIATION: People begin developing social finance and (family-related) financial relationships such as household budgeting, planning for their kids' education, and social activities (donations, for example). People now seek to build wealth, connect with financial communities, and follow the financial markets.

ESTEEM: People seek to build wealth, additional (discretionary) income and financial freedom. They can now begin investing in riskier securities (capital market instruments), real estate and buying luxury items. There is now higher demand for speculative trading, hedge funds and digital currencies, among others.

SELF-ACTUALIZATION: Humans now focus on financial freedom and the discovery of purpose by engaging in investment activities such as impact (social and ethical) investing, life fulfillment and philanthropy. Specifically, humans achieve high net worth, build legacies, and seek long-term impact.

Test your understanding 2

1. What would be one solution if corporations and governments sometimes need to get their hands on funds quickly?
2. How can money market securities be used to enhance liquidity?
3. How do investors behave during periods of heightened uncertainty about the economy? What would be the consequences for risk premia?
4. Provide some reasons for an individual investing in the money market instead of opening a plain bank savings account.

Solutions appear at the textbook's website.

Summary

- We cast a short look inside the global money market.
- We listed and briefly explained the characteristics of the money market such as short-term life, low or no risk, high liquidity, wholesale market, global presence, organized banking system, and determination of interest rates.
- We identified and discussed some risks in the money market.
- We mentioned and elaborated on the functions of the money market including warehousing funds, financing national and international trade, monetary policy implementation, federal funds market and economic functions.
- We looked at some money market functions focusing on monetary operations, shadow banking, and ended with some global trends in the international money markets.
- We finished the chapter by presenting some reasons why and ways of using the global money market.

Questions and problems

1. As of August 2023, the money market funds in the US were paying slightly above 5%. Discuss your options to invest your money when your investment horizon is one year or less.
2. Is a money market fund a good investment? Present some arguments in favor of and against it.
3. Can you explain the shift in investing toward money market funds caused by financial market volatility?
4. How does the money market contribute to or facilitate the conduct of monetary policy?
5. Why do asset price correlations typically rise during financial stress periods?
6. What are the pros and cons of money market accounts?

Notes

1. https://cranedata.com/
2. https://www.wsj.com/livecoverage/stock-market-today-dow-jones-08-08-2023/card/money-market-fund-yields-soar-to-16-year-high-qs3m1fYgvhRFr8ZMbfHR
3. https://fortune.com/2023/05/12/phillip-galles-former-chicago-commodities-trader-arrested-ponzi-scheme-fake-billionaire-hedge-fund-manager-122-luxury-cars/
4. See https://www.newyorkfed.org/markets/domestic-market-operations/monetary-policy-implementation
5. https://www.newyorkfed.org/markets
6. https://www.imf.org/external/pubs/ft/fandd/2013/06/basics.htm
7. https://finance.ec.europa.eu/capital-markets-union-and-financial-markets/financial-markets/financial-supervision-shadow-banking_en
8. https://www.newyorkfed.org/medialibrary/media/research/epr/2013/0713adri.pdf. See also the references therein for a more detailed look at the shadow banking system.
9. https://www.fsb.org/2022/12/global-monitoring-report-on-non-bank-financial-intermediation-2022/
10. https://www.fitchratings.com/research/fund-asset-managers/global-money-market-funds-outlook-2023–08–12–2022.

11. https://www.imf.org/en/Publications/GFSR/Issues/2023/04/11/global-financial-stability-report-april-2023
12. https://www.ecb.europa.eu/press/key/date/2020/html/ecb.sp201123~8d9573b1b1.en.html
13. https://ideas.repec.org/a/oec/dafkad/5jg0097l3qhl.html
14. https://www.globalbankingandfinance.com/the-future-of-global-money-movement-5-trends-for-2023-and-beyond/
15. https://www.bankofengland.co.uk/explainers/what-is-islamic-finance
16. In Chapter 5 we discuss additional participants in the money market.
17. https://www.nytimes.com/2023/04/21/business/money-market-funds.html

References

Pozsar, Zoltan, Tobias Adrian, Adam Ashcraft, and Hayley Boesky (2013). Shadow Banking. FRBNY *Economic Policy Review*, (December), 1–16.

Watkins, James Simon (2022). *Religion and the Global Money Markets: Exploring the Influence of Christianity, Islam, Judaism and Hinduism*. Palgrave MacMillan. Springer International Publishers.

Chapter 5

Money market instruments and intermediaries

Introduction

We saw in the previous chapter that the main function of the money market is to facilitate the transfer of funds from one agent to another. These agents can be households (or retail investors), businesses (including institutional investors), the government (at all three levels, namely federal, state and local) and foreign entities and individuals. More specifically, the major participants in the money market are commercial banks, insurance companies, pension funds, finance companies, investment companies, government-sponsored enterprises, money market mutual funds, futures market exchanges, brokers and dealers, and the Federal Reserve.[1] Specifically, the government sells Treasury securities (to all other participants) to fund the national debt. The central bank (the Federal Reserve in the US) buys and sells these securities to conduct monetary policy. Commercial banks buy government securities in order to make short-term loans and serve the short-term investment needs of their depositors. Businesses buy and sell government and other short-term securities (to be discussed below) as part of their typical cash management. Institutional investors such as investment/brokerage companies trade on behalf of commercial accounts, leasing or finance and companies lend funds to individuals, and pension funds and insurance companies also buy Treasury securities in order to maintain liquidity ready to be redeemed to their clients or policyholders. Finally, individuals buy money market funds as part of their short-term investment strategy. However, it is rational to assume that investors always hold some cash – on money market funds – so as to include in their investment portfolios which comprise riskier assets, maintain liquidity and exploit any new investment opportunities that may come along.

DOI: 10.4324/9781003677161-7

All above participants – also known as financial institutions – except the government and the individuals, serve the purpose of being financial intermediaries. These are institutions that pool funds from savers – people and firms – and lend them to those who need to borrow – people, firms and governments – thereby transforming assets and providing access to financial markets. This is indirect finance, as we learned in Chapter 3. Note that financial intermediaries are also involved in direct finance, when borrowers sell securities directly to lenders in the financial markets. These financial intermediaries strive to allocate funds to their best uses so as to increase overall efficiency translating to increase in investments and economic growth while, at the same time, mitigating risk(s).

In what follows next, we will list and explain all money market instruments and then proceed with some discussion on some financial intermediaries (financial institutions).

1 Money market instruments

There are several money market instruments. The most important ones, that we will discuss here, are the following: Treasury bills, Commercial paper, Negotiable certificates or orders of deposit, Repurchase agreements (repos), Federal funds, Banker's acceptances, and the Eurodollar market.

1.1 Treasury bill market

Treasury bills (T-bills) represent a short-term claim of the federal government (the Department of the Treasury) in the United States. The Treasury issues T-bills with maturities ranging from 4 to 26 weeks, corresponding to 28, 91, and 182-day maturities, respectively, on a weekly basis. On a monthly basis, one-year maturity T-bills are also issued. Finally, the Treasury occasionally issues T-bills with even shorter than four weeks, which are called *cash management bills*. Such bills are designed to bridge the government's gap between the Treasury's flow cash balances, meaning they help finance the Treasury's payment obligations until tax payments are received. Cash Management bills are only available through a bank, broker or dealer. T-bills are the most widely held and most liquid securities in the money market. Individuals, businesses and foreign governments are all investors in the T-bill market. An individual investor can purchase T-bills directly from the government. Their appeal is based on four characteristics that no other money market security possesses.

First, the risk (of non-repayment) is nil and that such securities are known as risk free. T-bills are backed by the federal government and are therefore free of default (credit) risk. Later in the chapter and the book, we will call them the *risk-free rate* (instrument). Second, T-bills are highly liquid which means that an investor can easily and quickly sell them to other investors. How is this done? Government securities dealers, who serve as intermediaries in the secondary market, buy existing T-bills from investors who want to sell them, or sell them to those who want to buy them. The dealers' profit comes from the slight difference between the sale price of the bill and the purchase price. Third, although the interest income that you may receive from a T-bill is exempt from any state or local income taxes, you will still need to report interest income on your federal tax return and you may pay taxes (based on your marginal tax rate). Hence, in essence, this makes T-bills partially tax-exempt. Finally, the last desirable feature of the T-bills are their relatively low minimum denomination, $1,000, which allows small private investors to invest their limited funds.

The federal government issues T-bills at a discount from par (the maturity value, usually $1,000), which means that it does not actually pay interest on them. Hence, the investor's yield comes from the increase in the value of the security between the time it was purchased and the time it matures (assuming they hold the bill to maturity). If the T-bill is sold prior to maturity, then its return is found by the difference between the selling price (sold in the secondary market) and the purchase price. There are two ways to compute the yield of the T-bill: the bank discount method (BDM) and the investment rate method (IRM). We illustrate both next using actual Treasury auction data (you can access the Treasury's website at *www.treasurydirect.gov* for a host of offerings and explanations). Table 4.1 shows selected results from the third week of October 2023 government auction results (CUSIP is the unique identification number assigned to each security registered in the United States and refers to the Committee on Uniform Securities Identification Procedures).

The bank-discount method calculates the T-bill *discount* (from par or face value) and is common to short-term securities. Thus, the T-bill discount represents the percentage discount of the purchase price from par value (Par) for newly issued T-bills, and is computed as follows:

$$BDM = \frac{Par\ value - Purchase\ price}{Par\ value} * \frac{360}{n} \tag{5.1}$$

where 360 represents the days in a year and n the number of days of the investment or the investor's holding period. The second fraction represents the annualization factor based on a 360-day year. Let us apply this formula to the data in Table 5.1.

Table 5.1 Selected T-bill auction results, October 2025

Security term	*CUSIP*	*Issue date*	*Maturity date*	*High rate*	*Investment rate*	*Price per $100*
4-week	912797RP4	10/21/2025	11/18/2025	4.030%	4.099%	99.686556
8-week	912797RX7	10/21/2025	12/16/2025	3.960%	4.040%	99.384000
13-week	912797PD3	10/23/2025	01/22/2026	3.810%	3.900%	99.384000
26-week	912797SM0	10/23/2025	04/23/2026	3.660%	3.781%	98.149667

Notes: CUSIP refers to the unique number of the T-bill; source: *www.treasurydirect.gov*

We will use the 4-week's T-bill data so we can verify the high rate of 4.030%. Using equation (5.1), we get

$$BDM = \text{high rate} = \frac{100 - 99.686556}{100} * \frac{360}{28} = 0.003134 * 12.85714$$
$$= 0.0403 \quad = 4.03\%$$

HOW AUCTIONS ARE ANNOUNCED

Each announcement includes this information:

What security is auctioned
The amount offered
The auction date
The issue date
The maturity date
Terms and conditions of the offering
Closing times for competitive and non-competitive bidding
Other relevant information

Four times a year, the first Wednesday in February, May, August, and November, the Department of the Treasury holds a press conference to discuss Treasury security auctions.

Source: https://treasurydirect.gov/auctions/how-auctions-work/

However, the investment rate is a more accurate representation of what an investor will earn since it uses the actual number of days per year, 365 (and in a leap year, the number is 366), and the true initial investment in its calculation (by dividing by the purchase price). Hence, the BDM underestimates the investor's return. So, the investment rate method (IRM) is expressed as follows:

$$IRM = \frac{Par\ value - Purchase\ price}{Purchase\ price} * \frac{365}{n} \qquad (5.2)$$

Using the same data as before, we have:

$$IRM = \frac{100 - 99.686556}{99.686556} * \frac{365}{28}$$
$$= 0.003144 * 13.03571429 = 0.04098$$
$$= 4.099\%$$

How does the government carry out auctions? The general terms are outlined in the nearby *sidebar* regarding the auctions' announcements. Bids can be competitive or non-competitive. Regarding *competitive bidding*, which is only applicable to institutional investors, the maximum is 35% of the offering amount by a single bidder. Bidders specify the rate, yield, or discount margin that they will accept.[2] For non-competitive bidders (that is, all of us individual investors) the maximum amount is $10 million per auction. We agree to accept the rate, yield, or discount margin determined at the auction. We can use our *TreasuryDirect* account (thus, bypassing broker) to purchase the securities, which will go directly into our bank account.

After the subscription books (recording all the bids received) at the various Federal Reserve Banks and branches are closed, the bids are submitted to the Treasury for allocation. Then, the Treasury first allocates the part of the total offering is needed to fill all the noncompetitive bids and the remainder is allocated to the competitive bidders. The allocation begins with those that have submitted the highest bids, going downward until the total amount offered is allocated.[3] The *stop-out price* is the lowest price, or highest yield, at which bills are awarded. The average issuing price is then computed as a weighted average of the competitive bids accepted. Thus, the price paid by competitive and noncompetitive bidders reflects the lowest price of the competitive bids. Finally, note that the prices paid for 6-month T-bills are significantly lower than the prices paid for 3-month T-bills, because the investment term is longer (see last column of Table 5.1).

1.2 Federal funds

The term *federal funds* (or fed funds) is a misnomer as such funds have nothing to do with the federal government. Simply, the term comes from the fact that these funds are held at the 12 district Federal Reserve banks. Hence, they represent the funds that depository institutions can lend to or borrow from, on a short-term basis, from each other. In other words, the federal funds market is also known as the *interbank funds* market. The *federal funds rate* is the rate charged on federal funds transactions. The *effective federal funds rate* is essentially determined by the market but is influenced by the Federal Reserve through open market operations to reach the federal funds rate target. Though this rate directly affects few businesses or consumers, analysts view it as an important indicator of the direction in which the Fed wants the economy to move. Figure 5.1 shows the *effective federal funds rate*, calculated as a volume-weighted median of overnight federal funds transactions, from January 2006 to October 2023, on a weekly basis. The two light gray shaded regions represent recessions, the 2007/8 global financial crisis and the 2020 mini contraction.

According to the Federal Reserve (the Fed), the federal funds market consists of domestic unsecured borrowings in US dollars by depository institutions from other depository institutions and government-sponsored enterprises. But, what is the purpose of the federal funds market? The main purpose of this market is for

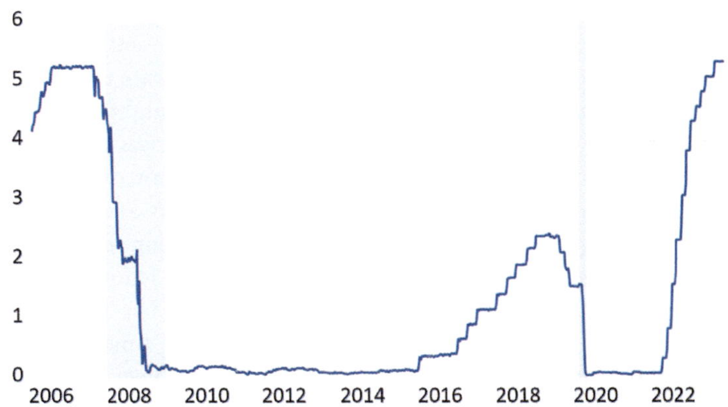

Figure 5.1 The effective federal funds, 1/1/2006–10/15/2023

Note: the shaded regions show recessions, the 2007/8 global financial crisis and the 2020 3-month mini contraction.

commercial banks to borrow funds from each other so as to meet certain reserve requirements set by the Fed.[4] To meet these reserve requirements, banks must keep a certain percentage of their total deposits (their excess reserves) with the Fed.

1.2.1 The federal funds market during the 2007/8 financial crisis

Although the fed funds market was significant before the 2007/8 global financial crisis, the latter changed the market fundamentally. There were three key developments responsible for that: The Fed's balance sheet expanded in size during the crisis, the Fed began paying interest to banks on funds they held in their reserve accounts at the Fed, and a set of new banking regulations were enacted. The reason for the Fed's rapid increase in its balance sheet was the application of *quantitative easing* (QE) programs whereby the Fed purchased large amounts of longer-term securities including US Treasury debt and mortgage-backed securities. As a result, there was a reduction in the supply of these securities, and this caused their prices to increase and their yields to decline. All this, in an effort to prop up the depressed housing and mortgage markets and boost recovery. A number of QE programs were introduced, with the first in 2008 and the next two in 2010 and 2012. The QE programs flooded the banking system with liquidity and made it less necessary for banks to borrow in the federal funds market.

During the height of the financial crisis, the Fed began paying interest of 25 basis points on excess reserve balances in December 2008, increasing the rate to 50 basis points in December 2015. The idea and expectation was that a bank that wished to lend in the federal funds market and earn interest could always hold its reserves with the Fed (effectively "lending" to the Fed) and earn interest on their excess reserves (IOER). Naturally, this action removed the incentive of the commercial banks to accept a rate lower than that in the federal funds market. Finally, a set of new rules and regulations were put in place. For example, Congress responded to the financial crisis with the Dodd–Frank Act. Included in this large act were small changes to the Federal Deposit Insurance Corporation's regulatory standards, changes which have had a direct effect on the incentives that banks have to hold cash assets. For example, the FDIC levied charges on banks when it provides them with deposit insurance for their depositors' funds (up to $250,000). Presently, the depository institutions can receive IOER and the effective federal funds rate is below the IOER rate. Therefore, they have largely ceased lending in the overnight market. This role is now mainly played by the government-sponsored enterprises (GSEs), especially those dealing in the housing and mortgage market. On the borrowing side, domestic institutions are oversupplied with reserves from the Fed's asset purchases, and the FDIC's new capital requirements penalize them for holding reserves.

What is the relationship or linkage between the effective federal funds rate and the equally widely watched by the market 3-month T-bill? The federal funds rate is normally slightly higher than the T-bill rate at any given time (see Figure 5.2). The reason is that a lender in the federal funds market is subject to credit (default) risk, since it is possible that the financial institution borrowing the funds could default on the loan. How does one rate affect the other? Two reasons can exist. First, T-bills yields are more closely influenced by the fed funds rate. Second, T-bill yields can swing up or below the fed funds rate depending on whether the US Treasury Department is issuing more or fewer bills than investors want. This is clearly shown in Figure 5.2.

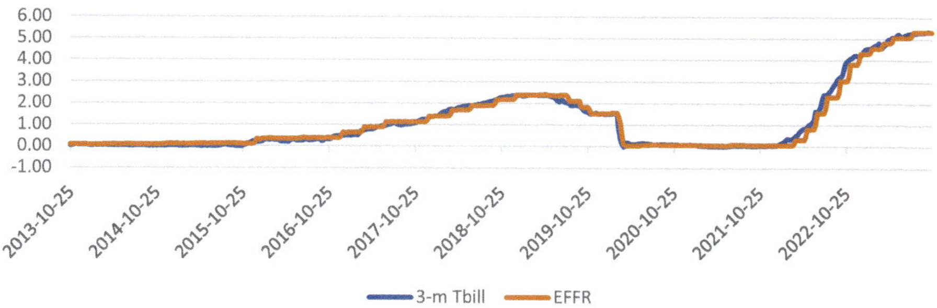

Figure 5.2 The effective federal funds rate and the 3-month T-bill, weekly

Source: Federal Reserve Economic Data

1.3 Repurchase agreements

The market for *repurchase agreements* (repos) works much the same as the fed funds market except that other than banks can participate. For example, a firm can sell Treasury securities in a repo whereby the firm agrees to buy back the securities at a specified future date. In essence, a repurchase agreement transaction represents a loan backed by the (US Treasury) securities, usually T-bills. Hence, a repo is essentially a short-term collateralized loan. Because repos are collateralized with Treasury securities, they are usually low-risk investments and thus have low interest rates. A *reverse repo* refers to the purchase of securities by one party from another with an agreement to sell them. The volume of trade is in the low trillions of US dollars and the most common maturities range from 1 to 15 days and for 1, 3, and 6 months.[5]

Who are the main participants in this market? Government securities dealers (also known as primary dealers) frequently engage in repos. Financial institutions such as banks, savings and loan associations, money market funds as well as non-financial institutions often participate in the repo market. Primary dealers use the repo to manage their liquidity and to take advantage of anticipated changes in interest rates. The Fed also uses repos in conducting monetary policy by adjusting bank reserves on a temporary basis. To achieve this adjustment, the Fed will buy or sell Treasury securities in the repo market. However, the maturities of Fed's repos do not exceed 15 days. Repo transactions are conducted via a telecommunications network where dealers and brokers create repos for firms with excess or deficiency of funds (for a fee).

How can we estimate the yield of repurchase transaction? Understand that the repo rate is determined as the difference between the initial selling price of the securities and the agreed-on repurchase price, annualized to a 360-day year. The relevant formula is below.

$$Repo\ rate = \frac{Repurchase\ price - Selling\ price}{Selling\ price} * \frac{360}{n} \tag{5.3}$$

So, for example if an investor initially purchased securities at a price $9,995,000 while agreeing to sell them back at a price of $10,000,000 at the end of a 30-day period, his yield (or repo rate) on this repurchase agreement would be 0.60%, obtained as follows:

$$\text{Repo rate (yield)} = \frac{10{,}000{,}000 - 9.995{,}000}{9{,}995{,}000} * \frac{360}{30} = 0.006003 = 0.60\%$$

1.3.1 Characteristics of the repo market

What are the main features of repurchase agreements (RPs)? First, the maturity. Although, as mentioned earlier, RPs are typical for overnight or a few days, they can last for up to six months. In addition, RPs with longer *tenors* (tenor is like the maturity date) are usually considered higher risk. During a longer tenor, more factors can affect the counter party's creditworthiness, and interest rate fluctuations are more likely to have an impact on the value of the repurchased asset. *Open* or *continuing* overnight RPs are those that are renewed each day with the repo rate or the amount of funds invested adjusted to reflect the prevailing market conditions. Other types are the *term* RPs, which have specified maturity dates that can range from overnight to several months, and *third-party* RPs, in which the securities are not delivered to the transferee rather they are held by a custodian such as a clearing bank) and is subject to an agreement signed by all three parties to the transaction.

Second, the principal amounts in RP transactions are usually arranged in large dollar amounts, typically beginning with 10 million dollars. Third, the yields in the repo market are low (but still above the T-bill rates) because they are collateralized with Treasury securities. The interest rate paid on RP funds is negotiated by the repo counterparties and is set independently of the coupon rate or rates on the underlying securities. In general, repo interest rates are influenced by overall money market conditions, the rates paid for comparable funds in related markets, and the availability of eligible collateral.

Fourth, since RPs are close substitutes for federal funds borrowings, the activities of institutions that have direct access to both markets should keep the rates on RPs and federal funds transactions in close relationship to each other. For example, the interest rate on an open repo is generally close to the federal funds rate. The overnight fed funds rate typically exceeds the overnight RP rate, reflecting the return investors require for lending unsecured in the fed funds market rather than investing in a collateralized RP agreement. Hence, the spread between the federal funds rate and the RP can vary on economic conditions, the availability of eligible collateral, the amount of securities held in dealers' inventories and more.

Fifth, the valuation of collateral – typically Treasury securities or agency securities and mainly T-bills – depends on the length of the contract length and the type of the collateral because RPs entail both credit and interest-rate risks. The securities used as collateral are valued at the current market price, plus accrued interest (calculated to the maturity date) *less* a margin of overcollateralization or *haircut* for term agreements. In other words, the initial RP price is less than the market value of the underlying securities, which reduces the lender's exposure to market risk. To mitigate interest-rate risk, parties adjust the collateral value (the underlying securities) daily – *marking it to market* – to reflect changes in market prices and to maintain the agreed-upon margin. Changes in the market value of these positions can give rise to a *margin deficit* or a *margin excess*. For example, if the market value of the RP securities declines significantly, the borrower may be asked to provide additional collateral. In contrast, if the market value of the securities rises substantially, the lender may be required to return the excess collateral to the borrower.

1.3.2 Other insights about the repo market

What was the impact of the 2007/8 global financial crisis on the repo market? The crisis caused the value of mortgage securities to decline and thus, financial institutions participating in the housing market became more exposed to risk. As a result, those financial institutions that relied on the repo market for funding were not able to obtain funds. Investors also grew more concerned about the (quality of the) securities that were posted as collateral as well as the underlying securitized securities. According to the Securities and Exchange Commission (SEC), repo liabilities reached the all-time high at close to $5.1 trillion in March 2008 and declined sharply during the 2008–2009 financial crisis.

The crisis shattered the trust between the two parties, in other words, and each party became wary of the other's intentions and actions. Prior to the crisis, major investment houses such as Bear Stearns, Lehman Brothers, Morgan Stanley, and Merrill Lynch, were at the heart of the repo market. But when the subprime real estate market weakened early in 2007, repo market buyers became nervous about the quality of the securitized assets and the increasing haircuts on deals. Then, beginning in March 2008 Bearn Sterns declared financial stress which forced the government to rescue, followed by the default of Lehman Brothers in September and the failure of AIG. All these and more events during that year caused a *run* on the repo market.

What is the general role of the repo market in any advanced economy? According to the International Capital Markets Association (ICMA), the repo market is essential in the efficient functioning of the financial market.[6] Specifically, apart from its basic role of providing an efficient source of short-term financing, some other roles of this market are as follows.

To facilitate central bank operations: Enables central banks to implement monetary policy more efficiently under normal market conditions and to quickly act as lenders of last resort during periods of market stress. Central bank RPs can penetrate swiftly into the interdealer repo market through which liquidity can be efficiently redistributed to banks and non-banks.

To finance leverage and hedge debt issuance: Specialized institutional investors such as hedge funds borrow cash in the repo market to fund leveraged investments on a cost-efficient basis and also borrow securities to allow them to take short positions. Primary dealers also rely on this market to hedge the interest rate risk on a long position in a new issue, while taking an offsetting short position in an existing issue with similar risk. Also fundamental to the hedging and pricing of derivatives.

To promote price discovery: The repo market promotes price discovery by facilitating primary market activity as well as feeding liquidity in the secondary market, which fosters trading and arbitrage.

To prevent settlement failures: Confidence of investors in the securities market is pivotal to the efficient functioning of the market, as we saw earlier. Where an intermediary has sold securities to one party (perhaps purchased from another), but the delivery fails to arrive on time, the intermediary can borrow those securities in the repo market to ensure that it can make timely delivery to the first party until the second party delivers. Without the ability to borrow securities, delivery failures may lead to disorderly conditions, thus interrupting the flow of trading and damaging further investor confidence.

1.3.3 The role of the MMF in the Fed repo market

The importance of the money market funds (MMFs) as cash investors in repos has increased over the last 25 years. One major reason is the growth of assets under management in government MMFs, which are required to invest at least 99.5% of their assets in cash, US government securities, or repos collateralized by cash and government securities. For these funds, the latter investments were more appealing. Assets in government MMFs increased considerably in the first half of 2020, when demand for government assets surged amidst the COVID-19 pandemic.[7] MMFs conduct their repo investments with securities dealers (the primary dealers) but also with insurance companies, endowments funds, government-sponsored enterprises (GSEs), and the Federal Reserve.

More specifically about the Fed's participation in the repo market, the Fed introduced a new monetary policy tool – an overnight reverse repo facility (RRP) – in 2013 intended to improve control over short-term interest rates. The RRP provides an opportunity to invest cash on a collateralized basis at a rate set by the Fed. Although RRP has been actively utilized by MMFs in the first half of the 2010s, their use sharply declined during the second half of the decade. However, as clearly seen in Figure 5.3, it has substantially picked up since then. In the graph, the (weekly) series is constructed as the aggregated daily amount value of the RRP transactions reported by the New York Fed as part of the Temporary Open Market Operations (TOMO). These operations involve short-term repos and reverse repos that are designed to temporarily add or drain reserves available to the banking system as well as influence daily trading in the federal funds market.

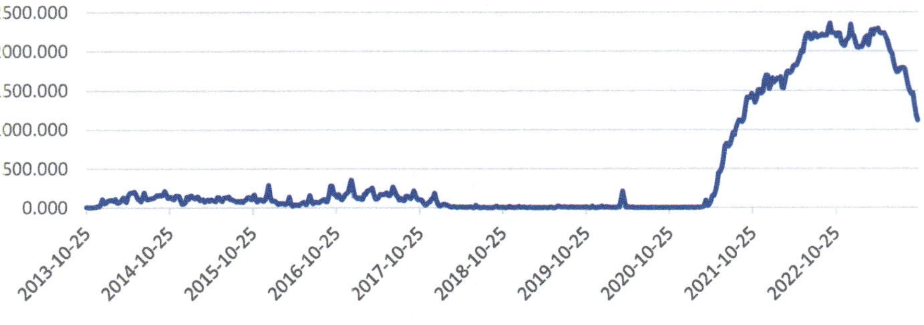

Figure 5.3 Overnight reverse repo agreements by the Federal Reserve, weekly

Source: Federal Reserve Economic Data

Notice from the graph, that at the end of 2022, the daily volume of the overnight reverse repos reached a new record high. Analysts noted that the persistent presence of the Fed in such private short-term financial transactions, both during quantitative easing (QE) and the current quantitative tightening (QT) period, reflects the preference of financial institutions (and other companies) to deal with the Fed rather than conducting businesses among themselves. This situation has a positive and a negative side.[8]

On the positive side, the Fed has been able to meet the demand for cash (or government securities, in general) by MMFs. At the same time, the Fed avoids the need for emergency interventions to ease turmoil such as those during the September 2019 – when overnight money market rates spiked and exhibited significant volatility, amid a large drop in reserves due to the corporate tax date and increases in net Treasury issuance – and March 2020 – when economic disruptions associated with the COVID-19 pandemic sparked a global dash-for-cash as investors sold securities rapidly.[9] On the negative side, the Fed "forced" MMFs and other participants to use its overnight repo and reverse repo facility, while enjoying zero counterparty risk and high-quality collateral. The cost is that these players reduce their dealings with other private sector entities thereby sidelining the role of private markets for short-term funds. The consequences of that would be the weakening of their role (and presence) and ultimately undermine the efficiency and robustness of the market economy. This new way of the Fed to conduct monetary policy makes it as the lender (or market maker) of the first resort rather than the lender of the last resort.[10]

1.4 Commercial paper

Commercial paper represents unsecured promissory notes, issued by large and creditworthy corporations, that have a maturity date of up to 270 days. Most commercial paper (CP) actually matures in 20 to 45 days. The purpose of issuing a CP is to provide liquidity or to finance a firm's investment in inventory and accounts receivable. Nonbank corporations such as the General Motors Acceptance Corporation and GE Capital use CP notes extensively to finance the loans that they extend to their customers. Finance companies provide consumers with home loans, automobile loans, and unsecured personal loans. Some other types of CP are promissory notes (legally binding agreements that one party writes to another, promising to pay a specified amount of money on a predetermined future date), checks (issued on-demand through banks according to instructions from the issuing company) and drafts (a draft is an agreement between the drawer (bank), drawee (company), and payee (investor) and the bank writes the agreement and instructs the company to pay the investor a specified amount of money at a predetermined time). A certificate of deposit (CD) is also a form of CP. We discuss CDs in the next subsection.

Issuing CP is an alternative (or cheaper) to short-term bank loans. The rate charged by banks to their best customers is known as the *prime rate*. The cost of bank loans rose sharply in the 1980s and as a result, corporations turned to CP issuance and financing. Figure 5.4 shows the return on CP against the bank prime rate (PR) for the period January 1990 to February 2010. As is clearly shown, the prime rate has consistently been above the CP yield throughout the 2013–2023 period.

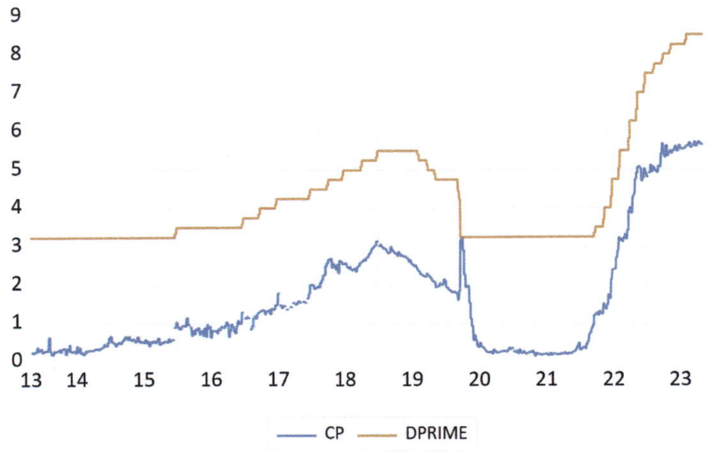

Figure 5.4 Commercial paper (CP) yield and bank prime rate (PR), weekly

Source: Federal Reserve Economic Data

CP is placed (sold) either directly or through independent dealers to a varied pool of institutional buyers. Investors in CP earn competitive, market-determined yields in notes whose maturity and amounts can be tailor-made. Although the Securities Act of 1933 requires that securities offered to the public be registered with the Securities and Exchange Commission, CP can be exempted from registration requirements – which is a very costly and time-consuming task – as long as they abide by certain requirements such as their maturity being less than 270 days and that the paper is not available to individual investors (or general public).

The minimum denomination of CP is usually $100,000, and typical denominations are in multiples of $1 million. Individual investors wishing to participate in the CP market can do so indirectly through investing in mutual funds such as money market funds (MMFs are major investors in the CP market). Just like T-bills, CP is typically a discount security where the investor purchases notes at a discount (or less than face value) and receives the face value at maturity. The difference between the purchase price and the face value is the interest received on the investment. The yields in CP are always a bit higher than those of the T-bills to reflect the credit risk of the CP issuer and lower liquidity. Formula 5.3 can be used to compute the CP's yield.[11]

1.4.1 Some considerations in the commercial paper market

It is important to note that only large corporations with high credit ratings (*blue-chip* companies) will be able to sell the instrument at a reasonable rate. Nonfinancial firms also issue commercial paper. Nonfinancial issuers include public utilities and industrial and service companies. The latter use CP to finance their working capital (accounts receivable and inventory) either on a permanent or seasonal basis, and to finance, on a temporary basis, construction projects. Public utilities also use commercial paper to fund nuclear fuels and construction. Many types (categories) of investors participate in this market besides MMFs and commercial banks. Nonfinancial corporations including life insurance companies and private and government pension funds are also large purchasers of CP notes.

Historically, and before WWII, banks were the main investors in CP and used the paper as a reserve asset for diversification purposes. In the 1950s and 1960s, industrial firms began holding CP as an alternative to bank deposits, which were subject to Regulation Q. The high and variable interest rates in the 1970s forced households and businesses to hold more of their funds in short-term in the form of MMFs (as mentioned earlier). Similarly, many large businesses found that they could borrow in the CP market at less expense than they could borrow from banks. As a result of the above forces, the CP market grew fast and by the early 1990s, MMFs were holding 42% of their assets in CP. Figure 5.5 illustrates the volume of CP outstanding since 2001 (COMPOUT). By 2007, CP reached its highest point of $2.23 billion.

A special type of commercial paper, an innovation in the market, the *asset-backed commercial paper* (ABCP), which refers to short-term securities with more than half having maturities of 1 to 4 days, became instrumental in the global financial crisis of 2007/8. 2008. ABCP differs from CP in that it is backed (secured) by some bundle of assets such as securitized mortgages and trade receivables. ABCP is issued by a company, called a *special purpose entity*, which purchases receivables from one firm or a group of firms, and finances the purchase with funds raised in the CP market. Although the risk of most CP depends on the entire firm's operating and financial risk, ABCP's risk is tied directly to the creditworthiness of pledged specific financial assets. To add to that, the credit rating (by a credit-rating agency) of the securitized (underlying) asset plays a role in its marketability.

Beginning in 2007, when the quality of the subprime mortgages used to secure ABCP was exposed, a run on ABCPs started and panicky investors began selling them at very low prices. The sharp dip in the volume of these two securities is clearly shown in Figure 5.5. In addition, there was no deposit insurance backing

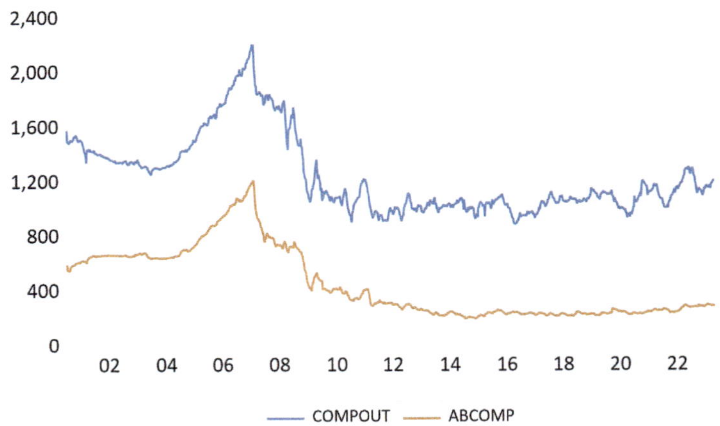

Figure 5.5 Volumes of CP and asset-backed CP outstanding, weekly

Source: Federal Reserve Economic Data

these investments, as in the case of commercial banks. The Fed had to intervene (in September 2008) and guarantee these assets to prevent the collapse of the MMF market and permit a quiet liquidation of their ABCP holdings.

1.5 Negotiable certificates of deposit

A *certificate of deposit* (CD) is simply a document documenting a time deposit by a customer within a bank (credit union or other depository institution) and specifies the amount, the maturity date, the locked interest rate and the method to compute the interest. A *time deposit* implies that the depositor leaves a lump-sum that cannot be withdrawn for a certain period of time. CDs are considered safer investment alternative than bonds, stocks, and other asset classes due to the predetermined and fixed interest rate that eliminates any risk of returns. CDs generally offer a higher interest rate than a bank savings account or money market fund. CDs' two main disadvantages are: first, they cannot be liquidated before maturity without a penalty, and second, the depositor will earn lower returns (interest) during a time period of rising interest rates. A variant of CDs is the variable-rate CD, as explained in the nearby *sidebar*.

A *negotiable certificate of deposit* (NCD) – also known as *jumbo CD* – is a certificate of deposit with a minimum par value of $100,000, although they can carry a face value of $10 million. Typical maturities for NCDs are up to 4 months and, occasionally, up to 6 months. In view of the large minimum amounts a small depositor must have to invest in an NCD, these instruments are sometimes purchased by MMFs which, in turn, allow individuals to indirectly invest in the NCD market thus, making it a very active primary market. A secondary market for NCDs also exists, and provides investors with some liquidity.

The rates paid on NCDs, as the term implies, are agreed between the bank and the depositor and are similar to the rate paid on other money market instruments (due to their low level of risk). The latter is also enhanced from the investors' implicit assumption that the government would never allow a large bank to fail. The result of this is for such banks to offer lower interest rates on NCDs. NCDs provide a return in the form of interest along with the difference between the price at which the NCD is redeemed and the purchase price. NCDs offer

VARIABLE-RATE CD

Variable-rate CDs (VRCDs) have the feature that their maturity is divided into equally long rollover periods, also called legs, in each of which the interest rate is set anew. The interest accrued on a leg is paid at the end of that leg.

The interest rate on each leg is set at some fixed spread to a certain base rate which is usually either a secondary market CD rate, T-bill rate, LIBOR or the prime rate.

Popular maturities of VRCDs are 18 months and 2 years, and roll periods are 1 and 3 months. VRCDs are used by banks because they improve their liquidity positions by providing funds a slightly higher yield than T-bills (with the same maturity) because of less liquidity and safety. Note also that the premiums increase during recessionary periods since they reflect the market's perception of the financial system's safety. This is clearly shown in Figure 5.6, where the 3-month NCD and 3-month T-bill rates are exhibited. Interest rates on NCDs are generally quoted on an interest-bearing basis with the interest computed on the basis of a 360-day year. So, for example, a \$1 million, 60-day NCD with a 2 percent annual interest rate would entitle the NCD holder to: \$1,000,000 * [1+ (60/360) * 0.02] = \$1,003,333.

for relatively long periods. VRCDs are purchased by money market investors who want to invest in instruments with long-term maturities but be protected from loss if interest rates increase. The largest investors in VRCDs are money market funds.

Some related bank accounts – or *transactions deposits* – are the demand deposits and the negotiable orders of withdrawal (NOW) accounts. A *demand deposit* account is a typical bank account that requires a small minimum balance and pays no interest. They are also known as *checking accounts* and their purpose is to serve customers who wish to write checks against their account. By contrast, a type of transaction deposit that pays interest, provides checking services and requires a larger balance amount is the *negotiable order of withdrawal* account. Another difference between the two accounts is the length of time of notice you need to give to the bank before you make a withdrawal. Despite their features, NOW accounts are not that popular compared to the traditional demand deposit accounts.

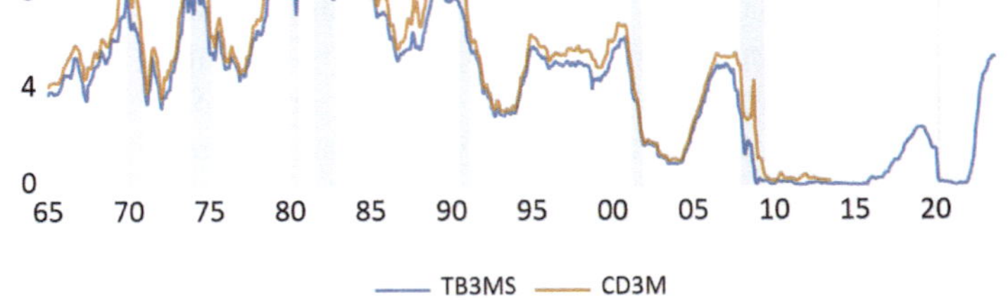

Figure 5.6 3-m negotiable certificates of deposit and 3-m T-bill rates, monthly

Note: NCD data was discontinued after July 2013
Source: Federal Reserve Economic Data

1.6 The Eurodollar market

The *Eurodollar* (or *Eurocurrency*) *market* is a market originally located in European financial centers (primarily in London) for lending and borrowing the world's major convertible currencies. A *Eurodollar* refers to a time-deposit account that is denominated in US dollars but held outside the US or in foreign banks. Over time, non-European countries were included as destinations for the US dollar deposits, including the Bahamas and Cayman Islands. However, offshore locations subjected the market to political and economic risks in the country of their domicile. The main currency is the US dollar, but other currencies such as the Euro, pound sterling and the Japanese yen are also used. The participants in that market are commercial banks, private banks, and some investment banking firms.

The Eurodollar market has grown rapidly primarily because depositors earned a higher rate of return on a dollar deposit in the Eurodollar market than in the domestic market. The origins of the Eurodollar market date back to the period after World War II. The US provided funds – via the *Marshall Plan* – to rebuild the war-ravaged continent and this led to the wide circulation of dollars overseas, and the development of a separate, less regulated market for depositing those funds. Other reasons for the market's growth were, first, the fact that multinational banks were not subject to the same US regulations restricting local banks (the Regulation Q) and second, because they are willing to accept narrower spreads between the interest paid on deposits and the interest earned on loans. The Eurodollar market facilitates international trade, provides greater flexibility to manage financial positions and offers a greater source of funds than otherwise from the home market.

Eurodollars are an alternative to fed funds where US banks lend to and borrow from each other on an overnight basis receiving or paying the fed funds rate. Banks from around the world buy and sell overnight funds in this market and the rate they pay (when they buy) is known as the *London interbank bid rate* (LIBID), and the rate for funds offered for sale as the *London interbank offer rate* (LIBOR). The overnight LIBOR and the fed funds rate tend to be very close to each other. If, at a particular point in time, the fed funds rate exceeds LIBOR, banks that need to borrow funds will borrow at LIBOR, thus raising rates, and banks with funds to lend will lend at the fed funds rate, thus tending to lower rates. These demand-and-supply pressures will drive the two rates together.

The British banks Barclays, UBS, and Royal Bank of Scotland. some of the world's largest and most important banks, began manipulating LIBOR to boost profits and/or limit losses from derivative trades from 2005 to 2009. The world learned of that scandal in 2012. Specifically, the bank had made fraudulently low LIBOR submission rates to dampen market speculation and negative media comments about the firm's viability during the financial crisis. In settling with UK and US regulators the firm agreed to pay $450 million in fines.[12] The LIBOR scandal had broader consequences for the financial industry and investor trust. The revelation that major banks had been manipulating a key benchmark rate shook investor confidence and led to a decline in the stock market. The scandal also led to a renewed focus on the need for stronger regulation and oversight of the financial industry.[13]

In the US, for US dollar-denominated financial products, LIBOR was replaced (in 2023) by the Secured Overnight Financing Rate (SOFR) as the primary benchmark interest rate. SOFR is based on actual transactions in the US Treasury repurchase market, making it a more reliable and transparent benchmark than LIBOR. In the UK, the *Sterling Overnight Index Average* (SONIA), which is the effective overnight interest rate paid by banks for unsecured transactions is now used in lieu of LIBOR. The ESTR, which stands for the Euro Short-Term Rate, is the benchmark rate at which European banks engage in unsecured euro-denominated short-term lending. This rate replaced the Euro Overnight Index Average (EONIA) rate in 2022.

1.6.1 Instruments in the Eurodollar market

Some instruments are the Eurodollar time deposits, CDs, Notes, and Commercial paper. *Eurodollar time deposits* are intrinsically different from dollar deposits held at US banks in that the former are liabilities of banks located outside the US. Similarly, a Eurodollar CD is a large (1$ million) negotiable receipt for a dollar deposit at a bank located outside the US. In view of the US dollar's dominance in world transactions (trade and investments), some firms overseas receive US dollars as payment for exports and invest in Eurodollar CDs. Since the Eurodollar market is located outside the US, banks there and instruments such as Eurodollar CDs are not subject to reserve requirements. Effectively, this means that banks can lend out 100 percent of their (new) deposits. The immediate and important consequence of that is the very narrow spread (difference) between the rate banks pay on large Eurodollar deposits and what they charge on Eurodollar loans is relatively small. This implies that interest rates in that market are attractive for both global depositors and borrowers.

In the late 1970s, Eurodollar floating-rate CDs (FRCDs) and Eurodollar floating-rate notes (FRNs) made their appearance in an effort to protect borrowers and lenders against interest rate risk (*interest-rate risk* means that higher/lower interest rates decrease/increase asset principal values). By making their coupon payments go with market interest rates, these floaters stabilize the principal value of the instrument. The rate adjusts periodically to the LIBOR. The rate on FRCDs ensures that the borrower's cost and the investor's return reflect prevailing market interest rates. A similar idea is for a variable-rate CD. The market for FRCDs is no longer active.

Finally, *Euro commercial paper* (ECP) is a type of unsecured, short-term loan issued by corporations and can be tailored to satisfy investors' needs. *Unsecured* means that interest or principal payment obligations on the paper are not guaranteed by collateral, which makes ECPs an attractive source of financing. An interesting feature of ECPs is that the currency in which they are denominated differs from the currency of the market where the bond is issued. For example, if a US company issues a short-term bond denominated in Euros to finance its inventory through the international money market, it has issued ECP.

The ECP's rate is typically between 50 and 100 basis points above LIBOR. ECPs are usually issued in denominations of $100,000, with a minimum investment amount of $500,000. Hence, this market is dominated by institutional investors.

Although this instrument has a tiny market in the US, in Europe it is more significant as European companies that want short-term funding in dollars can place their papers.

1.7 Bankers' acceptances

A *Banker's Acceptance* (BA) implies that a bank accepts responsibility for a future payment to the bearer on a given date. The BA was created in 1913 by the Federal Reserve Bank to help US banks compete with London banks in the international financing arena. Since this instrument originated in international trade, as a means of financing international trade, the following example reflects that. Assume that a liquor store owner in Greece wishes to buy a case of Scotch whiskey from a company in Scotland. The Scottish whiskey company does not want to ship the case of whiskey without being paid because it has never heard of that liquor store in Greece and realizes that it would be difficult to collect if payment were not forthcoming. Similarly, the Greek liquor store is unwilling to send money to Scotland before receiving the liquor. In this case, each party's bank can intervene to resolve this issue by issuing a BA (with a stamp of *accepted* on the letter of credit) where the bank in essence substitutes its creditworthiness for that of the purchaser.[14]

BAs have an active secondary market where the exporters can sell the acceptance before then at a discount to obtain cash immediately. The purchaser of the BA (an investor) then receives the payment guaranteed by the bank at some later date. The investor's return on a BA is derived from the difference between the discounted price paid for the acceptance and the amount to be received in the future. Hence, BAs are sold on a discounted basis like commercial paper and T-bills. Their maturities typically range from 30 to 270 days. BAs are relatively safe investments because both the bank and borrower are liable when the BA matures.

How can one calculate the size of the discount, price and the cost of a BA? Assume that you have \$1 million CP due in 182 days at 1.00% discount. How can we find its price? Its cost? It appears that we are using a rearrangement of the BDM formula (5.1). So,

$$Price = \$100 * \frac{n}{360} * 1\% \tag{5.4}$$

and thus

$$\text{Price} = 100 - (182/360) * 1 = 100 - 0.50555 = 99.494444$$

Consequently, the cost of the BA would be \$994,944.44 (= 1,000,000 *x* 0.9949444).

Before we leave this section, it would be interesting to link Management – corporate culture, in particular – to some money market instruments. The question is what does corporate culture have to do with the issuance (or even the efficient use) of some money market instruments? We suspect that corporate culture influences a firm's financial performance, risk profile, and stock liquidity and this, in turn, affects its access to short-term loans in the money market. Box 5.1 explains this linkage in some detail.

Box 5.1

How does corporate culture affect a firm's use of the money market?

FINANCIAL PERFORMANCE: A strong corporate culture can lead to better financial outcomes, lower default risk, and greater investor confidence, making the firm a more attractive and trustworthy borrower in the money market.

RISK PROFILE: A corporate culture that relies on strong internal controls, accountability and ethical behavior/standards enjoys lower risk. As a result, financial institutions are more likely to extend loans, and the firm is more trusted to issue money market securities such as commercial paper or engage in repo agreements.

INVESTOR CONFIDENCE: Strong and transparent culture by a firm creates trust and credibility among investors who will be more willing to lend to or invest in the firm and, consequently, the firm enjoys lower cost of financing or investing.

LIQUIDITY: A company with a healthy corporate culture enjoys higher liquidity and marketability for their common stock (shares) simply because investors actively and frequently engage in their trading. As a result, the company will be able to have easier access to short-term credit and enjoy overall high financial quality.

Test your understanding 1

1. You submit a noncompetitive bid in October 2023 to purchase a 28-day $1,000 T-bill, and you find that you are paying $999.8671. What are the yields based on the bank discount method and investment rate method?
2. Explain the relationship between the fed funds rate and LIBOR and discuss what would happen if these rates were out of line at any given point.
3. Why are rates in CDs and T-bills very closely held? What is the market's implicit assumption?
4. Why do large companies issue commercial paper?
5. Can you mention some risks of Banker's Acceptances, from the perspective of the bank?

Solutions appear at the textbook's website.

2 The financial intermediaries

A vibrant and healthy economy requires a financial market (system) that effectively and efficiently moves funds from people who save to people who have productive investment opportunities. Such a system includes financial intermediaries or financial institutions (as we first mentioned in Chapter 3). The use of an intermediary in financing (or raising funds externally) is indirect finance. Of all the financial intermediaries, commercial banks take the prize in indirect finance. In what follows below, we will discuss some fundamental traits of, or that plague, financial intermediaries and then proceed with the brief discussion of the most important ones.

2.1 Characteristics of the structure of the financial system

In this subsection, we will discuss the roles of transactions costs, information costs and the free-rider problem on the functioning of the financial market and, especially, how these problems affect the financial intermediaries. Allen and Santomero (1998) discussed the theory of intermediation focusing on transaction and information costs.[15] They argued that transaction costs have fallen and information has become cheaper and more available, as financial markets became more integrated, globalized and changed structure. They also conceded that standard theories of intermediation based on transaction costs and asymmetric information are difficult to reconcile with the changes that have taken place in the financial markets. Financial intermediaries need to do more to ensure well-functioning financial markets. We begin with how transactions costs influence financial decisions.

2.1.1 Transactions costs

As we mentioned in Chapter 3, financial markets have many functions including the provision of liquidity and disseminating information. Recall that liquidity refers to the ability of a financial asset to be converted into cash easily, fast and with no loss of value. A closely related concept to liquidity are *transactions costs*, which represent the cost of buying and selling financial instruments (when you use a broker or dealer). Financial markets need to ensure that transactions costs are kept very low and to minimize any frictions in the market. Transactions costs can be substantial in financial markets especially when the initial investment budget is very low.

Consider, for example, the cost of buying 10 stocks via an online broker who charges \$0 per stock, and your investment budget is \$1,000.[16] However, even if there are no brokerage fees, there are several other fees for the trade: trade commissions, sales load, management fees and more. Also, keep in mind that many online brokers state that the standard online \$0 commission does not apply to over-the-counter (OTC) equities, transaction-fee mutual funds, and fixed-income investments, but service charges of \$25 apply for trades placed online through a broker and/or \$5 by automated phone. If you decide to buy a bond instead, the problem would be even worse because the smallest denomination for some bonds is as much as \$10,000, and your investment budget is only \$1.000.

Just assume that the broker will charge you \$6.95 per trade, per stock for your 10 OTC stocks plus the \$25 service fee.[17] You understand that the total cost of the 10 stocks (ignore the min and max number of shares, just buy one share) would be: 10 shares x \$6.95 + 25 = \$94.5. This amount represents 9.45% reduction of your \$1,000 budget which, as you can image, is quite hefty. However, if you join a mutual fund (we will discuss this investment company category in the next chapter) your cost would have been much smaller because of the efficiency these companies achieve when polling together small investors' funds and invest them in a greater variety of stocks (your familiar from economics concept of *economies of scale*). The fact that almost half of Americans own financial securities attests to the low cost of transactions via such investment means.

An alternative way that you can reduce your transaction costs is by purchasing the securities directly from the company or the government. In the first case, we are talking about a *Direct Stock Purchase Plan* (DSPP) which refers to the opportunity that individual investors have to buy stocks directly from a company thereby avoiding a broker. However, even though DSPPs minimize commission fees, there could be other explicit charges such as initial set-up fees, purchase requirements (which depend on the company to provide dividend reinvestments and price discounts) and transfer fees (which are payments to third-party institutions that record transactions, issue certificates, etc.). For more information on DSSPs, visit the SEC's webpage.[18]

Finally, as we have learned in subsection 2.1 earlier, you can invest in government securities such as T-bills by purchasing them directly from the government (through *Treasurydirect*) thus, bypassing a broker and its fees. For example, investment banks such as Fidelity charges a flat fee of $19.95 per trade in government securities (notably bonds, not bills) and a bank may charge you fees or commissions for the T-bill transaction.

2.1.2 Information costs

Another characteristic of financial markets (via their instruments) is that they communicate *information,* summarizing certain essential details about the issuer. For example, how much do you want to learn about the issuer of a stock or bond? Or if you are purchasing an existing instrument, how much do you need to know about the person who is selling it to you? Finally, if you wish to buy a used car, how much information do you must have about the car?

In addition to simply summarizing information, financial instruments are designed to address the problem of *asymmetric information*, which refers to the fact that some people (for example, borrowers or sellers) have some information they don't disclose to other people for example, lenders or buyers). This problem is also widely known as *agency theory* (or agent–principal problem), where the agent (a manager of a corporation) may not act in the best interest of the owners (the principal) and thus conflicts arise between these parties. By the way, conflicts can also arise between shareholders and credit holders of a company as with the company's manager and credit holders (or debt holders). Hence, information plays a central role in the structure of financial markets and their constituents (financial instruments and institutions). Markets require access to information in order to function well and so, when the cost of obtaining that information is too high, they cease to work. It follows then that information costs make the financial markets among the worst functioning of all markets.

Asymmetric information poses two significant obstacles to the smooth flow of funds within financial markets, *adverse selection* and *moral hazard.*

THE PRISONER'S DILEMMA AND THE TRAGEDY OF THE COMMONS

The prisoner's dilemma refers to a decision-making paradox in which two rational players when looking after their own self-interest cannot achieve an optimal solution. Each player seeks his welfare at the other player's expense.

The first arises *before* the transaction occurs. Just as a potential buyer of a used car needs to know the relative trustworthiness of the car's seller, the lender (for example, an insurance company) needs to know how to distinguish good credit risks from bad. The second problem occurs *after* the transaction. Just as buyers need reassurance that sellers will deliver their purchases after receiving payment, lenders need to find a way to tell whether borrowers will use the proceeds of a loan as intended. We will see these two problems again in Chapter 6 when we discuss the insurance industry.

Fortunately, the markets have found ways to reduce transactions costs and smooth out the flow of funds. In the above example of the used car, the buyer could hire a mechanic to take a look at the car before he buys it. This would raise the cost of buying the car and may not be worth it in the end. Even worse, the seller may refuse to allow the mechanic to inspect the car. That is why, the seller may resort to cheaper alternatives such as free online used-car reviews, subscription to magazines such as the *Consumer Reports* (in the US) and other (typically free) services such as *CARFAX* (also in the US) in order to learn about the reliability and safety of particular car makes and models. In the case of potential financial investments, and in hopes of distinguishing between good and bad firms or financial issues (such as bonds), market participants may subscribe to the services produced by credit-rating agencies such as *Standard & Poor's*, *Moody's*, *Fitch & Associates* and *Value Line* which gather information on firms' balance sheet positions and investment activities. Finally, when it comes to evaluating the creditworthiness of individuals (as potential borrowers), several consumer reporting companies such as *Equifax*, *Experian* and *Transunion* exist to sell their data and credit scores to various providers of household credit.

As a result, they avoid cooperation in the decision-making process and end up in a much worse condition. A real example would refer to the arms races that nations embark in, individually, instead of cooperating and abandoning arms altogether.

The tragedy of the commons describes a situation in which individuals with access to a public (shared) resource act in their own interest and, in doing so, ultimately deplete or destroy the resource. For example, overfishing or overhunting have the potential to push many species into extinction such as the Pacific bluefin tuna and the elephant (for ivory), respectively.

2.1.3 The free rider problem

What about the private collection and sale of information, as mentioned above? You might get the impression that asymmetric information problems would just disappear, but reality is that they do not! That is because such information does not really exist because such information is sold directly to a payer, can be expensive to an average person like you and me and also because of the free-rider problem. The *free rider problem* occurs when people take advantage of the information that other people have paid for but they did not. The problem of free riding occurs when goods (products or services) are *non-excludable*. Sharing a public park with others, you fishing with other people in the same coast, animals freely grazing in a parcel of land, enjoying national defense and so on are examples of goods that are not excludable. In addition, you should have realized that such goods are *non-rivalrous*, meaning that one's consumption or enjoyment does not diminish another's consumption or enjoyment. For example, does your fresh-air breathing diminish your neighbor's fresh-air breathing? An example from finance would be financial stability which can be enjoyed by everyone if market agents – except you – act in good faith.

Two very important situations that appear in financial markets can help explain the free rider problem: *the prisoner's dilemma* and *the tragedy of the commons*. A well-known game, the prisoner's dilemma, best explains the reason why you might be a free rider even though it benefits you to pay, and the tragedy of the commons, explains the depletion or destruction of common resources if left to individuals for free. The nearby *sidebar* discusses both situations.

We witness abundance of cases where these two issues happen daily in the world. We hear of some of OPEC members' cheating on their oil production quota, on the unwillingness of some shoppers to buy online for fear of being cheated by the online company, we typically see trash all over a park we frequent. How can society mitigate these two problems? The obvious solutions would be to appeal to human nature by giving incentives to the free riders. For example, you would be willing to pay some money to keep your neighborhood clean (when others do that as well) if you are offered a higher price for your house when you sell it. Alternatively, we can appeal to people's altruism. Second, via enforcement or punishment. Collective action to enforce cooperative behavior through rules, laws, democratic or other collective decision-making procedures, and/or explicit social punishment for free riding may transform many people to behave toward the more collectively beneficial cooperative outcomes. Third, if we are talking about a public good, then the obvious solution would be to convert it into a private good so excludability and rivalry exist. Finally, government intervention by providing information – for free – so people 'distinguish' bad-credit and good-credit individuals so as to ensure all citizens or residents in a neighborhood keep their yards, sidewalks in front of their house clean, pay for incidental neighborhood needs, for example, for everybody's benefit.

Mitigating the free rider problem in financial markets would also entail some of the suggestions mentioned above. For example, the government or a private company would provide information about firms that have done wrong things (despite the potential political costs) or an arm of the government such as the SEC in the US or the Financial Services Authority (FSA) in the UK, could require securities firms to have independent audits (where accounting firms certify that the firms are abiding by standard accounting principles and disclosing accurate information about their sales, assets, and earnings) and do not mislead the public.

2.2 Financial intermediaries

In this section, we will discuss some major financial intermediaries that are crucial for the functioning of the financial markets (not that the others are not, however): the depository institutions such as commercial banks, savings banks, and credit unions. In the next chapter, we will present the non-depository institutions namely, investment banks and investment companies, insurance companies and pension funds. We begin with commercial banks.

2.2.1 Commercial banks

As you already know, commercial banks (or depository institutions) supply credit in the economy by providing loans to businesses to expand their business and individuals to buy goods and services, students to pay for their college education and several services such as checking and savings accounts. All these activities aim at financing and boosting economic growth. Just like any other business, a bank has assets and liabilities where their sum is the total assets and their difference is what we call *net worth*. Some examples of assets are loans, investments in government securities and physical capital. Examples of liabilities are checkable and time deposits and borrowings (from other banks or the Fed). A bank's assets are referred to as *uses of funds*, whereas its liabilities are the *sources of funds*. Figure 5.7 displays the sources (Panel A) and uses of funds (Panel B) of all commercial banks in

Panel A: sources of funds

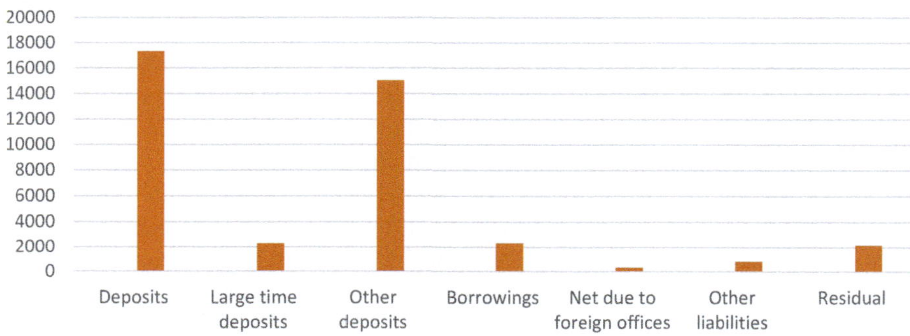

Panel B: uses of funds

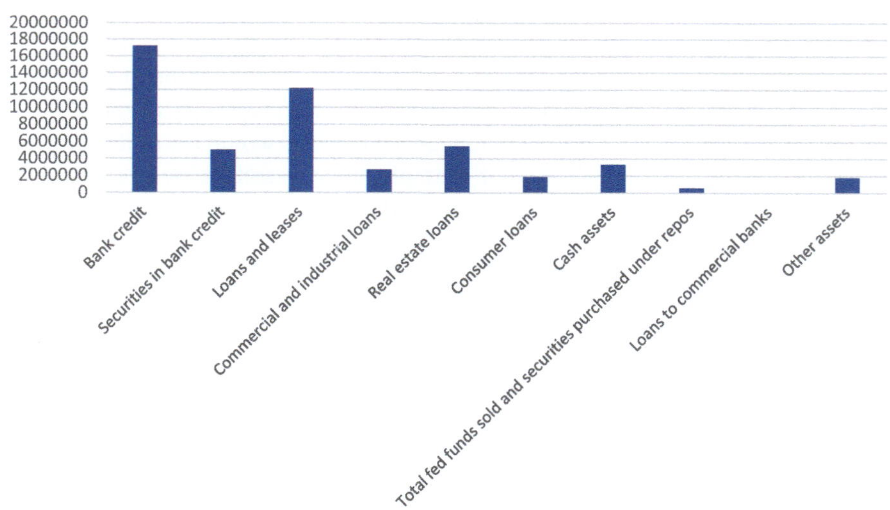

Figure 5.7 Sources and uses of funds of all commercial banks in the US, September 2023

Source: Federal Reserve, *H.8 publication*, October 2023.

the United States on September 2023. As is clearly shown from Panel A, the deposits make up the largest chunk of all commercial banks' liabilities of which the large deposits amount to a small fraction of traditional deposits, as mentioned earlier. The residual is the difference between assets and liabilities. From Panel B, where the uses of funds are shown, it is evident that a big portion of these banks' uses of funds go to bank credit, of which the securities in bank credit such as Treasury and agency securities and mortgage-backed securities hold a sizable amount (although not shown in the graph). Next, comes loans and leases (to non-depository institutions and other unclassified institutions) and, a distant one, real estate loans (both residential and commercial). Finally, the cash assets include vault cash, cash items in process of collection, balances due from depository institutions, and balances due from Federal Reserve banks.

The interest payments earned on the assets are a bank's profits. Banks make profits by selling liabilities and using the proceeds to buy assets, a process known as *asset transformation*. For example, savings deposits enable the bank to make a mortgage or car loan, if the interest rate the bank pays to the savings account exceeds that it charges for the loan. A bank can also make a profit if it holds short-term liabilities such as checkable deposits and uses the proceeds to buy longer-term assets such as loans with higher interest rates, that is, it borrows short and lends long.

In addition to the above, regular balance sheet entries, banks engage in off-balance sheet activities, which generate (fee) income. Even though such activities do not require an investment of funds, they do create a contingent obligation for banks. Some popular off-balance sheet items include letters of credit, loan commitments, forward contracts on currencies and types of swaps (interest-rate and credit default swaps). In general, off-balance sheet items are typically those not owned by, or are a direct obligation of, the bank. These items may expose depository institutions to credit, liquidity, or counterparty risks and, experts say, that they should not be separated from the on-balance sheet activities. For example, when bank loans are securitized and sold off as investments, the secured debt is often kept off the bank's books, which, in turn, exposes the bank to some of the above risks.

Off-balance sheet activity of commercial banks in the US has grown tremendously due to various reasons such as financial deregulation (which enabled the creation of more instruments), technological advances, shrinking profit margins and market competition changes. These events have provided new opportunities for banks (as well as non-banks) to engage in such activities in an effort to maintain decent margins and survive competition. Finally, capital adequacy requirements put additional pressures on banks which were required to keep more capital aside. Figure 5.8 shows the rapid growth of off-balance sheet activity in the US since 1990.

In general, a bank must be able to manage efficiently its assets and liabilities in order to make profits. What's hidden behind this *asset-liability management process* are the ability of the bank to have enough cash in hand to meet deposit outflows (referred to as *liquidity management*), possess assets that are not in danger of default (known as *asset management*) and the amount of capital it needs to acquire and maintain to avoid failure (or *capital adequacy management*). Although more liquid assets tend to earn lower returns, banks still desire to hold them (mainly as excess reserves) to provide insurance against the costs of deposit outflows. Banks manage the amount of capital they hold to prevent bank failure as well as meet bank capital requirements set by the regulatory authorities, but may not keep too

Figure 5.8 Off-balance sheet commercial bank activity in the US, 1990–2023

Source: Federal Reserve Economic Data

much capital because they may risk lowering their shareholders' returns. In addition to these, a financial institution must be able to manage credit or default risk and interest-rate risk or the risk of decreases in earnings and asset returns that result from interest-rate changes (we discus interest rate risk in the next section). These will be discussed in a later chapter.

The commercial banking sectors in the European Union and the United States have gone through major changes and consolidation in recent years. Consolidation over time was in order to achieve economies of scale and become more efficient. According to a speech by a member of the Supervisory Board of the ECB in 2021, the profitability of European banks fell from just under 6% at the end of 2018 to around 1.5% at the end of 2020, and remained well below that of US banks, whose return on equity stood just below 8% at the end of 2020.[19] In addition, the European banking sector has too many banks with heavy cost structures compared to that in the United States where the number of banks fell threefold as much as in Europe between 2009 and 2011.[20] However, consolidation in the European banking sector is lagging. Reasons for such delays include the complexity of the process, regulatory impediments as well as several home and national biases.

2.2.2 Savings banks

Savings banks are also known as *thrift institutions* and include *Savings & Loan* institutions (S&Ls) as part of savings institutions. All these types offer similar services as a regular commercial bank and rely on the federal funds market to transact (lend excess funds or borrow, if in short of funds). Savings institutions can be mutual, that is, owned by depositors, or owned by shareholders. The majority of these institutions uses of funds are on residential mortgage loans. The 1980s had been a turbulent period of the S&Ls because of two reasons. First, since the 1970s, the interest rates were capped by the government substantially below what could be earned elsewhere, thus leading savers to withdraw their funds. In addition, inflation was a problem due to various supply shocks such as the oil shocks. Second, when interest rates rose, the mortgages that the S&Ls had underwritten lost a considerable amount of value and this essentially destroyed the S&L industry's net worth. This came to be known as the *S&L debacle*. By the late 1980s, Congress decided to address the thrift industry's problems and passed the *Financial Institutions Reform, Recovery and Enforcement Act* of 1989 that instituted a number of reforms. In addition, the *Resolution Trust Corporation* was established and funded to resolve the remaining troubled institutions (by closing hundreds of S&Ls). The final cost to taxpayers was estimated to be higher than $120 billion.

In Europe, German savings banks were under fire by the ECB's regulators (and also by the German financial regulators) as they urged the savings banks to overhaul their sector's safety net in an effort to protect individual lenders from collapse. According to a 2020 *Financial Times* article, savings banks (known as *Sparkassen*) in Germany have been forcefully resisting (through vigorous lobbying) the German government's proposals for a pan-eurozone deposit insurance scheme, which they fear would supersede their own support system.[21] Sparkassen have been operating under a so-called institutional protection scheme whereby the main concern was to prevent the collapse of an individual lender, rather than just to guarantee clients' deposits in case of the demise of a Sparkasse. Institutional protection schemes link banks within a financial group (the so-called, *Cooperative Financial Group*) and allow a member bank in stress to receive financial support from the scheme's other members. Austria and Spain have similar institutional protection schemes between groups of cooperative and savings banks.[22]

2.2.3 Credit unions

Unlike commercial and savings banks, *credit unions* are nonprofit institutions, are smaller than other depository institutions and restrict their business to credit union members who share a common bond. Common bond may be defined as members having a common community, occupation or place of work. Examples include members' affiliations with a church, university or a labor union. Because they do not issue stock, they are essentially owned by their members (depositors) and receive a share (dividend). Because they are not taxed (due to their nonprofit status), when credit unions accumulate earnings, they can use them either to offer higher rates on deposits or to reduce rates on loans. These are major advantages of credit unions compared to commercial banks. In addition, they do not have to achieve a desired return for shareholders, which means that they may not be managed efficiently. Further, the strength of the common bond (an employer) may turn disadvantageous if that employer faces financial difficulties and lays off workers, which, in turn reduce liquidity of the credit union. To avoid being overly dependent on a particular employer and face credit and liquidity risks, credit unions have responded by merging with others as well as diversify their sources of funds.

According to the *World Council of Credit Unions*, the mission is to promote more equitable and resilient communities through financial inclusion.[23] The latter means that the organization strives to provide access to affordable, reliable and self-sustainable financial services so as to improve the lives of people of all income levels. According to the organization's Annual Report, over 300 technical assistance programs in 90 countries have been implemented comprising of financial inclusion through digital solutions and formal financial services, empowering women by addressing gender disparities in accessing financial services, improving the socioeconomic integration and security of migrants and refugees via entrepreneurship and employment programs, and promoting growth and increased access to responsible finance through advocacy for legal and regulatory reforms.[24]

In Europe, credit unions operate in a number of European countries including in the Republic of Ireland, Estonia, Romania, Poland, the United Kingdom, The Netherlands and the Republic of North Macedonia. Albania, Latvia, Lithuania, Ukraine, Croatia and Moldova also have credit unions. In Europe, these institutions make an important contribution to the European social economy by supporting thousands of communities and more than seven million European households with affordable financial services.[25]

3 Using the money market instruments

In this section, we will discuss how individual and institutional investors use the money market instruments. Obviously, the common reasons by both market players are that they desire to earn a near-certain rate of return (keep in mind that some individual investors cannot participate in some money market instruments like commercial paper and the federal funds markets) and maintain liquidity. For individual investors, liquidity is achieved by converting a money market instrument (such as a T-bill or a Banker's Acceptance) into cash (by selling it). For institutional investors, in addition, by issuing or exchanging new short-term securities such as commercial paper, NCDs and repos.

The growing pace of globalization and international integration, sped up the flow of funds across national borders making investments – financial and real alike – as well as speculation faster and more effective. As a result of global financial integration, the money market rates are influenced by not only domestic factors but also international factors (through the forces of demand and supply). For example, if the demand for short-term funds (denominated in a particular currency) is high relative to the short-term funds that are available in that currency, then the money market interest rates will be relatively high in that country. An implication of these relationships is also the high correlations/covariances among international money market rates. The money market rates of Canada, China, Europe 19, Great Britain, Japan and US, shown in Figure 5.9, from January 2000

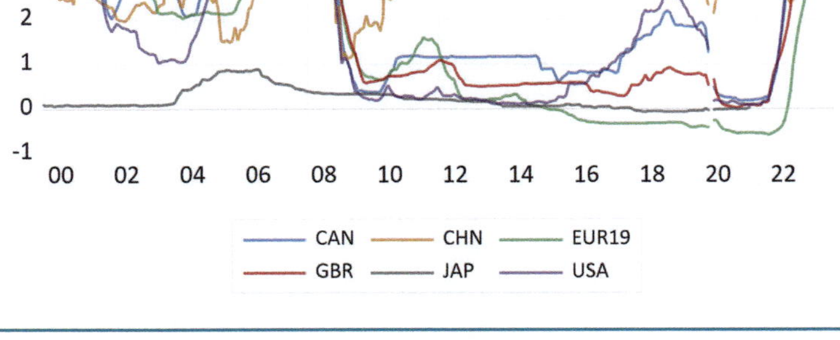

Figure 5.9 International money market rates, 2000:01–2023:10

to October 2023, illustrate this point. High rates are seen (implied) during the early 2000s, then during the 2005–2008 period and finally as recently as 2021. Economic growth was mostly responsible for such high rates. The prolonged period from 2019–2020 witnessed low rates – due to weak economies – but with high correlations because they tended to move together.

How can a retail (like you and me investor) exploit changes in interest rates? Recall that when interest rates rise, then investors require a higher rate of return on money market instruments causing a decrease in their prices. However, due to their short-term nature, the sensitivity of these instruments to changes in interest rates is not as high as that for longer-term securities such as bonds. Hence, you can reasonably expect the repayments and investment income during the period of your investment. The only thing that happens during the investment period is the inverse effects of *price* (or interest-rate) *risk* and *reinvestment risk*. Without getting into a specific example, when rates go up, the value of an asset goes down (due to the present value formula) and so you lose on the principal (capital). That's the price risk. But, at the same time, you gain interest income because you reinvest the proceeds (income) at a higher rate. This is the reinvestment rate risk. In general, these two effects balance each other out and so, if you hold the instrument to maturity, you will not lose. You may lose only if you sell it before its maturity. However, these two risks are not very serious in money market instruments.

Some additional insights regarding yields and rates of return on money market instruments are necessary so you can understand the differences between them and also be able to compare among rates and yields of various money market instruments. Let us begin with recalling the holding-period return, *HPR*, which we first learned in Chapter 2 (as the rate of return). The formula is below.

$$\textit{Holding-Period Return} = \frac{P_1 - P_0 + \textit{Distributions}}{P_0} * 100 \tag{5.5}$$

where distribution means anything that you receive from that instrument such as interest income. As an example, if you hold a T-bill for which you paid \$98.80 and has 270 days to maturity, its HPR would be HRP = (100 – 98.80)/98.80 = 0.0121 or 1.21%. HPR is also known as the *yield to maturity* (YTM) if you hold the fixed-income security (such as a bond) until it matures.

If we wish to find the money market yield or *holding period yield*, *HPY*, the formula would be

$$\textit{Holding-Period Yield} = \textit{HPR} * (360/t) \tag{5.6}$$

where t is the time period and so, with the values above it would have been HPY = 0.0121 * (360/270) = 0.0161 or 1.61%. The *money market yield* is the annualized HPR based on the 360-day year convention. It is also known as the *CD equivalent yield*.

What if you wish to invest in a foreign money market instrument? What would be your rate of return (or yield)? In this case, we need to include the exchange rate or, more specifically, the percentage change in the exchange rate. For example, if you, the US investor, want to obtain Euros at \$0.91 and invest in a one-year money market instrument in Greece yielding 10% (in Euros), what would be the *effective yield* (or the exchange rate-adjusted yield) when the (assumed) spot exchange rate is 0.92? The understanding here is that you want dollars at the end of the investment period and thus you need to convert the Euros into dollars. To answer this problem, we need to apply the following formula:

$$Effective\ Yield = (1 + HPR_f) * (1 + \%\Delta ER) - 1 \qquad (5.7)$$

where HRP_f is the yield earned on a foreign money market instrument (actually equ. 5.5 without the distributions) and ΔER the percentage change in the exchange rate. The percentage change in the exchange rate is 1.0109 [= 1 + (0.92 – 0.91)/0.91]. So, using our values we get:

$$EY = (1.10) * (1.0109) - 1 = 0.1119$$

which means that the effective yield would be 11.20% from this foreign investment. Needless to say, that if the exchange rate was \$0.90, then EY would have been 8.79% (you can check that).

A related rate of return is the effective annual rate, EAR, which we first encountered in Chapter 2. The formula is EAR = $[1 + (APR/n)]^{n} - 1$, where APR is the annual percentage rate, defined as number of periods *x* periodic rate, and *n* is the number of periods. In Chapter 2, we used this formula to compare among interest rates offered by a bank. When we substitute the term *HPY* for APR in the EAR equation and make an exponent adjustment (where *t* is the time period again), we derive the *effective annual yield*, EAY:

$$EAY = [(1 + HPY)]^{365/t} - 1 \qquad (5.8)$$

The EAY adds 1 to the HPY and compounds the whole quantity one year forward and then subtracts the result from 1 to obtain the annualized return.

In general, when you shop around for the best investment for your money and consider a bank certificate of deposit (CD) or other fixed-income investment, you will need to go beyond the stated or quoted interest rate. If both instruments offer the same interest rate, what other information do you need to know before making your decision? You need to know the frequency of compounding (or the number of compounding periods) because this separates the two investments (*ceteris paribus*). Then, you need to compute the effective (annual) yield of each. For example, if these two investments offer an interest rate of 6% and mature in one year, but one compounds annually while the other compounds semi-annually, which one is better?

Assume you have \$1,000 to invest in the annually compounded investment, then the return is simply 6%, because it is annual. Specifically, multiply it by \$1,000 by 6% and you will get \$60 in interest. At the end of the year, you'll have \$1,060. Your effective yield is the \$60 gain divided by the \$1,000 investment, or 6%. The semi-annually compounding investment is a little different. At the end of six months, you take half the annual interest rate, 3%, and multiply it by \$1,000 (the principal amount). Then, you will have \$1,030 at the end of the six months. Then, after six more months, you multiply again the new \$1,030 balance by 3%, which yields an interest payment of \$30.90. So, the new total you get \$1,060.90 and when you divide it by \$1,000, you get 6.09%. This is higher than the 6% for annual compounding. Now, you can make a decision based on your needs, as an investor.

Finally, investors use specific money market instruments such as T-bills or other cash equivalents when constructing basic investment portfolios along with the other major asset classes, equities and fixed income (mostly bonds). We can show a simple example here using two stocks and the T-bill but when it comes to forming a more realistic risky portfolio we need additional tools and insights that we will learn in a later chapter when we are done with these major asset classes. Assume that we wish to invest in two stocks, *X* and *Y*, with expected returns of 10% and 20%, respectively and risk (standard deviation) of 15% and 25%, respectively. Next, we will to pair each of these stocks with the T-bill which offers a (certain) return of 3%, *F.* If we allocate equal weights – 50–50 – to each of these instruments, what would be the rate of return and risk of each two-asset portfolios?

We begin with the expected return of the *XF* and *YF* portfolios. Denote as w the weights for each instrument, w_X and w_F, and w_Y and w_F, respectively. The formula then is as follows:

$$E(R_{XF}) = w_X\, E(r_X) + w_F\, r_F \tag{5.9}$$

where r_F is the risk-free asset's return. Plugging in the above numbers, we get

$$E(R_{XF}) = 0.50 * 10\% + 0.50 * 3\% = 5\% + 1.5\% = 6.5\% \text{ and}$$
$$E(R_{YF}) = 0.50 * 20\% + 0.50 * 3\% = 10\% + 1.5\% = 11.5\%$$

Next, we need to compute the risk (variance or standard deviation) for each of the two portfolios. The formula is as follows:

$$\sigma_{XF} = w_X * \sigma_X \tag{5.10}$$

because there is no risk for the risk-free rate instrument. Plugging in the values from above, we get

$$\sigma_{XF} = 0.5 * 15\% = 7.5\% \text{ and}$$
$$\sigma_{YF} = 0.5 * 25\% = 12.5\%$$

So, let us see what we have here and evaluate each portfolio. The XF portfolio yielded 6.5% with a risk of 7.5%, whereas the YF portfolio, yielded 11.5% with 12.5% risk. Which is better? In the XF portfolio, the risk is half compared to the YF portfolio, but that came with a cost! The cost is the reduction in the expected return. Would you say that XF is preferred to YF because of its lower risk?

One tool that allows us to compare investments with different expected returns and risk levels is the *coefficient of variation*, *CV*. Its formula is

$$\textit{Coefficient of Variation} = \sigma_{XF} / E(R_{XF}) = \sigma / \mu \tag{5.11}$$

which shows the risk per (one) unit of return. In the above example, would you consider the YF portfolio riskier than the XF portfolio? Let us put them on an equal basis for proper comparison.[26] Let us compute their CVs.

$$CV_{XF} = 7.5\% / 6.5\% = 1.15 \quad \text{and} \quad CV_{YF} - 12.5\% / 11.5\% = 1.08$$

We see that XF portfolio actually has a higher risk per unit of return than XF! So, we should not prefer XF portfolio just because it happens to have a lower standard deviation, but YF because of its relatively more favorable risk-return relationship. This is the proper way to compare two securities that have different levels of risk.

Test your understanding 2

1. Classify the following situations moral hazard or adverse selection cases. (a) Misuse of office supplies by employees, (b) Taking excessive risks with the money that your parents give you, (c) When you wish to buy a used car and do not know as much for it, (d) Making frequent visits to your doctor even for minor things, (e) The potential differences in the required rates of return for equity and debt, (f) When you go to your bank to apply for a personal loan.
2. Explain what is implied behind the following two situations: (a) you are driving on the highway and suddenly the truck in front of you overturns and wads of money are spread on the street and (b) you are an underage student and drink alcohol in your dorm.
3. What are some fundamental differences between savings banks and credit unions?
4. What is the difference between the holding-period return and the holding-period yield?

Solutions appear at the textbook's website.

Summary

- We discussed a number of money market instruments such as the Treasury bill, the federal funds market, repurchase agreements, commercial paper, negotiable certificates of deposit, the Eurodollar market, and bankers' acceptances.
- Next, we briefly presented the characteristics of the depository institutions (or financial intermediaries) such as transactions costs, information costs and the free rider problem.
- Then, we discussed some financial intermediaries such as commercial banks, savings banks and credit unions.
- We ended the chapter with some ideas on how one can exploit the money market via computing yields and rates of return and comparing various risky instruments.
- In this vein, we derived formulae for the rate of return, yield, expected return and the coefficient of variation.

Questions and problems

1. Compute the bank-discount and investment rates of return of a 26-week Treasury bill priced at \$99.5655. Explain the outcomes from your perspective, as an investor.
2. What was the purpose of quantitative easing by the Fed during the 2007/8 global financial crisis?

3. What is the relationship or linkage between the effective federal funds rate and the equally widely watched by the market 3-month T-bill?
4. How does the Federal Reserve (Fed) use a repo?
5. What is the Fed's role when the repo market became malfunctional in 2019? What was the situation during the 2020 global health pandemic? What are some implications of this situation for firms and consumers?
6. As an investor, you have the following investment options. (1) a stock of a well-known company, whose expected return is 14% and risk 10%; (2) a bond of a creditworthy issuer with expected return of 3% and risk of 2%; (3) an indexed (to the S&P500 stock market index) portfolio of securities with expected return of 13% and volatility (risk) of 7%. Which one would you choose and why?

Notes

1. Other potential users of the money market are universities, endowment funds, charities, authorities, and nonprofit organizations.
2. Competitive bidders such as financial institutions can submit their bids for all Treasury securities online using the Treasury Automated Auction Processing System (TAAPS).
3. An interesting concept – *the winners' curse* – arises from such auctions. Winners of T-bill auctions are those who submit the highest bids. Given that the T-bills are worth the same to all bidders, they differ only by their respective bids. If we consider the average bid as final and accurate, then the highest bidders overestimated the T-bills' value meaning that winners overpaid!
4. Banks can also borrow directly from the Fed, but it discourages banks from regularly borrowing from it.
5. According to the Fed, the total repo liabilities (or repo borrowings) at around $4.1 trillion as of September 30, 2020.
6. https://www.icmagroup.org/market-practice-and-regulatory-policy/repo-and-collateral-markets/icma-ercc-publications/frequently-asked-questions-on-repo/3-what-is-the-role-of-repo-in-the-financial-markets/
7. https://www.sec.gov/files/mmfs-and-repo-market-021721.pdf
8. https://www.atlanticcouncil.org/blogs/econographics/fed-reverse-repos-hit-a-new-record-an-unhealthy-development/
9. https://www.federalreserve.gov/econres/notes/feds-notes/what-happened-in-money-markets-in-september-2019–20200227.html and https://libertystreeteconomics.newyorkfed.org/2022/07/the-global-dash-for-cash-in-march-2020/
10. https://www.atlanticcouncil.org/blogs/econographics/fed-reverse-repos-hit-a-new-record-an-unhealthy-development/
11. Also, formula 5.2 – used to find the yield on a T-bill – can be employed but with a 360-day year entry.
12. https://www.hbs.edu/faculty/Pages/item.aspx?num=43888
13. https://www.learnsignal.com/blog/libor-scandal-overview/
14. A letter of credit (L/C) represents a commitment by that bank to back the payment owed to the Scottish exporter.
15. Allen, Franklin and Anthony M. Santomero, (1998). The Theory of Financial Intermediation. *Journal of Banking & Finance* 21, 1461–1485.
16. The move toward zero trading fees began in the United States in 2019 with giant brokerage houses such as Charles Schwab, TD Ameritrade, E-Trade, Fidelity, Robinhood and Interactive Brokers among others.
17. These are actual values taken from Charles Schwab's website on November 13, 2023: https://www.schwab.com/pricing
18. https://www.investor.gov/introduction-investing/investing-basics/glossary/direct-investment-plans-buying-stock-directly

19. https://www.bankingsupervision.europa.eu/press/speeches/date/2021/html/ssm.sp210611~87256e1f4b.en.html
20. https://www.bankingsupervision.europa.eu/press/speeches/date/2021/html/ssm.sp210611~87256e1f4b.en.html
21. https://www.ft.com/content/b90e3848-fe9a-427e-8a17-3facd01ff4be
22. https://www.ft.com/content/b90e3848-fe9a-427e-8a17-3facd01ff4be
23. https://www.woccu.org/
24. https://www.woccu.org/documents/2022_Annual_Report_English
25. http://www.creditunionnetwork.eu/
26. This is not normally applied to portfolios but this is a simple illustration.

Chapter 6

Investment companies and investment bankers

Introduction

In the previous chapter, we presented and discussed at length the main instruments of the money market. In this chapter, we conclude the presentation of the money market by discussing one very important instrument, the money market fund(s). This is part of an investment company, otherwise known as a mutual fund. There are other types of investment companies – more specialized or sophisticated – that assist individual investors fulfill their investment needs such as hedge funds, exchange-traded funds, real estate investment trusts and more. The main role of an investment company is to serve the needs of retail investors through a truly wide variety of financial investment opportunities. Investment companies also can design portfolios specifically for large retail investors with specific goals. We elaborate on the role of these financial (or non-depository) institutions and their characteristics and list the main types of mutual funds.

The second part of the chapter deals with another financial industry, the investment banking industry, which is also very important in the money as well as the capital markets (we discuss this market in the next chapter). This segment of the financial services industry is key to serving the needs of institutional investors such as firms, governments and companies when these investors need to engage in mergers, acquisitions or raise capital. This industry has been one of a many key players leading up to 2008 Global Financial Crisis because of its involvement with mortgages and securitized products. In addition, the crisis changed the face and nature of the commercial banking (depository institutions) and investment banking (non-depository institutions) industries when the Federal Reserve permitted investment banks to become commercial banks and accept deposits so they could survive the crisis. In discussing this industry, we will present the process of a typical

DOI: 10.4324/9781003677161-8

initial public offering (IPO) and some basics on mergers and acquisitions, which are the two main services of investment bankers.

1 The investment company industry

In this section, we present the investment companies by discussing the following: their purpose, structure, investment types, taxation, performance and future trends. We also include some basic research on some characteristics of this industry.

1.1 The nature of an investment company

Let use start with a simple question for you, the small, retail investor. How many individual financial assets can you invest in with your small investment budget (say, $1,000, $2,000, or $3,000)? The answer is simple and obvious: not many! Now, what if a company approaches you and says that if you entrust me with your money, I would pool every small investor's funds to come up with a greater amount and invest that amount to various financial assets, what would you say? It sounds like a good idea and, in fact, it is. Hence, a company (or financial intermediary) that pools together small funds and invest those funds in a wide range of securities or other assets is called an *investment company* (IC). An IC will earn returns on its portfolio in the form of interest or dividends which, in turn, are forwarded to the individual investors, based on their share of the total investment fund. Immediately, you understand that this way of investing has more benefits than doing it yourself. Let us list some of these potential advantages of pooling small amounts and investing them in many more financial assets.

1.1.1 Diversification

Taking advantage of a greater variety of financial assets (and real assets) implies *diversification*, which is the spreading of funds across various financial products and services so as to reduce risk, and this is one of greatest advantages of investing through an investment company. It also implies that you have own *fractional shares*, that is, a portion of a share if you cannot afford to buy one (with your own money). By pooling funds, every small investor can behave like a large investor. Holding fractional shares is also known as *divisibility*.

1.1.2 Professional management

Given that you are a small investor and do not have the expertise and knowledge to manage your own investments, going through an IC you can exploit the full benefits of professional managers (portfolio managers, investment analysts and more) who would strive to achieve superior investment results for their investors. Professional investment managers do that via constant searches of sectors/financial assets that they expected to growth in the future, avoid investments in riskier or volatile financial assets (if that is their mandate, which we will discuss shortly), and apply a variety of investment strategies.

1.1.3 Low transaction costs

Being part of a pool of funds with one manager who trades large blocks of securities, the investor can enjoy substantial savings on brokerage fees and commissions.

1.1.4 Administrative services

ICs keep records of trades and issue periodic reports based on capital gains/losses from the accounts (funds), dividends, and redemptions, and may reinvest dividend and interest income for shareholders.

1.1.5 Other benefits

ICs offer investment vehicles that cater to all types of investor risk appetites (low, medium or high), provide advice and analysis on combinations of investments such as the stock market, real estate, commodities and options, are qualified to offer professional investment management services thus allowing investors to reach their investment goals quickly and with minimal risk.

Who are the main participants in an IC? In general, in the investment management industry the key players (agents) are the professionals, the investors and the intermediaries. The *professionals* comprise investment/portfolio managers and research/financial analysts and provide the following: emphasis on the risk and return profiles of financial assets across markets and allocate funds accordingly; facilitation of the flow of funds to those sectors that are expected to grow so as to exploit them profitably; offering of custom-made advice and opinions to the investor so he can best fulfill his investment objective; and in the process of allocating capital across markets and asset classes, they are aiding in price discovery and transparency. These professionals can also be asset managers working at brokerage houses, buy-side analysts, risk managers, quant analysts, insurance companies, banks and many more. The *investors* can be either retail or institutional: small investors like you and me or wealthier individuals; institutional investors such as pension funds, foundations/endowments funds, sovereign wealth funds and the like. The financial *intermediaries* can be specialized finance companies, investment bankers, commercial bankers, traders, sell-side analysts, among other categories; they provide investment services and products to clients.

Which bodies regulate or oversee the investment company industry? A number or government and professional bodies ensure that an ICI strives to achieve the highest benefit of an individual investor. First, the Securities and Exchange Commission (SEC), a US federal agency, is responsible for overseeing the securities industry, including the registration and regulation of investment companies, investment advisers and brokers/dealers. Second, the Financial Industry Regulatory Authority (FINRA) oversees the regulation of brokerage firms and their registered securities representatives. Because SEC-registered brokers and dealers must generally become members of FINRA, in essence the SEC permits FINRA to assume primary responsibility for reviewing broker/dealer registration applications. Third, the Commodity Futures Trading Commission (CFTC) is an independent agency responsible for regulating commodity futures and options markets in the US. Investment managers of funds that invest in commodity futures and options must generally register with the CFTC.

Fourth, the National Futures Association (NFA) is the self-regulatory organization for the US futures industry. Commodity trading advisors who are registered with the CFTC must also be members of the NFA. Fifth, in the US each of the 50 states and Washington D.C. regulates activities by investment funds, investment advisers and broker-dealers within their jurisdiction. Related to state regulation the North American Securities Administrators Association (NASAA) represents state and provincial securities regulators in the US, Canada and Mexico. NASAA members are the closest regulators to local communities, small businesses and the investing public throughout North America. NASAA's members mission is to protect investors from fraud and abuse, conduct investor education, provide guidance and assistance via the established regulatory framework, and ultimately help power the North American economy by ensuring the integrity of the financial markets.[1]

Finally, the IC industry itself safeguards the rights of investors. According to its mission "For more than 80 years, its purpose has been to support regulation that strengthens the foundation of investment companies and asset managers more broadly for the ultimate benefit of the long-term individual investor."[2] Some of its priorities, according to its website, are fund governance, fund regulation and retirement security. It often writes letters to the SEC offering suggestions on the above subjects in an effort to improve outcomes.

The National Association of Investment Companies (NAIC) is the largest industry association for diverse-owned alternative investment firms. The association provides education, advocacy and industry events, and focuses on "increasing the flow of capital to high-performing diverse investment managers often underutilized by institutional investors. Their members represent a broad spectrum of backgrounds and investment strategies."[3] Finally, in the United Kingdom (UK), the Association of Investment Companies (AIC), founded in 1932 to represent investment trusts (the oldest form of collective investment), has greatly evolved today with many more and diverse investment companies and funds. Its mission is "to support and promote the long-term benefits of investment companies by engaging with members, investors, and the wider financial community."[4]

1.2 Classes of investment companies

According to the US *Investment Company Act of 1940*, investment companies are divided into three principal classes:5

(1) *Face-amount certificate company*, which implies an investment company which is engaged or proposes to engage in the business of issuing face-amount certificates of the installment type, or which has been engaged in such business and has any such certificate outstanding.[6]

(2) *Unit investment trust* (UIT) means an investment company which (1) is organized under a trust indenture, contract of custodianship or agency, or similar instrument, (2) does not have a board of directors, and (3) issues only

redeemable securities, each of which represents an undivided interest in a unit of specified securities; but does not include a voting trust.

(3) *Management company*, which suggests any investment company other than a face-amount certificate company or a UIT.

Further, management companies are divided into these two main categories:

(a) open-end and closed-end companies, defined as follows:
   (1) *Open-end company* means a management company which is offering for sale or has outstanding any redeemable security of which it is the issuer.
   (2) *Closed-end company* means any management company other than an open-end company.

(b) Diversified and non-diversified companies, defined as follows:[7]
   (1) *Diversified company* means a management company which meets the following requirements: At least 75 per centum of the value of its total assets is represented by cash and cash items (including receivables), Government securities, securities of other investment companies, and other securities for the purposes of this calculation limited in respect of any one issuer to an amount not greater in value than 5 per centum of the value of the total assets of such management company and to not more than 10 per centum of the outstanding voting securities of such issuer.
   (2) *Non-diversified company* means any management company other than a diversified company.

It is also interesting to mention that other publications about the IC industry (ICI Factbook) classify another type as a managed company (besides the closed-end and open-end funds), that of an Exchange-Traded Fund. In what follows below, we will present only the most important types of ICs, namely UITs, open- and closed-end ICs. The open-end type is what we commonly call a mutual fund.

1.2.1 Unit investment trust

A *unit investment trust* is a type of *unmanaged investment company* (and SEC-registered) in the sense that once the portfolio of a fixed number of securities is selected, it stays fixed, no one manages it (and hence, there is no trading), and then the UIT will make a one-time public offering of this portfolio. A UIT buys a relatively fixed number of securities and holds them for the life of the UIT with little or no change in between. Hence, investors know more or less what they are investing in for the duration of their investment. Like a mutual fund (which we will discuss on p. 146), UITs issue redeemable shares (or units), and like closed-end funds (which we discuss next), they typically issue a specific, fixed number of shares. However, unlike mutual funds or closed-end funds, UITs have a preset termination date based on the portfolio's investments and investment goals. In other words, a UIT will terminate and dissolve on a date that is specified at the time the UIT's creation. When a UIT terminates, any remaining investment portfolio securities are sold and the proceeds are paid to the investors. Finally, a UIT does not have a board of directors, corporate officers, or an investment adviser to render advice during the life of the trust. UITs themselves are registered with the SEC and subject to SEC regulation.[8] The characteristics of an UIT are described in its *prospectus* (we fully define it in the mutual funds subsection).

As mentioned earlier, a UIT typically issues redeemable units which means that the UIT will buy back an investor's units at their approximate *net asset value* (NAV). Let us define NAV more precisely because it is used for the other two types of ICs. We begin with the formula:

$$\textit{Net Asset Value} = \frac{\textit{Market value of Assets} - \textit{Liabilities}}{\textit{No. of shares outstanding}} \tag{6.1}$$

To apply the formula, you should remember that is on a per-share basis. Here's an example. If a mutual fund has a NAV of $100 million and investors own 10,000,000 of the fund's shares, the fund's per share NAV will be $10. What if during a holding period the value of the stock portfolio increased to $110 million while the fund incurred $1 million in trading expenses and management fees (the Liabilities)? If no new shares were sold during the period, the new NAV of the total investment company is $9.9 million. Because per share NAV is based on NAV, which changes daily, and on the number of shares held by investors, which also changes daily, per share NAV also will change daily.

UITs hold a variety of securities and each UIT may have different investment objectives, strategies, and investment portfolios. They also can be subject to different risks and fees and expenses. Fees reduce returns on fund investments and are an important factor that investors should consider when buying shares. Fees can be categorized as those on the distribution of the trust (sales charges on units purchased including initial and deferred charges as well as a fee for the creation of the trust) and on the operation of the UIT (operating expenses including general administrative costs). Investors can obtain UIT price quotes from brokerage or investment firms and investment company websites. Even though a fixed number of units of a UIT are sold in a public offering, a trust sponsor probably maintains a secondary market, where investors can sell their units back to the sponsor and other investors can buy those units.

Figure 6.1 shows the total net assets (in $billions, year-end) of UITs (left scale) and the number of UITs (right scale) in the US from 1990 to 2024. *Total net assets* comprise equity trusts, debt trusts and tax-free debt trusts, of which since 2000 the equity trusts had the lions' share (reaching 93% of the total assets by 2021) followed by tax-free debt trusts (not shown in the figure). The number of trusts outstanding (no. of UITs) has been sharply decreasing as sponsors were reduced and created fewer new trusts and existing trusts reached their preset termination dates.[9]

1.2.2 Closed-end funds

This type is one whose funds are actively managed by professional investment managers for a fee. Typically, the management company is the firm that organizes the fund. Initially, a closed-end fund holds an initial public offering (IPO, which we discuss later in the chapter) and the money raised is used by portfolio managers to buy securities. Future capital raising within the fund can happen either from issuance of common shares via secondary offerings, at-the-market offerings, or

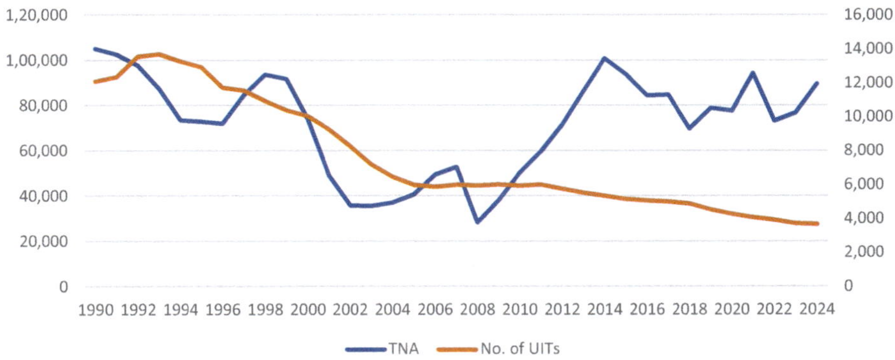

Figure 6.1 Total net assets and number of trusts in the US, 2000–2024

Notes: Total Net Assets, left scale; No. of UITs, right scale
Source: ICI Factbook 2025; author's graphical representation

Table 6.1 Selected closed-end funds data

Fund	*NAV*	*Market Price*	*Disc/Prem*
Guggenheim Enhanced Equity Income (GPM)	$9.08	$9.43	3.85%
Liberty All-Star Equity	$6.79	$6.57	−1.94%
Gabelli Dividend and Income Trust	$25.58	$21.64	−15.40%

dividend reinvestments, or issuance of debt and preferred shares. A *closed-end fund* does not redeem or issue shares. Instead, an investor who wishes to cash out must sell his shares to other investors in the open market. Closed-end funds' shares are traded on organized exchanges (or in the over-the-counter market) and can be purchased through brokers just like other equity share (common stock). The market price of this fund's share fluctuates just like any other publicly traded securities and is determined by market demand and supply forces.

Just like UITs, closed-end funds witnessed continuous declines since 2017 (from 532 in that year to 441 in 2022) despite the majority of them being in bonds over the same period, which saw marginal increases from 2018 to 2021 (*ICI Factbook* 2023). Table 6.1 shows three closed-end funds with some information on their NAVs, market prices, and the discount/premium percentages. The premium or discount values are found by taking the percentage difference between market price and NAV [(Price – NAV)/NAV]. Discounts to NAV, shown by negative differences, are more common than premiums. Wide-margin deviations of the market prices from NAVs is a puzzle in finance because discounts imply that the fund sells for less than NAV. Using sound economic analysis, if the fund sold all of its the assets in the portfolio, it would realize proceeds equal to NAV, thus instantly increasing the wealth of its investors. Related to this puzzle, is also the enigma that in some closed-end funds, like the Guggenheim fund, the prices when initially issued were above NAV (Inception NAV: $19.10 and Inception Price: $20.00).[10] In other words, it is unclear why investors would purchase these newly issued funds at a premium to NAV when the shares tended to fall shortly thereafter.

Closed-end funds make distributions to shareholders in three different forms: (1) as *income* from payments from interest and dividends that the fund earns on its investments in securities, (2) as realized *capital gains* and (3) as *return of capital*. Income distributions accounted for the majority of closed-end fund distributions, followed by return of capital and capital gains.[11]

1.2.3 Open-end funds (mutual funds)

Open-end funds are what we typically call *mutual funds* (MFs) and are defined as those that issue new fund shares (or units) and redeem existing shares (or units) on demand. They are the dominant type of ICs. Such funds are typically regulated with respect to disclosure, the form of organization (corporations or trusts); custody of fund assets; minimum capital; valuation of fund assets; and restrictions on fund investments (such as limits on leverage, types of eligible investments, and diversification of portfolio investments).[12] In contrast to the closed-end funds, MFs allow existing fund investors to sell their shares back to the fund when they wish to cash out at NAV (which is computed every trading day at 4:00 pm in the US). Also, unlike closed-end funds, the price of these funds will never fall below NAV because they stand ready to redeem shares at NAV. The offering price will exceed NAV, however, if the fund carries a load (we will discuss this shortly). Finally, another difference from closed-end funds is that MFs do not trade on organized exchanges and thus the number of outstanding shares changes daily.

The first and most important thing a prospective investor must do is to read the fund's prospectus. A *prospectus* is a booklet or leaflet that fully describes the fund. The information contained in it comprises the following items: (a) investment objectives/goals; (b) fee table; (c) investments, risks, and performance; (d) investment advisers and portfolio managers; (e) purchase and sale of fund shares; (f) tax information; and (g) financial intermediary compensation.[13] Let us briefly explain each of these items. The investment objectives, constraints and the investor's risk tolerance must be defined first. These are part of an investor's investment policy statement (IPS), which also includes the role(s) of the portfolio manager. An example of an investment objective would be this: "The financial plan developed for NTL in 2010 indicates a required real growth rate of 5% to satisfy his future obligations and retirement in 2028, as expected." An example of constraints would be the following: "Any dividends from stocks and coupon payments from bonds should be split 50–50 for reinvestment purposes and transferring to his checking account, at the end of each quarter." Finally, an example of defining the investor's risk tolerance would be to fill out an online risk-tolerance questionnaire or answer the portfolio manager's specific questions on the amount of risk that he wishes to assume in his portfolio. The IPS should acknowledge that the portfolio will be subject to many relevant risks including liquidity, legal, regulatory, mortality, business, and a myriad of other risks which would negatively or positively impact the portfolio's expected return.

Who are the investors in MFs? First, the small, retail investor who held almost 88% of the $22.1 trillion in US mutual fund net assets in 2022. These investors invest in both ends of the mutual fund, the long-term and short-term (money-market).

The second category of investors are the institutional investors (nonfinancial businesses, financial institutions, and nonprofit organizations), which at year-end 2022 held a relatively small portion of mutual fund net assets. Specifically, institutions invested 64% in money market funds because these investors see mutual funds as a conduit for managing their cash balances (see subsection 1.2.4).[14]

The fee structure of the fund must be clear to the investor as well. There are several types of fees such as shareholder fees and annual fund operation expenses. Specifically, the shareholder fees include loads, redemption fees, exchange fees, account fees and purchase fees. A *load* is the amount that investors pay when they join the fund (*front-end load*) or exit (*back-end load*) the fund and resemble commissions. There are also funds that do not change a load or a sales charge, known as no-load funds. You would then wonder how these funds cover the cost of an investor buying or redeeming his shares to the fund. These funds charge other types of fees, as mentioned above. A *redemption fee* is similar to the back-end load (also known as a deferred sales load), but it is paid directly to the fund and not to the broker (in which case it would have been treated a back-end load). An *exchange fee* is one charged when the investor switches funds within the same fund's family of funds. An account fee is imposed on the maintenance of an investor's account especially when it falls below some min amount. Finally, a *purchase fee* is assessed on the investor upon joining the fund (similar to the front-end load).

The second category of MFs' fees concerns the general operation of the fund. First, there are *management fees* which paid out of fund assets to the fund's investment adviser for managing the fund's investment portfolio and for administrative fees payable to the investment adviser. Then, there are the soc-called "*12b-1 fees*," which are fees paid by the fund out of fund's assets to cover distribution expenses and shareholder service expenses. Finally, there are *other general expenses* which include custodial expenses; legal expenses; accounting expenses; transfer agent expenses; and other administrative expenses.[15]

Another item the investor must pay attention to, is the fund's turnover rate. *Turnover* is the ratio of the trading activity of a portfolio to the assets of the portfolio. It measures the fraction of the portfolio that is "replaced" each year. For example, a $10 million portfolio with $5 million in sales of some securities and purchases of other securities would have a turnover rate of 50%. High turnover means that capital gains or losses are being realized constantly, and therefore that the investor cannot time the realizations to manage overall tax obligation.

The obvious question is now this: given so many fees, how would an individual investor decide which fund is the best for him/her? It is important to understand that the fee structure differs from fund to fund due to competition and plethora of different fund offerings. To assist the retail investor, FINRA has created an online fund analyzer software (or cost calculator) so you use it and select the best fund in line with your objective, constraints and risk tolerance parameters.[16]

Finally, MFs come in practically thousands of varieties in each asset class. Asset classes are the general types of MFs such as equity, bond, foreign, hybrid, commodity, index and so on. In turn, each of these asset classes are categorized by market capitalization (small, mid and high), diversification (value, focused and more), sector or industry (dividend, tech, pharma and more), issuer (corporate or government) and many, many more. MFs, however, have an underlying structural liquidity mismatch because they invest in securities across a range of liquidities, including securities that are costlier or take more time to sell. A *hybrid MF* is one that combines equity and debt securities. There are many types of it such as aggressive, conservative, and asset allocation (which implies an adjustment of the securities weights based on market conditions). An *index fund* is an important class because it tracks an equity or a bond index such as the S&P500 equity index or its counterpart bond index. A related product is an exchange-traded fund (ETF). We'll discuss this in subsection 1.2.5. Some index funds invest in all of the securities in a market index, whereas others in a sample of the securities included in a market index. Index funds have generally followed a passive style of investing which means they aim to maximize returns over the long run by not trading (i.e., buying and selling securities) frequently. Index funds, typically but not always, have the lowest cost among all other MFs.

1.2.4 Money market mutual funds

Money-market mutual funds or *money-market funds* (MMFs) are the most important class of MFs because they are targeted by all types of investors. Such funds play a critical role in managing these investors' short-term money needs or their cash flow. MMFs participate in the repo market by investing cash in repos alongside other types of firms. MMFs in the United States are classified by investment focus, tax status and type of investor and are taxable. By contrast, MMFs in the Eurozone contribute mostly to the short-term funding of banks (that is, they fulfill the role of an intermediary) because banks are traditionally the main providers of credit to non-financial borrowers. In 2023, new deposits can earn 2.31% in the Eurozone, on average, compared with a European Central Bank interest rate of 3%, whereas in the US, one-year deposits return 2.24% compared with the Federal Reserve's interest rate range of 4.75% to 5%.[17]

Where do MMFs invest in? They invest in a wide variety of financial – money and debt – instruments such as these we discussed in the previous chapter, namely certificates of deposits, time deposits, repurchase agreements, and commercial paper (CP) and the following ones; *floating-rate notes*, which are simply medium-term debt instruments with variable interest rates, *asset-backed commercial paper*, which resembles the traditional CP in that it is issued for up to one year but they represent an obligation of the issuing company (vs. being unsecured as the CP), and *government-backed securities*, which are debt instruments issued by the federal government or its agencies. MMFs do not invest in riskier securities such as derivative or other structured products.

Who uses MMFs? Retail investors use this market to invest in Treasury bills, earn some interest in their idle cash by opening up savings and checking accounts, and, in general, enjoy the yields, liquidity and safety of their money in times of financial stress in the stock and bond markets. Institutional investors (or money managers) create such funds and use these short-term money

GREEN FINANCE SUFFERS

In February 2024, investment firms JP Morgan Chase and State Street and dozens of other giant companies have pulled out of the world's largest coalition of groups waging financial war on fossil fuels, products as part of their well-diversified asset portfolios as well as when designing client portfolios. Businesses make extensive use of MMFs in managing their daily operations and investments. For example, when companies have a temporary cash shortfall, they often turn to commercial paper, repurchase agreements and so on to bridge the gap. By contrast, when they have excess cash and no immediate need for it, they invest it in MMFs. The federal, state and local governments are heavy users of, and investors in, such funds when they experience cash fluctuations due to the timing of tax receipts. For example, municipalities invest their excess cash in MMFs by selling municipal bonds are sold to these funds. The proceeds are then used to pay for building schools, repairing roads and bridges, creating jobs, and more. Finally, other organizations such as endowment funds, universities, charities, and nonprofit organizations use MMFs as a safe, liquid, and affordable cash management tool.

What are some trends in the global MMF industry? Figure 6.2 compares the net asset growth in the three largest countries/regions in quarters 3 and 4 in 2023. The total value of worldwide investment fund net assets measured (in trillion Euros) increased to €67 in 2023Q3 relative to €62.48 in 2023Q4, or a 4.2% increase (EFAMA Factbook 2025).[18] The Asia-Pacific region (which includes Japan) remained stagnant. An emerging trend in this market is the growth of mutual fund assets in developing nations. This growth can be attributed to the strong performance of these countries' equity markets. Perhaps one of the most significant global trends is the increasing attention being paid to environmental, social, and governance (ESG) issues. Topics included are related to climate change, diversity and inclusion, human rights, the rights of company shareholders, and company compensation structures. The MMF industry is responding to increased investor interest in ESG investing by creating ESG-tailored funds (ICI 2023 Factbook, p. 31). Giant investment banks are part of the world group Climate Action 100+, an investor-led initiative to ensure the world's largest corporate greenhouse gas emitters take necessary action on climate change. Recently however, bid finance firms are

Climate Action 100+. This group/coalition aims to use its "environmental, social and corporate governance" (ESG) metrics to decide what money goes where in the global investment world. Given that an asset management firm must make its top priority the best interests of its investors, the firms that left the group were not prepared to let the radicals from Climate Action 100+ scrutinize their books and analyze decisions in light of their supposed harm to the environment. This would effectively undermine these banks' independence and authority. It remains to be seen what happens next, as Black Rock has also made similar decisions.

Source: https://www.reuters.com/sustainability/sustainable-finance-reporting/jpmorgan-fund-arm-quits-climate-action-100-investor-group-2024-02-15/#:~:text=JPMorgan%2C%20State%20Street%20quit%20climate%20group%2C%20BlackRock%20steps%20back%20%7C%20Reuters

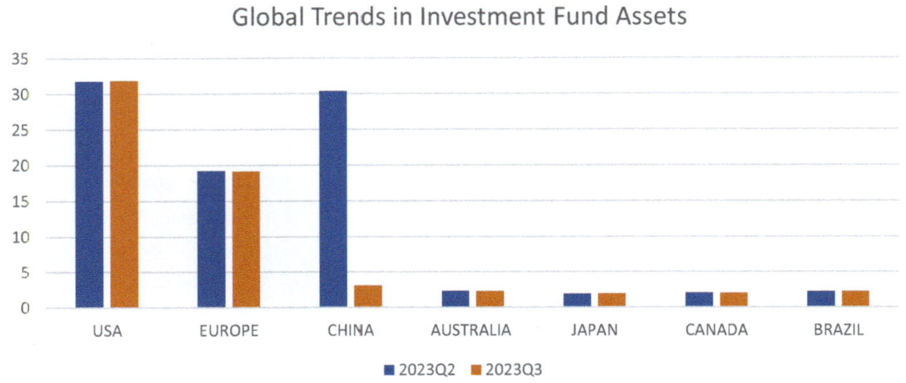

Figure 6.2 Regional growth of investment funds, 2023:II–2023:III
Source: ICI Factbook 2025; author's graphical representation.

pulling out of the group, as the nearby *sidebar* indicates. It is interesting to note that some ESG MMF categories include religious and social funds. Finally, another recent trend is the shifting of funds from standard bank deposits into MMFs by depositors in search of higher yields given that such funds invest in medium-term securities including bonds. One more reason for this shift is the fact that MMFs offer wider diversification, liquidity and ease of trading in them.

1.2.5 Exchange-traded funds

Just like an open-end fund (or mutual fund, an *exchange-traded fund* (ETF) is an SEC-registered company which pools retail investors' funds and invest in stocks, bonds, or other assets. ETFs, unlike mutual funds, are traded daily on a stock exchange at a market-determined prices, can be sold short and are more tax efficient than actively managed mutual funds. Investors may buy or sell ETF shares through a broker or in a brokerage account. In general, exchange-traded products (for stocks, bond, commodities etc.) carry some risks such as credit, liquidity and market risks. How do ETFs work? The fund provider (like an institutional investor or a broker) owns the underlying assets, designs a fund (basket of assets) to track their performance and then sells shares in that fund to investors (just like buying shares of a company). Shareholders now own a portion of an ETF, but they do not own the underlying assets in the fund. However, investors may get dividend payments for any dividend stocks in the index fund.

ETFs are governed by the same regulations as mutual funds when they invest equities. However, ETFs investing in commodities, currencies, and futures have different structures and are subject to different regulatory requirements. Some additional advantages of investing in ETFS include diversification, lower costs and trading flexibility. Although ETFs may trade like stocks, in reality they also resemble index funds and can vary greatly in terms of their underlying assets, investment goals and fee structure (especially the fund's expense ratio, or the fee the fund charges to manage and maintain the ETF). That is why it is instructive to read the prospectus before engaging in an ETF. There are various other types of ETFs (besides stock and bonds or notes, such as Exchange-Traded Notes) such as commodity, international, cryptocurrency, leveraged among others.

So, ETFs, MFs or stocks? As mentioned above, an ETF is a much better choice than an MF because of its advantages: lower costs, tax-efficiency (which means that the investor now can time his gains/losses), and daily management (selling it short, for example, to take advantage of intraday price fluctuations). Just like stocks, ETFs can have unique ticker symbols that let you track their price activity daily. Unlike stocks, ETFs represent a basket of stocks and thus may provide better diversification than a single stock. That diversification can help reduce your portfolio's exposure to risk.

Test your understanding 1

1. What are some of the traditional and distinguishing characteristics of closed-end funds?
2. In 2022, the SEC considered whether to propose amendments to enhance the liquidity risk management of open-end funds. An appealing feature of open-end funds is the ability for shareholders to redeem their shares daily, in both normal times and times of stress. What problem(s) could this possibly have for investors?
3. Can you explain why ETFs (and other related funds) have liquidity and market risks?
4. Can you explain why a retail store may need the money market by investing in an MMF?

Solutions appear at the textbook's website.

2 The investment banking industry

Unlike the investment company industry, which serves all types of investors, retail and institutional, the *investment banking industry* serves primarily legal entities such as commercial companies, financial institutions and governments to raise funds in the capital markets (a process known as *underwriting*) through the means of initial public offerings (IPOs) and performs other activities such as mergers and acquisitions (M&A). Investment banks (IBs) may also provide related services such as market-making and securities trading for both equities and their derivatives, commodities as well as fixed income (known as FICC, or fixed income, currencies, and commodities). Some top IBs globally are Goldman Sachs, JP Morgan Chase, Credit Suisse, Barclays, UBS. Investment banks are frequently divided by size (the largest global banks that offer all products and services and operate in all regions), status (boutique or middle-market banks), region (tend to operate in specific locations), and industry focus (healthcare, technology etc.).

There is some confusion between the term investment bank and the investment banking division of a bank. According to the corporate finance institute (CFI), "full-service investment banks offer a wide range of services that include underwriting, M&A, sales and trading, equity research, asset management, commercial banking, and retail banking. The investment banking division of a bank provides only the underwriting and M&A advisory services."[19] Let us briefly describe the IPO and the M&A processes next.

2.1 Initial public offering

When a privately held company wishes to go public, it initiates an IPO process and (typically) hires investment bankers to assist the company in going public. Why would a private company want to become a public company? Plenty of reasons, some of which are: by selling shares to the public provides the company with additional capital, to increase liquidity and access since its shares can be traded on a stock exchange, to attract top talent with greater job security and stability and more. Before the company can go public, a number of steps must be performed, which are listed and briefly explained next. To learn more about IB, you may wish to download the CFI's Investment Banking Manual from their website.[20]

2.1.1 Planning phase

A few months to a year may be required to arrange the IPO event. First, the company must select and hire the underwriters (investment bankers or the syndicate), the lawyers from both sides (the company and the underwriting team), the certified public accountants and the Securities and Exchange Commission (SEC) experts. Second, the SEC requires a filing of the registration statement (known as *Shelf Registration*) and conduct due diligence. In addition, the SEC requires the *S-1 registration statement*, which includes the prospectus (see p. 146) and private information that is not required to be disclosed to investors. Third, the company must prepare a preliminary prospectus (known as *red herring*) for investors to see in order to get some idea about the company before they invest in it (but without any share or pricing information). Additional paperwork includes the *engagement letter*, which includes a reimbursement clause, which holds the issuing company accountable to covering the underwriter's out-of-pocket expenses, the *gross spread* (or the underwriting discount intended to cover the underwriter's fee), and the *letter of intent*, which states the underwriter's commitment to the company and the company's agreement to cooperate (see the pricing item below), provide all information, and offer the underwriter a 15% overallotment option.[21] Fourth, the marketing of the upcoming IPO to investors (see next).

2.1.2 The roadshow

Once the IPO has been approved by the SEC, representatives from the company and the syndicate (the underwriting team) travel the country to meet with prospective investors and "sell" the company to them. Nowadays, roadshows are done also online to save time and money. The idea is to get the intention by these investors to commit purchasing shares of the company. Their intentions are then recorded in the order book where the objective is *oversubscription* (or more demand for shares than the planned supply) by the public investors. Note that it would be of interest to investors to reveal their true intentions so as to get their demanded (desired) share allocation later.

2.1.3 Pricing

After the investors' interest has been recorded, the company and the underwriters sit together to discuss how the sale of the shares will be conducted. There are three main ways that this can be done: *firm commitment*, which implies that the underwriter will purchase all shares from the issuing company and resell them to the public; *best efforts agreement*, which states the underwriter will not guarantee a specific amount of money but will sell the shares on behalf of the company, and *all or none agreement*, which states that unless all of the offered shares can be sold, the offering is canceled. The factors that affect the price of a share include the state of the economy (an expanding economy is preferred to a contracting economy to launch the IPO), the company's goal and the success (or failure) of the roadshow. In other words, it is possible that the company may defer the launching of its IPO based on weak demand or investor interest at the roadshow.

Typically, IPOs are underpriced to ensure that the issue is (over)subscribed by the investors, even if it results in the company not receiving the full value of its shares. Underpricing is a strategy because (a) investors of the IPO expect a rise in the price of the shares on the offer day and (b) it compensates them for the risk that they take by investing in the IPO. So, at that stage the exact price and number of issues to be sold are set.

2.1.4 Launching of the IPO and beyond

In about a month after the IPO is launched, the underwriter provides analysts' recommendations, after-market stabilization guidance, and creates a market for the stock issued. During this period, the underwriter has the freedom to trade and influence the price of the issue as prohibitions against price manipulation are suspended.[22] In addition, during this period, investors no longer rely on the prospectus but on the market forces for information regarding their shares.

2.2 The M&A process

The M&A concept refers to an agreement between two companies to consolidate functions and assets and then continue as one united company (the *merger*) or the purchase by a company of another company and its assets (the *acquisition*). It is important to mention that mergers and acquisitions can take many forms. For example, mergers can be *conglomerate* (when two companies are completely unrelated), *statutory* (where merging companies remains in existence as a legal entity), *triangular* (which involves a third party such as a subsidiary of the buyer) and *market- or product-extension* (where the first merger occurs between companies that deal in similar products but different markets, and the second merger occurs between companies that offer similar products and occupy similar markets). Examples of different types of acquisitions are *friendly* (when the acquiring company purchases another company with the approval of the target company's shareholders and board of directors), *hostile* (the opposite of friendly, which is also known as a tender offer), *leveraged buyout* (when the acquiring company purchases the target company using borrowed money), and *asset or stock deals* (where in an asset sale, the acquirer purchases the target company's assets, whereas in the stock deal the buyer purchases the target company's stock and assumes ownership of all its current assets and liabilities).

According to CFI, the M&A process involves a number of steps, from both the buy- and sell-sides. Let us only focus on the buy-side process below.[23]

2.2.1 Beginning phase

Define your M&A goals, acquire information on potential targets and set the search criteria.

2.2.2 Acquisition planning

At this stage, you can make the first contact with the target(s), draft the letter of intent (*teaser*), in which you express interest in pursuing a merger or acquisition and provide a summary of the proposed deal, and take care of some items such as competition/antitrust law implications, employment law considerations, and licensing matters, among others.

2.2.3 Due diligence

Perform valuation of the target company (SWOT analysis can also be conducted), create financial modeling and operational analysis including an assessment the culture fit of the two firms, and cater to legal and fiscal matters to identify the key risks that may arise from the potential transaction, determine fair pricing and increase bargaining power.

2.2.4 Negotiations and closing

This is the point where you make a "go/no go" call based on previous analysis, create an initial deal (including price of shares or the business) and present it to the target company, and if all parties agree, then the deal is closed and the acquirer firm can begin the integration process (dealing with finances, organizational structure, roles and responsibilities, culture, etc.).

2.3 Investment banking trends

As the world becomes more and more financially integrated, the IB industry will constantly face new challenges emanating either from global events such as the global pandemic crisis, regional wars, the advancement of technology or country/regional-specific changes in regulations, market-specific changes (digital transformation) and others. The latter includes the growing sophistication of clients as well as other workplace arrangements (including remote work). More specifically, a number of trends are emerging which are certain to transform (if not already by the time you read this) the IB industry worldwide.

First, the rapid rise of *artificial intelligence* (AI) or *generative AI* enables routine tasks to be completed faster and data analysis to be done on a more timely, precise and comprehensive manner than before. This will cause IBs to adopt such technology to deliver more effective, quicker and efficient service to their clients. Second, the emergence of sustainable finance and related concepts such as environmental, social and governance (ESG) is forcing the IB industry to implement solutions to the satisfaction of their socially conscious clients. Add to that the global drive, from the EU Commission or the SEC, for example, towards sustainable finance through regulatory changes which requires investment funds to, at least, match 80% of the asset's name.[24]

Another trend relates to climate change regarding global efforts (led by the US, China and other major countries) to reduce carbon emissions from fossil-fuel sources (coal, oil etc.). The transition requires massive amounts of resource reallocation, new technologies, and innovation such as green bonds (green finance) all of which are definitely going to affect the IB industry of the future. A fourth trend relates to the digitalization of finance including the blockchain technology and distributed ledgers, digital wallets, cuber-security, big data analytics and *regulatory technology* (RegTech) and *supervisory technology* (SupTech), among many others. RegTech is an emerging platform that combines technology and financial regulations to facilitate compliance with regulations in various industries, especially banking, finance, communication, as well as energy.[25] We will encounter these concepts again in Chapter 13.

A final emerging trend is geopolitics which includes tensions, wars, conflicts, threats and the like. As of 2024, we are still witnessing a number of geopolitical events such as the (still ongoing) 2022 Ukraine–Russia war, the 2023 Israeli–Gaza conflict, armed acts of violence in the wider Middle-East, the Arabian Peninsula, and elsewhere. These uncertainties compel IBs to reassess their risk management strategies and the makeup of their portfolios, under scenarios of potentially sudden market shifts and economic instability. McKinsey has developed a list of the five major trends and challenges for IBs, some of which have been mentioned above.[26]

Test your understanding 2

1. Can you identify some major investment banking trends (conditions) that boost the industry and some that pull back the industry?
2. What are the main functions of an investment bank? Explain briefly each function.
3. Nick sets up a start-up but he is still searching for investors to raise capital. Being a novice in the market, he connects with an investment banking firm, which has an established history of helping businesses to operate well. The firm buys the securities from Nick and sells the same to investors to raise funds. Which IB function is described here?

Solutions appear at the textbook's website.

3 Insurance companies and pension funds

In this section, we discuss two non-depository financial institutions that play a major role within the financial market. Recall that in Chapter 5, we discussed two very important challenges for the financial intermediaries namely, adverse selection and moral hazard. Briefly, the insurance industry faces an adverse selection problem, which means that those who are most likely to need insurance are most likely to purchase it. For example, someone with chronic health problems is more likely to purchase a life insurance policy than someone in very good health. Also, insurance can cause the insured to take more risks because they are protected, which is known as the moral hazard problem. For example, moral hazard exists when the parties involved in a potential deal are not responsible for bearing costs arising from the deal. Doctors and insured patients, for instance, agree to extra tests, which may or may not be necessary but the cost is borne by the insurance company.

A *pension fund* is a financial institution that accumulates large sums of money to invest into the capital markets to generate profit and then pay out – in the form of pension – to employees when they retire. In that way, they resemble insurance companies and mutual funds. Pension funds are typically managed by employers (companies) and their main goal is to ensure there will be enough money to cover the pensions of retirees. *Pension plans* refer to a savings plan for employees that can be used for retirement. The amount of money in the fund comes from the following sources: (1) new contributions by the employee sponsored by the pension plan; (2) new contributions by the employer sponsored by the pension plan on behalf of the employee; (3) dividends or interest earned by the fund; and (4) capital gains of the securities in which the fund has invested. Let us look in more detail at each financial institution. We begin with the insurance industry.

3.1 Insurance companies

Insurance companies provide financial protection to agents (people and institutions) against hazards for a premium. The two main types of insurance are life, and property and casualty. Other types include health (care), business services (such as credit default swaps), bond, and mortgage insurance. In what follows next, we briefly describe some activities of insurance companies as related to setting premia, investments and regulation. Some discussion on life insurance policies is also found in section 5.

Insurance companies employ financial specialists (actuaries and underwriters) to calculate the risk of specific insurance policies and adjusters (to determine the amount the insurance company should pay for the loss) so they can set the insurance premium. An *insurance premium* is the money an individual or business pays for an insurance policy. In general, insurance premiums

ADVERSE SELECTION AND INSURANCE PREMIA

Assume that a group of students is made up of two types, those who are diligent and work to prepare the assignment and those who do not (free ride). The grade for the assignment will be the same for everyone in the group since the professor is not aware of who worked and who did not. This is a example of adverse selection for the professor, a cost to those students who really worked for the assignment and a benefit to the free riders. Similar situations are faced by an insurance company.

When some residents in a particular neighborhood lock their house are based on the probability that the company will have to pay to the insured and the potential amount of the payment as well as by the extent of competition within the industry for the specific type of insurance offered. More specifically, the actuary estimates the amount of losses an insurance company can expect to face in the coming year based on previous years using statistical methods, risk theory and macro trends such as inflation. The underwriter conducts various scenarios (assessments) to select the types of insurance to be provided based on the underwriters' specialized knowledge in risk and the benchmark rates supplied by the actuaries. Finally, the adjuster will determine how much the insurance company should pay for the loss using information gathered by investigators in order to develop recommendations for the payout. Viewed in another way, insurance companies can estimate the present value of a payment that they will have to make and the premium charged for that insurance is affected by the present value of the expected payment (plus some markup to cover additional expenses and their profit). The nearby *sidebar* links the adverse selection problem with setting the right premiums using a real example about student groupwork.

door while others do not, the insurance company will not know this and thus will charge the same premium to both types of residents. The company will base its premium calculations on past police reports showing break-ins because if it did not, the premium would have been too low and entail a loss to the company.

The follow-up problem, however, is that once people have insurance they are likely to change their behavior. For example, if I insure my bike I will not "lose sleep over it" any longer even though I was very careful before! This behavior is well understood by the insurance company and this results in higher insurance premia. This situation is the moral hazard part of setting insurance premia. Consequently, insurance companies typically assess the probability of a loss incurred by the people who obtain insurance instead of relying on the general population (as in the cases described in the sidebar where the insurance company looks at general police reports about incidents of that sort). This means that insurance companies can charge premiums that more closely fit the likelihood that insureds will file claims to cover their losses.

Insurance companies invest the funds they receive from premiums. As a result, they are dependent on the income from (or the performance of) these investments and must carefully balance liquidity and risk. Finally, the insurance industry is highly regulated by state agencies (or commissions), which varies by state, in the US. According to the Insurance Information Institute (III), regulation stems from the McCarran–Ferguson Act of 1945, "which describes state regulation and taxation of the industry as being in 'the public interest' and clearly gives it preeminence over federal law. State insurance departments oversee insurer solvency, market conduct and, to a greater or lesser degree, review and rule on requests for rate increases for coverage, among other things. In addition, in commercial insurance, workers compensation is the most highly regulated."[27] In the European Union, there is the Directive 2009/138/EC on the taking-up and pursuit of the business of insurance and reinsurance (Solvency II). *Solvency II* requires insurance and reinsurance companies in EU to hold sufficient financial resources, and sets out governance, risk management, transparency and supervisory rules.[28]

Finally, the insurance industry in general is faced with any of the same general risks and trends mentioned in the previous subsection for the IB industry. The frequency and severity of global risks necessitates a swift and agile response from the insurance industry in order to properly react as society's financial safety nets. Insurance technology companies (*InsurTech*) remain at the center of merger and acquisition activity to seek solutions across the value chain. According to Deloitte, another area where the insurance industry could face significant disruption is "the opportunity and potential threat posed by the growth in *embedded insurance...* what's changing rapidly is the volume of insurance premiums for major lines likely to be built into other types of third-party transactions, bypassing traditional sellers, such as insurance agents, upending direct-to-consumer sales from insurers."[29] Insurers are also expanding their policy portfolios to cover renewable energy projects and green finance projects. Finally, "due to technology and culture transformations most carriers have transformed their finance systems to meet the January 1, 2023 effective date for new accounting rules for reporting on long-term insurance and annuity contracts."[30]

3.2 More on insurance companies

Insurance companies try to reduce both the adverse selection and moral hazard problems. Screening insurance applicants reduces adverse selection because a person who wants to buy a life insurance policy, for example, may be required to pass a physical evaluation (weight, blood pressure, blood tests, etc.). It makes sense, in this context, for an insurance company to deny medical/health coverage to a terminally ill person. Also, one who wants to purchase auto insurance must provide driving records, which include accidents and traffic violations/citations, and may have to pay more compared to an applicant with a spotless driving record. Similar actions are taken to mitigate the effects of moral hazard as well. Policies, for example, may restrict the insured person from engaging in certain risky activities, require some policy holders to secure their establishment with preventive measures (i.e., sprinkler system or fire stations), include deductibles (where the insured pays the initial cost of some repair up to some maximum amount), or add coinsurance (where a significant percentage of the cost is covered by the insurance company and the rest by the insured).

What is a *cat(astrophe) bond*? Assume that insurance companies sell flood or earthquake insurance to an area (or region) where earthquakes and floods are typical. Given that when one such natural disaster (catastrophe) occurs all insureds will file claims simultaneously, the insurance companies will go out of business because of the immediate large payouts. A solution to this problem is providing insurance to insurance companies, and this is done by *reinsurance companies*. Such companies are global in scope in order to spread risks and remain solvent even in the event of catastrophes. The financial industry has designed catastrophic bonds (cat bonds), which allow individual investors to share a portion of the reinsurance risk. So, an insurance company will sell some cat bonds and invest the proceeds in low-risk financial instruments like US Treasury bonds. If a catastrophe occurs, these bonds are sold so as to pay the claims the insurance company faces. But if no such event took place during the investment period, the cat bond owners receive a decent return which is typically several percentage points above the yield on US Treasury bonds (of equal maturity).

According to the *Reinsurance News* website, "Catastrophe bond issuance in the first quarter of 2024 reached a huge $4.23 billion, which is a record for the opening quarter of the year".[31] Following the same news report, "Last year saw cat bond spreads hit new heights,... investors continue to benefit from favourable pricing dynamics. The report shows that the average spread above expected loss in Q1 2024 was 6.42%, which is down on Q4 2023's 6.7%, and also the high of 9.41% in Q1 2023."[32] According to the Swiss Re Institute (a major, global reinsurance company), "Record-high catastrophe bond issuance in 2023 is a sign of attractive conditions for investors as well as the growing demand for transfer of peak risks such as large natural catastrophes."[33] Cat bonds have a solid track record despite above-average global natural catastrophe losses (due to damaging thunderstorms and hurricanes) annually in recent years, according to the same source.

Finally, insurance companies are exposed to additional risks such as credit, liquidity, market and interest rate. For example, in view of the rise in interest rates after a prolonged period of low interest rates, it is expected that insurance companies who have invested a large proportion of their funds in long-term debt securities they will be highly exposed to interest rate risk. Also, the 2008 global financial crisis hit insurance companies hard because that had invested some of their funds in mortgage-backed securities or in junk bonds, both of which collapsed during that period. Other insurance companies incurred losses from their credit default swaps and from their stock holdings. Recall the bailout of the American International Group (AIG), the largest insurance company in the world, which would have a devastating effect on the insurance industry and the rest of the financial sector, if not rescued. In September 2008, the Federal Reserve bailed out AIG with the support from the US Treasury (the "too big to fail" argument was advanced for the rescue).

3.3 Pension funds

Pension funds are unique, however, in that they offer savings plans through which fund participants accumulate tax deferred savings during their working years before withdrawing them during their retirement years. Although funds originally invested in and accumulated in a pension plan are exempt from current taxation, tax payments are made when funds are actually distributed to the fund participant. The pension fund industry comprises two distinct sector, private and public pension funds. *Private pension funds* are those funds administered by a corporation such as an insurance company or a mutual fund. *Public pension funds* are those funds administered by a federal, state, or local government such as Social Security, in the US.

Pension funds (plans) are commonly categorized as defined-benefit or defined-contribution plans depending on how contributions are made and on the level of benefits provided. In a *defined benefit pension fund*, the fund sponsor agrees to provide the employee a specific cash benefit upon retirement, based on a formula that considers factors such as years of employment, life expectancy and salary during employment. Complications arise when funds overestimate the rate of return on their investments thus permitting them to reduce their contributions to the plan so as to increase their earnings. However, this led to these pension funds becoming underfunded and incapable of covering future payment obligations. A prime example is that of the state of California (the well-known California Public

Employees' Retirement System, or CalPERS, the nation's largest pension fund for government workers) when it set generous defined benefits for its state employees without raising the required employee contributions. But, when its projected rate of return from investments came in short and thus the value of its pension fund contributions did not grow over time as expected the fund became deficient (from 2000 to 2012).[34] Some pension funds made risky investments in real estate, junk bonds, hedge funds and international securities in order to justify their high projected rates of return. Other solutions to the underfunding problem are raising taxes or modifying the formula for employee contributions.

A *defined-contribution plan* provides benefits that are determined by the accumulated contributions and the fund's investment performance. With this plan, the company knows with certainty the amount of funds to contribute, contrary to an unknown amount under the defined-benefit plan. The final retirement benefit is then based on total employer contributions and any gains or losses on the investments purchased by the fund with these contributions. Some employers match a portion of the contribution made by their employees.

Private defined benefit and defined contribution pension funds come in various types such as 401(k) and 403(b) plans, individual retirement accounts (IRAs), and Keogh plans. A *401(k)* plan is a company-sponsored retirement account in which employees can contribute a fraction of their income with employers often matching at least some of these contributions. Two basic types of 401(k) s exist, the traditional and Roth, and differ primarily in how they're taxed. The *403(b)* is only for government and non-profit employees. A *Keogh* plan is a retirement plan for the self-employed or unincorporated small businesses and categorized either as defined contribution or defined benefit plans. Figure 6.3 shows the values of these main private plans from 2021 to 2023:III for the US (in billions of dollars; quarterly figures are seasonally adjusted annual rates).

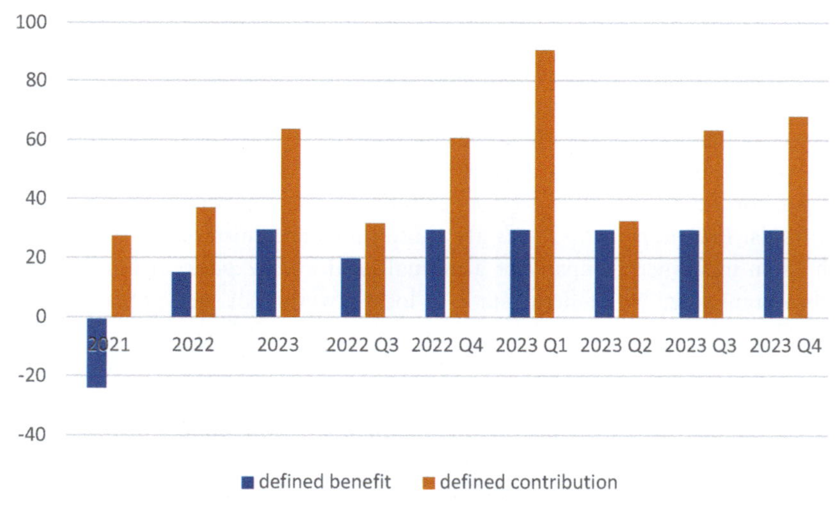

Figure 6.3 Private pension funds defined benefit and defined contribution plans

Source: www.federalreserve.gov, Tables F.118.b, c.

From the graph, it is evident that defined benefit funds experienced a reduction in new assets held, while defined contribution funds saw a general increase in new asset investments (from 2021–2023). This shift in assets resulted in a huge shift in the risk of retirement benefits, from employers to employees, during the 2008 global financial crisis.

Public pension funds include state and local government pension funds and the federal government pension fund. Employees of state or local governments may contribute to pension funds sponsored by these employers via the "pay as you go" system, meaning that contributions collected from current employees are the source of payments to the current retirees. The federal government sponsors two types of pension funds. The first involves funds for federal government employees (civil service, military personnel, and railroad). The second type of fund, and the largest federal government pension fund, is Social Security. Social Security is funded on a pay as you go basis, whereby current employer and employee Social Security taxes are used to pay benefits to current retirees.

The regulation of pension funds depends on the type of plan but all plans must comply with the relevant Internal Revenue Service tax rules. The *Employee Retirement Income Security Act* (ERISA) of 1974 (and 1989 revisions) regulates the defined-contribution plans and requires a pension fund to choose one of two vesting schedule options, which determine when an employee has a legal right to the contributed funds: (1) 100% vesting after five years of service or (2) graded vesting, with 20% vesting in the 3rd year, 40% in the 4th, 60% in the 5th, 80% in the 6th, and 100% in the 7th year. A component of ERISA is the Pension Benefit Guaranty Corporation, which is set to provide insurance on pension plans. The PBGC will step in to make up the deficiency if the pension fund is incapable of fully providing the benefits promised. The PBGC is not government-funded, but is financed by annual premiums and income from invested assets.

Pension fund portfolio managers are concerned about interest rate risk (the possibility that higher interest rates reduce the value of their holdings). If they hold long-term, fixed-rate bonds, the market value of their portfolio will decrease during periods when interest rates increase. They may periodically hedge against interest rate movements by selling bond futures contracts. Many portfolio managers periodically sell futures contracts on stock indexes to hedge against market downturns. Finally, portfolio managers of pension funds can obtain various types of insurance to limit the risk of the portfolio.

4 Investor investment perspectives

If you are an individual seeking services from insurance companies and pension funds, you are now aware of what's offered and covered from the discussion above. If you wear your investment hat, however, how can you exploit these two financial institutions? In addition, is it possible to have both types of services, as a policy-holder and investor? In other words, should protection be combined with wealth (value) creation? Here are some investment and insurance plans offered by insurance companies.

One important plan, which combines both services, insurance and investment, is the *insurance-cum-investment* plan. Variants of this plan include traditional products such as guaranteed-return plans and riskier ones such as *unit-linked insurance plans* (ULIPs). The first type works well with all investors, depending on their risk-return profile, and are tax-free (under certain circumstances). ULIPs fulfill one's long-range goals, come with a life insurance cover and under favorable market conditions, they can fetch a hefty return. Of course, this means that they carry investment risks in a volatile market. Other services include economizing (saving) on taxes, permission to invest regularly (say, every year put new money in), the offering of annuities and the offering of products such as permanent life insurance policies. *Permanent life insurance* – either whole life or universal life – policies enable you to invest in conservative investments like mutual funds or ETFs and allow you to curate your policy to meet your risk tolerance and goals. Put differently, permanent life insurance can serve as a hedge against market risk.

Other important services of life insurance plans are: (1) ability to take a loan from your policy (borrow against the cash value of your permanent life insurance policy); (2) use it as collateral for a loan (which facilitates getting approved or getting you a better rate on the loan); (3) withdraw funds (withdrawals are typically tax-free up to your policy basis, which is the amount you've paid in premiums so far); (4) collect dividends (the money an insurance company distributes to eligible clients when the company performs better financially than it expected for the year); (5) receive accelerated benefits (if unexpected or extreme medical emergencies arise); (6) cash out the policy (terminate it so you get back the cash value you put in, less any fees the insurance company may charge). However, read the fine print in the contract (assuming you will take out one because you need it) because permanent life insurance policies generally carry higher premiums and some involve managing various investments and fees. Thus, they may not be the right choice for everyone.

Insurance companies offer *guaranteed investment contracts* (GIC), which are agreements between investors and an insurance company, typically used in retirement plans. The term "guaranteed" suggests that the company guarantees the investor a certain rate of return in exchange for holding the deposit for a specified period. A GIC functions similarly to a bond with varying maturity up to 20 years. At maturity, the investor receives both the principal investment and any accrued interest. Some GICs offer periodic disbursements of the built-up interest over the contract's life. Typically, highly risk-averse investors prefer such contracts as they are looking for a conservative investment to counter out the more volatile portion of their portfolio. A major disadvantage of such contracts is that the rate of return may be less than inflation thus, returning funds with lower purchasing power and that they carry risk.

A variant of GIC is the *synthetic* GIC. According to the Financial Accounting Standards Board (FASB),

> A synthetic GIC is a contract that simulates the performance of a traditional GIC through the use of financial instruments. A key difference between a synthetic GIC and a traditional GIC is that the policyholder (such as a benefit plan) owns the assets underlying the synthetic GIC. (With a traditional GIC, the policyholder owns only the contract itself that provides the plan with a call on the contract issuer's assets in the event of default.) Those assets may be held in a trust owned by the policyholder and typically consist of government securities, private and public mortgage-backed securities, and other asset-backed securities, and investment grade corporate obligations.[35]

Finally, another variant of the basic GIC is a bullet GIC. A *bullet GIC* is a guaranteed investment contract that is paid out as a lump sum as opposed to a series of cash flows (as in a regular GIC). Consequently, a bullet GIC resembles a zero-coupon bond, but with deferred repayment of principal and interest.

Although pension funds represent an investment asset for employees, it can be a potential source of funds (financing) for an (the) employer, especially if traditional loans fall out of favor with some business owners. Funding your business using your pension pool may be an alternative option compared to the traditional ones and may be well worth considering it. In the United Kingdom, for example, pension-led financing can be done either using a self-invested personal pension (SIPP) or a small self-administered scheme (SSAS). A SIPP acts like a tax-efficient wrapper for all your investments, where you choose what shares, funds and other investments to place in your SIPP and the government automatically adds tax relief at the rate you pay tax. So, your business to take a commercial loan from your pension (following the approval of the trustee) via a SSAS. Also, since pension funds can own intangible assets such as patents, trademarks, designs, copyrights, and more, your SIPP or SSAS can purchase the needed intellectual property and lease it back to your business at some commercial rate.[36] In general, for business owners with a significant amount of savings in their pension, this could be a profitable and flexible finance option. As another example, take the experience of Brazil in the 1990s when, following the country's pension fund reforms, such funds became important potential suppliers of long-term non-inflationary financing to productive investment.[37]

How would you pick the best pension plan's payout? We believe that the right alternative would depend on your current status (single, married, family) as well as on factors such as your sources of income, your comfort level with investment risk and even your health. Regarding pensions, you may have at least two options upon retirement: (1) take a pension annuity and receiving a monthly check; (2) if permitted, take a lump-sum distribution, which you will need to invest and manage. With an annuity, you need not worry about outliving your pension payments. Because you know that the same amount is coming in on a regular basis, budgeting for everyday and unusual expenses may be easier. According to FINRA, if you decide to take a pension annuity, you then must decide how you want the pension to be paid. You may have three options.

1. The single-life, where you might choose a payout that lasts for your lifetime only. With a single-life annuity, when you die, the payments stop even if you die soon after they start.
2. You could choose an annuity to be paid out over your lifetime plus the lifetime of another person, usually your spouse, in what's called a joint-and-survivor payout. The amount of your monthly check is less than what you'd receive with a single-life annuity, and after death your survivor will get the percentage of your pension you specified up front every month for life.
3. The option of a period-certain payout with a joint-and-survivor annuity, which provides income to a beneficiary you name for a specific period if both you and your spouse die before the period ends.

The downside of the annuity options, however, is that inflation can erode the purchasing power of these payments over time and that the income depends on the viability and financial strength of the payer.

With a lump sum, you can roll it into an individual retirement account (IRA), where you are taxed only on money you decide to take out. Your employer calculates the amount you receive based on (1) what the plan would have paid you as an annuity over your projected life expectancy, and (2) the current interest rate, which determines what the plan would have earned on the lump sum if it had been paid out in increments over your lifetime.

The lump-sum amount will vary with the prevailing interest rates. If interest rates are high, you'll receive a smaller lump sum than you would if rates were low. FINRA lists a number of risks with this option: (a) responsibility for providing lifetime income; (b) taxes due immediately on cash-payouts and annual tax on investment earnings; (c) danger of spending assets too fast; and (d) danger of significant investment losses.[38]

If you wish to invest in a mutual fund, you should also be aware of the various share classes such as A, B, C and so on. For example, Class A shares charge upfront fees and have lower expense ratios (including lower 12b-1 fees), so they are better for long-term investors, and reduce upfront fees for larger investments, so they are a better choice for wealthy investors. Class A shares also possess voting power. Class B shares charge exit fees and have higher expense ratios but convert to A-shares if held for several years. Class C shares have higher expense ratios than A-shares and a small exit fee (typically usually waived after one year) and are popular with retail and short-term investors. Class D shares have no include front- or back-end loads, and have the lowest expense ratio compared to other share classes. These are usually available through discount brokers, and fees are charged per transaction. Class M shares carry lower front-end loads than A shares and are available to investors with larger initial investments. The maximum front load is either 0% or between 1% and 3.5%, the maximum deferred load is 0%, the maximum 12b-1 fee ranges from 0% to 25 basis points (bps) up to 100 bps, whereas the min investment is $50,000 or more. For more information on many more class shares, see Morningstar.[39]

Let's explain and work out an example from the ABC mutual fund. The information is in Table 6.2. The investor ponders of making a $10,000 lump-sum purchase of a Class A share or another $10,000 lump-sum purchase in Class C shares of the same mutual fund. Both funds earn an annual rate of return of 5%. Compare the hypothetical account balances over time. A-class shares assess a 5.25% front-end load and 0.87% annual operating expenses, whereas B-class shares do not have a front-end load but charge a 1.62% fee to cover the fund's

Table 6.2 Some information on the ABC mutual fund

Fund	*Initial Investment*	*Account balance after 1 year*	*Account balance after 5 years*	*Account balance after 10 years*	*Account balance after 20 years*
A-class	$9,475	$9,862.20	$11,576.04	$14,147.86	$21,125.26
B-class	$10,000	$10,231.28	$11,769.83	$13,852.89	$19,190.26

annual operating expenses. The values below show the two accounts' balances at the end of 1-, 5-, 10- and 20-year horizons.

The initial investment is found by simply subtracting the front-end load of $525 (=$10,000–5.25%), for the A-class share, and the $10,000 is the same, for the B-class share investment. The account balance of $9,822.52 after one year for the A-class share is found as follows: $9,475*1.05 = $9,948.75, which is the 1-year return of the invested funds. Then, subtract the 0.87% fee of $86.55 (=$9,9948.75*0.87%) from the invested funds to get to the $9,862,20 value. Then, repeat the same steps (n-year return minus the operating expense) for each subsequent year (to get to 5, 10 and 20 years) to see the values in the table. To assist you with the 5-year value, start with the return of the next amount ($9,862.20) and add the yield of 5% (=$9,862.2*1.05) to get to $10,355.31 and the subtract the 0.87% fee (=$10,355.31*0.87%) or $90.1, to arrive at the net value for year 2 (=$110,355.31- $90.1) of $10,625.22. Continue in the same manner (for 3 more years) to get to the $11,576.04 value shown in the table (or very similar to that). The same process applies to the other values in the table.

The main point from this example is for the investor to compare the two investments based on his/her investment horizon. As you can see, Class-B share performed better in the short term (5 years or less), and the Class-A share surpassed it over a longer period of time (10+ years) mainly due to the lower annual operating expenses despite the $525 front-end sales load paid at the start of the investment. In general, each investor must choose the best combination of fees. Many investors are willing to pay for financial advice, while others may choose to hire a financial manager who charges directly for services instead of collecting commissions. If you do buy a fund through a broker, the choice between paying a load and paying 12b-1 fees will depend primarily on your expected time horizon. Loads are paid only once for each purchase, whereas 12b-1 fees, for example, are paid annually. Thus, if you plan to hold your fund for a long time, a one-time load may be preferable to recurring 12b-1 charges. If a class share has the structure that an exit fee or back-end load (as opposed to front-end load) of, say, 5%, is reduced by a certain percentage (say, 1%) every year until the sale (5th year), then the ending value can be found by multiplying the initial investment by the (*1 + growth rate of the investment*) in the power of *n* term (*n* being the years and declining) by the (*1 – back-end load*) term.

As a retail investor, you can exploit investment bankers' services via their broker-dealer services. Recall that a broker brings buyers and sellers of securities together, whereas a dealer sells securities from its own inventory. So, you would go through a broker – discount or full-service – if you wish to buy/sell stock unless you do it directly. Then, your broker will contact his dealer at the exchange (organized such as the New York Stock Exchange, or over-the-counter such as NASDAQ) in order to fulfill the order. Also, the retail divisions of IBs extend loans to individuals (as well as businesses).

How can you compare among various mutual funds (and, by extension, evaluate fund managers)? Although there are several measures to assess (evaluate) any mutual fund (some of them we learned in Chapter 2), here we will use another measure known as the information ratio (IR) or *tracking error* or *appraisal ratio*. This metric measures a portfolio's average return in excess of that of a comparison or benchmark portfolio divided by the standard deviation of this excess return. Formally, the information ratio is calculated as:

$$IR_{MF} = \frac{R_{MF} - \bar{R}_b}{\sigma_{er}} \tag{6.2}$$

where:

IR_{MF} = the information ratio for the specific mutual fund portfolio
R_{MF} = the average return for the mutual fund during the specified time period
R-bar$_b$ = the average return for the benchmark portfolio during the period
σ_{er} = the standard deviation of the excess return during the period

Notice that the numerator records the mean *excess return* and reflects the investor's ability to use talent and information to generate a portfolio return that differs from that of the benchmark against which their performance is being measured (e.g., the market index). The denominator measures the amount of residual (non-systematic or non-diversifiable) risk that the investor incurred in pursuing those excess returns. The coefficient σ_{er} (obtained from regression and referring to the standard error of the regression or the residual standard deviation) is sometimes called the tracking error of the investor's portfolio and represents an "uncertainty cost" of active management in the sense that fluctuations in the periodic excess return values represent randomness which is beyond an investor's control and could possibly hurt performance. It is also important to mention that other analysts define the information ratio as the alpha of the fund and use the appraisal ratio to refer to the ratio of *alpha* to nonsystematic risk, as follows:

$$IR_{MF} = \alpha_{MF} / \sigma_{MF} \tag{6.3}$$

To annualize IR, just multiply the IR value by the square root of time. A variant of the IR metric is one that improves upon the Sharpe ratio by adding the fund's information ratio, as follows:

$$S^2_{MF} = S^2_B + [\alpha_{MF} / \sigma_{MF})]^2 \tag{6.4}$$

where S_B is the benchmark (market) index. This version is most appropriate for a hedge fund. However, there are instances that other funds such as a pension fund, which is largely passive and with a well-diversified position (just like an index fund), may wish to add a position in an active portfolio to its current position such as a hedge fund. IR is another version of a reward-to-risk trade-off and, in this context, the reward is the alpha of the active position. Put differently, it is the expected return on that incremental portfolio above the risk premium that would normally correspond to its systematic risk. Hence, IR quantifies the trade-off between alpha and diversifiable risk. IR is a central concept in mutual funds and not just index funds of exchange-traded funds (ETFs). Depending on an investor's investment horizon, this uncertainty cost can be even greater than the expense ratio or trading spreads. In other words, while a low expense ratio is important, a lower tracking error suggests a reduced likelihood of incurring costs from volatile performance, regardless of your investment horizon. Low errors indicate that the performance of the portfolio is close to the performance of the benchmark.

Here's an example with hypothetical data for two mutual funds' (MF) returns, A and B, over five periods for which you are asked to apply the IR and decide which one had achieved a better performance (compared to the market, S&P):

MF A	11%	3%	12%	14%	8%
MF B	10%	4%	11.5%	13%	9%
S&P	12%	5%	13%	9%	7%

To begin solving it, we must first compute the excess returns (fund's return *minus* the market's returns) for each fund for each period. These are shown below.

MF A	−1%	−2%	−1%	5%	1%
MF B	−2%	−1%	−1.5%	4%	2%

You may be tempted to conclude that MF A's performance was better because you might have added each fund's periodic excess returns (for A, for example, −1%−2%−1%+5%+1%) and get 2%, whereas you would get 1.5% for MF B. However, one must compute each fund's standard deviation to get an accurate picture of how consistent each fund's performance was to its benchmark. The formula is the typical standard deviation formula and one would obtain a value of 2.5% for MF A and 2.31% for MF B.[40] Hence, fund B achieved more consistent performance to its benchmark index (the opposite conclusion reached earlier).

At this point, it is important to mention that a small tracking error indicates that a fund does not significantly outperform its benchmark (as in passive investments). This suggests that the investor may consider withdrawing his money from that fund and putting it into other, more promising fund. Tracking errors tend to be small, but they can still adversely affect your returns.

We end this chapter with an important question for students in finance-related disciplines such as management and marketing: what is the relationship between PESTEL Analysis with the mutual fund industry? *PESTEL* is the acronym for Political, Economic, Social, Technological, Environmental and Legal factors that affect the economy and its specific areas. The nearby *box* explains how PESTEL is linked with the mutual fund industry. In general, such analysis helps mutual fund managers (and firms) to identify macroeconomic and regulatory risks, align products with market trends and investor sentiment and adapt investment strategies to external changes.

Box 6.1

PESTEL analysis and the mutual fund industry

POLITICAL: the government's policies (taxation, spending, regulation) influence capital markets. Political uncertainty can increase market volatility, prompting fund managers to adjust portfolio allocations or hedge risks.

ECONOMIC: Macroeconomic factors such as interest rates, inflation, GDP growth, and unemployment affect returns across asset classes. For example, during periods of economic expansion, equity mutual funds may outperform, whereas during recessions, bond or money market funds become more attractive.

SOCIAL: In general, changing demographics, investor preferences, and attitudes toward sustainability shape fund flows. For instance, increasing investor demand for specific funds can lead mutual fund companies to develop sustainable or ethical investment products.

TECHNOLOGICAL: Technological factors such as advances in financial technology enhance fund distribution, data analysis, and portfolio management. In addition, the emergence of robo-advisors and algorithmic (program) trading has changed how mutual funds are marketed and managed.

ENVIRONMENTAL: Such factors including climate change and green finance influence long-term asset valuations and regulatory expectations. As a result, mutual funds increasingly integrate environmental risk assessment to manage exposure to carbon-intensive industries (many investors now invest in Environmental, Social and Governance, ESG, funds).

LEGAL: Legal factors such as securities laws, investor protection regulations, and disclosure requirements shape fund governance and transparency. For example, specific financial regulations such as MiFID II in Europe or the SEC's rules in the US, affect fund operations, costs, and reporting obligations of mutual funds.

Test your understanding 3

1. ABC Fund sells Class A shares with a front-end load of 4% and Class B shares with 12b-1 fees of.5% annually as well as back-end load fees that start at 5% and fall by 1% for each full year the investor holds the portfolio. The investor has a 5-year investment horizon and his investment budget is $10,000. Assume the rate of return on the fund portfolio net of operating expenses is 10% annually.
   a. What will be the value of the investment in Class A and Class B shares if the shares are sold after 1 year?
   b. after 4 years?
   c. after 10 years?
   d. Which fee structure provides higher net proceeds at the end of each investment horizon?

2. Can you link the concept of risk aversion to insurance buying? Provide some examples.
3. Which general types of investments do pension funds prefer?
4. Can you lists some considerations when selecting the right pension plan for you?

Solutions appear at the textbook's website.

Summary

- We discussed the investment company (mutual fund industry) industry by discussing the following: their purpose, structure, investment types, taxation, performance and future trends.
- Potential advantages of pooling small amounts and investing them in many more financial assets: diversification, professional management, low transaction costs, administrative services, other benefits.
- Investment companies are divided into three principal classes: (1) Face-amount certificate company; (2) Unit investment trust (UIT); (3) Management company.
- Other categories include open-end and closed-end companies.
- An open-end company means a management company which is offering for sale or has outstanding any redeemable security of which it is the issuer.
- A closed-end company means any management company other than an open-end company.
- A UIT typically issues redeemable units which means that the UIT will buy back an investor's units at their approximate *net asset value* (NAV).
- A closed-end fund does not redeem or issue shares. Instead, an investor who wishes to cash out must sell his shares to other investors in the open market.
- Open-end funds are what we typically call *mutual funds* (MFs) and are defined as those that issue new fund shares (or units) and redeem existing shares (or units) on demand.
- There are several types of fees such as annual fund operation expenses and shareholder fees such as loads, redemption fees, exchange fees, account fees and purchase fees.
- Money-market mutual funds or money-market funds (MMFs) are the most important class of MFs because they are targeted by all types of investors.
- MMFs invest in a wide variety of financial instruments such as certificates of deposits, time deposits, repurchase agreements, commercial paper, asset-backed commercial paper, and government-backed securities.
- Retail investors use this market to invest in Treasury bills, earn some interest in their idle cash by opening up savings and checking accounts, and, in general, enjoy the yields, liquidity and safety of their money.
- Institutional investors create such funds and use these short-term money products as part of their well-diversified asset portfolios when designing client portfolios.
- An exchange-traded fund (ETF) is an SEC-registered company which pools retail investors' funds and invest in stocks, bonds, or other assets.

- ETFs, unlike mutual funds, are traded daily on a stock exchange at a market-determined prices, can be sold short and are more tax efficient than actively managed mutual funds.
- The investment banking (IB) industry serves primarily legal entities such as commercial companies, financial institutions and governments to raise funds in the capital markets (*underwriting*) through the means of initial public offerings and performs other activities such as mergers and acquisitions (M&A).
- When a privately held company wishes to go public, it initiates an IPO process and (typically) hires investment bankers to assist the company in going public.
- The M&A concept refers to an agreement between two companies to consolidate functions and assets and then continue as one united company (the *merger*) or the purchase of a company of another company and its assets (the *acquisition*).
- The IB industry will constantly face new challenges emanating either from global events such as the global pandemic crisis, regional wars, the advancement of technology or country/regional-specific changes in regulations, market-specific changes and others.
- A pension fund is a financial institution that accumulates large sums of money to invest into the capital markets to generate profit and then pay out – in the form of pension -to employees when they retire.
- The pension fund industry comprises two distinct sector, private and public pension funds.
- Private pension funds are those funds administered by a corporation such as an insurance company or a mutual fund. Public pension funds are those administered by a federal, state, or local government such as Social Security, in the US.
- Pension funds (plans) are commonly categorized as defined-benefit or defined-contribution plans depending on how contributions are made and on the level of benefits provided.
- Insurance companies provide financial protection to agents (people and institutions) against hazards for a premium.
- The two main types of insurance are life, and property and casualty. Other types include health (care), business services (such as credit default swaps), bond, and mortgage insurance.
- Insurance companies try to reduce both the adverse selection and moral hazard problems.

Questions and problems

1. How do insurance companies reduce their exposure to various types of insurance? What role would credit default swaps on mortgages play?
2. Explain how a strong economy, a low risk-free rate and industry conditions affect an insurance company.
3. In which financial instruments do typical pension funds invest in?
4. Which type of risk do pension funds typically face? How do they hedge that risk?

5. Suppose today a mutual fund contains 1000 shares of ABC currently trading at \$35, 2,000 shares of QRS currently trading at \$40, and 1,500 shares of XYZ currently trading at \$45. The mutual fund has no liabilities and 15,000 shares outstanding held by investors.
   a. What is the fund's net asset value (NAV) today?
   b. If tomorrow ABC's shares increase to \$45, QRS's shares increase to \$48, and XYZ's shares increase to \$50, recompute NAV. Assume the no. of shares outstanding remains the same.
6. Following on the previous problem, assume that today 1,000 additional investors buy one share each of the mutual fund at the NAV you found in part (a).
   a. How much more funds does the fund manager have to invest?
   b. Suppose that the fund manager decides to use these additional funds to buy additional shares in ABC stock. At today's market price, how many shares could he buy?
   c. What would be the composition of the new portfolio in shares?
   d. Given the same rise in share values as in the problem above, what will be tomorrow's NAV?
   e. To which factors (magnitudes) does the fund owe its change in value? Compare with the previous result in problem 6.
7. Suppose an individual invests \$10,000 in a front-end load mutual fund. The load fee entails a charge of 4 percent of the amount invested.
   a. What is the investor's actual investment?
   b. Assume further that the annual fund operating expenses are 0.85 percent. If the investor reinvests the annual returns paid on the investment (5 percent annually), what would be the value of the investments after one year with the operating fees deducted? [**Hint**: compute the annual operating expenses by multiplying the *average* NAV by the annual operating expenses].
   c. What would be the investor's return on the mutual fund investment after 1 year?
   d. Compute the investor's dollar proceeds after 2 years (following the above steps).
   e. What was the total value of expenses this investor paid to the fund and dollar proceeds (in 2 years)? Can you derive his (implied) annual rate of return? [**Hint**: use the PV formula= $FV/(1+r)^n$ and solve for r. For FV, use the value you derived in part (d)].
8. An employee with 20 years of service at a company is considering retiring within the next 10 years. The employer uses a simple (flat) benefit formula by which the employee receives an annual benefit payment of \$1,500 *times* the number of years of service. Compute the employee's annual retirement payment(s) when he retires now, in 5 years, and in 10 years.
9. Following-up on problem 8, assume now the employer uses a benefit formula by which the employee receives an annual benefit payment of 3 percent of his career average salary *times* the number of years of service. Assume an average salary of \$45,000 until today, \$50,000 in 5 years and \$60,000 in 10 years. Recompute the employee's annual retirement payment(s) when he retires now, in 5 years, and in 10 years.

10. Assume we have two fund managers, A and B, and have the following rates of return and tracking errors: A has an (annualized) return of 10% and a tracking error of 5% and B has an annualized return of 11% and a tracking error of 4%. The relevant benchmark index has an annualized return of 8%. Compute the Information Ratios for both managers and conclude as to which manager was more effective in beating the benchmark.

Notes

1. https://corporatefinanceinstitute.com/resources/wealth-management/north-american-securities-administrators-association-nasaa/
2. https://www.ici.org/about-the-investment-company-institute
3. https://naicpe.com/about-us/
4. https://www.theaic.co.uk/about-us
5. https://www.law.cornell.edu/uscode/text/15/80a-5
6. A face-amount certificate company is a type of corporation that raises money by issuing investors debt securities of a specified value.
7. https://www.law.cornell.edu/uscode/text/15/80a-5
8. https://www.investor.gov/introduction-investing/investing-basics/glossary/unit-investment-trusts-uits
9. ICI Factbook 2025 data tables: https://www.icifactbook.org/25-fb-data-tables.html
10. https://www.guggenheiminvestments.com/cef/fund/gof
11. ICI Factbook 2025.
12. ICI Factbook 2023, p. 11.
13. https://www.investor.gov/introduction-investing/investing-basics/glossary/mutual-fund-prospectus
14. ICI Factbook 2023, p. 26.
15. https://www.investor.gov/introduction-investing/investing-basics/glossary/mutual-fund-fees-and-expenses
16. https://tools.finra.org/fund_analyzer/
17. https://www.reuters.com/markets/why-european-money-market-funds-inflows-are-lagging-behind-us-torrent-2023–04–11/
18. https://www.efama.org/newsroom/news/record-net-sales-global-money-market-funds-2023#:~:text=Net%20assets%20of%20worldwide%20investment,EUR%2099%20billion%20in%20Q3
19. https://corporatefinanceinstitute.com/resources/career/investment-banking-overview/
20. https://corporatefinanceinstitute.com/resources/valuation/investment-banking-book-pdf/
21. The gross spread is defined as the sale price of the issue sold by the underwriter *minus* the purchase price of the issue bought by the underwriter.
22. https://corporatefinanceinstitute.com/resources/equities/ipo-process/
23. The sell-side essentially refers to a similar approach but the seller must prepare some additional documents, participate in the bidding process and receive the letter of intent and then negotiate. See previous footnote.
24. https://www.reuters.com/sustainability/us-sec-poised-ban-deceptive-esg-growth-fund-labels-2023–09–20/
25. https://www.esma.europa.eu/sites/default/files/trv_2019_1-regtech_and_suptech_change_for_markets_and_authorities.pdf; and https://www.bankingsupervision.europa.eu/press/publications/newsletter/2023/html/ssm.nl231115_2.en.html
26. https://www.mckinsey.com/industries/financial-services/our-insights/five-big-shifts-shaping-a-new-world-for-corporate-and-investment-banks
27. https://www.iii.org/publications/commercial-insurance/how-it-functions/regulation

28. https://eur-lex.europa.eu/EN/legal-content/summary/insurance-and-reinsurance.html
29. https://www2.deloitte.com/us/en/insights/industry/financial-services/financial-services-industry-outlooks/insurance-industry-outlook.html
30. https://www2.deloitte.com/us/en/insights/industry/financial-services/financial-services-industry-outlooks/insurance-industry-outlook.html
31. https://www.reinsurancene.ws/q124-catastrophe-bond-issuance-rises-30-year-on-year-to-record-4–23bn-report/
32. https://www.reinsurancene.ws/q124-catastrophe-bond-issuance-rises-30-year-on-year-to-record-4–23bn-report/
33. https://www.swissre.com/our-business/alternative-capital-partners/ils-market-insights-august-2023.html
34. https://www.city-journal.org/article/the-pension-fund-that-ate-california
35. https://www.fasb.org/page/PageContent?pageId=/Archive/superseded-standards/derivatives-statement-implementation/fasb-definition-of-a-derivative-synthetic-guaranteed-investmentcontracts.html&isStaticPage=true
36. https://www.whitehallgroup.co.uk/wp-content/uploads/2024/03/Property-Purchase-Guideline-1.pdf
37. https://www.cepal.org/sites/default/files/publication/files/5079/S00070645_en.pdf
38. https://www.finra.org/investors/learn-to-invest/types-investments/retirement/managing-retirement-income/selecting-retirement-payout-methods
39. https://morningstardirect.morningstar.com/clientcomm/Share_Class_Types.pdf
40. One can do this in excel using the =*STDEV.P* formula (function).

References

Investment Company Institute (ICI) 2023. Factbook. https://www.ici.org/system/files/2023-05/2023-factbook.pdf.

Corporate Finance Institute (CFI). https://corporatefinanceinstitute.com/

Insurance Information Institute (III). https://www.iii.org/.

Part III

The capital market

The capital market is another important financial market and includes equities (stocks), fixed-income (bonds and related) and hybrid (mixture of equity and bond) securities. The main role of the capital market is to facilitate the trading of securities such as stocks and bonds so that agents such as households, businesses and governments can raise capital for their own objective(s) (borrowing, investing, hedging and more). In contrast to the money market, where if a company needs money for business operations it borrows it from households or individuals, in the capital market, the money from individual investors or households is invested in a company's shares or bonds resulting in profits (or losses) as well as the production of goods and services. In general, capital markets facilitate the process by which businesses raise long-term funds via the provision of a market for debt and equities. The objective here is for companies to expand their productive capacity (via investment or other forms) and, in general, to promote economic growth and development. The main characteristics of the capital market are exactly the opposite of the money market: long-term, less liquid (and marketable) and high risk. In addition, the capital market (through its financial markets and institutions) plays two critical roles in an economy: allocation of risk capital through saving mobilization and risk pooling/sharing, and promotion of responsible governance and control through the provision to outside investors a variety of mechanisms for monitoring inside decision makers.

Furthermore, the capital market is made up of *public* and *private* markets. For example, companies which sell shares to the general public belong to the public capital market. Also, when someone invests in the stock market, individually or through an employee-sponsored retirement plan, they own a small portion of the public companies they have invested in. The private markets, by contrast, comprises of companies that are not publicly traded, but they still provide investors with an opportunity to acquire equity in exchange for providing capital. Examples of investors in the private market are venture capital firms – which invest in young companies or startups – and private equity firms – which invest in more established

DOI: 10.4324/9781003677161-9

companies. Unless one is a wealthy individual (professional investor), one cannot invest in the private markets. The capital market can also be distinguished between *primary* (where new securities are sold to investors) and *secondary* markets (where existing securities are traded). In the primary market the key players are firms, financial institutions (the fund managers or the "buy side"), investment banks (the "sell side") and public accounting firms. In the secondary market, the players are investors (of all types) and investment banks.

In this Part, we will discuss the equity and the fixed-income markets. Chapter 7 explains in detail the equity market, its characteristics and trends/developments, while Chapter 9 discusses the same for the fixed-income market. Chapters 8 and 10 analyze the two markets, from both the inside and outside perspectives, and present investment activities that an investor can pursue in order to exploit these markets. In addition, we will be presenting economic and financial analyses of major news in these markets so as to understand how they react (though their instruments) to news and situations.

Chapter 7

The equity market

Introduction

In general, the equity (stock) market provides the venue for two important functions: (1) the facilitation of the flow of funds from investors (individual or institutional) to corporations so the latter can finance their investments in new or expanded business projects, and (2) the allocation of equity investments between investors. Hence, companies use the equity market to perform a number of functions such as capital raising (for growth and investment), raising their public image, engaging in activities such as mergers and acquisitions, providing liquidity to investors (existing and new alike), and offering remuneration services (through stock offerings, for example).

How does the stock market operate? The stock market helps companies raise money to fund operations by selling shares of stock as well as create wealth for individual investors. Companies raise money on the stock market by selling ownership stakes to investors. In exchange for that, companies are required to disclose information to shareholders on how their businesses are run. Investors, on the other hand, benefit as their shares of stock become more valuable over time because companies put investors' money to work to grow and expand their businesses. Companies list their shares on the stock exchange in order to get access to the capital they need to operate and expand their businesses.

An efficiently functioning stock market serves important social and economic purposes. Apart from the above, a company's shares provide investors a way to save for the future that has historically yielded higher returns than bank deposits (given risk) and share prices (determined by trading in the stock market) serve as signals that help allocate society's scarce savings to the best investment projects (the allocative function). In addition, share prices help discipline managers to make the best use of the productive capacity already under their control and enables an investor to moderate the risk involved without sacrificing expected return via diversification.

DOI: 10.4324/9781003677161-10

In this chapter, we will explain the types of equity, their characteristics, how one can purchase equity, how we value equity, the theories underlying stock markets and the trends and developments in that market.

1 Equity investments

An *equity investment* is money invested in a publicly traded firm through the purchase of shares of that firm. These shares are typically traded on a stock exchange. By purchasing stocks, an investor becomes a shareholder with entitlement to a portion of the assets and profits of the firm. Investors purchase shares of a company so they can benefit from a (possible) rise in value – capital gain – and/or from dividends. Equity determines the valuation of a company as it represents the company's assets *minus* its liabilities and is a key indicator of the financial health of the company. In contrast to the above – the public equity – there is also *private equity*, which is a longer-term investment (typically with a fixed term of ten years or more) and investors are required to be high net worth individuals.

There are several types of equity investment with distinct rewards and risks. These are common stocks, preferred stock, equity warrants, restricted stock and convertible debt. We discuss them on p. 180–181. Figure 7.1 shows the growth of equity holdings by households in the United States from 2000 to 2023. From the graph, it is clear that households drastically increased their equity holdings since the late 2010s. Also, it seems that in the first quarter of 2020 and the second quarter of 2022, households shed their equity holdings, presumably in response of world events such as the COVID-19 pandemic and the Russian–Ukraine war and rising inflation, respectively. Regarding the first world event, consider some facts. Specifically, on Monday, March 9, 2020, the Dow Jones Industrial Average

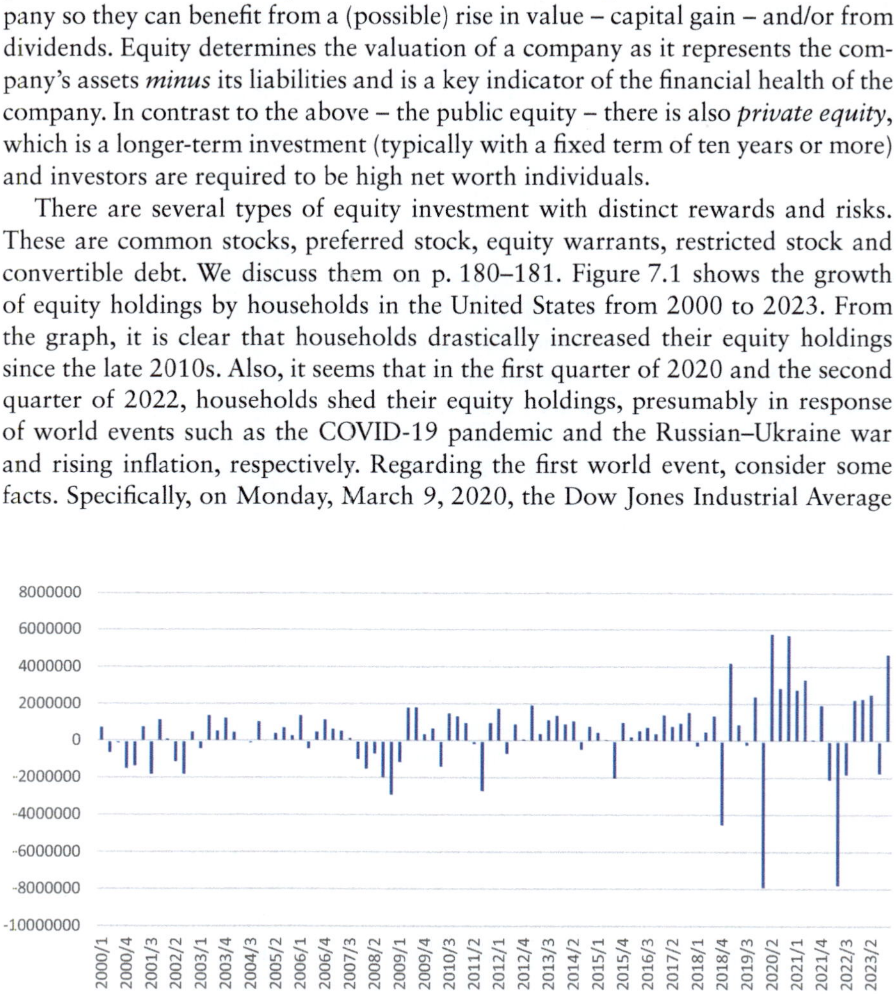

Figure 7.1 Direct and indirect holdings of corporate equity by households

Data source: millions of US dollars; Financial Accounts of the United States, Federal Reserve Board.

equity index fell 7.79%, a few days later, the index set another record by falling by almost 10%, and gain on March 16, it dropped by almost 13%. This led the New York Stock Exchange to suspend trading several times during those days. Between mid-February and March, the Dow lost 37% of its value. The rapid rise in inflation and subsequent interest-rate increases shattered the equity (as well as the bond) market worldwide.

1.1 Private equity

An *equity fund* offers accredited investors a diversified investment option typically for a minimum initial investment amount. Investors may also increase investment through rights shares, should a company wish to raise additional capital in equity markets. Accredited investors include institutional investors (insurance companies, university endowments and pension funds), and high income or net worth individuals. There is a number of different types of equity funds, each with their own characteristics and level of risk such as value, growth, blend (value-growth), and low volatility. What are some disadvantages of equity funds? First, there is the requirement that an investor keep his funds for a long period of time before some return is realized and thus, these investments are illiquid. Second, an equity fund may impose high fees and expenses some of which may be hidden from investors. The SEC imposes strict requirements and guidelines regarding the fee structure.[1] Third, private equity firms may have interests that are in conflict with the funds they manage and, by extension, the limited partners invested in the funds. They may also be managing multiple private equity funds as well as a number of portfolio companies. All these entail conflicts of interest.[2]

Private equity firms are investors that provide capital to private companies in exchange for an ownership stake in the business. Private equity (PE) firms have a lot of experience and expertise in helping businesses grow, so they can be a valued source of funding for companies. However, it is important to understand the different types of PE firms and what they offer before you decide to partner with one as each type of firm has its own strengths and weaknesses. PE firms typically invest in companies that are undervalued and have the potential to generate high returns. If PE firms invest in companies when stock prices are very high, they may be subject to large losses (if stock market conditions deteriorate or correct) even if they can improve operations.

There are two types PE firms: venture capital and real estate. *Venture capital* (VC) firms invest in companies that are in their early stages of development, typically providing seed money or first-round financing. VC firms tend to invest in companies with high growth potential that are in industries such as technology, healthcare, and biotechnology. In exchange for their investment, VCs typically receive a minority stake in the company, which offers them a financial interest in the success of the business and allows them to participate in its growth. According to the *Financial Times*, the average VC fund did not reliably outperform the average stock over the past 20 years. In addition, "the medium-term median returns have been no better than mediocre".[3]

Real estate private equity firms invest in all types of real estate, including office buildings, apartments, warehouses, and retail centers. These firms often invest in properties that need renovation or development. These firms typically purchase equity in these companies and then work to improve their operations and increase their value. A study by Riddiough and Da (2023) examined the longitudinal performance of 2,738 liquidated PE funds, and found that real estate PE funds underperformed both the (alternative) buy-out and VC investments as well as the public market alternative.

1.2 Common stock

Common stock is a type of security that represents partial ownership in a company. Owning common stock of a company entitles the owner a number of things. First, common shareholders have the right to vote in elections pertaining to company leadership, which can affect a company's operations. Other rights under this privileged include authorization to issue new shares of common stock, approval of amendments to the corporate charter, and adoption of bylaws. Many small (individual) investors may wish to assign their vote to management through the use of a *proxy* or may not even exercise their right to vote. As a result, management normally receives the majority of the votes and can elect its own candidates as directors.

Second, common stockholders enjoy limited (legal) liability, which essentially means that they are not responsible beyond the amount of their investment if the company suffers losses or is liquidated. Put differently, *limited liability* means that if the firm cannot pay its debts, the firm's creditors may attach only the firm's assets and not go after (or sue) the corporation's equity holders for further payment. For example, if you paid $100 for a company's share which subsequently was liquidated, the max amount you could lose is just the $100. Third, common shareholders are *residual claimants* which essentially means that they are the last in line of all those who have a claim on the assets and income of the corporation in the event of liquidation of the firm's assets. Hence, all other claimants (debtholders, tax authorities, lawyers and other stakeholders) are first in line for payments. If the firm is not in liquidation, shareholders have claim to the part of operating income left over after interest and taxes have been paid. Finally, some companies may offer shareholders *preemptive rights*, which give them the opportunity to purchase additional shares before they are offered to the public. This can be a valued benefit for investors who want to maintain their ownership stake in the company.

Other characteristics of common stock include fungibility, volatility, liquidity and continuous existence. *Fungibility* means that (all) shares of a company's common stock are worth the same amount at any given time, and each share represents ownership of the underlying company in the same amount. So, any one share of common stock could be replaced by another without any change in value. *Volatility* means that common stock prices are more likely to change significantly (upwards and/or downwards) over time. Note that common stock is more volatile than preferred stock (discussed next) or corporate bonds (discussed in Chapter 9). *Liquidity* (or marketability) means that can efficiently buy and sell their shares anytime. Finally, common stocks do not have a maturity date and thus, shareholders can (in theory) hold their shares indefinitely, allowing for perpetual (ongoing) ownership.

When you wish to buy shares of a public company, you should know that all shares are not all created equal. In other words, there are different classes of shares often designated as Class A and B. For example, some companies give shareholders greater benefits or voting rights than owners of other classes of stock. The corporation's owners can create the number and nature of share classes in almost any manner they see fit. A company's Board of Directors might set different share classes for many reasons such as to keep voting control of the company in a few hands by establishing different voting rights for different shareholders. For example, a company might issue ordinary (common) stock with one vote per share, designated as Class A-shares, then also issue executive stock with 100 votes per share, designated as Class B-shares. The repayment priority for Class B-shares could also be on the lower side, in case of bankruptcy. The rights, however, are set by the company's Board of Directors, as mentioned above. Below are a couple of examples of companies that have issued different class shares.

Facebook has what's called a *dual class structure* of Class A-shares and Class B-shares. The Class A-shares are the typical ones where investors have one vote per share. The Class B-shares, however, are controlled by M. Zuckerberg (the CEO of Facebook) and just a small group of insiders. Every Class B-share gets 10 votes. B. Ford, Ford Motor Company's CEO has amassed control of the company (since 2022) by owning Class B shares that carry super-voting powers and permitted the Ford family to retain control of the company. While the Class B shares account for 2% of Ford's outstanding stock, they control 40% of the voting power. A number of other companies have issued dual-class shares such as Nike, Visa and Alphabet.

In the United States, unequal voting structures (or dual-class shares) are commonly associated with technology and media companies, but in Europe there is no industry-specific structure. In Europe, the tradition is what they call "loyalty shares" and government ownership. According to the Investor Shareholder Services' website, a number of different structures are found in many countries. For example, while in France more than twice as many companies have unequal voting rights than those that don't have them, in Sweden is around split equally. In Greece and Portugal there are no companies with unequal voting rights. Loyalty shares are allowed in Finland, Italy, Sweden, Switzerland, Belgium, France and the UK. Finally, while loyalty shares are not allowed, other unequal voting practices are allowed in Denmark, Germany, Netherlands and Spain.[4]

1.3 Preferred stock

Unlike common stock, *preferred stock* represents (technically) an equity interest in a firm but does not allow for voting rights. Preferred shareholders are compensated (via dividends) only when earnings have been generated. In other words, if the firm does not have sufficient earnings from which to pay the preferred stock dividends, it may omit the dividend without fear of being forced into bankruptcy. Usually, preferred stock dividends are cumulative, which means that dividends (current and previously omitted) are paid first to preferred shareholders before being paid on common stock. Preferred stock owners do not have a claim on company's profits beyond the stated fixed annual dividend. All profits above those needed to pay dividends on preferred stock belong to the owners of common stock.

Preferred stock is a *hybrid security* – a mix of equity and debt – because the dividend is fixed (resembling a bond's payment) and because it can be *called away* (or redeemed by the company) on a prespecified date. As a result of the latter, there is a possibility the call price could be higher than the price the investor paid initially.

Unlike bonds, preferred stock is not debt that must be repaid. Also, income from preferred stock gets preferential tax treatment, since qualified dividends may be taxed at a lower rate than bond interest. Preferred stock performs better when interest rates decline (just like bonds, which we will discuss in Chapter 9). Preferred stock is also more likely to earn a higher yield than common stock. And preferred stock has a par value, unlike common stock, that is, a value it's issued at and can typically be redeemed at, when the preferred shares mature. Short-term investors who cannot bear the fluctuations in stock prices may view preferred stock as a better investment despite having less potential for long-term growth.

Another feature of preferred stock is its favorable tax treatment. First, dividends on preferred stock are not tax-deductible, and this reduces their attractiveness as a source of capital to issuing firms. By contrast, there is an offsetting tax advantage to preferred stock for corporations buying preferred stock of another company. In this case, it pays taxes on only half (50%) of the dividends received. As a example, assume that a firm's tax bracket is 20%, and it receives $20,000 in preferred-dividend payments. The firm's tax liability is only on half of that income, $10,000, and so total taxes are $2,000 (= 0.20 * $10,000 = $2,000). Note that the firm's effective tax rate on preferred dividends is therefore 0.20 * 50% = 10%. In view of this appealing feature of preferred stock tax treatment, it is not surprising that most preferred stock is held by companies.

Finally, another unique characteristic of some types of preferred stock is they can be converted into a fixed number of common shares (known as *convertible preferred stock*). For example, if your preferred stock has a conversion ratio of 5, then if you decided to trade in a share of preferred stock, you would get 5 shares of common stock. Let us do some basic economic analysis to see when it would be profitable for an investor to exercise the option to convert his preferred stock into common stock. First, check the conversion price, which is found by dividing the par value of the preferred stock by the conversion ratio. If the resulting number is not equal or higher than the current common share price, you will lose money converting your stock. This is called the *conversion premium*. For example, if you bought a preferred share for $50, the conversion price would be $10 ($50/5). To see if a capital gain from the conversion arises, and thus be worthwhile for you to convert, the stock needs to be trading above that price. If it is trading at $8 per share, your $50 share provides you $40 of common stock. In this case, the conversion premium can be computed using the formula below:

$$\textit{Conversion premium} = [(\textit{par value} - (\textit{current common stock price} * \textit{conversion ratio})]/100 \quad (7.1)$$

Hence, the conversion premium is 10% (= $50 – ($8 * 5)]/100.

In general, a company's common shares need to trade above the conversion price threshold for the conversion to be worthwhile for the investor. Even if the common shares are trading close to $10, it may not be worth it to convert especially if the preferred shareholder could be giving up some fixed dividend and a higher claim on company assets in the event of liquidation. If the convertible preferred stock is trading at $50 and the company's common shares are trading at $9, then the conversion premium would be $5 [= $50 – ($9 * 5)] or 10% ($5/$50). If the common shares move up to $9.5, the conversion premium shrinks to $2.5 or 5%. As the common shares increase in price, conversion becomes more attractive.

A high/low conversion price makes preferred stock act like a bond/equity. Therefore, the conversion premium affects the price at which the convertible preferred stock trades.

2 Equity market characteristics

It is important to note that the stock market is not the same as the stock of a particular company. The stock market comprises all publicly traded companies and their stock prices. When someone talks about the stock market going up or down, they are referring to the overall trend of stock prices across all companies. The equity market is affected by a number of factors and exhibits various characteristics. The factors that influence the equity market are numerous and can be small or large events. In this and the next chapter, we will mention and analyze some of these factors and events. Let us begin with some obvious features of an equity market.

When one wishes to measure the equity market, one may refer to the companies' *market capitalization* (market cap, for short) or size referring to the market value calculated by multiplying the companies' number of shares outstanding by the current stock prices. The main categories are large-cap ($10 billion or more), mid-cap and small-cap (less than $2 billion) companies. Table 7.1 shows the top ten US companies with the largest capitalization value along with their current stock price and number of shares outstanding.

Another feature of an equity market is *volatility*, defined earlier (in the case of single stock). One could write a book about stock market volatility and hundreds

Table 7.1 Ten largest US companies by market capitalization, as of April 2024

Company (ticker)	*Market cap*	*Price*	*Shares outst.*
Microsoft (MSFT)	$3.017 trillion	$405.98	7.43 billion
Apple (AAPL)	$2.852 trillion	$184.72	15.41 billion
Nvidia (NVDA)	$2.203 trillion	$881.50	2.50 billion
Alphabet (GOOG)	$2.054 trillion	$167.22	5.62 billion
Amazon (AMZ)	$1.940 trillion	$186.45	10.42 billion
Meta Platforms (META)	$1.144 trillion	$451.02	2.19 billion
Berkshire Hathaway (BRK-B)	$867.69 billion	$400.92	1.31 billion
Eli Lilly (LLY)	$698.64 billion	$735.10	950.42 *million*
Broadcom (AVGO)	$592.02 billion	$1,278	463.41 *million*
Tesla (TSLA)	$574.75 billion	$180.22	3.19 billion

Source: YahooFinance

of academic papers have been written about it. Stock price volatility often means risk and guides an investor to estimate potential future fluctuations. For example, it helps define whether a stock is cyclical or counter-cyclical, and whether it is defensive or not. High volatility indicates that the market index is fluctuating rapidly and unpredictably, while low volatility suggests a more stable and predictable index price. Historical or actual or past volatility can be computed in a number of ways such as by usual variance of a series (and its standard deviation) formula, the intraday (high/low) change in the stock market index's price (also known as range volatility), using some econometric model (some of which we will learn in Chapter 12 and explain in detail in Part B of the online Appendix), based on the prices of options contracts on an underlying asset (known as implied volatility) or actual volatility experienced by an investment over a given period of time (known as *realized volatility*) and is calculated by measuring the actual changes in the price of the investment over that period. The formula to compute the sample variance, s^2, is as follows:

$$s^2 = \Sigma (r_t - r\text{-}bar)^2 / (n-1) \qquad (7.2)$$

where r_t is the returns, *r-bar* is the mean return and *n* the number of observations.

Figure 7.2 shows the Standard and Poor's 500 (S&P500) index's daily log-returns, from January 2014 to April 2024. As is evident, we can see the high ups and downs in the index's returns during various periods especially during the early 2020s. The observation that there are tranquil (such as 2016 and 2017) and turbulent periods signifies *volatility clustering* (or bunching), whereby high/small returns alternate with high/small returns of either sign (positive or negative). Further, this graph implies that the ups and downs are not symmetric, rather they are *asymmetric* since the extent (magnitude) of negative returns is greater than that of the positive returns. This asymmetry can be verified by the two descriptive statistics – skewness and kurtosis – contained in Table 7.2 for the S&P500 stock market index and the other three stocks (randomly selected from Table 7.1).[5]

Notice that all except Amazon's stock returns display negative skewness but all financial assets have excess (above 3, the normal distribution's value) kurtosis.

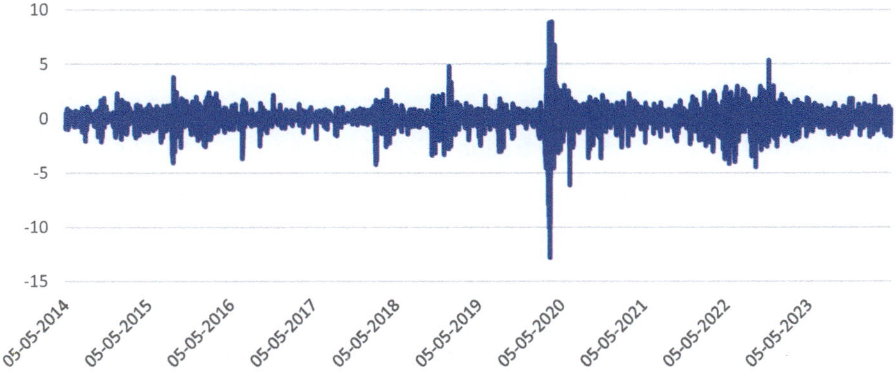

Figure 7.2 S&P500 index returns volatility, 2014:1–2024:4

Table 7.2 Descriptive statistics for the S&P500 index and three stocks

Index/stock	*Mean*	*Std Dev.*	*Skewness*	*Kurtosis*
S&P500	0.0390	1.1177	−0.8059	16.1991
MSFT	0.0431	0.7389	−0.1500	8.1976
AMZ	0.0429	0.8950	0.1224	5.9302
TSLA	0.0436	1.5195	−0.1434	4.5792

Notes: sample is from May 3, 214 to May 3, 2024; log-returns.

A *negative skewness* implies that the stock(s) experienced occasional but large negative returns and frequent small gains. Statistically speaking, a negatively (left-skewed) skewed distribution is one in which more values are concentrated on the right side (tail) of the distribution.

Kurtosis detects whether the tails of a given distribution contain extreme values. Distinguish between skewness, which is a measure of the symmetry of the distribution, and kurtosis, which determines the heaviness of the distribution tails. Financially speaking, kurtosis is a measure of financial risk and so, a large kurtosis value is associated with a high risk for an investment because it indicates high probabilities of extremely large and extremely small returns. By contrast, a small kurtosis value signals a moderate level of risk because the probabilities of extreme returns are relatively low. More specifically, financial assets exhibit *leptokurtosis*, which is positive excess kurtosis. The leptokurtic distribution shows heavy tails on either side, indicating large outliers (extreme values in returns). In conjunction with skewness, a leptokurtic distribution shows that the investment returns may be prone to extreme values on either side. Therefore, an investment whose returns follow a leptokurtic distribution is considered to be risky. Figure 7.3 displays such a situation for the stock market and Microsoft stock (with the normal distribution superimposed). As you can see, many values fall outside the normal curve (black curve).

Other general characteristics of the stock market refer to the way it functions. First, the market is made up of *organized* (or physical such as the New York Stock Exchange) and *over-the-counter* exchanges (or electronic such as the National Association of Securities Dealers Automated System, NASDAQ), where stocks are traded, traders on the exchanges are subject to the rules of the exchanges and trading on a stock exchange is restricted to stock brokers and traders who are members of the exchange. Individual investors must open up a brokerage account in order to participate in securities trading. Second, the price of each stock is determined by many factors but, in general, through the demand for and supply of shares by the companies and the market. Third, the stock market is a prime (or more precisely, a leading) economic indicator because it foretells what might happen in the economy. Share prices often reflect the overall economy and can be volatile as investors react to financial news and current events.

Fourth, the stock market is the dominant and ultimate place in the sense that in the long run it pays out. However, in the short-run, the market is dominated by

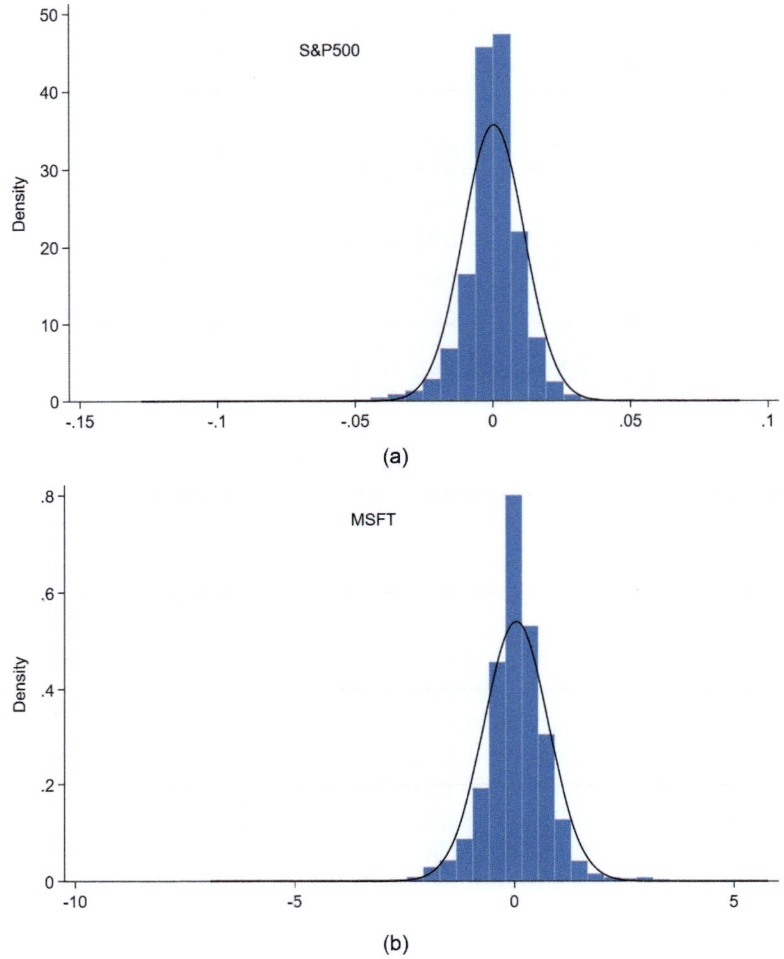

Figure 7.3 S&P500 and MSFT histograms with the normal distribution

Data source: *YahooFinance*

sentiments and many technical factors but in the long run, the fundamentals dominate. It punishes irrational investors and rewards smart investors. Put differently, rationality refers to making decisions based on facts and risk associated with it but not based on fads and emotions. The stock market has no emotions and does not care if you lose your wealth. It is necessary for an investor to have emotional stability in order to survive in the market. Fifth, the stock market rewards handsomely patient investors and in the words of Warren Buffett, "the stock market is a device for transferring money from the impatient to the patient" (investor).

Finally, the stock market ensures *transparency* and *continuity* via market makers. A *market maker* is a person who acts as the intermediary between buyers and sellers. This ensures there's always a marketplace for stocks on an exchange. Market makers can be brokers, dealers and designated market makers (DMM, see section 3 for more). A *dealer* is an intermediary who operates in the over-the-counter markets, whereas a *DMM* is one who operates in an organized exchange. Market makers buy and hold shares and continually list buy-and-sell quotations for shares so as to fulfill any order and thus ensure continuity in the market's trading process. The highest offer to buy shares listed from a market maker at any given time is known as the *bid*, and the lowest offered selling price is known as the *ask*. The difference between the two is called the *bid-ask spread*, which is a source of profit for the market maker. Because of market makers, you'll never have to wait to sell stocks at their full market value.

In general, the stock market is a continuously evolving and extremely complex dynamic system. It can be affected by small and large events alike because of the heterogeneity of investors and other participants. The stock market experiences advances (bull market) and declines (bear market). Stock markets move in tandem during certain periods and part during other periods. Many world equity markets are integrated, inter-dependent and exhibit persistence in the extent and nature of their reactions to various triggering local/global events such financial crises (1998 Russian crisis, 2007/8 global financial crisis), political shocks (Brexit/US elections), climate change and global health crisis (COVID-19). Stock markets are also characterized by *mean reversion*, which simply means that a stock's price cannot go up/down forever and at some point it will revert to its long-run average (that is, will go down/up).

3 How to invest in equity

To buy stocks, you need a broker or open up a brokerage account with a suitable financial institution. The broker can be a physical person at a financial institution such as a bank or an online one. Brokers typically charge trading commissions on stocks and have no account minimum to get started. Others, however, do not charge anything explicitly to trade. But you could also go with a trading app, especially if you want to trade occasionally via a mobile device. Then, once you have identified the stock you are interested in investing, get its ticker symbol (for example, MSFT if you want to buy Microsoft's stock) and enter an order with your broker. Your broker will then relay your order to the exchange where a market maker will sell you shares at the current market price. The shares are then delivered to your account.

There are two main types of order: market order or limit order. A *market order* lets you transact at whatever the best price currently (or at the moment you send in your order) but you will not have control over what price you transact at. A *limit order* permits you to transact only at the price you specify or better. If you can't get your price or better, the order won't execute. There are *limit-buy* (which

ROBO-INVESTING OR DIY?

Should you invest in an automated fashion or do-it- yourself (DIY)? When you sign up with a robo-advisor, you will need to fill out a questionnaire to find out your risk tolerance, goals and constraints. Robo-advisors may build your portfolio out of low-cost such as an equity index fund based on your answers to the questionnaire. You will pay the fees charged by those funds in addition to the robo-advisor's management fee.

If you prefer to pick your own investments, open up an online brokerage account and pick the stock(s). Many online stock brokers offer $0 account minimums and free trades. You need to do the research on stocks yourself, and manage your own portfolio, but you will skip some of the fees that can come with robo-advisors.

instructs the broker to buy shares if and when the shares may be obtained *at or below* a stipulated price) and *limit-sell* orders (which instruct the broker to sell if and when the stock price rises *above* a specified limit).

Brokers can be classified as discount or full-service. A *discount broker* allows you to buy and sell stocks online. It is like a self-service option for investors. Discount brokers tend to have low commissions and trading fees, and easy-to-use online trading platforms but do not offer investment advice. Most discount brokerages now offer their customers zero-commission stock trading. These companies make up for this loss of revenue from other sources such as payments from the exchanges for large quantities of orders and trading fees for other products like mutual funds. *Full-service brokerage* firms charge a fee or commission for the plethora of services they offer clients. They also provide investment advice or perform analysis on a client's behalf. Brokers may work for brokerage companies or operate as independent agents. A *robo-advisor* is an online investment platform that uses computer algorithms to implement trading strategies on behalf of its clients in an automated process. Because of this, they have very low entry fees and account balance requirements, most charge no annual fees, zero commissions, and more. The nearby *sidebar* contrasts robo-investing and do-it-yourself (DIY).

Note that there is a big difference between stock trading and stock investing. *Stock trading* refers to a short-term (perhaps days) activity whereby the person tries to take advantage of short-term events (at the company or in the market) to turn a short-term profit. This is known as active trading and can be categorized as speculation. *Day trading*, another variant of stock trading, refers to the buying and selling the same stock in a single day. Day traders care little about the inner workings of the businesses and try to make as much as possible in the next few minutes, hours or days based on daily price swings. *Investing* in stocks is a different matter altogether because it involves long-term endeavors, analyses and much more (we will discuss this in detail in Chapter 8).

There are several stock exchanges which you can follow to monitor the path of the stocks' prices you are interested in. Let us explain in brief some of them. The *New York Stock Exchange* (NYSE) index is another equity index that is widely followed. According to the NYSE's website,

> It's the world's most trusted equities exchange, with a market model designed to deliver optimal market quality to large corporates and investors... is the only exchange with a unique model which combines state-of-the-art technology with a human being at the point of sale — which together delivers the lowest levels of volatility and deepest pool of liquidity. During global events, turmoil and volatility, investors turn to the NYSE.[6]

NYSE operates four more equities exchanges (NYSE American, NYSE Arca Equities, NYSE national, and NYSE Chicago), each purpose-built to meet the needs of various institutional investors and offer greater choice to investors in how they trade. The NYSE's trading system is considered the most efficient one (relative to the over-the-counter or OTC market) because of the following reasons. First, at the heart of this market model is the DMM (formerly known as *Specialist*), who are obligated to maintain a fair and orderly market for their assigned securities. They facilitate price discovery during market openings, closings and during periods of substantial trading imbalances or instability. This personalized approach is instrumental to improving prices, dampening volatility, adding liquidity and enhancing value. Besides DMMs, the NYSE employs additional people to maintain their charge of a fair and orderly market. *Floor brokers* are employees of member firms who execute trades on the exchange floor on behalf of the firm's clients. *Supplemental liquidity providers* are electronic, high volume members incented to add liquidity on the NYSE.

The NASDAQ stock exchange is the most active stock trading venue in the US by volume, and ranked second behind NYSE. Unlike NYSE, the NASDAQ stock market conducts trades in the over-the-counter (OTC) system of trading. In NASDAQ, tech and information stocks are traded mostly. NASDAQ represents a serious competitor to NYSE because of its computerized system and relatively modern (FINRA, p. 2)[7]. It also offers lower listing fees than NYSE and includes some of the largest companies, such as technology giants Apple, Google, Amazon, and Microsoft. NASDAQ Inc. owns and operates two more stock exchanges in the US namely, the Philadelphia Stock Exchange and the Boston Stock Exchange, and seven European stock exchanges in Copenhagen, Helsinki, Stockholm, Iceland, Riga, Talliinn and Vilinius. The exchange's market cap was about $23.4 trillion, as of March 2024.

The *American Stock Exchange* (AMEX) was also a popular New York-based stock exchange, which was acquired in 2008 by NYSE American. Unlike the NASDAQ and NYSE, AMEX focuses on exchange-traded funds (ETFs). The AMEX was known as an exchange that introduced and traded new products and asset classes such as the options market in 1975 and ETFs in 1993. The AMEX also developed the reputation of listing companies that could not meet the strict requirements of the NYSE. Currently, a good portion of trading on the NYSE American is in small cap stocks. It operates as a fully electronic exchange.

There are more stock exchanges in the US and some of them are owned by NYSE or NASDAQ, the two main stock exchanges in the country. There are also some regional ones such as the *Miami Stock Exchange*, a regional exchange that offers stock, currency, and futures trading from its location of Miami, Florida, to Latin American and Caribbean countries; the *Philadelphia Stock Exchange*, the first stock exchange established in the US and the oldest stock exchange in the nation, headquartered in Philadelphia, PA, which is ow owned by Nasdaq; and the *National Stock Exchange*, an electronic stock exchange based in Jersey City, NJ, which was acquired by NYSE in 2018.

What about stock market indexes? There are several of them, some of which we mention below. Also, most major stock exchanges in the US have their own equity indices along with variants. The *Standard and Poor's 500 index* (S&P500) is a main stock market index tracking the stock performance of 500 of the largest companies listed on stock exchanges in the United States. It is one of the most commonly followed equity indices and is widely recognized as the leading indicator of US equity market performance. The index includes approximately 80% of the total market capitalization of US public companies, with an aggregate market cap of more than $43 trillion, as of April 30, 2024. This index is part of S&P Dow Jones Indices, a joint venture majority-owned by S&P Global, which comprises numerous financial indices, domestic and international alike. The S&P500 index is traditionally regarded as the main proxy for the equity market (as we will also see in Chapter 8). Furthermore, the S&P500 index has several variants representing sectors such as commodities, healthcare, consumer discretionary, communications, financial, energy and many more (see www.spglobal.com).

The NYSE also has several variants of its major equity index (the NYSE composite) such as the NYSE U.S. 100, energy, international commodity and many more (see www.ice.com). The Dow Jones (DJ) Averages are some of the world's oldest and most respected market indices. The *Dow Jones Industrial Average* (DJIA or Dow) is a major gauge of the US equity market but includes only 30 large companies. The index covers all industries with the exception of transportation and utilities, which are covered separately by the Dow Jones Transportation Average and Dow Jones Utility Average. The Dow's market cap, as of April 30, 2024, was approximately $40.1 billion. Some other DJ indices are the sustainability index (which tracks the performance of sustainability-driven companies around the world) and specialty indices (such as the economic stimulus and luxury indices).

How are the S&P500 and the DJIA indices constructed? Because DJIA corresponds to a portfolio that holds one share of each component stock, the investment in each company in that portfolio is proportional to the company's share price. Consequently, DJIA is a price-weighted average. The S&P500 index, by contrast, is called market (value)-weighted index because it reflects the relative weight of a company's capitalization value (the greater that market cap is, the more weight it has on the index's value). Let us exhibit the ways these two indices are constructed with an example (with hypothetical data). The data in Table 7.3 will be used for both indices.

In Table 7.3, we have the three companies, their beginning and ending stock prices and the number of shares outstanding. Then, the computed market values of each (share price *x* no. of shares) are displayed in the last two columns. To compute

Table 7.3 Hypothetical data to construct the S&P500 and DJIA indices

Company	*Beginning price*	*Ending price*	*No. of shares*	*Beginning value of stock*	*Ending value of stock*
ABC	$50	$55	20	$1000	$1100
DEF	$30	$35	10	$300	$350
GHI	$100	$85	2	$200	$190
Total				$1500	$1650

the *price-weighted index*, we first average the three companies' initial and final stock prices as follows.

Beginning price index: ($50 + $30 + $100)/3 = $60
Ending price index: ($55 + $35 + $85) / 3 = $58.33

The percentage change in the index is –2.78% (= –1.67/60). Notice that price-weighted averages give higher-priced shares more weight in determining the performance of the index. For example, although ABC increased by 10% and DEF by 16.67%, while GHI fell by only 15%, the index *dropped* in value. This is because the 10% increase in ABC and the 16.67% increase in DEF each represented a smaller price gain ($5 per share for each) than the 15% decrease in XYZ ($15 per share). Hence, it is concluded that a high-priced stock can dominate a price-weighted average.

To compute the market-(value-)weighted index, we use the last two columns of Table 7.3, where each company's stock value is computed and the market value totals. Setting the starting value of the index to 100, the index value would be 110 [= 100 x (1650/1500)]. This implies a 11% increase in the index from the previous period. The rate of return of the index equals the rate of return that would be earned by an investor holding a portfolio of all firms in the index in proportion to their market values (absent of dividends paid by those firms). So, the price-weighted index showed a decline, whereas the value-weighted index showed an increase. What is happening here? Simply, the price-weighted index placed more emphasis on the higher-priced stock (that of GHI company), while the value-weighted index placed more emphasis on the higher total market value stock (that of ABC company).

One important characteristic of both market-value-weighted and price-weighted indexes is that they reflect the returns to simple portfolio strategies. Specifically, if you buy shares in each firm in the index in proportion to its outstanding market value, your return will match that of the value-weighted index. Similarly, a price-weighted index tracks the returns on a portfolio comprised of an equal number of shares of each firm. To illustrate that, reconsider the data in Table 7.3 and add up the beginning and ending stock prices of each company to arrive at $180 (= $50 + $30 + $100) and $175 (= $55 + $35 + $85), respectively. The percentage change in the portfolio value would be exactly the same as in the index, namely –2.78% (=-5/180).

4 Stock market theories

A number of theories over time have been developed to explain the behavior of stock prices and, by extension, the stock market. Some of the theories are widely accepted today and some are not. Some theories have academic foundations and others reflect heuristics. Below, we briefly explain many of them with some basic examples.

4.1 The random walk theory

The *random walk theory* (RWT) posits that stock prices seem to follow a non-discernible trend or move (up and down) randomly over time. Consequently, any

Figure 7.4 Stock prices of Tesla corporation, 8/26/2019–8/26/2024
Data source: *YahooFinance*

attempt to predict stock prices would simply fail. Put differently, it would be impossible for traders to outperform (beat) the overall market other than by mere chance or luck. RWT was laid out by B. Malkiel (1973) in his influential book, titled "*A Random Walk Down Wall Street*".[8] Some other influential books/papers on the subject are those by P. Cootner (1964), titled "*The Random Character of Stock Market Prices*" and a series of academic papers by numerous financial economists. Look at Figure 7.4, where the daily stock prices of Tesla corporation are shown from August 26, 2019 to August 26, 2024. Pick a sharp rise in the stock price, say, October 19, 2021 starting with the price of $298 (where the arrow is). Could you have predicted that the stock price would further climb so rapidly during the full month of October (by almost 44%)? Consider the news around that day of reports of a large rental fleet order for Tesla's Model 3 sedans but Elon Musk took to Twitter to dispute that a contract had been signed! Would you take these conflicting reports are negative or positive? You would need more information, apparently, *ceteris paribus*. Musk had included some additional clarifications in his tweets which made shareholders confident about the deal, and that is why share prices soared (to a bit above $400). Would the average investor also interpret this as good news? In general, the point is that the evolution of stock prices is random and no one can predict their next value (unless illegal private/inside information is obtained). Hence, the random walk theory is the natural result of prices that always reflect all current information/knowledge, which gives rise to the efficient market hypothesis (see subsection 5.5).

4.2 The Dow theory

The *Dow theory* is made up of several beliefs, which include the idea that stock prices move in trends, which have distinct phases, and that volume is an important indicator of the strength of a trend. The theory was developed by Charles Dow, the founder of *Dow Jones & Co.* and *The Wall Street Journal* in the late 19th century. He believed that stock prices can be analyzed to predict future movements based on current trends relying on two broad indices, Industrials and Transports. An astute reader would immediately realize the limitation of this theory because of its reliance on just two sectors. The Dow theory runs contrary to the random walk theory. However, the Dow theory does not dispute the fact that stock prices are subject to random fluctuations in the short term, but it claims that long-run prices do reflect underlying economic trends and that these trends can be identified through technical analysis. We briefly present technical analysis (or chartism) in Chapter 8.

According to Dow theory, a bull market can be identified by the existence of higher highs and higher lows in the market. This reflects a positive signal for investors, as it indicates that the market is healthy and growing. In a bear market, investors should be cautious of any rally that occurs is likely to be a temporary correction rather than a sign of a trend reversal. The Dow theory contends that the primary trend cannot be easily reversed. As an example, if we observe *Industrials* (sector in the DJIA) to make a new relative high as did the *Transports*, then this would be considered a confirmation of the uptrend. Another requirement of the theory is that the movements of these two averages must confirm each other, along with their volumes. Note that these two indices have significantly changed since the theory was developed (more than a 100 years ago). Additionally, powerful market events such as Fed announcements about interest rate changes, inflation and unemployment news, geopolitical events and more may render the theory irrelevant.

4.3 The firm foundation theory

The *firm foundation* (or intrinsic value) *theory* posits that assets have an intrinsic value based on their present conditions and future potential.[9] The firm foundation proponent will calculate the stock's intrinsic value by summing the value of its present dividends and the estimated growth of its dividends in the future. Then, the investor will make buying and selling decisions based on the difference between the actual price of the stock and the intrinsic value. The theory also argues that the price will eventually revert to the intrinsic value. The problem is that forecasting the extent and duration of future growth (of the market as well as the stock's price and dividends) can be tricky.

The basic formula to find a stock's intrinsic value is as follows:

$$P_0 = \frac{P_1 + D_1}{1 + k} \tag{7.3}$$

where P_1 and D_1 are the stock's expected price and dividend (in the next period), respectively, and k is the discount rate or the investor's required rate of return. You can apply the capital asset pricing model (CAPM) to compute k (we first showed that in Chapter 2). You must also provide values for what you think the values of the stock's price and dividends would be in the next period. You could use a number of ways (formulas) starting with the simplest one, which is nothing else but the rate of growth of each magnitude based on the current and previous values. For example, if last month's stock price was \$50 and today is \$55, then the rate of growth would be 10% [=(55-50)/50]. You can apply the same with dividends. Another, more fundamental approach would be to use financial magnitudes of the company such as retained earnings and return on equity.

So, to apply the model in equation (7.3), assume that you expect the stock price to go to $60 next period (year) and the dividend to be $1.50. If you require a 10% rate of return from that stock, what would be its intrinsic value today, based on this particular information that you supplied? It would simply be $55.90 [= (60 + 1.5)/(1 + 0.10)]. If you observe today the stock's current price to be $52, what would you do? Buy more of it or sell it? This price, which is less than its intrinsic price, would provide better than a fair rate of return relative to its risk. Or, in the CAPM terminology, this stock is a positive-alpha stock, and you would want to buy more of it relative to a passive strategy. By contrast, if the intrinsic value turns out to be less than the current market price (of say, $58), you should buy less of it than under the passive strategy. It might even pay to go short on that stock!

4.4 The greater fool theory (castle-in-the-air theory)

The *castle-in-the-air theory* holds that an asset is only worth what someone else will pay for it. In other words, no asset has an intrinsic value that can be determined using fundamentals (earnings reports, valuation etc.) rather, the value of an asset is simply worth whatever the majority of investors think it is worth. Hence, it is a speculative strategy. The key to effectively applying this theory is timing, which means that the successful investor will buy an asset just before mass enthusiasm causes its price to rise and sell before that enthusiasm fades. It is also known as the *greater fool theory* and so, the less adjusted an investor is to the prevailing trends, the more likely he will have paid far more for it. Put differently, the investor will buy overvalued stocks and resell them at a higher price. He would think that there will always be a bigger fool (than he is) so as to pay for the stock at those high prices. Greater fool investors generally are impatient and are attracted to stocks that are popular or "hot".

A prime example of that was the 2007 subprime mortgage crisis, where people took mortgages in order to buy houses in hopes of finding a greater fool to whom they could sell the houses at a higher price and make substantial gains. While this may have worked for many years, eventually, the supply of fools began to dry up as more and more people began to see the reality that the houses were not worth that much or that they were (grossly) overpriced.

4.5 The efficient market hypothesis

This theory holds that stock prices reflect all available information and so there are fair (neither under- nor over-valued). The theory discards fundamental and technical analyses when investors employ them to properly value stocks and implies that no investor can beat the market in a consistent basis. We will not extend any further the theory here because it was first discussed in Chapter 2 and more will be said about in Chapter 8.

An interesting question arises at this point. How does marketing affect a company's stock price? Box 7.1 explains how. In general, long-lasting brands are valued by the market, generate loyal and repeat customers, are noticed by the investment community (retail and institutional investors) and rewarded at the end.

Box 7.1

How is a company's stock price affected by marketing activities?

ADVERTISING: Advertising boosts sales, company value, and enhances the company's brand name.

PROMOTIONAL CAMPAIGNS: Communicates new products or improvements in existing ones to the market, conveys information to consumers and investors.

OVERALL IMPACT: So, when all stakeholders notice the company's efforts to promote and inform their products or services, these activities have a positive image in the eyes of all people involved.

Test your understanding 1

1. a. If you buy 100 shares of HP stock, to what are you entitled?
   b. What is the most money you can make on this equity investment over the next year?
   c. If you paid $50 per share, what is the most money you could lose over the year?
2. If a stock's current market price is $50, what would be its intrinsic price if you expect a 10% increase in its price and dividend in the next period? Assume that you just received a $1.00 dividend and that you require a 12% rate of return from that stock. Would you buy more or less of it based on your valuation?
3. Assume that your preferred stock has a conversion ratio of 5. If you wanted to trade in a share of preferred stock, you would get 5 shares of common stock. If you bought a preferred share for $70, find the conversion price. If the stock trades at $10 per share, compute the conversion premium.

Solutions appear at the textbook's website.

5 Trends and developments in the stock market

The dynamic nature of the stock market implies that technological (artificial intelligence, blockchain technology, machine learning, to name but a few), institutional, policy-related and other news/developments must be internalized and exploited by an efficient stock market. We briefly discuss a few trends and developments that have impacted the stock market next.

5.1 Artificial intelligence

The widespread surge of *artificial intelligence* (AI), triggered by the rising popularity of ChatGPT, has substantially affected the stock market by creating trillions of dollars of market value. Giant tech companies such as Alphabet, Nvidia, Meta, Microsoft and many more have seen their stock prices sharply rise as a result of the implementation of AI technology. Analysts contend that AI will help boot worker productivity which, in turn, would further boost share prices. A recent study found that workers at a Fortune 500 software company who were given generative AI tools became 14% more productive and, for the least experienced workers, the gains approached 30%.[10] Even billionaire investors (such as Paul Tudor and Ed Yardeni) now say that the spectacular conventional popularity of AI has made them reevaluate their forecasts for inflation and the stock market. Of course, there is the negative side of AI as some significant financial players such as The Bank of America claim that stock rises due to AI may constitute a "baby bubble". You may also wish to read the SEC's report to the Congress on the impact of recent technological advancements in the securities market.[11]

In general, AI technology has reshaped the investment environment. For example, AI algorithms have the ability to analyze huge financial datasets in real time, thus enabling investors to make data-driven decisions. Further, this ability has enriched algorithmic trading (program trading by quantitative analysts) and made it easier to exploit market inefficiencies, capitalize on short-term price discrepancies and manage risks more efficiently. Finally, AI-driven investment platforms are now within reach by retail investors and these platforms can now create personalized investment portfolios based on individual investors' risk tolerance, financial goals and market conditions.[12]

The other side of the story is, as always, the negative side(s) of AI. For example, there is the danger that we may become overly reliant on AI models and as such, we may ignore certain aspects and overlook human judgment. In addition, since AI algorithms rely on historical data, keep in mind that they may not always capture the complex dynamics of the market or account for unexpected events. Keep in mind also that 'past returns do not guarantee future returns', a statement always made by mutual funds when selling products to investors. In the end, all AI systems can be susceptible to biases and so, investors beware. We discuss AI again in Chapter 13.

5.2 Institutional developments

A number of new developments such as technology, geopolitics, and social movements have forced institutional investors to rethink their investment strategies in the new era of world order. A recent report by McKinsey stated that global institutional investors are facing a new epoch marked by uncertainty, disruption, and radical shifts in public expectations of business and society. Global events such as the COVID-19 health crisis, wars in Europe and the Middle East, energy crisis, disruptions in global supply chains, inflation, and changing demographics are just a few signs of the current disorder.[13] As a result, these portfolio managers are revising their views on portfolio construction and management, as well as the responses of the stock market, so as to be pro-active and internalize global events.

A report by McKinsey mentioned that new regulations and rules by government authorities, after the 2007/8 global financial crisis, may not be in the best interest of pension funds, for long-term investments, but can benefit speculative funds such as hedge funds.[14] For example, regulators should not equate pension funds with hedge funds and apply the same policies as those for hedge funds. Pension funds are not as speculative as hedge funds and thus forcing them to put aside collateral (margin requirements or for specific asset classes imposed by Solvency II) for the same purposes as hedge funds are forced to do harms long-term investments and the individual investor. Other international bodies such as the Financial Stability Board and the World Economic Forum propose better and more efficient regulations for low-risk funds. They support the view that governments must ensure clear and stable regulations and begin eliminating fossil-fuel subsidies, higher prices for CO_2 emission rights, and increased support for research into cleaner energy, to make investments more attractive to pension funds and allow them to meet their sustainability goals.[15]

The SEC has approved a number of moves aimed at boosting transparency and fairness while increasing competition for individual investors' stock orders.[16] The proposals include requiring "retail stock orders to be sent to auctions before they are executed, a new standard for brokers to show they get the best possible executions for client orders, and lower trading increments and access fees on exchanges." Such interaction among brokers should enhance competition and result in better prices.

5.3 Other trends and developments

A recent study by Deloitte has identified a number of emerging trends in the global stock markets some of which are revenue pressures and margin squeezes (as mentioned in 6.2 subsection), operational inefficiencies, as older and traditional exchanges need to modernize to remain competitive, higher global regulatory activity, focusing on transparency, oversight, and risk management processes, continuous cybersecurity threats, and an evolving digital ecosystem incorporating blockchain, big data analytics, cloud, and other emerging technologies.[17]

We should also not forget the potent power of social media which have significantly affected the way stock markets operate and have altered the world of modern finance. The instant sharing of news, opinions, and real-time interactions on the social media platforms can have a big impact on market dynamics (if not already). A recent example of the role of social media is the situation with *GameStop*. Institutional investors were taken by surprise when a short squeeze on the company's stock was started by retail investors, who were grouped by *WallStreetBets* on the Reddit social media platform. GameStop's stock price experienced an outstanding increase as a result of this coordinated buying attempt. This case highlights the ability of virtual communities to question established market dynamics and the ensuing operation of market laws.

Finally, the environmental, social and governance (ESG) initiatives have been embedded in global stock markets. A 2023 survey by the *World Federation of Exchanges* (WFE) reported that the number of stock exchanges embracing this initiative has doubled and their ESG projects increased, that WFE members worked to create a global framework that individual exchanges can use to establish a *green offering* for listed equities, in order to ameliorate the flow of funding towards the financing of more sustainable economies, developed a comprehensive approach to measuring and managing their carbon footprint, taking into account the direct and indirect emissions impacts throughout their value chain, and the introduction of green bonds.[18]

Summary

We discussed the types of equity – common and preferred – along with private equity

- We explained several stock market characteristics including descriptive statistics such as skewness and kurtosis
- We also explained volatility and some of its versions
- We explored additional characteristics of the stock market such as the organized and over-the-counter types, some of its functions including transparency and continuity
- We showed how one can invest in equity including via a broker and some types of brokers
- We mentioned and briefly explained some important stock market exchanges such as the DJIA, NYSE, AMEX and NASDAQ
- We discussed the market makers in the stock exchanges such as dealers and specialists
- We explained how one can construct a stock market index
- We presented and briefly discussed some stock market theories including the random walk, the greater fool, the firm foundation and the efficient markets theories
- Finally, we mentioned a number of important trends and new developments in the stock market such as artificial intelligence, institutional and regulatory changes

Questions and problems

1. Below are three instances describing trading orders placed through a broker. Identify each one of them.
   a. You want to buy shares of ABC fast and believe the share price is approximately fair.
   b. For the same stock, you now think that its current price is too high given the firm's prospects. You aim at buying the shares at a price 5% lower than their current value.
   c. Now, you think that your shares of ABC are priced generously, and you plan to sell them. If the share price were to rise by $X, you are convinced that it would be greatly overpriced and want to sell it immediately.
2. A company receives dividends from preferred stock issued by another company in the amount of $10,000. If the receiving firm's tax rate on dividends is 18%, compute its taxes.
3. Below are actual values of Tesla corporation's stock (log)returns, for the 8/26/2019 – 8/26/2024 period.

   Kurtosis: 3.399

   Skewness : -0.1814

   Interpret the two statistics from the investor's point of view. Do you consider the stock risky?

4. What would mean for the stock market is stock price movements were predictable?
5. If you are a long-term investor, should you ever try to implement a greater fool strategy? Would GameStop and AMC stocks (known as *meme stocks*) be examples of this theory? Explain.
6. Explain what you would do, in terms of potential trading, if a stock's current price is $100 and you valued it at $80.
7. Which investment theory (from those we discussed here) was W. Buffett referring to when he called Bitcoin a 'rat poison squared'? Which investment theory does he believe in?
8. What is the relationship between the Dow Theory and technical analysis? Can the Dow Theory be applied to cryptocurrency exchanges?

Notes

1. https://www.investor.gov/introduction-investing/general-resources/news-alerts/alerts-bulletins/investor-bulletins/updated
2. https://www.investor.gov/introduction-investing/investing-basics/investment-products/private-investment-funds/private-equity
3. https://www.ft.com/content/2099d3c1–65ba-4c20-a50c-f730fd258f42
4. https://insights.issgovernance.com/posts/dual-class-share-structures-the-european-experience/
5. We discuss all descriptive statistics in Appendix A1.
6. https://www.nyse.com/markets/nyse
7. https://www.finra.org/sites/default/files/Corporate/p009760.pdf#:~:text=Based%20on%20Nasdaq%20and%20NYSE%20statistics%2C%20Nasdaq,an%20average%209%20out%20of%2010%20days.
8. At this point, it would instructive to read the book by Andrew Lo and Craig MacKinlay, *A Non-Random Walk Down Wall Street*, published in 1999. The authors claim that stock predictability is possible since markets are not completely random and that predictable components do exist in recent stock and bond returns.
9. Recall that we first encountered this notion in Chapter 2.
10. https://www.nber.org/papers/w31161
11. https://www.sec.gov/news/studies/techrp97.htm
12. https://www.forbes.com/councils/forbesbusinesscouncil/2023/07/17/how-artificial-intelligence-is-revolutionizing-stock-investing/
13. https://www.mckinsey.com/industries/private-capital/our-insights/performance-edge-investors-hone-their-strategies-for-a-new-era
14. https://www.mckinsey.com/capabilities/strategy-and-corporate-finance/our-insights/the-impact-of-regulation
15. https://www.mckinsey.com/capabilities/strategy-and-corporate-finance/our-insights/the-impact-of-regulation
16. https://www.reuters.com/markets/us/us-sec-vote-proposal-overhaul-stock-market-rules-2022-12-14/
17. https://www.deloitte.com/global/en/Industries/financial-services/perspectives/gx-future-of-global-securities-exchanges.html
18. https://wfe-live.lon1.cdn.digitaloceanspaces.com/org_focus/storage/media/WFE%20Annual%20Sustainability%20Survey%202024_v2_10%20year_pg_cb.pdf

References

Riddiough, Timothy J. and Li, Da (2023). Persistently Poor Performance in Private Equity Real Estate (May 3). http://dx.doi.org/10.2139/ssrn.4437519.

Tadesse, Solomon (2004). The Allocation and Monitoring Role of Capital Markets: Theory and International Evidence. *Journal of Financial and Quantitative Analysis* 39(4), 701–730.

Chapter 8

Analyzing and exploiting the equity market

Introduction

Analyzing the stock market is a daunting task! This endeavor involves various methods and tools to understand market trends, evaluate individual stocks, and make informed investment decisions. In this chapter we will offer an overview of the key approaches including fundamental and technical analyses, behavioral, econometric and more. Each approach has its own strengths and can be used independently or in combination with others for a more comprehensive analysis.

Next, we will show you how to interpret stock market movements and other equity-related news through the understanding the factors that influence price changes and how they reflect investor sentiment, economic conditions, and company performance. For example, we will explore how to assess different types of stock market movements such as short- and long-term movements, index movements and external events. Another important component of operating in the stock market is the ability to interpret financial news which is crucial for making informed investment decisions and understanding market dynamics. Examples of news we will be analyzing are company news, sector/industry news, macroeconomic and international news. In general, interpreting financial news requires a balanced approach that combines understanding the context, analyzing the potential impact, and applying critical thinking. By staying informed, using reliable sources, and maintaining a long-term perspective, you can make better investment decisions and navigate the complexities of the financial world.

Navigating the stock market successfully requires a clear plan, ongoing education, disciplined execution, and the ability to adapt to changing market conditions. By setting clear goals, diversifying your investments, and avoiding common pitfalls, you can increase your chances of achieving long-term financial success.

DOI: 10.4324/9781003677161-11

We will briefly present a guide to help you make informed decisions and navigate the complexities of the market. Some of the items that will be discussed are the investor's policy statement, apply diversification principles, avoid common pitfalls, leverage technology and manage risks.

Finally, we will show how you can use (exploit to your advantage) the stock market in an ethical, legal and prudent manner. Some ways we will present include spotting arbitrage opportunities, leveraging market inefficiencies, understanding investment strategies, and using available tools and information to maximize returns. While exploiting the stock market can lead to significant profits, it also involves risks. A balanced approach, informed by thorough research and disciplined execution, is essential for long-term success.

In discussing the above topics, we will include some important investment theories so you can better understand the consequences of your actions and guide you in your investment journeys in the stock market. In addition, we will present some basic individual investor investment strategies such as short sales, margin purchases, and dollar-cost averaging so as to get a better feel of the rewards and risks in investing in the stock market.

1 Analyzing the stock market

Conducting a thorough analysis of the stock market is nearly impossible. There is always an endless number of items to be looked at and evaluated and that would take an enormous amount of resources. The key is to identify which magnitudes are important and how to interpret them before making a decision. In this section, we will briefly present a number of economic and financial analyses that can be useful when trying to understand the stock market (to the extent possible, of course). We begin with fundamental analysis which includes examining macro, industry and firm magnitudes.

1.1 Fundamental analysis

The objective of *fundamental analysis* is to evaluate a business, its position within the industry and the general economic environment. To assess the financial condition of a firm (or its intrinsic value), one needs to conduct financial analysis. Such analysis comprises of the understanding of the four financial statements, construct and analyze key financial ratios and evaluate its management. The four financial statements are: the balance sheet, the income statement, the statement of cash flows, and retained earnings. Key financial ratios reflect the company's liquidity, profitability, asset management, debt management and market positions. Some representative ratios include the current ratio, the debt to equity, the price to earnings (P/E), the return to equity (ROE) and the return on assets (ROA) ratios. The idea is to assess the company's profitability, solvency and liquidity as well as view the company's trend over time and compare it with its peers (in the industry). Finally, it would be useful for an investor, or any other person interested in a company, to evaluate the competence and track record of its leadership team.

The evaluation of the company's industry reflects the company's competitive advantage, market share, and growth potential within that industry. There are several ways one can evaluate an industry. First, the investor can determine the industry's sensitivity to the business cycle. The *business cycle* is the irregular ups (advances) and downs (declines) in economic activity. It is composed of four distinct phases: expansion, peak, contraction and trough. The *expansion* phase is characterized by an increase in economic activity where many macro (GDP, incomes, inflation, employment etc.) and financial magnitudes (interest rates) go up. The transition point from expansion is the *peak*, or the transition from the end of an expansion to the start of a contraction. A *trough* occurs at the bottom of a recession just as the economy enters a recovery.

As the economy goes through different stages of the business cycle, the relative performance of different industries is expected to vary. For example, as the economy begins to recover from a contraction/recession, one would expect *cyclical industries*, those with above-average sensitivity to the state of the economy, to perform best. A prime example of a cyclical industry is durable goods such as vehicles. By contrast, *defensive industries* have little responsiveness to the business cycle. Defensive industries include food producers and processors and public utilities. These industries typically outperform others when the economy enters a recession.

Figure 8.1 plots the changes in retail sales (year over year) in total vehicle sales and grocery stores. Clearly, sales of cars, which is a durable good, fluctuate more widely than those of groceries. Vehicle sales jumped in 2021 (due to various reasons including the pandemic, low interest rates, fiscal stimulus package and more) but then fell steeply in subsequent years because of global supply-chain disruptions, high interest rates, inflation and other reasons. In contrast, sales growth in the grocery industry is relatively stable, with no years in which sales meaningfully decline. These patterns reflect the fact that vehicles is a discretionary good, whereas grocery products are staples and demand does not fall even during hard times.

Specifically, the sales of necessities show little sensitivity to business conditions but firms in heavy industries such as machine tools, steel and transportation are highly sensitive to the state of the economy. Another factor that determines how sensitive an industry is to the business cycle is operating leverage. Operating leverage refers to the division between fixed and variable costs. In general, the profits of firms with a lot of variable costs, relative to fixed costs, will be less sensitive to business conditions. The reason is that in economic declines, these firms can reduce

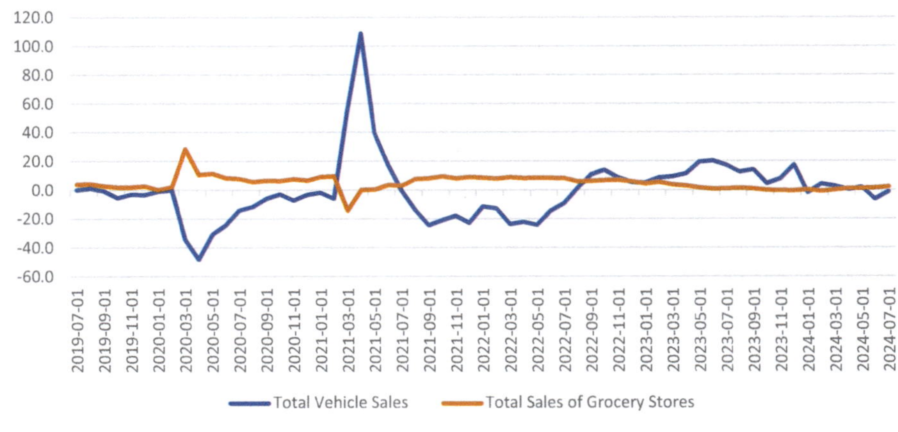

Figure 8.1 Cyclicality of industries
Source: Federal Reserve Economic Data

costs as output falls in response to falling sales. By contrast, profits of firms with high fixed costs will swing more widely with sales because such costs do not move to offset revenue variability. These are firms with high operating leverage and this can have large impacts on their profitability.

Finally, the conduct of general economic analysis entails the examination of macro magnitudes, financial magnitudes as well as economic policies. The usual macroeconomic magnitudes are gross domestic product (GDP), industrial production, unemployment, inflation, deficits and so on. In addition, one can look at the three major economic indicators namely, leading (which precede economic activity), coincident (which occur during a phase in the economy), and lagging (which trail economic activity). Examples of leading indicators are the stock market and manufacturers' orders, coincident indicators such as industrial production and manufacturing, and lagging indicators such as the average duration of unemployment and average prime rate charged by banks.

Finally, the investor performing fundamental analysis must go beyond the national economy and understand how foreign economies move and how they are likely to impact the domestic economy. That said, magnitudes such as stock and bond markets, interest rates, international trade, geopolitical events and more must be considered carefully.

1.2 Technical analysis

The other competing investment analysis to determine whether a stock's price is fair (correct), is technical analysis. The objective of *technical analysis* is to predict future price movements based on past market data, primarily stock price and volume. This is accomplished via inspecting charts (such as line, bar, candlestick and more) to visualize price movements and identify recurrent patterns and applying technical indicators like Moving Averages (MA), Relative Strength Index (RSI), and Bollinger Bands in an effort to identify trends and market momentum. For example, the spotting of chart patterns including head and shoulders, double tops/bottoms may indicate potential reversals or continuations in price trends, or support and resistance levels, which may determine key price levels where a stock has historically found support or faced resistance.

Let us present an example of the type of chart known as candlestick. Figure 8.2 shows IBM's stock prices for the period from 8/12/2024 to 8/30/2024. A *candlestick* is composed of three parts: the upper shadow, lower shadow and body. There are four data points in every candlestick: the open, high, low and close. The open is the very first trade for the specific period and the close is the very last trade for the period. The open and close are considered the body of the candle. The high is the highest priced trade and low is the lowest price trade for that period. The high is shown by a vertical line extending from the top of the body to the highest price called a shadow (or wick). The low of the candle is the lower shadow (or tail), is shown by a vertical line extending down from the body. Each candlestick represents a separate period of time. The body can have the color of green (representing a price gain) or red (reflecting a price loss). If the close is higher than the open, then the body is colored green, whereas if the open is higher than the close, then the body is colored red. Note also that if the real body is white (or green), it means the close was higher than the open, whereas when the real body is filled in or black (also red), it means the close was lower than the open.

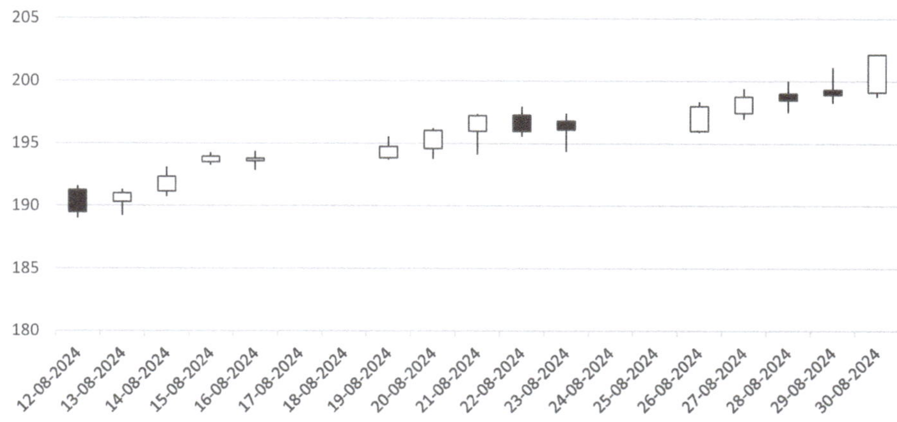

Figure 8.2 Candlestick chart for IBM stock
Data source: *YahooFinance*; Author created graph

Highlighting prices in color makes it easier for traders to view the difference between the open and close prices for that stock. Although price movements may sometimes appear random, to an untrained eye, they often form patterns traders use for analysis and/or trading purposes. These patterns are separated into bullish and bearish. Bullish patterns indicate that the price is likely to rise, while bearish patterns indicate that the price is likely to fall. In the candlestick chart shown in Figure 8.2, we observe both a bearish run, which develops in an uptrend when sellers outnumber buyers, and a bullish pattern, which takes place when buyers outpace sellers. The bearish action is reflected by a long black body engulfing a small white body and indicates that sellers are back in control and that the price could continue to decline. The bullish run is reflected by a long white body engulfing a small black body. So, since bulls have established some control, the price could head higher. Be careful, though, as candlestick patterns only represent tendencies in price movement, not guarantees.

Finally, there are some standard technical indicators (ratios) such as the trin statistic, the relative strength, and Bollinger bands. The *trin statistic* is defined as the ratio of average volume in declining issues to average volume in advancing issues. Ratios above 1 are considered bearish because the falling stocks would have higher average volume than the advancing stocks, indicating a net selling pressure. In the *relative strength approach*, the technical analyst (or chartist) compares stock performance over a recent period to performance of the market or other stocks in the same industry. A basic version of relative strength takes the ratio of the stock price to a market indicator. If the ratio increases over time, the stock is said to exhibit relative strength because its price performance has been better than that of the general market (such as the S&P500 index). If such strength continues for a long enough period of time it may offer profit opportunities.

Finally, the *Bollinger bands* are wrappers plotted at a standard deviation level above and below a simple moving average of the price. The bands adjust to volatility swings in the underlying price, that is they widen and narrow as the volatility of the underlying asset changes. Bollinger bands help determine whether prices are relatively high or low and are used in pairs, both upper and lower bands and in conjunction with a moving average. One can use the pair to confirm signals given with other indicators.

1.3 Quantitative analysis

Quantitative analysis employs statistical and mathematical models to analyze market data and predict price movements and optimize portfolios. The algorithms used are based on sophisticated and quite complex quantitative models. Such analysis also tests the performance of trading strategies on historical data to assess their effectiveness (what we call back-testing). Finally, risk management is practiced via tools such as Value at Risk (VaR) and Monte Carlo simulations.

Advances in quantitative analysis include Machine Learning (ML) and artificial intelligence (AI). The objective is to analyze vast amounts of data and identify patterns that human analysts might overlook. The main components of ML and AI include data mining, or the extraction of useful information from large datasets to predict market trends, algorithmic trading, that is, the implementation of automated trading strategies based on real-time data analysis, and predictive modeling, or the use ML models such as neural networks to forecast stock prices.

1.4 Sentiment analysis

Sentiment analysis seeks to gauge market sentiment by analyzing news, social media, and other sources of public opinion. The key components of it are news analysis (the monitoring of financial news and reports that could influence market perception), social media analysis (the tracking of sentiment on platforms like Twitter or Reddit for trends and public opinion) and surveys and indices (including the Consumer Confidence Index which reflects the overall mood of investors).

1.5 Behavioral analysis

BEHAVIORAL FINANCE and PROSPECT THEORY

The foundation of behavioral finance is that conventional financial theory ignores how people make decisions and that people make a difference.

The goal of *behavioral analysis* is to study investor behavior and psychological factors that can influence market movements. Investors suffer from hundreds of behavioral biases and informational processing errors as well as being confronted with several market anomalies. Errors in information processing can lead investors to misjudge the true probabilities of possible events or assets' rates of return. Examples of such errors include *overconfidence* (when people tend to overestimate the precision of their beliefs and tend to overestimate their abilities), *conservatism* (this bias means that investors are too slow in updating their beliefs in response to new evidence), and *representativeness* bias (which holds that people do not consider the size of a sample, or thinking that a small sample is just as representative of a population as a large one).

The term *behavioral biases* implies that individuals would tend to make less-than-fully-rational decisions using available information and this would lead them to incorrectly frame questions of the risk/return trade-offs. Examples of such biases include *framing* (depends on how one frames a situation, either in terms of gains or losses), *mental accounting* (which refers to a specific form of framing in which people separate certain accounts into being risky or conservative), *regret avoidance* (when individuals who make decisions that turned out wrong have more regret when that decision was more unconventional), *affect* (which is a feeling of good or bad that consumers/investors may attach to a potential purchase/stock), *confirmation bias* (when investors look for information that supports their prior opinion/decision and, as a result, they tend to mis-value the stocks of companies).

In general, behavioral biases would not matter for stock valuation (pricing) if rational arbitrageurs could fully exploit the errors of behavioral (biased) investors. Such investors would correct any misalignment of prices. Behavioral advocates argue, however, that in reality several factors limit the ability to profit from mispricing (this is known as *limits to arbitrage*). The nearby *sidebar* introduces behavioral finance and prospect theory which is a hot topic among business disciplines nowadays.

Economists now recognize that people may act irrationally. These irrationalities fall into two categories: first, that investors do not always process information correctly and second, that they often make inconsistent or systematically suboptimal decisions.

Prospect theory modifies the analytic description of rational risk-averse investors as treated in conventional financial theory.

Prospect theory posits two things: first, that a standard utility function is defined in terms of wealth and is concave, resulting in risk aversion, and second, that under loss aversion, the utility function is defined in terms of losses relative to current wealth. Further, it is also convex to the left of the origin, giving rise to risk-seeking behavior in terms of losses.

D. Kahneman and A. Tversky, Prospect Theory: An Analysis of Decision under Risk, *Econometrica* 47 (1979), 263–291.

1.6 Investment and portfolio analysis

In this analysis, the goal is to build and manage a diversified investment portfolio and maximize its return while controlling (or minimizing) risk. The two key elements of portfolio analysis are asset allocation and security selection. *Asset allocation* refers to the selection of major assets classes (equity, debt, commodities, etc.) that align with your IPS (your objectives, constraints and risk tolerance). *Security election* involves picking the right securities that would fulfill (hopefully) your investment goals. Related concepts around this analysis are *diversification* (the spreading of securities across various asset classes or sectors, geographic regions etc. to reduce risk), and *rebalancing* (the regular adjustment of your portfolio to maintain your desired asset allocation). In essence, investment and portfolio analysis involves the definition of your objectives (including your investment horizon), doing your homework by (applying a sensible investment analysis such as those we discussed above), keeping track (monitoring) of your investment portfolio and occasionally correcting if it goes off aim as well as adapting to market changes by adjusting your strategies.

2 Interpreting the stock market

Interpreting stock market movements involves understanding the factors that influence price changes and how they reflect investor sentiment, economic conditions, and company performance. Below, we offer a breakdown of how to interpret different types of stock market movements.

2.1 Short-term movements

Stock prices often move up or down on a daily basis due to supply and demand dynamics, influenced by news, earnings reports, or market sentiment. These short-term movements can be volatile and may not always reflect the long-term value of a company. Further, news, rumors, or changes in investor sentiment can cause rapid price changes. For example, positive news about a company can lead to a quick price increase, while negative news can cause a sharp drop. High trading volume often accompanies significant price movements and can indicate the strength of a trend. A price increase on high volume is typically seen as more sustainable than one on low volume.

2.2 Medium-term movements

Company quarterly earnings announcements can have a significant impact on stock prices. For example, if a company reports better-than-expected earnings, its stock price may rise; if earnings fall short, the price may drop. Data such as GDP growth, unemployment rates, and consumer confidence can influence stock prices over the medium term. Strong economic data generally leads to higher stock prices, while weak data can cause prices to fall. Stocks often move together within the same sector. For example, if the technology sector is performing well, individual tech stocks may rise, even if the broader market is not.

2.3 Long-term movements

Over the long term, a company's stock price tends to reflect its financial health, profitability, and growth prospects. Strong earnings growth, solid management, and a competitive advantage usually lead to sustained price increases. The stock market tends to move in cycles, following the broader economy. During periods of economic expansion, stocks typically rise, while during recessions, they often fall, as we mentioned earlier. Moreover, changes in interest rates set by central banks can have a long-term impact on stock prices. Lower interest rates tend to boost stock prices by making borrowing cheaper and encouraging investment, while higher rates can have the opposite effect. Finally, long-term trends, such as a bull market (rising prices) or a bear market (falling prices), can shape stock movements over years or even decades.

2.4 Market sentiment and behavioral factors

Extreme market sentiment, driven by fear or greed, can lead to significant market swings. For example, panic selling during a market crash can cause prices to plummet, while euphoria during a market bubble can drive prices to unsustainable highs. Investors often follow the crowd (herding behavior), which can amplify market movements. For instance, if a large number of investors start buying a particular stock, others may follow, driving the price up further, regardless of the stock's fundamentals. The stock market sometimes overreacts to news, leading to excessive price movements. These overreactions are often corrected over time as investors reassess the situation.

2.5 Interpreting stock index movements

Movements in major stock indices like the S&P 500, Dow Jones, or NASDAQ provide a snapshot of overall market performance. A rising index suggests broad market optimism, while a falling index indicates widespread concern. Investors may rotate between sectors (e.g., from technology to utilities) based on economic conditions or market sentiment. Observing these rotations can provide insight into broader market trends. Confidence in the stock market can also push up demand for individual stocks. If investors believe that stocks are a good investment, either because valuations are good or because the stock market has been trending upwards, higher demand for stocks can push up prices across the board.

2.6 The role of external events

Geopolitical events such as political instability, wars, or trade disputes can cause significant market volatility. For example, the announcement of trade tariffs or sanctions can lead to sudden drops in stock prices. Events like earthquakes, hurricanes, or pandemics can disrupt markets, especially if they affect major industries or economic hubs. Finally, new regulations or changes in government policy (e.g., tax reforms, environmental regulations) can have a profound impact on specific sectors and the broader market.

What is likely to be the behavior and views of "Gen Z" vs. the "millennials"? Gen Z, or people born from 1995 to 2010, is attuned to the digital age. Literally, after a few years after birth, they have been exposed to the internet, to social networks, and to mobile systems. In contrast, the millennials (the previous generation) enjoyed periods of economic prosperity and focused on the self. Millennials are said to be more idealistic, more confrontational, and less willing to accept diverse points of view. Members of Gen Z make decisions and relate to institutions in a highly analytical and realistic way. Armed with technological advances, this generation is seriously transforming the consumer and investment landscapes in ways that permeate all walks of life. They tend use information to comprehensively evaluate products and services by companies and seek employment even on a part-time basis. They tend to deviate from the established norms of social groups meaning that they are more likely to buy personalized items (and sometimes pay a premium for these). Hence, companies must now cater to the new consumption group and adjust their sales and production models. All these, of course, would have significant implications for their profits and stock prices.

Finally, what are some practical tips for interpreting the general stock market's movements? First, always consider the broader context when interpreting market movements. A single day's price change might be part of a larger trend or simply a reaction to short-term news. Second, avoid overreacting. Market movements can be unpredictable in the short term. Avoid making hasty decisions based solely on recent price changes. Third, diversifying your investments across different sectors and asset classes can help mitigate the impact of market volatility. Fourth, keep up with economic news, earnings reports, and geopolitical events, as these can provide valuable context for understanding market movements. Finally, use several tools and combine fundamental, technical, and sentiment analysis to get a more comprehensive view of what's driving market movements. By understanding the factors that influence stock market movements, you can better interpret changes in stock prices and make more informed investment decisions. So, do not fall for tips such as "this is a hot stock", "now it's the time to enter the stock market", "how to become a millionaire" and the like before you do your homework!

We end this section with this question: when an investor studies the stock market would it also be instructive to link it to a company's stock price movements? This is so because a company's actions, especially if it is a huge company, may affect the company itself as well as the general market. Recall from your Principles of Management course the functions of a manager. As a refresher, these are: planning, organizing (and staffing), leading, controlling and decision-making. You may wonder how these functions relate to a company's stock-market activity including the company's stock price. Box 8.1 explains these linkages. In general, managers play a critical role in shaping stock market activities through their strategic planning, leadership, financial controls, and investment decisions. Investors closely analyze management effectiveness, corporate strategies, and risk management to make informed stock market decisions.

Box 8.1

How do a manager's functions affect stock-market activities?

PLANNING: Managers set long-range plans such as corporate strategy, growth targets and make financial projections all of which affect stock valuations.

ORGANIZING: Managers decide how to allocate capital (resources), optimize their company's operations, and establish organizational efficiency which, in turn, influence profitability, costs and shareholder returns.

LEADING: A strong and reputable manager nurtures market trust, fosters innovation and enhances long-term value creation, which play a key role in his/her company's stock performance.

CONTROLLING: Managers monitor revenues, debt levels, and overall company operational efficiency along with transparency and effective risk management practices, all of which affect investor confidence.

DECISION-MAKING: Managers make key investment, merger and acquisition decisions that determine their company's position in the market and all these activities directly affect market share and investor perception.

Test your understanding 1

1. How do fundamental investors act when they observe a discrepancy between a stock's intrinsic price and its market price?
2. Why do some investors have the propensity to sell winner stocks and buy loser stocks too soon? Which theory explains this bias?
3. What is herding behavior and its implications for the stock market?

Solutions appear at the textbook's website.

3 Exploiting the stock market

In order to take advantage of the opportunities offered by the stock market, always within the legal and ethical contexts, you should be able to leverage market inefficiencies, understand investment strategies, and use all available tools and information to maximize returns. Here are some ways an investor can potentially exploit the stock market.

3.1 Finding arbitrage opportunities

Arbitrage involves the simultaneous buying and selling of the same asset in different markets to profit from price discrepancies without risk. Arbitrage typically requires quick execution, significant capital, and sophisticated trading systems to profit from small price differences. There are several types of arbitrage. *Spatial arbitrage* involves exploiting price differences of the same stock on different exchanges, *temporal arbitrage* entails taking advantage of price differences over time, such as during the closing of one market and the opening of another, *merger arbitrage* lies on betting on the successful completion of a merger or acquisition, where the stock of the target company might trade below the acquisition price.

We will mention one strategy (in subsection 3.6) on *statistical arbitrage*, which is a version of a market-neutral strategy. That strategy is pairs trading. Statistical arbitrage differs from pure arbitrage defined above in that it does not exploit risk-free positions but uses quantitative and often automated trading systems that seek out many temporary and modest price misalignments. Hence, the investor can take relatively small positions in many of these opportunities, and the law of averages would make the probability of profiting from all these bets very highly likely. Statistical arbitrage involves trading in hundreds of securities any given day with holding periods that can be measured in minutes if not seconds!

3.2 Exploiting market over- and under-reactions

Market over/under-reactions occur when prices move excessively/slowly in response to news, creating opportunities for investors who can correctly interpret the news. A number of strategies can be applied in these situations. You can continue the movement, bullish or bearish, and so engage in momentum trading.

Momentum investing involves buying stocks that have shown an upward price trend and selling those with downward trends. You could identify and invest in stocks that are trending upward, expecting the trend to continue in the short to medium term or invest in stocks that have outperformed their peers over a specific period, based on the idea that they will continue to outperform (the relative strength approach we mentioned earlier). Momentum investing relates to your microeconomics concept of "*the bandwagon effect*", whereby consumers simply jump on the opportunity to do whatever others do.

In contrast to momentum trading, you could buy stocks that have been excessively sold off due to temporary bad news or panic, or sell stocks that have surged on overly optimistic news. Further, you could trade on the idea that prices and returns eventually revert to their long-term average (the so-called *mean-reversion* principle). For example, buying undervalued stocks that are expected to return to their historical price range. All above strategies require patience, research, and the ability to withstand short-term volatility.

3.3 Value investing

Value investing involves buying stocks that are undervalued compared to their intrinsic value. For example, look for stocks that are trading at a significant discount to their book value, earnings, or cash flow and/or invest in companies with low price-to-earnings (P/E) ratios compared to their industry or historical averages, assuming the market has mispriced them. Ardent proponents of value investing include Benjamin Graham (the father of value investing), Warren Buffett, John Bogle, Charlie Munger, Peter Lynch, and Kenneth Fisher. The premises upon which value investing rests are that investors should focus on the business (analyzing the fundamentals of the company and not its stock price), that investors should believe in the company they wish to invest in, and understand its management principles (which should be good, ethical and strong).

3.4 Growth investing

Growth investing focuses on companies expected to grow at an above-average rate compared to other companies and/or the market. The idea here is to focus on industries with strong growth potential, such as technology, renewable energy, or biotechnology. Also, to identify and invest in companies that are in the early stages of their growth cycle but have a clear competitive advantage. Growth investors prefer capital appreciation rather than the steady streams of dividends (see subsection 3.5). Further, understanding the life-cycle of companies is key to practicing successful growth investing. The company *life-cycle hypothesis* states that companies go through four stages over their lives: start-up, consolidation, maturity and decline. So, in the start-up phase, business may be growing at a substantial pace, generating impressive gains in revenue and profits. At this stage, the company typically reinvests profits back into the business to drive further growth, rather than paying them out as dividends. Over time, as the company begins to mature, growth in revenue and profit slows and once it becomes fully mature, its growth slows further. At this point, most of these companies begin to distribute profits to investors in the form of dividends because investment opportunities available in their markets begin to diminish.

3.5 Dividend Investing

Dividend investing involves focusing on companies that regularly pay dividends, providing a steady income stream. So, you could invest in companies that have a long history of consistently increasing dividends (known as *dividend aristocrats*) or seek out stocks with a high dividend yield, but ensure the yield is sustainable based on the company's earnings and cash flow. This approach is suited for income-focused investors and can be less risky than growth investing. An alternative way that shareholders can get cash from the company (beyond the dividend) is when the company engages in *share repurchases* (that is, buying back some of its shares for existing shareholders in exchange for cash).

The dividend investing strategy is also known as *income investing* since investors choose stocks that provide regular income through dividends. This strategy is ideal for investors seeking steady returns with lower risk. Related to this is index investing, which entails investing in index funds or ETFs that track a market index. This strategy offers diversification and typically lower fees, making it suitable for long-term investors. Finally, an interesting strategy for retail investors is the *dollar-cost averaging* strategy. It involves regularly investing a fixed amount of money, regardless of market conditions. This strategy reduces the impact of market volatility and averages out your purchase price over time. Let us explain it in some detail with an example.

3.5.1 The dollar-cost averaging strategy

Dollar-cost averaging is the practice of investing a fixed dollar amount on a regular basis, regardless of the share price. It is designed to make you a disciplined investor and mind the costs. Let us assume that you invest $100 every month. When the market is up, your $100 will buy fewer shares, but when the market is down, you will buy more. Over time, this strategy could lower your average cost per share – compared to what you would have paid if you'd bought all your shares at once when they were more expensive than the average. Here's an example (see Table 8.1).

As you can see, you took advantage of the share's price decline in Month 3, significantly reducing the average cost per share. Despite paying $8 or more per

Table 8.1 Dollar-cost averaging example

Period	*Amount*	*Share price*	*Shares bought*
Month 1	$100	$10	20
Month 2	$100	$10	20
Month 3	$100	$7	50
Month 4	$100	$8	30
Month 5	$100	$10	20
Total invested:	**Average cost/share:**	**Total shares bought:**	
$500	$9.00	140	

share in four out of the five months, the average cost per share came out to \$9.00, and the investor was able to purchase a total of 140 shares. If, however, you had all \$500 been invested in Month 1, the average cost per share would have been \$10 for a total of 50 shares!

3.6 Other ways to exploit the stock market

The investor could exploit stocks' seasonal patterns (calendar effects) as some stocks or sectors tend to perform better at certain times of the year. For example, historically, small-cap stocks tend to outperform in January, possibly due to tax-loss harvesting in December and reinvestment in January (this the well-known market anomaly of *the January effect*). Another strategy is the "sell it in May and go away", which implies that stocks tend to perform better from November to April compared to May to October. Other well-known market anomalies are irregularities or patterns that deviate from the standard financial theories. For example, the *small-cap effect* (which entails investing in small-cap stocks, which have historically outperformed large-cap stocks over the long term) and the *value vs. growth* anomaly (which suggests that during certain market conditions, value stocks outperform growth stocks or vice versa, presenting opportunities for strategic shifts).

You could use financial tools such as derivatives (options and futures). These instruments allow investors to hedge, speculate, or enhance returns using leverage. For example, one could set up covered calls (or sell call options on stocks you already own), protective puts (by buying put options on your holdings) or even straddles and strangles (to speculate on high volatility by buying both call and put options on the same stock). Note, however, that such sophisticated strategies require a deep understanding of options pricing, risk management, and market conditions.

An investor (meaning an institutional investor, not a retail investor) could also apply algorithmic and high-frequency trading (HFT). *Algorithmic trading* involves using computer algorithms to execute trades at high speeds based on predefined criteria. Some strategies include *statistical arbitrage* (the use of algorithms to exploit small price discrepancies across different markets or securities), *market making* (the provision of liquidity by buying and selling large volumes of securities, earning the bid-ask spread) and *HFT* (by executing a large number of orders (blocks) at very fast speeds to take advantage of small price movements). Such strategies, obviously, require advanced technology, data analysis, and substantial capital investment.

One more recent trading strategy is the use of dark pools. Block trading is no longer desirable as many investors seek anonymity in their trading activities. *Dark pools* are private trading systems in which participants can trade blocks of securities without being identified. Hence, limit orders are not visible to the general public as they would be on a conventional stock exchange. Typically, dark pools accept unpriced orders and simply match buyers with sellers at the midpoint of the bid and ask prices conveyed on other markets. Because dark pools do not contribute to price discovery (assist the price to reflect all publicly available information about the security), they have been criticized as worsening the fragmentation of markets.

Finally, you could implement strategies based on behavioral biases to affect market prices (see subsection 2.4). Some strategies include *herd(ing) behavior* (the recognition of when the market is moving based on herd mentality and take the opposite position if it's unjustified), the use of indicators such as the *fear and greed index* (developed by *CNN Business*) which measures market sentiment to identify when the market is overly fearful – a buying opportunity – or greedy – a selling opportunity.[1] This index is based on seven underlying indicators (a few of which are stock prices breadth, strength and momentum, put and call options, market volatility and others). Needless to say, that applying these strategies necessitates deep insights into investor psychology and the ability to remain objective (cool) under pressure. It is certain that you encountered the notion of herding or crowd investing in a different context and course in your business studies. Specifically, such behavior is explained in microeconomics within the context of positive *network externalities* where consumers follow the trend and buy things that others buy (whether they need them or not).

3.7 Some actual examples

These examples are real (and drawn from the financial headlines on September 3, 2024) and seek your decision as to whether to buy the stock or not. The situation is in *italics* and the suggested answers below.

1. *Nvidia fell sharply below the 50-day moving average on Tuesday. Volume was tracking 17% higher than average. Earnings have moved the stock in 2023 and 2024. Shares fell 6.4% on Thursday after earnings even though the AI chip leader beat analyst estimates. Should you be buying or selling Nvidia stock now?*
   It is not easy to tell whether you should buy or sell the stock now. Chart signals and several technical measures can help you assess whether Nvidia stock is a buy now. Good earnings are excellent proof of why fundamental performance should be one of the guides of your investing methodology. Nvidia fell below its 50-day moving average in higher volume on Tuesday and that is a sell signal. The stock has to retake that level and build out its base before it becomes a buy.
2. *Investment management company T. Rowe Price has raised its dividend in all four recessions and for the last 38 years. T. Rowe Price pumps out cash profits and has few expenses. Shares trade at a forward P/E ratio of 12 today, below its decade average of 15. Analysts believe the company will still grow earnings by almost 7% annually over the long term. The stock's valuation is pretty reasonable for that expected growth. Would you buy the stock?*
   There are two possible outcomes. First, that the company could fall short of growth, and investors would get a high-yield dividend stock that will likely continue its payout. That would be a worst-case scenario. Or, that the stock could outperform the market if the business delivers as expected. This, heads or tails you win, investment scenario makes the stock a buy today.
3. *Super Micro Computer has been one of the biggest beneficiaries of the generative artificial intelligence (GenAI) boom. However, after rising by over 2,200% over the last five years, the company's share price growth began to stall. Super Micro's gross margin fell to 11.2% compared to 17% this time last year. In addition, the company is subjected to scrutiny about accounting manipulation, self-dealing, and sanctions evasion related to potential exports to Russia.*

In 2020, the company was fined $17.5 million by the SEC for accounting violations and improperly reporting revenue.

The company is not valued where one would expect for a tech company in a super-hot industry like GenAI. And the market might be pricing in the possibility that some of the allegations are true. Despite the huge rise in its stock price, one should consider avoiding Super Micro stock until more information becomes available.

4 Some investment and portfolio theories and strategies

We will discuss a number of concepts in this section on investment and portfolio theories as well as three simple investment strategies that an individual investor can undertake. We begin with the three investment strategies, margin purchases, short sales and pairs trading.

4.1 Some investment strategies

4.1.1 Purchases on margin

In a nutshell, ***buying stocks on margin*** means the investor borrows part of the purchase price of the stock from the broker in addition to his own money (the margin). In other words, you leverage the transaction. The broker, in turn, borrows money from banks at the *call money rate* to finance these purchases and then charge their clients that rate plus a service charge. An investor can engage in such a strategy if they are optimistic about the prospects on the stock, that is, they expect a big appreciation in the stock's price in the near future. Margin purchases are regulated by the Fed, which sets the so-called 50% *margin requirement,* and the SEC, which oversees the whole process. The margin requirement simply implies that the maximum amount the investor can borrow from the broker should be equal (or less) to their own amount (margin). So, for example, if the investor has $5,000 of own funds, they can borrow as much as $5,000, for a total of $10,000 for the investment (hence, $5,000/$10,000 is 0.50 or 50%).

To guard against the possibility that the investor's account falls below $5,000 (the loan amount), due to a decline (as opposed to an increase) in the stock's price, the broker sets a *maintenance margin*. If the initial (percentage) margin (of 50%) falls below the maintenance level (say, 30%), the broker will issue a *margin call*, which requires the investor to add new cash or securities to his margin account. If the investor does not respond, then the broker will sell securities from the account to pay off enough of the loan to restore the percentage margin to a suitable level. Let us work with an example.

Assume you contribute $6,000 toward the purchase of $10,000 worth of stock (100 shares at $100 each) and borrow the remaining $4,000 from your broker. The initial percentage margin is (equity in account/value of stock) or $6,000/$10,000 = 60%. This is acceptable because it is above the 50% margin requirement. Now, suppose your broker has a maintenance margin of 35%. How far could the stock price *fall* before you get a margin call? Denote as P be the price of the stock.

Therefore, the value of your 100 shares is 100P, and the equity in your margin account is 100P–4,000. The percentage margin is (100P – $4,000)/100P. Setting this equation equal to the maintenance margin of 0.35 and solving for P, we get a price of $61.53. If the price of the stock were to fall below $61.53 per share, you would get a margin call.

But why do investors buy securities on margin? They do so when they wish to achieve greater upside potential. This, however, comes with higher risks. Let us illustrate that so you can understand why margin purchases are said to be a "double-edged sword". Assume that you expect the stock's price to go up by 30% during the next year. Obviously, if you had invested your own money of $10,000 to buy those shares your expected return would have been 30%. But now, you wish to borrow another $10,000 from your broker so you can invest $20,000 and exploit even further that stock's potential. If a share costs $100, now you can buy 200 shares. If your broker charges you a 10% interest rate on the margin loan, what will your rate of return be if the stock price indeed increases 30% by the end of the year?

The 200 shares now will be worth $26,000 (= $130 x 200 shares). Paying off $11,000 of principal and interest on the margin loan leaves $15,000 (= $26,000 – $11,000). The rate of return will be 50% [= ($15,000 – $10,000)/$10,000]. Hence, you managed to magnify a 30% rise in the stock's price into a hefty 50% rate of return on your $10,000 investment! But what if the price actually fell by 30%? What would have been your rate of return in this case? In that case, the 200 shares will be worth $14,000 (= $70 x 200 shares), and you are left with $3,000 after paying off the $11,000 of principal and interest on the loan. The result is a big negative return of 70% [= ($3,000 – $10,000)/$10,000]. Notice also that the -70% return is much greater (in absolute sense) than the gain of 50%. That is why margin purchases are called a double-edged sword!

4.1.2 Short sales

The question now is this: How can you profit from a stock's price decline? From a short sale! A *short sale* permits investors to profit from a decline in a security's price. What is happening is this. You can borrow a share of stock from your broker today and immediately sell it in the market. Later, you must purchase a share of the same stock, when its price has sufficiently gone down, in order to return it to your broker (that is, to cover the short position). If the price decline was to your satisfaction (i.e., to generate a profit for you), then you were a successful short seller. Keep in mind that if the stock paid a dividend while shorted, you are responsible for that payment (to the lender or broker). Let us illustrate the strategy with a simple example.

Suppose you are bearish on ABC stock, whose current market price is $100 per share, expecting it to fall by 30%. You instruct your broker to sell short 100 shares. The $10,000 cash proceeds from the short sale are credited to your account. Your broker has a 50% margin requirement on short sales, which actually means that you must have collateral (cash or securities) in your account worth at least $50,000 that can serve as margin on the short sale. Let us say that you have that amount (of $50,000) in Treasury bills. Now, assume that you are right and ABC stock falls to $70 per share. To cover the short sale, you buy 100 shares to replace the ones you borrowed. Because the shares now sell for $70, the purchase costs only \$7,000. Since your account was credited for \$10,000, your (gross) profit is \$3,000 (which equals the decline in the share price *times* the number of shares sold short).

However, just like investors who purchase stock on margin, the short-seller must also be concerned about margin calls. By analogy, if the stock price rises, the margin in the account will fall and if it falls to the broker's maintenance level, the broker will give you a margin call. Suppose your broker has a maintenance margin of 30% on short sales. How much can the price of ABC stock *rise* before you get a margin call? Let P be the price of the stock. The value of the shares you must pay back is 100P and the equity in your account is \$15,000 – 100P. Your short position margin ratio would then be the application of the same formula we learned in margin purchases: *Equity in the account /Value of stock*. Therefore, setting this formula equal to 0.30, and plugging in the numbers, (15,000 – 100P)/100P, we get a price, P, of \$11.

4.1.3 Pairs trading

In subsection 3.1, we mentioned statistical arbitrage. One example of a statistical arbitrage strategy is *pairs trading*, where stocks are paired up based on an analysis of either fundamental similarities or betas (market exposures). The idea is to use statistics in order to pair up similar companies whose returns are highly correlated but where one company seems to be priced more aggressively than the other. Put differently, establish a market-neutral position by buying the relatively cheap firm (long position) and selling the expensive one (short position). Pairs trading is by no means a successful trading strategy and will have its ups and downs. Also, one needs to be very good with statistics and econometrics in order to identify the security pairs ranging from correlation, cointegration, copulas etc., analyses, to name a few.

Another way to see the power of pairs trading is that it can be implemented within and between asset classes, giving you the ability to capitalize on changes in relative values across global markets. Some of the popular types of pairs trades include stocks, indices and commodities. As one example, suppose that you have different opinions on the Eurozone countries. Then, you could place pairs trades on indices within the area such as the DAX, CAC, or other key indices. Further, if you have a different opinion between the UK and the Eurozone, then you can pair a European index against the FTSE, or even trading the foreign exchange pair Euro/British pound (EUR/GBP).

Let us say that you decide to open a long position for commodity X and short an equivalent amount of commodity Y in a pairs trade. Your returns would vary depending on how the two commodities perform relative to each other. Let us briefly explore some of them. So, if both commodities move up or down the same amount, the two positions hedge each other. If X moves up 10% and Y by 8%, the 10% gain on X would be partially offset by the 8% loss on Y, leaving you with a 2% gain. A loss would occur if the reverse took place. If both commodities fall by differing amounts, you would have a gain (if X fell by less than Y fell) or a loss (if X fell by more than Y fell). Now, if both commodities move in your way, where X advances by say, 10%, while Y declines by, say 8%, then the 10% gain on X's position, coupled with the 8% gain on the Y's short position, would leave you with an 18% return on the pairs trade. Finally, if both sides move against you, with X falls while Y rises (the opposite of what you expect for each commodity), and X's fall is greater than Y's rise, then you would end up with a loss on that trade!

4.2 The efficient market hypothesis

In Chapter 2, we briefly presented the efficient market hypothesis (EMH), and in Chapter 5, the random walk hypothesis. In this section, we cast a different look at EMH so we can provide more insights on how you can understand and use the stock market.

Recall that market efficiency refers to informational efficiency or how the stock market responds to new information. Here's an actual example. On September 5, 2022, CVS Health and Signify Health companies have entered into a final agreement under which CVS Health would acquire Signify Health for $30.50 per share in cash, which represented a premium over the prevailing current market prices.[2] If we plotted the price of the CVS stock a few months prior and after the acquisition announcement, we would have a graph like that shown in Figure 8.3. The vertical line in the graph shows the date of the announcement. So, the announcement of the merger action should cause the stock price to jump, if parties and the market viewed it as a good deal. The figure shows that stock prices jumped on the day the news became public and continued a couple days later. However, despite some days later the stock price's declines and rises, when the new year (2023) began the CVS stock price started to decline in a steep manner. This suggests that prices reflected the new information, including the likely impact of the merger premium, in the months that followed.

Another, more notable, example of dramatic change in stock prices on an announcement day, is shown in Figure 8.4. In that figure, the stock prices of Albertson's supermarkets a few months before and after the announcement of the merger with Kroger foods (on October 14, 2022) with that date shown by the vertical line. Immediately upon the announcement, Albertsons stock price declined dramatically but after this initial reaction, there is no further drift in prices, implying that prices

Figure 8.3 CVS daily stock prices around the acquisition of Signify Health date

Data source: *YahooFinance*; Author created graph

Figure 8.4 Albertsons's stock prices around announcement of merger with Kroger

Data source: *YahooFinance*; Author created graph

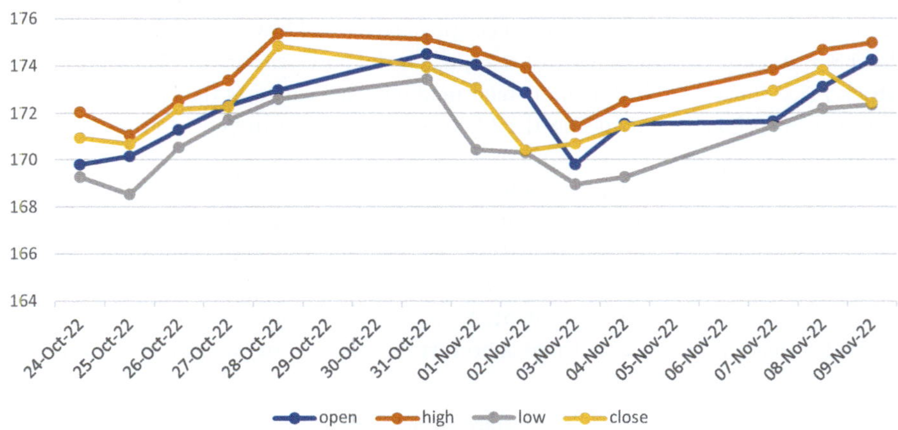

Figure 8.5 Intraday stock prices of JJ around acquisition of Abiomed date

Data source: *YahooFinance*; Author created graph

reflected the new information, including the likely magnitude of the takeover premium, by the end of the trading day.

Finally, another way of observing evidence of rapid response to new information may be found in intraday prices. On November 1, 2022, Johnson & Johnson announced the acquisition of Abiomed and completed the acquisition on December 22, 2022.[3] Figure 8.5 shows the intraday prices (open, high, low, close) a month before and after the announcement. On the announcement day, the spread between the high (and open) and low prices was the highest (over $4) among the days around the event.

But why should we expect stock prices to be informationally efficient? Investors will have an incentive to spend tangible and intangible resources to analyze and discover new information only if such activity is likely to generate higher returns. In addition, the activity may be worthwhile because the degree of efficiency differs across various markets, local and international alike. But let us be pragmatic. With so many well-backed, well-informed and well-financed financial analysts around willing to spend a lot of resources on financial research, it is not easy (for the rest of us) to spot profitable market inefficiencies. Furthermore, the additional return on research activity may be so small that only big portfolio managers will find them worth pursuing. Always recognize that information is the most precious commodity on Wall Street, and the competition for it is huge and ruthless. Nowadays, we have the so-called "expert networks" where you can hire vetted subject-matter experts for personalized (one-to-one) consultations on various topics. The advantages of using such platforms are that they help connect companies with subject matter experts, companies may need specialized knowledge that is unavailable in-house, and because investors may be looking to gain insights about specific industries or stocks that they are thinking of investing in.

It is important to mention that investors who are firm believers in market efficiency view investment analyses such as fundamental and technical are pure waste of time and resources. An efficient stock market would have instantly incorporated all available information (past and current public and private/inside) so that the prices of stocks we observe every minute are fair or correct. As a result, the EMH has never been widely accepted on Wall Street and by chartists (technical analysts). By contrast, it is important to state that even in an efficient market there is still the need for professional advice and guidance (on constructing and managing an investment portfolio) because of taxes, new financial instruments, changes in personal wealth and other unique investor characteristics (such as age, marital status on so on). Recall that fundamental analysis uses a much wider range of information to create portfolios (that is, looks at the economics of the firm, industry and economy) than does technical analysis, as we mentioned earlier. However, despite many easily available statistics such as a stock's price–earnings ratio or its market capitalization, investors tend to predict abnormal risk-adjusted returns. Such interpretations and findings do not sit well with the efficient market hypothesis and therefore are often referred to as efficient market *anomalies*. Let us briefly mention some of them next.

4.2.1 The P/E effect

It was discovered by Basu (1977, 1983) that portfolios of low price–earnings (P/E) ratio stocks have provided higher returns than high P/E portfolios.[4] Put differently, low P/E stocks will outperform high P/E stocks because growth companies enjoy high P/E ratios, but the market tends to overestimate the growth potential and thus overvalues these growth companies, while undervaluing low-growth firms. Does that mean that the stock market systematically misprices stocks according to this ratio? This would be a disturbing conclusion because P/E ratios are so easy to compute and observe. Another way to see such results is to assume that returns are not properly adjusted for risk. If, for example, two firms have the same expected earnings, the riskier stock will sell at a lower price and lower P/E ratio. Furthermore, because of its higher risk, the low P/E stock also will have higher expected returns.

4.2.2 The small-firm effect

Also referred to as the size effect, it was discovered that the risk-adjusted returns for extended periods (several decades) indicated that small firms consistently earned significantly larger risk-adjusted returns than larger firms. It was then argued that it was the size, not the P/E ratio, that caused the results discussed in the subsection above, but this contention was later disputed (that is, it was noted that the riskiness of the small firms was improperly estimated because such firms were not traded often).

4.2.3 The neglected-firm effect

Continuing from the prior subsection, Arbel and Strebel (1983) offered an alternative interpretation of the small-firm effect. Because small firms tend to be neglected by large institutional traders, information about them is less available and, by consequence, makes smaller firms riskier investments that command higher returns.[5] Furthermore, Merton (1987) provided a rationale for the neglected-firm effect. He showed that such firms might be expected to earn higher equilibrium returns as compensation for the risk associated with limited information (hence, any premium on such firms may not constitute a market inefficiency).[6]

4.2.4 Book Value–Market Value ratio

The Book Value–Market Value (BVMV) ratio relates the book value of a firm's equity to its market value. Rosenberg et al. (1985) found a positive relationship between current values for this ratio and future stock returns and argued that such a relationship between public information on the BVMV ratio and future returns was evidence against the EMH. Fama and French (1992) showed that this ratio is a powerful predictor of returns across securities.[7] This, essentially, means that, absent of beta, either that high BVMV firms are relatively underpriced, or that the ratio is serving as a proxy for a risk factor that affects equilibrium expected returns.

To summarize, studies that have used ratios to predict the cross section of expected stock returns have provided substantial evidence in conflict with the semi-strong form of market efficiency. Hence, significant results were found for P/E ratios, market value size, neglected firms, and BVMV ratios. Although the Fama and French work indicated that the optimal combination appears to be size and the BVMV ratio, a study by Jensen et al. (1997) showed that this combination only works during periods of expansionary monetary policy.[8]

4.3 Market efficiency vs. behavioral finance: some discussion

We have just finished discussing behavioral finance and the efficient market hypothesis. Let us spend some time in discussing these theories so you can understand where you stand. In our discussion, we will refer you to seminal papers for further insights. We pose some questions and then try to address them as objectively as possible.

How should the investor interpret such market anomalies (some of which were mentioned in subsection 4.6)? Does it imply that markets are grossly inefficient, so that simple trading rules can generate large profit opportunities? Fama and French (1993) argued that these effects are mere manifestations of risk premia.[9] By contrast, Lakonishok et al. (1995) counter-argued that these phenomena constitute evidence of inefficient markets, that is, of systematic forecast errors of stock analysts.[10] They believed that when analysts extrapolate past performance too far into the future, they overprice firms with recent good performance and underprice firms with recent poor performance. Later, when market agents recognize their mistakes, prices reverse (the so-called *reversal effect*). This is also reinforced by the small-firm and book-to-market effects because firms with sharp price drops may tend to be small or have high book-to-market ratios.

Do stock prices reflect fundamentals? This is (still) a hot topic! In 2013, the Nobel Prize in Economics was awarded to Eugene F. Fama and Robert J. Shiller, advocates of EMH and behavioral finance, respectively, and authors of two sharply differing Nobel-Prize lectures: "Two Pillars of Asset Pricing", by Fama, and "Speculative Asset Prices", by Shiller. Asness et al. (2019) found that the stocks of firms that are more profitable, growing at higher rates, tend to trade at higher relative prices. Such companies generally outperform the market, suggesting that investors are willing to pay a premium for them (also known as *quality stocks*). However, when stock prices are regressed against fundamentals, the authors found very low explanatory power (of less than 10% in the adjusted R-square). Then, they went ahead and examined the performance of some quality-sorted portfolios and found that they tended to offer significantly better absolute and risk-adjusted returns than the portfolios of low-quality stocks.[11] This, in essence, indicates that the market tends to undervalue stock fundamentals.

A more recent paper by Delao and Myers (2024) found that when prices of stocks (and bonds) diverge from their underlying fundamentals, it is because of errors investors make in their expectations of future cash flows or inflation. Prices for stocks, for example, seem to move around much more than their fundamentals.[12] The authors cited the earnings for the S&P 500 or dividends, and noted that these move around but relatively little over time, whereas prices for those stocks are volatile. Therefore, the authors asked if the fundamentals of these assets are relatively stable, why are prices moving around so much? Other notable economists such as Ritter (2003) and Barberis and Thaler (2003) have argued that stock markets are not efficient because they do not necessarily reflect economic fundamentals. Therefore, according to these authors significant and persistent deviations from the intrinsic value of a company's share price occur in market valuations.[13]

Using some actual examples to counter, consider the late 1970s and late 1990s in the US which generated significant deviations from intrinsic valuations. In the first case, the issue was inflation and so the market was probably undervalued. The second case took place because the market reached a P/E ratio of around 30 – an unsustainable level given a 3% real GDP growth or 13% returns on (book) equity. So, when these price deviations occurred, the stock market returned to its intrinsic-valuation level within 3 years. The point is that despite short-term deviations of valuation in the long-run the market (and economy) will have to fall back in line with economic fundamentals.

When deciding which stock to invest in, do you consider its past performance and if it is good/bad then you decide to buy/sell it? If so, then you would commit the "*gambler's fallacy*". This fallacy, which is similar to flipping coin and having a 50-50 chance of coming up with heads or tails, suggests that each outcome is independent of the previous one. However, in investing, individuals will fail to recognize that past events are independent of the future. Recall that the typical disclaimer in all investments is that "past returns do not guarantee future returns"! So, such investors biases lead to stock mispricing in a predictable way, giving confidence to an active manager's ability to identify sources of mispricing. Thus, markets clearly do not price assets as rationally as an efficient market would claim.

5 Correlations and equity portfolio construction

As we learned in Chapter 2, the correlations among asset classes (as well as among securities within each asset class) are crucial for achieving efficient portfolio diversification. So, when you are about to construct your financial asset portfolio you should first find the correlations (or covariances) and create a correlation matrix. Let us see how correlations can guide you in setting up a simple portfolio (without mixing any quantitative analysis (some of which was presented in Chapter 2). Some general rules are the following. First, negative correlations among pairs of assets hedge with each other and help the portfolio to navigate through many market crises and declines. Second, market correlations help traders find discrepancies between different markets that are moving together naturally. For example, when one market trails another, the lagging market could be seen as a divergence for a long opportunity to catch up to the other market(s).

Third, what if the two markets comove in a positive manner? This typically happens when national news breaks such as that by the Federal Reserve (following its Federal Open Market Committee, FOMC, meetings). For example, when the Fed takes a more accommodative policy stance (or is "*dovish*") the market interprets that as an impending decline in interest rates. This puts higher pressure on equity markets due to more money flooding the market, making money cheaper to borrow. In addition, it puts downward pressure on the US dollar implying increased supply, which helps commodities advance. When interest rates are lowered (or expected to drop), bond prices increase (that is, bonds are sold at a premium). Obviously, the opposite occurs when the Fed takes a more "*hawkish*" tone, with implied interest rate to increase. The result is a decrease in equities (as well as risk). Finally, when assets have high positive correlations (hence, in the language of financial econometrics, they are "*cointegrated*"), a low-correlation asset portfolio constructed to maximize diversification gains may not necessarily result in diversification gains in the long run.

Recent work on portfolio construction and positive correlations among its assets suggest that selecting a low-correlated portfolio to maximize diversification gains does not necessarily result in long-term diversification gains.[14] Other researchers contend that moving to a positive stock-bond correlation world will cause a balanced portfolio of stocks and bonds to deliver more volatile performance but with more extreme tail events. Further, they assert that when correlation is positive, the optimal allocation to stocks may be slightly different relative to when correlation is negative.[15]

Here's another word of wisdom from the market. Depending on your investment horizon, you (the investor) must have a good mix of asset classes in the portfolio. Specifically, if you are there for the long run then you should have more stocks than bonds (and other financial assets) in your portfolio. As you age and get closer to the end of your investment horizon, you should increase bond allocations (and other cash instruments) while reducing stock allocations, even though they may earn lower returns than stocks. Finally, if you need money in the near future, conservative investments would make more sense, because there is a smaller chance of suffering an upsetting short-term loss.[16]

Let us offer here a brief refresher on the relationship between portfolio risk/return tradeoff, investment strategies and the role of correlations. In general, the *risk/return tradeoff* means that higher/lower potential returns generally come with higher/lower risk. Hence, a direct relationship is implied. This concept relates to the indifference curve analysis we learned in Chapter 1. In this context, indifference curves represent an investor's preferences in the risk/return tradeoff. Each curve shows combinations of risk and return that offer the same level of utility to the investor, meaning they are equally satisfied with any point on that curve. The slope of the indifference curve reflects the investor's risk aversion, where a steeper slope indicates higher risk aversion, while a flatter slope suggests lower risk aversion.

In modern portfolio theory, portfolios are often constructed to achieve an optimal balance between risk and return. One of the key tools is mean-variance optimization, which relies heavily on asset correlations. The goal is to maximize expected return for a given level of risk. Correlations between assets are essential inputs in this optimization process, as they help determine the weight of each asset in the portfolio. The correlation between assets affects where a portfolio lies on the *efficient frontier* or the set of portfolios that offer the highest expected return for a given level of risk. Therefore, portfolios composed of assets with low or negative correlations can shift closer to the efficient frontier by achieving higher returns for the same level of risk or lower risk for the same expected return. Conversely, if assets in the portfolio are highly correlated, the potential for risk reduction is lower, making it harder to achieve an optimal portfolio position on the efficient frontier.

How do correlations affect[17] the portfolio's asset allocation strategy? Asset correlations influence decisions on asset allocation, which is the process of distributing investments across different asset classes (e.g., stocks, bonds, commodities, real estate) to achieve desired risk and return profiles. So, over the long term, investors may choose assets with historically low or negative correlations to build a well-diversified portfolio that can withstand various market conditions. By contrast, in the short term, correlations may shift due to economic cycles, geopolitical events, or other market factors. Portfolio managers may adjust allocations based on expected changes in correlations. For example, in times of a crisis, correlations between asset classes like stocks and bonds may increase, reducing the diversification benefit.

We understand that asset correlations change over time, especially during periods of market stress or volatility, and we call them dynamic correlations.[18] Specifically, in financial crises, previously low-correlated assets (such as stocks and bonds) may start moving together as investors sell off assets across the board. This phenomenon, known as *correlation breakdown*, can undermine diversification strategies (Loretan and English, 2000, and Li et al., 2024). As a result, due to the changing nature of correlations, investors need to regularly monitor the correlations between assets in their portfolio and rebalance the portfolio accordingly. This may involve shifting towards assets that offer better diversification potential as correlations evolve. Moreover, within an equity portfolio, sector-specific correlations can guide diversification decisions. Sectors like technology and healthcare might have low correlations with energy or utilities, offering opportunities to spread risk across sectors. Further, assets from different regions or countries often exhibit low correlations due to varying economic conditions, political climates, and market dynamics. Geographic diversification, therefore, allows investors to spread risk across different economies.

In sum, in portfolio construction, asset correlations influence the level of diversification, risk, and return trade-offs. Low or negative correlations between assets enhance diversification, reducing overall portfolio risk and stabilizing returns. High correlations, on the other hand, limit diversification benefits and make the portfolio more vulnerable to systemic risks. Because correlations change over time, portfolio managers must continuously monitor and adjust allocations to optimize performance and minimize risk under different market conditions.

Finally, what about augmenting your portfolio of domestic assets to include international assets at any level such as firm, industry (sector) or country (developed or emerging)? Research has indicated that the correlation between developed markets and emerging markets varies over time and is influenced by several factors, including global economic conditions, investor sentiment, and market-specific events. In general, historically, developed markets (DM) and emerging markets (EM) have exhibited lower correlations, which has made emerging markets attractive for diversification in global portfolios. Emerging markets typically have different economic drivers (e.g., commodity dependence, growth from industrialization) compared to developed markets, where economies are more mature and driven by consumption and services. However, over the past two decades, as globalization has increased, the correlation between developed and emerging markets has risen. As EMs have become more integrated into the global financial system, economic linkages, trade, capital flows, and investor behavior have contributed to higher correlations.

Today, developed and emerging markets typically show a moderate positive correlation. This means that while they often move in the same direction, they are still somewhat influenced by different factors, providing some diversification benefits. For instance, global events like monetary policy changes in developed economies (e.g., US Federal Reserve actions) can have spillover effects on emerging markets. During periods of global economic growth or optimism, both DM and EM equities tend to perform well, leading to a positive correlation. Conversely, in times of global financial stress, correlations tend to increase as investors reduce exposure to riskier assets, including EM assets, causing both markets to move down together.

Despite the increasing globalization, there are times when emerging and developed markets diverge due to differing economic cycles, policy responses, or regional events. For example, emerging markets can experience unique shocks, such as political instability, currency crises, or commodity price fluctuations, which might lead to periods of underperformance relative to developed markets. Many emerging markets rely on commodities (e.g., oil, metals, agricultural products) for economic growth. Fluctuations in commodity prices can lead to periods of divergence between EM and DM performance, especially if developed economies are less dependent on commodity exports. Finally, emerging markets often have significant levels of US dollar-denominated debt. A strong US dollar can increase the cost of servicing this debt, putting pressure on EM economies, while developed markets might not face the same level of stress.

In times of global financial crises or market turmoil (e.g., the 2008 Global Financial Crisis or the COVID-19 health pandemic), correlations between developed and emerging markets rose. This happens because investors tend to "sell everything" in risk-off scenarios, which reduces the diversification benefits that typically exist between the two markets. In addition, during such crises, investors often flee riskier assets (like emerging market stocks or bonds) and move into safer assets (like developed market government bonds or blue-chip stocks), causing emerging markets to decline more sharply than developed markets, but increasing the short-term correlation between the two.

Which factors affect the correlation between developed and emerging markets? A number of them, in reality, but below we only mention a few key ones. First, interest rate changes and quantitative easing policies in developed markets (e.g., the US or Europe) can impact capital flows into and out of emerging markets, increasing the correlation between these markets. Second, both DMs and EMs are affected by global trade dynamics. Trade tensions or commodity price swings (like oil price changes) can simultaneously impact both developed and emerging markets, raising correlation levels. Third, as foreign investors increasingly participate in emerging market investments (both equities and bonds), the performance of these markets becomes more influenced by global financial trends and risk appetite, linking them more closely with developed markets. On the stock-bond correlations, emerging market equities have a moderate to high correlation with developed market equities, particularly during global growth phases or risk-off periods. However, the correlation tends to be lower when the two markets are driven by idiosyncratic factors (e.g., local EM political changes, or regional economic shocks). Emerging market bonds, particularly sovereign debt, often have a lower correlation with developed market bonds. However, external factors like US interest rates or global risk appetite for yield can increase this correlation, especially during periods when US Treasury yields rise, putting pressure on EM debt markets.

What do the above factors have to do with an investor's long-term diversification potential? While correlations between developed and emerging markets have generally increased over time, the two markets do not move in perfect sync, and emerging markets still offer diversification benefits in a global portfolio. The long-term diversification potential exists due to (1) different economic drivers and growth patterns in emerging economies, (2) unique risks and opportunities related to demographic trends, industrialization, and technological catch-up in EM countries and (3) localized shocks that may not affect DMs in the same way. In sum, while EM markets provide diversification potential, their increasing integration with global financial systems has led to higher correlations with DMs over time, particularly in equity markets.

5.1 An example

In this subsection, we show that correlations among various financial assets – the Standard & Poor's Exchange Traded Fund (SPY), the 10-year Treasury Note (BOND), the Euro–US dollar exchange rate (EURUSD), and the emerging markets ETF (EM) – vary over time. Table 8.2 shows the correlation matrices for the whole period (9/16/2016 – 8/9/2024), first subperiod (9/16/2016 – 9/16/2021) and second subperiod (9/17/2021 – 8/9/2024). The two subperiods were chosen *ad hoc.*

We see that there are very low correlations among all assets during the entire period and one of them (exchange rate – SPY) negative. In the first subperiod, we

Table 8.2 Correlations among EURUSD, EM, BOND, SPY

Entire period (9/16/2016 – 8/9/2024)			
	EURUSD	EM	BOND
EM	0.0372		
BOND	0.0375	0.0236	
SPY	−0.0915	0.0789	0.0670
1st subperiod (9/16/2016 – 9/16/2021)			
EURUSD	EM	BOND	
0.0255	0.0986		
0.1490			
−0.1706	0.1135	0.1908	
2nd subperiod (9/17/2021 – 8/9/2024)			
EM	0.0479		
BOND	−0.0218	−0.0432	
SPY	−0.0341	0.0305	−0.0411

Notes: EURUSD is the Euro–US Dollar exchange rate; EM is the emerging markets equity ETF; BOND is the 10-year Treasury bond; SPY is the Standard & Poor's ETF.

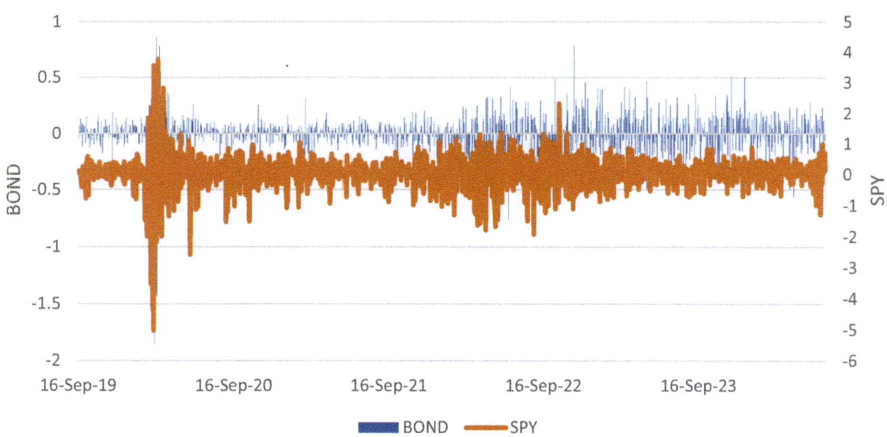

Figure 8.6 Bond – SPY returns
Source: Author created graph

see stronger correlations between many asset pairs. In the second subperiod, we see more negative correlations among pairs. Therefore, you now see the dynamic nature of the relationships among diverse financial assets and their implications for portfolio construction, as we discussed above. Some of these observations are also seen in Figures 8.6 to 8.8, where the returns of selected asset pairs are shown over the entire period only. We note that the BOND and the SPY returns and the

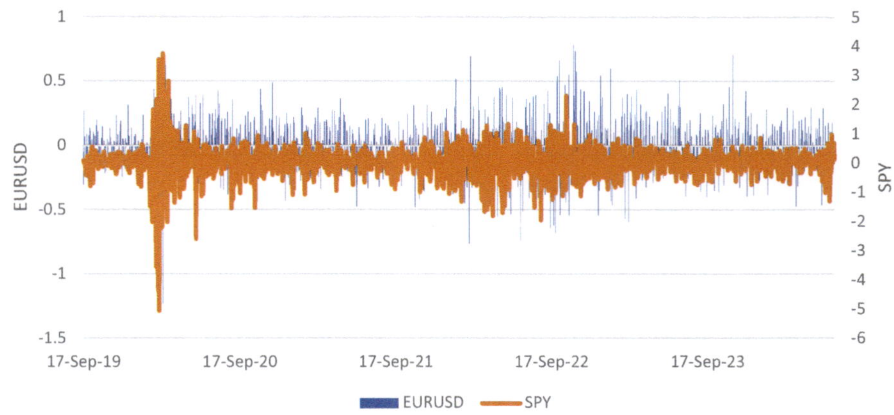

Figure 8.7 EURUSD – SPY returns
Source: Author created graph

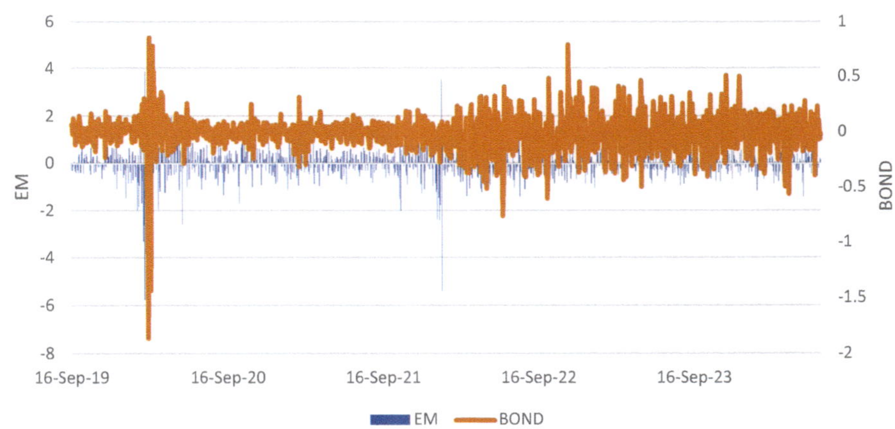

Figure 8.8 EM – Bond returns
Source: Author created graph

EURUSD and SPY returns are not correlated much and that the first pair's correlations are positive while the second pair's negative. The same degree of correlation is observed with the EM–BOND returns pair. However, in all cases we observe spikes of higher similar comovement (correlation) at various time frames, especially in the first subperiod and around the beginning of 2020. Note that a -1.0 correlation (between two assets) implies a risk-free portfolio.

So, if you were to build a portfolio containing all these assets, and applying equal weights, what would have been your return and risk? In addition, which period would have offered you a better risk/return payoff? To answer these questions, we need some additional information for each asset such as its descriptive statistics. In addition, we need to apply the risk and return formulae we first presented in Chapter 2. Selected statistics for each asset are shown in Table 8.3. We obtain the pairs' correlations from Table 8.1.

Table 8.3 Descriptive statistics for the four assets

Statistics	*EURUSD*	*EM*	*BOND*	*SPY*
WHOLE PERIOD				
Mean	−0.0008	−0.00174	−0.00569	0.02054
St. Dev.	0.0056	0.01776	0.00484	0.01622
1ST SUBPERIOD				
Mean	0.0049	0.01784	0.00271	0.02964
St. Dev.	0.0077	0.03224	0.00699	0.02972
2ND SUBPERIOD				
Mean	−0.0049	−0.01578	−0.01171	0.01404
St. Dev.	0.0080	0.01984	0.00661	0.01793

Recall the formulae (from Chapter 2) on the computation of the portfolio's return and risk, which we replicate here for convenience. The portfolio's return, R_p, is as follows:

$$R_p = w_{EURUSD}{}^*R_{EURUSD} + w_{EM}{}^*R_{EM} + w_{BOND}{}^*R_{BOND} + w_{SPY}{}^*R_{SPY}$$

and the portfolio's standard deviation as follows:

$$\sigma_p = sqrt[(w_{EURUSD}{}^*\sigma_{EURUSD})^2 + (w_{EM}{}^*\sigma_{EM})^2 + (w_{BOND}{}^*\sigma_{BOND})^2 + (w_{SPY}{}^*\sigma_{SPY})^2 + 2^*\, w_{EURUSD}{}^*w_{EM}{}^*\sigma_{EURUSD}{}^*\sigma_{EM}{}^*\rho_{EURUSDEM} + 2^*w_{EURUSD}{}^*w_{BOND}{}^*\sigma_{EURUSD}{}^*\sigma_{BOND}{}^*\,\rho_{EURUSDBOND} + 2^*\,w_{EURUSD}{}^*\,w_{SPY}{}^*\,\sigma_{EURUSD}{}^*\,\sigma_{SPY}{}^*\,\rho_{EURUSDSPY} + 2^*\,w_{EM}{}^*\,w_{BOND}{}^*\,\sigma_{EM}{}^*\,\sigma_{BOND}{}^*\,\rho_{EMBOND} + 2^*\,w_{EM}{}^*\,w_{SPY}{}^*\,\sigma_{EM}{}^*\,\sigma_{SPY}{}^*\,\rho_{EMSPY} + 2^*\,w_{BOND}{}^*\,w_{SPY}{}^*\,\sigma_{BOND}{}^*\,\sigma_{SPY}{}^*\,\rho_{BONDSPY}]$$

Let us apply these two formulae for the three periods. We begin with the whole period's analysis. We assume equal weights for each asset or 0.25. The portfolio's return is:[19]

$$R_p = (0.25^*\ -0.0008) + (0.25^*-0.00174) + (0.25^*\ -0.00569) + (0.25^*0.02054) = 0.003078$$

The portfolio's standard deviation is computed as follows:

$$\sigma_p = sqrt[(0.25^*0.0056)^2 + (0.25^*0.01776)^2 + (0.25^*0.00484)^2 + (0.25^*0.1622)^2 + 2^*0.25^*0.25^*0.0372^*0.0056^*0.01776 + 2^*0.25^*0.25^*0.0375^*0.0056^*0.00484 + 2^*0.25^*0.25^*-0.0915^*0.0056^*0.1622 + 2^*0.25^*0.25^*0.0236^*0.01776^*0.00484 + 2^*0.25^*0.25^*0.0789^*0.01776^*0.1622 + 2^*0.25^*0.25^*0.0670^*0.00484^*0.1622]$$

$= \text{sqrt}\ [0.00164 + 4.6247\text{E-}07 + 1.2705\text{E-}07 - 1.03889\text{E-}05 + 2.53577\text{E-}07 + 2.84106\text{E-}05 + 6.57478\text{E-}06] = 0.04113$

The portfolio's return and risk for the 1st and 2nd subperiods (see subscripts) are:

$R_{p1} = 0.013773 \qquad \sigma_{p1} = 0.012048$
$R_{p2} = -0.00459 \qquad \sigma_{p2} = 0.007458$

So, let us see what we got here. The highest return was obtained in the 1st subperiod and the worst in the 2nd subperiod. Obviously, we ignore the second subperiod where our return is negative. Looking at the whole period's and 1st subperiod's risk and return values, you could be tempted to infer that you would prefer the 1st subperiod's investment opportunity and not the entire period's. This is because you looked at the standard deviation of the whole period's returns and saw that is it higher than that of the 1st subperiod's. As a risk averse investor, you would think like that. This is the *absolute comparison* of the risk/return profiles of each investment opportunity.

But, relatively speaking were we better off during the whole period or the 1st subperiod? This can be answered by computing the coefficient of variation (CV), which measures the risk per unit of return, or the Sharpe ratio, which measures the extra reward per unit of risk (note that here we do not involve the risk-free rate so we can obtain the extra return). Let us apply these two metrics.

Coefficient of Variation for the whole period: $CV_w = \sigma_p/R_p = 13.3525$
Sharpe ratio for the whole period: $\text{Sharpe} = R_p/\sigma_p = 0.07483$
and
Coefficient of Variation for the 1st subperiod: $CV_1 = \sigma_{p1}/R_{p1} = 0.874755$
Sharpe ratio for the 1st subperiod: $\text{Sharpe}_1 = R_{p1}/\sigma_{p1} = 1.14317$

According to CV, you should prefer the 1st subperiod because your risk per unit of return is lower than that of the whole period. The Sharpe ratio confirms this choice because its value is higher than that of the whole period and suggests that you maximize the return per unit of risk. So, in this case your conclusion was correct, on a relative basis. What if you had the following values for investments A and B: $R_A = 0.070$ and $\sigma_A = 0.050$ and $R_B = 0.120$ and $\sigma_A = 0.070$. Would you still go with investment A because it has lower risk? Apply the CV metric and observe that $CV_A = 0.05/0.07 = 0.714$ and $CV_B = 0.07/0.12 = 0.583$. In this case, the conclusion is reversed and you would pick investment B because of its lower relative risk per unit of return (due to its higher rate of return)!

We end this section with a short discussion on the link between the investors' need to understand the equity as well as all financial markets and PESTEL analysis (which we first mentioned in Chapter 2). In general, such analysis assists in strategic planning, risk management, and investment decisions by offering insights on how external factors might influence market trends, asset prices, and investment returns Box 8.2 presents the components of PESTEL and then explains how they are related to the financial markets.

Box 8.2

How is PESTEL analysis related to financial markets?

POLITICAL: Politics or governmental decisions greatly affect financial markets via economic policies (such as spending and taxation), regulations (laws and anti-trust restrictions), geopolitical risks and foreign relations (including trade and investment policies). For example, companies can exploit these factors to determine if it is worthwhile invest abroad or not.

ECONOMIC: Economic factors relate to macro and micro policies including inflation, interest rates, and exchange rates. Investors can then form investment portfolios based on these factors and companies can use this information to value companies to see if they are under- or over-valued.

SOCIAL: Such factors refer to demographics, consumer tastes and preferences, investor appetite for yield and general lifestyle trends. Investors and management/marketing teams look at such factors to construct or tilt asset portfolios or promote products in an effort to exploit these conditions as profitably as they can. A prime example is the trends that emerged after the global health pandemic of 2020 (COVID-19) where technology products soared and lifestyles were drastically changed.

TECHNOLOGICAL: Technological factors refer to infrastructure, social media, cyber security and research and development, to name a few. Technological disruption can affect asset portfolios, financial and economic magnitudes or one's life entirely. Financial teams must incorporate these factors in their analyses to understand how entities and people behave. We discuss financial technology's impact on financial markets in Chapter 13.

ENVIROMENTAL: Environmental (along with technological) factors represent reality these days. The global trend towards carbon emissions reduction and transition to a green environment is the talk of the day referring to ESG factors. Global companies strive to reduce emissions and make production cleaner and investors seek socially responsible or environmental-friendly investments.

LEGAL: Finally, legal factors such as regulations, labor laws and intellectual property rights laws greatly affect the financial operations of companies as well as the composition of investors' asset portfolios. For example, understanding the legal side of a business helps with compliance and effective liability management. Also, the legal structure of a company defines the safety and precaution rules for it to deliver a safe and quality product.

Test your understanding 2

1. Assume you acquired 200 shares of a $50 stock for a total cost of $10,000.

   a. If the initial margin requirement is 50%, how much did you borrow?
   b. If the stock price increases by 20%, what are the total value of your position and margin?

c. What if the stock price decreased by 20%, what are now your total value of the stock and margin?d. Compute the rates of return on both situations.

2. Continuing with the above example, suppose your broker has a maintenance margin of 25%. How far can the stock price fall before you receive a margin call?
3. What is a short sale and why do investors engage in it? Which investors would engage in margin purchases?

Solutions appear at the textbook's website.

Summary

- We analyzed the equity market by explaining a number of theories and approaches.
- Fundamental analysis aims at understanding the economics and financial behind a company through the examination of five key aspects namely, liquidity, profitability, debt, asset and market.
- In addition, the national economy must be assessed by looking at macroeconomic magnitudes such as GDP, inflation, unemployment and more.
- Finally, the industry is evaluated in order to understand where the industry is headed and what the position of the company is within it relative to its peers.
- Technical analysis involves predicting future price movements based on past market data, primarily stock price and volume.
- Quantitative analysis employs statistical and mathematical models to analyze market data and predict price movements and optimize portfolios.
- Sentiment analysis seeks to gauge market sentiment by analyzing news, social media, and other sources of public opinion.
- Behavioral analysis studies investor behavior and psychological factors that can influence market movements.
- Investors suffer from hundreds of behavioral biases and informational processing errors as well as being confronted with several market anomalies.
- The two key elements of portfolio analysis are asset allocation and security selection.
- Asset allocation refers to the selection of major assets classes (equity, debt, commodities, etc.) that align with your objective, constraints and risk tolerance.
- Security election involves picking the right securities that would fulfill (hopefully) your investment goals.
- Interpreting stock market movements involves understanding the factors that influence price changes and how they reflect investor sentiment, economic conditions, and company performance.
- Extreme market sentiment, driven by fear or greed, can lead to significant market swings.
- Geopolitical events such as political instability, wars, or trade disputes can cause significant market volatility.
- Arbitrage involves the simultaneous buying and selling of the same asset in different markets to profit from price discrepancies without risk.

- Momentum investing involves buying stocks that have shown an upward price trend and selling those with downward trends.
- Value investing involves buying stocks that are undervalued compared to their intrinsic value.
- Growth investing focuses on companies expected to grow at an above-average rate compared to other companies and/or the market.
- Dividend investing involves focusing on companies that regularly pay dividends, providing a steady income stream.
- Dollar cost averaging is the practice of investing a fixed dollar amount on a regular basis, regardless of the share price.
- The investor could exploit stocks' seasonal patterns (calendar effects) as some stocks or sectors tend to perform better at certain times of the year.
- Buying stocks on margin means the investor borrows part of the purchase price of the stock from the broker in addition to his own money (the margin).
- A short sale permits investors to profit from a decline in a security's price.
- Pairs trading is applied when stocks are paired up based on an analysis of either fundamental similarities or betas (market exposures).
- Market efficiency refers to informational efficiency or how the stock market responds to new information.
- Portfolios of low price–earnings (P/E) ratio stocks have provided higher returns than high P/E portfolios.
- The correlations among asset classes (as well as among securities within each asset class) are crucial for achieving efficient portfolio diversification.
- The correlation between assets affects where a portfolio lies on the efficient frontier or the set of portfolios that offer the highest expected return for a given level of risk.
- Asset correlations influence decisions on asset allocation – the process of distributing investments across different asset classes to achieve desired risk and return profiles.
- Asset correlations change over time, especially during periods of market stress or volatility, and we call them dynamic correlations.

Questions and problems

1. The late Charlie Munger – a genius and his stock-picking skills, wisdom and life – said in 2017 that "Diversification is for those who don't know anything." Explain his argument and offer a counter.
2. What are some of the assumptions which imply an efficient capital market?
3. What are some of the implications of market efficiency? Answer with respect to portfolio/financial analysts, fundamental and technical analyses.
4. Consider a coin toss with a payoff of \$100 for heads. Now, consider a gift of \$100 combined with a bet that imposes a loss of \$100 if that coin toss comes up tails. Explain which one an investor might prefer and pair it with the relevant behavioral bias.

5. Suppose you are bearish (pessimistic) on XYZ stock, whose market price is \$100 per share. You instruct your broker to sell short 1,000 shares. Suppose the broker has a 50% margin requirement on short sales.
   a. What is your initial percentage margin?
   b. Suppose you are right and XYZ falls to \$70 per share. You can now close out your position at a profit. What is your (gross) profit?
   c. Suppose the broker has a maintenance margin of 30% on short sales. How much can the price of the stock rise before you get a margin call?
6. Assume the following information on two assets, X and Y: $E(r_x) = E(r_y) = 0.20$ and $\sigma_x = \sigma_y = 0.10$. Then, answer the following questions:
   a. Compute the corresponding covariances given the following correlation coefficients: $\rho_{xy} = 1$; $\rho_{xy} = 0.5$; $\rho_{xy} = -0.5$; $\rho_{xy} = -1$.
   b. What happens to the standard deviation of the portfolio under these four conditions? Assume equal weights. Briefly explain each result.

Notes

1. https://edition.cnn.com/markets/fear-and-greed
2. https://www.signifyhealth.com/news/cvs-health-to-acquire-signify-health#:~:text=Subscribe%20Here!,Lynch.
3. https://www.jnj.com/media-center/press-releases/johnson-johnson-to-acquire-abiomed
4. Basu, Sanjoy (1977). The Investment Performance of Common Stocks in Relation to Their Price-Earnings Ratios: A Test of the Efficient Market Hypothesis. *Journal of Finance* 32, 663–682. Basu, Sanjoy (1983). The Relationship between Earnings Yield, Market Value, and Return for NYSE Common Stocks: Further Evidence. *Journal of Financial Economics* 12, 129–156.
5. Arbel, Avner and Paul Strebel (1983). Pay Attention to Neglected Firms. *Journal of Portfolio Management* 9(2), Winter, 37–42.
6. Merton, Robert C. (1987). A Simple Model of Capital Market Equilibrium with Incomplete Information. *Journal of Finance* 42, 483–510.
7. Fama, Eugene F. and Kenneth R. French (1992). The Cross Section of Expected Stock Returns. *Journal of Finance* 47, 427–465.
8. Jensen, Gerald R., Robert R. Johnson, and Jeffrey M. Mercer (1997). New Evidence on Size and Price-to-Book Effects in Stock Returns. *Financial Analysts Journal* 53(6), November–December, 34–42.
9. Fama, Eugene F. and Kenneth R. French (1993). Common Risk Factors in the Returns on Stocks and Bonds. *Journal of Financial Economics* 33, 3–56.
10. Lakonishok, Josef, Andrei Shleifer, and Robert W. Vishny (1995). Contrarian Investment, Extrapolation, and Risk. *Journal of Finance* 50, 541–578.
11. Asness, Clifford S., Andrea Frazzini and Lasse Heje Pedersen (2019). Quality Minus Junk. *Review of Accounting Studies* 24, 34–112.
12. Delao, Ricardo, and Sean Myers (2024). Which Subjective Expectations Explain Asset Prices? *The Review of Financial Studies* 37(6), June, 1929–1978. See also a correction: *The Review of Financial Studies* 38(8), August 2025, 2515.
13. Ritter, Jay (2003). Behavioral Finance. *Pacific-Basin Finance Journal* 11(4), 429–437. Barberis, Nicholas and Richard H. Thaler (2003). A Survey of Behavioral Finance. In *Handbook of the Economics of Finance: Financial Markets and Asset Pricing*, G. M. Constantinides et al. (eds.), New York: Elsevier North-Holland, pp. 1054–1123.

14. Narayan, S.W., Rehman, M.U., Ren, YS. et al. (2003). Is a Correlation-Based Investment Strategy Beneficial for Long-Term International Portfolio Investors?. *Financial Innovation* 9(64), 2–26. https://doi.org/10.1186/s40854-023-00471-9
15. https://www.pgim.com/content/dam/pgim/us/en/pgim-multi-asset-solutions/active/documents/research/ias-pma-rebrand-papers/2024/PMA-Prospects-and-Portfolio-Construction-Implications-0324.pdf
16. Clements, Jonathan (1993) Recipe for Successful Investing: First, Mix Assets Well, *The Wall Street Journal*, October 6.
17. Appendix C constructs an efficient frontier using Excel.
18. In Part D6 of the online Appendix, we demonstrate the most basic econometric model of volatility.
19. Recall that if you do not have the correlations but only the covariances you can re-arrange the formula for the correlation which is $\rho_{12} = \sigma_{12} / \sigma_1 \sigma_2$, where σ_{12} is the covariance between the two assets.

References

Fama, Eugene F. (2013). Two Pillars of Asset Pricing, *American Economic Review* 104(6), June, 1467–1485.

Li, David, Fernando Cerezetti and Roy Cheruvelil (2024). Correlation Breakdowns, Spread Positions and Central Counterparty Margin Models. *Journal of Financial Market Infrastructures* 11(3), 1–22. DOI: 10.21314/JFMI.2024.006.

Loretan, Mico and William B. English (2000). Evaluating Correlation Breakdowns during Periods of Market Volatility. *International Finance Discussion Papers* (IFDP), February. https://www.federalreserve.gov/econres/ifdp/evaluating-correlation-breakdowns-during-periods-of-market-volatility.htm.

Rosenberg, Barr, Kenneth Reid and Ronald Lanstein (1985). Persuasive Evidence of Market Inefficiency. *The Journal of Portfolio Management* 11(3), Spring, 9–16.

Shiller, Robert J. (2014). Speculative Asset Prices. *American Economic Review* 104(6), June, 1486–1517.

Chapter 9

The fixed-income market

Introduction

The *fixed-income market* is a financial marketplace where debt instruments, also known as bonds or fixed-income securities, are issued, traded, and settled. In essence, fixed-income securities represent a loan made by an investor to a borrower (such as a corporation or government) in exchange for periodic interest payments and the return of the principal amount at maturity. This market is one of the largest financial markets globally and includes various types of instruments, such as government, corporate, municipal, and asset-backed securities. In addition, the fixed-income market is essential to all investors, retail and institutional alike, since it can be used for various investment activities, some of which we will discuss later in the chapter.

The fixed-income market has gone a long way. Before the 1980s, the securities in that market were simply viewed as long-term and predictable investment products. That is, investors held the bonds to maturity expecting a stable (and relatively guaranteed) income. Then, not long after that, fixed income securities became more complex and not as predictable in their promised cash flows. In addition, it became complex to determine the amount of interest that will be received and many institutional investors, unlike retail investors, began trading fixed-income securities instead of holding them to maturity. As a result, the fixed-income market became more involved and massive in terms of volume and issuance (from several entities).

Figure 9.1 shows the total fixed-income market outstanding value across major issuer nations (US, EU, China, Japan, UK, Emerging Markets or EM, Canada, Australia, Switzerland, Singapore, Hong-Kong and Developed Markets or DM) for 2013 and 2023. As is immediately obvious, even in 223 (relative to 2013) the US holds the reins in fixed-income products issuance (in trillions of US dollars, $T) followed by the European union (EU), China and Japan. However, in 2023 China overtook Japan and the market share by the Emerging Markets increased substantially since 2013. Canada, Singapore and Hong-Kong remained relatively stable withing the decade.

Figure 9.2 shows the segments of the US's fixed-income market (which we will briefly discuss later in the chapter) since 2014. The amounts shown are in trillions

DOI: 10.4324/9781003677161-12

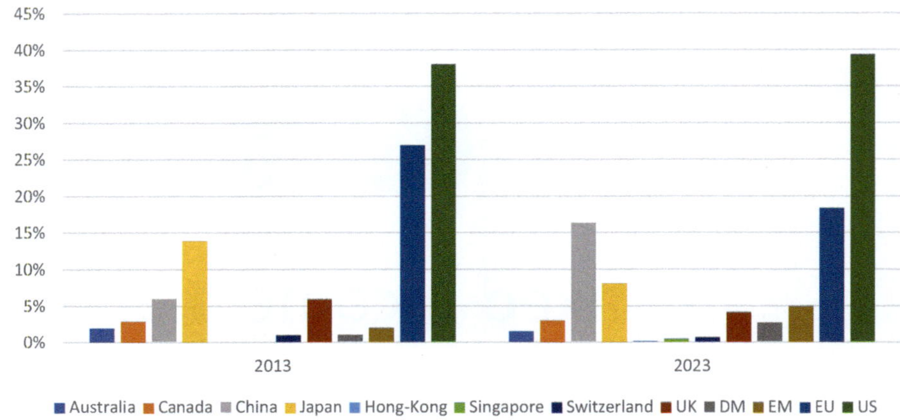

Figure 9.1 The global fixed-income market outstanding, 2013 and 2023

Source: SIFMA

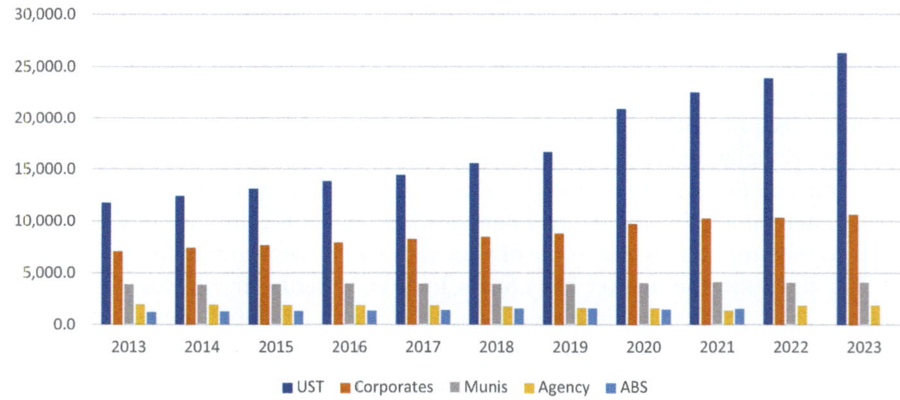

Figure 9.2 The evolution of the fixed-income market in the Unites States, 2014–2023

Notes: UST means US Treasuries, MBS = mortgage-backed securities, Corporates = corporate bonds, Munis = municipal securities, agency = federal agency securities, ABS = asset-backed securities

Source: SIMFA

of US dollars. As you see, US Treasuries (UST) and mortgage-backed securities (MBS) constitute a major (and growing over time) chunk of the market followed by the corporate bond market. Finally, asset-backed securities (ABS) entail the smallest place in the fixed-income market.

We will frequently use the terms fixed-income securities and bonds interchangeably in this chapter. What follows next are the main characteristics or properties of the bond market, the types of securities (and their issuers) traded in the market, some bond valuation methods and finally, how investors exploit the bond market.

1 The functions of the global bond market

The global bond market plays a critical role in the global financial system and economy by facilitating capital flow, providing a benchmark for interest rates, supporting monetary policy, and offering investment opportunities. Next, we list and briefly explain the primary functions of the global bond market. In our discussion, we will be referring to the main entities (issuers) of the bond market, namely governments and corporations. Later in the chapter we will decompose the government bond issuer.

1.1 Capital raising for bond issuers

A main reason (purpose) of the global bond market is to assist entities to raise capital for various purposes. For example, governments issue bonds to finance infrastructure, social programs, and other public expenditures. Sovereign debt issuance supports national budgets and provides a tool for managing economic growth. Finally, government institutions (related or not to the government) such as municipalities, agencies and international organizations (like the World Bank) use the global bond market to fund projects with public benefits, such as healthcare, education, infrastructure and sustainable development initiatives. In the US, Treasury bonds are typically the backbone of the bond market, as they provide a relatively low-risk investment option. Corporations also issue bonds to raise funds for business expansion, acquisitions, and capital investments. This provides a way for companies to access capital without diluting ownership through issuing stock. Corporate bonds give businesses flexibility in raising capital with specific terms and repayment schedules. In general, the bond market offers a cost-effective way to raise capital without diluting equity ownership.

More specifically, the global bond market provides access to global markets and foreign investments. The bond market facilitates cross-border capital flow, allowing investors to diversify internationally and countries to attract foreign capital. Developed economies and emerging markets alike use the bond market to access international investment, supporting economic growth and funding needs. International (foreign) bonds offer opportunities to diversify across currencies and regions, allowing investors to benefit from currency appreciation, interest rate differentials, and unique economic cycles. The bond market also supports environmental and social goals through sustainable finance instruments like green bonds, which fund climate-friendly projects, and social bonds, which finance initiatives such as affordable housing, healthcare, and education. Finally, environmental, social, and governance (ESG) considerations are increasingly important in global bond investing. Governments and companies issue bonds that align with ESG criteria, attracting a growing base of socially conscious investors.

In addition to developed economies, emerging markets rely on the global bond market to access capital for infrastructure, healthcare, and other critical sectors. By issuing bonds, these countries can attract foreign investment, support economic development, and fund growth projects. Supra-national institutions such as the World Bank and the Asian-American development bank issue bonds to fund projects in developing regions, supporting efforts to improve living standards, enhance resilience, and foster sustainable development.

1.2 Facilitating monetary policy transmission and economic growth

> **THE YIELD CURVE AS PREDICTOR OF ECONOMIC ACTIVITY**
>
> The Yield Curve (YC) is considered a good predictor of economic activity, particularly for future recessions. Specifically, an inverted YC has preceded every US recession since the 1970s. Recall that an inverted curve indicates that investors expect interest rates to fall and hence a recession, and as a result they demand higher (risk) premia. Thus, YC's predictive power stems from reflecting market expectations of future economic downturns. However, it cannot predict the timing and magnitude of a recession. Moreover, it is not immune to exogenous or unexpected events, and thus, its predictive power may be reduced.

The bond market is instrumental to a country's conduct of domestic monetary policy. Central banks conduct open market operations, such as buying or selling government bonds, to manage short-term interest rates and influence long-term rates. In periods of economic stress, central banks may buy government and corporate bonds to inject liquidity, lower borrowing costs, and stimulate the economy. The bond market enables these interventions, supporting monetary policy goals. Some central banks, like the Bank of Japan and the Reserve Bank of Australia (and the Fed in some instances), used bond purchases to maintain target yields for specific maturities, supporting monetary policy through targeted interest rate controls.

Fixed-income markets are sensitive to macroeconomic indicators and monetary policy. Apart from central bank policies, involving interest rate changes and quantitative easing (QE) to significantly impact bond prices and yields, inflation expectations influence the yields investors demand, as they seek to protect purchasing power. All these activities and considerations lead to strong economic growth accompanied with higher rates and yields. The opposite occurs (rate cuts and bond rallies) when economic contractions take hold.

A magnitude, known as the *yield curve* (YC), which exhibits yields across bond maturities, is a well-known indicator of economic expectations. Since longer-term bonds usually carry higher risk, they have higher yields than shorter-term bonds. Therefore, a normal yield curve reflects increasing bond yields as maturity increases. However, the yield curve can sometimes become flat or inverted. A steep YC often signals growth, while an inverted YC may indicate an impending recession. Bond yields additionally provide insight into investor views on inflation, economic growth, and geopolitical risks. For example, falling yields can indicate a *flight to quality* during uncertain periods, with investors moving capital into safer assets. Figure 9.3 displays the US yield curve as of October 28, 2024. We notice that it is a bit inverted since short-term securities (such as 1-month up to 1-year) have higher yields than the 30-year bonds. The nearby *sidebar* explains why the YC is a good predictor of economic activity.

The YC (of government bonds) serves as a benchmark for global interest rates. These rates influence lending rates for mortgages, corporate loans, and consumer credit, affecting financial conditions worldwide. When we take the difference in the yield of a Treasury's longer-term maturity (say, a 30-year bond) with that of a shorter-term maturity (say, a 1-year note), we construct a *term spread*. That is, we are moving along the YC. This indicates the spread between two same-quality and issuer securities. Figure 9.4 shows such a spread (the difference between the 10-year treasury bond at constant maturity minus the 2-year treasury bond at constant maturity for the 11-year period from 2014 to 2024, on a monthly basis). We notice that the spread became negative in September 2022 but rebounded into the positive territory just in September 2024. By contrast, when we take the difference between the yields of a corporate bond and a Treasury bond, we build a *credit spread*. Since corporate bond yields are priced relative to sovereign bonds, credit spreads reflecting credit risk (default) levels. This helps in pricing risk across the market, signaling economic health and investor sentiment about creditworthiness.

Some sources for further information: https://www.clevelandfed.org/indicators-and-data/yield-curve-and-predicted-gdp-growth

https://ig.ft.com/the-yield-curve-explained/#:~:text=As%20it%20turned%20out%2C%20a,of%20the%20curve%20so%20closely.&text=Even%20so%2C%20some%20sceptics%20say,yield%20curve%2C%E2%80%9D%20she%20said

In addition to enabling monetary policy, the bond market also supports the government's financial needs. Government borrowing and spending levels influence sovereign bond yields, and fiscal policies can affect the bond market's risk perception and overall demand for bonds. Sovereign bonds are bonds issued by a national government to raise money for government programs, debt repayment, and other uses. Buyers of sovereign bonds receive interest payments until the bond matures, when the government repurchases the bond. Some ways that government actions impact bond yields are: (a) risk, as a government's debt increases, the risk of default, inflation, and depreciation increases, which causes

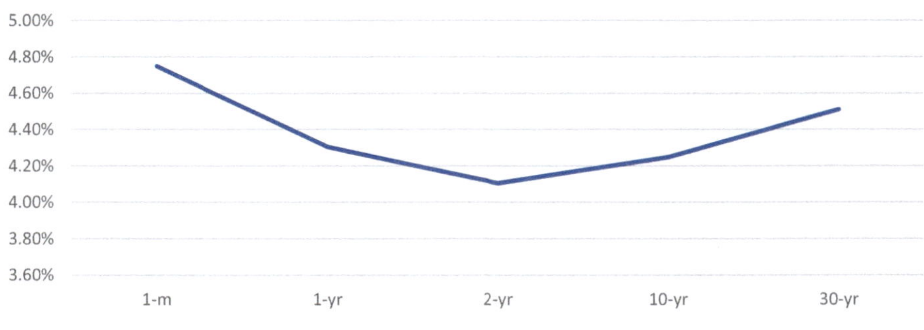

Figure 9.3 The US yield curve, 10/28/2024
Data source: Federal Reserve Economic Data.

Figure 9.4 A term spread: 10-yr Treasury *minus* 2-yr Treasury, 2014:9–2024:9

Data source: Federal Reserve Economic Data.

sovereign bond yields to rise; (b) the exchange rate, if a government borrows in a foreign currency, the devaluation of its domestic currency can make it harder to repay the debt; (c) fiscal expansion, which can lead to higher real interest rates (also known as the *crowding-out effect* of a government's huge effect on the bond market when raising capital). Finally, other factors that can affect sovereign bond yields include the money market rate, inflation shocks, temporary changes in fiscal balances, and output growth. In general, as government debt rises, sovereign bond yields should go up in recognition of the higher risk (default, inflation) carried by investors holding government securities.

1.3 Providing liquidity, safety and income

If you bought individual bonds and plan to hold them until maturity, you may not be concerned whether you would be able to sell them if you wanted to or how cost-efficient it is to do so when building a portfolio. This notion is known as liquidity. Government bonds, especially from developed markets (e.g., US Treasuries, German Bunds), are among the most liquid financial instruments, allowing investors to quickly buy or sell large quantities with minimal price impact. This liquidity supports the stability and efficiency of the broader financial market. In addition, such government bonds are viewed as low-risk investments and are in high demand during economic uncertainty, helping preserve capital and provide a safe place for investors. Furthermore, there is an active secondary market for Treasury bonds, making the investments highly liquid.

In general, liquid investments can be bought and sold with relative ease and without a significant change in price. Liquidity declines whenever it becomes more difficult to trade an investment due to an imbalance in the number of buyers and sellers or because of price volatility. In the case of bonds, investors should understand that the bond market is not always instantly liquid, and some bonds are easier to trade than others.

Bonds carry risks but some bonds offer protection against some risks such as inflation and interest-rate changes. Specifically, *Treasury inflation-protected securities* (TIPS) provide investors with protection against inflation, as their principal value adjusts with inflation rates. This helps preserve purchasing power in inflationary environments. Moreover, bonds are sensitive to interest rate changes, making them useful instruments for managing or hedging interest rate exposure. Investors and companies can use bonds, interest rate swaps, and options to hedge against rate fluctuations impacting cash flows or financial positions.

Finally, bonds provide a stable income stream for investors. In other words, bonds generate regular interest payments, appealing to investors seeking income, particularly retirees and institutions. The bond market allows for income generation at various risk levels, depending on the type of bonds (e.g., government, corporate, or high-yield). Also, bonds, especially high-grade government bonds, are generally seen as a low-risk investment that can preserve capital, making them suitable for investors focused on safety and income.

1.4 Supporting portfolio diversification and risk management

When an investor builds an investment (asset) portfolio, bonds are typically included in it. For example, a typical portfolio may have 60% allocation in equities, 30% in bonds and 10% in cash equivalents (such as Treasury bills or notes). Such a scheme implies asset class diversification. Bonds generally offer lower volatility than stocks and provide stable income, making them a fundamental component of diversified portfolios. Bonds help reduce overall portfolio risk and can improve risk-adjusted returns. In addition, government bonds, particularly those from advanced (mature) economies, often perform well when stocks decline, providing a counterbalance in portfolios during periods of financial market stress. The bond market and the stock market alternate between positive and negative correlations.

Figure 9.5 shows the simple correlations between the two asset classes for the US from December 2104 to August 2024. The equities are represented by the S&P500 (stock market) index and the bonds by the yields of the 10-year Treasury bond of constant maturity. We observe that the correlations ranged from positive to negative over the period but a negative correlation was most prevalent during the 2020s. The late 2010s period was characterized by very high positive correlation

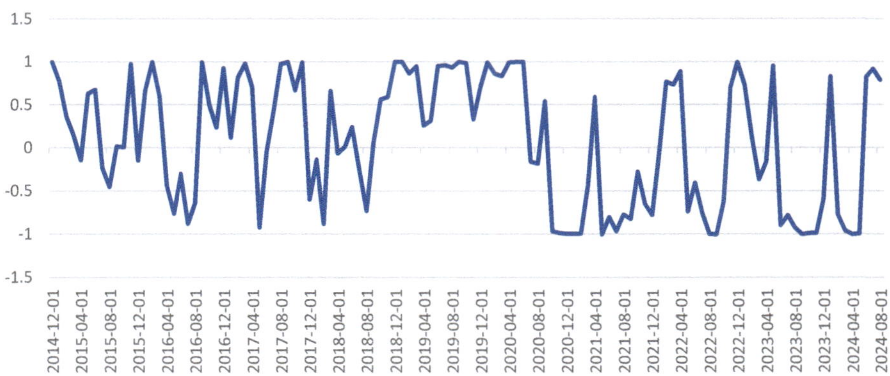

Figure 9.5 Simple correlation between US equities and bonds, 2014:12–2024:08

Data source: Federal Reserve Economic Data

between the two asset classes. These findings suggest that portfolio decisions must be updated to reflect the time-varying nature of stock-bond correlation. In general, stocks are considered high-risk, high-return securities, while government bonds are viewed as low-risk, low-return assets. More discussion on the role of correlation in a portfolio in subsection 5.7.

Finally, bonds serve the function of assisting institutional investors in conducting better asset-liability management. Insurance companies, pension funds, and other financial institutions use bonds to match the duration of their liabilities, ensuring they can meet future obligations to policyholders and beneficiaries. The mismatches are a result of changes to the financial conditions including changing interest rates (interest-rate risk) or liquidity requirements. For example, a bank typically makes long-term loans to people (for the purchase of cars and homes), while paying interest on short-term accounts. When interest rates rise, the banks will pay more in interest on accounts but receive the same on long-term loans because the interest rate is fixed.

In sum, the global bond market is crucial for raising capital, supporting economic growth, facilitating monetary policy, and providing a diversified range of investment options. It also plays a key role in enhancing liquidity, serving as a safe haven during market uncertainty, and offering tools for managing risk, income generation, and sustainability goals. Its depth and stability make it foundational to both financial markets and the global economy.

2 Characteristics of the fixed-income market

The fixed-income market is characterized by unique properties that distinguish it from other financial markets. These properties make it appealing for a wide range of investors, from conservative investors seeking steady income to those managing complex portfolios (the bond portfolio managers). Let us briefly explain some of the market's key properties.

2.1 The components of a bond and their features

By definition, a *bond* is a promissory note which 'promises' its holder a certain fixed stream of payments (the coupon income) for the duration of the life of the bond (maturity). A bond is a debt security or a loan that the bondholder makes to the bond issuer. The elements of a bond are the cash flows (the regular and predictable coupon or interest payments, at a fixed rate), the coupon interest (or the interest rate or yield used to compute the coupon payments), the principal repayment (or par or face value to be repaid at the end of the bond's life), the frequency of coupon payments (how often you will be receiving the coupon interest such as semi-annually or annually) and the maturity (or the length of time of the bond's life).

Here's an example. Assume you bought a 5-year bond at par value (here, $1,000), yielding a 5% interest and paying semi-annually, and plan to hold it to maturity. What are the cash flows over the 5-year period? First, compute the coupon interest or the payments: $1,000 x 0.05 = $50. Then, notice that the payments will occur semi-annually and so, this means that you will be receiving $25 ($50/2) every 6 months for 5 years for a total of $250 in 10 installments. Finally, on the fifth year, you will get back your principal, $1,000 (for a total cash flow of $1,250).

Most fixed-income securities provide regular interest payments to investors, but the coupon rate can be fixed or variable. A fixed rate means that coupons remain constant throughout the bond's life (as in our example above). Coupons fluctuate with changes in a reference interest rate (a floating-rate) such as the federal funds rate or the Secured Overnight Financing Rate (SOFR). Finally, there are bonds that do not pay periodic interest but are issued at a discount and mature at face value. These are known as *zero-coupon bonds*. Also, given that bonds repay the principal to investors at maturity, this property makes bonds a relatively predictable investment compared to equities, as the return of principal reduces uncertainty about future cash flows. Finally, the rate of return that investors earn on a bond, expressed as an annual percentage, is known as the *yield*. The yield depends on the coupon rate, purchase price, and the bond's maturity.

2.2 Bond determinants

In general, there is an inverse relationship between bond prices and yield (market rates). When interest rates rise, bond prices generally fall, and vice versa. This relationship is fundamental to bond pricing and affects how fixed-income securities are valued. This is clearly seen by the present value (PV) formula:

$$PV = FV / (1 + r)^t \tag{9.1}$$

where *FV* is the future value (such as cash flows), *r* the discount rate (or a market interest rate) and *t* the time period. Here's an example that highlights the price-yield inverse relationship. What would be the PV or price of a financial instrument today, P_b (that you are asked to pay), if it promises (with certainty) a FV or future sum of \$1,000 one year from now? Assume your opportunity cost of waiting for this sum is 10%. Note that this would also be the relevant discount rate. So, applying equation (9.1), we have

$$\text{PV} = \text{P}_b = \$1{,}000 / (1 + 0.1)^1 = \$1{,}000 / 1.1 = \$909.09$$

Now, if your opportunity cost changes to 9% and 11%, what would be the instrument's prices in each case?

$$@8\%\ \text{PV} = \text{P}_b = \$1{,}000 / (1 + 0.09)^1 = \$1{,}000 / 1.09 = \$917.43$$
$$@11\%\ \text{PV} = \text{P}_b = \$1{,}000 / (1 + 0.11)^1 = \$1{,}000 / 1.11 = \$900.90$$

As you see, a lower/higher rate (or yield) generated a higher/lower price. We will learn this process in greater detail in section 5 (on bond valuation).

In addition to this important relationship, we are interested in knowing how sensitive a bond's price is to changes in interest rates. This is known in the financial language as *duration*. In general, duration is a measurement of a bond's interest rate risk that considers a bond's maturity, yield, and coupon among other things. So, using our examples above, we notice that a 1% increase in yield (from 10% to 11%) resulted in a 1% change in the price (from \$909.09 to \$900.90). Longer-duration bonds are generally more sensitive to interest rate movements.

Other determinants of bond prices include credit ratings and liquidity. Bonds are rated by agencies like Moody's, S&P, and Fitch, assessing the issuer's ability to make timely payments of interest and principal. Investment-grade bonds (rated BBB/Baa and above) have lower risk, while high-yield or junk bonds carry higher credit risk. Recall that the difference between yields on corporate or riskier bonds and safer government bonds reflects the market's assessment of credit risk (see subsection 2.2). A widening spread indicates higher perceived risk, while a narrowing spread suggests lower risk.

Liquidity levels differ across the fixed-income market. For instance, government bonds are often highly liquid, as they are actively traded and generally viewed as low-risk. Corporate bonds, on the other hand, are typically less liquid, especially high-yield or lower-rated bonds, as they attract a smaller pool of buyers. Finally, municipal bonds (munis, see subsection 3.1.3) are often less liquid, especially in the secondary market, due to niche investor demand.

Finally, there are several additional risks plaguing the bond market. First, as mentioned earlier, we have interest-rate risk (whereby bond prices are inversely related to interest rates, so when rates rise, bond prices fall, and vice versa), credit risk (or the risk of issuer default and so lower-rated bonds carry higher credit risk, leading to higher yields), inflation risk (where rising inflation erodes purchasing power and reduces the real return on fixed-income investments) and currency risk (for bonds issued in foreign currencies, exchange rate fluctuations can impact returns for international investors).

In sum, the fixed-income market's properties – predictable cash flows, credit quality, interest rate sensitivity, diversification benefits, and economic indicators – make it a vital component of financial markets. Its stability and income generation appeal to conservative investors, while its sensitivity to interest rates and economic conditions attracts those managing more complex portfolios. Together, these properties make the fixed-income market essential for both issuers seeking capital and investors balancing risk and return.

Test your understanding 1

1. What is the purpose of the global bond market? What are its main roles/functions?
2. How does the bond market also supports the government's financial needs?
3. How do bonds serve the function of assisting institutional investors in conducting better asset-liability management?
4. Suppose you are offered a chance to buy a bond today at $943.39 for $1,000 one year from now. Assume that this is a safe investment opportunity. If you could put that amount to a savings account at your bank, earning 6% annually, would you accept this offer? Explain.

Solutions appear at the textbook's website.

3 Types of securities in the fixed-income market

After having a general discussion of the bond market, in this section we will review the major sectors of a country's bond market and the securities issued. This includes sovereign bonds, semi-government bonds, municipal or province securities, corporate debt securities, mortgage-backed securities, asset-backed securities, and collateralized debt obligations. Our discussion is limited to their descriptions only.

3.1 Sectors of a country's bond market

One classification is to separate a country's bond market into internal and external bond markets. The *internal bond market* of a country (also called the national bond market) is divided into two parts: the domestic and the foreign bond market. The *domestic bond market* is where issuers domiciled in the country issue bonds and where those bonds are subsequently traded. The *foreign bond market* of a country is where bonds of issuers not domiciled in the country are issued and traded. For example, in the US the foreign bond market is the market where bonds are issued by non-US entities and then subsequently traded domestically. In the United Kingdom (UK), a sterling-denominated bond issued by a Japanese corporation and subsequently traded in the UK bond market is part of the UK foreign bond market. Bonds in the foreign sector of a bond market have colorful (nick) names. For example, foreign bonds in the US market are called *Yankee bonds* and sterling-denominated bonds in the UK foreign bond market are known as *Bulldog bonds*.

The *external bond market* (also called the *international bond market* or more importantly, the *Eurobond market*) includes bonds with the following features:

- they are underwritten by an international syndicate
- at issuance, they are offered simultaneously to investors in many countries
- they are issued outside the jurisdiction of any single country
- they are in unregistered form

Eurobonds are classified based on the currency in which the issue is denominated. For example, when Eurobonds are denominated in US dollars, they are referred to as Eurodollar Bonds, whereas Eurobonds denominated in Japanese yen, are referred to as Euroyen bonds. A *global bond* is a debt obligation that is issued and traded in the foreign bond market of one or more countries and the Eurobond market.

In many countries, the largest sector is often bonds issued by a country's central government and these bonds are referred to as *sovereign bonds*. A government can also issue bonds in the Eurobond market or the foreign sector of another country's bond market, denominated in any currency.

In general, the sectors of a country's bond market represent bonds issued by the federal government, the state and local governments, the government agencies and the corporate sector. Note that not all governments have agencies that issue securities (like the US), only a couple of major economies such as Canada and Germany (but limited). Figure 9.6 shows the value (in $T) of the outstanding securities in the United States such as Treasuries (UST), municipal securities (Munis), corporates and agency debt (Agency), from 2013 to 2023. As is clear from the graph, Treasury bonds entail the largest chunk in the market and sharply rising over time) followed corporate bonds (which slowly increase over time). Agency bonds make up the smallest share in the bond market and is seen to remain relatively stable over the 11-year period. We briefly discuss each bond issuing entity next.

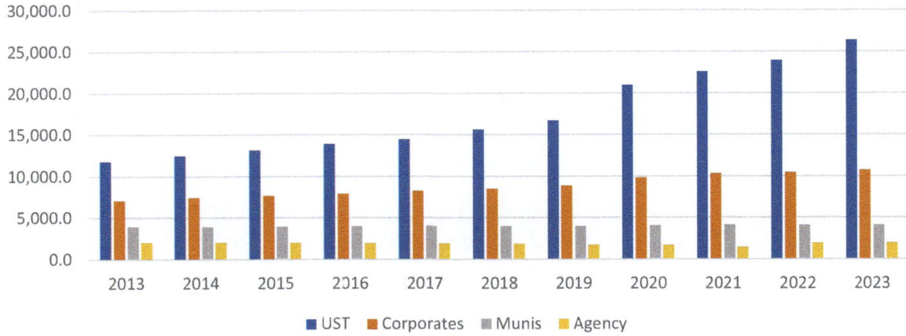

Figure 9.6 Volume of outstanding bond securities in the United States, 2013–2023

Notes: UST are United States Treasury bonds; source: SIFMA

3.1.1 The federal government

The US federal government issues Treasury notes (T-notes), bond (T-bonds) and Treasury-inflation protected securities (TIPS) in an electronic form now. T-notes mature in 2, 3, 5, 7, or 10 years, whereas T-bonds in 20 or 30 years. The interest rates on either are fixed at auction and do not change over the life of the note or bond. For both issues, the interest rate is never less than 0.125%. Interest is paid every 6 months until maturity. The minimum purchase (for an individual investor) is $100 up to a max of $10 million. For TIPS, the amount you get is based on the principal at the time of each interest payment and the principal can go up or down. The principal amount on TIPS is adjusted in proportion to increases in the Consumer Price Index. Therefore, they provide a constant stream of income in real (inflation-adjusted) dollars, and the real interest rates you earn on these securities are risk-free if you hold them to maturity. For more information on these issues visit www.treasury.direct.gov.

In this subsection, we will illustrate how TIPS work. Assume that you are thinking of purchasing a newly issued bond with a three-year maturity, with a par value of $1,000, and a coupon rate of 5%. For simplicity, assume the bond makes annual coupon payments. Assume that inflation turns out to be 2%, 2.5%, and 1% in the next 3 years. Table 9.1 shows how the bond cash flows will be calculated.

Table 9.1 Illustration of how TIPS work

Year	*Inflation*	*Par value*	*Coupon payment*	*Principal repayment*	*Total payment*
0		$1,000.00	$0	$0	$0
1	2%	$1,020.00	$51.00	$0	$51.00
2	2.5%	$1,045.50	$52.275	$0	$52.275
3	1%	$1,055.95	$52.797	$1,055.95	$1,108.753

Let us see how the values are calculated. The first payment comes at the end of the first year, at *t=1*. Because inflation over the year was 2%, the par value of the bond increases from $1,000 to $1,020; since the coupon rate is 5%, the coupon payment is 5% of this amount, or $51. Notice that principal value increases by the inflation rate, and because the coupon payments are 5% of principal, they too increase in proportion to inflation. Hence, the cash flows paid by the bond are in real terms. The remaining values for the coupon payments and principal repayment for years 2 and 3 are similarly computed. However, when the bond matures, the investor receives a final coupon payment of $52.797 plus the (price-level-indexed) repayment of principal, $1,055.95 or a total of $1,108.753.

Next, it would be instructive to verify your rates of return, nominal and real. The nominal rate of return on the bond in the first year is:

> *Nominal return = (Interest + Price appreciation) / Initial price* = ($51.00 + $20) / $1,000 = 7.10%.

The real rate of return is precisely the 5% real yield on the bond and found as follows:

> *Real return = ((1 + Nominal return) / (1 + Inflation)) – 1* = 1.071 / 1.02 = 0.05 or 5%

Other major countries issue Treasury-type (government) bonds. Germany, for example, issues bonds (*Bunds*) with maturities from 8–30 years and notes with a maturity of 5 years. The 10-year Bunds are the largest sector of the German government securities market in terms of amount outstanding. The UK also issues bonds, known as *gilts*. The French Treasury issues long-dated bonds (*Obligation Assimilable du Trésor*), with maturities up to 30 years and notes with maturities between 2 and 5 years. The Canadian government bond market is closely related to the US government bond market and has a similar structure, including types of issues. Finally, in Japan there are 2 types of government securities (referred to as JGBs): medium-term bonds and long-dated bonds.

3.1.2 Government agencies

It is possible for a central government to establish an agency or organization that can issue bonds. Therefore, the bonds of such entities are not issued directly by the central government but may have either a direct or implied government guarantee. These bonds are generically referred to as semi-government bonds or *agency bonds*. In the US, such bonds are referred to as federal agency securities and can be categorized by issuers called federally related institutions and government-sponsored enterprises. *Federally related institutions* are arms of the US federal government. Some of them are: the Export-Import Bank, the Commodity Credit Corporation, the Farmers Housing Administration, the Government National Mortgage Association (GinnieMae), the Private Export Funding Corporation, and the Small Business Administration.

By contrast, the *government-sponsored enterprises* (GSEs) are privately owned, publicly chartered entities and were created by Congress to reduce the cost of capital for certain sectors of the economy deemed to be important enough to require financial assistance. These sectors are agriculture (farmers), housing (homeowners), and education (students). Six such entities issue securities: Federal National Mortgage Association (FannieMae), Federal Home Loan Mortgage Corporation (FreddieMac), Federal Agricultural Mortgage Corporation (Farmer Mac), Federal Farm Credit System, Federal Home Loan Bank System, and Student Loan Marketing Association (Sallie Mae). These GSEs issue two types of bonds: debentures and discount notes. Each does not have any specific collateral backing the debt obligation, rather the ability to pay debtholders depends on the ability of the issuing entity to generate sufficient cash flows to satisfy the obligation. The two GSEs charged with providing liquidity to the mortgage market (Fannie Mae and Freddie Mac) also issue securities backed by the mortgage loans that they purchase. These securities are called agency mortgage-backed securities (MBS) and include mortgage passthrough securities, collateralized mortgage obligations (CMOs) and other variants.

Other countries also issue agency debt. For example, Canada has agency bonds, issued by government agencies and fully guaranteed by the Canadian government. An example is the *Crown Corporation bonds*, issued by agencies such as the Export Development Canada, Farm Credit Canada, and Canada Housing Trust. The issuer pays interest on the number of bonds purchased, and the principal is returned at the maturity date. Germany's agency bonds include those issued by a group of German regional development banks. An example is the *Joint Agency Social Bond*. In September 2022, three German regional development banks issued a EUR500 million Joint Agency Social Bond with a triple-A credit rating (by Fitch Ratings) in 2024. In Australia, there are the bonds issued by a State electric power supplier such as Pacific Power. These bonds are guaranteed by the full faith and credit of the Commonwealth of Australia. Finally, government agency bonds are issued by Germany's Federal Railway (*Bundesbahn*) and the Post Office (*Bundespost*) with the full faith and credit of the German central government.

3.1.3 Municipal securities

Municipal securities (or munis, for short) are issued by non-central governments. The greatest market is in the United States. There are both tax-exempt and taxable munis. *Tax-exempt* means that interest on a municipal security is exempt from federal income taxation. However, this feature applies to interest income, not capital gains. There are two main types of municipal security structures: general-obligation (or tax-backed) debt and revenue bonds. *Tax-backed debt* comprises of instruments issued by states, counties, special districts, cities, towns, and school districts that are secured by some form of tax revenue. This represents the strongest form of the obligation because it is secured by the issuer's unlimited taxing power. Tax revenues can come from individual and corporate income taxes, sales taxes, and property taxes. Because investors pay neither federal nor state taxes on the interest proceeds, they are willing to accept lower yields on these securities.

The second type of a municipal security structure is the revenue bond. *Revenue bonds* are issued for enterprise financings that are secured by the revenues generated by the projects themselves, or for general public-purpose financings. Revenue bonds can be classified by the type of financing and include utility revenue bonds, transportation revenue bonds, housing revenue bonds, higher education revenue bonds, and many more.

Let us perform some basic economic analysis to decide whether a muni is (should be) preferred to a taxable bond (such as a corporate bond discussed in section 3.2). In general, the investor choosing between taxable and tax-exempt bonds needs to compare after-tax returns on each bond. The correct comparison requires the computation of after-tax rates of return with the accounting of taxes on income and realized capital gains. However, here we will apply a rule of thumb. Let t denote the investor's marginal tax rate (the federal plus local marginal tax rate) and r_c the total before-tax rate of return available on taxable bonds. Consequently, $r_c\ (1 - t)$ represents the after-tax rate. If this value exceeds the rate on municipal bonds, r_m, the investor does better by holding the taxable bonds. Otherwise, the muni provides higher after-tax returns.

More formally, we have the following equations to determine the interest rate on taxable bonds that would be necessary to provide an after-tax return equal to that of a muni.

$$r_m = r_c\ (1 - t) \tag{9.2a}$$

$$\text{or} \quad r_c = r_m\ /\ (1 - t) \tag{9.2b}$$

$$\text{or} \quad t = 1 - (r_m\ /\ r_c) \tag{9.2c}$$

The first equation sets the two returns equal to each other for determining the indifference between a muni and the corporate bond. The second equation is the rate a taxable bond would need to offer in order to match the after-tax yield on the tax-free municipal bond (known as the *equivalent taxable yield*). The third equation shows the *yield ratio*, $r_m\ /r_c$, as a key determinant of the attractiveness of munis. The higher this ratio, the lower the cutoff tax bracket, and the more investors will prefer to hold municipal debt.

Let us work with an example. If your tax bracket is 28%, would you prefer to earn a 5% taxable return or a 3% tax-free yield? What is the equivalent taxable yield of the 3% tax-free yield? A 5% taxable return is equivalent to an after-tax return of 5(1 – 0.28) = 3.6%. Therefore, you would be better off in the taxable bond. The equivalent taxable yield of the tax-free security is 3/(1 – 0.28) = 4.16%. So, a taxable bond would have to pay a 4.16% yield to provide the same after-tax return as a tax-free bond offering a 3% yield.

In general, municipal bonds are high-quality investments that may be able to weather potential economic and financial downturns. However, individual municipal bonds can be less liquid than other assets, and it can be time-consuming and expensive to diversify across individual bonds. Investors who would prefer this market are those in high-tax brackets and those who invest for the long run.

3.2 Corporate bonds

Just like the federal and state/local governments and its agencies, corporations borrow money by issuing bonds. Unlike equities, most bonds are traded over the counter (the OTC market) via an electronic communications network (ECN) of bond dealers around the country. In practice, the bond market can be *thin*, in the sense that there are few investors interested in trading a specific issue at any particular time. Corporate bonds carry credit ratings and several provisions. The ratings on an estimate of bond safety are produced and published the three major bond rating agencies (Moody's, Standard & Poor's, and Fitch Ratings). So, corporate bonds with A (AAA, AA and A) ratings are safer than those rated B or below. As a general rule, safer bonds have lower yields to maturity.

Some corporate bonds carry a number of clauses such as call and put provisions. *Call provisions* allow the issuer to repurchase the bond at a specified call price before the maturity date. For example, if a company has issued a bond with a high coupon rate, when interest rates fall later, the firm might like to retire the high-coupon debt and issue new bonds at a lower coupon rate to reduce interest payments. The dollar proceeds from the new bond issue are used to pay for the repurchase of the existing bonds at a call price (the process is known as *refunding*). Economically speaking, a bond call option is valuable to the firm because it allows it to buy back the bonds and refinance at lower interest rates when market rates fall. Hence, investors lose in this case. To compensate investors for this risk, callable bonds are issued with higher coupons and promised yields to maturity than noncallable bonds.

Just like corporations view a call provision as valuable to them, investors (bondholders) view a *put provision* as valuable. So, if market yields are higher than those bondholders currently earn from a bond, they have the option to sell their bonds back to the issuer so they can purchase the new bonds with the higher coupon rate. However, in order to entice issuers (corporations) to take their bonds back, bondholders can sell the bonds at the put price.

Finally, another useful bond provision is convertibility. *Convertible bonds* give bondholders an option to exchange each bond for a specified number of shares of common stock of the firm. The *conversion ratio* is the number of shares for which each bond may be exchanged. Here's an example. Assume that a convertible bond (issued at par value, $1,000) is convertible into 45 shares of a firm's stock. If the current stock price is $20 per share, the option to convert is not profitable now (because the bond's conversion value would be $900 (=45 shares *x* 20)). If the stock price later rises to $25, then each bond may be converted profitably into $1,125 worth of stock. The *conversion premium* is the excess of the bond price over its conversion value. So, in this example, if the bond were selling currently for $950, its premium would be $50. In general, convertible bondholders benefit from price appreciation of the company's stock. But this comes at a price: convertible bonds offer lower coupon rates and stated or promised yields to maturity than nonconvertible bonds.

Finally, there are *floating-rate bonds* (floaters) which make interest payments tied to current market rates. For example, the rate might be adjusted annually to the current T-bill rate plus a premium implying that the bond always pays approximately current market rates. The main risk involved in floaters refers to changes in the firm's credit status. If the financial health of the firm deteriorates, then investors will demand a greater yield premium than is offered by the security (because the yield spread is fixed over the life of the security). The result would be a fall in the corporation's bond price. Note also that while the coupon rate on floating-rate bonds adjusts to changes in market interest rates, it does not adjust to changes in the firm's financial condition.

4 Bond valuation

In this section, we present how an investor can value (or price) a bond. Recall that a bond promises certain fixed (even) cash flows (the coupon payments) during its life and at the end the principal (par value) is returned. Therefore, the investor must discount all these future cash flows in order to find the security's price. We discount its expected cash flows by an appropriate discount rate. So, if we call the discount rate *r, and* maturity date *T,* then the bond value can be written as:

$$PV = P_b = \Sigma^T_{t=1} [Payments / (1 + r)^t] + Par / (1 + r)^T \qquad (9.3)$$

The summation sign means that we add the present value of each coupon payment, which is discounted based on the time until it will be paid. Then, the magnitude in the brackets is simply the present value of an annuity, whereas the second term is the present value of a single sum, the final payment of the bond's par value. An *annuity* is just a fixed, even stream of cash flows. Note that we first encountered part of this formula in section 2.2 (equation (9.1)).

There are two ways you can apply this formula, either by using the short-cut or the formula approach. The formula method uses the following expressions:

For an annuity: $(1/r)\ [1 - 1/(1 + r)^T]$ (9.4a)
For a single sum: $1/(1 + r)^T$ (9.4b)

We can call (9.4a) the *present value interest factor of an annuity* (PVIFA), with r and T as coordinates, and (9.4b) the *present value interest factor of a single sum* (PVIF), with the same coordinates. Consequently, equation (9.3) can be rewritten as

$$PV = P_b = C * [(1/r)\ [1 - 1/(1+r)^T)] + M * [1/(1+r)^T] \qquad (9.5a)$$
$$\text{or} \quad PV = P_b = C * (PVIFA_{r,T}) + M * (PVIF_{r,T}) \qquad (9.5b)$$

where *C* represents the coupon payments and *M* the par value of the bond. Let us show how you can apply these formulae to price a bond.

Assume that you wish to buy a 5-year bond with a coupon rate of 10% and a par of $1,000 making annual coupon payments. Using equation (9.5a), we have:

$$P_b = \$100\ [(1/.10) * (1 - 1/(1.1)^5] + \$1,000\ (1/1.10)^5 = 379.0787 + 620.9213 = \$1,000$$

where the coupon payment is $100 (=$1,000 * 0.10). So, the price of the bond currently is $1,000. We can also say that the bond sells at par.

Using the short-cut formula, equ. (9.5b), we have:

$$P_b = \$100\ (3.79079) + \$1,000\ (0.62092) = \$1,000$$

where the PVIFA value (3.79079) was found by the cross of the period (5) on the vertical axis, and discount rate (10%) on the horizontal axis of the first table in Table 9.2, and the PVIF value (0.62092) from the second table in Table 9.2. So, both approaches gave the same value for the bond. The $1,000 reflects the price that investors should pay for that bond, right now.

Corporate bonds are typically issued at par value. This means bond issuers (underwriters, or firms that market and sell the bonds to the public) are careful to choose a coupon rate that very close to current market yields. After the bonds are issued, bondholders may buy or sell bonds in secondary markets. This is where bond prices fluctuate inversely with the market interest rate. Interest rate

Table 9.2 Present value tables

PRESENT VALUE OF AN ANNUITY

n/i	1.0%	1.5%	2.0%	2.5%	3.0%	3.5%	4.0%	4.5%	5.0%	5.5%	6.0%	7.0%	8.0%	9.0%	10.0%	11.0%	12.0%	20.0%
1	0.9901	0.9852	0.9804	0.9756	0.9709	0.9662	0.9615	0.9569	0.9524	0.9479	0.9434	0.9346	0.9259	0.9174	0.9091	0.9009	0.8929	0.8333
2	1.9559	1.9559	1.9416	1.9274	1.9135	1.8997	1.8861	1.8727	1.8594	1.8463	1.8334	1.8080	1.7833	1.7591	1.7355	1.7125	1.6901	1.5278
3	2.9410	2.9122	2.8839	2.8560	2.8286	2.8016	2.7751	2.7490	2.7232	2.6979	2.6730	2.6243	2.5771	2.5313	2.4869	2.4437	2.4018	2.1065
4	3.9020	3.8544	3.8077	3.7620	3.7171	3.6731	3.6299	3.5875	3.5460	3.5052	3.4651	3.3872	3.3121	3.2397	3.1699	3.1024	3.0373	2.5887
5	4.8534	4.7826	4.7135	4.6458	4.5797	4.5151	4.4518	4.3900	4.3295	4.2703	4.2124	4.1002	3.9927	3.8897	3.7908	3.6959	3.6048	2.9906
6	5.7955	5.6972	5.6014	5.5081	5.4172	5.3286	5.2421	5.1579	5.0757	4.9955	4.9173	4.7665	4.6229	4.4859	4.3553	4.2305	4.1114	3.3255
7	6.7282	6.5982	6.4720	6.3494	6.2303	6.1145	6.0021	5.8927	5.7864	5.6830	5.5824	5.3893	5.2064	5.0330	4.8684	4.7122	4.5638	3.6046
8	7.6517	7.4859	7.3255	7.1701	7.0197	6.8740	6.7327	6.5959	6.4632	6.3346	6.2098	5.9713	5.7466	5.5348	5.3349	5.1461	4.9676	3.8372
9	8.5660	8.3605	8.1622	7.9709	7.7861	7.6077	7.4353	7.2688	7.1078	6.9522	6.8017	6.5152	6.2469	5.9952	5.7590	5.5370	5.3282	4.0310
10	9.4713	9.2222	8.9826	8.7521	8.5302	8.3166	8.1109	7.9127	7.7217	7.5376	7.3601	7.0236	6.7101	6.4177	6.1446	5.8892	5.6502	4.1925
11	10.3676	10.0711	9.7868	9.5142	9.2526	9.0016	8.7605	8.5289	8.3064	8.0925	7.8869	7.4987	7.1390	6.8052	6.4951	6.2065	5.9377	4.3271
12	11.2551	10.9075	10.5753	10.2578	9.9540	9.6633	9.3851	9.1186	8.8633	8.6185	8.3838	7.9427	7.5361	7.1607	6.8137	6.4924	6.1944	4.4392
13	12.1337	11.7315	11.3484	10.9832	10.6350	10.3027	9.9856	9.6829	9.3936	9.1171	8.8527	8.3577	7.9038	7.4869	7.1034	6.7499	6.4235	4.5327
14	13.0037	12.5434	12.1062	11.6909	11.2961	10.9205	10.5631	10.2228	9.8986	9.5896	9.2950	8.7455	8.2442	7.7862	7.3667	6.9819	6.6282	4.6106
15	13.8651	13.3432	12.8493	12.3814	11.9379	11.5174	11.1184	10.7395	10.3797	10.0376	9.7122	9.1079	8.5595	8.0607	7.6061	7.1909	6.8109	4.6755

(Continued)

PRESENT VALUE OF $1

n/i	1.0%	1.5%	2.0%	2.5%	3.0%	3.5%	4.0%	4.5%	5.0%	5.5%	6.0%	7.0%	8.0%	9.0%	10.0%	11.0%	12.0%	20.0%
1	0.9901	0.9852	0.9804	0.9756	0.9709	0.9662	0.9615	0.9569	0.9524	0.9479	0.9434	0.9346	0.9259	0.9174	0.9091	0.9009	0.8929	0.8333
2	0.9803	0.9707	0.9612	0.9518	0.9426	0.9335	0.9246	0.9157	0.9070	0.8985	0.8900	0.8734	0.8573	0.8417	0.8264	0.8116	0.7972	0.6944
3	0.9706	0.9563	0.9423	0.9286	0.9151	0.9019	0.8890	0.8763	0.8638	0.8516	0.8396	0.8163	0.7938	0.7722	0.7513	0.7312	0.7118	0.5787
4	0.9610	0.9422	0.9238	0.9060	0.8885	0.8714	0.8548	0.8386	0.8227	0.8072	0.7921	0.7629	0.7350	0.7084	0.6830	0.6587	0.6355	0.4823
5	0.9515	0.9283	0.9057	0.8839	0.8626	0.8420	0.8219	0.8025	0.7835	0.7651	0.7473	0.7130	0.6806	0.6499	0.6209	0.5935	0.5674	0.4019
6	0.9420	0.9145	0.8880	0.8623	0.8375	0.8135	0.7903	0.7679	0.7462	0.7252	0.7050	0.6663	0.6302	0.5963	0.5645	0.5346	0.5066	0.3349
7	0.9327	0.9010	0.8706	0.8413	0.8131	0.7860	0.7599	0.7348	0.7107	0.6874	0.6651	0.6227	0.5835	0.5470	0.5132	0.4817	0.4523	0.2791
8	0.9235	0.8877	0.8535	0.8207	0.7894	0.7594	0.7307	0.7032	0.6768	0.6516	0.6274	0.5820	0.5403	0.5019	0.4665	0.4339	0.4039	0.2326
9	0.9143	0.8746	0.8368	0.8007	0.7664	0.7337	0.7026	0.6729	0.6446	0.6176	0.5919	0.5439	0.5002	0.4604	0.4241	0.3909	0.3606	0.1938
10	0.9053	0.8617	0.8203	0.7812	0.7441	0.7089	0.6756	0.6439	0.6139	0.5854	0.5584	0.5083	0.4632	0.4224	0.3855	0.3522	0.3220	0.1615
11	0.8963	0.8489	0.8043	0.7621	0.7224	0.6849	0.6496	0.6162	0.5847	0.5549	0.5268	0.4751	0.4289	0.3875	0.3505	0.3173	0.2875	0.1346
12	0.8874	0.8364	0.7885	0.7436	0.7014	0.6618	0.6246	0.5897	0.5568	0.5260	0.4970	0.4440	0.3971	0.3555	0.3186	0.2858	0.2567	0.1122
13	0.8787	0.8240	0.7730	0.7254	0.6810	0.6394	0.6006	0.5643	0.5303	0.4986	0.4688	0.4150	0.3677	0.3262	0.2897	0.2575	0.2292	0.0935
14	0.8700	0.8118	0.7579	0.7077	0.6611	0.6178	0.5775	0.5400	0.5051	0.4726	0.4423	0.3878	0.3405	0.2992	0.2633	0.2320	0.2046	0.0779
15	0.8613	0.7999	0.7430	0.6905	0.6419	0.5969	0.5553	0.5167	0.4810	0.4479	0.4173	0.3624	0.3152	0.2745	0.2394	0.2090	0.1827	0.0649

Notes: n is the period, *i* is the discount rate, PVIFA is the first table.

fluctuations represent the main source of risk in the bond market but also the bond's maturity. In general, the longer the maturity of the bond, the greater the sensitivity of its price to fluctuations in the interest rate, *ceteris paribus*. Let us see what would happen to a bond's price when interest rates change.

Using the previous example, assume now that, *one year after the bond was issued*, market interest rates (or yields) dropped to 8%. What would be the price of that bond? Before applying the short-cut formula and using the tables in Table 9.2, we need to recognize three things: first, that we have lost one period in the valuation process and so, now we have 4 years until the bond matures, second, that the bond's coupon rate remains the same and third, and more importantly, that we need to value the bond at the current market yield. Therefore, we have:

$$P_b = \$100(3.31213) + \$1{,}000(0.73503) = \$1{,}066.243$$

As you see, the new price is higher than the initial price and sells for a premium (or extra amount) of $66.243. We say that the bond sells at premium. Why is the bond selling at a higher price now? Notice that new bonds now will carry a lower coupon rate (8%) and thus annual coupon payments are $80. So, ask yourself what you would like to earn on a yearly basis, $100 or $80? Naturally, you would prefer to earn $100 and so, your bond is more valuable than newly issued bonds! That is why these bonds sell at a premium from par.

Do you recognize that the opposite occurs when market rates rise? If they rise to 12%, what would be the new bond price, again one year after the bond was issued? Using the same formula, we obtain a price of $939.255, derived as follows:

$$P_b = \$100(3.03735) + \$1{,}000(0.63552) = \$939.255$$

In this case, the bond sells at a discount (from par). The reason is that newly issued bonds will provide $120 in annual payments and thus, older bonds will not be as preferred to the new ones forcing their market prices to go down. This is a capital loss on the bond.

Before going any further, you need to know what would happen to the components of the formulae (equations 9.5a and 9.5b), when payments are made semi-annually (which is the norm in the United States). In this case, three adjustments must be made: (1) the coupon (C) will be halved (C/2), (2) the discount rate (r) will be halved as well (r/2) and (3), the time period (T) will double (2T). The latter is because there are two payments within a year, every six months.

Now, let us understand how maturity affects the bonds' prices using various coupon rates. Since the prices will not be calculated here, you can verify them yourself as practice. Table 9.3 displays some examples of bonds at various maturities (1 year, 10 and 20 years) and three coupon (or market) rates, 2%, 6% and 10%. Assume that the bond sells at par when the discount rate is 8%. As you see, when interest rates depart from the coupon rate (of 8%), the change in the bond price is greater for longer times to maturity. You can see this by observing the 1st column of prices in the table. The longer the period your money is tied up, the greater the loss and, hence, the greater the drop in the bond price. In addition, the row for 1-year maturity bonds shows little price sensitivity to changes in interest rates. But for 20-year maturity bonds, interest rate changes have a large impact on bond prices. Therefore, the effect of discounting is greatest for the longer-term bonds.

Table 9.3 Bond prices under various maturities and discount rates

Maturity		*Discount rates*	
	2%	6%	10%
1 year	\$1,059.12	\$1,019.14	\$981.40
10 years	\$1,541.37	\$1,148.77	\$875.39
20 years	\$1,985.05	\$1,231.15	\$828.41

In general, a bond's maturity significantly impacts its price, meaning longer-term bonds experience greater price volatility and are typically more sensitive to interest rate changes compared to shorter-term bonds; this is often referred to as *price convergence to par* as the maturity date approaches.

Finally, it is interesting to find the (holding-period) rate of return on a bond, if we sell it at any time before maturity. Using the above example's data, assume that you bought the bond upon issuance (at the par), kept it for one year, and then sold it, at the price of \$1,066.243 or, in the other case, a price of \$939.255. What would be your holding-period rates of return (HPR)? The formula is as follows:

$$HPR = (Selling\ price - Purchase\ Price + Coupon)\ /\ Purchase\ Price \qquad (9.6)$$

Plugging in the values, with the premium bond, we have:

$$\text{HPR} = (1066.243 - 1{,}000 + 100)\ /\ 1000 = 0.166 \text{ or } 16.6\%$$

Now, plugging in the values, with the discount bond, we have:

$$\text{HPR} = (939.255 - 1{,}000 + 100)\ /\ 1000 = 0.0392 \text{ or } 3.92\%$$

So, changes in market rates will result in changes in bond returns rendering a bond's HPR better or worse than the original yield (10%). A decline in yield to maturity (8%) results in a holding-period return greater than the initial yield. Conversely, an increase in the bond's yield to maturity (12%) reduces its price, which means that HPR will be less than the initial yield. This is exactly what we see here.

Test your understanding 2

1. What is the yield ratio, when we are referring to the relative desirability of a muni versus a corporate bond?
2. What is the fundamental difference between a nominal and real rate of return? What type of inflation is used?
3. When would it beneficial (i.e., profitable) to exercise the bond conversion option?
4. Explain how maturity affects a bond's price

Solutions appear at the textbook's website.

5 How investors use the bond market

Institutional and retail investors can exploit the bond market by using strategies that leverage interest rate movements, credit spreads, yield curves, and bond market inefficiencies. Let us briefly explain some of them.

5.1 Interest-rate anticipation strategies

Many investors need to forecast interest rates in order to adjust or insulate their bond portfolios from adverse interest-rate movements. One important notion of interest-rate anticipation strategies is duration. *Duration* has a couple of different meanings. One is from its investors, Frederick Macaulay, who explained it as a measure of the effective maturity of a bond. The effective maturity was defined as the weighted average of the times until each payment with weights proportional to the present value of the payment. In plain terms, the Macaulay duration formula is expressed as:

$$D = \Sigma^{T}_{t=1} (w_t * t) \tag{9.7}$$

where w_t is the weight and t the time period.

Another way to explain duration, more useful for our discussion here, its description as a measure of the interest-rate sensitivity of a bond portfolio.[1] To express this notion algebraically, we note that the proportional change in a bond's price, $\Delta P/P$, is linked to the change in its yield to maturity (ytm), y, according to the rule below:

$$\Delta P/P = -D * [\Delta(1+y)/(1+y)] \tag{9.8}$$

However, a short-cut formula is more practical and is defined as:

$$\Delta P/P = -[D/(1+y)] * \Delta y \tag{9.8a}$$

which is defined as *modified duration*, MD. So, because the percentage change in the bond price is proportional to MD, the latter is a natural measure of the bond's exposure to interest rate volatility. Here's an example.

Assume a bond with a 30-year maturity, with a coupon rate of 8%, making annual payments and with a yield to maturity of 9%. What will happen to the bond price if the bond's yield to maturity increases to 9.1%? First of all, we need to derive the bond's price and duration. Using Excel's *PRICE* function, we obtain the sum of $89.726, and using the *DURATION* function, we get a duration of 11.373.[2] Then, using equation (9.8a), which tells us that an increase of.1% in the bond's yield to maturity (Δy =.001 or 1/100) will result (after taking the P into the right-hand side of the formula) in a price change of

$$\Delta P = -[D/(1+y)] * \Delta y * P = -(11.373/1.09) * 0.001 * 89.726 = -0.9362\%$$

So, returning to our strategy we say that if investors expect rates to increase, they might shorten duration (buy shorter-term bonds) to benefit from price increases. Conversely, if they expect rates to fall, they might lengthen duration to limit potential losses. This what is known as the *duration positioning strategy*. Therefore, the longer the duration, the more sensitive the bond is to interest rate changes, meaning longer-duration bonds tend to be riskier in an environment of rising rates.

Some factors that affect duration are the bond's maturity, where longer-term bonds generally have higher duration, the bond's coupon rate, and so bonds with lower coupon rates typically have higher duration, as a larger portion of their value is tied up in the principal repayment at maturity, and the yield to maturity, where a higher *ytm* generally results in a lower duration.[3]

In addition to duration, investors look at the yield curve (YC) and its shape in order to devise and apply investment strategies. The shape of the yield curve changes with economic cycles. Investors can take positions based on anticipated shifts in the yield curve. So, a steepening YC suggests buying long-term bonds or sell short-term bonds to profit from an expected rise in long-term yields relative to short-term yields. By contrast, a flattening YC implies buying short-term bonds and sell long-term bonds if the expectation is that short-term rates will rise or long-term rates will fall.

5.2 Credit spread strategies

Credit spreads (the difference between yields on corporate bonds and government bonds) fluctuate with economic conditions and credit risk sentiment. If an investor anticipates a reduction in credit spreads (e.g., improving economic conditions), they might buy higher-yielding corporate bonds to capture the spread compression. Conversely, if they anticipate a recession or increased default risk, they may avoid high-yield bonds or short credit to profit from widening spreads.

Another related strategy is *sector rotation*. The idea is to tilt (shift) the portfolio more heavily into industry or sector groups that are expected to outperform based on one's assessment of the state of the business cycle. For example, during economic expansions, corporate bonds and high-yield bonds often outperform due to improved credit conditions, while during recessions or market downturns, investors might shift to safer government bonds or investment-grade corporate bonds. It is important to mention that such a strategy, which falls into the general investment strategy of *market timing*, will be successful only if one anticipates the next stage of the business cycle better than other investors. In reality, it is never as clear how long each phase of the cycle will last.

5.3 Bond ladder, bullet and barbell strategies

Bond laddering is a strategy that involves purchasing bonds with staggered maturities, allowing investors to reinvest maturing bonds at prevailing rates. This approach reduces (diversifies) interest rate risk across different time horizons and helps investors manage cash flow needs. A *barbell strategy* is one in which an investor holds bonds with very short and very long maturities, minimizing exposure to intermediate maturities. If interest rates rise, the short-term bonds will mature quickly, allowing for reinvestment at higher rates, while the long-term bonds benefit if rates fall. Finally, in a *bullet strategy*, the portfolio is constructed so that the maturities of the bonds in the portfolio are highly concentrated at one point on the yield curve.[4]

5.4 Exploiting market inefficiencies and mispricing

Relative value trading (strategies) involves identifying pricing inefficiencies between similar bonds (e.g., bonds from the same issuer with different maturities or structures). By buying the undervalued bond and selling the overvalued one, investors can profit as prices converge. *Yield-pickup strategies* entail investors comparing (and swapping) bonds with similar credit ratings but different yields (e.g., municipal bonds vs. corporate bonds) and opt for those offering a higher yield while managing the associated risks. The *pure yield pickup* swap is an exchange of a shorter-duration bond for a longer-duration bond. This swap is pursued as a means of increasing return by holding higher-yielding, longer-maturity bonds and the investor is willing to bear the interest rate risk.

This strategy can be illustrated using the Treasury yield curve, as of November 8, 2022, shown in Figure 9.7. You can see from that graph that longer-term T-bonds offered higher yields to maturity than shorter ones. So, if an investor swaps the shorter-term bond for the longer one, he will earn a higher rate of return as long as the yield curve does not shift upward during the holding period. Of course, if it does, the longer-duration bond will suffer a greater capital loss.

Finally, taxable investors, for instance, might favor municipal bonds due to their tax advantages relative to taxable corporate bonds. Investors in high tax brackets often purchase municipal bonds because the interest is generally exempt from federal (and sometimes state) income taxes. This can lead to a higher effective yield than taxable bonds, making municipals particularly attractive to investors seeking tax efficiency.

5.5 Active vs. passive investing

Investment strategies can be generally categorized as passive or active. Passive investing simply means following a market index an earning its rate or return (with virtually minimal commission fees or other expenses). By contrast, active investing entails significant costs in hopes of earning a return (far) above the market (or index). Active bond managers seek to exploit short-term fluctuations in bond prices, credit spreads, or interest rates. They adjust portfolio allocations dynamically, hoping to outperform passive benchmarks. Alternatively, investors may use

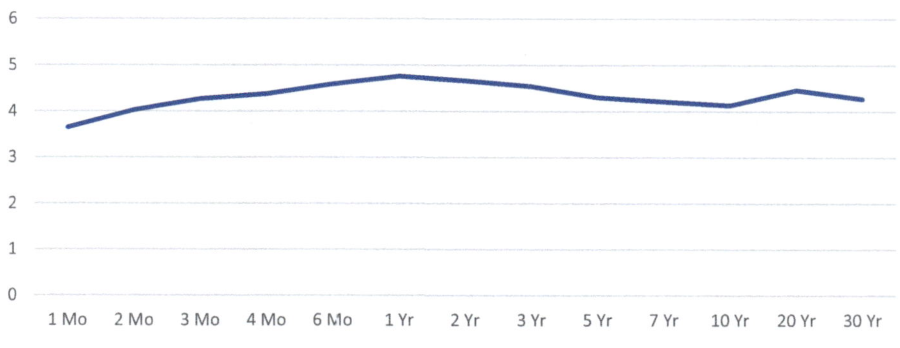

Figure 9.7 The US Treasury yield curve, 11/08/2022
Data source: www.treasurydirct.gov

bond index funds or ETFs to gain exposure to a diversified range of bonds at a low cost. Passive investing in bond indices can be a simple way to achieve market-average returns with less effort, though it may miss opportunities for excess return.

5.6 Hedging and junk bonds strategies

Finally, bond investors can exploit the bond market by applying risk management and hedging strategies. One such instrument for risk management (and hedging) is a credit default swap, CDS. A CDS is a financial derivative that provides insurance against the default of a bond issuer. Investors who believe a company's credit risk is mispriced can either buy or sell CDS protection. For example, they might buy CDS on an issuer they expect to default or sell protection if they believe the issuer's credit rating will improve. Investors can use interest rate swaps to hedge against rising rates or to adjust portfolio duration without selling underlying bonds. Options on interest rates (e.g., swaptions) can provide leverage to benefit from anticipated rate movements without holding actual bonds.

Risk-tolerant investors can also invest in high-yielding or junk bonds in an effort to enhance their yields. *High-yield bonds* offer the potential for higher returns, albeit with greater default risk. These bonds may perform well during economic growth periods when companies' ability to meet debt obligations is strong. Also, *convertible bonds* offer an option to convert the bond into stock at a later date, allowing investors to participate in equity upside while receiving bond interest payments. They are attractive in rising markets where the issuing company's stock is expected to perform well.

In sum, investors can exploit the bond market by anticipating interest rate changes, managing credit risk, capitalizing on yield curves, and leveraging global opportunities. Strategies such as bond laddering, duration adjustments, inflation protection, and hedging provide ways to enhance returns, manage risk, and diversify portfolios. Each strategy carries unique risks, and investors should carefully assess the macroeconomic environment and individual bond characteristics to optimize their bond market exposure.

5.7 How are stock-bond correlations affecting your investment portfolio?

At the heart of an efficient portfolio construction are the correlations among the assets that comprise the portfolio. In our case, stock-bond correlation can have a significant impact on your investment decisions. A negative correlation means that bonds can play their traditional role of potentially hedging against weak economic growth and mitigating stock market volatility. Therefore, a negative stock-bond correlation strengthens portfolio diversification and gives you better potential opportunities to meet your long-term investment goals. See Figure 9.5 on the stock-bond correlation for the 2014–2024 period.

The wild card in this relationship, however, is inflation. While bonds can hedge against growth shocks, they cannot protect against unexpected inflation shocks. Figure 9.8 displays the S&P500 stock market index, the 10-year Treasury Note and the rate of inflation for the past 11 years (2014–2024), on a monthly basis. The correlation between the stock market and the bond rate is 0.163, the correlation

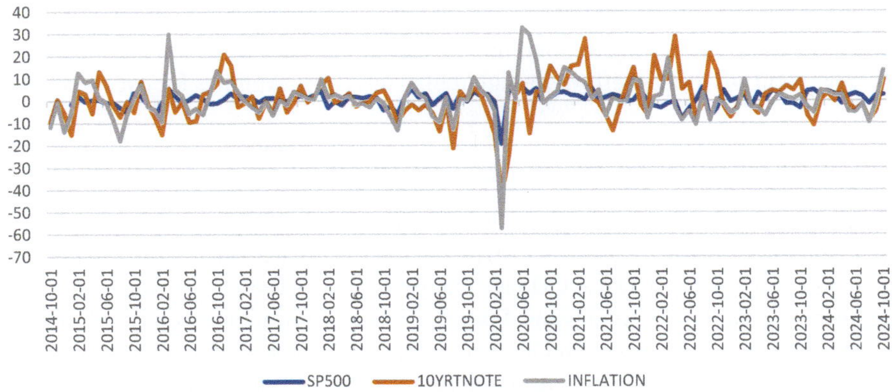

Figure 9.8 S&P500, 10-year T-note and inflation, 2014:01–2024:10
Data source: Federal Reserve Economic Data

between the stock market and inflation is 0.637 and that between inflation and the bond rate is 0.481. However, in the past there were periods of negative stock-bond correlations, according to research by Ilmanen (2003).[5] Specifically, the author found a negative correlation during the 1929–1932, 1956–1965 and 1998–2003 periods. However, most of the period under examination (which began in 1926) witnesses positive stock-bond correlations. Historically, when inflation is above 3% the correlation between equities and bonds tended to be positive as both asset classes struggle.

Ilmanen explained that the bond-to-stock causal direction (relationship) is positive (because falling bond yields tend to also reduce equity discount rates), but the stock-to-bond causality is negative (because a slow or weak equity market can trigger monetary policy easing and a bond market rally). In addition, this correlation is impacted by other variables such as macroeconomic and financial and mainly by inflation. Ilmanen stated that the stock-bond correlation is typically low when inflation and economic growth are low and when equities are volatile. The latter situation resembles the "flight-to-quality" phenomenon.

In general, even if correlations are positive, it can be shown that the portfolio standard deviation will be less than the weighted average of the component standard deviations, as long as the assets are not perfectly positively correlated (that is, have a correlation +1). Thus, portfolio diversification is of value as long as assets are less than perfectly correlated. Furthermore, the contribution of an asset to portfolio variance (risk) depends on its correlation with the other assets in the portfolio, as well as on its own variance (risk). Similarly, it can be shown that an asset that is perfectly negatively correlated with a portfolio can reduce the portfolio variance to zero. Therefore, we say that it can serve as a perfect hedge.

We end this chapter with a question: what would be the link between the fixed-income market and a company's marketing (advertising) efforts? You may think that these are unrelated but academic research has revealed that a firm's marketing campaigns are very much tied to its ability to tap the fixed-income market and raise capital. Box 9.1 explains how.

Box 9.1

How is the fixed-income market related to marketing?

CREDIT STATUS: A firm's marketing strategy can affect how investors view its creditworthiness and financial stability which, in turn, influences the company's demand for bonds.

PUBLIC IMAGE: If a company has and maintains a trustworthy and positive public image through its marketing efforts, then it will be easier for it to raise capital in the fixed-income markets.

INVESTOR RELATIONSHIPS: Marketing materials that go to investors contain information about the company, including potential bond issuance, which reinforce a positive investor perception about the company.

ADVERTISING: Research has shown that by boosting visibility, advertising improves stock returns, bond issuance at lower cost and liquidity.

Nejadmalayeri, A., I. Mathur, and M. Singh (2013). Product Market Advertising and Corporate Bonds. *Journal of Corporate Finance* 19 (February), 78–94.

Summary

- The global bond market plays a critical role in the global financial system and economy by facilitating capital flow, providing a benchmark for interest rates, supporting monetary policy, and offering investment opportunities.
- A main reason (purpose) of the global bond market is to assist entities to raise capital for various purposes.
- The bond market is instrumental to a country's conduct of domestic monetary policy.
- Fixed-income markets are sensitive to macroeconomic indicators and monetary policy.
- The yield curve (YC), which exhibits yields across bond maturities, is a well-known indicator of economic expectations.
- The YC of government bonds serves as a benchmark for global interest rates.
- Government bonds, especially from developed markets, are among the most liquid financial instruments, allowing investors to quickly buy or sell large quantities with minimal price impact.
- This liquidity supports the stability and efficiency of the broader financial market.
- Bonds provide a stable income stream for investors.
- Bonds help reduce overall portfolio risk and can improve risk-adjusted returns.
- Government bonds, particularly those from advanced (mature) economies, often perform well when stocks decline, providing a counterbalance in portfolios during periods of financial market stress.
- Bonds serve the function of assisting institutional investors in conducting better asset-liability management.

- The fixed-income market is characterized by unique properties that distinguish it from other financial markets.
- A bond is a promissory note which "promises" its holder a certain fixed stream of payments (the coupon income) for the duration of the life of the bond (maturity).
- The elements of a bond are the cash flows (the regular and predictable coupon or interest payments, at a fixed rate), the coupon interest (or the interest rate or yield used to compute the coupon payments), the principal repayment (or par or face value to be repaid at the end of the bond's life), the frequency of coupon payments (how often you will be receiving the coupon interest such as semi-annually or annually) and the maturity (or the length of time of the bond's life).
- There is an inverse relationship between bond prices and yield (market rates).
- Duration is a measurement of a bond's interest rate risk that considers a bond's maturity, yield, and coupon among other things.
- Duration measures how sensitive a bond's price is to changes in interest rates.
- The major sectors of a country's bond market and the securities issued include sovereign bonds, semi-government bonds, municipal or province securities, corporate debt securities, mortgage-backed securities, asset-backed securities, and collateralized debt obligations.
- The internal bond market of a country (also called the national bond market) is divided into two parts: the domestic and the foreign bond market.
- The foreign bond market of a country is where bonds of issuers not domiciled in the country are issued and traded.
- The external bond market is also called the international bond market or more importantly, the Eurobond market.
- It is possible for a central government to establish an agency or organization that can issue bonds.
- The bonds of such entities are not issued directly by the central government but may have either a direct or implied government guarantee and are generically referred to as semi-government bonds or agency bonds.
- Municipal securities are issued by non-central government and can be both tax-exempt and taxable.
- Some corporate bonds carry a number of clauses such as call and put provisions and convertibility options.
- To value a bond, one needs to discount all expected cash flows with an appropriate discount rate.
- Institutional and retail investors can exploit the bond market by using strategies that leverage interest rate movements, credit spreads, yield curves, and bond market inefficiencies.
- Many investors need to forecast interest rates in order to adjust or insulate their bond portfolios from adverse interest-rate movements using duration.
- Credit spreads (the difference between yields on corporate bonds and government bonds) fluctuate with economic conditions and credit risk sentiment.
- Bond laddering is a strategy that involves purchasing bonds with staggered maturities, allowing investors to reinvest maturing bonds at prevailing rates.
- A barbell strategy is one in which an investor holds bonds with very short and very long maturities, minimizing exposure to intermediate maturities.

- A bullet strategy entails a portfolio's construction so that the maturities of the bonds in the portfolio are highly concentrated at one point on the yield curve.
- Yield-pickup strategies entail investors comparing (and swapping) bonds with similar credit ratings but different yields and opt for those offering a higher yield while managing the associated risks.
- Passive investing simply means following a market index an earning its rate or return (with virtually minimal commission fees or other expenses), whereas active investing entails significant costs in hopes of earning a return above the market.
- High-yield bonds offer the potential for higher returns, albeit with greater default risk.
- A credit default swap is a financial derivative that provides insurance against the default of a bond issuer.

Questions and problems

1. Suppose you belong to the 18% tax bracket. Would you prefer to earn a 5% corporate bond return or a 4% tax-free yield? What is the equivalent taxable yield of the 4% tax-free yield?
2. Assume you have an 8% coupon, 5-year maturity bond paying coupons semi-annually. Compute the value of the bond under the following three interest-rate scenarios: market interest rates remain the same, rise to 9% and fall to 7%. What happens to the bond's price as it approaches maturity? What price will be reached at maturity?
3. Assume that you wish to invest in a Treasury Inflation Protected Securities (TIPS). Then, consider the following information on one security: the coupon rate is 4%, the maturity is 3 periods and the expected inflation rates are 2%, 3% and 1% for each of the three periods. Compute the total payment, your nominal and real rates of return *after year 1*. What do you conclude?
4. Assume a bond with a 20-year maturity, with a coupon rate of 8%, making annual payments and with a yield to maturity of 9%. What will happen to the bond price if the bond's yield to maturity increases to 9.1%? Can you (approximately) prove it in another way?
5. Explain what would happen to bond yields (and spreads relative to a safe benchmark) in each of the following situations, if you wish to buy: (a) a corporate bond from a not-so-familiar company; (b) a sovereign bond from a country that is experiencing an economic contraction; (c) a corporate bond from a global company that is experiencing more growth; and (d) a sovereign bond from a country that is experiencing an economic boom.
6. Given two identical bonds with respect to coupon rates and maturity dates, when one bond is callable but the other is not, which bond will sell at a higher price?
7. Calculate the price of the 30-year, 8% coupon bond, making semi-annual payments when market yields are 6%. Compare the capital gains for the interest rate decline to the losses incurred when the rate increases to 5%.
8. Explain the relationship among the coupon rate, current yield, and yield to maturity (ytm) for discount bonds. Prove it using the 8% coupon bond, making semi-annual payments and selling at ytm of 10%.

9. If an investor bought a bond (with a coupon of 7%) at $974.23, kept it for one year, and then sold it at $982.17, what would be his holding-period return? Can you explain this rate of return? Assume that three years were left to the bond's maturity when you bought it.
10. What is a credit default swap? Who pays a premium and who collects payments in the event of a loan loss, for example?

Notes

1. Recall, that we briefly touched upon that in our discussion of Table 9.3.
2. When using the =PRICE and =DURATION functions, enter the following in each cell: 1/1/2000, 1/1/2030, 8%, 9%, 100, 1, 0). Note that we used the 100 as the bond's redemption price (not 1000).
3. To complement duration, investors compute the bond's convexity measure. We discuss that in Chapter 10.
4. We discuss at length these strategies in Chapter 10.
5. Ilmanen, A. (2003). Stock-Bond Correlations. *The Journal of Fixed Income* 13(12), September, 55–66.

Chapter 10

How do investors exploit the global bond market?

Introduction

In the previous chapter, we explored the details (characteristics) of the global bond market and illustrated some basic bond valuation techniques and some general ways of using the global bond market. In this chapter, we go deeper in showing how one can exploit the bond market by providing strategies, market analyses, algebraic examples and more. In general, investors can use the global bond market to achieve a variety of financial goals, including income generation, portfolio diversification, capital preservation, and hedging, against various types of risks. Essentially, leveraging the vast and diverse global fixed-income landscape to find opportunities offering higher yields or better risk-adjusted returns compared to their domestic market alone.

The global bond market offers opportunities across different sectors, maturities, currencies, countries, and risk profiles, enabling investors to optimize their strategies. In other words, fixed-income investors can benefit from expanding into global markets, where enhanced yield can be found. Some key performance drivers include the premia in foreign and foreign currency bonds, geographic diversification, and currency hedging strategies. Global bonds can be less volatile than a particular country's bonds when hedged. In addition, irregular economic growth and inflation across countries present great opportunities for global bond investors.

As of August 2020, ICMA (International Capital Market Association) estimated that the overall size of the global bond markets in terms of USD equivalent was approximately \$128 trillion. Of this amount, \$87.5 trillion (68%) were SSA bonds and \$40.9 trillion (32%) corporate bonds.[1] The SSA bond markets are dominated by the US (\$22.4tn), China (\$19.8tn), and Japan (\$12.4tn). Sovereign bonds constitute 73% (\$63.7tn) of the global outstanding SSA market.[2]

In sum, the global bond market offers a vast array of opportunities for investors with varying risk appetites and financial goals. By understanding market dynamics, leveraging tools like diversification, duration management, and arbitrage, and

DOI: 10.4324/9781003677161-13

staying informed about global economic trends, investors can exploit the global bond market to enhance returns, manage risks, and achieve long-term financial objectives.

In what follows next, we cast a detailed look on how investors exploit the global bond market, specify the ways and steps to build a bond investment portfolio, provide some specific examples of building bond portfolios, explain the various ways to assess a bond portfolio's performance, and show how an investor can interpret and act on various news from central banks, the government, the corporate sector and the rest of the world.

1 How can an investor use and exploit the global bond market?

Investors can use and exploit the global bond market to achieve a variety of financial goals, including income generation, portfolio diversification, capital preservation, and hedging against economic risks. The global bond market offers opportunities across different sectors, maturities, currencies, and risk profiles, enabling investors to optimize their strategies. Below, we list and elaborate on many ways investors can utilize and exploit the global bond market.

1.1 Generate regular income

Recall that bonds provide regular interest payments (coupons), thus making them an attractive option for income-focused investors such as retirees or those seeking predictable cash flows. Consequently, the appropriate strategy would be to in invest in investment-grade bonds for stable, lower-risk income. *Investment-grade bonds* are those with ratings of As and Bs, according to the three credit-rating agencies, Standard & Poor's, Moody's and Fitch & Associates. Specifically, bonds that are believed to have a lower risk of default and receive higher ratings by the credit rating agencies, are the investment-grade bonds. As a result, these bonds tend to be issued at lower yields than less creditworthy bonds. By contrast, *high-yield bonds* (junk bonds) are those offering higher returns, but come with increased credit risk. Table 10.1 contains the letter designations of the investment-grade and the non-investment grade ratings.

In general, for convenience investors typically group bond ratings into two major categories: Investment-grade rated Baa3/BBB– or better. Non-investment-grade (high yield or junk bonds) rated Ba1/BB+ and lower.

1.2 Diversify your investment portfolio

Given that bonds generally have lower volatility and a low correlation with equities, they tend to offer diversification benefits in a portfolio. We had discussed this in Chapter 9. The strategy in this case would be to include in your stock portfolio bonds such as government bonds for safety and stability as well as corporate bonds and emerging market debt in order to diversify across sectors and regions/countries.

Table 10.1 Credit ratings of bonds by the three credit-rating agencies

Investment grade	*Moody's*	*Standard & Poor's*	*Fitch*
	Aaa	AAA	AAA
	Aa1	AA+	AA+
	Aa2	AA	AA
	Aa3	AA-	AA-
	A1	A+	A+
	A2	A	A
	A3	A-	A-
	Baa1	BBB+	BBB+
	Baa2	BBB	BBB
	Baa3	BBB-	BBB-
Non-investment-grade			
	Ba1	BB+	BB+
	Ba2	BB	BB
	Ba3	BB-	BB-
	B1	B+	B+
	B2	B	B
	B3	B-	B-
	Caa1	CCC+	CCC+
	Caa2	CCC	CCC
	Caa3	CCC-	CCC-
	Ca	CC	CC

Sources: Moody's, Fitch Ratings, Standard & Poor's

There are various ways that you can exploit the international bond market. For example, you can take advantage of the yield differentials across regions. Bond yields vary significantly across countries and regions due to differing economic conditions, central bank policies, and credit risks. Thus, by investing in higher-yielding bonds from countries with strong economic fundamentals but relatively high interest rates (e.g., emerging markets or regions with higher risk premiums) you may pick up additional yield with less risk. You can leverage emerging market bonds because such bonds often provide higher yields than developed market bonds due to perceived higher risks. That is why you need to diversity across multiple emerging markets to reduce risk exposure to any single country. You can consider both sovereign and corporate bonds from emerging markets to exploit growth opportunities.

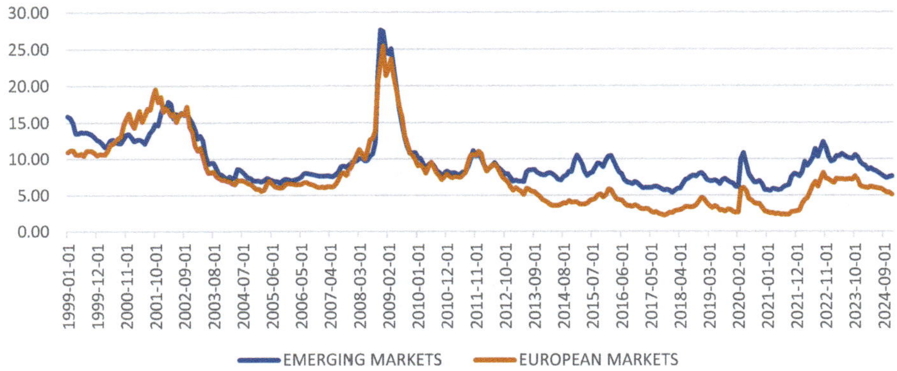

Figure 10.1 Emerging and European bond yield indices, 1999:01–2024:09

Source: Federal Reserve Economic Data

Figure 10.1 exhibits the monthly bond yield indices of emerging economies and European economies, from 1999 to 2024 (source: *FRED*). As you observe, there is a very close relationship between the two yields. In addition, before 2012, the European markets delivered often higher yields compared to the emerging markets, but after that year, the reverse was the norm. The correlation using this entire dataset is 0.907. Arbitrarily splitting the sample into 1999–2011 and 2012–2024 subperiods, we computed the correlations as 0.932 and 0.754, respectively.

You can also monitor the macroeconomic indicators as well as keeping an eye on central bank policies, inflation rates, GDP growth, and geopolitical developments, as these factors influence bond yields and credit spreads. Therefore, you could adjust bond (and other assets') allocations based on economic cycles and/or increase exposure to safe-haven bonds (e.g., US Treasuries) during recessions or market turmoil. More on this advice later in the chapter.

1.3 Hedge your bond portfolio

> **HEDGING INSIGHTS**
>
> Market wisdom suggests that domestic bond hedging can take various forms such as with Treasury futures (for interest-

When investing in foreign bonds, you can use currency hedging to mitigate exchange rate risk, but that would be a riskier strategy not suitable for conservative investors. First, you need to understand the nature of currency risk you wish to mitigate. *Currency risk* (or foreign exchange risk) arises when the value of one currency changes relative to another. So, for example, if an investor holds assets denominated in euros while their base currency is USD, a depreciation of the euro against the dollar reduces the value of the investment in USD terms. Currency hedging can be applied since international bonds provide exposure to foreign currencies, allowing investors to hedge or speculate on currency movements. Second, there are several financial instruments and strategies for currency hedging. For example, you can use forward contracts. A *forward contract* locks in an exchange rate for a specific amount of currency on a future date. Here's an example. You expect to receive €1,000,000 in 3 months. Then, enter a forward contract to sell €1,000,000 at a locked-in rate of 1.05 USD/EUR regardless of the market conditions later (after 3 months). The nearby *sidebar* discusses some additional ways an investor can hedge currency risk (and some ways for domestic bonds).

rate risk) and S&P futures (for credit risk). By engaging in currency swaps, the investor can hedge against that type of currency risk. Specifically, by swapping cash flows in the foreign currency with domestic at a predetermined rate. Finally, using currency options which give investors the right, but not the obligation, to buy or sell a particular currency at a pre-specific exchange rate before the option expires.

Alternatively, you could hedge against economic risks via inflation and deflation hedging strategies. *Inflation-linked bonds* (such as TIPS) adjust their principal and interest payments based on inflation, helping preserve purchasing power. *Deflation hedging* entail holding long-term government bonds which can perform well in deflationary environments as interest rates fall.

Furthermore, apart from investing in typical (conventional) bonds, you could invest in green and sustainable bonds within the context of exploiting environmental and social impact. Green bonds and social bonds finance environmentally friendly or socially impactful projects. According to the S&P's Global webpage, "The S&P Green Bond Index is designed to track the global green bond market. This pioneering index maintains stringent standards in order to include only those bonds whose proceeds are used to finance environmentally friendly projects."[3] So, add green bonds for socially responsible investing while earning stable returns and/or target bonds from issuers with strong ESG (Environmental, Social, Governance) ratings to align investments with your personal (or institutional) values.

Moreover, you could focus on inflation-protected bonds or securities (Treasury Inflation-Protected Securities, TIPS) which adjust for inflation, preserving purchasing power. You can include other countries' inflation-linked bonds so you can realize further diversification and inflation protection. Also, you can optimize tax efficiency by investing in tax-exempt bonds such as municipal bonds (in the US) because they often provide tax-free interest income at the federal level, and sometimes at the state level, making them attractive for high-income investors. Hence, you can include such bond in your portfolio (for tax savings) and hold taxable bonds in tax-advantaged accounts (e.g., IRAs or 401(k)s) to maximize after-tax returns.

Finally, you could leverage technology and data through the use of analytics platforms (tools) to track yield spreads, duration, credit ratings, and market trends. A simple strategy would be to identify undervalued bonds using quantitative models and track global macroeconomic indicators to predict interest rate movements.

1.4 Engage in other activities with bonds

If you have very good market understanding and perception as well as good forecasting skills, you could perhaps take advantage of *interest-rate trends*. Bond prices and yields are sensitive to interest rate changes, creating opportunities for investors who can predict rate movements. So, a strategy could be to buy long-duration bonds to capitalize on price appreciation, when rates are expected to decline, and shift to short-duration bonds to minimize interest rate risk, when rates are expected to rise. Perhaps, you are willing to monitor credit cycles so as to shift between investment-grade and high-yield bonds based on credit market conditions.

Also, you could engage in *arbitrage opportunities*. For example, you could take advantage of pricing inefficiencies between credit default swaps (CDS) and bond yields by buying bonds and simultaneously purchasing CDS protection if spreads diverge. You could execute relative value trades if you are able to identify mispricings within the bond market (e.g., between bonds of the same issuer with different maturities or structures) and trade to exploit these differences. Let us illustrate this with a simple example.

Taking advantage of pricing inefficiencies between CDS and bond yields involves strategies that exploit the misalignment between the credit risk premium implied by CDS spreads and the credit spreads embedded in bond yields. First, understanding the relationship between CDS and Bond Yields. A *CDS spread* reflects the cost of insuring against the default of a bond issuer, whereas a bond yield spread (over a risk-free rate) compensates for credit risk, liquidity risk, and other factors. In an efficient market, the bond yield spread is approximately equal to the CDS spread. Hence, pricing inefficiencies arise when the CDS spread and bond yield spread deviate due to market imbalances or liquidity conditions.

Then, identify possible pricing inefficiencies. For example, if the CDS spread is lower than the bond yield spread, it would suggest that the market underprices credit risk in the CDS market (this is known as Cheap CDS vs. bond yield spread). By contrast, if the CDS spread is higher than the bond yield spread, then this means that the CDS market overprices credit risk relative to the bond market (Expensive CDS vs. bond yield spread).

How to apply the arbitrage strategy. Understand what the basis and a basis trade are. The *basis* is the difference between the CDS spread and the bond yield spread. *Basis trades* aim to profit from the convergence of this difference. A *positive basis trade* occurs when the CDS spread is higher than the bond yield spread. So, buy the bond to earn the higher yield spread. Sell protection via a CDS contract to hedge credit risk. Then, the profit arises from the difference between the bond yield and the CDS premium. A negative basis trade occurs when the CDS spread is lower than the bond yield spread. In this case, sell the bond or short it. Buy protection via a CDS contract to hedge credit exposure. The profit arises from the cheaper CDS cost relative to the bond spread. Here's a numerical example.

Example of a positive basis trade: Bond yield spread: 4%. CDS spread: 3%. Hence, the basis is 4% – 3% = 1%. The strategy then would be to buy a bond yielding 4%, sell CDS protection at 3%, and pocket a net profit of 1% (ignoring transaction and funding costs).

In conclusion, the global bond market offers a vast array of opportunities for investors with varying risk appetites and financial goals. By understanding market dynamics, leveraging tools like diversification, duration management, and arbitrage, and staying informed about global economic trends, investors can exploit the global bond market to enhance returns, manage risks, and achieve long-term financial objectives. You should always, however, keep in mind the risks to these activities some of which are the following. *Interest Rate Risk*: Rising rates reduce bond prices, impacting portfolio values; *Credit Risk*: Risk of default by issuers, especially with high-yield and emerging market bonds; *Currency Risk*: For foreign bonds, exchange rate fluctuations can impact returns; and *Liquidity Risk*: Some bonds, especially in niche markets, may be harder to sell quickly.

2 Building a bond portfolio

Building a bond portfolio requires a structured approach to align investments with your financial goals, risk tolerance, and time horizon. Below are the key steps to construct a bond portfolio.

2.1 Set up your investment policy statement for bonds

As we have explained in an earlier chapter, the investor must set up (define) his/her investment policy statement (IPS) for the overall portfolio. Here, we apply this task to the bond component of the overall portfolio. The investor can define a number of objectives depending on various constraints and degree of risk tolerance, as we will explain below. Some examples of objectives are: *Income Generation*: Focus on bonds with regular coupon payments; *Capital Preservation*: Prioritize high-quality bonds with minimal credit risk; *Growth*: Seek bonds with capital appreciation potential (e.g., falling interest rate environments); *Diversification*: Add bonds to balance equity market risks; *Tax Efficiency*: Consider municipal bonds or tax-advantaged accounts for minimizing tax impacts.

Next, assess your risk tolerance. In this case, the investor can consider the types of risks that are relevant to bonds, such as credit risk, where the investor must decide how much exposure you are comfortable with to lower-rated bonds (e.g., high-yield or junk bonds), interest rate risk, so as to determine his willingness to take on long-duration bonds that are sensitive to interest rate changes, and currency risk, in order to decide if he is comfortable with currency exposure from foreign bonds or if he will hedge the risks.

Finally, determine your time horizon. Match the bond maturities to your investment timeline: *Short-Term Goals*: Use short-duration bonds (maturities < 5 years); *Medium-Term Goals*: Use a mix of intermediate-duration bonds (maturities 5–10 years); and *Long-Term Goals*: Consider long-duration bonds (maturities > 10 years). Finally, choose the bond types that are in line with your IPS. Select bonds based on your goals and risk profile: *Government Bonds*: Low risk, backed by governments (e.g., US Treasuries, UK Gilts); *Corporate Bonds:* Higher yields but with credit risk; *Municipal Bonds*: Tax-free income for US investors; *Emerging Market Bonds*: High yields but higher risks; *Inflation-Linked Bonds*: Protection against inflation (e.g., TIPS, UK Index-Linked Gilts); and *Floating-Rate Bonds*: Adjusting to interest rate changes.

2.2 Select a portfolio strategy

Decide on a strategy that aligns with your goals. A number of strategies are available. For example, the *ladder approach* entails building a portfolio with staggered maturities for regular cash flow and reinvestment flexibility. The benefits of this approach are: regular cash flow as bonds mature; reduces interest rate risk since maturing bonds can be reinvested at prevailing rates; and is best for investors seeking steady income and flexibility. The *barbell strategy* combines short-term bonds for liquidity with long-term bonds for yield. Its benefits include: stability of short-term bonds with the higher yields of long-term bonds, flexibility in adjustments as interest rates change, and is designed to manage interest rate uncertainty while earning moderate returns. Figure 10.2 shows these three bond-portfolio building strategies. The *core-satellite strategy* contains high-quality bonds as the core and riskier bonds as satellites for higher returns. The strategy's structure is as follows: *Core*: US Treasuries, municipal bonds, or high-quality corporate bonds for stability; *Satellite*: High-yield, emerging market, or inflation-linked bonds for diversification and yield enhancement. It is best for balanced investors seeking moderate growth with lower risk. And the bullet strategy focuses on bonds maturing around a specific target date. The strategy's benefits are that it aligns investment with a fixed timeline and reduces reinvestment risk. It is suitable for investors that have targeted goals requiring lump-sum payouts at a specific time (e.g., saving for a child's college education or a large purchase). Later in this section we exhibit the laddering, bullet and barbell bond portfolio construction strategies with examples.

There are some other bond portfolio construction methods namely, the total return, passive and income-focused strategies. Needless to say, that the most basic, intuitive strategy would be to buy the bonds and hold them to maturity (the so-called *buy-and-hold* strategy). You eliminate at least two important risks that come with bonds: interest-rate (price) risk and liquidity risk. The *total return strategy* focuses on both interest income and capital appreciation by actively managing bond selection and timing. To apply this approach, buy undervalued bonds or those with improving credit profiles, monitor interest rate trends to adjust duration exposure and expect maximum return (if you are an active investor). The *passive bond investing* approach rests on building a diversified bond portfolio that mimics the performance of a bond index (e.g., Bloomberg Barclays Global Aggregate Bond Index). The benefits of this approach are low-cost with minimal management and broad diversification across issuers, sectors, and geographies. This is best suited for long-term, risk-averse investors seeking market-level returns.

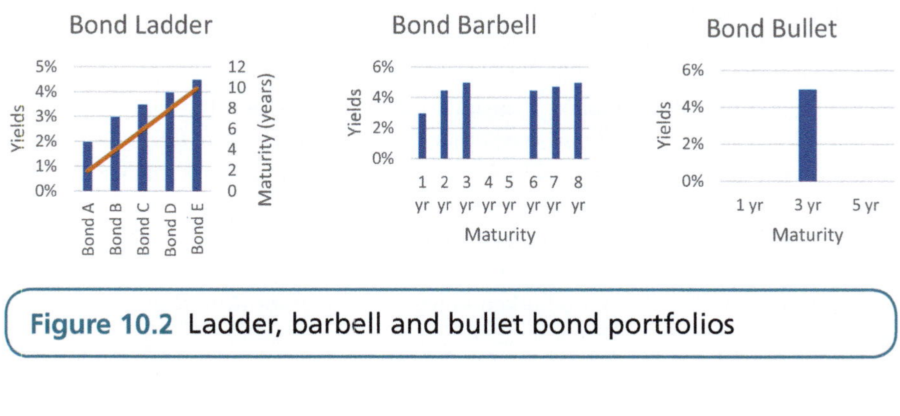

Figure 10.2 Ladder, barbell and bullet bond portfolios

Finally, *the income-focused strategy* entails prioritizing high-yielding bonds for regular income. So, invest in corporate bonds, preferred securities, or high-yield ("junk") bonds and include emerging market bonds for additional yield opportunities. This approach may work best for income-focused investors comfortable with higher risk.

In tune with the above bond portfolio construction strategies, you should consider the economic and market conditions. More specifically, monitor the interest-rate environment for rising and falling rates. So, for rising rates focus on short-duration or floating-rate bonds, whereas for falling rates, include long-duration bonds for potential price appreciation. Watch the rate of inflation and include inflation-linked bonds to protect purchasing power. Stay informed by monitoring macroeconomic indicators (e.g., inflation, GDP growth, central bank policies and currency fluctuations for foreign bonds). Manage costs by minimizing transactions costs via low-cost bond or ETF funds or mutual funds (for better diversification). Finally, as mentioned earlier, monitor the credit cycle and shift between investment-grade and high-yield bonds based on credit conditions. Regularly review the portfolio to ensure it aligns with your goals and market conditions and apply rebalancing. For example, replace maturing bonds to maintain strategy (e.g., ladder or barbell) and adjust allocations if credit quality or interest rate conditions change.

2.3 What are some specific ways to build a bond investment portfolio?

As mentioned earlier, building a bond investment portfolio involves a structured approach to meet specific financial goals, risk tolerance, and time horizons. In this subsection, we illustrate the three approaches mentioned in subsection 3.2 (ladder, barbell and bullet) with some examples.

2.3.1 The ladder bond portfolio

Recall, that a ladder bond portfolio is a strategy where bonds with staggered maturities are purchased to provide steady cash flow and mitigate interest rate and reinvestment risk. The steps are listed below.

Step 1: Define your investment goals

First, determine the portfolio's *purpose* (e.g., income generation, risk management, or capital preservation). Then, identify your *investment horizon* or how long you want the ladder to run (e.g., 5, 10, or 20 years). Finally, assess your *risk tolerance*, that is, decide on the mix of bond types (e.g., government, corporate, or municipal bonds) based on risk appetite.

Step 2: Determine your total investment

Decide how much capital you want to invest. For example, you may want to allocate $100,000 for this purpose.

Step 3: Choose maturity intervals

Here, you must decide the spacing of bond maturities (e.g., every year, 2 years, or 5 years). Here's an example: A 5-year ladder with annual intervals will require bonds maturing in 1, 2, 3, 4, and 5 years.

Step 4: Allocate funds across maturities

Divide your total investment equally (or as desired) across the maturities. For example, with your $100,000 amount, consider the bonds maturing in 1, 2, 3, 4, and 5 years, and compute the investment per maturity: $100,000/5=$20,000 per maturity.

Step 5: Select bonds for each maturity

Choose bonds based on issuer type (government, corporate and municipal), coupon rate (pick bonds with competitive coupon payments) credit quality (ensure a minimum credit rating, e.g., investment grade for corporate bonds) and liquidity (opt for bonds that are easier to trade, if needed).

Step 6: Reinvest as bonds mature

When a bond matures, reinvest the principal into a new bond with the longest maturity in your ladder. This ensures the ladder remains consistent. Here's an example. When the *1-year bond* matures, reinvest the proceeds into a new *5-year bond*, maintaining the staggered structure. Below is a more detailed example of a laddered bond portfolio construction. Its assumptions are: total investment of $100,000, maturity of 1 year and ladder length of 5 years. Table 10.2 below shows some specifics (hypothetical values):

Therefore, by following this structured approach, a ladder bond portfolio can provide a balance of steady income, risk mitigation, and flexibility to adapt to changing interest rate environments.

Table 10.2 An example of a laddered portfolio

Maturity (Years)	*Investment*	*Bond Type*	*Coupon Rate (%)*	*Annual Income*
1	$20,000	US Treasury	2.5%	$500
2	$20,000	Corporate Bond	3.5%	$700
3	$20,000	Municipal Bond	3.0%	$600
4	$20,000	Corporate Bond	4.0%	$800
5	$20,000	US Treasury	2.5%	$500
Total annual income:				**$3,100**

2.3.2 The barbell bond portfolio

Recall that building a barbell bond portfolio involves a strategy that combines short-term bonds for stability and liquidity with long-term bonds for higher yields and potential capital appreciation. The absence of intermediate-term bonds creates a "barbell" effect, balancing risk and return by exploiting the characteristics of both ends of the yield curve. Below are the steps to build a barbell bond portfolio.

Skipping steps 1 and 2 (since they are the same as for the ladder portfolio), we start with step 3.

Step 3: Allocate funds across bond maturities

In this case, pick short-term (1 to 3 years) and long-term bonds (7+ years), and decide on their allocation. Remember that short-term bonds offer lower yields but are less volatile and provide liquidity, and use them as a hedge against rising interest rates since they can be reinvested at higher yields as they mature. By contrast, the long-term bonds provide higher yields and potential capital gains if interest rates fall, but are more sensitive to changes in interest rates but can lock in favorable rates. For short-term bonds, opt for high-quality government bonds (e.g., US Treasuries, sovereign bonds) as well as floating-rate bonds, whereas for long-term bonds select investment-grade corporate bonds for higher yields, sovereign bonds with strong credit ratings, or even high-yield or emerging market bonds (if you are an aggressive investor). Finally, a simple allocation example would be to equally split your investment budget into these maturity bonds or apply your risk tolerance profile to change the allocations.

Step 4: Consider the economic conditions

As a prudent investor, you must consider economic conditions and, particularly, rising interest rates. So, in rising interest rates rely more on short-term bonds to minimize duration risk, and reduce exposure to long-term bonds unless yields are very attractive. In contrast, in a falling interest-rate environment, favor long-term bonds for price appreciation; short-term bonds still provide liquidity but may earn less income.

Step 5: Reinvest short-term maturities

When short-term bonds mature, reinvest proceeds into either new short-term bonds to maintain liquidity or long-term bonds if interest rates are favorable or the yield curve steepens. Furthermore, monitor the yield curve as the barbell strategy thrives on exploiting shifts in the yield curve: Specifically, in a steepening yield curve long-term bonds become more attractive as yields rise, whereas in a flattening (or inverted) curve short-term bonds gain appeal as their yields approach or surpass long-term bonds.

Step 6: Regularly review and rebalance your portfolio

Adjust allocations between short- and long-term bonds based on changing market conditions (e.g., interest rates, credit spreads), and your financial goals or liquidity needs. Consider selling long-term bonds if they appreciate significantly due to falling interest rates.

Example of a barbell portfolio

Investment Amount: \$100,000, denote it as *V*.

Allocation (50-50): \$50,000 in short-term US Treasuries or investment-grade corporate bonds (1–3 years), denote them as *Vs* and \$50,000 in long-term municipal bonds, corporate bonds, or government bonds (10–30 years), denote them as *Vl*.

Bond characteristics: Short-term bonds yield, *Ys*=3%; Long-term bonds yield, *Yl*=6%.

Let us now construct an algebraic example of a *barbell bond portfolio* to illustrate how allocations work and the potential income generated.

Calculate the income from each bond

Annual income from short-term bonds, *Is*: *Is* = *Vs* * *Ys* = \$50,000 * 0.03 = \$1,500

Annual income from long-term bonds, *Il*: *Il* = *Vl* * *Yl* = \$50,000 * 0.06 = \$3,000

Total portfolio income: *Is* + *Il* = \$1,500 + \$3,000 = \$4,500

Compute the overall yield of the portfolio

The overall yield of the portfolio, *Yp*, is a weighted average based on the allocations and is expressed as follows:

$Y_p = (Vs/V * Ys) + (Vl/V * Yl)$

Y_p = [(\$50,000/\$100,000) * 0.03] + [(\$50,000/\$100,000) * 0.06] = 0.045 = 4.5%

Adjust for reinvestment

Assume that short-term bonds mature in 2 years and interest rates rise to 4%, Y's. You can now reinvest the \$50,000 in higher-rate short-term bonds and earn the following income:

New short-term bond income: I's = Vs * Y's = \$50,000 * 0.04 = \$20,000

Total new income: \$2,000 + \$3,000 = \$5,000

New portfolio yield: Y'p = [(\$50,000/\$100,000) * 0.04] + [(\$50,000/\$100,000) * 0.06] = 0.05 = 5%

So, what have we learned from this strategy? The barbell strategy allows flexibility since short-term bonds protect against rising rates, enabling reinvestment at higher yields and long-term bonds lock in higher yields for the long run, benefiting from stability and capital appreciation if rates fall. The portfolio's yield adjusts dynamically based on interest rate movements, providing both liquidity and growth potential. This example demonstrates the barbell strategy's balance between income and adaptability to changing market conditions.

2.3.3 The bullet bond portfolio

A *bullet bond* portfolio focuses on bonds with maturities that cluster around a specific target date. This strategy is often used to match liabilities or achieve a specific investment goal at a future date. Let us go through the steps of this strategy.

Step 1: Setup the portfolio

Objective: Achieve a target amount in *10 years* by investing in bonds maturing around this date.
Total Investment: V=$100,000
Bond Characteristics:
All bonds mature in *10 years*.
Bonds have a coupon rate of *5% annually*.
The bonds are purchased at *par value* (P=100% of face value, $1000).

Step 2: Determine the cash flows

Each bond provides the following cash flows:
Coupon payments: C = *face value* * *Coupon rate*
So, with the face value of $1,000, each bond pays C = $1,000 * 0.05 = $50 per year. Do not forget to include the principal repayment of $1,000 at maturity (or 10 years).

Step 3: Allocate the investment funds

To allocate the portfolio, first divide the total investment ($100,000) by the face (or par) value of each bond: *N* = *V/Face value* = $100,000/$1,000 = 100 bonds. Hence, the bond portfolio will consist of 100 bonds, *N*, that mature in 10 years.

INVESTMENT STRATEGIES AND GOALS

Depending on the investor's goal, a bond portfolio construction method is better.

If the goal is to earn predictable income, then the best strategy would be a bond ladder. If the goal is to earn (capture) higher rates, then a barbell is suitable. Finally, if the investor wishes to save for some expense in some future time, the bullet bond portfolio is the best.

Obviously, investors do not need to apply a single method. They can always mix and match or apply a combination of these strategies.

Step 4: Calculate annual income

The portfolio earns coupon income every year for 10 years, as follows: Total annual income, I: $I = N * C = 100 * \$50 = \$5{,}000$ per year.

Step 5: Compute total return at maturity

At the end of 10 years, the total coupon payments would be $I * 10 = \$5{,}000 * 10 = \$50{,}000$, and the principal repayment of \$100,000 (or $N * \textit{Face value} = 100 * \$1{,}000$). Therefore, the total bond portfolio's return at the end of 10 years would be *Total coupons* + *principal repayment* = \$50,000 + \$100,000 = \$150,000.

The advantages of the bullet bond portfolio are that maturities are aligned to meet a specific future need it provides steady annual income and a big sum at the end of the investment horizon and that you may have control over duration which reduces reinvestment risk (simply because duration matches the portfolio's investment horizon).

Comparison with the other two strategies

Unlike a *ladder* or *barbell*, the bullet strategy concentrates on a single time horizon, making it ideal for specific goals but less flexible in adapting to interest rate changes. For instance, if interest rates rise, the bullet portfolio can't reinvest cash flows at higher rates (as in a ladder strategy), and if interest rates fall, the portfolio benefits less from capital gains compared to a barbell strategy. The nearby *sidebar* explains which technique is preferred under several investor goals.

Test your understanding 1

1. Name some ways that you can exploit the international bond market.
2. Assume you have the following data on yield spreads: Bond yield spread is 4% and the CDS spread is 3%. Compute the basis and outline a strategy (ignore transaction and funding costs).
3. Explain the usefulness of the barbell strategy.
4. Compare the ladder strategy to the bullet strategy.

Solutions appear at the textbook's website.

3 How can we assess a bond portfolio's performance?

Assessing a bond portfolio's performance involves evaluating various metrics and factors that reflect returns, risks, and alignment with investment objectives. Here are some ways.

3.1 Total return

The *total return* measures the portfolio's overall performance, including income, price changes, and reinvestment of coupons. The formula is simple (just like the rate of return formula we learned in Chapter 9):

$$\textit{Total Return} = \frac{\textit{Ending value} - \textit{Beginning value} + \textit{Coupon Income}}{\textit{Beginning value}} \qquad (10.1)$$

The components are the coupon income, price changes and any reinvestment of coupons.

3.2 Yield analyses

The *current yield* (CY) focuses on the income generated relative to the bond's price and is expressed as *CY = Current coupon income/Current price.*

The current yield will be greater/lower than the coupon rate when the bond sells at a discount/premium, but for a bond selling at par, CY will be equal to the coupon rate. The disadvantage of this yield measure is that it considers only the coupon interest ignoring any other source for an investor's return. For example, it ignores any capital gains/losses when a bond purchased at a discount/premium is held to maturity. Finally, no consideration is given to reinvestment income.

The *yield to maturity* (YTM) is the expected return if the bond is held to maturity, accounting for coupon payments and price changes. To compute YTM, first determine the expected cash flows and then search, by trial and error, for the interest rate that will make the present value of cash flows equal to the market price plus accrued interest. This is a special case of an internal rate of return (IRR) calculation where the cash flows are those received if the bond is held to the maturity date.

Consider an 8-year, 7% coupon bond, making *semi-annual payments* valued at the 8% market rate. The price of this bond (using excel and assuming a $100 face value) is $94.17.[4] Hence, the 4% interest rate is the semi-annual yield to maturity.[5] The market convention, however, is to double that (for annual basis) to 8% (also known as the *bond-equivalent yield*). A limitation of YTM (albeit an improvement over CY) is that it assumes that the coupon payments can be reinvested at an interest rate equal to YTM.

When a bond is callable, investors calculate a yield to call as well as YTM. *The yield to call* (YTC) assumes the issuer will call a bond on some assumed call date and that the call price is the price specified in the call schedule. When a bond is puttable, the yield to the first put date is calculated. The *yield to put* (YTP) is the interest rate that will make the present value of the cash flows to the first put date equal to the price plus accrued interest. YTP assumes that any interim coupon payments can be reinvested at the implied (calculated) yield. Finally, the yield to worst (YTW) is the lowest potential yield among YTM, YTC and YTP.

3.3 Benchmark comparison and measurement of the portfolio's exposure

You can compare the portfolio's performance to relevant benchmarks such as the Bloomberg US Aggregate Bond Index, ICE BofA Global Broad Market Index.

You can also evaluate returns relative to volatility using the Sharpe ratio or the *Sortino ratio* (defined as $(R_p - R_f)/\text{downside deviation}$, where R_p is the portfolio's return, R_f is the risk-free rate, and downside deviation is a measure of the investment's downside volatility or losses).

In addition, you can assess the portfolio's exposure to different types of risks using some risk metrics such as those we learned in Chapter 9 namely, duration, convexity and some qualitative measures for credit and liquidity risk. Recall that duration measures sensitivity to interest rate changes. Longer durations indicate higher interest rate risk. *Convexity* adjusts for non-linear price changes due to large interest rate shifts. Credit risk analyzes the portfolio's credit quality (e.g., average credit rating, credit spread changes). Liquidity risk evaluates ease of buying/selling bonds without impacting prices.

We now illustrate how to compute convexity. *Convexity* measures how the duration of a bond changes as interest rates fluctuate. It helps capture the curvature in the price-yield relationship, improving estimates of bond price changes when rates change. The formula is below.

$$C = (1/P) * \Sigma\, [(CF_t * t(t+1)/ (1+ytm)^{t+2}] \qquad (10.2)$$

where C is convexity, P is the bond price, CF_t are the cash flows at time t, y is the yield to maturity and t the time period of each cash flow.

An alternative way to express the convexity formula is by augmenting the duration formula, as follows:

Duration rule	$\Delta P/P = -D * \Delta y$	(10.3)
Augmented equation	$\Delta P/P = -D * \Delta y + 0.5 * C * (\Delta y)^2$	(10.4)
Convexity	$[1/ (P * (1+y)^2\,] * \Sigma^n_{t=1}\, [\, \{CF_t/(1+y)^t\} * (t^2 + t]\}]$	(10.5)

where D is modified duration. Use interest rates (yields) as decimals in the equations. Equation (10.4) is often referred to as *the duration-convexity rule*. You understand that the term (t^2+t) is the same as $t(t+1)$ in (10.2) above.

Assume a $1,000 bond, with a 5% coupon rate, 3 years to maturity, a YTM of 6%, and making annual payments. The current price of that bond is $972.77. This is shown in Step 1.

Step 1: Compute cash flows and the price of the bond

Year (t)	*Cash Flow*	*Discount Factor*	*PV of Cash Flow*	*t(t+1)*
		(1.06)^t	*$CF_t/(1.06)^t$*	
1	$50	1.06	50/1.06 = 47.17	1(1+1)= 2
2	$50	1.1236	50/1.1236 = 44.49	2(2+1) = 6
3	$1,050	1.1910	1,050/1.1910 = 881.11	3(3+1) =12

Total bond price: P = 47.17 + 44.49 + 881.11 = 972.77

Step 2: Compute convexity

To compute convexity, we set up another table as follows.

Year (t)	*CF_t * t(t+1)*	*Discount Factor $(1.06)^{t+2}$*	*PV of Weighted Cash Flow*
1	50 * 2 = 100	1.1236	100/1.1236 = 88.99
2	50 * 6 = 300	1.1910	300/1.1910 = 251.88
3	1,050 * 12 = 12,600	1.2625	12,600/1.2625 = 9,980.20

Hence, C = (88.99 + 251.88 + 9,980.20)/972.77 = 10.61.

An intersing question emerges here. Why do investors desire convexity? The simple reason is that bonds with greater convexity (curvature) gain more in price when yields fall than they lose when yields rise. If bond A is more convex than bond B, then Bond A would enjoy larger price increases and smaller price decreases when interest rates fluctuate by larger amounts. You understand that this feature is more valuable during a volatile interest-rate environment and consequently, investors must pay a fee to enjoy this benefit.

3.4 Apply the immunization technique

An *immunized bond portfolio* is designed to shield investors from interest rate fluctuations by matching the portfolio's duration with the investment horizon. This ensures that changes in interest rates have minimal impact on the portfolio's value, balancing reinvestment risk and price (or interest-rate) risk. Below, we illustrate a simple case of immunizing a 2-bond portfolio using durations.

Step 1: Define your investment objective

Assume that a pension fund needs to pay $100,000 in 5 years. The goal is to construct a bond portfolio that ensures this payment is met regardless of interest rate changes.

Step 2: Choose the bonds for the portfolio

We select two bonds: *Bond A:* A 2-year Treasury bond with a 3% coupon and *Bond B*: A 10-year corporate bond with a 5% coupon. Both bonds have a face value of $1,000 and pay annual coupons.

Step 3: Calculate the duration of bonds

Using the Macaulay Duration for bond A, duration (D) is approximately 1.92 years. For bond B, D is approximately 7.8 years.[6] The target duration for immunization is 5 years, which perfectly matches the liability.

Step 4: Solve for the portfolio weights

We now need to allocate X% in Bond A and (1–X)% in Bond B so that the portfolio duration, D_p, equals 5. This is done as follows:

$$X * D_A + (1-X) * D_B = D_p \tag{10.6}$$
$$X * 1.92 + (1-X) * 7.8 = 5$$

Solving for X, we obtain 0.476. So, 47.6% of the portfolio is invested in Bond A, and 52.4% in Bond B.[7]

Step 5: Construct portfolio

- Investment Amount: $100,000
- Bond A Allocation: $47,600
- Bond B Allocation: $52,400

This ensures the portfolio's duration is exactly 5 years, immunizing it against interest rate changes.

Therefore, by carefully selecting bond weights to match duration with the investment horizon, this immunized portfolio ensures that regardless of interest rate movements, the portfolio will meet the future obligation of $100,000 in 5 years.

3.5 Perform attribution analysis

Performance attribution analysis seeks to answer several questions such as the bond portfolio manager's performance in relation to the portfolio objectives and constraints. Also, attribution analysis is a process of breaking down the portfolio's return into different factors that explain the portfolio's performance. For example, which factors were responsible for the portfolio's performance? Sector allocation, security selection, manager's skill (style)? In other words, would a manager's over- or under-allocation in a particular sector be responsible for the portfolio's return in excess or short of the benchmark portfolio's return? Let us illustrate the analysis using hypothetical data (as shown in Table 10.3).

Assume that the overall asset portfolio consists of equities (70% allocation), bonds (25% allocation) and cash (5% allocation). The rate of return of this managed portfolio was 6%. Now, we need to establish the benchmark (or bogey) portfolio so we can compare the manager's (managed) portfolio to it. The benchmark (passive) portfolio also consists of equities (60% allocation), bonds (30% allocation) and cash (10% allocation). Next, we compute the total return of the benchmark portfolio (as shown in panel A of the table) by multiplying each portfolio's component allocation by its respective return:

Benchmark portfolio's total return: 0.60 * 6% + 0.30 * 2% + 0.10 * 0.5% = 4.25%

Table 10.3 Performance attribution analysis

Panel A: initial return data

Managed, Benchmark Portfolios (MP, BP)	*MP's weights*	*BP's weights*	*BP's return*
Equities	0.70	0.60	6%
Bonds	0.25	0.30	2%
Cash	0.05	0.10	0.5%

Benchmark portfolio's total return = 4.25%
Managed portfolio's total return = 6%
Excess return of the managed portfolio – return of the benchmark portfolio = 6% – 4.25% = 1.75%

Panel B: asset allocation analysis

Component	*MP's weights*	*BP's weights*	*Excess weights*	*BP's return*	*Contribution to performance*
Equities	0.70	0.60	0.10	6%	0.10 * 6% = 0.6
Bonds	0.25	0.30	–0.05	2%	–0.05 * 2% = –0.1
Cash	0.05	0.10	–0.05	0.5%	–0.05 * 0.5% = –0.025

Total contribution due to asset allocation = 0.6 – 0.1 – 0.025 = 0.475%

Panel C: sector and security selection analyses

Component	*MP's return*	*BP's return*	*Excess return*	*MP's weight*	*Contribution of sector allocation*
Equities	7.85%	6%	7.85% – 6% = 1.85%	0.70	1.85% * 0.7 = 1.295
Bonds	1.937%	2%	1.937% – 2% = –0.062%	0.25	–0.062% * 0.25 = –0.0156

Total contribution of security selection = 1.295% – 0.0156% = 1.279%

So, given that the bond portfolio manager's portfolio earned 6% over the same period, the excess return of this (managed) portfolio is 1.75% (6% – 4.25%). The next question is more interesting: what can we attribute this managed portfolio's excess (superior) performance to? To the over-weighing of the equities component (from 60% to 70%) or to the under-weighing (from 30% to 25%) of the bonds component, that is, to the differential asset allocation? As seen from Panel B of Table 10.3, we computed the total contribution of the managed portfolio's return due to asset allocation as 0.475% by multiplying the excess weights (the difference between the MP's and BP's weights) by each portfolio's component return. The major contribution of this asset allocation to superior performance came from the excess weighting of the equity market when the equity market had a hefty return of 6%.

The third and final question is even more interesting: what do we attribute the remaining return of 1.275% (=1.75% – 0.475%) to? To sector selection and security selection within each market! Let us see how we can determine this. We ignore the cash component of each portfolio. Panel C of the table contains the analysis. After taking the difference in the returns of the equities and bonds between the managed and benchmark portfolios, so as to produce the excess returns, we multiply these by MP's weights (0.70 and 0.25) to arrive at the following values:

Equities: 1.85% * 0.7 = 1.295
Bonds: –0.062% * 0.25 = –0.0156

Then, the total contribution of security selection is 1.279% (= 1.295% – 0.0156%). Therefore, we conclude that most of the managed portfolio's excess return was due to the manager's skill in over-allocating funds to the equities sector and (slightly) under-allocating funds to the bonds sector.

4 Analyzing real bond market news

In this section, we present several real news (such as announcements, policy changes, meetings) from four major world central banks (Federal Reserve Bank, the Bank of England, European Central Bank and the Bank of Japan) and analyze them with respect to the economy and the bond market, in particular.

4.1 Interpreting news from the central banks

4.1.1 From the Fed

On February 7, 2025, the news about the US economy was as follows: healthy US job growth (non-farm payrolls); rising inflation expectations (up to 4.3%); lower unemployment rate (to 4%).[8] What could all that mean for the Fed with respect to interest rates? Analysts are saying that this economic environment supports the Fed's inclination to keep interest rates steady (for now), and that the new administration's priorities (on international trade, thus affecting the dollar's value) are still uncertain which, in turn, makes the Fed adopt a wait-and-see policy. The Fed's Monetary Policy Report (Feb. 2025) suggested that the financial system is still sound and resilient despite high valuations in equity, corporate debt, and residential real estate.

Why would the Fed continue keeping interest rates steady (at around 4.25%) despite rising inflation expectations and a strong labor market? First, the Fed could perhaps want to avoid endangering (hurting) the labor market by raising interest rates too soon. Second, the Fed wants to watch inflation data to see if it creeps up in the next couple of months before its next meeting and then decide on rate changes. Third, the Fed gets pressure from the federal government to lower rates and so it adopts a cautious stance currently. Finally, the current US government administration imposed hefty tariffs (on imported goods from selected nations) in March 2025 and this would further (and significantly) elevate inflation rate. As a result, the Fed wants to wait and see the effect of this policy.

What would be the impact of tariffs on the US economy and what would the Fed's response to that policy be? In general, tariffs boost inflation at home because domestic importing firms will pay the duty. Economists generally see tariffs as having a one-time impact on prices, affecting particular goods where the duties are imposed on. In addition, tariffs do not boost economic growth. Therefore, just like the Fed ponders, the impact may not be widespread so as to alter the fundamental drivers of inflation. If the latter is true, then the Fed may be forced to raise interest rates. Even any indication that the tariffs are presenting longer-lasting pressure in prices could prompt the Fed to raise interest rates.

What about the impact of rate changes on the US dollar? Lower interest rates cause a depreciation of the US dollar thus making it weak against other currencies. A weak currency is usually inflationary because it makes imports, particularly energy, more expensive. However, a weak currency boosts exports by making US products cheaper for foreign markets. The ECB, the Bank of England, and the Bank of Canada have all cut interest rates in February 2025 even after the Fed said it was not in a hurry to move.

By contrast, when the Fed raises rates, it becomes more attractive for international investors to hold US dollars, leading to increased demand and a stronger currency. Hence, the dollar appreciates against the other currencies. In this case, imports are boosted but exports are depressed.

Finally, what would Fed rate changes mean for the bond markets? We will analyze the impact of an interest-rate rise on the bond market since the opposite happens in an interest-rate cut. First of all, when the Fed raises interest rates, bond prices fall and yields rise. Bond prices and interest rates have an inverse relationship. Higher rates make newly issued bonds more attractive, causing existing bond prices to fall. Here's a simple example. If the Fed hikes rates by 0.50% (or 50 basis points), a 10-year bond paying 3% becomes less attractive compared to newly issued bonds offering 3.5% or higher, leading to a price drop for the 3% bond. Second, short-term bonds react faster than long-term bonds. Specifically, short-duration bonds (such as the 2-year Treasury notes) adjust quickly to Fed rate hikes. Longer-term bonds (e.g., 10-year, 30-year Treasuries) are influenced by future inflation expectations. Third, credit markets tighten and corporate borrowing costs rise. Higher Fed rates increase borrowing costs for corporations issuing bonds, leading to higher credit spreads (corporate bond yield minus Treasury yield). Also, high-yield (junk) bonds suffer more as investors demand higher compensation for risk. Finally, the impact on the yield curve is noteworthy. If short-term rates rise faster than long-term rates, the yield curve may invert, which is often a recession indicator.

Some additional considerations include the following. The bond market reacts based on future rate expectations and, as a result, if the Fed signals future hikes, bond yields may rise. Inflation and economic data become key drivers of bond yields in a steady-rate environment. How do rising inflation and interest rate rises impact bond prices? Inflation expectations are generally negative for bonds, as when inflation is rising, central banks tend to raise interest rates to try and control inflation. Higher interest rates make the fixed return or coupon of bonds become less appealing to investors also because of higher inflation which erodes the purchasing power of those fixed coupon payments. By contrast, signs of decelerating inflation can push bond yields lower. Persistently below-target inflation can trigger a loosening of monetary policy, meaning lowering the interest rates, in an effort to encourage borrowing and spur growth.

Fed rate changes influence credit spreads between Treasuries and corporate bonds, affecting investment decisions in riskier assets. Finally, Fed policies impact global yields, particularly in emerging markets that rely on dollar-denominated debt.

4.1.2 From the Bank of England

In February 2025, the Bank of England (BoE) cut interest rates by a quarter-point (to 4.5% from 4.75%).[9] The BoE said it would be careful about further moves in the face of an expected inflation spike and global economic uncertainty. The BoE halved its 2025 growth outlook and said inflation would be almost double its 2% target this year. The central bank said it was unclear exactly how any future US trade tariffs would affect inflation in Britain. In general, higher global tariffs (including retaliatory ones) are likely to cause slower growth. The outlook for Britain's economy is bad. First, inflation (above target at 2.5%) is expected to get higher later this year due to higher energy prices and expected increases in regulated utilities. The unemployment rate rose to 4.4%. The economy stagnated in the third quarter of 2024 and growth in the second quarter had been 0.4%. The value of the pound has sunk sharply as the Bank of England signaled there would be more interest rate cuts later this year.

In response to the interest-rate cut, the yield on UK 2-year gilts (government bonds) fell to 4.09%, representing a fall of 0.05 percentage points. This caused the British pound to depreciate against a trade-weighted basket of currencies. Signs of UK's stock market softening also contributed to the pound's depreciation. Those fluctuations show that investors are demanding more compensation (that is, a higher risk premium), to buy UK assets. In addition, rising UK bond yields are pushing up government spending on interest expense and that could put the government's budget plans at risk. A weaker currency could also drive inflation higher.

We mentioned earlier that BoE signaled that a rate cut could finally be coming later this year. While the Bank of England decided to cut rates this on February 5, 2025, the Fed kept them on hold. In this case, expectations matter for bond investors. This signal was interpreted as good news for US bonds, and so yields across the Atlantic also fell. The 10-year US bond yield has now fallen below 4%, similar to that in the UK (compared to 4.3% a week ago).

4.1.3 From the European Central Bank

The European Central Bank (ECB) cut its key interest rate by another 0.25 percentage points to 2.75% early in February 2025 amid an uncertain economic outlook and sticky inflation.[10] Eurostat data indicated that the bloc's economy unexpectedly stagnated in the fourth quarter of 2024 (mainly due to the German economy's economic woes). The German bond market is nervous as the ECB hints at possible interest rate cuts to boost the Eurozone's sluggish economic growth. The chance of a further significant rate cut has stirred speculation impacting bond yields across

Europe. Germany's 2-year bonds, which represent a key indicator for ECB rate shifts, dropped in yield, while the country's 10-year bonds also dipped slightly. Germany's bond performance sets the tone for the Eurozone's financial markets.

European bonds are primed to outperform in 2025 because of the US's threats about imposing trade tariffs (on the European Union as well), forcing the European Central Bank (ECB) to slash interest rates. This will weigh on the region's export-oriented economy at a time when it is already experiencing sluggish growth and declining inflation. That will force the ECB to cut rates from 2.75% to 1.5%. This repricing toward more ECB cuts will trigger a rally in European bonds relative to US Treasuries. Strategies say that this could be the year for European government bonds. Furthermore, deeper interest rate cuts will push the Euro back through parity with the dollar (the pair was trading about $1.04 in early February 2025). With the ECB cutting interest rates faster than the Fed, this has placed further pressure on the euro, which has fallen sharply.

4.1.4 From the Bank of Japan

There is a new era looming for Japanese bonds. Investors worldwide are watching the Japanese market, as the Bank of Japan (BoJ) ponders rate hikes amid rising yields. This runs contrary to other major central banks which reduce interest rates. With the five-year Japanese government bonds yield at 0.985% and the 30-year at 2.285%, Japan's decades of low rates could be ending. The yen touched high versus the US dollar early in February 2025 after BoJ advocated continued interest rate hikes. The yen is on track for its fourth straight weekly gain against the dollar amid Donald Trump's tariff threats and as spending data added to signs that the BoJ will raise interest rates again. This was a widely expected move by the BoJ as global investors move from the deflation and stagnant economic growth that plagued Japan for decades.

Low interest rates for decades meant cheap borrowing costs for domestic Japanese companies as well as for global borrowers who held *samurai bonds* (that is what foreign bonds issued by Japan are called outside Japan). But now, a new era emerges and markets price this in their future valuations. Investors become cautious and raise their demand for bonds towards the shorter end of the yield curve. This is so because they want to avoid the risk that comes from longer-duration bonds.

Another interesting feature of samurai bonds, for global investors, is that they pay small premia over the local currency bonds and this is attractive to asset managers worldwide so they can swap to their local currencies and pick up some extra yield. This however, is not appealing for domestic investors. For investors, the Japanese bond markets should start offering a higher risk premium and higher yields in response to the BOJ's continued policy adjustments. As the market digests the new policy stance, there will be tactical opportunities for asset managers to exploit the inefficiencies in the Japanese bond and interest rate swap markets during this period of increased volatility.

4.2 Interpreting and exploiting global news for bond investments

Interpreting bond market news effectively helps investors make informed decisions about fixed-income investments, interest rate trends, and broader economic conditions. Here is how to analyze key factors in bond market news (from the central banks and the government).

4.2.1 Central Bank policy news

A number of key indicators are worth regularly watching. For example, the policy statements published by the Fed, the ECB, the BoE and the BoJ on interest rate hikes or cuts. Also, their' forward guidance on future monetary policy announcements, where *forward guidance* is a means to tell the public about the likely future course of monetary policy. Specifically, when central banks provide forward guidance, market agents can use this information to make decisions about spending and investments. So, when rate hikes/cuts are announced, bond prices fall/rise and yields rise/fall. Higher rates make existing bonds less attractive, lowering their prices. Short-term bonds react faster than long-term bonds. Finally, sectors like tech and high-yield bonds underperform.

Lower rates increase demand for existing bonds with higher yields. Long-term bonds benefit more than short-term bonds. Corporate bonds and emerging markets gain appeal. So, investor action could take the following forms: If rates are expected to rise, shift toward short-duration bonds to reduce risk, and if rates are expected to fall, hold longer-duration bonds to benefit from price appreciation.

Finally, keep an eye on government bond auctions (US Treasury, European bonds) as well as on foreign demand for bonds. Further, read about central bank bond-buying programs at auctions as well as for continuation of quantitative easing, QE, or tightening, QT. How to interpret such news. If there is weak demand for bonds (low auction bids, Fed selling QE Assets), then bond prices would be expected to fall and yields to rise. By contrast, a strong bond demand (due to high foreign buying or further QE programs), is expected to raise bond prices (and cause yields to fall). In terms of investor actions, in high-demand environments, bond market stability favors long-term positions, whereas in weak demand situations, be (remain) cautious as rising yields may hurt bond prices.

4.2.2 Inflation news and economic data

The key indicators to watch are the CPI (Consumer Price Index), PPI (Producer Price Index), wage growth, employment reports, and GDP growth figures. So, rising inflation causes bond prices to fall and yields to rise. Higher inflation erodes real returns of fixed-income investments. In this case, central banks may tighten their monetary policies, making bonds less attractive. Bonds regain appeal as real returns improve, when inflation is lower. Central banks may keep or cut rates, further supporting bonds.

So, what kind of action(s) would an investor take? If there are inflation concerns, go for TIPS (Treasury Inflation-Protected Securities), while for no worries, increase exposure to long-term bonds for better returns.

4.2.3 Yield curve movements

Recall that there are three types of shape of the yield curve (YC): normal (implying that long-term yields higher than short-term and, thus, a healthy, growing economy; inverted (where short-term yields higher than long-term, thereby signaling a contraction and possibly a recession in the economy; and flat (where short- and long-term yields are roughly similar suggesting economic uncertainty as to where the economy is headed.

So, how would you interpret the positions of YC and what actions could you take? A YC inversion may suggest a high recessionary economic environment and thus you should switch to safer assets such as Treasuries or gold (*flight to safety* effect). A steepening YC insinuates expectations of economic growth thus, favoring riskier assets such as corporate bonds or equities. Finally, a flattening YC would mean taking caution as a potential economic slowdown may lie ahead.

4.2.4 Credit market and default risk news

You should also follow news from the credit (bond) market as they affect the yields and riskiness of fixed-income securities (including structured products, not just bonds). The indicators to watch are corporate bond spreads (for example, investment grade vs. high-yield bonds), Credit Default Swap (CDS) spreads and sovereign debt ratings and downgrades.

So, how would you interpret such news and what actions could you take? Widening spreads and rising CDS prices imply higher default risk (for bond issuers). Investors demand more compensation for risk, pushing yields higher. Stick to high-quality government or AAA-rated corporate bonds. In addition, higher spreads could signal economic downturns or credit stress. Additionally, watch the earnings reports of major bond issuers (banks, energy firms, tech giants) and in case of poor earnings or high debt, credit spreads would widen (implying higher risk) causing bond yields to rise.

Obviously, strong earnings reports imply lower risk (or tighter spreads) causing bond yields to fall. In case of tightening (smaller) spreads, that would mean improved credit conditions and a lower risk perception, hence favoring corporate bonds. It also indicates economic stability or recovery. In this case, investors should consider corporate or emerging market bonds for higher yields.

4.2.5 Global geopolitical news

Geopolitical risks are many these days and more emerge continuously. Some key indicators to watch are global (regional) wars, conflicts, global instability, commodity shocks (oil prices surging, supply chain issues), sovereign and banking crises in advanced and emerging markets. You can interpret such news as being cautions and given that you are a risk-averse investor (by default, this is the assumption), you should switch investments to safe-haven bonds (such as US Treasuries or German Bunds). You may witness high-yield and emerging market bonds selloffs.

What about general investor sentiment? *Investor sentiment* refers to the overall attitude of investors towards a particular market or asset, essentially reflecting their perception of future price movements. Hence, investors can be optimistic (bullish) or pessimistic (bearish) depending on their expected direction of the market. So, risk-on sentiment (based on economic recovery or additional government stimulus measures) would entice investors to move to equities and riskier assets including corporate and emerging-market debt.

In sum, interest rate news determines bond price direction, inflation data erodes the purchasing power of stable incomes (hurting bonds), widening credit spreads means riskier environment (tightening shows confidence) global economic and financial risk events recommend investments in safe-haven bonds and finally, corporate news on earnings and debt levels impact corporate bond yields. So, the best strategy under uncertain markets would be to hold diversified bonds (government + corporate), add TIPS for inflation protection and short-duration bonds if rates rise, and watch credit spreads and central bank policy for directional trends.[11]

One last question: How is a company's management linked to the global fixed-income market? You know from your finance courses that a (chief) financial manager is charged with his company's capital structure (proportions of debt and equity). What would be some other corresponding roles for a manager in a company? Box 10.1 explains which ones.

Box 10.1

Which manager's roles are related to the fixed-income market?

CONTROLLING: A manager's role is to monitor and control debt levels, in relation to equity, in order to maximize the use of borrowed funds.

DECISION-MAKING: Managers ensure that their decisions achieve their goals with the overall goal of shareholder wealth maximization in mind; hence, managers should tap the global fixed-income market **guided** by these goals so as to balance (optimize) their company's debt and equity levels.

BUDGETING/TREASURER: Managers often handle budgets, control costs, and report on financial performance including direct oversight of fixed-income investments and liquidity management.

Test your understanding 2

1. What is a bond's total return? When do you omit the coupon income from the formula?
2. What is the purpose of immunizing a bond portfolio?
3. What are some of the questions that performance attribution analysis seeks to answer?
4. What would be the impact of interest-rate rate changes by the Fed on the US dollar?

Solutions appear at the textbook's website.

Summary

- Investors can use and exploit the global bond market to achieve a variety of financial goals, including income generation, portfolio diversification, capital preservation, and hedging against economic risks.
- The global bond market offers opportunities across different sectors, maturities, currencies, and risk profiles, enabling investors to optimize their strategies.

- When investing in foreign bonds, you can use currency hedging to mitigate exchange rate risk, but that would be a riskier strategy not suitable for conservative investors.
- TIPS adjust their principal and interest payments based on inflation, helping preserve purchasing power.
- Bond prices and yields are sensitive to interest rate changes, creating opportunities for investors who can predict rate movements.
- Taking advantage of pricing inefficiencies between CDS and bond yields involves strategies that exploit the misalignment between the credit risk premium implied by CDS spreads and the credit spreads embedded in bond yields.
- An investor must set up his/her investment policy statement (IPS) for the overall portfolio.
- The IPS contains information on the investor's objective, constraints, degree of risk tolerance and time horizon.
- The bond ladder approach entails building a portfolio with staggered maturities for regular cash flow and reinvestment flexibility.
- The bond barbell strategy combines short-term bonds for liquidity with long-term bonds for yield.
- The core-satellite strategy contains high-quality bonds as the core and riskier bonds as satellites for higher returns.
- A bullet bond portfolio focuses on bonds with maturities that cluster around a specific target date.
- The current yield (CY) focuses on the income generated relative to the bond's price.
- The yield to maturity (YTM) is the expected return if the bond is held to maturity, accounting for coupon payments and price changes.
- Convexity measures how the duration of a bond changes as interest rates fluctuate.
- An immunized bond portfolio is designed to shield investors from interest rate fluctuations by matching the portfolio's duration with the investment horizon.
- Performance attribution analysis seeks to answer several questions such as the bond portfolio manager's performance in relation to the portfolio objectives and constraints, and the effectiveness of his asset allocation in the portfolio.
- Interpreting bond market news effectively helps investors make informed decisions about fixed-income investments, interest rate trends, and broader economic conditions.

Questions and problems

1. List the main bond portfolio construction strategies and mention the two main risks that each eliminates (or minimizes).
2. Consider an 8-year, 7% coupon bond, making *semi-annual payments* valued at the 8% market rate. The price of this bond (using excel and assuming a \$100 face value) is \$94.17. Compute its yield to maturity.

3. Assume that you have a 3% coupon, 10-year bond making annual payments. Its par value (and initial price) is \$100. Currently, it sells for \$88.13 because its yield to maturity is 4.5%. Compute:
   a. the bond's modified duration, *at the initial yield*
   b. its convexity
   c. Now, assume that that its yield increases to 5% and the bond now sells at \$84.556 (verify this). What percentage decline did this bond's price suffer (from par)? Compute the predicted price decline using the duration rule. Explain.
   d. Now, use the duration-convexity rule and explain the result.

4. Why do investors like convexity?
5. Assume that an insurance company must make a payment of \$12,762 in five years. The market interest rate is 5%. The portfolio manager wishes to fund the obligation using three-year zero-coupon bonds and perpetuities (making annual payments). Compute:
   a. The present value of the obligation
   b. The durations of the obligation, the zero-coupon bonds and the perpetuity
   c. The duration of the asset portfolio. Interpret the allocations.

6. Assume that a portfolio manager's asset portfolio consisted of 80% equities, 15% bonds and 5% cash. The rate of return of this managed portfolio was 7%. The benchmark portfolio's asset allocations were 60% in equities, 35% in bonds and 5% in cash equivalents. Each component in the benchmark portfolio yielded 6%, 2.5% and 1%, respectively. Conduct performance attribution analysis by computing the following:
   a. The benchmark portfolio's total return
   b. The excess return of the managed portfolio
   c. The total contribution due to asset allocation
   d. Interpret what you found

7. Below are two actual statements from Bank of England's officials around mid-February 2025: "The macroeconomic news over recent months has been uncomfortable, pointing to the higher-than-expected inflation and flatlining growth." "[P]oor growth has been more because of weakening demand relative to supply in the economy." Interpret these two statements and explain how the BoE would respond, with respect to changing interest rates.
8. In the United States, bond spreads have remained remarkably stable since the beginning of 2025. Inflationary pressures (such as those coming from the country's imposition of tariffs on several countries) would make it harder for the Fed to proceed with new interest rate cuts. What should investors do regarding bond investments?
9. Here is an interesting, yet perplexing, question: What if tariffs are lifting inflation while they are hindering the economy? Should the Fed raise, lower or keep steady interest rates?

Notes

1. https://www.icmagroup.org/market-practice-and-regulatory-policy/secondary-markets/bond-market-size/

2. https://www.icmagroup.org/market-practice-and-regulatory-policy/secondary-markets/bond-market-size/
3. https://www.spglobal.com/spdji/en/indices/sustainability/sp-green-bond-index/#overview
4. The details are: 1/1/2000, 1/1/2008, 7%, 8%, 100, 2, 0, corresponding to the excel function =*PRICE*(settlement, maturity, rate, yield, redemption, frequency, basis) in that order.
5. To compute YTM, just apply Excel's function =*YIELD* with its arguments.
6. If a portfolio manager wishes to fund such obligations with perpetual bonds, the perpetuity duration formula would be (1+y)y, where y is yield.
7. We show how to compute portfolio's weights in Part C2 of the online Appendix.
8. https://www.reuters.com/markets/us/us-job-growth-misses-expectations-january-unemployment-rate-40–2025-02–07/
9. https://www.bankofengland.co.uk/monetary-policy-summary-and-minutes/2025/february-2025#:~:text=Monetary%20Policy%20Summary%2C%20February%202025&text=The%20MPC%20adopts%20a%20medium,percentage%20points%2C%20to%204.5%25
10. https://www.ecb.europa.eu/press/pr/date/2025/html/ecb.mp250417~42727d0735.en.html
11. We discuss geopolitics in Chapter 14.

Part IV

Other financial markets

This part primarily deals with the derivative securities, foreign exchange and commodities markets. The objective is not to fully describe each of these markets. Rather, to provide a brief but essential coverage of the operations, risks, opportunities and future trends of these markets.

Chapter 11 presents, in brief, the first two markets so the reader gets a rudimentary understanding of their functions. Some specific questions that are addressed in that chapter are the following. First, what the key features and functions of the derivatives and commodities markets are. Second, what the determinants of each of these markets are. Third, how and why do people trade in these markets? Finally, what are some actual examples of dealing in each of these markets?

Chapter 12 discusses the foreign exchange market and extends the analysis to how investors exploit this market. Specifically, some strategies are described and applied with hypothetical data. Some actual examples will also be mentioned and analyzed. For example, some ways of hedging and speculating in the foreign exchange market will be presented.

Chapter 13 discusses the financial technology and its impact on these financial markets as well as the global financial markets. We will also dedicate a section on artificial intelligence (AI) and trace its profound and permeating effects on the global financial markets. The cryptocurrency market will also be discussed.

Chapter 14 deals with the various global risks that affect the global financial markets. We identify a number of global risks and classify them into short-term and long-term. Then, we trace the implications of these categories of risk on the financial markets. Finally, we discuss how retail investors cope with these global risks.

DOI: 10.4324/9781003677161-14

Chapter 11

The derivatives and commodities markets

Introduction

The derivatives market is vast and plays a significant role in global finance. While it can help manage risks, it also involves significant complexities and potential for financial instability. The derivatives market refers to the financial market where derivative contracts are bought and sold. A *derivative* is a financial instrument whose value is derived from the value of an underlying asset such as a financial asset, index or interest rate. Common types of derivatives include futures, options, swaps, and forwards. *Futures* are contracts to buy or sell an asset at a predetermined price and date. *Options* are contracts that give the right, but not the obligation, to buy or sell an asset at a specified price within a specific time frame. *Forwards* are tailor-made (customized) contracts between two parties to buy or sell an asset at a future date for a price agreed upon today. Finally, *swaps* are agreements to exchange cash flows or liabilities between two parties, often used to exchange interest rate payments or currencies. Some other types of derivative securities are weather, currency and credit. In this market, investors and companies can hedge against risks, speculate on price movements, or gain exposure to various assets without directly owning them. Let us briefly explain each of them next.

Derivatives are often used to reduce the risk of price fluctuations in assets, that is, for hedging. For example, a company that exports goods might use derivatives to lock in exchange rates to avoid losses if the currency fluctuates. Traders can use derivatives to bet on the future price movements of an asset, such as stocks, commodities, interest rates, or currencies. This activity is referred to as speculation. This can lead to higher returns, but also carries higher risk. Derivatives also allow investors to control a large position with a relatively small amount of capital, increasing potential gains (or losses). Hence, they can use them as leverage.

The derivatives markets serve the fundamental function in the growth of economies and the efficient operation of companies. Specifically, they permit price

DOI: 10.4324/9781003677161-15

discovery, which is vital for informing current decisions about investments and resource allocation. Therefore, these markets provide a critical risk management function by allowing any player with exposure to an asset to hedge that exposure across various maturities over time. In general, there are two types of derivatives markets: the *over-the-counter* (OTC) markets and the exchange-traded derivatives markets. Recall that OTC refers to trading among decentralized networks of buyers and sellers, scattered throughout the country, usually liaised by few highly unified financial institutions such as brokers. OTC trading can also take place directly, whereby the counterparties have direct relationships with each other. By contrast, *exchange trading* takes place in a centralized order book and on a multilateral basis, where all traders interact with each other at the same time and in physical location.

1 Characteristics of the derivatives markets

Global over-the-counter (OTC) derivatives notional amounts outstanding grew to $730 trillion at the end of June 2024, according to the Bank of International Settlements (BIS) (see Figure 11.1). While, interest-rate (INTRATE) derivatives' notional outstanding amounts expanded over the period, the foreign exchange (FOREX) derivatives (mainly those denominated in Japanese yen) slightly increased to $129.9 trillion from $118.5 trillion. The other (OTHER) derivatives category (which includes equity and commodity derivatives), remained rather flat over the period shown in Figure 11.1. The exchange-traded (ET) derivatives shows an alternating pattern over the same 3-year period, with a peak in the second quarter of 2023. Following BIS, "the exchange-traded derivatives cover the turnover and open interest of foreign exchange and interest rate futures and options". Some exchange-traded instruments include ETF futures and options, and stock index options and futures. These instruments were much larger than OTC derivative contracts (forwards, swaps and options) for the 2021, 2022 and 2023 years.[1] The key differences between OTC and ET Derivative markets are: (1) the OTC

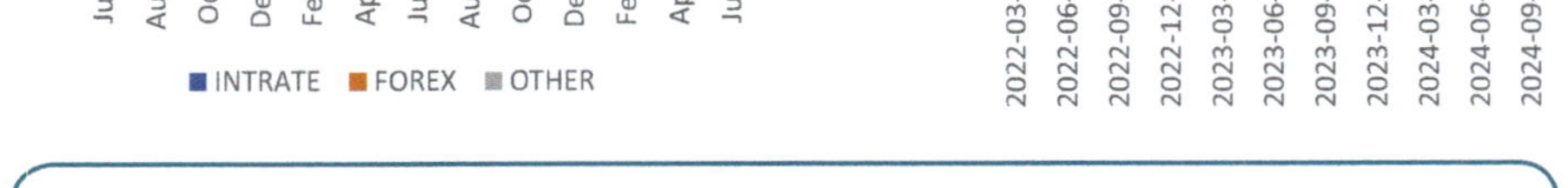

Figure 11.1 Volume of global OTC and exchange-traded derivatives

Notes: half-year values for OTC derivatives; quarterly for the exchange-traded derivatives; in millions of USD; source: BIS data.

market offers more flexibility and customizability, (2) the OTC market is less transparent than the ET market, and (3) the OTC market involves more counterparty risk, and it is less liquid than ET.

1.1 Determinants of the derivatives markets

The derivatives market is influenced by several key determinants, which affect the demand and supply of derivatives. These factors influence how participants in the market (such as investors, traders, and companies) use derivatives to manage risks, speculate, or achieve other financial goals. A real example of hedging with derivatives is the actions of Southwest Airlines which used derivatives to implement a price hedging strategy in 2008. This permitted the company to buy jet fuel at a low fixed price even as energy prices reached record highs. More specifically, the derivatives market is influenced by a mix of economic factors, market conditions, regulations, and investor behavior. Understanding these determinants helps market participants navigate the complexities of derivative pricing, risk management, and speculation strategies. Below are the main determinants of the derivatives market with a brief discussion for each.

1.1.1 Underlying asset price

The value of the underlying asset is one of the most important factors affecting derivative prices. For example, the price of a stock affects the value of options or futures contracts based on that stock. Hence, if the price of the underlying asset rises or falls, it will directly impact the value of the derivative. For example, if the price of oil rises, the value of oil futures contracts would generally rise as well.

1.1.2 Volatility

We have discussed volatility a number of times thus far. Recall that *volatility* refers to the degree of variation in the price of the underlying asset over time. High volatility typically leads to higher derivative prices because there is greater uncertainty about future price movements. In options markets, for example, implied volatility, which is a measure of expected future volatility, is a key input in determining option premiums. The more volatile an asset is expected to be, the higher the price of options linked to that asset. Derivatives can be volatile contracts with a high degree of leverage, which can result in big gains and losses. The exchanges mitigate credit risk through clearinghouses (which guarantees payment to both parties).

1.1.3 Interest rates and macro indicators

The level of interest rates has a significant impact on the derivatives market, particularly for interest rate derivatives like swaps and futures. Higher interest rates generally reduce the present value of future cash flows and can affect the pricing of derivatives, particularly those tied to bonds or currencies. Conversely, lower interest rates may increase the demand for derivatives that offer returns based on interest rate changes.

Also, economic conditions and indicators, such as inflation, GDP growth, unemployment rates, and other macroeconomic data, can have a direct or indirect effect on the pricing of derivatives. For example, a strong economy may increase demand for equity-related derivatives, while economic downturns might lead to more hedging activity using derivatives tied to commodities or currencies.

1.1.4 Supply and demand and market sentiment

The basic economic principle of supply and demand impacts derivative prices. If there is greater demand for a specific derivative, its price may increase, while an oversupply can push prices down. For instance, if more investors or traders are hedging against price movements in a particular market (such as oil), the demand for oil-related futures or options will increase. Higher demand for a derivative contract pushes up its price, while lower demand leads to lower premiums or spreads. So, when demand surges such as during financial crises, derivative premiums spike due to heightened uncertainty and risk aversion. High trading volume in derivatives markets enhances liquidity, reducing bid-ask spreads. A case in point is the 2008 financial crisis, during which the demand for credit default swaps (CDS) on subprime mortgage bonds skyrocketed, increasing CDS spreads.

Supply in these markets depends on the willingness of market makers, institutional traders, and speculators to take the opposite side of a trade. Supply constraints (e.g., few sellers of CDS, for example) can cause derivative prices to move sharply. In general, the derivatives market is highly sensitive to supply and demand conditions, impacting pricing, volatility, and liquidity. A surge in demand for risk protection or speculation can significantly affect derivative valuations, often leading to market distortions during crises or speculative bubbles.

Market sentiment (or the collective attitude of investors toward a market or asset) can drive speculative activity in the derivatives market. If investors are optimistic about a particular asset's price, derivatives based on that asset may see an increase in demand. Finally, speculators use derivatives to bet on the direction of price movements without necessarily owning the underlying asset.

DERIVATIVES REGULATION

In the United States, the following bodies regulate the derivatives market: the Commodity Futures Trading Commission, the Securities and Exchange Commission, the Financial Industry Regulatory Authority and the national Futures Association. Regulation was the consequence of the passing of the Dodd–Frank Wall Street Reform and Consumer Protection Act of 2010, which implemented new regulations after the deregulation of the industry in the 1990s and 2000s and the ensuing 2008 global financial crisis.

In the European Union, legislation was passed under the European Market Infrastructure Regulation (2012) and the regulatory authority is the European Securities and markets Authority.

The appetite for speculation can greatly influence derivative prices.

> In the United Kingdom, the legislation is the 2021 UK Securities Financing Transaction Regulation and the regulatory authority is the Financial Conduct Authority.

1.1.5 Market liquidity

Recall that liquidity refers to how easily an asset or derivative can be bought or sold without affecting its price. Highly liquid markets, where many participants are buying and selling derivatives, tend to have tighter bid-ask spreads and lower transaction costs. The liquidity of the underlying asset also impacts the derivatives market. For example, if an asset is illiquid, the corresponding derivative might have lower liquidity, making it harder to enter or exit positions.

1.1.6 Time to maturity

The time until the expiration or settlement of a derivative contract also plays a crucial role in determining its price. This is particularly relevant for options, where the *time value* (the value derived from the remaining time until expiration) can be significant. As the expiration date approaches, the time value decreases, and this is reflected in the pricing of the derivative.

1.1.7 Regulation and the legal framework

The regulatory environment can also shape the derivatives market. For example, regulations regarding margin requirements, leverage, and reporting requirements can influence how market participants engage with derivatives. Legal constraints on certain types of derivatives (such as bans on particular speculative instruments) or new regulatory requirements (like post-2008 financial crisis reforms) can alter market behavior and derivative pricing. Futures, options, and certain swaps are traded on exchanges regulated by the Commodity Futures Trading Commission (CFTC) or the SEC, depending on the underlying asset. Swaps were traded over the counter, however. The nearby *sidebar* contains the regulatory bodies of the US, European Union and UK.

1.1.8 Various risks

A number of risks affect the derivative instruments. The risk that the counterparty (the other party to a contract) may default on their obligations affects the value and structure of derivatives. Higher counterparty risk can make derivatives more expensive, as market participants may demand higher returns or premiums to compensate for the potential for default. This risk has become more important in the OTC derivatives market, which involves customized contracts between two parties. Also, leverage risk is important in this market. A poorly timed leveraged trade can wipe out an investor's capital, and an unregulated OTC derivative contract carries the risk of default by the counterparty. Political instability, wars, sanctions, and other geopolitical events can have a significant impact on the derivatives market, especially those related to commodities (such as oil or gold), currencies, or government bonds. For example, an oil crisis or conflict in a major oil-producing region can lead to increased demand for oil-related derivatives as investors hedge against rising prices.

1.1.9 Exchange rates

For derivatives based on foreign currencies, the exchange rate between two currencies is a key element. Currency derivatives like forwards and options are impacted by changes in exchange rates and interest rate differentials between countries. Fluctuations in exchange rates can lead to changes in the pricing of currency derivatives as traders anticipate future movements in exchange rates. Arbitrage involves exploiting price discrepancies between markets. When there are inefficiencies between the price of a derivative and its underlying asset, traders will use arbitrage strategies to profit. These actions can influence the pricing and liquidity of derivatives.

1.1.10 Technological advancements

Finally, technological changes, particularly in trading platforms, algorithmic trading, and data analysis, can affect the efficiency and accessibility of the derivatives market. The rise of electronic trading and high-frequency trading (HFT) has increased market activity, creating new opportunities but also potential risks.

1.1.11 Margin requirements

Derivatives are subject to margin requirements, which means that investors who trade derivatives are often required to post *margin*, which is a deposit of (own) funds that serves as collateral against potential losses. Margin requirements vary depending on the type of derivative and the exchange or broker through which it is traded. For futures contracts, derivatives exchanges set initial margin requirements as low as 5% or 10% of the contract to be traded. However, during periods of market volatility, futures exchanges may increase initial margin requirements to any level they deem necessary.

1.2 The put-call parity relationship

A formal relationship that must exist between put and call options in efficient capital markets is the *put-call parity*, which states that the price of a call option implies a specific fair price for the corresponding put option with the same underlying asset, strike price and expiration date. It depends on the assumption that financial markets are free from arbitrage opportunities, suggesting that securities offering identical payoffs with identical risks must sell for the same current price. This parity applies only to European (put and call) options, which must be exercised at expiration date. The basic equation is as follows[2]:

$$C + PV_k = P + S \tag{11.1}$$

where C is the price of the European call option, PV_k is the present value of the strike price *k*, discounted from the value on the expiration date at the risk-free rate,

P is the price of the European put, and *S* is the spot price or the current market value of the underlying asset.

Here is a simple example of using this parity. Assume that we want to know if the price of a 6-month European 50-strike put option on ABC stock at \$6.50 is correct, given that the current price of the stock (S) is \$45, the strike price of the options (k) is \$50, the present value (PV) of k is \$49.50 and the price of a 6-month European call option (C) on the stock is \$3.00. Plugging these into (11.1), we have:

$$\$3 + \$49.50 = P + \$45 \text{ and so } P = \$52.50 - \$45 = \$7.50 = P$$

Therefore, the price of this put option on ABC stock should be \$7.50 according to the put-call parity principle. Hence, all prices are in equilibrium.

But what would happen if there were a mismatch in the equation? This would immediately open up an arbitrage opportunity! Let us say the market price of the put option is actually \$8.00 instead of \$7.50. In this case, the equation would look like this:

$$\$3 + \$49.50 \neq \$8 + \$45 \text{ or } \$52.50 \neq \$53$$

This means the put option is *overpriced* relative to the call option and the underlying stock. Traders can exploit this discrepancy by simultaneously buying and selling the options in a way that locks in a risk-free profit. Here, an arbitrageur could exploit this mispricing by selling the put option for \$8, buying the call option for \$3, and shorting the underlying stock at \$45. This would result in an immediate cash inflow of \$5 (= \$8 – \$3) and, at expiration, a guaranteed profit of \$0.50 (\$53 – \$52.50) because the short stock position would cancel out the exercise of either the put or call option.

Some additional conditions that must be present for the parity to hold are that the stock does not pay dividends, interest rates remain unchanged until the expiration date and there are no brokerage fees.

What if you need to compute the PV(k), the present value of the strike price? The formula for that is

$$k = e^{-rT} \qquad (11.2)$$

where r is the risk-free rate and T the time to maturity. For example, if the current stock price is \$30, the current risk-free rate is 3% and the time to maturity is 0.5 years, we would get a value of k equal to 29.553 [= 30*exp(–0.03*0.5)].

2 Trading in the derivatives market

As mentioned earlier, the derivatives market allows investors to trade financial instruments like futures, options, swaps, and forwards that derive their value from underlying assets (stocks, bonds, commodities, interest rates, etc.). However, trading in derivatives requires understanding market mechanisms, risk management, and execution strategies. Consequently, the following steps must be taken by the investor. But before you undertake this activity, you must open an account with a broker who has access to the derivatives market.

Step 1: Understand the different types of derivatives

Before trading, an investor must know the key types of derivatives: *futures contracts*, which are agreement to buy/sell an asset at a future date for a set price; *options contracts*, which give you the right but not obligation to buy/sell an asset at a predetermined price; *swaps*, or contracts exchanging cash flows (e.g., interest rate swaps, currency swaps); and *forwards*, which refer to customized, non-exchange-traded contracts (similar to futures).

Step 2: Understand the trading details

Once you have an active account, you must meet margin requirements as derivative trades often require leverage. Then, you should understand trading fees and the contract specifications such as lot size, expiration dates, etc.

Step 3: Analyze the market and develop a strategy

In general, investors use different strategies based on risk appetite and market outlook. For example, a hedging strategy can be used to protect against price movements (e.g., an airline buying oil futures to hedge fuel costs). A *speculative strategy* aims to profit from price movements (e.g., buying call options if expecting a stock to rise). *Arbitrage* involves exploiting price differences between markets (e.g., buying a commodity in one market and selling in another). Finally, *spread trading* refers to simultaneously buying and selling related contracts to capitalize on price spreads. For example, you might buy an S&P 500 futures contract if you expect the index to rise.

Step 4: Execute trades and manage risk

Once your strategy is in place, you can place trades via your broker's platform. For example, you may specify a market order, a limit order, or a stop-loss order. You must be aware of margin calls when your account's value falls below some pre-determined level. Since derivatives are often leveraged, small price movements can lead to large gains/losses. To hedge risk, apply a stop-loss order, enhance portfolio diversification, and/or use key risk management tools. As an example, you may use options to implement a protective put strategy to limit downside risk in your stock portfolio.

Step 5: Wrap-up the trade

Derivatives have expiration dates, so investors must monitor positions and decide when to exercise options contracts or sell before expiration, roll over futures contracts to avoid delivery obligations or close losing positions to limit downside risk. For example, a trader holding a short futures position may close it early if the market moves against him.

Before going any further with a simple example of trading in the derivatives market, it is important to go through some essential concepts regarding options. An *option premium* is the price a trader pays to exercise the option. It is comprised of the intrinsic and the extrinsic values. The *intrinsic value* is the difference between the actual value or current market price of the stock and the strike price. The *strike price* or the *exercise price* is the price at which you can buy or sell a security when you purchase an options contract. The intrinsic value of a call option is current stock price *minus* strike price, whereas that for a put option is the reverse. Only in-the-money (or positive value) options have intrinsic value. In other words, intrinsic value exists if the strike price is below the current market price in regard to calls and above for puts.

The *extrinsic value* is made up of time until expiration, implied volatility, dividends and the cost of carry. *Time value* is any premium in excess of intrinsic value before expiration. Often traders view the time value as the amount they are willing to pay for an option above its intrinsic value. So, *time value = extrinsic value = the option premium – intrinsic value*. The *time until expiration* affects the time value component of an option's premium. In general, as expiration approaches, the levels of an option's time value decrease (time decay factor) for both puts and calls. Put differently, as expiration nears, extrinsic value decays to zero, leaving only intrinsic value if the option is in the money. Higher volatility indicates greater expected fluctuations (in either direction) in underlying price levels, which results in higher option premiums for puts and calls. Finally, the underlying security's dividends and the current risk-free interest rate are important for option premiums. This reflects the cost to carry shares in an underlying security, where *cost of carry* is the potential interest paid for margin or received from alternative safe investments (T-bills) and the dividends from owning shares outright.

Now, we are ready to illustrate with an example using options how one can trade a company's stock or the trading stock options, a common derivative instrument. We build two real scenarios with the actual price of that company's stock. We use Apple's (AAPL) stock price which, as of March 11, 2025, it was trading at (approximately) $220.

Scenario 1: You are bullish (optimistic) on Apple stock

This means that you expect it to rise to $240 in the next month. Instead of buying 100 shares (which would cost $22,000), you buy a call option as a leveraged bet on the stock's price increase. So, you purchase one (1) option contract on AAPL with the following terms: Option type: Call; Strike price: $230; Expiration date: 1 Month later; Premium paid (or the cost per contract): $5.00 per share. So, 1 contract equals 100 shares, totaling $500. This contract gives you the right to buy 100 shares of AAPL at $230 per share before expiration.

Three weeks later, AAPL stock rises to $238, exceeding the strike price of $230. The call option's value increases because the contract now allows you to buy shares below market price. So, what would be the stock's intrinsic value and your profit?

Intrinsic value: Since AAPL is now $238, the option's intrinsic value = $238 – $230 = $8 per share. Given that you bought 1 contract or 100 shares, the total intrinsic value = $800.

Profit Calculation: Initial cost (premium paid) = $500; Current value of option = $800; Net profit = $800 – $500 = $300

Now, you can close your position by selling the call option before expiration at its new price ($8 per share). The total profit: $300. The return on investment (ROI) is 60% on the initial $500 investment (= 300/300). Note that if you had bought 100 shares of AAPL at $220, your profit would have been $1,800, but you would have to shell out $22,000 in capital instead of just $500 for the options trade.

Scenario 2: You are bearish (pessimistic) on Apple stock

If AAPL's stock had fallen below $220, the call option would expire worthless, and you would lose the $500 premium paid.

So, what are the main takeaways from this simple options trading? First, understand how options allow investors to control large positions with less capital (leverage). Second, compute the maximum loss is the option premium ($500) which implies limited risk-taking. Third, a high reward potential since the profit in this trade was 60% ROI in three weeks. Finally, observe time sensitivity as options lose value as expiration approaches.

One more example of trading a stock option. Assume that you are analyzing XYZ stock, which is currently trading at $50. You decide to buy a call option with the following details: Strike price = $55; the option premium = $3 per share; the contract size = 100 shares; the expiration date = 1 month from today. At expiration, the stock price could be $50, $55, $58, or $60. What could your profits or losses be at each stock price scenario?

First, calculate the call option's payoff, using the standard payoff formula for a call option:[3]

$$max\ (0, S_T - K) \tag{11.3}$$

where S_T is the stock price at expiration and K the strike price ($55). At $50, the payoff is zero (or negative and so, the option expires worthless); at $55, the payoff is zero (we say that it is *at-the-money*, with no intrinsic value); at $58, the payoff is $3 and at $60, it is $5.

Now, let us calculate the total profit/loss. You paid $3 per share for the option, so your net profit/loss is found by using this formula:

$$Total\ Profit/Loss = Call\ Payoff - Option\ Premium \tag{11.4}$$

Therefore, for 100 shares per contract, the total profit/loss is:

At stock price of $50: the cost of option is –$300 and so the net profit/loss is –$300
At stock price of $55: the cost of option is –$300 and so the net profit/loss is –$300
At stock price of $58: the cost of option is –$300 but the payoff is $300, and so the net profit/loss is $0 (break-even point)
At stock price of $60: the *cost* of option is -$300 but the total payoff is $500, and so the net profit/loss is $200 (profit)

Let us summarize what we have found. The break-even price is $58 (strike price + premium). If the stock stays at or below $55, the investor loses the entire $300 premium. If the stock rises to $60, the investor makes a $200 profit. Higher stock prices mean greater profits. This is a *bullish strategy* where the investor earns positive profits if XYZ stock rises above $58 before expiration.

Test your understanding 1

1. How are demand and supply conditions affecting the derivatives markets?
2. What are the intrinsic and extrinsic values in a derivative? What happens as expiration nears?
3. Suppose a call option on ABC stock has an intrinsic value of $10; the total premium is $15. What is the stock's extrinsic value?
4. What are the conditions for the put-call parity to hold?

3 The characteristics of the global commodities market

The global commodities market is a massive financial marketplace where raw materials and primary goods are bought, sold, and traded. It is divided into two major categories: *hard commodities* – natural resources that must be extracted or mined (e.g., oil, gold, metals), and *soft commodities* – agricultural or livestock products (e.g., wheat, coffee, cotton). The global commodities market is valued in the trillions of dollars (projected to reach a nominal value of US$123.04 trillion in early 2025, according to *Statista*) with daily trading volumes exceeding hundreds of billions. The major commodity exchanges facilitate trading, include the CME Group (Chicago Mercantile Exchange, USA), the London Metal Exchange (LME, UK), the New York Mercantile Exchange (NYMEX, USA) and the Shanghai Futures Exchange (SHFE, China). Figure 11.2 shows the evolution of selected commodity price indices (annual basis) from 2000 to 2024. As you can see *Energy* had its ups and downs much more that *Non-energy* commodities (such as agriculture, beverages, food, and raw materials including timber), whereas the *Precious metals* commodities were on the rise since 2000.

The types of commodities traded are:

Energy Commodities such as Crude oil (WTI, Brent), Natural gas, Coal and Electricity. Oil alone has a daily trading volume of over $2 trillion.

Metals such as precious metals (Gold, Silver, and Platinum), *Industrial Metals* (Aluminum, Copper, Nickel, Zinc), and *Rare Earth Elements* (Rocks, Ores). Gold is one of the most actively traded commodities, with a daily turnover exceeding $100 billion.

Agricultural Commodities such as Grains (Wheat, Corn, Soybeans, Rice), Softs (Coffee, Cocoa, Cotton, and Sugar), and Livestock (Cattle, Pork Bellies). Agricultural commodities play a key role in global food security and inflation trends.

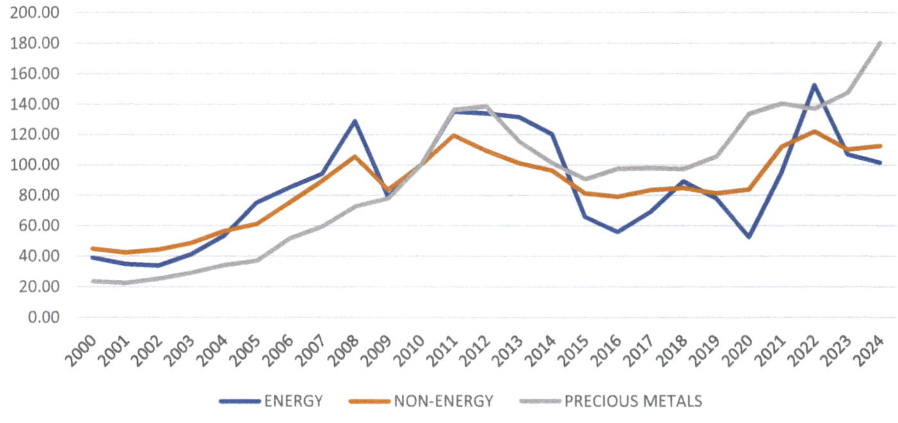

Figure 11.2 Selected commodity indices, 2000–2024
Source: World Bank

What are the common characteristics of commodities? They can be physically delivered worldwide (via ships, in bulk) and at low cost (due to economies of scale), can be stored for a long time (even liquid commodities like crude oil) and, in some cases, for a very long time and can be exchanged with other commodities of the same type (such as oil and livestock). Also, some commodities are known as *primary commodities* or natural products that can be extracted in their raw form and can vary (in quality) among them (crude oil, for example), and *secondary commodities*, which are produced from primary commodities (gasoline, for example). It is these characteristics that make commodities suitable for trading in global markets.

In the next subsection (3.1), we explain how the commodities markets operate using examples. In subsection 3.2, we show how hedging is practiced in this market and in subsection 3.3, how speculation is implemented (through hypothetical and real examples).

3.1 How the commodities market works

The modern commodities market relies on derivative securities, such as futures and forward contracts. Buyers and sellers can transact with one another easily and in large volumes without needing to exchange the physical commodities themselves. Commodity trading is a two-sided business, bringing buyers and sellers together in over-the-counter deals. This trading cannot be done through centralized exchanges because physical commodities vary in grade and quality (as well as location). By contrast, oil futures are traded on an exchange such as the Intercontinental Exchange (Brent crude oil is traded there) and the New York Mercantile Exchange (where the West Texas Intermediate is traded.)

We begin with the *spot market*, in which buying and selling physical commodities for immediate delivery. The *futures and options market* involves trading contracts that allow investors to speculate on future price movements. Related to the spot and forward markets (prices), we have the notions of contango and backwardation. Traders monitor whether futures are trading at a premium (*contango*) or a discount (*backwardation*) to the spot price. This provides an indication of whether inventories are rising or falling. When markets are in contango there may be an opportunity to conduct a cash-and-carry arbitrage. Very briefly, a *cash-and-carry arbitrage* strategy involves buying the underlying asset in the spot market and simultaneously selling a futures contract, aiming to profit from the price difference at the expiration of the futures contract.[4] Finally, the *Exchange-traded funds* (ETFs) and *Mutual funds* are investment vehicles that give exposure to commodity price movements without physical ownership.

The key factors that influence commodity prices are supply and demand (for example, weather conditions, mining output, oil production cuts), geopolitical events (such as wars, trade sanctions, OPEC decisions), currency strength (since commodities are often priced in US dollars, affecting global demand) and inflation and interest rates (rising inflation typically boosts demand for gold and oil). The biggest commodity trading countries are the USA (crude oil, corn, gold), China (iron ore, copper, coal), Saudi Arabia (crude oil), Russia (natural gas, wheat) and Brazil (soybeans, coffee, sugar).

3.2 Examples of hedging in the commodities market

The available opportunities in the commodities market are *hedging* – companies and governments use commodities to protect against price volatility, *speculation* – traders profit from price swings in oil, gold, and agricultural products, and *inflation hedging* – commodities often retain value during inflationary periods. Below is an example of hedging in the commodities market. In general, hedging in this market helps producers, consumers, and traders reduce their exposure to price fluctuations. One common method is using *futures contracts* to lock in prices. Sometimes, this is also known as a forward contract, which is a way to minimize the risk that the price of a commodity might go down before a farmer sells. A *forward contract* is an agreement to deliver a specific amount of a specific commodity at a specific time in the future. Because no one really knows whether prices will go up or down, a forward contract locks-in a price that is higher than the current cash price. One difference between the two contracts is that forward contracts are not standardized and tradable on an exchange, but can be traded in over-the-counter (OTC) markets, whereas futures contracts, are standardized legal agreements to buy or sell a specified quantity of a commodity for an agreed price, with delivery at a particular future time. These actually reflect the advantages of futures or forward contracts.

The example is of a farmer, attempting to hedge against falling corn prices. Consider this scenario: The corn farmer expects to harvest 10,000 bushels of corn in three months. However, he is concerned that corn prices might drop before he can sell his crop. The current corn futures price is $4.5 per bushel and the farmer wants to secure this price to avoid potential losses. His hedging strategy would be as follows:

Sell corn futures contracts today at $4.5 per bushel for delivery in three months. If corn prices drop to $3.5 per bushel, he still sells at the agreed $4.5 per bushel (via the futures contract). If prices rise to $6 per bushel, he will miss out on higher profits but is protected against losses. What are the outcomes? If prices fall, the farmer avoids losses, but if prices rise, he will not benefit but has guaranteed income. This type of hedging provides price stability and ensures farmers can cover production costs, even in volatile markets.

Here are two more examples of hedging in the energy and metal markets. Let us begin with hedging in the energy market (using an oil producer). A crude oil producer plans to sell 1 million barrels of oil in 6 months but fears that oil prices may drop. The current price of crude oil is $80 per barrel and the producer wants to lock in this price to protect against a decline. His hedging strategy would be as follows:

Sell crude oil futures contracts at $80 per barrel for delivery in six months. If oil prices fall to $70 per barrel, he can still sell at $80 per barrel (thanks to the futures contract). If prices rise to $90 per barrel, the producer misses out on higher profits but is protected from losses. So, the possible outcomes are: If prices fall, the producer avoids revenue losses, but if prices rise, the producer still benefits from stable pricing and predictable revenue.

The example of hedging in the metal market using a gold jewelry manufacturer is as follows. A jewelry manufacturer needs 500 ounces of gold in three months to produce jewelry. He fears that gold prices will rise, increasing his production costs.

The current gold price is $2,990 per ounce and the manufacturer wants to secure this price to control costs. His hedging strategy is as follows:

Buy gold futures contracts at $2,990 per ounce for delivery in three months. If gold prices rise to $3,100 per ounce, he still pays $2,990 per ounce (via the futures contract). However, if prices fall to $2,800 per ounce, the manufacturer overpays but has ensured cost stability. Overall, if prices rise, the manufacturer avoids increased costs, but if prices fall, he would have paid a premium but have secured predictable expenses.

For whom does hedging matter? *For producers*: hedging protects revenue from price declines; *for consumers*: hedging controls production costs and protects against rising prices; and *for traders*: hedging reduces risk in volatile markets.

3.3 Examples of speculating in the commodities market

In this subsection, we present a simple example of speculation in the commodities market. *Speculation* in this market involves buying or selling commodities with the expectation that prices will move in a favorable direction, allowing the trader to profit from price changes. Unlike hedging, speculators do not have a direct interest in the physical commodity – they are purely looking to profit from price movements.

Here's a simple scenario. Assume that an investor believes that crude oil prices will rise in the next three months due to rising geopolitical tensions in the Middle East. He will want to profit from this potential price increase. The price of Brent crude oil is currently $70 per barrel. The speculator expects a price increase to $75 per barrel within the next three months due to supply concerns. So, the strategy for this speculator would be to *buy* crude oil futures contracts at $70 per barrel for delivery in three months. Note that the speculator does not intend to take delivery of the oil, rather plans to close the position before the contract expires. The possible outcomes are the following:

> *Price rises:* After three months, geopolitical tensions escalate, and crude oil prices rise to $75 per barrel. The speculator sells their futures contract at $75 per barrel to make a profit of $5 per barrel. Note that for 1 contract (representing 1,000 barrels), the profit would be $5 × 1,000 = $5,000.
>
> *Price falls*: If the geopolitical tensions actually de-escalate, the price of crude oil falls to $65 per barrel. Then, the speculator sells their futures contract at $70 per barrel for a loss of $5. For 1 contract, loss = $5 × 1,000 = $5,000.

What are some key points of speculation? First, speculation carries significant risk. In this case, if the market moves against the speculator's prediction, they could face substantial losses. Futures contracts allow speculators to control a large amount of a commodity (e.g., 1,000 barrels of oil) with a relatively small margin deposit, which amplifies both potential profits and losses (leverage). Finally, speculators are usually concerned with short-term price movements, not long-term changes in supply or demand and so time-sensitivity is important in this market.

Obviously, someone can speculate in Gold, when he buys gold futures contracts believing that the price will rise due to an economic crisis or in agricultural commodities, where a trader might buy wheat futures contracts, speculating that adverse weather conditions will reduce the harvest and push prices higher. In sum, speculating in commodities involves making educated guesses about future price movements and taking positions in futures, options, or ETFs to profit from these changes. The risks are high, but so are the potential rewards.

An actual example of speculation in the commodities market is that by Amaranth Advisors (AA) LLC., a hedge fund (based in Greenwich, Connecticut) that suffered significant losses in 2006 due to speculative trading in natural gas futures. AA, founded by N. Maounis, was a multi-strategy hedge fund managing approximately $9.2 billion at its peak in August 2006. The fund engaged in various trading strategies, including significant positions in the natural gas market. The fund's head energy trader, Brian Hunter, anticipated that natural gas prices would rise due to expected supply constraints. To capitalize on this forecast, Amaranth amassed large positions in natural gas futures contracts, betting on a price increase. At one point, the fund's positions for January 2007 delivery were so substantial that they equaled the entire amount of natural gas used by US residential consumers in that month.

Contrary to AA's expectations, natural gas prices declined sharply in 2006, dropping from over $11 per million BTU to about $5. This adverse movement led to losses exceeding $6 billion, effectively wiping out nearly two-thirds of the fund's assets. By September 21, 2006, AA announced it had lost almost 65% of its assets due to these speculative bets. The collapse of AA prompted regulatory scrutiny. In 2007, the Commodity Futures Trading Commission (CFTC) charged the fund and B. Hunter (and fining them by $7.5 million) with attempting to manipulate natural gas futures prices.[5]

This incident underscored the risks associated with speculative trading in commodity markets and highlighted the need for effective risk management practices. This real-world example illustrates how speculative positions, especially when highly leveraged and concentrated, can lead to catastrophic financial outcomes if market movements contradict the trader's expectations.

Another means of speculating in this market is via a *contract for difference* (CFD). A CFD is a derivative contract where two parties agree to exchange the difference in the value of an underlying asset between the time the contract opens and the time it closes. In essence, this trading activity focuses on the price movement of the asset/commodity, without actually owning the asset. Such trades can be leveraged so as to magnify potential returns and can be sold short. For example, say you have bought a US Crude Oil CFD future believing the price of oil will rise. If you are correct, your profit would be calculated based on the difference from when you entered the position, to when you closed it. So, if you entered the CFD at $60 per barrel, and closed it when the market reached $65, the market would have moved $5 in your favor. However, if your prediction is incorrect, and the market moves against you instead, you make a loss.

Recall that futures traders are not required to pay the entire value of a contract. Instead, they are required to post an initial margin (specified by the exchange), ranging between 2 and 10% of the total value of the contract. Thereafter, the position is marked to market daily. Why? Because traders and exchange (clearinghouse) agents wish to know what the value of the contract is. For example, if the futures position loses value when the market moves against it (if you are buying and the market goes down), then the amount of money in the margin account will decline accordingly. So, if the amount of money in the margin account falls below the specified maintenance margin (set at a level around the initial margin), the futures trader will be required to post additional funds (margin) to bring the account up the initial margin level.[6] By contrast, if the futures position is profitable, the profits will be added to the margin account. Here is an example.

Suppose the initial and maintenance margins on a wheat contract are $500 per contract. A farmer who sells 10 contracts must deposit at least $5,000 with the clearing house to cover the margins. Each day the position is marked to market. If the market moves in the farmer's favor, for example, the futures price declines on a particular day, the farmer's margin account is credited with the accrued profit for that day. On the other hand, if the futures price rises, the margin account is debited with the accrued loss. So, on any day when the margin account falls below $5,000, the farmer is required to post variation margin to bring the account back up to at least $5,000.

3.4 Example of inflation hedging

A standard example of inflation hedging in the commodities market is investing in gold, which historically tended to maintain or increase in value during periods of rising inflation, serving as a store of value and a hedge against the erosion of purchasing power. In general, precious metals such as gold have been historical favorites for hedging against inflation due to their scarcity, physicality (tangibility), and negative correlation to money. Commodities (including oil) provide a direct hedge against negative commodity supply shocks, which lead to increase in interest rates and cause bond and stock returns to decline. Also, they provide a hedge against lower stock returns as rising prices cause GDP growth to slow. Due to their inflation hedging ability, precious metals (and industrial commodities) are valued portfolio components. Historically, gold and oil have been strong inflation hedges because their prices tend to rise when inflation increases. Figure 11.3 displays the changes in

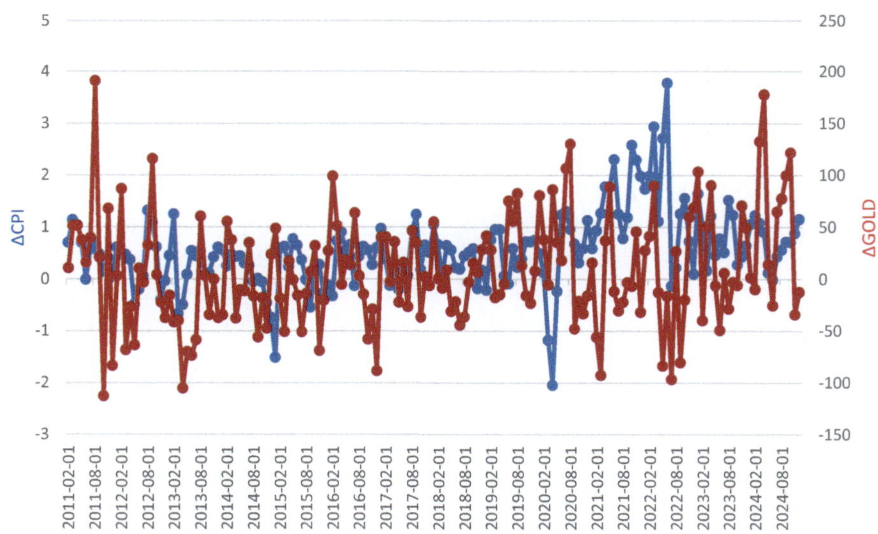

Figure 11.3 Changes in US CPI and gold prices, 2011:02–2024:08
Data sources: FRED and Statista

the US consumer price index (ΔCPI) and gold prices (ΔGOLD) from February 2011 to August 2024. We can easily observe that ups and downs in gold in synch with inflation. The correlation between the two series (in changes) is 8%. Hence, lately this linkage is weak and gold may not really entail a good inflation hedge.

Here's a simple example using two commodities (in a portfolio), gold and crude oil. An investor is concerned about rising inflation and wants to hedge against its impact using commodities. The investor has $1,000,000 in cash and expects inflation to rise over the next 12 months. He decides to invest in gold and crude oil futures to protect purchasing power. Assume that, currently, gold is trading at $3,100 per ounce and crude oil at $70 per barrel. The investor allocates $500,000 to gold and $500,000 to crude oil. At the end of 12 months, inflation has increased significantly, and commodity prices have reacted as follows:

> Gold rises to $3,400 per ounce (+9.6%), and crude oil rises to $90 per barrel (+28.5%). What are the rates of return from each investment?
> *Gold investment returns*: Initial investment: $500,000; Percentage increase: 9.6%; Final value: $500,000 * (1 + 0.096) = $548,000. The profit from gold investment is $48,000.
> *Crude oil investment returns*: Initial investment: $500,000; Percentage increase: 28.5%; Final value: $500,000 * (1 + 0.285) = $642,500, a profit of $142,500.

What is portfolio's rate of return? Total portfolio value after 12 months: $548,000 + $642,500 = $1,190,500. The total profit from commodities hedge: $190,500. The total percentage return of the portfolio is then 19.05% (= $190,500/$1,000,00). Hence, by investing in commodities, the investor gained 19.05% while inflation eroded the purchasing power of cash. This simple example demonstrates how gold and oil act as effective hedges against inflation in the commodities market.

3.5 Trends in some commodities markets

As of late March 2025, commodity prices have been plunging, and investment banks are slashing their forecasts for 2025. According to *Oxford Economics*, "Demand has been weaker than investors anticipated in 2024, especially in China.... Strong supply from commodities such as wheat, steel, and crude oil has also weighed heavily on prices and contributed to inventory build. The exception has been gold, with central banks driving its price higher and making it a bright spot for the whole sector."[7]

There are huge changing patterns in global trade. Global markets allow new expert trading firms to step in and conduct trades. China has been the engine for growth in commodity trade among the BRIC countries (Brazil, Russia, India and China) by drawing iron ore from Brazil and India, and oil and gas from Russia. Chinese demand has accelerated development in resource-rich, emerging economies in Africa and Latin America. Economic fundamentals matter a lot in the global commodities market by linking markets and routes. A case in point is the US shale revolution, which had a big impact on the pattern of global energy trade. It enabled the US to reduce its oil imports, increased its exports (of US refined products including Liquified Natural Gas, LNG) and prompted traditional suppliers of the US (example, Nigeria), to find alternative markets. Recall that one common characteristic of commodities is storage. Storage promotes market stability because inelasticity in the supply and demand for commodities increases the potential for volatility in these markets.

The global energy landscape is rapidly shifting towards renewable resources. In 2024, the US saw significant growth in renewable energy capacity, with wind power reaching 153.8 GW and solar power expanding by a record-breaking 38.4 GW to 128.2 GW.[8] In addition, there is a decline in coal usage. Market dynamics have led to a decrease in coal consumption, as natural gas and renewables become more cost-effective and efficient. Since 2005, coal's share in US electricity generation has declined from 42% to 15% by late 2023. The US has achieved record levels of oil and natural gas production, contributing to a surge in electricity demand and a boom in renewable energy growth.[9]

The metals market has experienced fluctuations, with carbon metal prices recently dipping, while stainless steel remains stable. High demand for red metals has led to longer lead times. Manufacturers are exercising caution regarding large investments amid high interest rates and political uncertainties in the US[10] Furthermore, the global metal market is on an upward trajectory, expected to grow from $4.39 trillion in 2024 to $4.65 trillion in 2025, at a compound annual growth rate (CAGR) of 5.9%. This growth is driven by construction, infrastructure development, and industrialization. These trends and figures underscore the dynamic nature of the energy and metals markets, shaped by a complex interplay of economic, technological, and geopolitical factors.

A 2024 article by UNCTAD (United Nations Conference on Trade and Development), on the recent developments, challenges and opportunities in commodity markets suggested the following trends on specific commodities markets[11]:

On commodity price trends

Fuel prices decreased in 2023 due to improved global supply and lower demand, but saw a surge in late 2023 due to OPEC+ supply cuts. Minerals prices of critical minerals like cobalt, lithium, and nickel decreased in 2023 due to oversupply and reduced demand. Food commodities prices generally decreased in 2023, except for tropical beverages like cocoa and coffee, which saw significant price increases due to weather conditions and geopolitical factors.

On geopolitical and trade tensions

The war in Ukraine and instability in the Middle East have impacted commodity prices, particularly precious metals like gold, which increased due to geopolitical uncertainty.

On policy issues

EU regulation on deforestation-free products: Introduced mandatory due diligence for commodities like palm oil, coffee, cocoa, and soy, requiring traceability to ensure they are produced on land not subject to deforestation. More agreements to ensure stable supply chains for minerals essential for the energy transition, such as cobalt, copper, lithium, and nickel were put in place.

On renewable energy growth

R enewable energy consumption and capacity have surged, with significant growth in solar photovoltaic and wind power additions, particularly in China.

On economic implications

Declining prices of critical minerals have positive impacts for consumers, making clean energy technologies more affordable, but may discourage investment in new mining projects and affect economies dependent on mineral exports.

In sum these points highlight the complex interplay between market dynamics, geopolitical events, and policy measures in shaping commodity markets and their implications for global trade and development. In addition, prolonged periods of political instability can lead to permanent changes in consumer and producer behavior, potentially intensifying the impact on commodity markets.

Test your understanding 2

1. What is the main economic function of the commodities futures market? How do the two transaction parties – producers and consumers – benefit?
2. What is the purpose of "marking-to-market" of a futures position every day?
3. What is the difference between hedging and speculation in the commodities market?

4 The roles of management and marketing in the derivatives and commodities markets

We conclude this chapter with a set of interesting questions for readers across the management and marketing disciplines. What are the relationships between management and the derivatives and commodities markets? What is the role of marketing in these two financial markets? You may be inclined to say that there is little or no connection, but the narrative which follows will prove otherwise.

4.1 The role of management in the commodities and derivatives markets

We begin with management's role in the derivatives market. Recall that one function of a corporation's manager is decision-making. In general, management plays a crucial role in the derivatives market by ensuring risk control, strategic decision-making, regulatory compliance, market development, and financial innovation. The involvement of managers spans across financial institutions, investment firms, exchanges, and regulatory bodies. More specifically, one of the most critical roles of management in the derivatives market is risk assessment and control. Managers use derivatives to hedge against market uncertainties, such as interest rate changes, currency fluctuations, and commodity price volatility. CFOs and treasury managers use interest rate swaps to protect against rising borrowing costs. We mentioned earlier that, managers such as fund and pension managers use derivatives to hedge stock market downturns or interest rate derivatives to manage long-term liabilities. Also, risk managers continuously analyze Value-at-Risk (VaR), stress testing, and scenario analysis for exposure control.[12]

Senior management in financial institutions and investment firms incorporate derivatives into strategic planning, decide on capital allocation (using derivatives to enhance returns while balancing risk), portfolio managers integrate derivatives for tactical asset allocation, adjusting exposures based on macroeconomic conditions and, finally, investment banks create new derivative products, such as ESG-linked derivatives, volatility ETFs, or synthetic options to set proper asset allocation and trading strategies.

In conclusion, managers use derivatives to hedge financial and market risks, investment firms and financial institutions utilize derivatives for strategic risk management, for market development (by promoting liquidity, efficiency, and innovation in the derivatives market) in an effort to balance profitability, stability, and regulatory compliance while driving financial innovation for their companies.

Regarding the commodities market(s), management also plays a crucial role via influencing pricing, risk management, supply chains, investment strategies, and market stability. The relationship between management functions and commodities markets can be examined from different perspectives, including corporate, investment, risk, and regulatory management. For example, companies that produce, consume, or rely on commodities must effectively manage their procurement, production, and financial strategies to navigate price fluctuations. Companies in sectors like energy, agriculture, and mining need to secure raw materials at optimal prices to control costs. As an example, consider the airline industry: an airline needs to hedge against rising oil prices by securing long-term fuel contracts. Furthermore, managing production levels in response to commodity price changes helps businesses optimize profitability. For example, oil companies adjust drilling activity based on crude oil prices to maximize margins. Finally, many corporations hedge commodity price risks using futures, options, or swaps to ensure stable costs. For instance, a steel manufacturer hedging against iron ore price swings to protect production costs.

Institutional and individual investors use commodities as part of a diversified portfolio to hedge against inflation, currency risks, and geopolitical instability. Commodities like gold, oil, and agricultural products serve as alternative investments for diversification. Asset managers create commodity-focused funds (e.g., SPDR Gold Shares) to give investors exposure to commodities without direct trading. Moreover, risk management in commodities entails hedging price risk (a coffee producer, for example, hedging against declining coffee bean prices by selling futures contracts). Commodity prices are highly sensitive to geopolitical tensions (e.g., Russia–Ukraine war impacting oil prices). Since commodities are priced in US dollars, fluctuations in exchange rates impact their value. For example, emerging market companies adjust hedging strategies to counter currency depreciation risks.

Finally, governments and regulatory agencies influence commodities through trade policies, taxation, and environmental regulations. Governments sometimes impose export bans or subsidies to protect domestic markets. Regulatory bodies enforce sustainability practices in commodity extraction and trading. For example, carbon pricing affecting coal and oil production costs. Agencies like the CFTC (Commodity Futures Trading Commission) regulate derivatives trading to prevent market manipulation (for instance, imposing stricter margin requirements for speculative commodity trading).

4.2 The role of marketing in the commodities and derivatives markets

In general, marketing plays a critical role in the derivatives market by helping financial institutions, exchanges, and investment firms promote their products, attract investors, and educate market participants. It also enhances liquidity, market transparency, and investor confidence in derivative instruments such as futures, options, swaps, and structured products.

Given that derivatives can be complex, marketing plays a crucial role in explaining their purpose, benefits, and risks. For example, Exchanges and financial firms offer seminars, webinars, and online courses on derivatives trading. The CME Group and Nasdaq regularly publish educational content on futures, options, and hedging strategies. Online brokerages market user-friendly derivative platforms (e.g., Robinhood, Interactive Brokers, E*TRADE). Banks and hedge funds use white papers, research reports, and expert analyses to attract institutional clients.

Marketing also helps differentiate derivative instruments and trading platforms in a competitive financial environment. The Chicago Mercantile Exchange (CME) and Intercontinental Exchange (ICE) promote themselves as trusted global platforms for derivatives trading. Nowadays, mamy exchanges advertise derivative product innovation such as for ESG-linked derivatives (e.g., carbon futures, green bonds) or promote unique trading platforms such as algorithmic trading, or AI-driven risk management tools. High-frequency trading firms and market makers advertise their role in ensuring tight spreads and deep liquidity. Banks and asset managers package derivatives with structured investment products to attract institutional clients. Influencers and financial educators promote options and futures trading on YouTube, Twitter, and Reddit. Online brokers promote zero-commission derivatives trading through mobile apps (e.g., Robinhood Options Trading).

In view of the risks of derivatives, marketing must also ensure compliance with financial regulations. Derivatives marketing campaigns must highlight risk factors and disclaimers. Firms must comply with SEC, CFTC, and ESMA rules regarding fair advertising of derivative products. Finally, green derivatives (e.g., carbon credit futures) are marketed for sustainable investing.

In sum, marketing simplifies derivatives for retail and institutional investors. Marketing enhances the accessibility, trust, and efficiency of the derivatives market, driving participation from hedgers, speculators, and institutional investors.

Finally, what is the linkage between marketing and the commodities market? Marketing plays a vital role in the commodities market, even though commodities are often seen as standardized, undifferentiated goods. Marketing helps in branding, price differentiation, demand forecasting, supply chain optimization, and hedging strategies. It enables producers, traders, and financial institutions to strategically position commodities in global markets.

First, for branding and differentiation: commodities are typically homogeneous (e.g., crude oil, wheat, gold), making branding more challenging. However, marketing strategies can create perceived differentiation and value. For branded commodities: for example, Starbucks markets its coffee as "premium" by focusing on single-origin beans and sustainability. Some companies promote their low-carbon aluminum or "green steel" to appeal to environmentally conscious buyers. Organic and Fair-Trade certifications add value to products like coffee, cocoa, and tea. "Kobe Beef," "Champagne," and "Jamaican Blue Mountain Coffee" use geographical identity to increase market appeal. Second, for price differentiation and marketing strategies: even in a market where prices are influenced by supply and demand, companies use marketing tactics to achieve better pricing power. Companies sell "carbon-neutral" oil, recycled metals, or responsibly sourced diamonds at a premium. Marketing promotes commodity ETFs, futures, and structured products to institutional and retail investors. Example: SPDR Gold Shares (GLD), a gold-backed ETF, is marketed as a safe-haven investment.

Third, for forecasting demand and related market research. Marketing departments help commodity firms understand demand patterns by analyzing consumer trends, economic indicators, and geopolitical events. Also, analyses of consumer behavior/demand such as veganism or increased demand for plant-based commodities like soybeans and almonds or shifts to electric vehicles which, in turn, lead to higher demand for copper, lithium, and nickel. Marketing insights help optimize distribution channels for global commodity exports. For example, shipping route adjustments based on real-time market data for crude oil and LNG transport. Finally, for trend forecasting where agriculture marketing plans for seasonal price fluctuations in crops like wheat and corn. Hence, energy marketers adjust pricing strategies based on winter demand for natural gas.

Fourth, for hedging and risk management strategies. Marketing teams within a corporation work with risk managers and traders to protect against price volatility through hedging strategies. Fifth, for the provision of digital and content marketing. Technology has transformed commodity marketing through digital platforms, AI-driven pricing models, and direct-to-consumer strategies. Companies use blockchain tracking to market supply chain transparency (e.g., ethical gold sourcing). Other companies utilize social media analytics to track consumer sentiment on food prices. Finally, platforms like ICE (Intercontinental Exchange) and CME Group use digital marketing to attract commodity investors and traders.

In conclusion, marketing is a crucial driver of growth and stability in the commodities market, influencing everything from branding and pricing to risk management and digital engagement.

Summary

- The derivatives market refers to the financial market where derivative contracts are bought and sold.
- The derivatives markets serve the fundamental function in the growth of economies and the efficient operation of companies.
- The derivatives market is influenced by several key determinants, which affect the demand and supply of derivatives.
- Some determinants include a mix of economic factors, market conditions, regulations, and investor behavior.
- Supply in the derivatives markets depends on the willingness of market makers, institutional traders, and speculators to take the opposite side of a trade.
- The risk that the counterparty (the other party to a contract) may default on their obligations affects the value and structure of derivatives.

- Currency derivatives like forwards and options are impacted by changes in exchange rates and interest rate differentials between countries.
- Derivatives are subject to margin requirements.
- The call-put parity states that the price of a call option implies a specific fair price for the corresponding put option with the same underlying asset, strike price and expiration date.
- Trading in derivatives requires understanding market mechanisms, risk management, and execution strategies.
- The intrinsic value is the difference between the actual value or current market price of the stock and the strike price.
- The extrinsic value is made up of time until expiration, implied volatility, dividends and the cost of carry.
- Time value is any premium in excess of intrinsic value before expiration.
- The global commodities market is a massive financial marketplace where raw materials and primary goods are bought, sold, and traded.
- It is divided into two major categories: Hard Commodities and Soft Commodities.
- The modern commodities market relies on derivative securities, such as futures and forward contracts.
- Buyers and sellers can transact with one another easily and in large volumes without needing to exchange the physical commodities themselves.
- The spot market is one in which buying and selling physical commodities for immediate delivery takes place.
- The futures and options market involves trading contracts that allow investors to speculate on future price movements.
- The key factors that influence commodity prices are supply and demand, geopolitical events, currency strength and inflation and interest rates.
- The available opportunities in the commodities market are hedging, speculation and inflation hedging.
- Hedging helps producers, consumers, and traders reduce their exposure to price fluctuations.
- Speculation involves buying or selling commodities with the expectation that prices will move in a favorable direction, allowing the trader to profit from price changes.
- An example of inflation hedging in the commodities market is investing in gold, which historically tended to maintain or increase in value during periods of rising inflation, serve as a store of value and a hedge against the erosion of purchasing power.
- The global energy landscape is rapidly shifting towards renewable resources.
- The metals market has experienced fluctuations, with carbon metal prices recently dipping.
- Managers use derivatives to hedge financial and market risks, investment firms and financial institutions utilize derivatives for strategic risk management, for market development in an effort to balance profitability, stability, and regulatory compliance while driving financial innovation for their companies.
- Marketing plays a critical role in the derivatives market by helping financial institutions, exchanges, and investment firms promote their products, attract investors, and educate market participants.

Questions and problems

1. Please answer the four questions below:
   a. How can investors use derivatives to hedge risk?
   b. How do investors profit from arbitrage in the derivatives market?
   c. What is the difference between speculation and hedging in derivatives?
   d. What is the role of derivatives in portfolio diversification?
2. An investor buys a call option on XYZ stock with a strike price of $100 for a premium of $5 per share. The option expires in one month. At expiration, XYZ stock is trading at $110.
   a. How much profit or loss does the investor make from this trade? What would be the total profit if the contract size was 100 shares per option?
   b. What would happen if the stock price had closed at $95?
3. An investor is analyzing stock ABC, which is currently trading at $50. He observes the following derivative prices:
   European Call Option with a strike price of $50: $7
   European Put Option with a strike price of $50: $4
   The risk-free interest rate is 5% per year, and the option expires in 6 months (0.5 years). The investor wants to check if the put-call parity holds and whether there is an arbitrage opportunity.
   a. Does put-call parity hold?
   b. If not, how can the investor exploit arbitrage?
4. An investor is analyzing stock ABC, which is currently trading at $40. The investor decides to buy a call option with the following details:
   Strike price = $45
   Option premium = $3 per share
   Contract size = 100 shares (standard option contract)
   Expiration date = 1 month from today
   At expiration, the stock price could be $40, $45, $48, or $50.
   What would be the investor's profit or loss at each stock price scenario? What kind of strategy would that be for the investor?
5. Define intrinsic and extrinsic values for an option. What are the key differences between the two?
6. A farmer is about to harvest 10,000 bushels of wheat but he is concerned that the price of wheat might drop significantly between now and harvest, impacting his profits. He wants to sell his wheat at a good price, but not to speculate on the market. How can he protect himself from a potential price decline? Assume that the current price of a wheat futures contract (for delivery at harvest time) is $6.00 per bushel. Explain what would happen if the price of wheat drops to $5 or rises to $7.
7. Define speculation in the commodities market and explain how a speculator (in oil, for example) profit if he expects the price of oil to go up or down.
8. How could political unrest and instability affect the commodities markets?
9. In early 2025, the US government-imposed tariffs on several nations (China, Mexico and Canada) it trades with. How could such trade tensions affect the global commodities market?
10. What could be the impact of trade wars on gold as commodity?

Notes

1. https://www.lseg.com/content/dam/data-analytics/en_us/documents/charts/lseg-size-of-global-market-2024-in-charts.pdf
2. Read the seminal paper: Stoll, Hans R. (1969). The Relationship Between Put and Call Option Prices. *Journal of Finance* 24(5), 445–457.
3. For a put option, the formula is $max(0, K - S_T)$, as you might have imagined.
4. We discuss a carry trade in Chapter 12.
5. https://www.cftc.gov/PressRoom/PressReleases/5692–09?utm_source=chatgpt.com
6. This resembles the process of *purchases on margin*, we discussed in Chapter 8.
7. https://www.oxfordeconomics.com/resource/five-key-commodity-trends-to-watch-for-in-2025/
8. https://www.deloitte.com/us/en/insights/industry/renewable-energy/renewable-energy-industry-outlook/2025.html
9. https://www.eia.gov/energyexplained/us-energy-facts/imports-and-exports.php
10. https://www.meadmetals.com/
11. https://unctad.org/system/files/official-document/c1mem2d62_en.pdf
12. *Value at Risk* (VaR) is a statistical measure that estimates the potential loss in value of an investment over a specific time period (usually a day), given a certain probability.

Chapter 12

The foreign exchange market

Introduction

The *foreign exchange (forex or FX) market* is the global marketplace where currencies are traded. It is the largest and most liquid financial market in the world, with daily trading volume exceeding \$7.5 trillion, according to the Bank of International Settlements (2024, BIS). In the forex market, participants buy, sell, and exchange currencies at current or determined prices. The value of a currency in relation to another is called the *exchange rate*. For example, if you are buying US dollars with Euros, the exchange rate will determine how many Euros you need to purchase one dollar. As of April 18, 2025, the USD–Euro exchange rate was 0.88 Euros or that 1 Euro would buy \$1.14 (= 1/0.88). A *direct quotation* expresses the value of a foreign currency in dollars (or the number of dollars per currency, \$1.14), whereas quotations that express the number of units of a foreign currency per dollar are referred to as *indirect quotations* (0.88). You must have noticed that the indirect quotation is the reciprocal of the corresponding direct quotation.

All players in any economy (households or individuals, businesses and the government) use the forex market. For example, commercial banks serve this market by holding inventories of each currency so that they can accommodate requests by the other agents. Companies including multinational corporations tap the forex market when they conduct business overseas and in different currencies. Individuals also rely on the foreign exchange market when they travel to foreign countries or make foreign purchases. Finally, governments exploit the forex market when they borrow funds internationally, and central banks which may buy or sell their own currency to influence its value and stabilize the economy.

This market is not physically located in a building or country so that traders can exchange currencies. Instead, agents exchange one currency for another through a commercial bank (known as foreign exchange dealers or intermediaries) in the over-the-counter (OTC) market via electronic telecommunications networks (ECNs). So, if anyone wants to buy Euros right now, this transaction calls for immediate execution and takes place in the *spot market*. It follows that the current exchange rate (in the spot market) is called the *spot rate*.

What if you wish to see the exchange rate between two other currencies, and not against the US dollar? For example, if a Greek company does business with Canada, the company would like to know the Canadian dollar relative to the Euro.

DOI: 10.4324/9781003677161-16

This type of exchange rate is known as the *cross* (exchange) *rate*. As an example, consider the spot exchange rates between the US dollar ($) and the Euro (€) and the US dollar vs. the Canadian dollar (C$), $1.14 and $0.72, respectively. What would be the value of the € in C$? Simply, take the ratio of (€/$) to (C$/$) or $1.14/$0.72 = C$1.58. Thus, one Euro is worth C$1.58.

Furthermore, what if you expect to receive some payments in a foreign currency at a future point time and wish to eliminate the risk of a(n) (unfavorable) change in the exchange rate. In this case, you need to lock in the spot exchange rate at which you can obtain that currency in the future via a forward contract. A *forward contract* is an agreement between two parties (you and a foreign exchange dealer, for instance) that specifies the currencies to be exchanged, the exchange rate (known as the *forward rate*), and the transaction's date.[1] It is obvious that such an arrangement serves the need to hedge future payments and not worry about fluctuations in the spot rate until the time of their future payments.

Other major foreign exchange markets are the futures, swap and option markets. Briefly, the futures market, which is similar to the forward market, involves trading of standardized contracts which are traded on an exchange. The swap market entails a derivative contract which permits two parties to exchange cash flows or liabilities from different financial instruments. Finally, the option market allows investors to buy and sell financial instruments underlying securities at a specific price over a specific period.

Commercial banks charge fees for conducting forex transactions. In essence, they buy currencies from agents at a slightly lower price than the price at which they sell the currencies. Therefore, at any given point in time, a bank's buy quote for a foreign currency (*bid*) will be less than its sell quote (*ask*). The *bid–ask spread* represents the differential between the two quotes and serves to cover the costs of the transaction (and is a source of profit for the bank). Obviously, competition and volume are two important factors that affect how narrow or wide the bid-ask spread is. The more intense the competition among banks is, or heavier the volumes of currencies are, the narrower the spread would be.

In what follows next, we will explore the determinants of the foreign exchange market, list the factors that influence exchange rates, derive and discuss some important international economic parities, provide some simple examples of forex trading and conclude with the presentation and application of some exchange rate forecasting techniques.

1 Characteristics of the foreign exchange market

The forex market is a 24-hour market across different time zones (Asia, Europe, and North America). The forex market is bigger than the stock market with global stock market trades approximating $200 billion daily, and highly liquid, meaning large transactions can occur with minimal price impact. The most traded currencies are the US Dollar (USD), Euro (EUR), the Japanese Yen (JPY), British Pound (GBP) and the Chinese Yuan (CNY). According to 2025 *Statista*, the USD was involved in over 88% of all forex transactions, the EUR entailed 30% of transactions, JPY around 17% of global forex turnover, GBP of approximately 13% of forex trades and CNY about 7% (closely followed by the Australian and Canadian dollars). Major forex trading hubs are found in New York, London, Tokyo, and Sydney.

Some additional key features of the forex market are. First, it is a decentralized market which, as mentioned earlier, operates in the OTC market, meaning that transactions occur directly between parties (such as through banks, brokers, or financial institutions) rather than through a central exchange. Second, the participants include central banks and commercial banks, governments, corporations, investors, retail traders as well as hedge funds which speculate on currency price movements for profit. Third, this market is famous for its high liquidity, meaning there are a large number of buyers and sellers readily available to trade currencies. This permits traders to easily enter and exit positions without significantly affecting the market price. In addition, high liquidity deters market manipulation by traders (something that regularly occurs in stock or futures markets).

Fourth, the forex market is known for its volatility, meaning exchange rates can fluctuate significantly and rapidly. This volatility presents both opportunities for profit and risks for those who do not manage their positions effectively. Fifth, forex trading allows traders to use leverage, which means they can control large positions with relatively small amounts of capital. Leverage can amplify both profits and losses, so it's crucial for traders to understand and manage leverage effectively. Sixth, relative to other markets, forex trading typically has low transaction costs, often reflected in the difference between the buying and selling prices of a currency pair, known as the spread. Seventh, while decentralized, the forex market generally maintains a high level of transparency, with information about market conditions readily available to everyone. Finally, one more feature of the forex market is that currencies are traded in pairs, meaning that the value of one currency is expressed relative to another, as mentioned earlier. Major currency pairs are the EUR/USD, GBP/USD and USD/JPY.

Despite being a global decentralized market, the forex market is regulated by governments and other regulatory organizations around the world. These regulatory bodies ensure that the forex market operates with integrity. For example, the major forex regulators are the National Futures Association (NFA) and the Commodity Futures Trading Commission (CFTC), in the US, the Financial Conduct Authority (FCA) in the United Kingdom, and the European Securities and Markets Authority (ESMA) is the financial markets regulator and supervisor for the European Union. Then, there are some secondary global regulators such as Japan's Financial Services Agency (FSA), Canada's Investment Industry Regulatory Organization (IIROC), Singapore's Monetary Authority of Singapore (MAS) and Hong Kong's Securities and Futures Commission (SFC).

As mentioned, the global foreign exchange market is dynamic, highly liquid and transparent. So, what are some functions of the forex market? First, it enables participants to exchange their currencies in the global market and trade seamlessly and efficiently. This primary function of the foreign exchange market is also known as the *transfer function*. In other words, the market facilitates the transfer of purchasing power in terms of foreign exchange between the parties involved in the transaction. Therefore, it involves sending money or foreign currencies from one party to another to settle their accounts. The function is performed through credit instruments such as bank drafts, telephonic transfers and bills of exchange.[2]

Second, the forex market has an impact across international trade, investments and travel, hence encouraging companies to invest in foreign markets. Foreign trade (just as domestic trade) depends on credit. The *credit function* of the forex market implies the provision of credit in terms of foreign exchange for the export and import of goods and services. For this, bills of exchange are generally used for making payments internationally. The main purpose of credit is to help the importer in taking possession of goods, sell them next and obtain the money to pay the bills.

Third, it offers protection to traders and investors from fluctuating currency values. This is called the hedging function of the forex market. Essentially, it implies some protection against risks related to fluctuations in the foreign exchange rate. Under this system, buyers and sellers agree to sell and buy goods on a future date at some commonly agreed rate of exchange. The basic purpose behind this function is to avoid losses that might be caused because of variations in the exchange rate in the future.

Finally, it connects the worldwide economies to promote financial growth to achieve global economic stability. International capital flows are the lifeblood of global economic activity. The market's liquidity empowers businesses to access the necessary foreign currency to import or export goods and services, governments to borrow funds denominated in foreign currencies from international investors, and investors to benefit from diversification of their portfolios by investing in foreign currency-denominated assets.

What are some disadvantages of the foreign exchange market? First, as mentioned on p. 327, the high volatility of the foreign exchange market can be felt by traders, which means that prices fluctuate quite frequently and are unpredictable. Thus, anyone dealing in this market may face higher risks. Second, despite global regulation, the global presence of this market increases its chances of facing associated frauds and scams. Therefore, an investor must be cautious when selecting a trading platform as well as (online) brokers. Third, and also related to its regulation, the forex market in some big countries is not regulated and so some currency pairs involving, for example, the Indian Rupee may encounter additional risks (including fraudulent activities). Fourth, the forex market is not for the novice investor because of its complexity. For starters, you need to be thorough with your knowledge and expertise. If you are new to trading, you may initially need guidance, before you can grasp the key concepts. Finally, excessively fluctuating exchange rates could result in significant losses especially during the times of geopolitical upheaval and central bank announcements. Consequently, before trading you should consider all the risk factors. The next section lists and explains the various economic and political risks the forex market faces.

How do we measure an exchange rate's movement (change)? In general, as economic conditions change, exchange rates can change significantly. Specifically, a decline in a currency's value is often referred to as depreciation (devaluation), whereas an increase in a currency value is referred to as appreciation (or revaluation). For example, when the Euro depreciates against the US dollar, this means that the US dollar is strengthening relative to the Euro. So, comparing a foreign currency's spot rate at two specific points in time would enable us to compute the change or the percentage change in the value of the foreign currency, as follows:

$$\%\Delta \textit{ in foreign currency value} = (S_t - S_{t-1})/S_{t-1} \qquad (1)$$

where S_t is the current spot rate and S_{t-1} is the previous period's spot rate. By dividing by the previous period's value, we obtain the percentage change ($\%\Delta$).

It follows that when you compute the change in one USD vis-à-vis on currency and another USD vis-à-vis another currency, the resulting changes are not the same. For example, the USDJPY spot exchange rates for April 17 and 18, 2025, were 141.928 and 142.15, respectively, whereas the USDGBP spot exchange rates (for the same days) were 0.7556 and 0.7521, respectively. Hence, the percentage change in the USDJPY spot rate was –0.00156 and that for the USDGBP rate it was 0.00465. Consequently, we say that in the first case the JPY depreciated (or that the USD appreciated) and in the second case that the USD appreciated (or the British Pound depreciated). Depreciation of a currency, in essence, implies paying more to exchange it with another currency. Exchange rates change almost every second given the global, 24/7/365, operation of the forex market. Therefore, one cannot truly speak of an "equilibrium" exchange rate because it is simply elusive (fluid). In the next section, we explore the factors (reasons) why exchange rates fluctuate (or deviate from some "equilibrium" point or value).

Is the forex market efficient? There is an ongoing debate on this question. On one hand, the market's high liquidity (meaning trades are easily executed without significant price fluctuations), the large number of participants, and the constant flow of information (which immediately leads to price adjustments that reflect new information) enable it to be highly efficient. On the other hand, the market was rocked during various (specific) time periods such as the COVID-19 global health pandemic[3], and that it may be more efficient in the long term than in the short term, given that short-term trading strategies and news events can lead to temporary deviations from efficiency[4]. See also subsection 2.4.

2 Factors that affect the exchange rate

In general, the factors that affect an exchange rate rest with the reasons which affect the demand for, and supply of, currencies (see subsection 3.6). These factors shift the two schedules (or sides of the market) either to the right – which is an increase – or to the left – which is a decrease. For example, the more valued a currency is (as perceived by participants), the greater the demand for it will be, shifting the curve to the right. Hence, if no other factors change, the currency's value (against another currency) will increase (or appreciate). A number of other factors affect the two schedules, which we list and briefly explain next. For the analyses, assume two countries, UK and Canada, and that, initially, their interest rates, inflation rates and income levels are equal. The home country is the UK.

2.1 Interest rates

Interest rate changes between two countries affect their currencies' exchange rate. The channel of influence is via the demand for and supply of international financial investments (foreign securities) in each country. For example, if the UK's interest rates rise relative to the Canadian rates, *ceteris paribus*, then investors in the UK will reduce their demand for Canadian dollars because Canadian investments are not attractive right now. At the same time, Canadian investors will increase their demand for British pounds in order to invest in the UK, which means that there will be an increase in the supply of Canadian dollars to be exchanged for

British pounds. So, in a demand–supply schedule where the vertical axis denotes the value of the British pound (relative to the Canadian dollar) and the horizontal axis shows the quantity of pounds demanded and supplied, a decrease in demand for Canadian dollars and an increase in supply of Canadian dollars will decrease the exchange rate making the pound more valuable (hence, it would appreciate) and the dollar less valuable (hence, it would depreciate).

2.2 Inflation rates

When a country's inflation rate changes against another country's inflation rate (assumed to remain the same), the exchange rate changes because of the inflation rates' impact on international trade (exports and imports). Assume a sudden increase in inflation in the UK, *ceteris paribus*. This should cause some UK consumers to switch to Canadian products instead of their domestic products. At any given exchange rate, this would reflect an increase in the UK's demand for Canadian dollars. By the same token, the spike in UK inflation should reduce Canadian's desire for British goods and therefore reduce the supply of dollars at any given exchange rate. The combined effects of the increased UK demand for dollars and the reduced supply of dollars for sale place upward pressure on the value of the Canadian dollar. Hence, the Canadian dollar appreciates and the British pound depreciates.

2.3 Income levels

Using the same analogy as above, a rise in the UK's income level, *ceteris paribus*, would cause the demand schedule for dollars to shift outward, reflecting the increase in UK income and therefore increased demand for Canadian goods, and the supply schedule of dollars for sale to stay the same. Therefore, the equilibrium exchange rate of the Canadian dollar is expected to rise (that is, to appreciate).

2.4 Expectations

Recall that the foreign exchange market is continuous and has many salient (attractive) characteristics one of which is efficiency. This means that news of a potential surge in UK inflation, for example, may cause currency traders to sell pounds, anticipating a future decline in the pound's value. This response places immediate downward pressure on the pound. Other participants (individuals and institutional investors), also can place pressure on the equilibrium value of any exchange rate. Needless to say that institutional investors (banks, speculators, day traders) can exert greater influence on exchange rates compared to individual investors' actions.

2.5 Government and central bank actions

Finally, government actions can add to fluctuations in an exchange rate. For example, governments can impose foreign exchange and trade barriers, and central banks can intervene (by buying and selling currencies) in the foreign exchange markets, in addition to the above factors. More specifically, increased government spending can lead to higher demand for goods and services (in our discussion, imports), potentially increasing demand for foreign currencies and leading to home currency depreciation. Also, changes in taxation can affect income, saving, and investment, which can indirectly influence exchange rates. Finally, governments can impose restrictions on the flow of capital into and out of the country by limiting the amount of foreign currency that can be exchanged or transferred. Central banks can intervene by buying or selling their currency in the foreign exchange market to influence its value. For example, buying their own currency can increase its value, while selling can lower it.

According to a 2015 Bank of International Settlements (BIS) paper, foreign exchange intervention has been actively used as a policy tool in many economies in Asia and other emerging economies.[5] Two frequent intervention rules were "leaning against exchange rate misalignment" and "leaning against the wind". Leaning against the wind is a type of intervention that entails a systematic intervention against the direction that the exchange rate is moving, whereas leaning against the exchange rate misalignment entails central banks' stepping into the foreign exchange market if they see that the current exchange rate appears to be either overvalued or undervalued. These types of intervention were used by agents such as fundamentalists, speculators and the central bank. The authors did not find any strategy that is superior to (or dominates) another.

In sum, the above factors can affect exchange rates but not in isolation. This means that many factors are likely at play at any point in time making the prediction of the exchange rate's movement, up or down, not always clear cut. For example, if there is a sudden increase in the UK inflation and interest rates (see section 4 to understand why these two typically go together), relative to the Canadian inflation or interest rates, we have two possible effects. On one hand, the increase in UK inflation will place upward pressure on the Canadian dollar's value because of its impact on international trade, but on the other hand, the increase in UK interest rates will place a downward pressure on the dollar's value because of its impact on capital flows! This means that the relative impacts (or sensitivities of the exchange rate to each of these factors) depends on the relative importance of (the volumes of) trade vs. capital flows. For instance, if international (or bi-lateral) trade (export and impot) volumes are higher (in values) than bi-lateral capital flow volumes, then the Canadian dollar might appreciate – because the relative inflation rates will likely be more influential – rather than depreciate. Lately, however, international capital flows are greater than international trade flows and so one needs to carefully examine the likely impact of these factors on exchange rates.

2.6 The balance of payments

Records of a country's demand for and supply of currency are known as the *balance of payments* accounts. Essentially, these accounts are primarily to report the country's international performance in trading with other nations, either in physical forms – exports and imports – or financial form – capital in- and out-flows. The principle of balance-of-payments accounting reflects the need to record the flow of payments between the residents of a country and the rest of the world during a given time period. The balance-of-payments (BoP) account records all transactions that affect the supply of or demand for a currency in the forex markets.

In general, when an international transaction triggers demand for a currency (say, US dollars), it is recorded as a credit in the country's (here the US) BoP. By contrast, any transaction that gives rise to a supply of a currency is recorded as a debit in BoP account(s). For example, in order for foreign buyers to pay for US goods and services, which are invoiced in dollars, the foreign buyers must purchase dollars, hence a demand for dollars in the forex market.

Some factors that affect exports are the ones we mentioned earlier (inflation rates, interest rates and more) plus the worldwide prices of goods and services that the country exports. In this case, we are referring to the *terms of trade* (ToT, the ratio of exports to imports prices), which measures how many imports a country can obtain with a given amount of exports. Therefore, a favorable ToT means a country can purchase more imports with the same amount of exports. Along with physical exports, there are exports of services such as spending by foreign tourists in the US, for example, which also give rise to a demand for US dollars. The other side of the international transactions is the imports of goods and services (including income payments). By now you should be able to understand why the quantity of US imports of goods increases when the US dollar is worth more in the foreign exchange markets (because a more valuable dollar makes imports cheaper).

BoP contains a number of accounts, two of which are the current and capital accounts. The *current account* represents a summary of the flow of funds between one country and all other countries due to purchases of goods or services, or income on financial assets. The *capital account* represents a summary of the flow of funds resulting from the sale of assets between one country and all other countries over a specified period of time.

3 Some international parities

We explained in the previous section that a number of economic and financial magnitudes affect the exchange rate. Certain magnitudes, however, are more important than others because they additionally combine to form important financial and/or economic relationships, parities or conditions. We will identify a number of them in this section and provide a brief discussion for each.

3.1 The interest-rate parity

This parity (to be defined shortly) combines exchange rates and interest rates "forcing" them into an equilibrium or parity. To understand the parity, we need to first understand the notion of arbitrage in the foreign exchange market. Recall that arbitrage refers to the realization of a riskless profit. Specifically, a trader can exploit a discrepancy in quoted prices (in our context, to the foreign exchange market) and earn a sure profit (without committing funds). The empirical literature has identified three main types of such arbitrage: locations, triangular and covered interest arbitrage.

Very briefly put, *locational arbitrage* is the process of buying a currency at one location cheap and, simultaneously selling it at another location at a higher price. For example, if the bid prices of an Indian rupee are \$0.401 and \$0.399 at Bank A and B, respectively, while the ask prices are \$0.403 and \$0.400 in the same banks, would locational arbitrage be possible? Yes, you could buy Indian rupees at Bank B for $0.400 and sell them to Bank A for $0.401. So, if you had $1 million you could buy them at Bank B and sell them at Bank A for a profit of $1,000 (= $1,000,000*0.401 – $1,000,000*0.400).

Triangular arbitrage involves using cross-(exchange) rates and can be executed by transacting in one currency (in the spot market) to capitalize on a rate (value) differential (discrepancy) in the cross-rates between the two currencies. A simple example can clarify this process. Assume the following information: the (quoted) price of Canadian dollar (CAD) in US dollars (USD) is $0.96; the price of Malaysian ringgit (MR) in US dollars is $0.24; and the price of CAD in Malaysian ringgits is MR4.15. Assume that you have $1,000,000 to invest in this transaction. Given this information, how can you perform triangular arbitrage?

First, realize that the correct (appropriate) cross exchange rate should be 1 Canadian dollar = 4 Malaysian ringgit (= $0.96/$0.24). Thus, the actual value of CAD in terms of MR is more than what it should be, which implies potential arbitrage gains. You could obtain CAD with USD, sell them for MR and then exchange them for USD. With $1,000,000, this strategy would generate $1,037,500, representing a profit of $37,500. The algebraic execution is below:

> [USD$1,000,000/$.96 = CAD$1,041,666.667 * 4.15 = MR4,322,916.67 * $.24 = $1,037,500]

Interesting question: What should happen to eliminate any further triangular arbitrage? The value (price) of the CAD with respect to USD would rise, the value of CAD with respect to MR would decline, and the value of MR with respect to USD would fall. More specifically, the first implication is due to the banks' raising their ask (sell) prices due to excess demand for the foreign currency (CAD). Then, the banks reduce their bid (buy) prices of CAD with respect to MR (stated differently, they reduce the number of ringgit to be exchanged for CAD). Finally, the banks reduce their MR bids with respect to USD.

Finally, we need to explain the covered interest arbitrage condition. Here, we need the concept of the forward rate, which we first defined earlier. In general, *covered interest arbitrage* (CIA) is the process of taking advantage of discrepancies between two countries' interest rate differentials, while covering (securing or hedging) your (exchange rate) risk with a forward contract. Let us see that through a simple example. Assume the following information which relies on the interest-rate differential between the UK and the US and the prevailing spot exchange rates (your investment budget is $150,000):

- The current spot rate of the pound is $1.50.
- The 90-day forward rate of the pound is $1.50.
- The 90-day interest rate in the US is 3%.
- The 90-day interest rate in the UK is 5%.

How should you proceed? First, convert today the $150,000 to £100,000 (= $150,000/$1.50) and deposit them in a UK bank. Then, immediately sell £105,000 90 days forward and, by the time the deposit matures, you will have £105,000 [= £100,000 * (1 + 0.5)]. Finally, 90 days later you can fulfill your forward contract obligation by converting your £105,000 into $157,500 (based on the forward contract rate of \$1.50 per pound, found by multiplying £105,000 by \$1.50). This results in a 5% return over this 90-day period, which is higher by 2% than the US interest rate.

There is version of CIP, the *uncovered interest rate parity* (UIP), which states that the expected difference in exchange rates should reflect the difference in interest rates between two countries. This basically means that if a country has a higher interest rate than another country, then the first country's currency is expected to depreciate in the future to account for the higher return.

Now that we have presented the covered interest rate arbitrage, we are ready to present the *interest-rate parity* (IRP) condition. IRP simply states that when interest rates and exchange rates adjust such that CIA is no longer feasible, then an equilibrium condition prevails. Put differently, the forward-spot rate differential is just enough to offset the interest rate differential between two currencies. We can derive this important condition algebraically as follows.

Denote as i_h the home (domestic) interest rate, i_f the foreign interest rate and f_p the forward rate (premium) of the foreign currency so as to have

$$f_p = [(1 + i_h)/(1 + i_f)] - 1 \qquad (2)$$

Alternatively, we could redefine equation (2) as follows:

$$f_p = (F - S)/S \cong i_h - i_f \qquad (2a)$$

which suggests that the forward premium is approximately equal to the interest-rate differential. It follows that when the foreign interest rate is less/higher than the home interest rate, the IRP relationship suggests that the forward rate should exhibit a premium/ discount. You may also realize that in such cases there may be potential for CIA!

You need to understand that IRP does not imply that investors from different countries will earn the same returns! Rather, it compares a foreign and a domestic investment in risk-free interest-bearing securities by an investor. For example, if country A has a 5% interest rate and country B has a 7% interest rate, country A's investors will earn 5% at home or engage in CIA. If they do the latter, when IRP is valid, then they would simply earn a 5% return just like the one in their home country. The same holds for country B's investors (they would earn the 7% return). Thus, each investor does not achieve the same nominal return here, even though IRP exists. Put differently, investors cannot use CIA to achieve higher returns than those achievable in their respective countries.

Does IRP (or CIP) hold? A plethora of academic work exists but the results are still mixed. Some reasons as to why this parity may not hold are transaction costs (that is, commissions and fees associated with currency exchange which reduce potential profits), market imperfections (because not all markets are perfectly efficient due to differences in liquidity, information asymmetry, and risk aversion among investors), default risk (as investors perceive differences in default risk between countries, this leads to risk premia that impact interest rates), and capital controls (as some countries restrict capital flows, which can affect exchange rates and thus, IRP). In general, the validity of IRP was solid prior to the 2007/8 global financial crisis (GFC). For example, Akram et al. (2008, 2009) and McBrady et al. (2010) found a general validity of CIP.[6]

Borio et al. (2016) found that CIP failed to hold since GFCs due to the cross-currency basis' persistence. The authors stated that the "cross-currency basis indicates the amount by which the interest paid to borrow one currency by swapping it against another differs from the cost of directly borrowing this currency in the cash market. Thus, a non-zero cross-currency basis indicates a violation of CIP."[7] Baba and Packer (2009) and Coffey et al. (2009) suggested that funding shortages in the US financial markets and counterparty risk led to a deterioration in liquidity and observed deviations from covered interest parity in the USD–EUR pair.[8]

THE THREE PARITIES

According to Roll and Solnik (1979), all three parities – IRP, PPP and IFE – are implied by a consumer who can invest both at home and abroad and who can import goods for his own consumption. In other words, they all apply under complete certainty.

However, under uncertainty, IRP remains unchanged, but more complex equations involving risk premia are required for PPP and IFE. Specifically, under uncertainty, PPP would be biased due to consumer risk preferences. However, in the long run PPP may hold as agents exploit internationally divergent real prices.

Roll, Richard and Bruno Solnik (1979). On Some Parity Conditions Encountered Frequently in International Economics, *Journal of Macroeconomics* 1(3), (Summer), 267–283.

3.2 Purchasing power parity

Another important relationship is the purchasing power parity (PPP), which simply explains the nature of the relationship between prices of the same goods (or basket of goods) across nations. There are two versions (forms) of PPP: the absolute and relative. The *absolute form of PPP* implies that in the absence of international barriers and other limitations (such as tariffs and quotas), consumers will buy the cheaper product. In other words, prices of the same basket of products in two different countries should be equal when measured in a common currency. If price differences exist, then the demand should work to equalize the prices. The *relative form of PPP* acknowledges that because of market imperfections, prices of the same basket of products in different countries will not be the same when measured in a common currency. Hence, an exchange-rate adjustment is needed for the relative purchasing power to be the same whether buying the goods at home or from overseas.

We can derive algebraically PPP, capitalizing on equation (2), as follows:

$$e_f = [(1 + I_h)/(1 + I_f)] - 1 \cong I_h - I_f \qquad (3)$$

where I is the inflation rate for home (h) and foreign (f) country, and e_f is the percentage change in the value of the foreign currency. It is easy to see that when $I_h > I_f$, e_f would be positive implying the foreign currency's appreciation.

Does PPP hold? Again, the evidence is mixed. Early work (Froot and Rogoff, 1995; Frankel and Rose, 1996; Abuaf and Jorion, 1990; and Taylor, 2006) indicated that PPP holds in the long run but not in the short run.[9] Recent studies, however, rejected PPP. Crucini et al. (2010), Crucini and Yilmazkuday (2014), and Crucini and Telmer (2020) reported deviations from PPP due to various reasons such as market segmentation and transaction costs.[10]

It is interesting to mention a rule of thumb or an informal measure of PPP, published by *The Economist* periodical in 1986 and which continues to date. This measure is known as "The Big Mac Index". This index measures whether the market exchange rates for different currencies are under- or over-valued by measuring each currency against a common standard, the Big Mac hamburger sold by McDonald's restaurants globally. For example, a Big Mac costs £4.59 in Britain, about 6 US dollars in the Euro area and US$5.79 in the United States, as of end of January 2025. The implied exchange rate is 0.79. The difference between this and the actual price reflects the differences in the purchasing power of each currency. Switzerland has the most expensive Big Mac in the world, at over 8 US dollars.

One final comment about PPP. Some empirical tests relied on testing the exchange rates for unit root(s) and then for cointegration. Existence of a unit root (or following a random walk) in an exchange rate implies absence of PPP in the long run. A cointegration test (that is, testing for a long-run relationship between two or more exchange rates that contain a unit root) would indicate absence so as to suggest invalidity of long-run PPP. We illustrate such tests in Part D of the online Appendix.

3.3 The international Fisher effect

When one combines the relationships between the exchange rate and interest-rate and inflation-rate differentials, we arrive at another major equilibrium condition or parity known as the international Fisher effect (IFE). Recall the standard Fisher effect (which we learned in Chapter 3), where the nominal interest rate is equal to the real rate plus expected inflation. IFE extends this equation to express an exchange rate's appreciation or depreciation to inflation and interest rate differentials. More specifically, using equation (2), we could substitute the percentage exchange rate change, e_f, for the forward premium, as follows:

$$e_f = [(1 + i_h)/(1 + i_f)] - 1 \qquad (4)$$
$$e_f \cong i_h - i_f \qquad (4a)$$

In essence, equation (4) or (4a) or IFE theory all imply that when $i_h > i_f$, the e_f will be positive or appreciate because the (relatively) low foreign interest rate reflects (relatively) low inflationary expectations in the foreign country. This appreciation will improve the foreign return to investors from the home country, thus equalizing foreign and home securities' returns.

In general, PPP's main theme is on how a currency's spot rate will change over time following inflation differentials. IRP theory emphasizes why the forward rate differs from the spot rate and the extent of the differential that should exist, at a specific point in time. Finally, IFE focuses on how a currency's spot rate will change over time in accordance with interest-rate differentials. Note, however, that PPP is related to IFE because expected inflation differentials influence the nominal interest rate differentials between two countries. The nearby *sidebar* presents a historical account of the three parities suggesting that they differ under certainty and uncertainty conditions.

We conclude this section with the question of how the exchange rate affects a firm's marketing operations (functions). The general answer is that it affects pricing, demand, budgeting, supply chains, and promotional strategies. Box 12.1 explains how in some detail.

Box 12.1

How does the exchange rate affect a firm's marketing operations?

PRICING: Exchange rate fluctuations directly affect the cost of goods sold and the final price to consumers in foreign markets. You already know that if the domestic currency strengthens, exports become more expensive abroad, making products less competitive. Consequently, firms may need to adjust prices or offer discounts to remain competitive internationally.

PROMOTION: Fluctuations in the exchange rate can influence a company's promotional efforts and its brand position in different markets. For example, a company may promote itself as a premium brand in markets with strong currencies and as a value brand where the local currency is weaker. Therefore, companies need to adapt to foreign markets to optimally exploit differences in purchasing power of its international customers.

BUDGETING: Global (multinational) companies face currency translation risks when converting foreign revenues into domestic currency. For example, an American company operating in Europe and earning Euros may face a conversion of lower dollar profits if the Euro weakens (vis-à-vis the dollar). The marketing implication is that budget planning, promotional spending, and profitability analyses must account for exchange rate fluctuations (volatility).

Test your understanding 1

1. What would be the gains from locational and triangular arbitrage?
2. Explain the similarities and differences among locational arbitrage, triangular arbitrage and covered interest arbitrage.
3. Explain the impact (effects) of the trade-related and financial factors on the Euro-USD exchange rate. Be general in your analysis.
4. Identify the key magnitudes (main themes) in the IRP, PPP and IFE theories.

4 Examples of foreign exchange strategies

In this section, we present very basic foreign exchange transactions that can be undertaken by the average (as well as institutional) investor in an effort to exploit price discrepancies, in addition to the above ones we presented within the context of the parities. Let us begin with trading currency futures.

4.1 Trading currency futures

Recall that currency futures contracts are contracts specifying a standard volume of a particular currency to be exchanged on a specific settlement date. The goal of trading such contracts is to hedge foreign currency positions. A buyer/seller of a currency futures contract locks in the exchange rate to be paid for a foreign currency/exchanged for the home currency at a future point in time. Individuals or firms can execute orders for currency futures contracts via a broker who serves as the intermediary.

As an example, assume that on March 1, a futures contract on 50,000 British pounds with a September settlement date is priced at $1.60 per pound. The buyer of this currency futures contract will receive £50,000 on the settlement date and will pay $80,000 for the pounds (= £50,000 * $1.60 per pound) *plus* a commission paid to the broker. At the same time, the seller of this contract is obligated to sell £50,000 at a price of $1.60 per pound and therefore will receive $80,000 on the settlement date, *minus* the commission owed to the broker.

If you believe that a currency futures price will be different from the spot rate, then you can earn arbitrage profits. For example, you observe the currency futures price on the British pound to be $1.60 and that forward contracts for a similar period are available for $1.58. You may attempt to purchase forward contracts and simultaneously sell currency futures contracts. If you can exactly match the settlement dates of the two contracts, you can earn a guaranteed gross profit of $.02 per unit. What if you speculate in these markets and expect a change in an exchange rate? You wish to exploit this by trading currency futures contracts. How could you profit from such a situation?

Assume that as of May 10, a futures contract specifying 100,000 Brazilian reais and a June 19 settlement date is priced at $0.18. On May 10, you (the speculator) expect the real to decline and so, you sell futures contracts on reais. Assume also that on June 19, the spot rate of the real is $0.175. How should you proceed? First, the US dollars from the contract to sell are $18,000 (= BR100,000 * $0.18). Second, buy reais in the spot market and pay $17,500 (= BR100,000 * $0.175). Finally, sell reais for $18,000 to fulfill the futures contract and reap $500 profit. The $500 gain on the futures position reflects the difference between the amount received ($18,000) when selling the reais in accordance with the futures contract relative to the amount paid ($17,500) for those reais in the spot market.

4.2 Speculating with currency options

Just like using futures or forward contracts to hedge a position in a foreign currency, firms can use currency options to cover such open positions. More specifically, multinational corporations employ (buy) call options on a currency to hedge future payables. An investor can speculate with currency options by taking positions based on his/her expectations of future exchange rate movements. Recall that (currency) options give the investor the right, but not the obligation, to buy (call) or sell (put) a currency at a specified exchange rate (strike price) before or on the option's expiration date. Let us begin with a demonstration of buying a call option, which means that the investor is bullish or optimistic on a foreign currency.

Specifically, the investor expects the foreign currency to appreciate vs. the domestic currency. So, they buy a EUR/USD call option if they expect the Euro to rise. They would profit if the spot rate exceeds the strike rate *plus* the premium (they paid to buy the call option). For example, assume that the EUR/USD is 1.10. Then, buy 1-month EUR/USD call option, with a strike price of 1.12, and pay the premium of \$0.01. If EUR/USD rises to 1.15, then the profit would be \$0.02 per unit (= 1.15 – 1.12 – 0.01). By contrast, if the EUR/USD stayed at 1.10, the loss would have been just the premium you paid (\$0.01).

If the investor is bearish on a foreign currency, that is, he expects it to depreciate, he can buy a GBP/USD put option. A profit is realized if the spot rate is less than the strike rate *minus* the premium. Finally, the investor can sell options in speculations that the currency will not move as much. The objective is to collect premiums! This is a risky strategy, however, because of high potential losses (if there is actual sharp move in the currency's value) and is not advised for the individual investors. There are other types of strategies involving options but they are beyond the scope of this section.[11]

In general, if the speculator is risk-neutral (ignoring transaction costs), he will want to buy pounds *n* years forward if $F_n^{\$/£} < S_n^{\$/£}$ and sell pounds *n* years forward if $F_n^{\$/£} > S_n^{\$/£}$. If transaction costs are included, then we can amend the above by saying that he would buy pounds forward if the price is les than his expected future selling price. By contrast, a risk averse speculator would not trade (buy or sell forward) unless the expected return is sufficient for the systematic risk taken. Obviously, this risk depends on the correlation of the exchange rate with the values of other assets and liabilities. If the exchange-rate risk is not diversifiable, there may be a risk premium in the forward rate.

4.3 Carry trade in forex

Carry trading is a long-term foreign exchange strategy that takes advantage of interest rate differentials between two currencies, the "carry". Traders profit from earning interest on the currency they hold while paying a lower interest rate on the borrowed currency. Let us show with an example.

First, pick a high-yield and low-yield currency pair. The Japanese yen (JPY) is notorious for conducting carry trades. Then, go long on (buy) a currency with a high interest rate. Assume that currency is the Australian dollar (AUD). Sell (short) the currency with a low interest rate. So, you buy AUD/JPY, where AUD has a higher interest rate than JPY. The Australian interest rate is 4%, the Japanese interest rate is 0.1%, and so the two countries' interest-rate differential would be 3.9%. If you buy one standard lot (100,000 units) of AUD/JPY and hold it for a year, you could earn 3.9% in interest alone. In other words, borrow in JPY, convert JPY to AUD, and invest in Australian assets to earn 4% (holding the position for a year and assuming no change in the exchange rate). So, if you borrow ¥10,000,000, with an 1AUD = 100JPY exchange rate, you would exchange AUD100,000 (= ¥10,000,000 ÷ 100). Invest this amount in Australian bonds at 4% annual return and earn AUD 4,000. After one year, convert back to JPY (assuming no change in exchange rate).

Obviously, the longer you hold the trade, the more interest you accumulate. Also, additional profit comes if the currency pair moves in your favor. Some important risks include the exchange rate risk, if the currency pair moves against you, losses can exceed interest earnings, interest-rate changes, high volatility, which can cause sharp price changes, and (do not forget!) broker fees! Carry trading is ideal for patient investors who can handle long-term positions and market fluctuations. It works best in stable economic conditions with minimal rate changes.

4.4 The golden cross and death cross

Finally, you could apply some other types of strategies such as the popular trend-following foreign exchange strategy. This resembles more of a technical analysis rather than fundamental analysis where economic and financial magnitudes are examined to derive forecasts and or expectations about exchange rates (or currencies). Some tools could be moving averages or momentum indicators such as the relative strength indicator (RSI). The idea behind trend-following is that you should trade in the direction of an established currency trend, upward or downward.

More specifically, let us select two currency pairs, the EUR/USD and USD/GBP. We will employ the 50-day and the 200-day simple moving average (SMA) techniques. The rule would then be to buy when the 50-day SMA crosses above the 200-day SMA. This is known as the "golden cross", which implies a bullish signal. The signal suggests that the pair may be for an upward trend or in strength. Traders identify three stages in the golden cross technique. The first one the downtrend which is not expected to last long. The second one is the beginning of the uptrend, where the short- and long-term moving averages are expected to cross. The final stage is the prolonged uptrend, which confirms the bull market and entails gains. In general, traders can utilize this technique to determine when to enter and exit the market. The indicator can also be used by traders to understand when it makes sense to sell, buy or hold.

By contrast, when the MA indicators show a transition from a bull market to a bear market, we are talking about the "death cross". As you may have guessed, this is the exact opposite to the "golden cross". So, this means that the 50-day MA (the short-term one) crosses from above the 200-day MA (the long-term one). As with the golden cross, the death cross has three stages (phases). The first phase is the uptrend in the security's price (value) until it peaks (buying momentum tapers off). The second phase marks the decline in the security's price, where the actual "death" cross occurs and signals a bearish state. The third and final phase sees a continuation in the downtrend until it rebounds.

Using real data for one year (5/2/2024 to 5/2/2025), we computed the two moving averages and plotted the resulting graphs, as shown in Figure 12.1. You

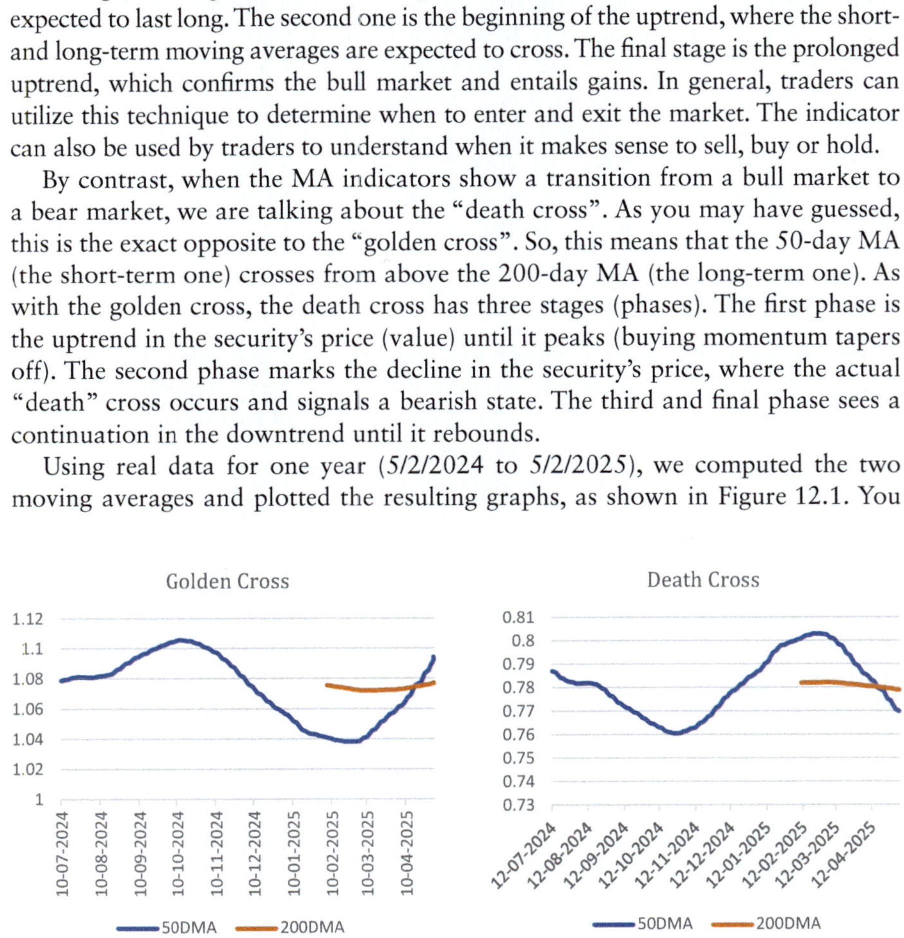

Figure 12.1 50-day and 200-day moving averages, EUR/USD, USD/GBP

Data source: *YahooFinance*; Author-created graph

can clearly see the three stages identified above. Looking at the first graph, we can see that the cross over date is 4/23/2025 and, according to this technical indicator, a trader should expect an uptrend. This reflects the "golden cross" state. Inspecting the second graph, we see exactly the reverse and the date where the cross took place was 4/8/2025 for the USD/GBP exchange rate. This the "death cross" situation.

In general, one can use these technical indicators in conjunction with other indicators and, perhaps, along with some fundamental analysis. This advice is not just for mere confirmation purposes but also for plausible interpretation purposes.

5 Exchange-rate forecasting

Exchange-rate forecasting – the prediction of the future spot exchange rate – is essential for all market agents because it assists them in making informed decisions for borrowing and investing, managing capital flows, capital budgeting, as well as for policy formulation. In the preceding sections, we discussed some strategies involving exchange rates such as speculation and hedging. However, if agents are able to forecast future rates, then it can be said that the market is inefficient. An inefficient market permits abnormal returns (the difference between the actual return and an expected return) or gains to be realized from using information. In Chapter 2, we first discussed market efficiency and its three forms (weak, semi-strong and strong, based on the availability of information).

In subsection 4.2, we discussed the actions of speculators, if they were risk neutral (in the absence of transaction costs), and concluded that they would buy or sell forward if the forward rate equals the expected spot rate. The question that arises is whether all available information used by the speculators (or the market, in general) to derive the forward rate was used effectively or efficiently. There are ways to test for that (that is, if there is some bias in the forward rate, as predictor of the market's expected spot rate) using regression analysis (we discuss regression analysis in the online Appendix B). Let us simply express one model next.

$$S^{\$/£} = \alpha_0 + \alpha_1 F^{\$/£} + \alpha_2 X + u \quad (5)$$

where $S^{\$/£}$ is the actual (realized) spot rate, $F^{\$/£}$ is the forward rate and X any relevant information for the exchange rate. The u term is the error term. Using daily or weekly data, you could estimate this regression model and obtain values for the slope parameters (α_1 and α_2) of interest. How would one interpret the results?

First, if relevant information were not incorporated in the forward rate by the market, the market would be inefficient. In this case, the estimate of α_2 would be significantly different from zero. In theory, the value of that coefficient should be zero, which would suggest market efficiency. Similarly, we should expect the value of the α_1 coefficient to be one, suggesting that (on average) the forward rate would correctly predict the realized spot rate. In the opposite case, we would interpret its value as that the forward rate is a biased predictor of the future (realized) spot rate.

Finally, we should expect the value of the constant term (α_0) to be zero. But what would other values mean? If $\alpha_0 > 0$, then the forward price of the pound, is less than the realized spot value of the pound. Hence, buying the pound forward allows the speculator to earn a positive return, on average. This is known as a risk premium. On the other hand, if $\alpha_0 < 0$, there is a premium for going short on pounds – or long on the dollar. Ample early empirical evidence suggests there is a risk premium in the forward rate, and that it is time-varying. For example, Baillie et al. (1983), Fama (1984) and Wolff (1987), to name just a few, all reported such risk premia. Recent work on the topic corroborated these early findings. See for example, Landon and Smith (2003) and Miah and Altiti (2020).

Next, we continue with a brief description of the two main techniques of foreign-exchange forecasting.

5.1 Fundamental forecasting

In section 2, we discussed the major factors that affect an exchange rate. When we include these – and possibly more – factors in a regression model, we would apply the fundamental forecasting technique. In essence, such a regression specification would resemble equation (5) on p. 341. Once you estimate the model, you could then use it to derive forecasts for the exchange rate (your dependent variable) using actual values for all independent variables.

In general, fundamental forecasting involves several steps. First, select the model based on what you seek to explain and forecast. For example, you could test theories such as PPP or IRP. Second, collect the relevant data for the independent and the dependent variables. In our example, the dependent variable would be the exchange rate(s) and the independent variables would be the interest rates, inflation rates and income levels, for example, between any two countries. Then construct their differentials (your home country's interest, inflation rates or income level *minus* those of the foreign country). Third, estimate the model using some econometric method (mainly through simple or multiple regression). Then, test the model. Fourth, generate forecasts from your estimated regression equation (after making some assumptions about the explanatory variables). Finally, evaluate your model's forecasting accuracy using metrics such as the Mean Square Error (MSE) or the Absolute Forecast Error (AFE). Both metrics rely on the *forecast error,* defined as

(Forecasted or Predicted value – Realized or Actual value)

and so, MSE and AFE (as a percentage of the realized value) are defined as:

$$MSE = (1/n)\ \Sigma^{n}_{i=1}\ (Actual\ value - Predicted\ value)^2 \quad (6)$$
$$AFE = (Predicted\ value - Realized\ value)/\ Realized\ value \quad (7)$$

Let us demonstrate regression and forecasting with some actual data. The dependent variable is the percentage change in the EUR/USD exchange rate ($\%\Delta ER$) over the period from January 1999 to January 2025. The two independent variables are the inflation rate (INF) and interest rate (IR) differentials (US *minus* EU, European Union). The results from the regression are below (with t-stats in parentheses).

$$\%\Delta ER = \underset{(0.278)}{0.0515} - \underset{(-1.334)}{0.0824\ IR_t} + \underset{(1.078)}{0.020\ INF_t} \qquad \text{R-square} = 0.03$$

As we see, neither variable is statistically significant [since t-stats are below (the absolute value of) 2], which means that neither PPP nor IRP hold (for this dataset). The R-square is very low, which also supports the above conclusion. A graphical illustration is shown in Figure 12.2, where the fitted (predicted) and actual points are shown (for each independent variable).

To forecast the value (or %change) in the exchange rate in the next period, assume that IR and INF diffs are 2% and 1.8%, respectively. Then, plugging these values into the estimated regression equation above, we obtain the forecasted value of –0.0773 as follows:

$$0.0515 - 0.0824 * (2) + 0.020 * (1.8) = -0.0773$$

What if we wanted to predict the change in the exchange rate when we believe that interest rate differentials would change by 1%? In this case, the answer is the following:

$$0.0824 * 0.01 = 0.000824$$

meaning that it would change by 0.0824%, *ceteris paribus*. The key is to assume that all other variables remain the same (the *ceteris paribus* assumption). The same can be done when we believe that the change in inflation rate differentials would be 1%. In this case, you would use the variable's coefficient only.

How could one test PPP using simple regression? Just construct the independent variable to reflect inflation rate differentials between two countries and estimate

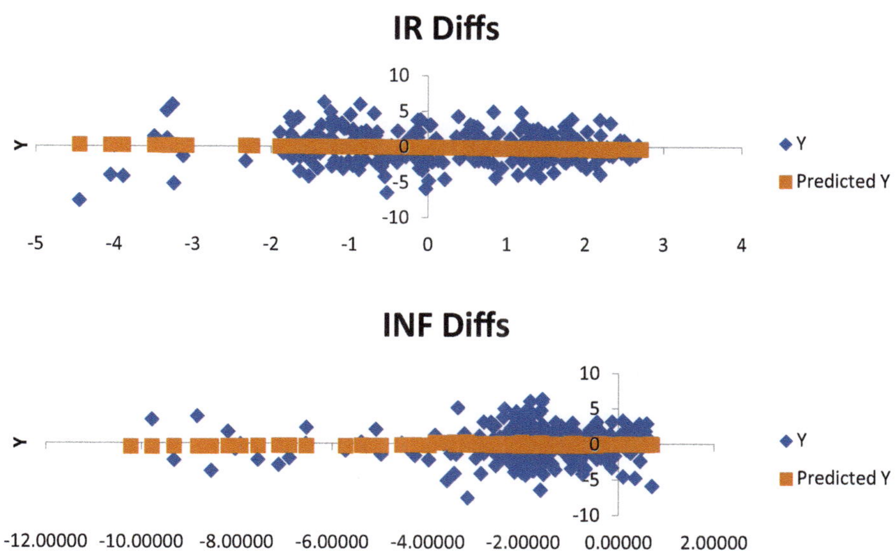

Figure 12.2 Line fit plots from multiple regression testing PPP and IRP

Notes: IR are interest-rate differentials and INF are inflation-rate differentials between the US and EU

Data source: *YahooFinance*; Author-created graph

the model. Inspect the constant (alpha) and slope (beta) terms. If beta equals 1, then a 1% increase in PPP rates should result in a corresponding 1% increase in spot exchange rates. When beta > 1, then spot rates overreact to changes in PPP, while if beta < 1 this would suggest an underreaction to changes in PPP. The alpha should be zero.

5.2 Technical forecasting

Technical forecasting involves the use of a series' own historical data to predict its future value(s). This method abstracts from other variables as in fundamental forecasting. For example, in our case there may be a trend of successive daily exchange rate adjustments in the same direction, which could lead to a continuation of that trend. Figure 12.3 shows such a trend for the daily USD/GBP exchange rate from May 13, 2024 to May 13, 2025. As you see, the series went through two different phases, an upward and two downward ones. So, one could use a simple econometric model such as trend or autoregressive to derive the relevant coefficients and use them for forecasting. Let us demonstrate these two regression-type methodologies.

Trend analysis is simply the raw series over time, as in the following model:

$$ER_t = a + b\,t \tag{8}$$

where t is time. So, one would obtain the series and regress them against time.[12] Using excel (after generating a column from 1 to n observations, here 251), and leaving the most recent data point out of the sample used for the regression (for forecasting purposes), we obtain the following estimated model (t-stats in parentheses):

$$ER = 0.7801 - 0.0045 * t \quad \text{R-square} = 0.0003$$
$$(367.4)\ (-0.312)$$

Figure 12.3 Plot of daily USD/GBP values, 5/13/2024–5/13/2025
Data source: *YahooFinance*; Author-created graph

As you suspect by now, this is *not* a good model. If we plug in the next time period, 252, we get the predicted value of –0.3539 for the exchange rate as follows: 0.7801 – 0.0045 * 252. The predicted or forecasted value is far away from the actual one and so, the forecast error is very big.

Let us see if we have better luck with the autoregressive model, known as *autoregression* (AR) in the econometric literature.[13] Here, we simply regress the series against its own previous (lagged, t-1) values, as follows:

$$ER_t = a + b\, ER_{t-1} + u \tag{9}$$

The estimated model (leaving out the last data point again) is below:

$$\underset{}{ER_t} = \underset{(1.524)}{0.0159} + \underset{(72.90)}{0.9792} * ER_{t-1} \quad \text{R-square} = 0.9542$$

As you see, we obtained a much better fit based on the two metrics. Using it to forecast, we get a forecast of the exchange rate of 0.7529, when the previous value was 0.7527, as follows: 0.0159 + 0.9792 * 0.7527. As you can see, the forecast is much closer to the actual one, which validates the model.

At this point, it is instructive to explain one thing. These two models just presented are not "technically" classified as technical models. They are either simple regression models or univariate models (especially the autoregressive one). Examples of technical forecasting models are moving averages (MA) and the two technical indicators (which we first mentioned in Chapter 8 and discussed in subsection 4.4), and exponential smoothing (ES) which we present next along with the MA technique.

You can apply both techniques in Excel, as follows. We will use the same data as in the previous subsection. When you go to *Data>Data Analysis>Moving Average* OR *Exponential Smoothing* in Excel, highlight the column of the series (exchange rate) and plug in any value you wish for the interval or damping factor (speed coefficient) and finally, check the "Chart Output" box. Both techniques "smooth out" the series. Let us try with 7, 14 and 21 days, for MA, and 0.5 and 0.7 for ES. We will demonstrate this in Part D4 of the online Appendix.

Briefly, *exponential smoothing* calculates a weighted average of past data points, with the weights decreasing exponentially as the data points get older. The smoothing constant (or dumping factor), α, controls the rate (speed) at which the influence of past observations decreases. A higher α means more recent observations are given greater weight, while a lower α means more of the distant data is considered. So, it all depends upon the judgment (beliefs) of the investigator. The ES formula is as follows:

$$\hat{y}_{t+1|T} = \alpha y_t + (1 - \alpha)\, \hat{y}_{T|T-1} \tag{10}$$

where $0 \leq \alpha \leq 1$ is the smoothing (damping factor) parameter and $\hat{y}_{t+1}$ the estimated next period's ($t+1$) value.

Figure 12.4 displays the three versions of the MA technique. As is clearly evident, the 7-day model performed better given that the forecasted points (orange squares) are very close to the actual points (blue diamonds), compared to the 14- and 21-day models. It is sensible to remark that the shorter the forecast horizon, the more accurate the forecast is. Moving on the two ES models, seen in

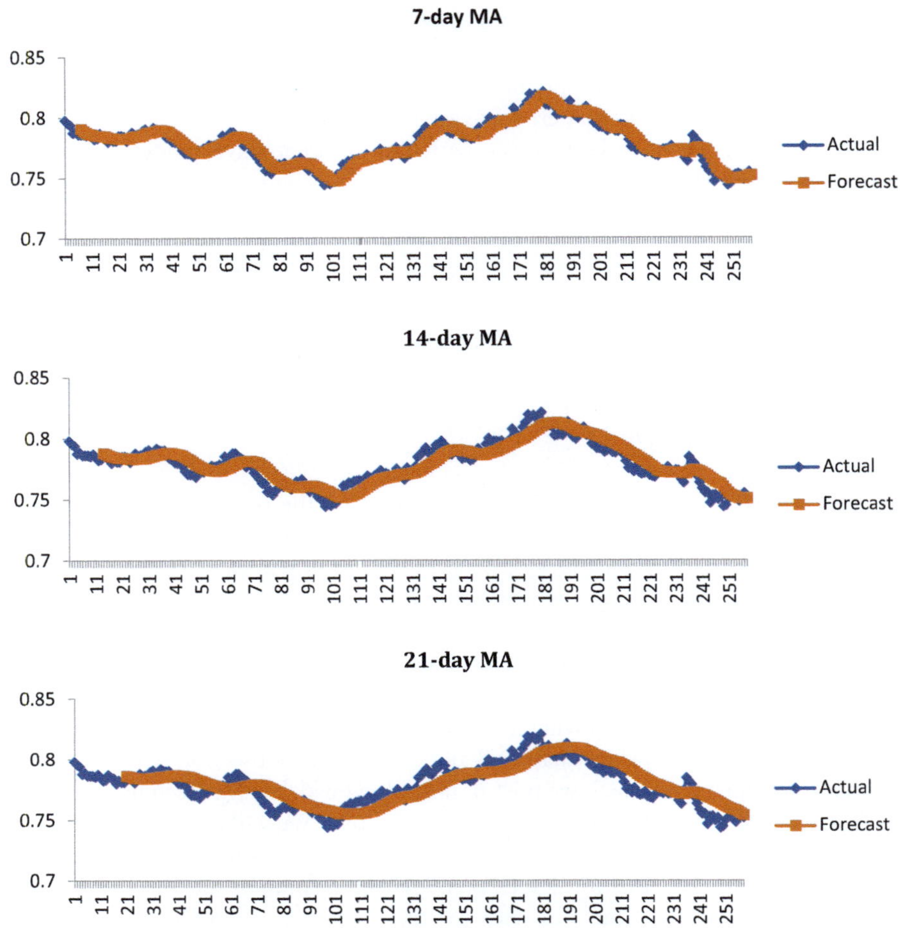

Figure 12.4 7-, 14- and 21-day moving averages for the USD/GBP exchange rate

Source: Author-created graph

Figure 12.5, we that the 0.5 damping factor (value) performed much better than the 0.7 one, given the closeness between the two lines.

5.3 Additional models and insights

One other (version of the) model that resembles the AR one we discussed in the previous subsection, is the so-called random walk (RW) model. We first encountered the notion of the random walk in Chapter 7, where we discussed some equity-market theories. As a refresher, we had defined the random walk theory as one which claimed that stock prices seem to follow a non-discernible trend or move (up and down) randomly over time. Here, we can define *random walk* (RW) as a process where the current value of a variable is composed of the past value plus an error term (known as *white noise*).[14]

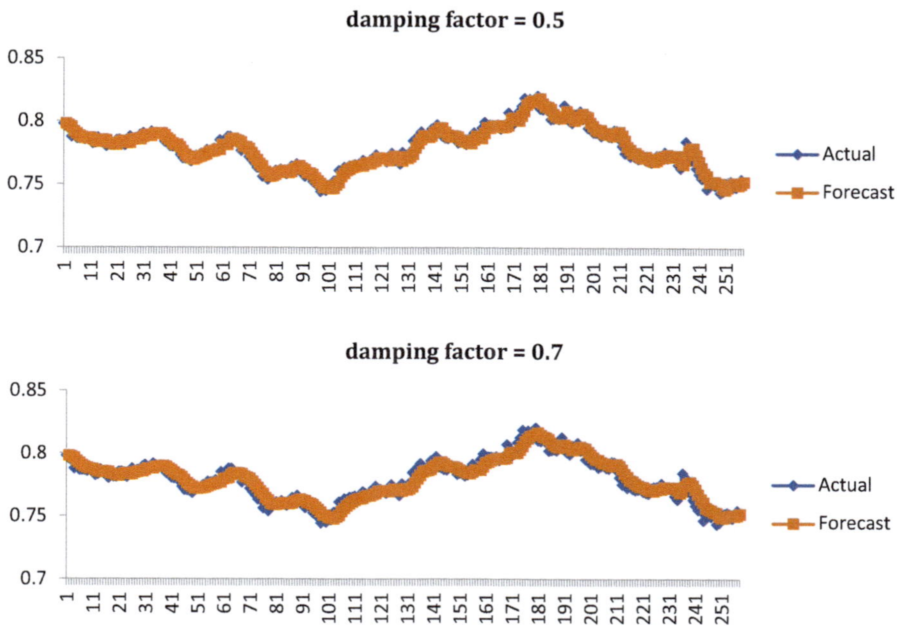

Figure 12.5 Exponential smoothing forecasts of the USD/GBP exchange rate

Source: Author-created graph

Algebraically a random walk is represented as follows:

$$y_t = y_{t-1} + \varepsilon \tag{11}$$

This process implies that the best prediction of y for next period is the current value, or that it does not allow to predict the change $(y_t - y_{t-1})$. That is, the change of y is absolutely random. In practice, the presence of a random walk process makes the forecast process very simple since all the future values of y_{t+n} for $n > 0$, is simply y_t. The term ε is the error term.

If we add a constant term, α, in equation (11), we obtain the random walk with a drift model. This resembles equation (9) above. If $\alpha > 0$, then the process will show an upward trend.

What if we add an error term to equation (8), so that the new specification would like this:

$$y_t = y_0 + a^*t + \Sigma^n{}_{t=1}\, \varepsilon_t \tag{12}$$

This process shows both a deterministic trend $(y_0 + at)$ and a stochastic trend (due to the error term). The significance of the RW model is that many economic time series follow a pattern that resembles a trend model.

One important concept (from financial econometrics) is that of a mean reversion. A *mean-reverting* series is one that reverts back to its historical average, at some point in time. In other words, it never continues upward or downward for a very long time and such deviations are transitory. Traders use mean reversion to identify potential buy and sell opportunities based on deviations from the mean. In addition, there is ample empirical evidence that, for developed countries, real exchange rates are reverting to the level implied by PPP theory. In addition, for major currency pairs, long-run PPP holds and that the nominal exchange rate is the main driver of this adjustment process (for some evidence, see Goldberg et al., 1997).

Finally, some thoughts about using theory. Theory often instructs which fundamental macroeconomic variables should be relevant to exchange rate determination. However, it remains on the size of the relationship, that is, the (true) coefficient in a regression of the exchange rate on the fundamental variable. Thus, it will always be necessary for the researcher when attempting to produce an accurate forecast of an exchange rate's future level, to empirically re-estimate the relationship (between the exchange rate and the fundamental variables). Then, they can use these historical estimates to inform their forecasts. This process entails several difficulties – economic and econometric alike – and so the researcher must possess knowledge and use any information correctly. The relevant literature has come a long way since the early studies of determining the best model based on its ability to predict assuming correct values of the independent variables (see Meese and Rogoff, 1983a, b). New forecasting techniques have been developed, many of them quite technical and sophisticated, but it still remains unclear as to whether these advances in econometric modelling have been able to beat the RW model, on a consistent basis. However, the reader should read the paper by Moosa and Burns (2014) who found that exchange rate models outperform the random walk, in terms of direction accuracy and profitability, but the RW cannot be outperformed in terms of the magnitude of error.

Test your understanding 2

1. What are the objectives and key differences (risk profile and time frame) between hedging and speculation in the forex markets?
2. What are the differences between fundamental and technical forecasting in the forex markets?
3. What is the random walk and what is its main implication?

Summary

- The foreign exchange (forex) market is the global marketplace where currencies are traded.
- Other major foreign exchange markets are the futures, swap and option markets.
- The characteristics of the forex market are, first, that it is a decentralized market which operates in the OTC market, that the participants include central banks and commercial banks, governments, corporations, investors, retail traders as well as hedge funds which speculate on currency price movements for profit, that the market is famous for its high liquidity, that it is known for its volatility, that it uses leverage, and that it has low transaction costs.

- Some functions of the forex market are: (1) it enables participants to exchange their currencies in the global market and trade seamlessly and efficiently; (2) it has an impact across international trade, investments and travel; (3) it offers protection to traders and investors from fluctuating currency values; and (4) it connects the worldwide economies to promote financial growth to achieve global economic stability.
- The factors that affect an exchange rate rest with the reasons which affect the demand for, and supply of, currencies.
- Some specific factors that affect the exchange rate are interest rates, inflation rates, incomes, expectations, government and central bank actions and the country's balance of payments.
- Locational arbitrage is the process of buying a currency at one location cheap, and simultaneously selling it at another location at a higher price.
- Triangular arbitrage involves using cross-(exchange) rates and can be executed by transacting in one currency (in the spot market) to capitalize on a rate (value) differential (discrepancy) in the cross-rates between the two currencies.
- Covered interest arbitrage is the process of taking advantage of discrepancies between two countries' interest rate differentials, while covering (securing or hedging) your (exchange rate) risk with a forward contract.
- Uncovered interest rate parity states that the expected difference in exchange rates should reflect the difference in interest rates between two countries.
- The interest-rate parity condition simply states that when interest rates and exchange rates adjust such that it is no longer feasible, then an equilibrium condition prevails.
- The purchasing power parity explains the nature of the relationship between prices of the same goods (or basket of goods) across nations.
- The absolute form of PPP implies that in the absence of international barriers and other limitations (such as tariffs and quotas), consumers will buy the cheaper product.
- The relative form of PPP acknowledges that because of market imperfections, prices of the same basket of products in different countries will not be the same when measured in a common currency.
- The international Fisher effect theory implies that when the home interest rate exceeds the foreign interest rates, the exchange rate change will be positive or appreciate because the (relatively) low foreign interest rate reflects (relatively) low inflationary expectations in the foreign country.
- Some foreign exchange trading strategies include trading currency futures, speculating with currency options, engage in carry trades, and determining the golden cross and death cross.
- Exchange-rate forecasting – the prediction of the future spot exchange rate – is essential for all market agents because it assists them in making informed decisions for borrowing and investing, managing capital flows, capital budgeting as well as for policy formulation.
- There are two main approaches to exchange rate forecasting: fundamental and technical.
- Some econometric models employed in exchange rate forecasting are trend analysis, autoregressions, moving averages, exponential smoothing.

Questions and problems

1. Explain the concepts of locational and triangular arbitrage and the conditions for them to be reasonable.
2. You are a US investor and you observe the following information:

	Quoted price/rate
Spot rate of Euro	\$.95
90-day forward rate of the Euro	\$.94
90-day Euro interest rate	5%
90-day US interest rate	3%

   What would be your rate of return if you used covered interest arbitrage? Assume that you invest \$1,000,000. Explain the implications of the process.
3. Assume that the Canadian dollar's forward rate currently exhibits a premium of 4% and that interest rate parity exists. If US interest rates decrease, how must this premium change to maintain interest rate parity?
4. Compare IRP, PPP, and IFE.
5. Canada and Japan typically had lower inflation than the United States. How would you expect this to affect the Canadian dollar's or the Japanese yen's values? Explain.
6. Explain the fundamental and technical approaches to forecasting exchange rates. What are some limitations of using either approach to predict exchange rates?
7. Assume that you have estimated the following model of exchange rate percentage change, $\%\Delta ER_t$:

   $$ER_t = 0.045 - 0.0745\ IRD_t + 0.0150\ INFD_t + 0.125\ INCD$$

   where IRD is the interest-rate differentials, INFD the inflation rate differentials, and INCD the income level differentials between two countries.
   a. Make a forecast of the $\%\Delta ER$ if IRD = 1.5%, INFD = 2% and INCD = 3%.
   b. What would be your forecast of the $\%\Delta ER$ if IRD = 2%?
   c. What would be your forecast of the $\%\Delta ER$ if INCD = 4%?

8. US-based ABC Co. exports TVs to British manufacturers invoicing them in US dollars. The company plans to keep its price over the next year. ABC Co.'s competitors, by contrast, bill their products in British pounds (GBP) and will not be changing their prices over the next year either. The US risk-free interest rate is presently 5%, whereas that in the UK is 3%. Today the spot rate of GBP is \$0.95. The company's revenues from its TV exports to the UK will be approximately \$1 million over the next year.
   a. If the company decides to use the international Fisher effect rather than the spot rate to forecast the exchange rate of the Australian dollar over the next year, will its expected revenue from its exports be higher, lower, or unaffected? Explain.

9. This question involves evaluation of forecasting using the purchasing power parity (PPP) relative to the forward rate. You believe that the Canadian dollar's

movements are mainly due to PPP. You observe that today's (nominal) annual interest rate in Canada is 8%, compared to 5% in the US In addition, you expect that annual inflation to be roughly 3% in Canada and 1% in the US Finally, you believe that the interest rate parity holds. If Canadian dollar's current spot rate is $.98, do you think the one-year forward rate would underestimate, overestimate, or be an unbiased estimate of the future spot rate? Explain.

10. Can you suggest some ways of determining whether PPP holds? Describe one limitation in testing whether PPP holds.

Notes

1. We discuss the forward rate again in Section 3.
2. A bill of exchange is a written order that one party receives from another requiring a specific amount of money to be paid or received, either immediately or at a later date. It is legal document and serves as legal evidence of debt.
3. Azzam, I., A.A. El-Masry, and E. Yamani (2023). Foreign Exchange Market Efficiency During COVID-19 Pandemic. *International Review of Economics & Finance* 86, 717–30. doi: 10.1016/j.iref.2023.03.043. Faheem Aslam, Saqib Aziz, Duc Khuong Nguyen, Khurrum S. Mughal, and Maaz Khan (2020). On the Efficiency of Foreign Exchange Markets in Times of the COVID-19 Pandemic. *Technological Forecasting and Social Change* 161, 120261. https://doi.org/10.1016/j.techfore.2020.120261.
4. Namhoon Lee, Wonseok Choi, and Yuntaek Pae (2021). Market Efficiency in Foreign Exchange Market. *Economics Letters* 205, 109931. https://doi.org/10.1016/j.econlet.2021.109931.
5. Chutasripanich Nuttathum and James Yetman (2015). Foreign Exchange Intervention: Strategies and Effectiveness. *BIS Working Papers* no. 499.
6. Akram, Q. Farooq, Dagfinn Rime, and Lucio Sarno (2008). Arbitrage in the Foreign Exchange Market: Turning on the Microscope. *Journal of International Economics* 76, 237–253. Akram, Q. Farooq, Dagfinn Rime, and Lucio Sarno (2009). Does the Law of One Price Hold in International Financial Markets? Evidence from Tick Data. *Journal of Banking & Finance* 33(10), (October), 1741–1754.
7. Borio, Claudio, Robert N. McCauley, Patrick. McGuire, and Vladyslav Sushko (2016). Covered Interest Parity Lost: Understanding the Cross-Currency Basis. Bank of International Settlements, September. https://www.bis.org/publ/qtrpdf/r_qt1609e.htm.
8. Baba, Naohiko and Frank Packer (2009). Interpreting Deviations from Covered Interest Parity During the Financial Market Turmoil of 2007–08. *Journal of Banking and Finance* 33, 1953–1962. Coffey, Niall, Warren B. Hrung and Asani Sarkar (2009). Capital Constraints, Counterparty Risk, and Deviations from Covered Interest Rate Parity. *Federal Reserve Bank of New York Staff Reports*, no. 393 (September).
9. Froot, K.A., and Rogoff, K. (1995). Perspectives on PPP and Long-Run Real Exchange Rates. In *Handbook of International Economics* (pp. 1647–1688). http://www.sciencedirect.com/science/article/pii/S1573440405800127. Frankel, J.A., and A. K. Rose (1996). A Panel Project on Purchasing Power Parity: Mean Reversion within and between Countries. *Journal of International Economics* 40(1), 209–224. http://www.sciencedirect.com/science/article/pii/0022199695013962. Abuaf, N., and P. Jorion (1990). Purchasing Power Parity in the Long Run. *Journal of Finance* 45(1), 157–74. https://www.jstor.org/stable/2328814. Taylor, M.P. (2006). Real Exchange Rates and Purchasing Power Parity: Mean-Reversion in Economic Thought. *Applied Financial Economics* 16(1–2), 1–17. http://www.tandfonline.com/doi/abs/10.1080/09603100500390067.
10. Crucini, M.J., M. Shintani, and T. Tsuruga (2010). The Law of One Price without the Border: The Role of Distance versus Sticky Prices. *Economic Journal* 120(544),

462–480. https://doi.org/10.1111/j.1468-0297.2010.02354.x. Crucini, M.J., and H. Yilmazkuday (2014). Understanding Long-Run Price Dispersion. *Journal of Monetary Economics* 66, 226–240. http://www.sciencedirect.com/science/article/pii/S0304393214000701. Crucini, M.J., and C.I. Telmer (2020). Microeconomic Sources of Real Exchange Rate Variation. *Review of Economic Dynamics* 38, 22–40. https://www.sciencedirect.com/science/article/pii/S1094202520300090.

11. For example, there is the straddle strategy whereby the investor expects high volatility but does not know which way (higher or lower). A straddle uses both call and put options with the same strike price.
12. This is known as a deterministic trend model, because there is no error term. See also subsection 5.3.
13. This is part of the general class of models, known as autoregressive [integrated] moving average (AR[I]MA) models. We explain this model in Part D5 of the online Appendix.
14. In econometrics, a normal variable with zero mean and variance one is white noise.

References

Baillie, Richard T., Robert E. Lippens, and Patrick C. McMahon (1983). Testing Rational Expectations and Efficiency in the Foreign Exchange Market. *Econometrica* 51(3), 553–563.

Fama, Eugene F. (1984). Forward and Spot Exchange Rates. *Journal of Monetary Economics* 14(3), 320–338.

Goldberg, Lawrence G., Thomas F. Gosnell and John Okunev (1997). Purchasing Power Parity: Modeling and Testing Mean Reversion. *Journal of Banking & Finance* 21, 949–966.

Landon, Stuart and Constance E. Smith (2003). The Risk Premium, Exchange Rate Expectations, and the Forward Exchange Rate: Estimates for the Yen–Dollar Rate. *Review of International Economics* 11(1), 144–158.

McBrady, M., S. Mortal and M. Schill (2010). Do Firms Believe in Interest Rate Parity? *Review of Finance* 14(4), 695–726.

Meese, Richard, and Kenneth Rogoff (1983a). Empirical Exchange Rate Models of the Seventies: Do They Fit Out of Sample? *Journal of International Economics* 14, 3–24.

Meese, Richard and Kenneth Rogoff (1983b). The Out-of-Sample Failure of Exchange Rate Models: Sampling Error or Misspecification? In J. Frankel (ed.), *Exchange Rates and International Macroeconomics* (Chicago: Chicago University Press), 67–105.

Miah, Fazlul and Omar Altiti (2020). Risk Premium or Irrational Expectations? An Investigation into the Causes of Forward Discount Bias Across 27 Developed and Developing Economies Forward Rates. *The North American Journal of Economics and Finance* 51, 100847. https://doi.org/10.1016/j.najef.2018.09.005.

Moosa, Imad and Kelly Burns (2014). The Unbeatable Random Walk in Exchange Rate Forecasting: Reality or Myth? *Journal of Macroeconomics* 40, 69–81. https://doi.org/10.1016/j.jmacro.2014.03.003.

Wolff, Christian C.P. (1987). Forward Foreign Exchange Rates, Expected Spot Rates and Premia: A Signal-Extraction Approach. *Journal of Finance* 42(2), 395–406.

Chapter 13

Financial technology and financial markets

Introduction

Financial technology (fintech) is simply the use of technology by companies and financial institutions to deliver financial products and services to people and financial markets. The companies that rely primarily on technology, known as *fintechs*, conduct fundamental functions affecting how users borrow, save, borrow, pay, and protect money (or financial wealth) globally. The origins of fintech trace back to 1990s but fintech became important a decade later and particularly during the 2007/8 global financial crisis, primarily in the payments zone. Early fintechs such as *E-Trade*, *Paypal*, and *Square*, enabled individuals and small companies to trade stocks online or accept credit cards via a mobile device (smart phones). Fintech disruptions have since been rapidly expanding to every corner of finance. Just think of Bitcoin, which was born in 2009 and rapidly followed by other cryptocurrencies using blockchain technology. A 2023 McKinsey report (*Fintechs: A New Paradigm of Growth*) stated that "fintechs have entered a new era of value creation focusing on sustainable, profitable growth."[1]

What are some key aspects of fintech? First, innovation, in an effort to improve and automate financial services. Second, the use of digital tools/technologies like mobile apps, software, and online platforms to manage financial services. Third, expansion in the online banking sphere to conduct digital payments, lending, investing, and insurance. Some fintech apps enable access of financial account data such as transactions and account balances or allow users to track their investments across multiple platforms. Some examples include apps like *Venmo* and *Zelle*, and automated investment platforms like robo-advisors. Other fintech apps permit users to trade stocks or cryptocurrencies. *Robinhood* and *Coinbase* are classic examples of executing a wide variety of investments quickly and easily.

Fintech has grown tremendously over the past decade, according to data from *DocuClipper*.[2] Specifically, the North American region led the global fintech market with a value of $112.91 billion in 2024, accounting for 34.05% of the total market share. This region continues to dominate in funding, innovation, and adoption of digital financial solutions. The Asia Pacific (APAC) region is expected

DOI: 10.4324/9781003677161-17

to dominate the US as the world's largest fintech market by 2032. The region's economies are increasingly facilitating access to all sorts of financial transactions. Europe (and especially The Netherlands and the UK) captured 20% of total global fintech investment in 2020, with strong regulatory frameworks supporting *RegTech* and digital banking growth. Additionally, the rapid growth of the EU FinTech industry has been accompanied by significant policy efforts such as the 2018 *FinTech Action Plan* aimed at fostering a more competitive and innovative European financial sector, the launch of the *EU Digital Finance Platform* and the adoption of additional legislation, such as the proposed financial data access and payments package.[3]

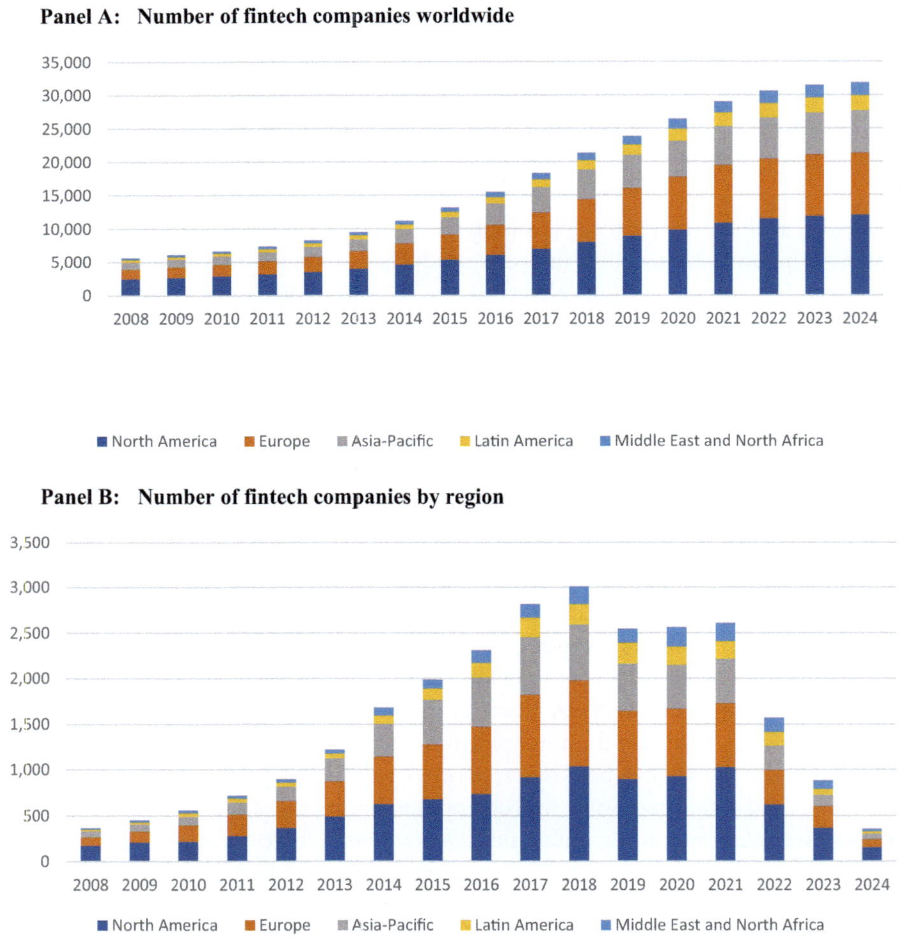

Figure 13.1 Number of fintech companies worldwide and by region, 2018–2024

Panel A: Number of fintech companies worldwide

Panel B: Number of fintech companies by region

Source: *Statista*

The Middle East and Africa regions (combined with Latin America and APAC excluding China) represented 15% of fintech global revenues in recent years and are projected to grow to 29% by 2028. McKinsey estimates that the recent surge in investor funding has been particularly strong in the Kingdom of Saudi Arabia, United Arab Emirates, Egypt, and Bahrain.[4] Finally, Latin America (LA) saw notable investment growth in 2023, with fintech funding rising from $28.9 billion in 2022 to $36 billion in H1 2023. According to the Inter-American Development Bank, LA's fintech ecosystem recorded 340% growth from 2017 to 2023. Brazil, Mexico and Colombia account for 57% of total companies' in digital payments and lending.[5]

Figure 13.1 shows the number of fintech startup worldwide from 2008 to 2024 (Panel A), and the number of fintech companies by region (Panel B) during the same period. From Panel A, it is clear that the number of fintechs was rising sharply during the 2019–2022 period but growing slowly after 2023. Panel B reveals the rapid growth of these companies in the Europe and North America regions followed by the Latin America and Asia-Pacific region. The growth of these companies echoes what we described above. Some major reasons for the drastic decline in these companies were the 2021 FX meltdown, the 2022 market correction, adverse economic fundamentals (rising inflation and interest rates) were among the main roots of the decline.

1 Categories of financial technology products

Fintech covers a wide range of uses across business-to-business/consumer (B2B, B2C), peer-to-peer (P2P) markets. Some other types include internet of things, AI and ML and Blockchain technology. Below, we present and briefly discuss these and more key elements of fintech that are changing the financial landscape.

1.1 Business-to-business

Business-to-business (B2B) simply reflects wholesale transactions between two or more businesses such as selling products or services to other businesses. Just think of a company (business) selling a product to another company (business) such as transportation equipment (a car, for example) or raw materials rather than to a consumer (which we explore next). Examples of B2B companies are wholesalers and shipping companies. Essentially, B2B involves exchange of goods, services, or information between businesses, thus forming a crucial part of the economy and global supply chain.

1.2 Business-to-consumer

Business-to-consumer (B2C) pertains to direct transactions that take place between a business and an individual, the consumer or end user. This is usually done without an intermediary such as a retailer. For example, when you buy a piece of clothing online this would be a B2C transaction. It is not hard to see that the emergence and growth of B2C was due to the growth of electronic commerce (e-commerce) and Amazon in the late 1990s. Other examples of B2B businesses are *Shopify* and *Cisco*. There are some key differences between B2B and B2C, however.

First, the volume of transactions is much higher in B2B than in B2C, for obvious reasons. Second, B2B sales often require administrative processes including approvals by several stakeholders. Third, prices of products (or services) are more competitive and lower for consumers than for businesses. In other words, in B2C, consumers pay the same price for the same products. By contrast, in B2B pricing, businesses negotiate prices and payment terms and may or may not pay upfront. Third, both B2B and B2C may charge a fee or subscription for access to content or consumable products. Think of online streaming TV services where you need to subscribe to view content.

1.3 Peer-to-peer

Peer-to-peer (P2P) is a networking and business model where individuals interact directly with each other, thus bypassing intermediaries such as retailers/wholesalers or a bank. P2P transactions involve direct money transfers (loans) between individuals, facilitated by apps like *PayPal*, *Google Pay* or *Apple Pay*. Sometimes, P2P is called "crowd-funding" or "crowd-lending". Individual investors (lenders) who typically want a better return on their cash savings than they would earn with a bank account or money market fund engage in P2P transactions. So, lenders can open accounts on the relevant P2P websites and deposit various amounts of money to fund potential loans. Then, loan applicants can post their financial risk profiles and funding needs, to determine the interest rate they will have to pay to borrow. Applicants may then receive loan offers from one or more investors and accept one of them. It is also possible to haggle the terms of the loan online. Finally, the money transfers to the borrowers and the monthly loan payments to the lender(s) are handled through the platform. Investors earn returns on their investments when borrowers make repayments, usually in the form of monthly instalments. It is instructive to mention that any potential investor considering P2P lending should check the site's transaction fees as fees vary across platforms.

In general, apps for making payments are easy to use because you simply tap your smartphone on a suitable point-of-sale (POS) terminal and can make payments and securely save your debit and credit card information. Furthermore, such apps reduce (or eliminate) the need to use physical (debt/credit) cards thus moving into a cashless society. Finally, you can use cryptocurrencies to make online payments.

1.4 The Internet of Things

The Internet of Things (IoT) is a network of real-world devices, gadgets, and appliances that are equipped with sensors, connections, and software to collect and share data online with other devices. Examples of such devices or gadgets include smartphones and smartwatches. IoT relies on various technologies like Wi-Fi, Bluetooth, and cellular, to connect devices and collect and share data, thus enabling remote monitoring and control. When applied to fintech, the collected data can include information about customer behavior and transactions history. For instance, smart wearables and connected devices can monitor user activity, location, and biometric data, all of which can potentially be useful to financial applications.

Furthermore, IoT data can be exploited to assess risk and prevent fraud. For instance, banks and insurance companies can use IoT data to evaluate the risk associated with insuring a property via the monitoring of environmental factors like temperature and humidity in real time. Financial lenders can leverage IoT data (from connected vehicles or smart homes) to assess a borrower's creditworthiness, potentially leading to more accurate lending decisions and better terms for borrowers. Finally, IoT devices are used to monitor high-value assets such as vehicles, equipment, and inventory. This is particularly relevant in industries like supply chain finance and asset-based lending, where tracking and managing assets is essential.

1.5 Artificial intelligence and Machine Learning

Artificial intelligence (AI) and Machine Learning (ML) are transforming the fintech sector by offering innovative solutions and opportunities for financial institutions, startups, and customers. *Artificial intelligence* is technology that focuses on creating machines and computers capable of performing tasks that are typically done by humans (and human intelligence). It encompasses various technologies like Machine Learning, Deep Learning, and Natural Language Processing (NLP), enabling computers to learn, reason, solve problems, and make decisions.[6] By 2024, AI gave rise to *generative AI* (gen AI), a technology that can create original content such as text, images, and video. The technologies on which gen AI tools are built are Machine Learning (ML) and Deep Learning.

Machine Learning allows computers to learn and make predictions from historical data by training an algorithm. ML encompasses a several algorithms (or Machine Learning techniques) such as the familiar linear regression, the logistic regression, decision trees, random forest, clustering and more. Perhaps, the most popular type of ML algorithm is a *neural network* (NN) or artificial neural network. An NN consists of interconnected layers of nodes (analogous to a human's neurons) that work together to process and analyze complex data. Neural networks are well suited to tasks that involve identifying complex patterns and relationships in large amounts of data.[7] *Deep Learning* (DL) is a subset of Machine Learning that uses multilayered neural networks. DL tools trigger most of AI applications.

By contrast, the simplest form of ML is known as *supervised learning*, which involves the use of labeled data sets to train algorithms to classify data or predict outcomes accurately. The objective is for the model to learn the linkages between inputs and outputs in the training data (by identifying patterns in the data), so it can predict the labels of new, unseen data. A prime application of supervised learning is recognizing spam (junk) email. Other important applications include image and speech recognition and fraud detection.

Both AI and ML algorithms analyze huge datasets to identify potential risks and detect fraudulent activities in real-time by spotting unusual patterns in transactions and flag suspicious activities. This allows for more accurate risk assessment and personalized lending decisions, expanding access to credit for underserved populations. How can these be leveraged in fintech? First, through algorithmic trading, which analyzes market trends and executes trades at high speeds. ML models can adapt to changing market conditions, improving trading strategies and increasing profitability. Second, via AI-powered *Chatbots*, which provide efficient customer support. One example of a Chatbot is *ChatGPT* developed by OpenAI and can engage in conversational exchanges and generate human-like text responses. Banks also use such chatbots such as *Erica* by the Bank of America. Using a Natural Language Processing system, it can answer user questions, write articles, and even generate creative content. In addition, it guides customers through transactions and can even identify potential issues before they escalate. Finally, by the use of AI-driven *robo-advisors*, which offer personalized investment advice, automatically rebalance portfolios, and provide cost-effective solutions for investors.

1.6 Cloud computing

Cloud computing is the supply of computer services via the internet (also known as the *cloud*), rather than on local hardware (computers). This service includes servers, storage, databases, software, and many more, in on-demand and on pay-as-you-go bases. Put differently, instead of owning and maintaining actual hardware and software, you can use cloud service providers to access these resources from anywhere and any type of device. Besides offering greater flexibility, scalability (due to fluctuations in demand) and convenience, cloud computing reduces capital expenditures and operational costs associated with managing own hardware and software. In addition, such services speed up the deployment of fintech applications to the market and enable companies to bring new products and services to market more quickly and boost their profits. There is also greater security as leading cloud services companies (such as *Amazon Web Services* and *Google Cloud*) invest heavily in security, offering robust measures to protect data and applications and, in the event of a disaster, solutions include built-in disaster recovery and backup options.

1.7 Blockchain technology

A *blockchain* is a digital, decentralized distributed ledger system that enables secure data storage over a network of computers. It uses a distributed database to store data in blocks, linked together chronologically, making it very difficult to alter without consensus from the network.[8] This secures data integrity and provides a tamper-proof record, making blockchain ideal for digital applications such as cryptocurrencies and financial services (like retail companies tracking the movement of goods between suppliers and buyers and media by managing and enforcing copyrights). Consequently, you can use blockchain technology to create an immutable ledger for tracking orders, payments, accounts,

FINTECH AND EU REGULATIONS

The European Union (EU) has created various directives such as PSD II for payment services and GDPR for data protection. PSD I established SEPA in 2007; PSD II (effective in 2017) expands payment service definitions and mandates banks to provide third-party access to customer data. Regulatory Technical Standards (RTS) were adopted to facilitate secure communication between banks and third-party providers. GDPR replaced Directive 95/46/EC, enhancing personal data protection since May 2018. Current regulations are seen as adequate, but there are calls for clearer definitions regarding big data.

and other transactions. In addition, by streamlining transactions and procedures, it is possible to cut costs and eliminate middlemen.

1.8 InsurTech

Fintech is also transforming the insurance industry, known as *InsurTech* (insurance technology) with new products and services emerging to meet changing customer needs. Essentially, insurtech companies use various technologies to automate processes, analyze data, and develop new products. This process can employ AI, data analytics, blockchain and IoT. According to the Corporate Finance Institute, Insurtech "fosters greater efficiency, transparency, and accessibility within the industry, benefitting both insurance providers and customers. By automating processes, improving risk assessment accuracy, and offering tailored coverage, Insurtech disrupts the conventional insurance model to meet evolving consumer demands and expectations."[9]

Insurtech assists insurance companies to lower their costs, improve efficiency, and stay competitive. It also allows them to offer more personalized and convenient insurance products to customers such as distribution, underwriting, claims management, and product design enabling them to boost revenues. Insurtech has many insurance applications some of which are auto, home, health, life insurance, worker's compensation and cyber. A simple example is the use of wearable fitness devices which provide the insurance company a wide and growing range of possible data on behavioral and health metrics of an insured person. Similarly, plug-in car monitoring devices track your driving behavior using telematics, which utilizes technology from your car to collect and transmit data to the insurance company in real time.

> The EU has not yet established specific regulations for crypto-assets. Crypto-assets qualify as financial instruments under Markets in Financial Instruments Directive II. The Commission is monitoring developments in crypto-assets and aims to standardize APIs for open banking by mid-2019.
>
> Carla Stamegna and Cemal Karakas, (2019). Fintech (financial technology) and the European Union. EPRS | European Parliamentary Research Service.

2 Financial technology and financial markets

The relationship between fintech and global financial markets is increasingly tight and transformative. Fintech is redesigning how financial services are created, delivered, accessed, and regulated across borders. The nearby sidebar discusses the efforts the EU has taken to regulate financial services and cryptocurrencies. Here's a breakdown of the key relationships.

2.1 Key relationships

2.1.1 Market access and inclusion

Fintech expands finance by enabling broader access to global markets, especially for retail investors and underserved populations. Examples include robo-advisors like Charles Schwab, Fidelity Investments, Betterment and E-Trade allow low-cost investing in global ETFs, and mobile banking and payments in emerging markets bring new participants into formal financial systems.

2.1.2 Capital market efficiency

Fintech improves market efficiency and transparency in a variety of ways by enhancing algorithmic trading, reducing bid-ask spreads, offering real-time market data and analytics via Application Programming Interface (API) and AI tools.

2.1.3 Cross-border payments and currency markets

Fintech firms like *Wise* (previously TransferWise) and *Ripple* offer faster and cheaper foreign exchange and remittance services. This affects FX market structure and liquidity, as well as the nature and extent of monetary policy transmission in small and open economies.

2.1.4 Disintermediation

As we saw earlier, P2P lending, decentralized finance (DeFi), and crowdfunding platforms reduce reliance on traditional banks. The implications include a shift in credit origination and loan pricing and great competition for deposits, affecting banks' role in monetary transmission.

2.1.5 Market volatility and new asset classes

Fintech enables new financial instruments such as cryptocurrencies and tokenized assets and digital securities traded on blockchain platforms. These asset classes may introduce volatility or correlation shocks in global markets and pose problems in complicated regulatory coordination.

2.1.6 Regulatory spillovers and financial stability

Global fintech developments (e.g., Libra/Diem, CBDCs) force cross-border regulatory collaboration and impact financial stability. Some risks that can be easily identified are cybersecurity threats, shadow banking or unsupervised financial innovation and systemic risk in highly interconnected digital platforms.

In sum, fintech acts as both a driver and disruptor in global financial markets. It increases access, transparency, and speed, but it also introduces new risks and regulatory challenges. Finally, its global reach is reshaping how capital flows, risk is priced, and financial markets operate.

2.2 Examples of fintech's application to financial markets

Below are some specific real-world examples of how fintech is applied to financial markets, across asset classes and financial activities.

2.2.1 Equities and equity markets

Several brokerage firms offer commission-free apps, making trading more accessible to a wider audience. Some popular ones are *Robinhood*, *Charles Schwab*,

Fidelity Investments, *E*TRADE*, and *Interactive Brokers*. These online companies enable real-time trading in US stock markets, fractional share purchases, and options trading for retail investors. The impact is to unfetter access to stock trading, thus significantly increasing retail participation.

Other types of fintech companies are those offering/using algorithmic trading platforms (proprietary or not). Examples of such companies include *Thomson Reuters*, *Refinitiv Ltd*, *TD Ameritrade*, *E-Trade*, and *IG Group*, where investors use Python-based strategies to back-test and automate trades in equity markets. This enables retail and institutional investors to implement hedge fund-style strategies.

Financial institutions such as investment banks, hedge funds, mutual funds, and insurance companies frequently use algorithmic trading to manage large orders efficiently, reduce trading expenses, and execute trades faster than human traders. Specifically, hedge funds rely on algorithmic traders to deploy sophisticated strategies like statistical arbitrage, high-frequency trading, and trend following. Apart from institutional investors, some retail investors also use algorithmic trading platforms to automate their trades and potentially improve their trading performance.

2.2.2 Fixed-income markets

In these markets, electronic bond trading platforms also exist facilitating institutional trading of corporate and government bonds with transparency in pricing. A pioneering blockchain use in sovereign bond markets was the World Bank's *bond-i*, which was a blockchain-based 2-year bond and issued in 2018. The two-year bond raised 110 million Australian dollars, marking the first time that investors have supported the World Bank's development activities in a transaction via blockchain technology.[10]

2.2.3 Monetary policy

Fintech can impact the extent and nature of monetary policy. Specifically, fintech through lower search costs can make lending more accessible, potentially diminishing the impact of traditional interest rate adjustments on credit availability. Moreover, fintech apps and online platforms can facilitate faster deposit outflows from traditional banks, potentially destabilizing the banking sector during times of monetary tightening. The European Central Bank has published a number of studies on the impact of fintech on monetary policy transmission mechanism. Franco (2024) shows that fintech lenders tend to accelerate the monetary policy transmission to mortgages rates, whereas they lessen the pass-through to mortgage volumes (the fintech channel of monetary policy).[11] Erel et al. (2023) report that online banks react to changes in the federal funds rate. The authors find that a 1% increase in the federal funds rate leads to a 0.3% larger increase in the deposit rates of online banks relative to traditional banks. Thus, online bank deposits experience inflows, while traditional banks experience outflows.[12]

2.2.4 Foreign cross-border transfers

A number of financial technology companies focus on global money transfers and foreign exchange trading. These fintechs represent a better alternative to international business banking in terms of cost and speed. One such company is *Wise* (formerly TransferWise) and aims to make the international transfer process cheap and easy. It was founded in 2011 and headquartered in London. If you travel, live and work internationally and need to send money overseas, this company is right for you because it can be up to 8 times cheaper than banks, it is fair and easy way to manage your money across borders.[13] In 2024, the company was rocked by a data breach but continues to expand to other parts of the world such as Tallin (Estonia) and Singapore.

Another fintech company is *Revolut* (UK), which offers digital bank and currency exchange apps. It empowers travelers and global investors to hedge FX risk. According to *Forbes* magazine, Revolut is a "low cost and easy to use,... is among the top digital-only financial providers for regular travelers and those sending money overseas. It comes with a transparent fee structure and transfers are safe and secure."[14]

2.2.5 Other international investments

Some fintechs with applications in commodities and real assets are *Paxos Gold* and *AgUnity*, which use tokenized gold on blockchain. In the first fintech, each token represents one fine troy ounce of London Good Delivery gold and allows micro-investments in gold and instant settlement globally. In the second fintech, it tracks crop inputs and outputs for smallholder farmers in developing countries thereby increasing transparency in agricultural commodities and access to micro-financing. In derivatives and risk management, companies such as *Deribit* and *Numerai* specialize in crypto derivatives exchange and hedge fund using encrypted data. Deribit offers futures and options on Bitcoin and Ethereum and thus, enables institutional-grade hedging and speculation in digital assets, while Numerai crowdsources AI models to trade equities and derivatives, hence innovating portfolio construction using collective intelligence. In sustainable and ESG investing, *Clarity AI* and *Carbonplace* are two fintechs that offer platforms for ESG analytics and carbon credit trading. Both companies help investors evaluate companies' environmental and social performance and enhance trust and efficiency in these markets.

2.2.6 Central Bank Digital Currencies

Central Bank Digital Currencies (CBDCs) are digital forms of a country's official currency, issued and regulated by its central bank (unlike cryptocurrencies). Central banks issue such forms of money in place of printing money (fiat money). CBDCs function as a digital claim on the central bank, offering a safe and stable form of digital money. CBDCs offer a number of advantages (besides being government-backed and regulated): they are safe and liquid, represent a digital form of the official currency, have the potential of increasing the efficiency of a payments system, and could foster new financial innovations and services.

Several countries have already launched CBDCs, including the Bahamas (*DCash*), Jamaica (*JAM-DEX*), Lithuania (*LBcoin*) Nigeria (*eNaira*), and China (e-CNY). The European Central Bank is actively working on developing a digital euro. CBDCs are also being considered in other jurisdictions, such as the US. Some of the challenges associated with CBDCs include cybersecurity risks, privacy concerns, and potential impacts on monetary policy and the financial system.

2.3 Linkages between fintech and financial services worldwide

The relationship between financial technologies and global financial services is very close. More and more people are now using this disruptive technology to carry out their business in a fast, secure and economical way. Fintech is transforming the financial sector landscape and is obscuring the boundaries of both traditional (brick and mortar) financial firms and the financial sector. Consumer banking and fund transfers (payments) are the most vulnerable sectors to disruption from fintech applications. In addition, the asset (wealth) management sector is shifting towards fintech solutions, exploiting data analytics to enhance client relationships. In what follows next, we will provide some academic empirical evidence on the linkages between fintech and the financial services industry, understand the role of fintech to developing nations and people (especially women) worldwide, and end with a look at some risks of the fintech revolution.

2.3.1 Academic evidence on the fintech–financial markets linkage

The emergence of fintech and its relationship with traditional financial markets and institutions have increasingly been the focus of academic research. Berg et al. (2022) find that cooperation between the two is getting closer fast. Kommel et al. (2019) and Saklain (2024) report that fintechs compete with traditional financial institutions in similar market segments and business areas. Lee and Shin (2018) corroborate the evidence that traditional financial institutions are increasingly investing in fintechs. Zhang, Hung, and Chang (2017) demonstrate that causality between bank loans and Peer-to-Peer (P2P) loans varies across regions in China. Jagtiani and Lemieux (2018) provide evidence that fintech lending penetrated areas that lack banking services in the US. Lee and Shin (2018) discuss the advantages of fintech in providing financial services and the challenges for traditional financial institutions.

Other related studies also suggest that fintech activities may exacerbate risk contagion and asset volatility in the financial system (Benoit et al., 2017). Anagnostopoulos (2018) admits that the traditional financial sector faces new risks connected with the emergence of fintech startups. The *Financial Stability Board* (2017)[15], He et al. (2017) and Li et al. (2020) acknowledge that fintech activities could intensify risk contagion and assets volatility in the financial system, thereby undermining financial stability.

What about the relationships between fintech and other, traditional financial instruments or magnitudes such as exchange rates, oil or stock prices? Afshan et al. (2024) find that fintech has a statistically significant positive relationship with digital currencies and exchange rates, verifying co-movement and mutual influence. The authors interpret this result as that fintech innovations can reshape traditional financial markets and enhance international trade and cross-border remittances. Furthermore, the authors report that fintech innovations help stabilize risks associated with oil price volatility and financial markets, thus lessening their adverse impacts. Carlini et al. (2022) investigate the dynamics between fintech and bank stock returns and report that banks' equity investments in fintechs are associated with negative abnormal stock market returns suggesting that such investments are unfavorable (perhaps due to perceived risks and uncertainties). Moreover, the authors find that European banks experience more significant negative stock market reactions compared to North American banks.

What about the contribution of fintech to environmental sustainability and green finance? The extant empirical evidence suggests that fintech positively contributes to green innovation in polluting industries in China (Song and Hao, 2024) and Udeagha and Ngepah (2023), in examining how green finance and fintech can contribute to the BRICS nations' goal of achieving carbon neutrality, report that all promote environmental sustainability. In addition, they find support for the so-called *Environmental Kuznets Curve* theory, which states that as a nation becomes mature (advanced), its reliance of environmentally harmful energy (fossil fuels) diminishes in favor of greener technologies. Finally, Tang et al. (2024) report the results of the study that fintech can provide the necessary funding for green growth, while green finance can also be used to promote green investment and develop green and sustainable projects in ASEAN countries.

Finally, what about the role of fintech to the segment of society that prefers Sharī'ah-compliant financial services? Evidence has indicated that mobilizing funds for a common or communal cause through crowdfunding, for example, which resembles donation or interest-free loans, mirrors the traditional Islamic principles of social finance. In addition, it is believed fintech has the potential of promoting financial inclusion in Islamic economies. The reader can learn more about the linkage between fintech and Islamic finance through these sources: a book, titled *Fintech and Islamic Finance: Theory and Practice* (Umar A. Oseni and S. Nazim Ali, eds., Routledge, 2019), and research papers by Hasan et al. (2020) and Qudah et al. (2023), to name just a few. In addition, a recent *FINTECH* journal Special Issue, titled *Trends and Developments in FinTech*, discusses fintech trends such as the aspects of the regulation of digital activities, the implementation of technologies on reducing carbon emissions, ESG investments by FinTech, the trend towards asset tokenization and related banking activities in relation to FinTech, and the development of central bank digital currencies assisted by FinTech.[16]

2.3.2 The role of fintech in developing nations and women

Fintech can play a pivotal role in all sectors of developing economy. First, it reduces under-banking conditions, especially in regions with limited traditional banking infrastructure. For example, mobile money platforms can provide basic financial services like payments and savings at reduced costs. Second, fintech can drive innovation and entrepreneurship, leading to the creation of new businesses and job opportunities in all sectors of a developing country. It can also facilitate trade and investment by using digital payments which are more convenient and secure relative to the conventional cash-based systems. In addition to empowering investment decisions, financial technology can help raise consumer awareness about the environmental and social implications of consumption decisions, and incentivize them to more resource-efficient and sustainable choices.[17] Third, fintech can streamline financial processes, making them faster and more efficient, which can boost productivity and economic growth. At the same time, fintech can support a country's transition to a sustainable, low-carbon economy. Finally, fintech can also play a role in improving financial literacy by providing access to educational resources and tools.

Fintech offers banking services to people in remote communities, especially women. According to the *World Economic Forum*, digital tools (accounts) can boost women's autonomy and status within a household, offer women greater and easier access to credit, and can access government services (including payments) faster and more efficiently.[18] All these amenities imply great news for economic growth and the reduction of inequality, poverty, and informality. Bryan Zhang, Co-Founder and Executive Director at the Cambridge Centre for Alternative Finance, has stated that "By using digital platforms, women can access capital, engage in crowdfunding and manage their finances with greater ease. This democratization of financial services is levelling the playing field, allowing more female-led businesses to emerge and flourish."[19]

2.3.3 Additional risks of the fintech revolution

In addition to benefits, fintech brings new risks and challenges for consumers, producers, and the wider financial system. We mentioned some risks in earlier subsections. Some other risks include over-indebtedness among poor(er) populations, impediments to future competition (due to sector concentration), potential abuses of power and services by unregulated fintechs, and the marketing of existing and new digital assets to people without basic financial literacy. Therefore, it is possible that the losses from the digital revolution may overshadow the gains that it provides if regulators do not change the way they oversee the financial system. Financial authorities may need a more structured framework to identify fintechs large enough to undermine the health of the financial system and devise plans on how to deal with potential failures of such firms.

A 2018 *KPMG Report* on emerging risks of fintech companies identified the need to address important questions about accountability and regulation, since customer data becomes simultaneously more available and more valuable. In addition, increased dependence on fintech and big data could distance firms from their customers when they need to be closer to them (especially in poor nations) and may result in an ecosystem that can become opaque.[20]

Finally, according to McKinsey & Company research, three trends will shape the next phase of fintech growth. First, fintechs will continue to benefit from the radical digital transformation of the banking industry and e-commerce growth around the world. Second, fintechs still have room to achieve further growth in an expanding financial-services ecosystem. Finally, some fintechs are proving more resilient during the current market correction than others.[21]

We end this section with a look at the relationship between fintech and SWOT analysis—Strengths, Weaknesses, Opportunities, and Threats. Box 13.1 explains how each component of SWOT applies to fintech, either as an industry or as part of a financial institution's evaluation of fintech integration.

Box 13.1

How can fintech relate to SWOT analysis?

STRENGTHS: Fintech companies or financial institutions possess speed and efficiency, cost reduction capabilities, effective customer service (robo-advising), innovation and use of data analytics.

WEAKNESSES: Some limitations fintechs may face are cybersecurity risks, regulatory compliance, lack of trust and profitability pressures.

OPPORTUNITIES: Some external trends or developments that fintechs can leverage include financial inclusion, partnerships with financial institutions, blockchain technology and *regtech growth* (via AI and ML tools).

THREATS: External risks that may affect fintech firms' success or stability include regulatory scrutiny, *bigtech* competition (from Amazon or Google), economic cycles (particularly downturns), cybercrime and fraud and technological obsolescence.

Test your understanding 1

1. What are the differences between Business-to-business (B2B) and Business-to-consumer (B2C)?
2. How can you exploit artificial intelligence (AI) and Machine Learning (ML) in financial services?
3. How can fintech enhance women's status in developing nations?

Summary

- Financial technology (fintech) is the use of technology by companies and financial institutions to deliver financial products and services to people and financial markets.
- Fintech covers a wide range of uses across business-to-business/consumer (B2B, B2C) and peer-to-peer (P2P) markets.
- Some other types include the Internet of Things (IoT), artificial intelligence (AI) and Machine Learning (ML) and Blockchain technology.
- The IoT is a network of real-world devices, gadgets, and appliances that are equipped with sensors, connections, and software to collect and share data online with other devices.
- AI is technology that focuses on creating machines and computers capable of performing tasks that are typically done by humans.
- ML allows computers to learn and make predictions from historical data by training an algorithm.
- Cloud computing is the supply of computer services via the internet (also known as the *cloud*), rather than through local hardware (computers).
- The key relationships between fintech and financial markets are market access and inclusion, capital market efficiency, cross-border payments and currency

markets, disintermediation, market volatility and new asset classes, and regulatory spillovers and financial stability.
- Fintech can play a pivotal role in all sectors of developing economy.
- Fintech offers banking services to people in remote communities, especially women.
- Fintech brings new risks and challenges for consumers, producers, and the wider financial system.

Questions and problems

1. Can you identify some ways that financial technology (fintech) can affect consumer behavior?
2. Can you identify some ways that artificial intelligence (AI) can affect consumer behavior?
3. Do you think that financial technology is making consumers more complacent? What could be some risks?
4. How can central bank digital currencies promote financial inclusion?
5. What is the fintech lending channel of monetary policy?
6. How can fintech affect minority populations worldwide? List some positive and negative effects.
7. Explain some ways that fintech and traditional financial institutions are interconnected. Any implications?
8. How can fintech create financial market volatility?

Notes

1. https://www.mckinsey.com/industries/financial-services/our-insights/fintechs-a-new-paradigm-of-growth.
2. https://www.docuclipper.com/blog/fintech-statistics/#:~:text=Top%20Fintech%20Statistics&text=There%20are%20now%20over%2030%2C000,deals%2C%20the%20highest%20ever%20recorded.
3. https://www.ecb.europa.eu/press/fie/box/html/ecb.fiebox202406_08.en.html
4. https://www.mckinsey.com/industries/financial-services/our-insights/fintech-in-menap-a-solid-foundation-for-growth
5. https://www.iadb.org/en/news/study-fintech-ecosystem-latin-america-and-caribbean-exceeds-3000-startups
6. https://www.ibm.com/think/topics/artificial-intelligence#:~:text=Program%20Manager-,What%20is%20AI?,and%20respond%20to%20human%20language.
7. https://www.ibm.com/think/topics/artificial-intelligence#:~:text=Automation%20of%20repetitive%20tasks.,automating%20processes%20without%20human%20intervention.
8. https://www.ibm.com/think/topics/blockchain#:~:text=Blockchain%20is%20a%20shared%2C%20immutable,making%20it%20resistant%20to%20tampering.
9. https://corporatefinanceinstitute.com/resources/career/what-is-insurtech/#:~:text=InsurTech%2C%20short%20for%20%E2%80%9Cinsurance%20technology,automate%20the%20traditional%20insurance%20industry.
10. https://www.worldbank.org/en/news/press-release/2018/08/23/world-bank-prices-first-global-blockchain-bond-raising-a110-million
11. Franco, Lavinia (2024). The Fintech Lending Channel of Monetary Policy. ECB (October 7).

12. Erel, Isil, Jack Liebersohn, Constantine Yannelis, and Samuel Earnest (2023). Monetary Policy Transmission Through Online Banks, ECB (April 25).
13. https://www.remitfinder.com/money-transfer-providers-Wise/pr/transferwise
14. https://www.forbes.com/uk/advisor/banking/revolut-review/
15. http://www.fsb.org/2017/06/financial-stability-implications-from-fintech/
16. https://www.mdpi.com/journal/fintech/special_issues/5PKAF5E8TF
17. https://www.weforum.org/stories/2020/11/sustainable-digital-finance-low-carbon-economy/
18. https://www.weforum.org/stories/2024/02/fintech-growth-customer-demand/
19. https://www.weforum.org/stories/2024/02/fintech-growth-customer-demand/
20. https://assets.kpmg.com/content/dam/kpmgsites/uk/pdf/2019/02/emerging-risks-and-evolving-responses.pdf
21. https://www.mckinsey.com/featured-insights/mckinsey-explainers/what-is-fintech

References

Afshan, Sahar, Ken Yien Leong, Arsalan Najmi, Ummara Razi, Bawani Lelchumanan, Calvin Wing Hoh Cheong (2024). Fintech Advancements for Financial Resilience: Analysing Exchange Rates and Digital Currencies During Oil and Financial Risk. *Resources Policy* 88, 104432. https://doi.org/10.1016/j.resourpol.2023.104432.

Anagnostopoulos, Ioannis (2018). Fintech and Regtech: Impact on Regulators and Banks *Journal of Economics and Business* 100, 7–25, 10.1016.

Benoit, S., J.E. Colliard, C. Hurlin, and C. Pérignon (2017). Where the Risks Lie: A Survey on Systemic Risk. *Review of Finance* 21(1), 109–152.

Berg, Tobias. Andreas Fuster, and Manju Puri (2022). FinTech Lending. *Annual Review of Financial Economics* 14, 187–207. http://dx.doi.org/10.1146/annurev-financial-101521-112042.

Carlini, Federico, Belinda Laura Del Gaudio, Claudio Porzio, and Daniele Previtali (2022). Banks, FinTech and Stock Returns. *Finance Research Letters* 45, 102252. https://doi.org/10.1016/j.frl.2021.102252.

Hasan, Rashedul, M. Kabir Hassan, and Sirajo Aliyu (2020). Fintech and Islamic Finance: Literature Review and Research Agenda. *International Journal of Islamic Economics and Finance* 1(2), 75–94.

He, Dong, Ross B Leckow, V. Haksar, Tommaso Mancini-Griffoli, Nigel Jenkinson, Mikari Kashima, Tanai Khiaonarong, Celine Rochon, and Hervé Tourpe (2017). Fintech and Financial Services: Initial Considerations. International Monetary Fund. *Staff discussion notes* no. 17/05.

Jagtiani, Julapa and Catharine Lemieux (2018). Do Fintech Lenders Penetrate Areas that Are Underserved by Traditional Banks? *Journal of Economics and Business* 100(C), 43–54.

Kommel, Karl Arnold, Martin Sillasoo, and Agnes Lubloy (2019). Could Crowdsourced Financial Analysis Replace the Equity Research by Investment Banks? *Finance Research Letters* 29, 280–284. https://doi.org/10.1016/j.frl.2018.08.007.

Lee, In and Yong Jae Shin (2018). Fintech: Ecosystem, Business Models, Investment Decisions, and Challenges. *Business Horizons* 61(1), 35–46. https://doi.org/10.1016/j.bushor.2017.09.003.

Li, Jianping, Jingyu Li, Xiaoqian Zhu, Yinhong Yao, and Barbara Casu (2020). Risk Spillovers Between FinTech and Traditional Financial Institutions:

Evidence from the US. *International Review of Financial Analysis* 71, 101544. https://doi.org/10.1016/j.irfa.2020.101544.

Qudah, Hanan, Sari Malahim, Rula Airout, Mohammad Alomari, Aiman Abu Hamour, and Mohammad Alqudah (2023). Islamic Finance in the Era of Financial Technology: A Bibliometric Review of Future Trends. *International Journal of Financial Studies* 11, 76. https://doi.org/10.3390/ijfs11020076.

Saklain, Md Sohel (2024). FinTech, Systemic Risk and Bank Market Power – Australian Perspective. *International Review of Financial Analysis* 95 (Part A), 103351. https://doi.org/10.1016/j.irfa.2024.103351.

Song, Yi and Yuqing Hao (2024). Understanding the Relationship Between Fintech, Natural Resources, Green Finance, and Environmental Sustainability in China: A BARDL Approach. *Resources Policy* 89, 104608.

Tang, Pengzhu, Houyun Ma, Yuanyuan Sun, and Xiaowan Xu (2024). Exploring the Role of Fintech, Green Finance and Natural Resources towards Environmental Sustainability: A Study on ASEAN Economies. *Resources Policy* 94, 105115. https://doi.org/10.1016/j.resourpol.2024.105115.

Udeagha, Maxwell Chukwudi and Nicholas Ngepah (2023). The Drivers of Environmental Sustainability in BRICS Economies: Do Green Finance and Fintech Matter? *World Development Sustainability* 3, 100096.

Zhang, Zan, Ken Hung and Tsangyao Chang (2017). P2P Loans and Bank Loans, the Chicken and the Egg, What Causes What?: Further Evidence from a Bootstrap Panel Granger Causality Test. *Applied Economics Letters* 24(19), 1358–1362.

Chapter 14

Global risks affecting the financial markets

Introduction

Global financial markets face a variety of risks that can impact their stability and performance. These risks are interconnected and often influenced by geopolitical events, economic policies, technological advancements, natural disasters and more. In the next section, we will explore these and more global risk factors that impact the financial markets. In general, global risks create higher volatility and declining financial asset prices as investors react to heightened uncertainty and risk. In addition, such risks raise borrowing costs (for all market agents) which embed risk premiums. Individual and institutional investors, during times of uncertainty, may engage in herd(ing) behavior, whereby they sell or buy assets as a group. This can also lead to a flight to safety or flight to quality, where investors shift to safer assets like US Treasury bonds and gold. Global risks can propagate across international financial markets through merchandise trade and financial linkages, potentially leading to financial instability, especially when economic and financial crises hit multiple countries simultaneously.

So, how would the financial markets respond to global risks? Investors, for example, attempt to price such risks into equity and option markets, but the uncertainties surrounding these events can lead to sudden, sharp reactions when they actually take place. Financial institutions and government authorities implement stress testing and scenario analyses to identify, quantify, and manage the potential impacts of global risks.

According to the IMF's 2025 *Global Financial Stability Report*, global financial stability risks have increased significantly, driven by tighter global financial conditions, heightened trade and geopolitical uncertainty. Their assessment is supported by three important challenges: (1) valuations remain high in some key markets; (2) highly leveraged financial institutions and their relationship with banking systems; and (3) risks of market turmoil and challenges to debt sustainability for highly indebted sovereigns. The top two global risks that markets consider are

DOI: 10.4324/9781003677161-18

State-based armed conflicts (proxy wars, civil wars, coups, terrorism, etc.) and extreme weather events. Furthermore, the report indicates that major geopolitical risk events can trigger a significant decline in stock prices and raise sovereign risk premiums, as mentioned earlier, thereby posing a potential threat to macro-financial stability.[1] It is interesting to mention that, according to the same report, 31% of the respondents anticipate turbulence for the next two years (2027) and an impressive 45% of them for the next 10 years. Both proportions have risen since last year.

Before we turn to the discussion of the various global risks, it is worth casting a critical look at the recent political developments in the US, following Donald Trump's return to the Presidency. One of Trump's key policy instruments was trade policy which culminated with the announcement of extensive tariffs on its trading partners beginning on April 2, 2025. As was expected, this announcement resulted in pronounced sessions of financial market stress in the days that followed. The *volatility index* (*VIX*), a widely recognized metric for investors' fear about uncertainty, which measures market expectation of short-term volatility conveyed by stock index option prices, rose sharply, reflecting an acute rise in uncertainty and heightened risk aversion among investors (see Figure 14.1). As you can see from the graph, the VIX rose a lot during the 2007/2008 global financial crisis (to above 60 points) and during the 2020 COVID-19 global health pandemic.

Typically, global risk-off episodes trigger safe-haven flows (what we named flight to safety earlier) into safe bonds (like US Treasuries) and currencies (the Swiss franc). In the past, such flows tended to temporarily lower yields on high quality sovereign bonds such as US Treasuries and/or German Bunds, while the US dollar and other safe-haven currencies typically appreciated. Furthermore, in the months that followed the April 2025 events, markets experienced another, albeit smaller and short-lived episode of uncertainty because of the escalation of the conflict in the Middle East.[2] Contrary to the April event, however, this adverse geopolitical risk event witnessed a slight appreciation of the US dollar.

Global financial markets have gone through sustained fundamental shifts, gradually integrating individual investors into the financial landscape. This transformation has reshaped how markets operate, establishing more accessible ways for

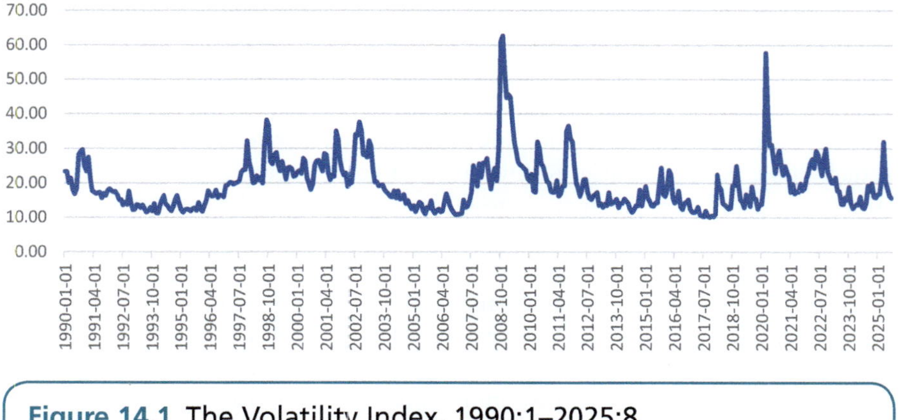

Figure 14.1 The Volatility Index, 1990:1–2025:8

Data source: Federal Reserve Economic Data

individuals to participate in activities traditionally reserved for institutional and professional investors. In the last section, we discuss how retail investors cope with the increasing complexity of the global money and capital markets.

1 Global risks and their implications for financial markets

This section lists and discusses the various global risks and traces the impacts of each one of them on the global financial markets. The analysis includes academic and practitioner research papers as well as other articles from global organizations.

1.1 Geopolitical risks

Broadly speaking, geopolitical risks are risks that arise from the interactions between or among countries which generate economic and financial instability. Interactions or relationships among countries include international trade, territorial disputes, supply chains and more. Elevated tensions among countries hurt stock markets, raise government borrowing costs, and pose risks to financial stability. For example, (armed) conflicts and regional wars such as the ongoing wars in Ukraine and the Middle East disrupt trade, energy supplies, and investor confidence, leading to market volatility. Also, political instability such as uncertainty in governments or sudden political/regime changes can destabilize markets, especially in emerging economies. Finally, trade wars including tariffs, sanctions, and protectionist policies can disrupt global supply chains, raising costs and affecting business profitability.

According to Chapter 2 of the IMF's 2025 *Global Stability Report* (mentioned on p. 371), geopolitical tensions also affect cross-border investments. These, in turn, hurt asset prices, negatively weigh on financial institutions, and curb lending to the private sector, thus posing a threat to economic and financial stability. The Report found that the average monthly drop in stock prices is about 1 percentage point across countries, but a much larger 2.5 percentage points in emerging market economies. In addition, the increase in sovereign risk premiums, as measured by prices for credit derivatives that protect against default, after geopolitical events was, on average, by about 30 basis points for advanced economies and 45 basis points for emerging market economies.[3]

An important step in understanding geopolitical risks is the construction of geopolitical risk indices by several researchers. One prominent index is that by Caldara and Iacoviello (2022).[4] According to the authors, their geopolitical risk index (GPR) "is based on searches of the archives of 10 newspapers: *Chicago Tribune*, the *Daily Telegraph*, *Financial Times*, *The Globe and Mail*, *The Guardian*, the *Los Angeles Times*, *The New York Times*, *USA Today*, *The Wall Street Journal*, and *The Washington Post*." The authors counted the number of articles related to negative geopolitical events in each newspaper for each month and expressed it as a share of the total number of news articles. Furthermore, the authors arranged the results of their search in eight categories: "Category1: War Threats; Category 2: Peace Threats; Category 3: Military Buildups; Category 4: Nuclear Threats; Category 5: Terror Threats; Category 6: Beginning of War; Category 7: Escalation of War; Category 8: Terror Acts". The main index's sub-indexes are the Geopolitical Threats (GPRT) index, which includes words from categories 1 to 5, and the Geopolitical Acts (GPRA) index, which includes words belonging to the remaining three categories.

Figure 14.2 shows the GPR index (Panel A) and its two components (Panel B) using data from January 2000 to August 2025.[5] We can clearly see the spikes in the main index during the early 2000s and 2020s. The main reasons for the 2000s spikes were the September 11 (9/11) 2000 terrorist attacks in the United States and the 2003 invasion of Iraq afterwards. The spikes in the early 2020s were due to the invasion of Russia into Ukraine and the smaller spikes in the index in the next couple of years were due to the Middle East conflict. Similar spikes are seen in the two components of the GPR index – threats and acts – shown in Panel B. In addition, you may observe higher turbulence in the threats sub-index compared to the acts sub-index during some periods and the reverse during other periods. It is assumed that geopolitical threats worry investors more than

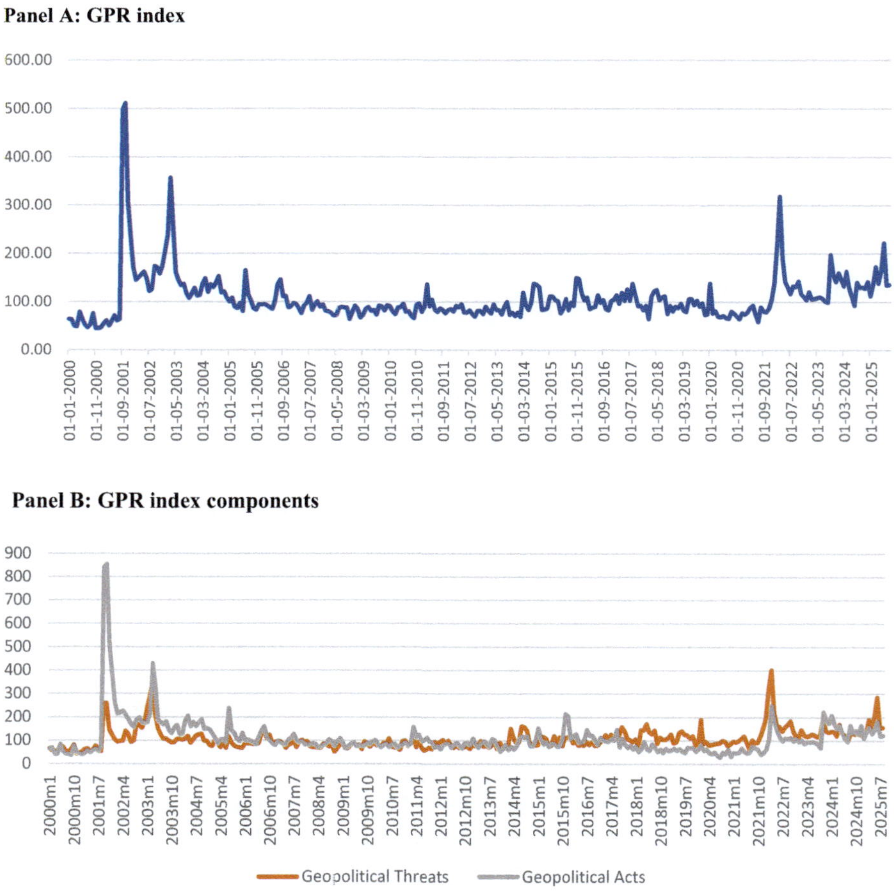

Figure 14.2 Geopolitical risk index and components
Data source: Caldara and Iacoviello's website (https://www.matteoiacoviello.com/gpr.htm)

acts since there is greater uncertainty around a threat which may or may not actually materialize.

It is important to state that the index is not complete in revealing the full spectrum of geopolitical risks, which may well be associated with other global threats such as climate change, water reserves and food security, cyber warfare, infectious diseases, technological advancements and more. According to a 2025 *S&P Global* Report, geopolitical risks have a significant impact on the global economic outlook, influencing economic growth, inflation, global financial markets, as well as global supply chains.[6] The same source classifies geopolitical risks into seven categories (political, economic, environmental, regulatory, cyber, security and competition for resources).

There is significant empirical academic work of the impact of geopolitical risks on the economy, financial markets and institutions, corporate policy, commodities and more. Some recent papers are those that examined the impact of geopolitics on stock markets (Agoraki et al., 2022), stock market volatility and spillovers (Zhang et al., 2023; and Salachas et al., 2024), the economy (Behn et al., 2025), corporate policy (Adra et al., 2023; Chowdhury et al., 2025), central banks (Salachas et al., 2025), commodities (Aizenman et al., 2024), and energy markets (Liu et al., 2025).

1.2 Economic and systemic risks

Economic (or macro) risks include recessions and economic slowdowns, at the regional and country levels, such as that of the 2008 financial crisis. Economic risks can lead to reduced consumer spending, falling corporate profits, and widespread unemployment, all of which hurt financial markets. Related risks include interest rates, inflation and currency depreciations. High inflation erodes purchasing power, leads to higher interest rates, and can cause market volatility, especially in emerging markets. High sovereign and corporate debt, especially in emerging markets, raises default risks when interest rates rise. Weakening demand in the US, Europe, or China ripples through trade, commodities, and capital markets.

Central banks raising interest rates to control inflation (e.g., the Fed, the Bank of England or the European Central Bank) can lead to lower asset prices, a higher cost of capital, and slower economic growth. Persistent inflation pressures can lead central banks (like the Fed, ECB, BoJ) to tighten monetary policy, raising borrowing costs and reducing liquidity. Finally, a sudden devaluation of a major currency (such as the US dollar, euro, or Chinese yuan) can create instability in foreign exchange markets and impact multinational companies.

Systemic risks refer to financial crises, global market liquidity squeezes and sovereign debt crises. For example, a collapse or failure of

THE GLOBAL SAVINGS GLUT

A global savings glut occurs when the desired global supply of savings exceeds the global demand for investment, leading to a surplus of capital. This, in turn, reduces interest rates and contributes to global financial imbalances. An actual situation was in 2005, when some nations had large savings, driven by their aging populations and weak local investments.

major financial institutions (e.g., banks or hedge funds) can lead to a loss of confidence in the entire financial system, as was seen during the 2008 global financial crisis. In times of crisis, markets may experience reduced liquidity, where assets cannot be sold or bought easily without significant price changes, leading to panic selling. Would more savings then be better for countries and the economy? The nearby *sidebar* explains that this may not actually be the case. Excessive national (sovereign) or corporate debt, not just in developing economies, can lead to defaults and subsequent credit crises (as in many European countries in the 2010s), destabilizing both local and global markets. A famous case in point is the European sovereign debt crisis of the 2010s which almost cost the breakup of the European Union.

> Some of the consequences of this savings glut were the housing bubble in the US, financial meltdowns (following asset bubbles) and reduced economic growth.
>
> Jørgensen, P.L. (2023). The Global Savings Glut and the Housing Boom. *Journal of Economic Dynamics and Control* 146, 104563. https://doi.org/10.1016/j.jedc.2022.104563.
>
> https://www.federalreserve.gov/boarddocs/speeches/2005/200503102/.

1.3 Environmental risks

Environmental risks refer to climatic changes such as extreme weather events, sea-level rise, natural disasters such as earthquakes, floods, and other natural events and human-induced risks such as pollution and deforestation. Such risks can disrupt supply chains, reduce agricultural output, and increase costs for businesses. Investors are increasingly focused on environmental risks (through ESG investing, for example). Environmental risks can have wider effects such as ecological damage, health issues and socio-economic consequences. For example, such risks can lead to loss of species, destruction of habitats, and damage to ecosystems. Furthermore, exposure to pollutants or poor environmental conditions can increase the risk of noncommunicable diseases and other health problems. Finally, environmental risks can cause water scarcity, food insecurity, involuntary migration, and economic losses.

1.4 Technological risks

Technological risks refer to potential adverse effects on an organization resulting from failures or inappropriate use of its technology systems, infrastructure, and data. Such risks, however, go beyond the organizations' control and include cybersecurity threats or attacks targeting firms, financial institutions or markets, and innovations like artificial intelligence (AI), blockchain, or cryptocurrency activities. All above risks can lead to the loss of sensitive data, financial fraud, and disruptions to the operations of global financial systems. Technological disruptions could also bring uncertainty, especially regarding regulation and systemic risk.

1.5 Behavioral risks

Apart from market risks, there are also market sentiment and investor behavioral risks as well as psychological factors risks. For example, mass panic selling, speculative bubbles, or irrational exuberance (e.g., the 2000 dot-com bubble or the late 2010s cryptocurrency hype) can create large market fluctuations. In addition, investors following trends or mimicking the actions of others (known as "herding behavior") can create volatility, particularly in smaller markets or niche assets. Finally, fear or (excessive) euphoria can drive markets away from their fundamental values, thereby creating instability.

1.6 Regulatory and legal risks

Global changes in regulation and taxation policies by nations and non-compliance entail such risks for the global financial markets. For instance, new regulations or changes in existing laws (e.g., tighter financial regulations after the 2008 crisis) can impact how businesses operate, which can, in turn, affect market performance. Changes in taxation (e.g., higher corporate taxes or wealth taxes) also can influence investor sentiment and corporate behavior. Such risks can potentially threaten businesses leading to financial losses, operational disruptions, reputational damage, and litigation. Legal risks typically involve non-adherence to existing laws and contractual obligations. Effective management of these risks requires proactive compliance, robust contract management, legal counsel, and integration into enterprise risk management (ERM) frameworks to ensure business resilience and continuity.

1.7 Sociocultural risks

Demographic shifts such as aging populations in developed countries can lead to slower economic growth, changing consumer preferences, and increased social spending. In addition, social unrest (protests, labor strikes, or civil disturbances) generate market instability and impact investor confidence. Poverty, inequality, poor access to healthcare and education, the erosion of social cohesion, negative stereotypes, and resistance to change, can all affect business success, public health, and the sustainability of communities. Some key aspects of sociocultural risks are societal structures (organization), cultural practices and beliefs (religious and traditional customs), and behavioral patterns (on consumption and new policies), and diversity and inclusion (racism and gender inequality).

1.8 Other global risks

These include health crises (pandemics), supply-chain disruptions and a multipolar world. The COVID-19 pandemic demonstrated how a global health crisis can disrupt economies, supply chains, and entire industries (e.g., travel, hospitality). The financial markets reacted with massive asset sell-offs followed by unprecedented government interventions. Events like these, regional wars/conflicts, piracy or natural disasters can severely disrupt supply chains, leading to shortages, increased prices, and production delays. These disruptions hurt global trade and economic growth. Disruptions in oil, gas, and electricity supply, either from geopolitical issues or natural disasters, can significantly affect financial markets and economies worldwide. Finally, the structural/economic shifts in many nations in forming new alliances or blocks [such as The Global South, which refers to a group of nations located in Africa, Latin America, Asia (excluding developed nations)] and Oceania (excluding Australia and New Zealand), the expanding of existing (BRICS+, OPEC+) blocs, the US–China rivalry, the emergence of Asia, and the rising trend of invoicing commodities outside the US dollar all suggest a multi-polar (or de-globalized) world.

2 Short- and long-term risks and their consequences

In this section, we will categorize the above-mentioned risks into short-term and long-term and trace the implications on the global economy and global financial markets. In doing so, we will identify the financial instruments that will be affected by these risks and determine where financial markets are mostly vulnerable or opportunistic.

2.1 Short-term global shocks

Short-term shocks typically last for a couple of years maximum (at the country level) and include macroeconomic and financial shocks. These risks trigger sudden market volatility and immediate repricing of assets. As mentioned on p. 375, sticky inflation and interest rates force central banks to act by keeping rates higher longer, thus hitting equity valuations and bond markets. You know that when interest rates increase, stock prices go down. There are also recession fears since weak consumer demand and slowing global trade raise risk of synchronized slowdown. Furthermore, emerging markets or highly leveraged corporates could face defaults if the US dollar remains strong. For example, at the retail investor level, as of September 20, 2025, the USD/EUR exchange rate was 0.85 Euros (per $1). This means that an American investor would be hesitant to convert dollars into euros because of this unfavorable exchange rate. However, a European investor may find it worthwhile to convert euros into dollars because they would exchange 0.85 of euro and receive $1.

Ongoing political and geopolitical shocks cause disruptions in global energy and grain markets, crude oil supplies and blockages of shipping routes (e.g., in the Red Sea and the Bab al-Mandab strait). Elections and political volatility in many advanced nations (the US, Germany, Italy and many more) generate global market instability. On market systemic risks, global private equity investors are facing a growing liquidity crunch as capital remains tied up in aging portfolios. This is part of the worldwide liquidity crunch that affects many countries as high interest rates cause higher debt-servicing costs and debt redemptions. According to the 2024 IMF Blog, higher interest payments and debt redemptions are stifling economic growth, employment and countries' public finances. This comes at a time when countries need critical investment to achieve sustainable economic growth and adapt to climate change. These liquidity pressures, if left unanswered, could lead to solvency problems for many vulnerable countries.[7]

The presence (and emergence of even more) external shocks from extreme weather such as hurricanes, droughts, or floods can disrupt agriculture and insurance. Although financial institutions have coped with extreme weather events before, this time the response to such events is different. First, the financial institutions are now global and complex and have affiliates or branches in many parts of the word. This implies that their exposure to such extreme events is higher than before. Second, the risk of physical damage to these financial institutions' fixed assets is real. The financial sector is nowadays affected by two key risk drivers: *physical risk* (destruction of crops, houses and agricultural infrastructure) and *transition risk* (the transition from a fossil-fuel-based economy to one powered by clean energy).

Finally, we should not forget cyberattacks, which disrupt exchanges, payment systems, or financial data. According to *Moody's Financial Cyber Risk Analysis Report*,

> The exponential rise of cyberattacks and ransomware has serious ramifications for businesses globally — costing them billions of dollars in losses, and threatening their long-term stability. The imperative for business leaders and boards to assess, quantify, and insure their cyber risk is clear. However, without a reliable means to measure cybersecurity risk, organizations are exposed to risks arising from customer, supplier, and partner relationships that are integrated into their ecosystems.[8]

Let us now map the short-term shocks to the asset classes they impact most so we can see where financial markets are weaker or stronger. Short-term shocks (e.g., geopolitical events, policy surprises, natural disasters, sudden market sentiment shifts) typically cause volatility spikes that hit certain financial assets more severely. Here are the main vulnerable asset classes and the reasons why.

The small-cap stocks appear to be more sensitive to funding constraints and investor risk aversion. They often lack global diversification, so they are hit harder by localized or even external shocks. For example, when the Russia–Ukraine war broke out, European equities (especially small caps and banks) witnessed sharp sell-offs (the Eurostoxx 50 index fell by approximately 15% in weeks) due to their direct exposure to war, sanctions, and energy dependence. Emerging market equities are also vulnerable to capital outflows when global risk sentiment worsens. Broad declines (such as the MSCI Emerging Markets index) dropped substantially due to capital flight to safe assets and uncertainty on global growth. Also, exchange rate volatility amplified losses as well. The Turkish lira, the Brazilian reai, the Russian ruble and the South African rand have all collapsed by more than 50% since the 2022 Russia–Ukraine war. Investors, additionally, quickly unwind during risk-off shocks, as they rush to safe haven currencies (USD, JPY, CHF). Finally, cyclical sectors (such as energy, airlines, and financials) quickly react to oil price spikes, interest rate shifts, or policy announcements.

Bonds also respond to short-term shocks. High-yield (junk) bonds and emerging markets sovereign debt respond by widening credit spreads as investors demand higher risk premiums (due to uncertainty) and flee to safe-haven bonds (US Treasuries, German Bunds). Long-duration bonds are more sensitive to sudden changes in interest rate expectations. Commodities (oil, industrial metals, and agricultural) are very sensitive to short-term shocks as well, and exhibit spikes on wars, geopolitics- and weather-driven events.

In sum, financial assets respond to short-term external shocks, such as interest rate changes or global risk aversion, by repricing and potentially triggering capital flows and exchange rate volatility. For example, a positive shock like a capital inflow can appreciate a domestic currency, while a capital outflow can lead to depreciation and a drop in asset prices. Both effects can potentially threaten financial stability. Inflows can lead to domestic asset appreciation and accelerated credit growth, but also raise concerns about a loss of competitiveness. Outflows can have the opposite effect, causing asset price declines and a sharp tightening of financial conditions. These events can also impact lending, investment, and overall economic output, with the specific impact depending on the asset class, the nature of the shock, and the country's financial structure. More specifically, an increase in short-term interest rates can lead to a contraction in the banks' total assets and investment funds, a persistent decline in lending to corporations and other financial institutions, and reduced investment demand. A broad shift in global risk aversion, like the one during the global health pandemic, can trigger capital outflows from emerging economies, leading to sharper currency depreciations and a tightening of domestic financial conditions.

What are some of the transmission channels regarding capital (in and out) flows? First, we have the credit channel where increases in short-term interest rates can lead to a negative and persistent decline in lending to non-financial corporations and other financial institutions, affecting their balance sheets. Second, the balance sheet channel, whereby external shocks can impact the profitability of banks, leading to higher leverage, may be at work. Third, the exchange rate channel occurs when shocks can cause exchange rate movements that affect the competitiveness of an economy and influence the cost of imports and exports. Finally, other potential channels of turbulence (or volatility) transmission may be at play such as currency and interest rate derivatives, which have grown significantly since the 2007/2008 global financial crisis.

2.2 Long-term risks

Long-term (structural) risks are those that last more than two years and entail structural or fundamental shifts. These risks evolve slowly but reshape markets fundamentally. For starters, the demographic and social country structures such as aging populations and migration and inequality are long-term risks. The former risk alters savings, pensions, and healthcare costs in advanced economies, whereas the latter causes great political instability affecting fiscal policy and globalization in these countries. A case in point are the (illegal and undocumented) migration (refugee) waves in (Southern) Europe from Africa and the Middle East since 2022 due to the existing (and continuing) regional conflicts and unrest (including poverty and inequality). Southern European countries (Greece, Italy, and Malta, primarily) are greatly affected by such flows. The cost is tremendous on infrastructure, and the financial pressures on smaller countries extraordinary. The problem is aggravated by the fact that many of these migrants do not seek employment in these countries (they are also asylum seekers) but intend to go deeper into Europe.

The climate and energy transition moves represent long-term risks. When countries apply decarbonization policies (imposing carbon taxes, prefer ESG investing, and regulatory pressures), this shifts capital away from fossil fuels and fundamentally alters the productive nature of resources at home. Greater investment in renewables, in an effort to secure energy efficiency and security, but reliance on critical minerals (lithium, cobalt) creates new supply risks. In general, climate and modern energy policies involve massive structural economic changes that risk causing job displacement, increased energy costs, financial instability from traditional investments, and disruptions to international trade and competitiveness, particularly for economies reliant on carbon-intensive industries. Financially speaking, countries may face investment gaps (or insufficient investment) in green infrastructure and technologies, which can hinder the clean energy transition. Also, limited access to capital for green energy investments, particularly for emerging market and developing economies, can impede decarbonization efforts and increase financial risks. Finally, structural economic changes during the transition period can affect the interest rate, thus requiring monetary policymakers to adapt to the new situation.

Technological and structural advancements such as artificial intelligence contribute to productivity boost but disruptions of labor markets and potential concentration of wealth are potential risks. The wider use of digital finance (cryptocurrencies) and the issuance of rival means of global payments including central bank digital currencies (CBDCs) fundamentally change the financial landscape and may cause volatility and uncertainty. Furthermore, the risks that come with that are cyberattacks and other fraudulent schemes, all of which create persistent vulnerability of the global financial infrastructure. Finally, geopolitical realignment in view of new country alliances, the ongoing decoupling in tech, trade, and financial flows and new preferences in reserve currencies, all lead to greater fragmentation of global capital markets.

In general, while short-term shocks cause volatility spikes in most of the financial assets, long-term structural risks determine strategic asset allocation not just for an investor's asset portfolio but also for a country's economic and financial infrastructure.

3 Retail investors and global risks

In this section we answer the following question: How do retail investors cope with global financial risks when dealing with the financial markets? The general answer is that retail investors can cope with global financial risks by diversifying their portfolios across different assets and geographic regions, adopting a long-term investment horizon, investing money they will not need in the short term, staying informed about market conditions, and managing emotional responses to crowd behavior and market volatility. For greater support, investors can also consider consulting a financial advisor and developing a comprehensive financial plan. More specifically, individual investors can address the following concerns.

First, apply appropriate portfolio management strategies relying on the diversification principle. Investors should spread investments across various asset classes, industries, and countries to reduce the impact of a downturn in one specific area.

The consequence of that would be higher expected return and lower risk. We have been mentioning this principle in many chapters in this textbook.

Second, start with the first step in the investment process: asset allocation. Recall that the second step is security selection. More precisely, be concerned with strategic asset allocation (as opposed to tactical asset allocation, which involves fine-tuning your objective in the short-run, see Chapter 2) so as to balance volatile assets, such as growth stocks, with more conservative choices like bonds and short-term investments. Strategic asset allocation protects you from making (unwise) temporary trades since it disciplines you and focuses on prioritizing long-term goals and aligning the asset mix with your risk tolerance and investment horizon.

Third, implement hedging techniques, if possible or applicable, by investing in assets that are expected to move in the opposite direction of your other investments to protect against losses. Perhaps, you could do your own financial analysis to identify those investment instruments that have the smallest correlation with the other assets in your portfolio for inclusion. In previous chapters, we mentioned such instruments (commodities, real estate, precious metals and so on) but you could uncover a few more. (Do not get your hopes high, though, in this highly integrated and connected world!) Furthermore, implement regular risk assessment by continuously assessing your investment risk to ensure it aligns with your goals and comfort level.

Fourth, it is important to maintain a sound behavioral and long-term approach by focusing on your own long-term financial goals, as a short-term view can lead to emotional decisions that are detrimental to investment performance. Also, avoid emotional investing and thus try to recognize and manage emotional impulses, like panic (selling) during market downturns, to maintain rational decision-making. Be smart about it and do not follow the herd! Invest in only for the long run assuming that you do not need funds in the near future, as this allows you to weather market volatility and avoid being forced to sell during a dip.

Finally, if you cannot manage most of your finances, hire a professional, seek guidance from a financial adviser who can help create a financial plan tailored to your goals, risk tolerance, and overall financial situation. Be aware that some money/portfolio managers may get you to alter your objective which may not actually align with what you really want. Be firm and challenge alternative advice. By hiring a professional you can leverage more resources including those provided by regulatory bodies, financial institutions, and investment platforms to stay informed.

In the World Economic Forum's 2024 *Global Retail Investor Survey* four structural shifts shaping individual financial behaviors, preferences and market activity are identified.[9] These are: new wave of retail investors; market volatility and cycles; innovations in financial products and platforms; and artificial intelligence. The survey (based on the 2022 survey) also revealed significant gaps in investor educations, trust and access to products, forcing calls to action for authorities and industry. Furthermore, retail investors have made substantial inroads into what was the exclusive space of professionals in the past thus enabling them to see a wider picture and make more informed decisions.

We end this chapter with a very general question: Which global risks affect a company's management and marketing functions (activities, operations)? The obvious answer is all of those we mentioned above can affect these (and more) functions of a company, but can we be a bit more specific? Box 14.1 attempts to answer this sub-question.

Box 14.1

Which functions of a firm's management and marketing are impacted most by global risks?

STRATEGY: Economic and market risks (aside from the typical ones such as recessions, inflation, currency fluctuations, energy prices and the like), technological advances, globalization and external events all affect a company's strategy and may make it harder for the company to achieve market leadership.

OPERATIONS: Macroeconomic, derivatives and commodities markets risks create challenges for a firm's operations including financial planning, cost management and market access; additional government-imposed risks such as politics, tariffs, sanctions etc. can disrupt a firm's (global) operations.

COMPETITION: Technological advancements, supply chain disruptions, social and environmental risks can impact a firm's competitive advantage through declines in production efficiency, logistic bottlenecks, resource scarcity, labor strife and unrest, and many more; the end result would be their negative impact on the company's bottom line.

Test your understanding 1

1. Where would investors shift their investments when there is turbulence in some parts of world that could have wider financial and economic implications? What could happen to some major exchange rates?
2. What are systemic risks? Name a couple and trace their implications.
3. What are some of the transmission channels of capital in- and out-flows?

Summary

- Global financial markets face a variety of risks that can impact their stability and performance.
- Global risks create higher volatility and declining financial asset prices as investors react to heightened uncertainty and risk.
- Such risks raise borrowing costs (for all market agents) which embed risk premiums.
- Individual and institutional investors, during times of uncertainty, may engage in herd(ing) behavior, whereby they sell or buy assets as a group.
- This can lead to a flight to safety or flight to quality, where investors shift to safer assets like US Treasury bonds and gold.
- Global risks can propagate across international financial markets through merchandise trade and financial linkages, potentially leading to financial instability, especially when economic and financial crises hit multiple countries simultaneously.
- Geopolitical risks are risks that arise from the interactions between or among countries which generate economic and financial instability.

- Economic (or macro) risks include recessions and economic slowdowns, at the regional and country levels.
- Environmental risks refer to climatic changes such as extreme weather events, sea-level rise, natural disasters such as earthquakes, floods, and other natural events and human-induced risks such as pollution and deforestation.
- Technological risks refer to potential adverse effects on an organization resulting from failures or inappropriate use of its technology systems, infrastructure, and data.
- Behavioral risks refer to those about market sentiment and investor behavioral risk as well as psychological factors risks.
- Global changes in regulation and taxation policies by nations and non-compliance entail such risks for the global financial markets.
- Demographic shifts such as aging populations in developed countries can lead to slower economic growth, changing consumer preferences, and increased social spending.
- Other global risks include health crises (pandemics), supply-chain disruptions and a multi-polar world.
- Short-term shocks typically last for a couple of years maximum and include macroeconomic and financial shocks, which trigger sudden market volatility and immediate repricing of assets.
- Long-term or structural risks are those that last more than two years and entail structural or fundamental shifts, which evolve slowly but reshape markets fundamentally.
- Retail investors can cope with global financial risks by diversifying their portfolios across different assets and geographic regions, adopting a long-term investment horizon, investing money they will not need in the short term, staying informed about market conditions, and managing emotional responses to crowd behavior and market volatility.

Questions and problems

1. How can financial stress in the foreign exchange markets spill over to financial assets? Are debt-ridden and emerging countries more or less vulnerable to such stress?
2. How do higher tariffs affect the global economy and global financial markets?
3. Which would be more relevant to investors? Short-term volatility in financial markets (say, following the bombing of Israeli/US on Iran) or long-term, structural changes (fundamentals) such as the COVID-19 health pandemic?
4. Explain how technological advancements and disruptions can create both new opportunities and risks for investors.
5. A June 3, 2025, OECD Economic *Outlook* Report, titled "Global Economic Outlook Shifts as Trade Policy Uncertainty Weakens Growth", found that "global economic prospects are weakening, with substantial barriers to trade, tighter financial conditions, diminishing confidence and heightened policy uncertainty projected to have adverse impacts on growth". Can you think of some risks that could validate these findings?
6. How can global uncertainty affect investors worldwide? Comment on investor behavior and their preferences between advanced and emerging economies.

Notes

1. https://www.imf.org/en/Publications/GFSR/Issues/2025/04/22/global-financial-stability-report-april-2025
2. At the time of writing, a historic peace agreement was signed by Israel and Hamas (to terminate the war in Gaza) through the auspices of the US President and some Arab nations.
3. https://www.imf.org/en/Blogs/Articles/2025/04/14/how-rising-geopolitical-risks-weigh-on-asset-prices
4. https://www.matteoiacoviello.com/gpr.htm
5. The index goes back to 1900 but we only show here since 2000.
6. https://www.spglobal.com/en/research-insights/market-insights/geopolitical-risk
7. https://www.imf.org/en/Blogs/Articles/2024/08/01/now-is-the-time-to-help-countries-faced-with-liquidity-challenges
8. https://www.moodys.com/web/en/us/capabilities/cyber-risk.html?cid=ppc-gglds-17386&gclsrc=aw.ds&gad_source=1&gad_campaignid=21355658581&gbraid=0AAAAAodz9IbCAAuxPP7wkt6r6h_0dHVpZ&gclid=Cj0KCQjwrc7GBhCfARIsAHGcW5WsUDewlB0WwJYfAedJfBsnXuh3E2RLmzMyjCoxb-CasLFsxsVMh-vMaAj-BEALw_wcB
9. https://www.weforum.org/publications/global-retail-investor-outlook-2025/

References

Agoraki, Maria-Eleni K., Georgios P. Kouretas and Nikiforos T. Laopodis (2022). Geopolitical Risks, Uncertainty, and Stock Market Performance. *Economic and Political Studies* 10(3), Special Issue on Politics and Finance, pp. 253–265.

Aizenman, Joshua, Robert Lindahl, David Stenvall, and Gazi Salah Uddin (2024). Geopolitical Shocks and Commodity Market Dynamics: New Evidence from the Russia–Ukraine Conflict. *European Journal of Political Economy* 85, 102574.

Behn, Markus, Jan Hannes Lang and Alessio Reghezza (2025). Geopolitical Risk and its Implications for Macroprudential Policy. European Central Bank, *Macro-prudential Bulletin* 28.

Adra, Samer, Yang Gao, Jin Huang, and Jiayi Yuan (2023). Geopolitical Risk and Corporate Payout Policy. *International Review of Financial Analysis* 87, 102613.

Chowdhury, Md Shahedur R., Mohsen Aram, Siamak Javadi, and Ali Nejadmalayeri (2025). Geopolitical Risk and Corporate Capital Structure. *Journal of Corporate Finance* 93, 102796.

Salachas, Evangelos, Georgios P. Kouretas and Nikiforos T. Laopodis (2025). Understanding Central Bank Responses to Geopolitical Risks: Evidence from the Fed and ECB. *Journal of Financial Stability* 80, September, 101452.

Salachas, Evangelos, Georgios P. Kouretas, Nikiforos T. Laopodis and Prodromos Vlamis (2024). Stock Market Spillovers of Global Risks and Hedging Opportunities. *European Journal of Political Economy* 83, June, 102533.

Liu, Zhenhua, Yushu Wang, Xinting Yuan, Zhihua Ding, and Qiang Ji (2025). Geopolitical Risk and Vulnerability of Energy Markets. *Energy Economics* 141, 108055.

Zhang, Yaojie, Jiaxin He, Mengxi He, and Shaofang Li (2023). Geopolitical Risk and Stock Market Volatility: A Global Perspective. *Finance Research Letters* 53, 103620.

Index